Criminal Investigation

An Analytical Perspective

Steven G. Brandl

University of Wisconsin—Milwaukee

PEARSON

Boston   New York   San Francisco
Mexico City   Montreal   Toronto   London   Madrid   Munich   Paris
Hong Kong   Singapore   Tokyo   Cape Town   Sydney

Series Editor: *Jennifer Jacobson*
Editorial Assistant: *Amy Holborow*
Senior Marketing Manager: *Krista Groshong*
Editorial-Production Administrator: *Anna Socrates*
Editorial-Production Service and Electronic Composition: *Stratford Publishing Services*
Text Design: *Stratford Publishing Services*
Photo Research: *Helane M. Prottas, Posh Pictures*
Composition and Prepress Buyer: *Linda Cox*
Manufacturing Buyer: *JoAnne Sweeney*
Cover Administrator: *Kristina Mose-Libon*

For related titles and support materials, visit our online catalog at www.ablongman.com.

Photo credits: Page 3, Associated Press/FBI; p. 30, © 2002 AP/Wide World Photos; p. 37, © Bettmann/CORBIS; p. 38, © GettyImages, Inc./Hulton Archive Photos; p. 52, © Evan Richman; p. 54, AP/Wide World Photos; p. 57, Kent Meireis/The Image Works; p. 58, Alan Mothner/AP/Wide World Photos; p. 66, Nick Ut/AP/Wide World Photos; p. 69, © Michael Newman/PhotoEdit; p. 90, © Bettmann/CORBIS; p. 95, Fred Greaves/AP/Wide World Photos; p. 101, © M. English/Custom Medical Stock; p. 109, AP/Wide World Photos; p. 145, AP/Wide World Photos/LAPD, LA Superior Court; p. 166, (top), © Bettmann/CORBIS, (bottom), Dan Loh/AP/Wide World Photos; p. 167, (left) Steve Jessmore/AP Photo/*The Flint Journal,* (right) Bill Cooke/AP Photo; p. 258, Mike Tripp/AP/*The Daily News-Record;* p. 284 (all) AP Photo/FBI; p. 286, Associated Press, AP/David Zalubowski; p. 296, Lui Kit Wong/AP/*The News Tribune;* p. 326, Associated Press, Pool, *The Union Tribune,* Dan Trevan; p. 385/Steve Helber/AP/Wide World Photos; p. 393, Sam Mircovich/Reuters Pool/AP Photo; p. 399, Don Halasy/AP/Pool/*New York Post;* p. 407, AP/Wide World Photos/Portland Police Department

Between the time Website information is gathered and then published, it is not unusual for some sites to have closed. Also, the transcription of URLs can result in typographical errors. The publisher would appreciate notification where these errors occur so that they may be corrected in subsequent editions.

Library of Congress Cataloging-in-Publication Data

Brandl, Steven G. (Steven Gerard)
    Criminal Investigation : an analytical perspective / Steven G. Brandl.
      p.   cm.
    Includes bibliographical references and index.
    ISBN 0-205-35947-7
    1. Criminal Investigation. I. Title.

  HV8073.B673 2003
  363.25—dc22   2203057965

Printed in the United States of America

10 9 8 7 6 5 4 3 2   08 07 06 05

*To those individuals who make,
or intend to make,
the world a more just place.*

*To Kara, Katie, and David,
who continually remind me of
the most important things in life.*

BRIEF CONTENTS

CONTENTS

PREFACE

Police work and criminal investigations are more complicated now than ever before. The work requires that individuals have a solid understanding of what they are reasonably expected to do, and the problems and pitfalls of the work. In particular, individuals who enter police work, or who already work in the field, should have an understanding of evidence, the strengths and weaknesses of different forms of evidence, and how different types of evidence can be used to establish proof. *Criminal Investigation* was written with these goals in mind. Accordingly, the basic and underlying theme of *Criminal Investigation* is that students should be able to think—and think critically—about important issues and problems in criminal investigation, and criminal justice in general. This knowledge represents a necessary foundation for an understanding of criminal investigation. This book is different from other criminal investigation texts primarily because of this emphasis: This book emphasizes analysis to a greater extent than other criminal investigation texts.

The emphasis on analysis is not to diminish the importance of investigative procedures. The procedures used to collect evidence are, indeed, an important aspect of criminal investigations. This book focuses on the most important, most frequently performed, and most complex evidence collection procedures but it is not a technically oriented training manual. For example, considerable attention is devoted to how to conduct proper and legally defensible lineups (Chapter 7). Most other books spend relatively little time on this issue. Lineups are a relatively complicated procedure and may produce extremely powerful evidence of guilt. *Criminal Investigation* provides instructions regarding lineups, and it also explains *why* these procedures are important in collecting valid eyewitness evidence. An explanation of complicated procedures often requires an *analysis* of the issue. *Criminal Investigation* will assist instructors in guiding their students through this process.

In addition, as another example, the book also devotes considerable attention to the procedures of collecting evidence as prescribed by law (Chapter 5). Of course, if evidence is collected in a technically proficient manner but without regard for procedural law, that evidence will not be able to be used to establish guilt. As such, an understanding of law as it relates to criminal investigative procedures is necessary if criminal investigations are to be effectively performed. *Criminal Investigation* can assist in this regard.

In short, *Criminal Investigation* offers several features to help establish an understanding of criminal investigation and the role of evidence in the process:

- *Detailed case studies* at the beginning of each chapter that can be used to analyze how evidence is (or could be) used to establish proof and to evaluate investigative procedures. Among the case studies are the Washington, DC, sniper case (Chapter 10), the investigation into the September 11 terrorist attacks (Chapter 14), the Unabomber case (Chapter 1), the Lindbergh baby kidnaping (Chapter 2), the case of Ernesto Miranda (Chapter 5), and the O.J. Simpson case (Chapters 6 and 8).
- *Detailed discussions of strengths and weaknesses of all major forms of evidence,* from DNA to other forms of physical evidence to eyewitness identifications to confessions to behavioral evidence and everything in between
- *Detailed discussions regarding the efficacy of various forms of evidence* in establishing proof
- *Information on and evaluation of proper evidence collection procedures;* procedures not limited to the collection of physical evidence
- *Numerous other case examples* to illustrate key points
- Text written in a *user-friendly, interesting, and conversational* manner

With regard to the organization of the text, the first three chapters provide a discussion of the basic issues of criminal investigation (e.g., organization, effectiveness, history, design). Chapters 4 and 5 discuss the role of evidence in criminal investigations, and the law as it relates to the collection of evidence. Chapters 6, 7, and 8 comprise, arguably, the most important chapters of the book. These chapters discuss the "big three" types of evidence in criminal investigations—physical evidence, eyewitness identifications (interviews), and confessions (interrogations). The next two chapters examine other sources of information in investigations including psychological profiling and other forms of behavioral evidence (Chapter 9), and the public, media, crime analysis, and databanks as sources of information (Chapter 10). Chapters 11 and 12 focus on issues that are unique to the investigation of particular types of crimes. The book concludes with a discussion of the documentation and presentation of evidence in court (Chapter 13) and the future of criminal investigations (Chapter 14).

Criminal Investigation: An Analytical Perspective provides the reader with a substantial and necessary foundation on which to base an understanding of the criminal investigation process.

ACKNOWLEDGMENTS

No person is an island, and nowhere is this more apparent than when writing a book. I would like to acknowledge the many people who assisted with this project. Jennifer Jacobson at Allyn & Bacon enthusiastically accepted my idea for this book and has been a delight to work with ever since. I would also like to acknowledge the hard work of all the others at Allyn & Bacon, especially Anna Socrates and Amy Holborow, as well as Kathy Glidden and Dennis Troutman at Stratford Publishing Services, and Cat Ohala.

This book has greatly benefited from the wise and kind assistance of numerous law enforcement officials, including Chief Tom Czarnyszka, Captain Larry Rittberg, Detective Gregory Lofy, and Detective Troy Nitschke of the Glendale, Wisconsin, Police Department; Lieutenant Peter Hoell of the Germantown, Wisconsin, Police Department; Chief Ken Mueller and Officer Kelly Scannell of the West Bend, Wisconsin Police Department; and Captain Brian O'Keefe, Captain Vince Vitalle (retired), Officer Alfonso Salinas, and the homicide detectives of the Milwaukee Police Department. Bradley DeBraska of the Milwaukee Police Association has also provided tremendous support over the years.

A small but energetic army of graduate assistants provided valuable assistance to me in the development of the text. Particularly noteworthy are the contributions of Melissa Loch, Jessica Berzowski, Mathew Bell, Sarah Kreitzer, Lisa Ruh, and Michelle Zerby.

I thank Professor Frank Horvath at Michigan State University, Professor Robert Worden at the University at Albany, and Professor Peter K. Manning at Northeastern University who first sparked my academic interest in criminal investigation and who guided my early research on the topic.

I also acknowledge the hundreds of criminal investigation students that I have had the privilege of instructing over the years. Their interest and excitement for this important material is a continuing source of motivation for me.

Finally, I thank the many reviewers who made constructive and useful suggestions that improved this book, including Jim Adcock, University of New Haven; Thomas Dreup, Clark State Community College; Daniel Hebert, Springfield Technical Community College; John Hill, Salt Lake Community College; Robert Lorinskas, Southern Illinois University; J. Gayle Mericle, Western Illinois University; Sarah Nordin, Solano Community College; Dale Nute, Florida State University; and Jill A. Shelley, Northern Kentucky University.

THE INVESTIGATION OF CRIME

OBJECTIVES

After reading this chapter you will be able to

- Summarize the Unabomber investigation
- Discuss the goals associated with the criminal investigation process
- Discuss the importance of criminal investigation in the criminal justice process
- Describe information theory as it relates to the criminal investigation process
- Discuss the role of luck and discovery in the criminal investigation process
- Discuss the criminal justice process as a filter
- Identify the most common reasons why crimes are not reported to the police, and the possible reasons why more crimes are not solved by the police

- Discuss the nature of criminal investigations at the local, state, and federal levels
- Compare state police agencies with highway patrol agencies
- Identify the major law enforcement agencies at the federal level and discuss their responsibilities
- Discuss the role and responsibilities of the International Police Organization (INTERPOL)

IMPORTANT TERMS

Criminal investigation

Criminal evidence

Criminal justice system

Information theory

Inductive and deductive reasoning

Service, order maintenance, law enforcement

Filter effect

Plea bargaining

Federal Bureau of Investigation (FBI)

Immigration and Naturalization Service (INS)

Drug Enforcement Administration (DEA)

United States Marshal Service (USMS)

U.S. Secret Service

U.S. Customs Service

Bureau of Alcohol, Tobacco, and Firearms (ATF)

INTRODUCTION

One of the longest criminal investigations in the history of the United States formally ended January 22, 1998, with a plea bargain that spared the life of Theodore J. Kaczynski, known in infamy as "the Unabomber." Ted Kaczynski, former professor of mathematics at the University of California at Berkeley, pled guilty to thirteen bombings that killed three people and injured twenty-three others. For more than seventeen years, a team of 100 FBI agents along with scores of personnel from other law enforcement agencies collected evidence in an attempt to solve the deadly mystery. During the course of the investigation, investigators gleaned much information about the bombs and how they were constructed, but they knew very little about the identity of the person or persons who made and sent the bombs. One thing that was clear was the bomber's modus operandi (MO), or method of committing the crime. Most of the packages were sent through the mail. The explosive devices were of similar construction, and they were often contained in a wood box or used wood as shrapnel. "Wood" was sometimes used as part of the fictitious return address, the name of the sender on the package, or the name of the recipient. The bombs became more sophisticated, powerful, and deadly as time went on. (The early bombs often contained miscellaneous "junk," such as furniture pieces, plumbing pipes, and sink traps. For this reason the Unabomber was first known as the "Junk Yard Bomber.") However, none of the components of the explosive devices were traceable. In addition, the bomber targeted similar groups of people—university professors (at University of Chicago, Northwestern, University of Michigan, Yale University, and University of California at Berkeley and San Francisco), airlines and airline executives (American and United Airlines), and computer technology firms (it was for the early targets, UNiversities and Airlines, that the FBI named this case *Unabom*).

In 1980, with the fourth bombing, investigators discovered what would become the bomber's signature initials (FC) on a metal part of the spent bomb. In 1987, an eyewitness came forward, stating that she saw an individual placing what appeared to be a bunch of wooden boards, which later turned out to be a bomb, in the parking lot of a Salt Lake City computer store. This information led to the creation of the then-famous composite sketch of the Unabomber.

During the next several years, beginning in 1993, the bomber sent a series of letters to various newspapers (primarily the *San Francisco Chronicle* and the *New York Times*). Some letters identified the crimes as the work of the "FC" terrorist group, some made general and specific threats, and one provided a social security number to authenticate future correspondence. As a possible lead, the agents checked the social security number and it belonged to a recently released convict from California (who, strangely enough, happened to have a tattoo that read "Pure Wood"). This individual was quickly cleared because it was determined that he had no knowledge or involvement in the crimes. One of the letters had a handwriting impression that read "call Nathan R Wed 7 pm." As another possible lead, investigators checked 10,000 people with the name

The FBI released this sketch of the Unabomber on April 25, 1995.

"Nathan R" in the United States, which yielded nothing. In April 1995, additional correspondence was made by the Unabomber to the *New York Times*. This letter provided a reason for a recent bombing, made more threats, and taunted the police (e.g., ". . . the FBI is a joke . . . "). The letter also specified the Unabomber's core demand: that his "manifesto" be published. The Unabomber promised that if the manifesto was published, the bombing would stop. With the recommendation of the FBI, the 35,000-word article titled "Industrial Society and Its Future" was published in *The Washington Post* on September 19, 1995. (www.unabombertrial.com/manifesto/index.html is one of the many sites on the Internet where the essay can be found.) Later, the manifesto was read by a man named David Kaczynski. David conducted his own investigation and came to the conclusion that the writing sounded very similar to the words and ideas of his brother Ted. Certain unique phrases used in the writing ("you can't eat your cake and have it too"), known to be used by Ted, made him all but certain that Ted was the author. In early 1996, David notified the FBI that he believed Ted, who was living in a shack outside of Lincoln, Montana, may have written the manifesto and may be responsible for the Unabomber bombings. The FBI found Ted Kaczynski at his cabin in the midst of bomb diagrams, explosives, other bomb-making materials, and a finished bomb ready to be mailed. After spending more than $50 million and a million work hours on the investigation, checking and rechecking 200 "good" suspects and hundreds of other suspects, conducting thousands of interviews, and fielding 20,000 calls placed to the FBI hotline (1-800-701-BOMB), the Unabomber was apprehended uneventfully outside his Montana cabin. The rest, as they say, is history. Ted Kaczynski was sentenced to life in prison with no possibility of parole (Douglas, 1996).

Criminal Investigation and Evidence Defined

Criminal investigation is the process of collecting crime-related information to reach certain goals. This simple definition has three important components: (1) the process, (2) crime-related information, and (3) goals. Each is discussed in the following paragraphs.

The process refers to the activities performed by the patrol officers, detectives, or other investigators who are responsible for the investigation. As discussed in detail in Chapter 3, criminal investigations usually consist of several stages, when certain activities are performed prior to other activities. The activities performed may be extensive or minimal depending on the nature of the crime being investigated. Clearly, the nature and seriousness of the crime, to a large extent, determine the activities that are to be appropriately performed during the investigation. The most common activities performed during investigations, even the most routine investigations, are searching for and interviewing victims and witnesses, and reading and writing reports (Greenwood et al., 1977).

Crime-related information is criminal evidence. It consists of supposed facts and knowledge that relate to a particular crime or perpetrator. It is what is obtained as a result of investigative activities and it is what is used to establish that a particular person committed a particular crime. Evidence is absolutely critical to an investigation. In fact, criminal evidence and criminal investigation are inseparable: Evidence is the basic substance of criminal investigation. Without evidence, an investigation can go nowhere; evidence is to an investigation as water is to life (Eck, 1983).

One of the major problems with evidence in criminal investigations, however, is that at the time the information is collected, investigators may not know whether it is relevant. In addition, in some investigations the police may be overwhelmed with massive amounts of information and, again, its relevance is unknown. Consider the information that was discovered during the course of the Unabomber investigation: the use and reference to wood, the signature initials FC, the composite sketch of the individual who was seen placing the wood boards/bomb in the parking lot, the social security number, the "call Nathan R" note, and the 20,000 telephone calls placed to the FBI hotline. As it turned out, none of this information was relevant or useful in the investigation or the eventual apprehension of Ted Kaczynski, although this was not known when the information was first discovered.

Another potential problem with evidence in criminal investigations is that it may not be accurate; but again, this may not be known when the information is first obtained. Compounding this problem is that even inaccurate information can be quite influential in making a determination or in drawing a conclusion. Perhaps the best example of this is eyewitness identifications. Eyewitness identifications have been shown to be extremely influential in the minds of jurors (and also for investigators and judges) in establishing that a particular person committed a particular crime; however, eyewitness identifications are often inaccurate (see Chapter 7). No question, these problems make the criminal investigation task much more difficult and complex.

Lastly, *a goal* is best considered a desired end or a future state. It is something that one wishes to achieve at some point in the future. Goals also assist in giving direction to activities to be performed. For example, if your goal is to get an A in a course on criminal investigations, this goal will hopefully lead you to certain activities such as reading the text, being attentive in class, and studying for the exams. Your ultimate goal might be to graduate and obtain an investigator position in a law enforcement agency, or get promoted.

Various goals have been associated with the criminal investigation process. Among the most common and significant are (1) to solve the crime, (2) to provide evidence to support a conviction in court, and (3) to provide a level of service to satisfy crime victims. Arguably, the most important and least questionable goal of the three is to solve the crime. To solve the crime, investigators must first determine whether a crime has been committed and ascertain the true nature of the crime, then identify the perpetrator, and then apprehend the perpetrator. Although the task of determining whether a crime has been committed and ascertaining the true nature of the crime may seem straightforward and relatively uncomplicated, oftentimes it is not. Investigators can often provide countless examples of when the crime was not really as it first appeared. In particular, "stories" told by certain victims, and incidents that involve certain circumstances, may be viewed as questionable in their truthfulness. Most fundamental, did a crime really occur? Or is this a phony report to defraud an insurance company? In the context of a robbery, did the "victim" pocket the money (or spend the money foolishly) and then claim to have been robbed? In one recent case, an employee of a tire store stole cash from the store, buried the cash in a jar (in his backyard), then returned to the store and hit himself over the head with a tire iron, causing unconsciousness. After other employees discovered the "victim" on the floor lying unconscious in a pool of blood, a "robbery" was reported. After some initial investigative activities (namely, an interview of the "victim"), the true nature of the crime became evident (Brandl, 1991). One might suspect that even with the Unabomber, the investigators had to question initially the true nature of the crimes. For example, was the individual who was injured as a result of the explosive blast really a victim, or was this person actually the person responsible for constructing the bomb and the explosion was just an unfortunate accident? If investigators do not question the true nature of the crime, serious problems can result (see the introduction to Chapter 3 describing the murder investigation of Carol Stuart).

After verifying the occurrence and the nature of the crime, investigators must then identify who committed the crime, and finally the perpetrators must be physically apprehended. To identify who committed the crime is to know with some degree of certainty (i.e., probable cause) who is responsible for the crime. To apprehend the perpetrator is to take this person into police custody (i.e., make an arrest). With the occurrence and nature of the crime verified, and the individual believed to be responsible for committing the crime identified and apprehended, the crime can be said to be solved. Often these three tasks—determining the occurrence and true nature of the crime, identifying the perpetrators, and apprehending the perpetrators—are related to each other and are worked on simultaneously.

A second goal often associated with the criminal investigation process is obtaining a conviction in court. The police are responsible for collecting the evidence that may be used to establish that the persons apprehended actually committed the crimes in question. The prosecutor presents the evidence collected by the police in court to prove to a jury (or a judge) beyond a reasonable doubt that the defendant is, in fact, guilty of the crime for which he is charged. In this sense, the police and prosecutor are on the same team, working toward the same end. There are many reasons to believe that the conviction standard is, and is not, an appropriate outcome on which to judge the performance of the police, and these issues are discussed in Chapter 3.

The third goal associated with criminal investigation is victim satisfaction. This outcome has taken on importance during the last few decades with the movement toward community policing. With the community policing philosophy, the police are supposed to be more concerned with how they are perceived by citizens and how they treat citizens (Goldstein, 1987). The idea is that satisfaction is a good thing, and something about which the police should be directly concerned. After all, citizens provide the resources (for example, pay taxes) necessary for the police to operate.

The ultimate goal of the criminal investigation process is the reduction in crime through either deterrence or incapacitation. To deter an individual from engaging in crime, punishment must be administered either to that person or to someone of whom that individual is aware. Of course, before punishment can be administered, an apprehension must be made. Similarly, before an individual can be incapacitated (by placement in prison or otherwise), and therefore not able to engage in crime, that individual needs to be identified and apprehended. Although deterrence and incapacitation are not within the complete control of the police, the police provide a critical ingredient in their achievement.

Types of Criminal Investigations

Generally, criminal investigations can be either reactive or proactive. Reactive investigations are the traditional manner in which police become involved in the investigation of crime. The crime occurs and then police respond or react to the crime. The police are typically in reactive mode when investigating crimes such as homicide, robbery, rape, and so forth. Reactive investigations are often divided into the initial (or preliminary) investigation and the follow-up investigation. In larger departments, uniformed police officers usually conduct initial investigations and detectives conduct follow-up investigations. In small departments, uniformed officers usually conduct initial and follow-up investigations.

Proactive strategies, which are often covert in nature, usually involve the police initiating investigative activities prior to the occurrence of a crime. Through proactive-type investigations, the police place themselves in a position to deal with crime before it happens. Proactive strategies are often used in investigating crimes such as prostitution, drug sales, and gambling. Investigators may also use particular proactive strategies in a primarily reactive investigation (e.g., surveillance to monitor the movement of a suspect in a robbery investigation). Common proactive strategies are those that require the police to go "undercover," when the police act in a covert manner and when the police are not easily recognizable as law enforcement officers. Such strategies include stings, decoys, undercover fencing operations, stakeouts, and surveillance (see Chapter 3). Typically, such investigations are most commonly conducted in police departments of moderate size with adequate personnel for such operations. State and federal agencies also commonly use such practices in collecting information in particular investigations.

Information Theory and the Criminal Investigation Process

Information theory is not so much an explanation of the criminal investigation process as it is a perspective from which to develop an understanding of it. According to information theory, the criminal investigation process resembles a battle between the police and the perpetrator over crime-related information (Willmer, 1970). In committing the crime, the perpetrator emits "signals" or information that the police attempt to collect through investigative activities. The information is "created" as a result of the commission of the crime. For example, the perpetrator may leave his fingerprints at the scene of the crime, the body of the murder victim may have traces of fibers from the perpetrator's clothing, or the perpetrator may be described by an eyewitness to the crime. In each case, the original source of the information (or evidence) is the perpetrator.

If the perpetrator is able to minimize the amount of information available for the police to collect, or if the police are unable to recognize the information, then the perpetrator will not be identified or apprehended. In this case, the perpetrator wins the battle. On the other hand, if the police are able to collect a significant amount of signals from the perpetrator, then the perpetrator will be identified and apprehended. As a result, the police win. Critical to the process are mistakes. Evidence is often left because the culprit made a mistake. The police must capitalize on these mistakes and collect the corresponding evidence. The bottom line, according to information theory, is that the source of all evidence is the perpetrator, and the fundamental task for the police in a criminal investigation is to find the evidence produced as a result of the crime.

Consider information theory in relation to the case of the Unabomber. Investigators had little information and few clues to guide their investigation of seventeen years. Investigators knew of the FC signature initials, they had the composite sketch, the social security number, the "call Nathan R" note, and the reference to wood. The Unabomber was, apparently, good at minimizing the amount of information available for the investigators to collect—until the publication of the manifesto in *The Washington Post*. The manifesto constituted a 35,000-word clue that came directly from the culprit. Indeed, as discussed earlier, the article proved to be the undoing of the Unabomber. The culprit made a mistake and the police capitalized on it. One can only speculate whether Ted Kaczynski would have been identified and apprehended if it was not for the publication of the manifesto.

The Role of Chance, Accident, and Discovery in Criminal Investigations

It is common to hear discussions about the role of luck and good fortune in solving crimes, and that the presence of good luck diminishes the efforts of investigators in solving crimes (e.g., detectives got lucky in solving the crime). The fact of the matter is that good luck should not diminish the work of the investigators or the quality of effort put forth during an investigation. Accident and good fortune are natural ingredients not only in many solved crimes but also in many other discoveries and breakthroughs.

There are countless examples: Consider the discovery of Post-it Notes, Velcro, Viagra, and even America, for that matter (see Jones [1991]). In the 1960s engineers at 3M were trying to develop a powerful glue. One formula that was tested would only weakly stick and could easily be pulled apart. The formula remained undeveloped. Years later, one of the engineers on the earlier project was trying to make a bookmark stick in his church songbook and in a flash he discovered a use for that weak glue: Post-it Notes. During the late 1940s, a Swiss engineer was trying to develop a better fastener for clothing. After a walk in the woods, he discovered burrs sticking to his clothes. After eight years of testing, he developed Velcro, which consists of fabric with hooks and loops that adhere when they touch but can be ripped apart. Viagra was developed by Pfizer Pharmaceutical Company as a treatment for heart-related ailments. In clinical trials, the male patients taking the medication often reported an unexpected and unusual side effect. Viagra is now prescribed as a treatment for male erectile dysfunction. As a last example, Christopher Columbus discovered America accidentally. He was on a mission to find India, and during the process prove that the world was round. What an "accidental" discovery he made!

The same sort of luck is often present in criminal investigations. Consider the role of luck in the investigation into the bombing of the Alfred P. Murrah Federal Building in Oklahoma City in 1995. Forty-nine hours twenty minutes after the bomb exploded (which killed 168 people and wounded more than 700), investigators found the culprit—Timothy McVeigh—sixty-three miles north of the scene of the crime in a small-town jail. He had been taken into custody by a state trooper for driving without a licence plate on his beat-up 1977 yellow Mercury Marquis and for carrying a loaded handgun. On April 19, 1995, at approximately twelve noon, three hours after the explosion, investigators from the FBI located a truck axle approximately 575 feet from the scene of the blast. It was figured that for this 250-pound piece of steel to be blown such a distance, it had to be at the center, or close to the center, of the explosion. Indeed, seconds before the explosion, a nearby security camera had filmed a Ryder truck in front of the Murrah building. On examination of the axle, a vehicle identification number (VIN) was discovered. Through a check of the National Insurance Crime Bureau database of vehicle numbers and their owners, the truck from which the axle belonged was traced to Elliot's Body Shop in Junction City, Kansas. It was learned that the truck was currently rented to an individual named Robert Kling. Investigators went to Elliot's and got a description and composite sketch of Kling. In showing the sketch to people in the area, several individuals recognized the man but no one had any further useful information about him—except the manager of a local motel who recognized the man in the sketch as her former guest. His name was not Robert Kling, she told investigators, it was Timothy McVeigh, or at least that was the name he used to register at the motel. With this name in hand, investigators checked a national criminal records database and it was learned that McVeigh was arrested two days earlier on gun and traffic charges and was currently detained in a jail in northern Oklahoma. A federal agent called the sheriff with an order to hold McVeigh for suspicion of bombing the Alfred P. Murrah Federal Building. If the agent would have waited another hour, McVeigh would have been free on bail and no longer in police custody (Serrano, 1998). So what was the role of luck in this investigation?

Just like the discovery of America and the invention of Viagra, it is quite common to find something when you are looking for something else. Have you ever misplaced your car keys and in the process of looking for them found something else you had been looking for earlier? The same phenomenon is present in criminal investigations. In investigating one crime, it is not uncommon to discover information that leads to another totally unrelated crime being solved. Case in point: the February 1993 explosion at the World Trade Center in New York City. The explosion killed six people, injured 1,042, and caused more than $500 million in damage. In investigating this bombing, federal agents discovered (and disrupted) a different group of Muslim fundamentalists that planned to blow up various places simultaneously in New York City: the Holland and Lincoln tunnels, the United Nations building, and the Jacob Javits Federal Building. Through the use of surveillance and undercover infiltration, eight suspects were arrested and eventually sentenced to prison for this plot (Morganthau and Masland, 1993).

The Role of Logic, Analysis, and Inference in Criminal Investigations

Criminal investigation has been likened to the game of chess: Each case to which the investigator is assigned is like a chess match in progress. Although many investigations are not as complicated as long, drawn-out chess matches, investigators who are actively working on as many as ten cases (or more) have potentially much information to remember and keep straight. Have you ever tried to play ten games of chess, or checkers, at the same time? Try it. As expected, there is a lot to keep track of, a lot of things to remember, and a lot of things to try to figure out. In trying to figure things out, logic, analysis, and inference are necessary. Logic refers to the process of reasoning, of drawing conclusions from statements of fact. In using logic to solve problems, one is required to analyze the dimensions of the problem and to make inferences to draw accurate conclusions.

There are two approaches to logical reasoning: the inductive approach and the deductive approach. With the inductive approach, one begins with particular facts or specific instances and draws general conclusions and explanations from these facts or instances. With the deductive approach, one begins with general premises and principles and, from these, specific conclusions are drawn. The conclusions that are drawn are often based on rules, laws, or other widely accepted principles. For example, the process of *developing* a psychological profile (Chapter 9) is an example of inductive reasoning. Based on specific crime scene characteristics, a general conclusion is drawn regarding the type of person most likely to have committed the crime. The process of *using* a psychological profile to focus an investigation is an example of the deductive approach. One begins with a summary description of the type of person most likely to have committed a particular crime and then draws a specific conclusion about who among the pool of potential suspects fits the profile most closely. One type of reasoning is not superior to the other; both are equally susceptible to error and success. Investigators use each approach to solve crimes.

Consider the following problems and the role of reasoning for each of them (www. school.discovery.com). First, see if you can figure out the answer to the following problem:

> After the bank robbery, two men ran out of the bank. One was seen wearing a red baseball cap and the other was seen wearing a blue baseball cap. The police did not know which one was the robber. Jake saw the robbery and could tell the police what color hat the robber was wearing. Jake's brother Joe later told their sister Jenny what happened. "Jake said the robber was wearing a red hat," he said. So, what color hat was bank robber wearing? It might be helpful to know that one of the brothers always tells the truth and the other one always lies, but we do not know which is which. (The solution is at the end of the chapter.)

For another problem that requires the use of logic for it to be solved, consider the following:

> Three playing cards—A, B, and C—from an ordinary deck of cards are facedown on a table. Can you identify each card as a queen or king and as a heart or a spade based on the following four pieces of information? (1) There is at least one queen to the right of a king, (2) there is at least one queen to the left of a queen, (3) there is at least one heart to the left of a spade, and (4) there is at least one heart to the right of a heart. What cards are A, B, and C? (See the end of the chapter for the solution.)

Understanding the importance of logic, analysis, and inference in conducting criminal investigations also raises important issues about the necessary qualities and characteristics of investigators. What makes a good investigator? Surprisingly, little research has addressed this issue. According to Cohen and Chaiken (1987), the qualities most important in investigators are good judgment, stability, stamina, persistence, intelligence, initiative, teamwork, involvement, and dedication. Fundamentally, investigators should have common sense and should be able to think through problems to their solution. In addition, motivation is widely perceived as one of the most crucial traits for effective investigators. This is in part because of the autonomy, or freedom, investigators often enjoy in performing their work. Because investigators are usually free of direct supervision, the opportunity for shirking, or simply avoiding work, is considerable. Integrity is also a critical quality. Cases can be lost when the honesty and integrity of investigators who collected the evidence during the investigation is effectively attacked by defense attorneys (e.g., see Chapter 6 and the discussion of the trial of O.J. Simpson). Identifying the desirable qualities of investigators is a first step, and the easy step. The challenge is to develop valid and reliable measures of these qualities to make appropriate and well-justified job selection decisions. In addition to personal qualities and traits, Cohen and Chaiken (1987) also explain that investigators should have a wide range of previous experience in law enforcement, that investigators should have solid street knowledge (i.e., knowledge of real-life criminal behavior), have knowledge of criminal statutes, and have excellent oral and written communication skills, as well as reading comprehension skills. The ability to read and write effectively is critical given the importance of reports in the investigative process. Reports provide continuity in investigations when several investigators are working on a case. They provide a basis on which to manage activities performed on the case, and they serve as the official record of how the investigation was conducted and how the information was collected. Simply stated, well-written, complete reports are critical in securing arrests and convictions. Similarly, much of investigators' time is spent interviewing victims, witnesses, and suspects. Victims, witnesses, and suspects are common and important sources of information about the crime and who committed it. Effective oral communication and human relations skills are extremely important in being able to obtain information from these sources. Training may be used to develop or refine these skills among investigators. Training in these and other areas (e.g., forensics, courtroom testimony, legal updates) may be beneficial in providing competent investigations (Kiley, 1998).

Criminal Investigation in the Context of the Criminal Justice System

The criminal justice system represents a societal-level response to crime (locking your doors at night is an example of an individual response to crime, and your neighborhood watch program is an example of a group-level response). By discussing the criminal justice system, we may come to an understanding of the importance of criminal investigation in the context of the overall system.

The Criminal Justice Process as a System

The criminal justice system, like any other system (e.g., the brake system on a car or the educational system), consists of a set of units (or subsystems). These units are related to each other, they are interconnected, and they depend on each other. The three components of the criminal justice system are police, courts, and corrections. A system is designed to reach some objective or goal. By most accounts, the primary goal of the criminal justice system is to reduce crime, and this is to be accomplished through deterrence or incapacitation of offenders. Furthermore, the units within the larger system have specialized functions that contribute to the attainment of the system's goals. Specifically, the specialized function of the corrections component is to maintain custody and control over offenders, and to punish or reform offenders. The specialized function of the court component is to determine the guilt or innocence of the accused. The specialized function of the police as it relates to the overall goal of the criminal justice system is to identify and apprehend criminals. Sound familiar? Sounds like criminal investigation.

It is also important to take note of where the criminal investigation process falls within the criminal justice process. As seen in Figure 1–1, "Investigation" is the second stage of the

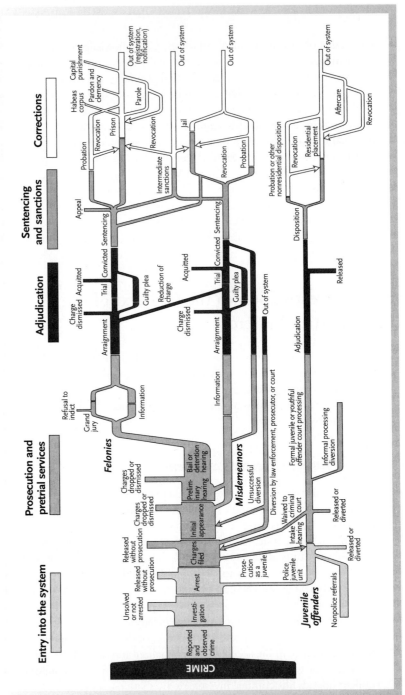

FIGURE 1–1 Sequence of events in the criminal justice process

Note: This chart gives a simplified view of caseflow through the criminal justice system. Procedures vary among jurisdictions. The weights of the lines are not intended to show actual size of caseloads. *Source:* Adapted from *The challenge of crime in a free society.* President's Commission on Law Enforcement and Administration of Justice, 1967. This revision, a result of the Symposium on the 30th Anniversary of the President's Commission, was prepared by the Bureau of Justice Statistics in 1997.

overall process. This is significant. If a criminal investigation is not successful (in this instance, if the perpetrator is not identified and apprehended), the rest of the criminal justice process is completely irrelevant. If the police are not able to identify and apprehend the perpetrator, then the courts cannot adjudicate, nor can corrections punish. In this case, criminals will not be deterred or incapacitated, and the amount of crime will not be reduced. As such, criminal investigation plays a critical and central role in the operation of the overall criminal justice process.

The Criminal Justice Process as a Filter

The criminal justice process can be portrayed as a filter or a funnel in which offenders (or cases) drop out of the process as their case progresses through the system. Figure 1–2 shows this filter effect with the processing of burglaries, robberies, and rapes. This figure is based on research that has examined case processing of more than 45,000 offenses in the seventy-five largest counties in the country (Bureau of Justice Statistics [BJS], 1999) as well as data

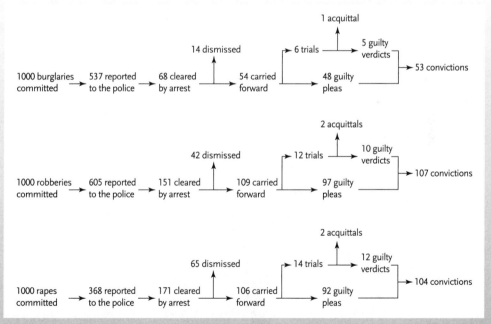

FIGURE 1–2 Filter effect of the criminal justice process

Adapted from the Bureau of Justice Statistics. (2002) *Criminal Victimization, 2001*. Washington, DC: U.S. Department of Justice.
Federal Bureau of Investigation. (2002) *Crime in the United States: Uniform Crime Reports*. Washington, DC: U.S. Department of Justice.
Bureau of Justice Statistics. (1999) *Felony Defendants in Large Urban Counties, 1996*. Washington, DC: U.S. Department of Justice.

from the National Crime Victim Survey (NCVS; BJS, 1997), and the FBI *Uniform Crime Report* (FBI, 2002).

Several aspects of Figure 1–2 are noteworthy. First, a substantial number of cases are immediately filtered out of the process because the crimes are not reported to the police. As seen in Figure 1–2, for burglary, robbery, and rape, the percentage of crimes not reported to the police ranges from sixty-one percent for rape to forty percent for robbery. It is often reported that, on average, approximately fifty percent of "all serious crimes" (i.e., index crimes) are *not* reported to the police (Cole and Smith, 2002). Although this statistic may be technically correct, it may be misleading for several reasons. First, in this statistic, larceny–theft is included as a "serious" crime, although one could argue that it really is not a serious crime or at least not as serious as many other crimes. Second, of all crimes that occur, a relatively large proportion are larceny–thefts. Larceny crimes are overrepresented among index crimes (FBI, 2002). Finally, it just so happens that of all the crimes analyzed by the NCVS, larceny–theft has the lowest reporting percentage (Figure 1–3). As a result of these three factors, the inclusion of larceny–theft in the calculation of the aggregate "serious crimes reported to the police" statistic drastically reduces, perhaps unjustifiably, the overall percentage.

So why are so many crimes not reported to the police? The answer to this question appears to relate somewhat to the type of the crime. For example, the most common reason given by rape victims regarding why the crime was not reported was that it was a "private or personal matter" followed by "fear of reprisal." For burglaries, the most common reasons were that "the property was recovered" or that "the offender was unsuccessful" or that there is "lack of proof." Not surprisingly, the most frequent reason cited *for* reporting a property crime (especially motor vehicle theft) was to recover the property or to allow for an insur-

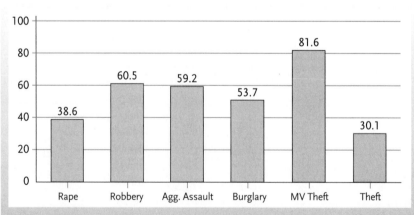

FIGURE 1–3 Percent of crimes reported to the police, 2001

Source: Bureau of Justice Statistics. (2002) *Criminal Victimization, 2001* Washington, DC: U.S. Department of Justice.

ance claim. The most common reason cited for reporting a personal crime was "because it was a crime" (BJS, 1997).

A second noteworthy aspect of Figure 1–2 is that many crimes, once reported, are not solved or cleared by arrest. Similar to the percentage of crimes reported to the police, it is commonly reported that, overall, approximately twenty percent of "all serious crimes" are solved (FBI, 2002). Once again, however, this may be misleading because of the strong influence of larceny–theft in this calculation. Nevertheless, there is significant variation in the success of the police in solving crimes: On the high end are murders with, on average, more than sixty-two percent solved; on the low end are burglaries, with less than thirteen percent solved (Figure 1–4).

So why are law enforcement agencies able to solve so few crimes? There are likely a multitude of factors that explain police lack of success in this regard. First and foremost may simply be the nature and structure of the crimes and how the police typically respond to them. The police are primarily reactive. Usually, it is only after a crime is committed that the police take action and, as such, the police are always trying to catch up to the culprit. The offender has the advantage in choosing the time and place of the crime as well as the method of committing the crime. In addition, given the structure of crimes, the necessary evidence to solve the crime may simply not exist. For example, it is not surprising that burglaries are the least likely to be cleared by an arrest. Typically, with the way burglaries are committed and the fact that there is usually no significant evidence left as a result of the crime (e.g., no eyewitnesses, no useful physical evidence), it is difficult to solve such crimes. On the other hand, with a crime such as homicide or even assault, there are often witnesses

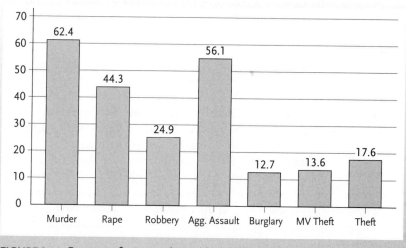

FIGURE 1–4 Percent of crimes cleared by arrest, 2001

Source: Federal Bureau of Investigation. (2002) *Crime in the United States: Uniform Crime Reports.* Washington, DC: U.S. Department of Justice.

to the crime. Furthermore, the perpetrator is usually someone known to the victim. These structural dimensions of the crime facilitate a higher rate of solvability.

A second factor that may help explain the limited success of the police in solving crimes is that the police have to follow certain rules in collecting evidence (see Chapter 5). Perhaps the police would be more effective in solving crimes if the law did not prohibit the police from torturing suspects or arresting and interrogating citizens without reason. Case in point is the investigation into the terrorist acts of September 11, 2001. During the course of the ensuing investigation, discussions arose regarding how to obtain information most effectively from individuals who were arrested in the United States and who were suspected of having links to Osama bin Laden, but who were not willing to talk to the authorities. Investigators reportedly considered using more extreme measures to extract information from these individuals, using "truth serum," and even moving the suspects to another country where "more rigorous interrogation techniques" could be used legally (Buncombe, 2001). As a society, we value our individual freedoms from government intrusion, but we must realize that this too has costs.

A third factor may be that the police operate with resource (time and money) constraints. With limited person power, many crimes simply cannot be investigated as thoroughly as they could be. Indeed, recent research shows that detectives spend, on average, less than four hours on each burglary and robbery investigation (Brandl, 1991). Perhaps with more resources, more crimes could be solved.

Finally, undoubtedly, investigators' mistakes can lead to offenders not being arrested. Investigators may overlook critical evidence or may engage in questionable procedures in collecting evidence (e.g., conducting unlawful searches, mishandling physical evidence). Although all of these factors may help explain why more crimes are not solved, probably the most significant explanation lies in the structure of the crimes. The police simply are at a disadvantage because of the manner in which they typically become involved in investigations.

The third noteworthy aspect of Figure 1–2 is the small percentage of cases that go to trial after screening. This is a result of plea bargaining. A plea bargain involves the defendant entering a plea of guilty in exchange for some consideration, usually a reduced sentence. For example, if the prosecutor charges the defendant with first-degree intentional homicide and intends to present evidence in court to prove the charge, the defendant may face a prison term of perhaps mandatory life in prison. Of course, if found not guilty, the defendant would not face any sanction. Realizing both possibilities, the defendant and the prosecutor may have some incentive to negotiate a plea, thereby reducing the uncertainty of the process. If the defendant agrees to plead guilty to second-degree homicide, the prosecutor still obtains a conviction and, at the same time, the defendant may face a prison term of perhaps only twenty years instead of life. The bottom line is that plea bargaining conserves resources and it reduces the uncertainty of the trial process for the defendant, the defendant's attorney, and the prosecutor.

Plea bargaining has its critics. The major criticisms of plea bargaining are, first, that the practice reduces the severity of appropriate punishments and thereby injects leniency into the judicial process. The argument goes that if a person committed first-degree homicide, then that person should be tried and punished for first-degree homicide. Plea bargaining prevents this from happening. Another major criticism is that plea bargaining may actually induce an innocent person to plead guilty. If a defendant did not commit a crime but believes that he may be proved guilty of that crime and face a stiff penalty, that person may be inclined to plead guilty to a lesser charge to lessen the associated sanction. In any case, for better or for worse, plea bargaining is a widely used practice in the criminal justice process.

Levels of Investigation

Governmental law enforcement services are provided at four levels: local, county, state, and federal. The nature and structure of criminal investigations at each of these levels are discussed next.

Law Enforcement and Criminal Investigation at the Local Level

As of 1999, there were more than 13,000 local police departments nationwide (BJS, 2001c). There is tremendous variation in the size of municipal police departments, with the New York City Police Department being the largest with more than 39,000 officers and 771 police departments with just one sworn officer. Most local police departments are quite small; more than 7,000 agencies employ less than ten sworn officers. However, a large percentage of sworn officers work in large departments. Twenty-three percent of all officers in the country are employed by the sixteen agencies that serve a population of one million or more citizens.

Municipal police departments have three primary functions: service, order maintenance, and law enforcement (or crime control). These functions also comprise the major categories of work activities within the organizations. "Service" refers to the provision of assistance to the public with regard to noncrime-related matters. Examples of such activities include getting keys out of locked vehicles and assisting motorists. "Order maintenance" involves activities oriented around maintaining the public peace. Order maintenance activities may include crowd control and responding to animal complaints. "Crime control" activities involve intervening in situations in which a law has been violated and the identity of the perpetrator needs to be determined. The criminal investigative process can be placed within the crime control aspect of the police mission. Different departments place different emphases on these functions. Although some departments emphasize service, others emphasize order maintenance, whereas others give priority to law enforcement activities. Research has shown that the emphasis is based on the preferences of the chief, which reflects the preferences of most community residents (Wilson, 1968). As such, although police in urban communities may most likely emphasize law enforcement activities and respond to situations with a law enforcement preference (e.g., give citations to juveniles out after curfew), police in suburban communities may most likely emphasize service-related tasks and show a preference for service dispositions (e.g., take juveniles home who are out after curfew). Local control of police departments allows citizens to have more direct input into how policing is conducted in their community, but also leads to a fragmented system of policing.

On average, approximately ninety percent of sworn officers in police departments (with ten or more full-time employees) are assigned to field operations, which includes patrol and investigative units. Approximately ten to twenty percent of sworn officers in police departments are assigned as investigators or detectives.

Law Enforcement and Criminal Investigation at the County Level

In most areas of the country, police services in rural or unincorporated areas of a county are provided by sheriffs' departments. In some places, like Georgia, sheriffs' departments exist alongside county police departments. The sheriff's department operates the county jail and provides services to the court, and the police department provides law enforcement in the county. As of 1999, there were 3,081 sheriffs' departments in the country (BJS, 2001d). As with local police departments, there is considerable variation in the size of county sheriff's departments. The largest sheriff's department in the nation is the Los Angeles County Sheriff's Department, with more than 8,000 full-time sworn personnel. The Cook County, Illinois, Sheriff's Department is the second largest, with 5,300 full-time sworn personnel.

Along with performing public service, order maintenance, and law enforcement activities in the county, most sheriffs' departments are also responsible for functions related to jail and court operations. Although approximately one quarter of all sheriffs' departments operate one or more jails, nearly all have court-related responsibilities such as serving court papers (e.g., eviction notices, notices of foreclosed property, subpoenas), and providing services to the courts (e.g., transporting prisoners to and from jail, courthouse security, bailiff duty).

Overall, on average, approximately forty-two percent of sworn officers in sheriffs' departments are assigned to patrol operations, thirty-one percent to jail operations, twelve percent to investigations, and eleven percent to court-related duties. Depending on the characteristics of the county, there may be considerable variation among sheriffs' departments in personnel allocation. For example, Cook County, Illinois, is quite urban, leaving little land area under the jurisdiction of the Cook County Sheriff's Department. As a result, in the Cook County Sheriff's Department, only four percent of officers are assigned to patrol and only three percent are assigned to investigations. Most personnel are assigned to jail and court duties.

Law Enforcement and Criminal Investigation at the State Level

State law enforcement agencies were created primarily to assist local police and county sheriffs' departments in carrying out their law enforcement functions. A primary reason for this perceived need was the effects of the automobile. With the introduction of the automobile, criminals had increased mobility and could easily travel across city and county jurisdictional lines, causing problems for enforcement efforts. In addition, with automobiles came highways and a need for automobile regulation and enforcement.

Today, states may have one of two arrangements. First, as is the case in Michigan, New York, Maryland, and Indiana, among others, a state may have a single unified state police agency. Other states, such as California, Georgia, and Florida, have a highway patrol along with another law enforcement agency to provide more comprehensive law enforcement services.

State police agencies have numerous organizational units to provide the broad spectrum of law enforcement services in the state. For example, the Michigan State Police has divisions that include traffic (to enforce traffic laws on state and interstate highways), criminal investigation (to provide investigative assistance to local and county agencies, and to initiate investigations of drug offenses, white-collar crimes, and other types of crimes), special operations (to assist with civil disturbances, disasters, and other exceptional law enforcement situations), training (to set minimum training and employment standards, certifying all police officers in the state), and forensic sciences (to provide crime laboratory and related resources to local and county agencies).

Highway patrol agencies specialize in traffic control and enforcement on the state and interstate highways. Generally their enforcement jurisdiction and authority is quite limited, and their services relate specifically to traffic matters. The complementary agency to the highway patrol has responsibility for the remaining general law enforcement tasks including investigations, training, and forensic sciences. These complementary agencies have various names (e.g., Georgia Bureau of Investigation, Florida Department of Law Enforcement, California Department of Justice).

Law Enforcement and Criminal Investigation at the Federal Level

At the time of the ratification of the U.S. Constitution, there was not a need or a desire for an elaborate system of policing in the United States. The enforcement of the few federal laws that were in existence at the time was the responsibility of a small corps of federal agents and marshals. Only limited enforcement powers were given to the federal government including "to lay and collect taxes," "to regulate commerce," "to establish post offices and post roads," and "to provide for the punishment of counterfeiting" (U.S. Constitution, Article 1, Section 8). Federal law enforcement authority also came from the power of Congress to enact all "necessary and proper" laws, the federal judiciary to interpret the Fourteenth Amendment and associated matters, and the need of the federal government to enforce new laws and court decisions. Throughout the years, these powers, and the expanding interpretation of them, have provided the mandate for the creation and further development of law enforcement agencies at the federal level.

Today there is often much confusion about the authority and jurisdiction of federal law enforcement agencies. Basically, these agencies have authority to enforce federal laws. They cannot enforce violations of state law any more than state or local authorities can enforce federal law. Federal laws are enforced by federal agencies, violators of these laws are adjudicated in federal courts, and those convicted of federal crimes are referred to the federal correctional system. What makes this seemingly simple system often rather confusing is that some acts are a violation of both federal and state laws (e.g., bank robbery, kidnaping) so that local and federal law enforcement agencies can be involved simultaneously in the investigation of these offenses. In addition, federal, state, and local law enforcement authorities may operate joint investigations or task forces directed at certain types of crimes (e.g., terrorism, drug trafficking). In such instances, clear lines of jurisdiction and authority may not be readily apparent. Furthermore, federal law enforcement agencies may, in certain instances, provide assistance to local authorities in investigations. For example, the FBI may assist local police departments in analyzing forensic evidence or in providing psychological profiles. Again, with several agencies involved in investigations, the lines of jurisdiction may not always be clear.

Most federal law enforcement agencies are specialized, focusing on a narrow range of federal laws. As federal laws were created, there needed to be an agency responsible for their enforcement. Although Congress could have continually assigned more enforcement responsibilities to a particular agency, like the FBI, this would have gone against the fundamental opposition to a strong, all-powerful, national police force. In addition, with the multitude of federal laws today, it would be impractical to expect a single agency, or even a few agencies, to be able to carry out such a mandate. In addition, such an arrangement would undoubtedly raise serious questions concerning control and accountability. As a result, we have what amounts to a fragmented system of federal law enforcement.

A multitude of federal agencies have law enforcement responsibilities, although in most of these agencies the responsibilities are quite limited. For example, while one does not typically think of the U.S. Department of Agriculture as a law enforcement agency, its Office of Inspector General has responsibility for investigating allegations of various crimes including food stamp fraud. Although the U.S. Department of the Interior is not a law enforcement agency per se, its Office of Inspector General has important criminal investigative responsibilities relating to theft and bribery involving programs receiving federal funds, mail fraud, and embezzlement and theft from Native American tribal organizations, among others. In addition, other federal agencies have sizable criminal investigation or other law enforcement divisions that are responsible for enforcing the laws that pertain to that particular agency (Table 1–1).

In the wake of September 11, 2001, President Bush proposed, and Congress passed, a massive reorganization of federal law enforcement efforts to provide more effective coordination of agencies responsible for domestic security. The center of this effort is the creation of a Department of Homeland Security. As of 2003, the exact configuration of this department is yet to be finalized. It is expected that the department will consist of existing agencies, and parts of existing agencies, being moved into the new department. The department will likely employ more than 170,000 people. This effort is the largest undertaking at the federal level since the creation of the Department of Defense in 1947. Some of the agencies that will become part of the new Department of Homeland Security are located in the Department of Justice and the Department of the Treasury.

TABLE 1–1 Federal Agencies Employing 100 or More Full-Time Officers Authorized to Carry Firearms and Make Arrests, 2000

Agency	No. of Officers
Primary Federal Law Enforcement Agencies	
Immigration and Naturalization Service	17,654
Federal Bureau of Investigation	11,523
U.S. Customs Service	10,522
Drug Enforcement Administration	4,161
U.S. Secret Service	4,039
U.S. Marshals Service	2,735
Bureau of Alcohol, Tobacco, and Firearms	1,967
Other Federal Agencies	
Federal Bureau of Prisons	13,557
Administrative Office of the United States Courts	3,599
U.S. Postal Inspection Service	3,412
Internal Revenue Service, Criminal Investigation Division	2,726
National Park Service	2,188
U.S. Capital Police	1,199
U.S. Fish and Wildlife Service	888
General Services Administration, Federal Protective Service	803
Bureau of Diplomatic Security, Diplomatic Security Service	617
U.S. Forest Service, Law Enforcement and Investigations	586
U.S. Mint	354
Veterans Health Administration	342
Amtrak	316
Bureau of Indian Affairs	281
Defense Protective Service	264
Department of Energy, Transportation Safeguards Division	214
Bureau of Engraving and Printing	211
Bureau of Land Management	197
Tennessee Valley Authority	190
Environmental Protection Agency	179
Library of Congress	147
Food and Drug Administration	133
National Marine Fisheries Service	125
Bureau of Export Administration	100

Source: Bureau of Justice Statistics. (2001) *Federal Law Enforcement Officers, 2000.* Washington, DC: U.S. Department of Justice.

DEPARTMENT OF JUSTICE

The Department of Justice is responsible for much of the enforcement efforts of the federal government. The law enforcement agencies within the Department of Justice are the FBI, the INS, the DEA, and the USMS.

Federal Bureau of Investigation

The FBI is the major investigative agency in the Department of Justice. Today, the FBI has broad authority and jurisdiction. It is responsible for more than 200 categories of federal offenses. The investigative responsibilities of the FBI fall into several main areas. The first and, during the last few years, the most visible area is domestic terrorism. Second, the FBI is the lead counterintelligence agency and has been given the responsibility for investigating foreign espionage, international terrorism, weapons of mass destruction, and attacks on the country's critical infrastructure (e.g., banking system, transportation system, mail system). Third is background investigations. The FBI conducts background investigations on all persons who apply for positions with the Department of Energy, the Nuclear Regulatory Commission, the Department of Justice, and the FBI. The FBI also oversees background investigations for presidential appointees and U.S. court candidates. The fourth area of responsibility relates to investigations of violations of the Civil Rights Act of 1964 and the Equal Credit Opportunity Act. Also included are investigations into police brutality and housing discrimination. Fifth, the FBI has enforcement responsibility for organized crime and drug trafficking. Sixth, the FBI has authority to investigate certain violent crimes, including kidnaping, sexual exploitation of children, extortion, bank robbery, and product tampering. The final area of enforcement responsibility for the FBI is white-collar crime such as money laundering, bank fraud, health care fraud, and public corruption.

The FBI also provides numerous types of assistance and support to local police agencies. For example, the FBI crime laboratory is a full-service forensic science laboratory that provides scientific examinations free of charge to any law enforcement agency. (Given the existence of state-operated and funded crime laboratories, local agencies do not rely on the FBI crime laboratory for their forensic analysis needs.) Analysis capabilities include documents, fingerprints, DNA, explosives, firearms, tool marks, toxicology, and tire treads, among others. The laboratory also maintains databases on everything from types of shoe prints and lipstick to types of feathers and rope (FBI, 1999b).

The FBI also maintains and operates the National Crime Information Center (NCIC). Established in 1967, its purpose is to maintain a computerized filing system of criminal justice information (e.g., stolen vehicles, guns, missing persons) available through a computer network. On average, approximately 1.3 million inquiries are made every day into the system from the more than 100,000 terminals located in police agencies across the country (FBI, 1999b).

The FBI offers training assistance to law enforcement agencies through the FBI National Academy and other training programs. The curriculum of the National Academy includes college courses in law, management, forensic science, and health and fitness, along with other topics. Since 1935, more than 30,000 students have graduated from the academy.

The FBI also provides other types of operational assistance to federal, state, and local law enforcement agencies (see FBI [1999b] for a complete list of services provided). For instance, through the Child Abduction and Serial Killer Unit, agents provide psychological profiles of offenders and offer other investigative assistance. The Critical Incident Response Group (CIRG) provides training and operational support in crisis management and hostage negotiations situations. The FBI Hostage Rescue Team and Special Weapons and Tactics programs are part of the CIRG. Evidence response teams are located in each field office and specialize in organizing and conducting evidence recovery operations from crime scenes.

Immigration and Naturalization Service

The INS is responsible for enforcing laws regulating the admission of foreign-born persons (i.e., aliens) to the United States and for administering the naturalization of applicants for U.S. citizenship. Specifically, there are four dimensions to the mission of the agency. First, the Border Patrol is responsible for preventing illegal entry of aliens across 6,000 miles of U.S. border with Mexico and Canada. This unit within the agency is growing fast. The Border Patrol has hired close to 2,500 new employees a year for the past several years. This rate of growth is likely to accelerate even further as a result of federal legislation related to the terrorist acts of September 11, 2001. Second, inspections are conducted of all travelers entering (or seeking to enter) the United States by land, air, or sea to prevent and detect illegal entry into the country. This is also an area of increased hiring in recent years. Third, the agency is responsible for regulating permanent and temporary immigration to the United States. Finally, the INS is responsible for deporting those individuals determined to be in the country illegally.

Drug Enforcement Administration

The DEA was created in 1973 with the merger of the former Bureau of Narcotics and Dangerous Drugs, the Office of National Narcotics Intelligence, the Office for Drug Abuse Law Enforcement, and the drug investigation and drug intelligence operation of the U.S. Customs Service. The primary function of the DEA is to control the distribution and use of narcotics and other dangerous drugs. The legal basis for the DEA is the Controlled Substances Act, Title II of the Comprehensive Drug Abuse Prevention and Control Act of 1970. Specifically, one of the main tasks of the DEA is to investigate violations of controlled substances laws at the interstate and international levels. Although the INS or U.S. Customs Service may seize drugs and apprehend drug violators, the persons arrested are referred to the DEA for investigation. In addition, the DEA manages a national drug intelligence program that involves collecting, analyzing, and disseminating drug intelligence information to other law enforcement authorities; seizes assets derived from or used for drug trafficking; regulates licensed drug manufacturing and distribution firms to prevent illegal diversion of drugs from these sources; and assists foreign governments in operating programs designed to reduce the availability of illicit drugs.

United States Marshal Service

The USMS is the oldest federal law enforcement agency, established in 1789. The agency was created to support the operations of the federal courts. In the beginning, the marshals served subpoenas, summonses, writs, warrants, and other processes issued by the courts. They were responsible for courtroom and jail space, they made sure jurors were available, and they ensured that witnesses were present. The agency was also responsible for conducting the national census every ten years (until 1870). Other tasks assigned to the agency over the years have included registering enemy aliens in time of war, capturing fugitive slaves, protecting American borders against armed expeditions from foreign counties, and swapping spies with the former Soviet Union.

Today, the USMS's primary responsibilities are providing security and protection for the federal judiciary (including the investigation of threats against federal court personnel and the physical security of federal court buildings), transporting federal prisoners to and from court proceedings and federal correctional centers, protecting endangered federal witnesses through the Witness Protection Program (which involves long-term protection of endangered witnesses, including identity change and permanent relocation when necessary), maintaining custody and control of assets seized from criminal activities, and serving subpoenas and other documents on behalf of the federal government. In addition, perhaps the USMS is most well-known for its responsibility in pursuing and locating federal fugitives. According to the USMS, the agency is responsible for arresting fifty-five percent of all federal fugitives—more than all other federal agencies combined.

DEPARTMENT OF THE TREASURY

Agencies within the Department of the Treasury also provide significant law enforcement and criminal investigative services. With a few exceptions, treasury enforcement agencies investigate violations of laws relating to the revenue-producing functions of the federal government—in particular, the failure to pay taxes and tariffs. The primary law enforcement agencies of the Treasury Department are the U.S. Secret Service, the U.S. Customs Service, and the ATF.

United States Secret Service

The U.S. Secret Service has two primary responsibilities: presidential protection and combating counterfeiting. The agency (originally known as the Secret Service Division of the Internal Revenue Service [IRS])was established in 1865 for the purpose of combating counterfeiting of U.S. currency. Throughout the years, the counterfeiting investigative jurisdiction of the agency has grown to include the area of counterfeit securities, forgery, altering government checks and bonds, thefts and fraud relating to electronic funds transfer, financial access device fraud, identity fraud, and fraud involving federally insured financial institutions.

After the assassination of President William McKinley in 1901, Congress assigned responsibility for the protection of the president to the U.S. Secret Service. This is the task most closely associated with the U.S. Secret Service today. The U.S. Secret Service is now authorized to protect

- The president, the vice president, the president-elect, the vice president-elect, and their immediate families
- Former presidents and their spouses for ten years from the date the former president leaves office
- Children of former presidents until the age of sixteen
- Visiting heads of state, foreign dignitaries, and their spouses while visiting the United States
- Major presidential and vice presidential candidates and their spouses within 120 days of a presidential election (Note: Other agencies such as the U.S. Customs Service and the USMS may provide protection of other presidential and vice presidential candidates during an election year.)

An important component of the U.S. Secret Service is the Uniformed Division. This unit is responsible for the protection of the White House complex (surveillance, entry control) along with the Treasury building; the residence of the vice president in Washington, DC; and foreign diplomatic missions in the Washington, DC, area and throughout the United States and its territories. The U.S. Secret Service currently employs more than 4,000 agents who are located in 125 offices throughout the United States and abroad.

United States Customs Service

The U.S. Customs Service has responsibility for collecting duties, excise taxes, and fees on imported or exported merchandise; seizing contraband (such as narcotics, tainted food, diseased plant products, and pirated merchandise); processing persons, baggage, cargo, and mail entering the United States; and enforcing regulations of other federal government agencies (such as the Department of Commerce) relating to international trade. Customs officers are located at every international airport, seaport, and land border crossing to interdict goods illegally entering the United States. Often customs officers work alongside INS agents. Although the INS is mostly concerned with *who* is entering the country, the U.S. Customs Service is mostly concerned with *what* is entering the country. As an example of efforts at controlling what enters the country, the U.S. Customs Service has recently received considerable criticism, as reported in the media, for its use of low-power X-ray machines located in several airports to search travelers. With the machine, inspectors can see through clothing to view items that could be detected only through a strip or body cavity search. Customs officials report that this device is to be used in place of many strip searches and therefore results in less intrusion (see Chapter 14).

Bureau of Alcohol, Tobacco, and Firearms

As its name suggests, the ATF enforces laws and regulations relating to alcohol, tobacco products, and firearms, as well as explosives and arson. The agency was created in 1862 as a unit of the IRS. It became famous when it was given enforcement responsibility for the Volstead Act (Prohibition) in 1919. Today, the ATF regulates the operations of domestic manufacturers, importers, and wholesalers of alcoholic beverages. The goal is to collect taxes on alcoholic beverages and to prevent tax fraud and smuggling in the alcoholic beverage marketplace. Enforcement activities relating to tobacco also are primarily to ensure the collection of tobacco excise taxes and to regulate the manufacture and export of tobacco products. The ATF has primary responsibility for enforcing federal firearms laws. Wherever illegal firearms are suspected, the ATF has jurisdictional authority. The ATF issues firearms licenses and conducts firearm licensee (those who sell firearms) qualification compliance inspections. The agency also conducts investigations to identify and apprehend individuals who illegally purchase firearms. Many of the ATF's activities are focused on the criminal use of explosives and arson. As such, the ATF plays a critical role in the investigation of arson and bombing incidents in the United States, and often serves as a resource to local agencies in investigating explosive incidents and arson schemes.

INTERNATIONAL POLICE ORGANIZATION

INTERPOL is not an agency of the U.S. government nor is it technically a law enforcement agency. It is worthwhile to mention here, however, because it has an important and close relationship with federal law enforcement agencies. INTERPOL, headquartered in Lyons, France, is an organization that has as its primary function the collection, analysis, and dissemination of criminal intelligence information on a worldwide basis. The agency facilitates communication between agencies in different countries and organizes meetings for investigators on specific cases. INTERPOL does not conduct investigations on its own initiative or without a request for assistance from a law enforcement agency of a member nation (Imhoff and Cutler, 1998). The agency is primarily concerned with terrorism, organized crime, economic and financial crime, and international drug trafficking. The agency maintains and operates various databases, including information on people linked to international crime, records of counterfeit currency seizures, theft of works of art, and fingerprints and photographs of people implicated in international crimes. These databases are designed to provide information to law enforcement agencies on people throughout the world. The point of contact for INTERPOL in the United States is the U.S. National Central Bureau of INTERPOL, located under the control and direction of the U.S. Departments of Justice and Treasury. This agency serves as the recipient of all investigative requests made by foreign law enforcement agencies as well as investigative requests to foreign law enforcement agencies.

Questions for Discussion and Review

1. What is the criminal investigation process and what is the role of evidence in the process?

2. What are the three major problems associated with evidence available in criminal investigations?

3. What does it mean to "solve" a crime? What subtasks have to be accomplished before a crime can be considered solved?

4. What are the two major types of investigations? What is the most significant way in which they differ?

5. How does information theory portray the criminal investigative process?

6. Why is luck and accident a common ingredient in criminal investigations?

7. What is the difference between inductive and deductive reasoning?

8. What are the most important qualities for an investigator to possess? Why?

9. Why are more crimes not solved by the police?

10. How is the criminal justice process like a funnel?

11. What are the primary differences between the state police and the highway patrol?

12. What are the primary responsibilities of each of the agencies within the U.S. Department of Justice? The U.S. Department of the Treasury?

13. What is the role of INTERPOL?

Related Internet Sites

www.crimescene.com

This site is designed to be a fun and educational site where you can view evidence of mock crimes and assemble the clues necessary to solve them.

www.usdoj.gov/dojorg.htm

This link gets you to the organizational chart of the U.S. Department of Justice. Click on an agency and you will be taken to that agency's web page. Agency web sites provide an excellent source of information about the agency, its operations, and employment opportunities.

www.ustreas.gov/bureaus/index.html

This link is similar to the Department of Justice link but it is for the agencies located in the U.S. Department of the Treasury.

www.whitehouse.gov/homeland

This site provides information on the Department of Homeland Security.

Answers to Logic Problems

1. The bank robber was wearing a blue hat. Say Jake is the liar and Joe is the truth teller. This means that Jake actually did say that the robber was wearing a red hat. However, whatever Jake says is false, so the robber's hat was blue. Now let's say that Joe is the liar and Jake is the truth teller. This means that Jake really said that the robber was wearing a blue hat. Because Jake always tells the truth, the robber's hat was indeed blue. The answer is blue, either way.

2. Card A = king of hearts, card B = queen of hearts, card C = queen of spades.

THE HISTORY OF CRIMINAL INVESTIGATION

OBJECTIVES

After reading this chapter you will be able to

- Summarize the Lindbergh baby kidnaping investigation

- Discuss the role of informers, thief-takers, and thief-makers in England in the 1700s and 1800s

- Discuss the forces that prompted the development of the London Metropolitan Police Department in the early 1800s

- Explain how the designers of the detective position accounted for the problems associated with the earlier systems of informers, thief-takers, and thief-makers

- Describe the nature of policing and criminal investigation during the political, reform, and community problem-solving eras of policing

- Discuss the drawbacks and problems with photography, Bertillonage, and fingerprints as methods of identification

- Discuss the advantages of fingerprints as a method of identification over photographs and Bertillonage

- Discuss the significance of *Brown* v. *Mississippi* to the tactics used in

criminal investigations—interrogations in particular

- Discuss the nature of the dragnet and the third degree as investigative tactics

- Discuss the creation and development of the FBI, and the contributions and role of J. Edgar Hoover in the process

- Discuss the role and importance of private detectives in the mid to early 1900s in America

- Discuss why gangsters, communists, and kidnaping became the dominant themes of the FBI in the 1920s and 1930s

- Discuss the meaning and goals of community policing

- Discuss the investigative strategies that are consistent with the ideals of community policing

- Discuss several recent high-profile successful and unsuccessful investigations of the FBI

IMPORTANT TERMS

Informers and
parliamentary reward

Thief-takers

Thief-makers

London Metropolitan
Police Department

Political era of policing

Reform era of policing

Community problem-
solving era of policing

Photography as a method
of identification

Rogues gallery

Bertillonage

Dragnet

The third degree

Bureau of
Investigation/FBI

Palmer raids

Pinkerton's Private
Detective Agency

Police professionalism

Community policing

Citizens as coproducers of
crime prevention

INTRODUCTION

The date was March 1, 1932. The place was Hopewell, New Jersey, and the home of Charles Lindbergh, the famed aviator who was the first man to fly over the Atlantic Ocean alone in a single-engine plane. Lindbergh was an American hero, a colonel in the U.S. Army Air Corps (the forerunner of the U.S. Air Force), and a wealthy aviation consultant. But on March 1, 1932, he was the father of a missing baby. The baby was taken from his crib between 8 PM, when his nursemaid, Betty Gow, last checked on him, and 10 PM, when she went to check on him again but discovered him missing. The baby's name was Charles A. Lindbergh, Jr., and he was just twenty months old.

The Hopewell Police and the New Jersey State Police were immediately notified. H. Norman Schwarzkopf, the chief of the New Jersey State Police (and the father of H. Norman Schwarzkopf, Jr., the commander of 1991 Desert Storm), took control of the investigation. Lindbergh reported to investigators that he and his wife were in the house between 8 PM and 10 PM, but the only memorable event was a "banging" noise at about 9 PM, and it seemed to come from the kitchen area. They thought something fell off a countertop or chair. At the time, it seemed of little significance. On checking the scene, footprints were discovered in the mud below the second-story window of the baby's bedroom but the police did not bother to measure, photograph, or take plaster casts of them. In the same area were two deep impressions in the dirt, and next to these impressions lay a carpenter's chisel. Approximately 100 yards from the residence the police found a wooden ladder that was in three separate sections. It was believed that the deep impressions came from the legs of the ladder, and that the ladder was used to gain entry into the second-story bedroom. On searching the baby's bedroom, an envelope was discovered on the window sill. Inside the envelope was a handwritten note that read:

> Have 50000$ redy with 25000$ in 20$ bills 15000$ in 10$ bills and 10000$ in 5$ bills. After 2–4 days we will inform you were to deliver the Mony. We warn you for making anyding public or for notify the polise the child is in gute care. Indication for all letters are signature and 3 holes.

On the bottom corner of the letter there was a design that consisted of two interconnected circles and three small holes.

One week after the kidnaping, an individual by the name of John F. Condon placed an open letter to the kidnapers in the *Bronx Home News* newspaper. The letter stated that he would be willing to serve as the go-between for the kidnapers and Lindbergh. The kidnapers agreed and so did Lindbergh. As instructed by the kidnapers, Condon then placed an ad in the *New York American* to notify the kidnapers that the money was ready to be delivered. "Mony is redy" was the message. On March 12, Condon received written instructions delivered by a cab driver to meet the kidnapers in a particular cemetery to deliver the money. Condon followed the directions and met with the supposed kidnaper at the cemetery. Condon told the man that he could not give him the money until he saw the baby. Condon later told the police that the man told him that his name was "John," and that he spoke with a German accent. On March 14, 1932, a second ransom letter was received and it increased the ransom by $20,000. Subsequent to the new ransom demand, the baby's pajamas were received by Condon in the mail. On April 2, 1932, "John" and Condon met again at another cemetery to exchange the money for the child. This time Condon had the money; however, under the direction of federal treasury agents, the serial numbers of the bills had been recorded. At the meeting, Condon gave the money to "John," was told that the baby was on a boat named "Nelly," and was given instructions on how to find the boat. The boat was located but there was no baby.

The house of Mr. and Mrs. Charles Lindbergh from which their child was kidnaped.

On May 12, 1932, the body of an infant was found four miles from the Lindbergh home. It was believed to be the Lindbergh baby. The body was in an advanced state of decomposition. The autopsy revealed that the baby died as a result of a blow to the head and that death had occurred at about the time the baby was reported missing. Investigators suspected that the baby may have been murdered in his room before he was taken or that he may have been dropped by the kidnaper as he was being carried down the ladder (which might have also explained the noise heard by the Lindberghs the evening of the crime). Meanwhile, the ladder was the focal point of interest and was analyzed by several wood experts. These experts were able to determine the kind of wood used to construct the ladder and the possible sources of the wood, but this information did not lead to any suspects.

Investigators believed that an employee at the house might have been responsible for the kidnaping because of the timing of the crime: The Lindberghs normally would not have been at the house during the week that the baby was taken but they decided to stay an extra day because the baby was not feeling well. With no other good leads, investigators focused their attention on Violet Sharpe, age twenty-eight, who was a maid at the residence. She did not have a solid alibi for the evening the baby disappeared and, according to the police, she appeared anxious when she was interviewed by them. With police pressure mounting, Sharpe committed suicide by drinking silver polish. The police later determined that she had been deceptive in answering their questions because on the night of the kidnaping she was on a date with another man even though she was engaged to be married to the butler who worked at the Lindbergh estate. Condon was also considered a possible suspect, but after intense scrutiny he was determined not to be responsible either. The police were beginning to be criticized for their handling of the investigation and their lack of progress in solving the most serious crime of the century. At this time, along with the New Jersey State Police and federal treasury agents, the FBI got involved as a result of Congress passing the "Lindbergh Law," which made kidnaping a federal offense and an FBI enforcement responsibility (as discussed later in this chapter, the FBI later made much of its role in the eventual successful apprehension of the suspected perpetrator, even though by most accounts, the FBI actually had little to do with solving the crime).

In mid 1934, ransom bills with the recorded serial numbers began to appear at various establishments in the New York and New Jersey area. The police recorded the locations in which the bills were being used but this strategy proved to be of little help. The investigation was still going nowhere. On September 15, 1934, the police got the break they were hoping for: An individual, described as speaking with an German accent, drove into a gasoline service station and proceeded to pay for his $.98 worth of gas with a $10 bill. The gas station manager, Walter Lyle, thought this was rather strange and alertly wrote on the $10 bill the license plate number of the vehicle driven by the man. Lyle then contacted the police. The police determined that the $10 bill was one of the ransom bills. Investigators checked the license plate number and learned that it was for a blue 1930 four-door Dodge that was registered to Richard

Hauptmann, a thirty-five-year-old German-born carpenter. The police staked out his apartment. When the police stopped and searched him, another ransom bill was discovered in his wallet. In his garage, the police found $14,000 of ransom money. On searching his home, police discovered a wooden rafter missing from the attic. The rafters were determined to be made from the same type of wood as the ladder, and the missing rafter appeared to be part of the ladder. With this evidence, Richard Hauptmann was arrested and charged with the kidnaping and murder of Charles A. Lindbergh, Jr.

During the trial, which was referred to at the time as the "trial of the century," the prosecution built their case on five critical pieces of evidence: (1) the money found in Hauptmann's garage was, as determined by the recorded serial numbers, part of the ransom money paid by Lindbergh; (2) the wood missing from the attic matched the wood in the ladder; (3) the handwriting on the ransom notes matched Hauptmann's handwriting; (4) witnesses reported seeing Hauptmann near the Lindbergh estate prior to March 1, 1932, the night of the kidnaping; and (5) Condon identified Hauptmann as "John," the person he met in the cemeteries. The fact that Hauptmann quit his job within days of when the ransom money was paid and that Condon's phone number was found written on a closet wall in Hauptmann's kitchen were also introduced at the trial.

The defense tried to counter several of these evidentiary items. The money found in Hauptmann's garage was claimed to have been given to him by a business associate before he left for Germany in 1933 (this man died before the discovery of the money by the police). It was claimed that because this individual owed Hauptmann money, Hauptmann decided to spend some of it. In addition, the defense questioned the handwriting match and the eyewitness identification. It was argued that the wood missing from Hauptmann's attic and used in the ladder was planted by the police. After twenty-nine court sessions, testimony from 162 witnesses, and the introduction of 381 exhibits, the case was given to the jury for deliberation on February 13, 1935. After eleven and one-half hours, the jury returned a verdict of guilty. Richard Hauptmann was sentenced to death and was executed April 3, 1936, in New Jersey's electric chair (Fisher, 1994; Waller, 1961).

The Importance of History in Understanding the Present and the Future

An understanding of history, the history of criminal investigations in particular, is important for at least three reasons. First, history provides a context in which to place modern criminal investigation and thus allows for an appreciation of how much or how little things have changed over time. Second, as the adage goes, those who do not remember the past are condemned to repeat it. To move forward, one must understand from where one has come. Accordingly, an understanding of history may provide insight into the previous attempts and new methods of solving persistent problems. And third, if history is cyclical, if it repeats itself, then we may be able to predict the future by knowing the past. It is with these understandings that attention is turned to the history of criminal investigations.

The Evolution of the Investigative Task: English Developments

American policing has its roots in English policing systems. As English society became more complex, and as traditional mechanisms (e.g., family, community) for controlling individuals' behaviors began to lose their effectiveness over time, there was a need for an increasingly sophisticated system of social control. When society was relatively simple, so too was the system of policing. Policing was first an individual responsibility, then a responsibility of the group. With the Frankpledge Model of 1100 AD, all males older than the age of twelve years were designated as responsible for the protection of the group. Then, the Parish Constable System of the 1200s required a constable to organize and supervise watchmen, who would protect members of the town or village. Variations of the watchmen arrangement lasted until formal police departments were created in the early 1800s.

Informers and Parliamentary Reward

A system of parliamentary reward operated during the 1700s and early 1800s. With this system, a reward was offered by the government to anyone who brought criminals to justice, or simply provided information that led to the apprehension of criminals. The more serious the crime, the larger the reward. Although this system may sound like a historical equivalent of a modern-day tip line (see Chapter 10), there were major differences, one of which was the legal context in which parliamentary reward operated. During the time of parliamentary reward, more than 200 offenses were punishable by death. These offenses included theft, vagrancy, forgery, and even cutting down a tree without permission. The methods of execution included hanging, burning at the stake, and drawing and quartering. Many referred to the laws of the time as the *bloody code*. Most people, however, did not support the legal system nor did they believe that the legal code was just. As a result, victims were often unlikely to pursue charges, witnesses often refused to testify, and juries were often not willing to convict. There was public sympathy for petty criminals who faced the possibility of execution (Klockars, 1985). The problem was that by benefiting from providing information that would lead to the apprehension of petty criminals, informers were viewed with the same contempt as the legal system. Informers were not the answer, they were part of the problem.

Thief-Takers

In the early 1800s, *thief-takers* appeared. A thief-taker was a private citizen who was hired by a victim to recover stolen property or to apprehend the criminal. The fee that the thief-taker charged was most often based on the value of the property recovered, and thief-takers only received compensation when the property was returned. The most desirable crimes to investigate, therefore, were ones that involved considerable property and ones for which the property was easily recovered. As such, thief-takers were not likely to spend much time on crimes for which the property was not likely to be recovered or on thefts that involved small amounts of property (Klockars, 1985). In essence, the thief-takers most often worked on behalf of the rich, not the poor. In addition to this "selective attention" problem, there was another even more serious problem with thief-takers: Thief-takers often worked in cooperation with thieves. Some thief-takers even employed thieves (Klockars, 1985). No question, the thief-taker arrangement was extraordinarily corrupt. The thief would steal from the victim, the victim would hire a thief-taker, the thief would sell the property to the thief-taker, and the thief-taker would then "sell" the property back to the victim. Everyone prospered at the victim's expense.

Agent Provocateur and Thief-Makers

Along with thief-takers there were thief-makers. A *thief-maker* was an individual who tricked another person into committing a crime and then would turn that person in for the parliamentary reward. Thief-makers were often thief-takers who resorted to deception, seduction, trickery, and entrapment to apprehend criminals and receive the monetary rewards (Klockars, 1985). These people essentially created criminals for their personal benefit. Not surprisingly, the methods used by these individuals were questioned and frequently viewed as outrageous.

London Metropolitan Police Department

With the 1800s came the Industrial Revolution and the dramatic and rapid increase in the population of cities, where people lived to be in close proximity to where they worked. Factory production was the new basis of the economy. With the Industrial Revolution also came an increase in wealth among some people and poverty among others. "Urban" problems were born—sanitation and health issues, ethnic conflict, and crime. With all the changes came political pressure for the government to institute a more formal, more sophisticated, and more effective system of property protection. It was in this context that in 1829 the London Metropolitan Police Department was established.

Introduced early in the London Metropolitan Police Department was the concept of the "plain clothes police officer"—a detective to some, a police spy to others. In designing the job of detective, tremendous public resistance had to be overcome. The resistance was caused, in large part, because of the problems associated with earlier investigative arrangements—the problems associated with parliamentary reward, thief-takers, and thief-makers. To overcome these obstacles, and to allow detectives to receive the support of the public, certain features were incorporated into the design of the detective position.

First, to address the problems of parliamentary reward (when petty criminals faced unjust punishment because of the actions of informers), detectives were linked to the crime of murder. There was no public sympathy for murderers. The "architects" of the detective position capitalized on stories of murder and offered "detectives" as a way to combat this horrific crime. In addition, detectives were to play a dual role: Not only were they to help bring punishment to the worst of criminals, they were also supposed to save the innocent from the worst of punishments (Klockers, 1985). One can see very clearly the direct association between detectives and murder in early detective fiction (e.g., Poe's *Murders in the Rue Morgue*, Doyle's *A Study in Scarlet*), and this likely helped sell the idea of the police detective.

Second, to address the problems associated with the thief-taker arrangement, the most significant of which was that thief-takers only worked on the behalf of the rich, detectives were to be given a salary (Klockers, 1985). If detectives were given a salary, it was argued, they could work on behalf of the rich and the poor alike. Ideally, they could investigate crimes for which the property loss was small. In addition, given the profitability of working on crimes for a fee in a private arrangement, detectives were to be paid more than police officers.

Third, to address the problems associated with thief-makers, particularly the practice of thief-makers tricking people into committing crimes for the thief-maker's benefit, detectives were made "reactive" and were assigned "cases" (Klockars, 1985). After crimes occurred, detectives were given the responsibility for investigating them. Because detectives were to become involved in investigations only after the crimes had already occurred, there was limited opportunity for thief-maker trickery. Detectives were to be evaluated in terms of their success in solving crimes. As a result, detectives were given more control over how they were to spend their working time and more discretion in determining how to investigate the cases they were assigned. These features—being responsible for the most serious of crimes, receiving a salary, and being reactive—eventually neutralized public resentment toward detectives.

The Evolution of the Investigative Task: American Developments

At the time of the ratification of the U.S. Constitution, there were few federal laws and, accordingly, the policing function was almost exclusively a responsibility of local government. Policing communities was quite informal, and consisted most often of volunteers assigned to the "watch" who would guard the village or town at night and later during the day. Local control of the police function was a desirable feature of American policing because, ideally, it allowed residents (and politicians) to influence more easily how policing was conducted in their community. The desire for local control also helped explain why the creators of the Constitution were resistant to the idea of an all-powerful national police force.

The First Police Departments and Detectives

It was not until the mid 1800s that formal municipal police departments were created. These institutions were primarily located in the large and rapidly growing cities of the eastern United States (e.g., Boston, Philadelphia, New York). The Industrial Revolution created similar problems in America as in England. Of particular significance were the violent labor protests and the rioting that stemmed from clashes between immigrants and native-born Americans (Conti, 1977). Municipal police detectives, those with primary responsibility for criminal identification and apprehension, did not appear until later in the 1800s, and this development occurred largely in response to public concern about the increasing amount of crime. For example, in most years of the early to mid 1800s, there were no homicides recorded in Suffolk County (Boston), Massachusetts. Between 1860 and 1869, however, seventy homicides occurred. During the 1870s, 107 homicides were reported (Lane, 1967).

The mid 1800s to the early 1900s has been characterized as the political era of policing (Kelling and Moore, 1988). As the name suggests, policing at the time was all about politics; the police organization was an arm of the political machine. Politicians, particularly mayors and ward politicians, controlled virtually every aspect of policing including who got hired, what work officers performed, and who got fired. Besides political connections, there were few selection standards. There were tremendous opportunities for corruption. Police supervisors were few, and their influence over beat officers was minimal because there was no mechanism to provide for supervision. There was little ability for citizens to summon the police when needed because there was no means of communication. Officers patrolled on foot. The police made few arrests. According to Lane (1967), more than half of all arrests made by the police during this time were for public drunkenness. This was an offense that beat cops could easily discover and no investigation was necessary. The police simply did not have the capability to respond to and investigate crimes. When an arrest was made, it was usually as a last resort. Making an arrest in the late 1800s usually involved a lot of work; officers would literally have to "run 'em in" to the police station or, when arresting a drunk, the officer would have to put the person in a wheelbarrow and wheel him in to the station (Haller, 1976). "Curbside justice" with a hickory baton was often perceived as an easier and more effective alternative by officers.

The political era of policing did not provide a large role for police detectives. Like the beat cops, detectives had limited capabilities in responding to criminal incidents and investigating crimes. During the late 1800s, Boston's politicians actually disbanded the police department's detective bureau because their contributions were viewed as minimal (Lane, 1967). Although important qualities for beat cops were size and fighting ability, the most important quality for detectives was a familiarity with criminals and their tactics. Many detectives were selected from the ranks of prison guards, and some were reformed criminals (Lane, 1967). With this specialized knowledge, detectives received more pay than beat cops. Detectives also received extra compensation through "witness fees," compensation received for providing testimony in court. Detective work was a clandestine activity. Detectives were often considered to be members of a secret service (Kuykendall, 1986). Detectives depended heavily on criminals for information to solve crimes. Detectives often worked in an "undercover" capacity to collect this information. Detectives never wore uniforms. Rather, they often wore disguises, even in court, to protect their identities. Sometimes detectives submitted their court testimony in writing so as not to reveal their identity (Kuykendall, 1986).

It was at about this time that identification systems began to be developed and applied to criminal investigations. The first technology that was used for this purpose was photography. By 1858, the New York City Police Department had on file 450 photographs of known crim-

New York City police officers pose in front of the 20th Precinct station in 1880.

inals. This collection of photographs was known as a *rogues gallery* (Dilworth, 1977). Although photographs were commonly used in "wanted posters" and assisted in the apprehension of criminals, photographs were extremely limited in their usefulness because criminals could easily alter their appearance either deliberately or simply through the passage of time. Of course, to be useful, authorities needed to have a photograph of the wanted person.

The most famous identification system of the time was the one developed by Alphonse Bertillon, a French criminologist who lived from 1853 to 1914. His system was known as Bertillonage and it was considered a major improvement over the use of photographs. The premise of the system was that the bone structure of an adult did not change over the course of a lifetime. Bertillon identified eleven measurements that could be taken, and these measurements, it was suggested, could be used to identify people and to differentiate one person from another. The measurements consisted of the following: the length and width of the head, the length of the left middle and little fingers, the length of the left foot, the length of the left forearm, the length of the right ear, the individual's height, the length of the outstretched arms, the measurements of the person's trunk, and notation of other descriptive information (e.g., eye color, hair color, nose shape, defining marks) (Muller, 1889). Bertillon estimated that the probability of two persons having the same eleven measurements was more than four million to one (Rhodes, 1968). Instruments and instructions were developed by Bertillon to make the measurement process as precise as possible. In addition, an elaborate filing system was developed to organize the classification of individuals from whom measurements were taken. Because it was difficult for the police to take measurements of criminals on the street, Bertillon also developed a scaled-down version of his system. Although the technique enjoyed initial success in confirming the identity of suspected and known criminals, and was used by police departments in many countries, by the early 1900s the deficiencies of the system were obvious. It was simply too cumbersome, error prone, and limited in its applicability to be viable as an identification strategy.

Wanted posters, such as this one that related to the assassination of President Lincoln, were one of the few investigative tools of the 1800s.

Along with the use of these identification methods, detectives at the time also used various "investigative" tactics to deal with crime and criminals. One common strategy was the dragnet roundup of suspects. When informed of a crime, the police would find and arrest all suspicious persons and would keep these people in custody until it could be determined that they did not commit the crime. In essence, the police would often resort to "rounding up the usual suspects."

Another commonly used investigative tactic at the time was *the third degree*, which was also known as *shellacking, messaging, breaking the news*, or *giving him the works* (Lavine, 1930). The origin of the expression "the third degree" is not clear, although some have speculated that the first degree was the arrest, the second degree was being transported to the police station, and the third degree was the interrogation (Kuykendall, 1986; Skolnick and Fyfe, 1993). A New York police reporter, Emanual Lavine, provided the following account of the administration of the third degree:

> The prisoner is tied to an armchair to prevent him from falling out and injuring himself. When he is safely and comfortably seated, he is struck on the side of the head with a piece of rubber hose or a piece of an automobile tire cut to a convenient size. The blows are not hard enough to produce unconsciousness but sufficiently vigorous to cause excruciating pain. The success of the treatment depends on the regularity of the blows. They are struck with a clock-like precision at regular intervals of about thirty seconds. . . . By using a rubber hose or tire no outward evidence of the punishment is discernible after a few hours, for the blows leave a red welt which quickly disappears. The point of contact, however, remains extremely sensitive for months (Lavine, 1930; pp. 51–52).

According to Haller (1976), the rubber hose was often known as *the gold fish* and the place where the beatings occurred was *the gold fish room*. Other common methods of administering the third degree involved placing a suspect in a *sweat box* for hours or days under constant questioning (Kuykendall, 1986), drilling teeth, burning with lit cigars or cigarettes, and beating with blackjacks or batons (Lavine, 1930). Many accounts suggest that the use of the third degree to obtain confessions was commonplace into the 1930s and beyond (Kuykendall, 1986). However, it is important to note that in 1936 the U.S. Supreme Court ruled in *Brown* v. *Mississippi* that prolonged beatings used to extract confessions were no longer a legally acceptable police practice. After the physical abuse of suspects abated, psychological coercion persisted, and in many situations this coercion has been approved by the courts (see Chapter 5).

Sheriff, State Police, U.S. Marshal, and the Bureau of Investigation

While police departments were being developed in the major cities in the eastern portion of the country, other areas were most likely to be served by sheriffs and marshals. In the western portion of the country, U.S. marshals were often the sole police power (Ball, 1978).

Marshals often employed deputies who also served as sheriffs, deputy sheriffs, or constables. With the appearance of automobiles and in the face of corrupt and ineffective municipal police agencies and sheriffs' departments, state police agencies were created to assist. In 1905, Pennsylvania created the first state police agency. It was designed to provide a police presence throughout the state, to assist the local police, and to provide police services in less populated, rural areas of the state (Conti, 1977).

Also of significance at this time was the development of the Bureau of Investigation, to be later known as the FBI. President Theodore Roosevelt initially asked the U.S. Congress to create a federal detective force in 1907. Congress opposed President Roosevelt's idea on the official grounds of the long-cited public disdain for an all-powerful federal law enforcement agency. However, unofficially, it was significant that in 1906 two members of Congress had been prosecuted for fraud, the investigation of which was conducted by the Justice Department using agents from the Department of the Treasury. As a result, many members of Congress were concerned about giving the executive branch of government more investigative power (power perhaps to initiate more investigations of congressmen). Along with denying President Roosevelt's request, Congress passed legislation that prohibited the Justice Department from using investigators from other federal agencies. Not to be stopped by Congress, in 1908 President Roosevelt created a *Bureau of Investigation* by executive order and directed Attorney General Charles Bonaparte to develop the agency within the Department of Justice. Twenty permanent and eighteen temporary investigators were hired.

With the turmoil surrounding its creation, it is not surprising that during the first years of its operation (1910s) the Bureau of Investigation was entrenched in scandal. However, at the same time, it was slowly becoming accepted as a law enforcement agency and was assigned law enforcement responsibilities. For example, in 1910 Congress passed the Mann Act, which prohibited the transportation of women across state lines for immoral purposes. Responsibility for the enforcement of the law was given to the Bureau of Investigation. Other statutes followed, prohibiting the transportation of stolen goods, vehicles, and obscene materials.

In 1916, with 300 agents, and in the face of war in Europe, the Bureau was given power to conduct counterintelligence and antiradical investigations. In 1919, the country experienced a series of bombings with targets ranging from police departments to banks (and including the residence of Attorney General A. Mitchell Palmer). These actions were believed to be the responsibility of communists and others who were "un-American." The bombings and their aftermath became known as the *Red Scare*. In response to the bombings, Attorney General Palmer established the General Intelligence Division (GID) within the Justice Department to increase significantly the ability to store information on radicals and those suspected of being sympathetic to radicals. An individual by the name of John Edgar Hoover was named the head of the GID. In 1920, using information from the GID, Attorney General Palmer authorized a series of raids (to be known as the *Palmer raids*) in thirty-three cities across the country that resulted in more than 5,000 arrests of people believed to be un-American or communists. The plan was to then deport the individuals who were arrested. The problem was that most of the people arrested were not radicals at all. The courts ordered many of those arrested to be released (Murray, 1955).

Private Detectives

In the mid 1800s and early 1900s, private detectives also played an important role in criminal investigations. In addition, many corporations (e.g., railroads, iron and coal mines) hired their own police forces for the primary purpose of dealing with their labor strikes (Conti, 1977). With regard to private detective agencies, the most prominent was Pinkerton's agency. Allen Pinkerton was a barrel maker turned Chicago deputy sheriff, turned Chicago detective. In 1850 he quit his job in the Chicago Police Department and established his own private detective agency. At first, most of the work of the agency involved protecting several midwestern railroads and railroad bridges from sabotage of the confederates as well as from striking laborers. Pinkerton and his associates' preferred method of operation was to mingle with known rebels and criminals in taverns, hotels, and brothels to learn of their plans. In 1861, Pinkerton learned of a plan to assassinate then president-elect Lincoln and was able to persuade Lincoln to alter his travel plans to disrupt the plot. Pinkerton was also hired to spy on the confederacy, to collect information on their strengths and weaknesses, and to apprehend enemy spies. Also at this time, the Justice Department, having no investigators of its own, used agents from the Pinkerton agency. Pinkerton had investigative and operational advantages over governmental agents; in particular, the agency operated without concern for cumbersome political jurisdictional lines. This capability made Pinkerton ideal for pursuing mobile criminals such as train robbers.

Pinkerton also had a well-developed system of internal communication, record keeping, and files on criminals. Police departments often relied on this information to learn what criminals were working in their area. By the turn of the century, the agency had a system in place to share information with the investigative services of foreign nations: Pinkerton operated on a global scale.

The Reform Era

With the problems of the political era policing system well noted, there were efforts made to reform the police; namely, to get the police out from the control of politicians. To do so required a new way of thinking about policing. This effort took the form of *police professionalism*. Forward-thinking police leaders such as O.W. Wilson, August Vollmer, and J. Edgar Hoover advocated a new philosophy and system of policing. This new way of thinking about policing was in direct reaction to the ugly politics of before. According to Kelling and Moore (1988), the system of policing from the early 1900s to the 1960s was known as the *reform era*.

The reform era was all about police professionalism and antipolitics. The police presented themselves as experts who had the specialized knowledge and capabilities to control crime. It was argued that if the police were able to distance themselves from citizens and politicians (i.e., professional autonomy) they would be the most efficient and effective. Crime control and criminal apprehension were viewed as the primary functions of the police. The new technology of the time contributed to and supported the ideals of the new way of thinking about policing. Specifically, the police patrol car allowed the police to increase their mobility and to respond quickly to crime scenes, random motorized patrol was viewed as a means of deterring criminals, and the patrol car provided separation between police officers and citizens. The two-way radio allowed police supervisors to be in constant communication with and to have constant supervision over beat officers. The two-way radio also allowed patrol officers to be directed to places where they were needed. The telephone turned police departments into twenty-four-hour-a-day agencies that were just a phone call away. With the telephone, citizens could easily summons the police when needed.

During the reform era, detectives became an important tool in police departments' efforts to enhance their professionalism and to deal with crime. Detectives were the ultimate professionals. They were highly paid and highly trained. The media at the time portrayed detectives as efficient and effective crime solvers. Similar to the police style in general, detectives often went about their work in a professional, aloof manner. *Dragnet*, a popular television show during the 1960s, captured this style well. The show was about two Los Angeles Police Department detectives and the investigations they conducted. They cut through the emotion of their work and became famous for their line, "Just the facts ma'am."

As a continuing attempt to provide organizational control over officers and detectives, detective work became much more removed from interactions with criminals. With scientific advances, more emphasis was placed on getting information from science (and from victims and witnesses) as opposed to from criminals. The rise of science was led in a large part by the FBI. Through the 1920s and 1930s, several initiatives were embarked on by the Bureau, each of which helped solidify its reputation as the top law enforcement agency in the country. First, the Bureau took the lead in the development of fingerprints as a method of criminal identification. In 1924 the Bureau's Identification Division was created. J. Edgar Hoover, who was now the director of the Bureau of Investigation, received authorization and funding for a national fingerprint identification service. The Bureau was to serve as the national repository and clearinghouse for fingerprint records. The Bureau began a campaign to collect fingerprints from every American. Representatives of the Bureau even went door-to-door in an effort to collect prints (FBI, 1990). Fingerprints were recognized to have numerous advantages over the earlier systems of identification (e.g., photography, Bertillonage). It was understood that fingerprints did not change, and could not be changed, from birth to death. In addition, fingerprints were unique. Furthermore, there was a uniform method of collection and classification, and this methodology was relatively simple. Fingerprint printing and storage systems were relatively inexpensive. Finally, fingerprints were useful not only for identification but also as evidence because fingerprints could be left by a suspect at a crime scene. Fingerprints could provide a clue regarding the individual who committed the crime. Photography and Bertillonage provided no such advantages. The major problem with fingerprints as a method of criminal identification was that matching a print of an unknown suspect to a potentially vast number of prints on file was a daunting and unproductive task. It was not until the development of the Automated Fingerprint Identification System (AFIS) in the 1980s that this limitation was addressed (see Chapter 6).

The second initiative of the Bureau was the development of a crime laboratory. In 1932, with a borrowed microscope and a few other pieces of equipment, the Bureau's laboratory opened. During its first year of operation, the laboratory conducted 963 examinations— nearly all of which involved examinations of handwriting in extortion cases (FBI, 1990).

Finally, in 1935 the Bureau began operation of the National Police Academy (to be known later as the *FBI National Academy*) to train select local police officers in investigative methods. Selection for and graduation from the National Academy was, and continues to be, a prestigious law enforcement accomplishment.

With these initiatives of the FBI, the agency took the lead in reform and crime fighting. It became the role model for other law enforcement agencies. Calvin Coolidge was elected president in 1923 and, in the aftermath of the Palmer raids, one of his first tasks was to reform the Justice Department, the Bureau of Investigation in particular. In 1924, Hoover was appointed the director of the Bureau of Investigation. In 1924, the Bureau had 441 agents. One of Hoover's first tasks was to upgrade the personnel standards of the FBI agents. Hoover fired about one quarter of all agents and mandated additional training for others. Hiring standards were raised, and training in law or accounting was required. A training school was established for various skills and for learning the procedures of the Bureau. According to Hoover, promotion was to be based on performance, not seniority. Control and standardization were the themes that reflected his management style.

During the late 1920s through the 1930s, numerous high-profile crimes and criminals took center stage with J. Edgar Hoover and his G-men. In particular, gangsters became larger than life, capturing the imagination of millions of Americans. The result was gangsters—like "Machine Gun" Kelly, "Pretty Boy" Floyd, "Baby Face" Nelson, John Dillinger, Al Capone, "Ma" Barker, and others—as heroes. Director Hoover saw the opportunity and rose to the challenge. With the assistance of Hollywood and detective fiction writers, he was able to portray his agents (and himself) at the same mythical levels as gangsters. Gangsters were portrayed as public enemies, the Bureau of Investigation's G-men were cop–heroes, and J. Edgar Hoover was the top cop.

Even beyond this skillful portrayal, J. Edgar Hoover was able to make the battle over good and gangsters personal, and use it to his and the Bureau's advantage. For example, in 1933 four of the Bureau's agents and several police officers were escorting bank robber Frank "Jelly" Nash to Leavenworth Prison when they were ambushed by three men with machine guns. Three officers and one agent were killed. At least in partial response to this tragic event, Congress passed nine major crime bills giving Hoover much more authority and power. Congress also gave agents of the Bureau authority to carry firearms for the first time (FBI, 1990).

In 1932 the nation was transfixed over the news of the kidnaping and murder of the infant son of Charles and Anne Lindbergh (see the introduction to this chapter). Kidnaping laws were passed by Congress, and the Bureau of Investigation was made responsible for this and other kidnaping investigations. As noted, when the kidnaper was apprehended, it was due more to the work of the Department of Treasury agents on the case and an attentive gas station worker than skillful investigative work on the part of the Bureau. Nevertheless, J. Edgar Hoover was able to take credit and reap the political rewards.

Even though the FBI was most often viewed as the ultimate scientific, professional law enforcement agency, the reality was that it was not immune from bungled investigations. Case in point: John Dillinger. When bank robber John Dillinger escaped from jail on March 3, 1934, the Bureau mounted a full-scale operation to catch him. For two months Dillinger escaped the Bureau's traps. Then Agent Melvin Purvis received a tip that Dillinger and members of his gang were hiding in Little Bohemia, a resort in Wisconsin. As agents converged on the lodge, several men ran from the area. As they drove away, agents fired on them, killing one and seriously injuring the others. As it turned out, these men were not part of Dillinger's gang. Dillinger and his associates escaped through a back window. This latest failed attempt to capture Dillinger was a major embarrassment to Hoover and the Bureau. Dillinger became public enemy number one. Several weeks later, Purvis got a tip that Dillinger was to be at a movie theater in Chicago the next evening. Dillinger was to be the one with the woman in the infamous red dress. Purvis had the theater surrounded. As Dillinger left the theater, he was shot and killed by Purvis (Theoharis, 1999).

Director Hoover was able to create convincingly the argument (and the imagery) that the Bureau of Investigation was what protected American citizens from the communists (i.e., the Red Scare), gangsters, and even kidnapers. By most accounts, it was masterful public relations. But there was more. Starting in 1935, a series of G-men movies was produced. Censorship laws only allowed gangsters in movies if they were being captured or killed by agents of the Bureau. Hoover became public hero number one (Gentry, 1991).

World War II brought new challenges. With the rise of totalitarianism abroad, a concern with internal enemies developed. By request of President Franklin D. Roosevelt in 1936, the FBI resumed with increased enthusiasm their information collection on the domestic activities of communists and radicals. By 1939, Hoover had reestablished the GID. The war years provided the FBI with a powerful rationale for monitoring political radicals. In addition, the passage of the Smith Act in 1940 provided a legal basis for FBI domestic security investigations. The Smith Act made it a crime to advocate or conspire to advocate the forceful overthrow of the government. During the early 1940s, the FBI underwent dramatic growth, with the number of employees increasing from 7,420 to 13,317, and the number of agents doubling to 5,702 (FBI, 1990).

In the early 1940s, the Bureau began resorting to more intrusive investigative techniques, wiretaps in particular, but also physical surveillance, elaborate record keeping, mail opening, and warrantless searches. Arguably, sometimes the Bureau's monitoring activities went beyond the expected targets (like communists) to less likely ones, like first ladies. Although President Roosevelt was quite supportive of Hoover and the FBI, Mrs. Roosevelt was not. In fact, Hoover considered her an enemy of the FBI and, little doubt, she considered the FBI an enemy of hers. As a critic of the FBI, the Bureau began to conduct investigations of First Lady Eleanor Roosevelt and her assistants. Despite her protests, the investigations continued and the FBI obtained information on Mrs. Roosevelt that included evidence of extramarital sexual relationships (Powers, 1983).

The fruits of this and other unofficial investigations by the Bureau became the basis of what was been referred to as Hoover's *secret files* (Gentry, 1991). The creation of these secret files got a boost with some official action in 1947. In 1947, the executive branch established the Federal Employee Loyalty-Security Program, which in its final form required that each federal agency conduct investigations of its personnel. This information was to be forwarded to the FBI for further investigative work or for filing. In addition, as part of this program, the FBI was given responsibility for conducting investigations of presidential appointees, supreme court nominees, and individuals in other high-level positions. With this responsibility, the Bureau exercised extraordinary influence in determining who filled high-level governmental positions; after all, investigations of some people could be (and were) more thorough than others.

The 1950s saw a decreasing concern with domestic communism and an increasing concern with organized crime. The event that focused public attention on the problem most directly was the discovery in 1957 of a meeting of major criminal figures in New York. Senate crime hearings were organized and the counsel for the investigating committee was Robert F. Kennedy. With his brother's election to the presidency in 1960 and his confirmation as attorney general in 1961, Kennedy was determined to increase law enforcement pressure on organized crime. Both Kennedys supported new crime laws that strengthened the Bureau's jurisdiction in organized crime cases. Aggressive use of wiretaps continued unabated.

The Community Problem-Solving Era

The 1960s was a troubling time for many Americans and the police. In the 1960s, America was in the grip of the Vietnam War. There were war protests across the country. It was the time of the civil rights movement, and the related demonstrations, marches, and riots. The police became viewed by many as an occupying army in the low-income, minority ghettos of urban cities. The police were called "pigs." In the 1960s, President John F. Kennedy was assassinated, as was Senator and presidential candidate (and former Attorney General of the United States) Robert Kennedy, and civil rights leader Martin Luther King, Jr. American society was in turmoil. Fear of crime was increasing dramatically. Actual crime was also increasing; the crime rate doubled from 1960 to 1970. Helter Skelter and Charles Manson were front-page news. The police were experiencing a crisis, yet they were supposed to have the knowledge and capabilities to control crime successfully. If the situation was not bad enough for the police, the U.S. Supreme Court rendered several landmark decisions (e.g., *Mapp* v. *Ohio*, *Miranda* v. *Arizona*; see Chapter 5) that were seen as "handcuffing" the police. In addition, in the late 1960s and early 1970s, several major research studies were conducted to examine the effectiveness of police operations. The Kansas City Preventive Patrol Experiment (Kelling et al., 1974) concluded that random motorized patrol did not deter crime. The RAND study on detectives (Greenwood et al., 1977) concluded that detectives contributed little to solving a crime and that many detectives could be replaced with clerical personnel.

In the face of this multifaceted crisis, the police realized that the old ideas of professionalism no longer worked. The police needed to get closer to the community to enlist their support and assistance in fighting crime. With this new way of thinking came the community problem-solving era of policing (Kelling and Moore, 1988), for which community policing is of central importance. A cornerstone of community policing is that police and citizens must be "coproducers" of crime prevention. Although the reform era emphasized police–citizen separation, the community era emphasized police–citizen cooperation.

Skolnick and Bayley (1988) identified four definitional elements of community policing. First and most important for the investigative function, community policing involves the community in efforts of criminal investigation and crime prevention. Second, community policing consists of a reorientation of patrol activities. It is realized that the patrol car is not the only means by which police services can be delivered. Community policing initiatives allow for the placement of police personnel in mini stations, provide for home visits, or provide for foot patrols (as well as patrol via bicycle, scooter, horse, roller blades, and so forth). Third, community policing requires increased accountability through citizen input into police practices and policy. Citizen satisfaction is a legitimate goal according to the community policing philosophy. Finally, with community policing, the police understand that different communities have different priorities and problems. Accordingly, community policing requires the decentralization of command and provision of services to individual neighborhoods.

All these features are supposed to result in several desired ends. First, such initiatives are supposed to reduce crime. Because community policing programs allow the police to have more interaction with the public, there are likely to be increased opportunities for the police to receive information that leads to crimes being solved (Sklonick and Bayley, 1988). Crime may also be reduced through citizen education and involvement in crime prevention programs. Crime may be reduced by paying attention to the conditions, the disorder, that may lead to an environment in which crime can flourish (Wilson and Kelling, 1982). Second, community policing programs are often expected to reduce fear of crime. This goal may also be attained through citizen education and involvement in crime prevention activities, as well as through the increased emphasis placed on reducing signs of disorder. Finally, because community policing programs enable citizens to have input into policing in their neighborhoods and make the police "easily accessible, frequently visible, and caring in their relationships with citizens" (Goldstein, 1987; pp. 8–9), community policing programs are often expected to improve citizen attitudes toward the police.

Although the research that has examined the effects of community policing has shown that it often does not work as expected (see Rosenbaum [1994]), the means and ends of community policing, in principle, seem to be quite congruent with the tasks of criminal investigation. The basic task of the police in a criminal investigation is to collect information that will lead to the identification, apprehension, and conviction of the subject who perpetrated the criminal act. Much of the research on the investigative function highlights the role of the public as suppliers of information to the police (Greenwood et al., 1977). Simply stated, the police are dependent on the public, and community policing makes this dependence explicit. However, the dependence of the police on the public is certainly not a new discovery. For example, in 1967, Reiss (1967) explained,

> The capacity of the police to solve any crime is severely limited by citizens, partly owing to the fact that there is no feasible way to solve most crimes except by securing the cooperation of citizens to link a person to the crime. (p. 105)

According to Kelling et al. (1974),

> Assigning the police full responsibility for the maintenance of order, the prevention of crime, and the apprehension of criminals constitutes far too great a burden for far too few. Primary responsibility rests with families, the community, and its individual members. The police can only facilitate and assist members of the community in the maintenance of order, and no more. (p. 533)

In short, given this realization, the community policing initiative seems to be congruent with the function of criminal investigation.

Strategies that provide an opportunity for community residents to share information with the police in solving crimes are particularly relevant in the era of community policing. For example, tip lines are quite common in criminal investigations today. The Crime Solvers and Crime Stoppers programs are supported by many communities across the country. In addition, police departments frequently establish designated tip lines for major investigations (see Chapter 10).

Along the same line, school liaison officers are located in a setting where they are available not only to assist students with questions or problems that they may have, but also to obtain information about crimes from the students. Similarly, police involvement with community watch groups provides a public service and also, arguably, makes it easier for residents to contact and provide information to the police that may assist in investigations. These strategies make police dependence on the public explicit and are congruent with the ideals of community policing.

Along with an explicit dependence on community residents for information, other developments in criminal investigation have occurred during the community problem-solving era of policing. Chief among these is DNA analysis as a method of identification (see Chapter 6). DNA analysis represents an extraordinary advance in science and in identification methods as applied to criminal investigations. The science of DNA, along with the introduction of computer technology to store, record, and match DNA prints across individuals, is potentially revolutionary in criminal investigative methods. In addition, other technology in the form of computer networks and databanks are also changing criminal investigations in dramatic ways (Chapter 10).

Once again, the FBI is often considered at the forefront of these changes. Today, the FBI crime laboratory is the most scientifically advanced and well-funded laboratory in the world, although it has recently been subject to severe criticism for its "sloppy" work in several cases (Kelly and Wearne, 1998). The FBI also operates the NCIC—a computerized network and storage system of crime information. The FBI continues to operate the National Academy and it provides many other types of operational assistance to federal, state, and local law enforcement agencies (see FBI [1999b]), including psychological profiling (Chapter 9). The FBI continues to enjoy high status and prestige at least in part because of the agency's involvement in high-profile (and successful) criminal investigations such as the terrorist acts of September 2001, the bombing of the Alfred P. Murrah Federal Building in Oklahoma City in 1995, the World Trade Center bombing in 1993, the bombing of Pan Am Flight 103 over Scotland in 1988, and the U.S. Embassy bombings in Kenya and Tanzania in 1998. Other high-profile but unsuccessful investigations serve as a reminder that the FBI is not immune from error. Consider the FBI involvement in the incident at Ruby Ridge in 1992, where agents mistakenly shot and killed the wife and son of Randy Weaver (who was believed to be a white supremacist and was wanted on gun violations); the catastrophic burning of the Branch Davidian compound in Waco, Texas, in 1993; and the investigation into the anthrax letters in 2001, which also remains unsolved.

During the course of history, police institutions and organizations have responded to a

EXHIBIT 2-1 Police request for information/Crime Stoppers release

CITY OF BROOKFIELD
POLICE DEPARTMENT

REWARD

The City of Brookfield Police Department in cooperation
with Waukesha County Crime Stoppers and the
Elmbrook School District is offering a reward for
information leading to the arrest of those responsible for
the vandalism reported October 2 at the new
Brookfield Elementary School under construction.

The reward amount is up to

$1,500.00

Anyone with information is asked to call the
City of Brookfield PD
at 414-782-6200 or
Waukesha County Crime Stoppers
at 1-888-441-5505.

*Police and citizens
must work together
to solve crimes.
The philosophy of
community policing
and police use of tip
lines make this clear.*

variety of external forces that have caused changes in their structure and function. Most people
would argue that much progress has been made. Ultimately, that is for the future to decide.

Questions for Discussion and Review

1. Can you think of any modern-day parallels to the Lindbergh baby kidnaping? The
   Palmer raids? The Red Scare? The expanding scope of jurisdiction for the FBI? Discuss
   the possibilities.

2. Why study history?

3. What problems resulted from the use of informers, thief-takers, and thief-makers?
   How were these problems addressed in designing the position of detective?

4. How did criminal investigation differ during the political era, the reform era, and the community problem-solving era?

5. What is Bertillonage? What are the system's major advantages and disadvantages?

6. What is the third degree? The dragnet?

7. How was the FBI created? What was the role of J. Edgar Hoover in the FBI?

8. What were the three criminal themes adopted by the FBI in the 1920s and 1930s?

9. What was the role of private detectives in the mid 1800s and the early 1900s?

10. During the reform era, what was the meaning of "professionalism"? How did detectives reflect professionalism?

11. Describe the crisis in policing in the 1960s.

12. What is the meaning of "coproduction"? Community policing? How does coproduction relate to the work of detectives and other officers in the era of community problem solving?

13. What are several of the high-profile success stories of the FBI? What are some of the high-profile lack-of-success stories of the FBI?

14. What might the future hold in terms of policing and criminal investigation? Explain.

15. What aspects of criminal investigation have changed much over the years? What aspects have changed little?

Related Internet Sites

www.sherlock-holmes.org.uk
This is the address to the web site of the Sherlock Holmes Society of London, "One of the foremost societies dedicated to studying and furthering interest in the career, life, and times of the famous consulting detective."

www.fbi.gov
This is the official FBI web site. The site provides information on the agency, its history, and its current operations.

www.ci.berkeley.ca.us/police/History/history.html
This link will take you to the history page of the Berkeley (California) Police Department, where the contributions of August Vollmer, the Father of American Policing, are discussed.

www.state.nj.us/lps/njsp/about/30s.html
This link takes you to the New Jersey State Police history web site. Changes in the agency from its creation to the present are discussed. The Lindbergh baby kidnaping of 1932 is also discussed

THE STRUCTURE AND CONTENT OF CRIMINAL INVESTIGATIONS

OBJECTIVES

After reading this chapter you will be able to

- Discuss the four types of police actions based on the typology of police activities
- Identify the four stages of the reactive criminal investigative process
- Differentiate between cold-case squads and investigative task forces
- Discuss why some cases receive more investigative attention from investigators than others
- Discuss the role of police response time in "on-scene" apprehensions
- Briefly summarize the research that examines the impact of the detective's effort on whether cases are solved
- Discuss how certain circumstances of crimes may influence whether crimes are solved
- Discuss the reasons for and against the use of "convicting suspects" as an indicator of investigative success

- Discuss the most significant reasons for case attrition
- Discuss the reasons for and against the use of victim satisfaction as an indicator of investigative success
- Discuss the factors that explain the increased use of undercover investigative strategies
- Discuss the relationship between undercover investigations and entrapment
- Discuss the research on the effects of undercover investigations
- Discuss the most significant unexpected or undesirable outcomes associated with undercover investigations
- Discuss the theory behind crackdowns, hot-spot patrol, and selective apprehension
- Discuss the research on the effects of crackdowns, hot-spot patrol, and selective apprehension

IMPORTANT TERMS

Differential police response

Case screening

Solvability factors

Task force

Cold-case squad

Triage hypothesis

Clearance rate

Arrest rate

Discovery crimes

Involvement crimes

Sting operation

Decoy operation

Undercover fencing operation

Surveillance

Stakeout

Entrapment

Displacement

Crackdown strategy

Hot-spot patrol

Selective apprehension

Initial and residual deterrence

Hangover effect

INTRODUCTION

On October 23, 1989, Charles Stuart and his pregnant wife, Carol, both thirty years old, left childbirth class at Boston's Brigham and Women's Hospital. Minutes later, Charles called 911 on his cell phone from his car to report that he and his wife had just been robbed and shot. Charles, seriously injured and bleeding from a gunshot wound to his abdomen, was unable to tell the police his location. Charles assisted the police in locating him and his wife by listening for the police sirens, judging the proximity of the police from the sirens, and then directing the police to where they were. After thirteen minutes, with Carol still clinging to life, the police located them. Charles immediately described the assailant as a young black man wearing a jogging suit. The search was on. Carol died that night of a single gunshot wound to the head, shortly after giving birth to her son by cesarean section; the baby died seventeen days later. Charles spent six weeks in the hospital including ten days in intensive care. During this time, the police launched a massive and, by many accounts, heavy-handed manhunt for the killer in the largely black Roxbury/Boston neighborhood. Police believed they found their killer with Stuart identifying William Bennett, age thirty-nine, as the man who looked "most like" his attacker in a police lineup. Bennett originally became a suspect when the police obtained information from some of his acquaintances that he bragged about the murder and that he said he saw Stuart look at him in his rearview mirror during the robbery (Stuart earlier told a similar story). In addition, Stuart recognized Bennett in a picture that was shown to him by the police while he was still in the hospital. On top of all this information, it was learned that Bennett had a long criminal record.

With Bennett in police custody, and most of Boston relieved that the killer was caught, the investigation took a wild and dramatic twist. Matthew Stuart, Charles' younger brother, came forward and told the police that on the night of the murder he met Charles, as planned, and that Charles, while still seated in his car, threw to him Carol's handbag. Matthew stated that inside the bag he found Carol's engagement ring, other items reported stolen, and a revolver. He told police that he threw most of the items into a river—except for the ring, which he kept and turned over to the police. As things began to unravel, and as it became more clear to the police that

Charles was, in fact, responsible for the murder of his wife, on January 4, 1990, Charles drove to the Tobin Bridge in Boston, stopped his car, got out, and jumped. The police later recovered his body along with a suicide note that read in part "I love my family . . . the last four months have been hell." On further investigation, the police learned that Charles was having an affair, he had significant financial problems, and that Carol had a sizable life insurance policy. It was also later determined that the police may have "coached" Stuart for the statement that he looked at the shooter in the rearview mirror (the same statement that the shooter allegedly made) and that Stuart may have recognized Bennett in the lineup because the police earlier showed a picture of Bennett to Stuart in the hospital. In addition, after Bennett's arrest, acquaintances of Bennett who reported that he was bragging about the crime recanted their statements (Alter and Starr, 1990; Baker, 1990) Without questioning the true nature of the crime, and in believing hook, line, and sinker the story told by Charles Stuart, the police opened themselves up to severe criticism regarding the investigation into the murder of Carol Stuart and the arrest of William Bennett.

The FBI's ABSCAM (for Abdul Scam; Abdul was the name of a fictitious sheik) undercover investigation began in mid 1978 with a focus on recovering stolen securities and paintings. Mel Weinberg, a convicted swindler, was recruited by the FBI to act as the middleman in the operation. Weinberg's role was to get thieves to bring stolen property to the FBI's undercover fencing operation, Abdul Enterprises, with offices located on Long Island, New York, and to a sixty-two-foot yacht in the nearby harbor. There,

The Charles and Carol Stuart crime scene. At crime scenes, things are not always as they first appear.

undercover agents posed as associates of a wealthy Arab sheik who was willing to purchase goods known to be stolen.

In late 1978, with information supplied to the agents by Weinberg, the ABSCAM investigation shifted focus from the investigation of stolen property in New York to a potentially more fruitful area of inquiry—political corruption in New Jersey. Undercover FBI agents approached the mayor of Camden, New Jersey, Angelo Errichetti, and informed him that a wealthy sheik was interested in investing in property located in Camden. Furthermore, the mayor was told by the agents that the sheik was willing to pay for political favors to accommodate his investment plan. As the mayor talked to people about the sheik and his plan, other public officials became interested in "helping," including several members of Congress.

In mid 1979, the focus of the FBI's undercover investigation shifted once again to an even bigger target—U.S. Congress. Several members of Congress were brought to a house in Washington, DC, a house rented by the FBI for purposes of this investigation. There the congressmen were told that an Arab sheik required assistance in gaining asylum in the United States. During the course of several meetings, the undercover agents were told that the cost of such assistance by the congressmen was

A still photograph from a videotape played at the ABSCAM trial. The envelope the congressman is holding contains $50,000.

$50,000. FBI agents videotaped these meetings, and lawyers for the Justice Department monitored the bribery negotiations through closed-circuit television from an adjacent room in the house.

The ABSCAM operation was terminated in early 1980, when the investigation was discovered by the press. Before it ended, however, twenty "bribe meetings" took place between undercover agents and public officials. These meetings, and the illegal actions that occurred during these meetings, ultimately resulted in twelve convictions, and included the conviction of one senator and six congressmen. Not surprisingly, on discovery, the U.S. Congress initiated an investigation into the ABSCAM operation. The Senate and House committees were critical of the investigation and noted in particular the problems with the selection and supervision of informants, the seemingly unlimited scope of the investigation, the misconduct by the informants, the reliance on corrupt middlemen, and inadequate management and supervision of the operation. Overall, ABSCAM raised numerous questions about the ethics and legality of undercover investigations and brought such operations into the spotlight of attention (see Theoharis [1999]).

Forms of Police Action

Criminal investigations, as well as other forms of police action, can be differentiated on the basis of two dimensions: whether police activities are overt or covert and whether activities are deceptive or nondeceptive (Marx, 1988). In putting these two dimensions of police work in a matrix, four types of police activities are identified (see Figure 3–1).

In Figure 3–1, cell A consists of actions that are overt and nondeceptive. Most police actions are of this nature. Included here are "reactive" investigations conducted by the police during which the police take action after a crime has been committed. Here, a witness or victim notifies the police of the crime and the police who respond can be readily identified as police investigators.

		Are police actions . . .	
		Overt?	Covert?
Does police action involve . . .	Nondeception?	A	C
	Deception?	B	D

FIGURE 3–1 Types of criminal investigations and activities
Adapted from Marx (1988)

Police actions that are overt but deceptive fall into cell B. Included here are actions during which the police, who are identified as the police, are not truthful in their interactions with citizens or suspects. For example, in an interrogation of a robbery suspect, the police may tell the suspect that his fingerprints were found on the cash register when in fact they were not. As another example, the police may advertise with street signs that certain areas are "high enforcement speed zones," when little traffic enforcement is actually conducted in such areas.

Cell C consists of actions in which the police are covert in their actions but do not attempt to be deceptive. An example would be passive surveillance or monitoring a suspect's actions or communications.

Undercover investigations are covert and deceptive, and are best placed in cell D of the matrix. In these actions, the police initiate action before a crime actually occurs and, as a result, they may actually *instigate* the crime. In these situations, the police cannot be immediately or easily identified as police officers nor can their true intentions be known. Clearly, as in the ABSCAM investigation, the public officials were not aware of the FBI's involvement in the situation, and certainly did not think that their "bribe meetings" were being secretly recorded by agents. The remainder of this chapter discusses the nature of overt, reactive investigations and covert, proactive investigations.

Stages of the Reactive Criminal Investigation Process

For purposes of definition, the reactive criminal investigation process as it exists in most police departments can be organized into several stages: initial discovery and response, preliminary investigation, follow-up investigation, and closure.

Initial Discovery and Response

In order for the criminal investigation process to begin, the police must discover that a crime has taken place and then notify the victim, or the victim or a witness must discover that a crime has occurred and notify the police. In the vast majority of cases it is the victim who first discovers that a crime occurred and who contacts the police. Then, in most cases, a patrol officer is dispatched to the crime scene. In the most serious cases (e.g., bank robbery, homicide), detectives may also respond to the scene and conduct investigative activities.

Some police departments use what are commonly referred to as differential police response (DPR) strategies (Worden, 1993). DPR involves responding to crime calls as well as other calls for service through means other than a traditional, immediate mobile police response. For instance, depending on the needs and resources of a police department, and based on policies created within a police department, certain crimes with certain characteristics may have a telephone report taken in lieu of a mobile police response. Other nontraditional responses could include asking complainants to walk or mail in their reports, or dispatching civilian personnel instead of sworn officers to handle the call. Worden (1993) reports that in Lansing, Michigan, most burglaries, larcenies, and vandalism complaints that involve property damage or loss less than $1,000 and for which there are no known suspects, no witnesses, no descriptions of suspects or their vehicles, and no other evidence, are simply reported over the telephone and do not usually receive any additional investigative attention. With no evidence available and with the crime being relatively minor, additional expenditure of resources is deemed unnecessary and unproductive.

Preliminary Investigation

If the matter is defined as a crime, and a telephone report or other alternative response is not viewed as appropriate, then an initial (or preliminary) investigation is conducted. The initial investigation consists of the immediate postcrime activities of the investigators who arrive at the crime scene. More specifically, three sets of tasks often comprise preliminary investigations: (1) coordination, (2) evidence collection, and (3) other investigative tasks. Coordination refers to the overall supervision of evidence collection and other investigative activities at the crime scene. The crime scene coordinator has responsibility for the investigation as it is conducted during the preliminary investigation. Evidence collection involves the processing of the scene and may include securing physical evidence and documenting the crime scene (e.g., taking photographs, making crime scene sketches). Other investigative activities include interviewing victims and witnesses, conducting neighborhood canvasses to locate additional witnesses, and making arrests. The specific activities performed by investigators may be a function of the particular case at hand. Most often, patrol officers have primary responsibility for all three aspects of preliminary investigations; however, with more serious crimes, police supervisors may have responsibility for the coordination of activities at the crime scene, evidence technicians may have responsibility for evidence collection tasks, and detectives may have responsibility for other investigative tasks. All the information collected as a result of a preliminary investigation would then be recorded in an initial investigative report and other related reports.

Follow-up Investigation

If a perpetrator is not arrested during the initial investigation, the case may be selected for a follow-up investigation. Typically, detective supervisors review the initial investigation reports from the case pool that appear relevant to their unit (e.g., Robbery, Crimes Against Property) and then decide which of the cases should be assigned to investigators for follow-up investigation. This process is known as *case screening*. The screening decision is usually based on two major factors: the seriousness of the crime and the evidence available as documented in the initial investigation report. The seriousness of a crime may be determined by the legally defined seriousness of the crime (e.g., felonies are more serious than misdemeanors), potential dangerousness of the culprit (e.g., a robbery during which the culprit used an Uzi machine gun may be more dangerous than one during which the culprit did not use a weapon), the actual harm that resulted from the crime (e.g., a robbery during which $10,000 was taken is more serious than one during which $5 was taken), and the characteristics of the victim (e.g., a robbery during which the victim is the mayor may be viewed as more serious

The activities of police officers during initial investigations are extremely important in solving crimes.

than a robbery during which the victim is a trouble-making teenager). Seriousness of a crime is always relative. What is serious in a suburban jurisdiction may not be serious in a large urban area; what is serious today may not be as serious tomorrow.

In making screening decisions, evidence considerations are often referred to as *solvability factors.* Solvability factors are key pieces of crime-related information that, if present, increase the probability that the crime will be solved. Not all evidence is equally valuable. Some types of evidence are more useful than others in solving crimes. Consider various types of information about a suspect and the possible source of this information: A suspect could be named by an eyewitness to the crime, a suspect could be named by an individual who saw the suspect with the stolen property or heard the suspect confess to the crime, a suspect could be named on the basis of a guess and supported by other witness information, or a suspect could be described (but not named or identified) by an eyewitness to the crime, and so forth. Clearly, some of this information would be better, or more valuable, than other information. One may also consider the potential value of other pieces of evidence such as license plate numbers, partial license plate numbers, vehicle descriptions, and physical evidence (e.g., fingerprints). Another critical solvability factor is the amount of time that has elapsed from when the crime occurred until it comes to the attention of the police. In homicides, for example, if a case is not solved within twenty-four hours of its occurrence, the chances of it ever being solved fall dramatically (Keppel and Weiss, 1994). One may reasonably expect the same to be true in other crimes as well.

In practice, solvability factors are often listed on the initial investigative report (e.g., is there a witness to the crime, can a suspect be named, is a significant MO present, is the stolen property identifiable) to keep the individuals who screen cases focused on these dimensions of the case. Some departments make solvability factors a more formal basis for case-screening decisions through the development of case-screening models. With formal case-screening models, predetermined, empirically calculated point values are attached to particular pieces of information that may be present after the preliminary investigation (e.g., presence of suspect information, fingerprints, etc.). The more useful the evidence, the higher the point value. For each case, the available evidence and corresponding points are tallied, and those cases with a point total higher than a predetermined score are selected for follow-up investigation; the othersare not (Gaines et al., 1983).

Detectives have considerable discretion in deciding what activities should be performed in follow-up investigations.

If a case is selected for a follow-up investigation, then the investigators assigned to the case must decide what activities to perform during the investigation. Depending on the particular case, the follow-up investigation may involve a variety of activities, ranging from recontacting and reinterviewing the victim, to submitting physical evidence to the crime laboratory, to seeking informants (Eck, 1983). The information that is cultivated as a result of these activities is recorded in follow-up investigative reports.

So what do detectives do when conducting follow-up investigations? Several studies have examined the activities performed during follow-up investigations and the amount of time detectives spend on cases during follow-up investigations. First, Greenwood et al. (1977), in their seminal research in Kansas City, Missouri, found that fifty-five percent of detectives' time was spent on case-related work, whereas forty-five percent was spent on activities that could not be attributed to any particular investigation. These researchers also point out that detectives spend considerable time on cases after they have been solved. This is time spent assisting the prosecutor in preparing the case for court and testifying in court.

With specific regard to activities performed, Ericson (1981) found that detectives interviewed one or more victims, complainants, or informants in thirty-two percent of the cases, and interrogated suspects in twenty-eight percent of the cases. Brandl (1991) found that the most common activities performed by detectives in burglary follow-up investigations were interviewing victims (sixty-seven percent of cases), interviewing witnesses (sixty percent), interviewing one or more suspects (thirty-seven percent of cases), and checking departmental computer files (twenty-three percent). During robbery follow-up investigations, the most common activities were interviewing victims (eighty-four percent of cases), interviewing witnesses (fifty-nine percent), conducting photo lineups of suspects (twenty-eight percent), and checking departmental computer files (twenty-six percent).

Eck (1983) examined activities performed by detectives during robbery and burglary investigations and found that as investigations progressed, the activities became less routine. The activities performed later in the investigation were more uncommon and less predictable than those performed earlier during the investigation. In addition, investigative activities usually first occur at or near the crime scene (interviewing victim, witnesses) and then expand to include other places and people. As an extraordinary example, consider the early stages of the massive investigation into the terrorist attack on the World Trade Center and Pentagon on September 11, 2001. After verifying that the planes were hijacked, the first task of investigators was to determine who hijacked the planes and flew them into the buildings. Within the first day of the incident, the FBI received information from an individual who had a verbal altercation with several Arabic men in the parking lot of Boston Logan Airport the morning of the hijackings. This individual thought that perhaps this altercation was relevant to the incident and he gave investigators a description of the vehicle these men were driving. Agents found this car parked in the parking lot of the airport. On searching the vehicle, investigators identified several names of the suspected perpetrators and found evidence that immediately led them to Florida, where some of the men had previously rented an apartment. It was also determined that luggage from one of the suspects did not make the connection to the flight out of Boston. With evidence obtained from the luggage, car, and apartment, the investigation led to, among other places, Germany, where other accomplices were discovered and where much of the planning for the attack allegedly occurred (Pope, 2001; Rising, 2002). As such, the initial activities of the investigation focused on where the suspects were last seen and then quickly moved to other places (see the introduction to Chapter 14 for a more detailed discussion of the September 11, 2001, hijacking investigation).

With regard to the overall amount of time detectives spend on follow-up investigations, Eck (1983) found that, on average, a total of 2.8 hours were spent on robbery follow-up investigations and 1.3 hours were spent on burglary investigations. Another study (Brandl, 1993) revealed that a mean of 3.7 hours was spent on burglary follow-up investigations and 4.5 hours on robbery cases. Ericson (1981) found that approximately thirty percent of all cases that came to the attention of the detective bureau received one or more hours of investigative time.

According to the study by Greenwood et al. (1977), less than half of all crimes "received serious consideration by an investigator" (p. 109). Specifically, it was found that sixty-three percent of robberies, thirty-six percent of nonresidential burglaries, and thirty percent of residential burglaries received at least one-half hour of detectives' time. Overall, it is probably safe to conclude that the amount of time spent on cases in various jurisdictions has much to do with the number of cases that need to be investigated and the resources that are available. Overall, the research suggests that with burglaries and robberies, relatively little time is spent on follow-up investigations.

Although detectives, on average, spend relatively little time on any particular follow-up investigation, it is reasonable to expect considerable variation among cases on the amount of time spent. Indeed, Brandl (1993) found that among burglary follow-up investigations, the amount of time spent by detectives varied from five minutes to more than fifty-two hours. With robberies, time spent varied from thirty minutes to more than fifty hours. With homicides, active investigations have lasted from one day to more than seven months (Brandl, unpublished manuscript). This variation begs the question: Why do some cases receive more investigative attention from detectives than others? Not surprisingly, the research that has addressed this question identifies two factors as being most influential: the seriousness of the crime and the evidence available (Brandl, 1993; Bynum et al., 1982). Specifically, burglaries and robberies that result in a large-value loss are usually investigated more extensively than those that involve a smaller loss. With regard to evidence, cases with promising leads receive more time than cases with no leads or cases for which the evidence is so strong that an arrest can be made immediately. If promising leads are available, detectives may reasonably believe that the case could be "broken" with only a little additional information. Cases with good leads are therefore considered more promising. However, if there are no leads, detectives may not expect much chance of an arrest clearance regardless of the time spent in the investigation. When the evidence is quite strong, little time may be needed to make an arrest.

Closure

At any time during the investigative process the case may be closed and investigative activities terminated. For instance, the case could be closed because of lack of leads or as a result of the perpetrator being identified and apprehended. In the latter situation, the crime would be considered "cleared by arrest" and primary responsibility for the case would shift from the police department to the prosecutor's office. However, the detectives assigned to the case would still have the responsibility of assisting the prosecutor in preparing the case for prosecution.

Other Reactive Investigative Strategies

Cold-Case Squads

Earlier it was noted that time is critical to solving crimes. In most solved homicides, for example, a suspect is taken into custody within twenty-four hours. If a case is not solved within this time frame, then the chances of it ever being solved fall drastically (Keppel and Weiss, 1994). In addition, caseload and corresponding time pressures often lead to old cases being set aside so that new cases with fresh leads can be investigated. Given the seriousness of some cases, however, it may not be desirable to suspend or terminate investigative activities on such cases. Cold-case squads address this dilemma. Cold-case squads are usually assigned murder and other high-profile crimes. They allow for "new eyes to be put on old cases." Regini (1997) describes the operation of the cold-case homicide squad in the Washington, DC, Police Department. The squad includes six homicide detectives, one detective sergeant, one detective lieutenant, eight FBI agents, and one FBI supervisor. The squad does not respond to fresh homicide scenes; rather, all cases that it investigates are at least one year old and could no longer be worked by the original investigators because of workload, time constraints, or the lack of leads. Cases are assigned to cold-case squad teams of at least one agent and one detective. According to Regini (1997), between 1992 and 1997, the squad solved 157 previously unsolved cases.

One case that was assigned to the Washington, DC, cold-case squad, and on which these investigators may still be working, is the disappearance of Chandra Levy, the 24-year-old University of Southern California student who was an intern at the Federal Bureau of Prisons. Chandra Levy vanished after leaving her apartment in Washington, DC, on the morning of May 1, 2001. This was, for all practical purposes, just another missing persons case in Washington, DC, until, that is, approximately one month after her disappearance when it was discovered that Ms. Levy and Congressman Gary Condit were having an affair at the time of her disappearance. Mr. Condit was less than forthcoming to investigators about his whereabouts during the time in question and his possible role in the disappearance. It was at this point that public pressure on the Washington, DC, Police Department became extraordinary and the investigation became intense. A massive foot search was conducted by the police of nearby parks, the fare log records of 1,600 taxicab drivers working in the city in early May were examined, Mr. Condit's apartment was searched, and countless other leads were followed—all to no avail. With good leads exhausted and with other cases needing to be worked, in July 2001, the case was assigned to the cold-case squad of the Washington, DC, Police Department (Lengel and Horwitz, 2001). On May 22, 2002, skeletal remains identified as those of Chandra Levy were discovered in a remote area of Rock Creek Park, one of the places searched earlier, by a man walking his dog. Women's clothing was found nearby. Given the condition of the remains and the circumstances of her disappearance, her death was determined to be a result of foul play, although no other details could be gleaned from the bones or the scene (Horwitz and Twomey, 2002). As of 2003, no arrests have been made.

Task Forces

In response to high-profile crimes, particularly those that involve several jurisdictions, investigative agencies may form task forces. Task forces are usually temporary in nature and bring together representatives of agencies to deal with a particular crime or crime problem. A task force is a highly visible investigative response. Task forces are particularly common in investigating drug trafficking and serial crimes (e.g., serial homicide). By bringing together representatives from various agencies, task forces can enhance cooperation, communication, evidence sharing, and person-power in an attempt to solve, or otherwise address, the crimes in question.

Outcomes of Reactive Investigations

As discussed in Chapter 1, three outcomes are commonly associated with the criminal investigative process: (1) solving crimes, (2) convicting suspects, and (3) satisfying victims. To appreciate more completely the reactive criminal investigation process, it is necessary to understand the particulars of each of these outcomes.

Solving Crimes

Clearance and arrest data are typically used to measure the performance of the police in solving crimes. According to the FBI (1999b), the police can clear a crime "when at least one person is arrested, charged with the commission of the offense, and turned over to the court for prosecution" or "by exceptional means when some element beyond law enforcement control precludes the placing of formal charges against the offender"(p. 211). On the basis of clearance data, the *clearance rate* can be calculated. The clearance rate refers to the number of FBI part I, or index, crimes (murder, rape, robbery, aggravated assault, burglary, larceny–theft, motor vehicle theft, and arson) that are cleared during a given period of time divided by the number of crimes known to the police in that same period. The *arrest rate* is similar to the clearance rate except that only crimes in which a suspect is taken "into custody" are included. Studies have shown that the difference between the number of clearances and the number of arrests can be substantial (Eck, 1983).

The limitations and criticisms of arrest and clearance rate measures are many. For instance, with regard to clearance data, police practices of "unfounding" crimes (i.e., determining that a reported crime did not actually occur) and attributing numerous crimes to a suspect in custody (often based on MO alone) may systematically and unjustifiably distort the data. With arrest statistics, there is variance across departments on what actually consti- tutes "in custody" or an arrest (Sherman and Glick, 1984). As a result, different rates of arrest could be obtained by departments that simply use different definitions of "arrest."

Although clearance and arrest data are imprecise measures of the crime-solving out- come, the appropriateness of the crime-solving outcome itself remains largely uncontested. It is, after all, a necessary condition for future criminal justice system processing. However, it is not a *sufficient* condition for future processing. The police may be able to make a sub- stantial number of arrests, or a dramatic increase in arrests, but that, by itself, is little guar- antee of future processing. It is important to realize that it is the steps taken after an arrest that lead to the attainment of other elusive outcomes like deterrence or incapacitation. In essence, the crime-solving outcome, at least as measured by clearance and arrest data, does not provide any indication of the *quality* of arrests or clearances.

The police have varying rates of success in solving crimes. In general, the police enjoy greater success in solving violent crimes (murder, rape, robbery, aggravated assault) than property crimes (burglary, motor vehicle theft, larceny). Within these crime categories, however, there is variation. This is particularly true for personal crimes, for which, nation- ally, more than sixty-two percent of homicides are solved compared with just less than twenty-five percent of robberies (FBI, 2002).

What determines whether a crime is solved? Some analysts have come to the conclu- sion that the *circumstances* that surround the incident (e.g., the evidence present in the case) largely determine the outcome of the case, whereas others argue that the *efforts* of investiga- tors are the most important. For example, personal crimes, by definition, involve contact between the victim and the offender *and* they also often involve offenders who are known to their victims. Accordingly, favorable circumstances (victim–offender contact and victim– offender relationship) often exist for personal crimes to be solved.

A number of studies have examined the relative contribution of circumstances and police effort in solving crimes. For instance, Spelman and Brown (1991) analyzed the role of police response time in making on-scene arrests in serious crimes (i.e., part I crimes not including homicide or arson). Overall, they found that only approximately three percent of all serious crimes reported to the police resulted in a response-related arrest.

Because approximately seventy-five percent of all crimes do not involve contact between the victim/witness and the offender (i.e., they are *discovery crimes*), often an extended period of time elapses between when the crime occurs and when the crime is dis- covered and reported. This, in turn, allows the offender to flee the scene of the crime and prohibits a fast police response from leading to an arrest. The remaining twenty-five percent of crimes (i.e., *involvement crimes*) actually involve a confrontation between a victim or wit- ness and the offender. However, a delay in reporting the crime to the police, even of a few minutes, often allows the suspect to flee the scene of the crime before the police arrive. As such, only when citizens immediately call the police to report involvement crimes can police response time make a difference. In short, from this research, it appears that police ability to make *on-scene* arrests is determined largely by circumstances (e.g., type of crime, citizen reporting time) outside their immediate control.

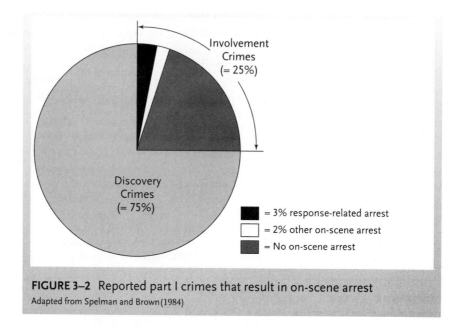

FIGURE 3–2 Reported part I crimes that result in on-scene arrest

Adapted from Spelman and Brown(1984)

Other studies have focused more directly on the role of information and investigative effort in solving crimes. For example, consider the landmark study conducted by Greenwood et al. of the RAND Corporation in 1977. Their findings were based on analyses of two sets of data. First, based on an analysis of the computer-readable case assignment file maintained by the Kansas City (Missouri) Police Department, the researchers provided insight into how detectives spend their working hours. These analyses included a wide variety of crimes including homicide, assault, rape, robbery, kidnaping, auto theft, and burglary. In comparing the amount of time spent on uncleared cases with the amount of time spent on cleared cases, they found that more time was spent on uncleared cases than on ones that were cleared. On this basis they concluded that "the cases that get cleared are primarily the easy ones to solve" (Greenwood et al., 1977; p. 112). (It should be noted here that nowhere in this study was an operational definition of "clearance" provided. Hence, it is not clear exactly what a "clearance" entails, or how [or if] a crime that is "cleared" differs from a crime that is "solved.")

Second, an analysis of cleared crimes (homicide, aggravated assault, felony morals, robbery, burglary, theft, auto theft, and forgery/fraud) from five police departments (Berkeley, Long Beach, Los Angeles, Miami, and Washington, DC) provided a means by which to describe how these cleared cases were cleared. The researchers found that approximately twenty-two percent (38 of 172) of the cleared crimes resulted from an arrest by a patrol officer at the scene of the crime. In another forty-four percent (76 of 172), the perpetrator was "known" (meaning not specified) when the crime report was first taken and, as described by the researchers, "the main job for the investigator in these cases [was] to locate and apprehend the perpetrator, and to assemble evidence adequate to charge him" (p. 135). The remaining thirty-four percent (58 of 172) of all cleared crimes were cleared primarily as a result of "simple routine actions" of detectives (e.g., showing mug shot books, acting on precise and detailed informant tips). According to Greenwood et al. (1977), only about three percent of these cleared crimes could be attributed to "special actions" of detectives.

Greenwood et al. (1977) explain that the overwhelming majority of solved cases are solved because of arrests by patrol officers or because the identity of the perpetrator is known when the crime report reaches the detective. "If information that uniquely identifies the perpetrator is not presented at the time the crime is reported, the perpetrator by and large, will not be subsequently identified" (Greenwood et al., 1976; p. 65). Thus, according to the researchers, "it is not true in general that the greater the investigative effort devoted to a crime the more likely it will be cleared" (p. 64). In short, according to the RAND study, the contributions of detectives in solving crimes is minimal.

One of the more recent studies to examine the relative impact of investigative effort and evidence on case outcomes was conducted by Brandl and Frank (1994). In this study, 292 robbery cases and 317 burglary cases from a medium-size midwestern municipal police department were analyzed. The analyses showed that in burglary and robbery cases with moderate suspect information, the probability of an arrest increased significantly with the more time detectives spent on the case, but this relationship did not hold true in cases with strong or weak suspect information. Hence, effort determined the outcome in cases with moderate suspect information, and circumstances determined the outcome in cases with weak and strong suspect information. In addition, it was found that most detective time was spent on cases with moderate suspect information. It was also found that significantly more time was spent on cases that were solved than on cases that were not solved. These findings directly contradict the conclusions offered by Greenwood et al. (1977) that first, "it is not true in general that the greater the investigative effort devoted to a crime the more likely it will be cleared" (p. 64) and second, that "the cases that get cleared are primarily the easy ones to solve" (p. 112).

Finally, a study of nearly 800 homicide investigations in four jurisdictions—Detroit, Baltimore, Los Angeles, and Milwaukee—found that the efforts of investigators and the circumstances of the incidents had an impact on whether cases were solved (Wellford and Cronin, 1999). As for the role of circumstances, it was found that a homicide was more likely to be solved if drugs were not involved in the crime, if a witness at the crime scene provided valuable information, and if the crime occurred in a private place. As for efforts of investigators, it was found that cases were more likely to be solved if three or more detectives were assigned to the case, and if detectives and evidence technicians responded quickly to the crime scene. As portrayed in this study, efforts *and* circumstances are important in solving crimes.

Convicting Suspects

Another standard on which to judge the performance of the police in investigating crimes is *convicting suspects* (Petersilia et al., 1990). Those who advocate the use of convicting suspects as an appropriate investigative outcome argue that the quantity of crimes solved is essentially meaningless if other outcomes (like punishment, deterrence, and so forth) are not achieved (Skogan and Antunes, 1979). These outcomes can only be attained if perpetrators are convicted. Moreover, it is argued that the police have a direct bearing on how far a case is processed, and what the disposition will be. As explained by Forst et al. (1982), "[t]here can be no doubt that the police do make a difference—they determine largely what happens after arrest" (p. 49).

Several arguments have also been offered against the use of "convicting suspects" as a measure of investigative success. First, in direct contrast to the argument just presented, it is suggested that the police have only minimal control over what happens during the adjudication process. Other actors within the process control charging and conviction decisions (e.g., prosecutor, judge, jury). Therefore, the police should not be evaluated on the abilities, practices, or policies of these other criminal justice actors.

Second, the use of convictions as a measure of investigative effectiveness assumes that the police make arrests for the sole purpose of convicting suspects. The conviction criterion does not allow for consideration of the arrest as a situational tool of the police—a means by which to induce information (i.e., develop an informant) or restore order (Petersilia et al., 1990).

Should investigators share the responsibility for whether defendants are convicted in court?

Third, use of the conviction measure as a standard on which to evaluate investigative success also assumes that the only purpose of submitting cases to the prosecutor is to bring charges against the suspect. It ignores other purposes such as reducing public pressure on the police or simply documenting the criminal behavior of a suspect even though it is recognized by the police that there is too little evidence for charges to be filed (Petersilia et al., 1990). To the extent that these arguments are valid, the use of convictions as a measure of investigative success is inappropriate.

Several studies have examined the causes of case attrition, or why convictions are not obtained. At the most simplistic level, cases are most often rejected and dismissed because it is perceived by the prosecutor (or judge) that a conviction is not likely or even possible. Research has found, not surprisingly, that the most important factor that contributes to this perception is the strength and quality of the evidence associated with the case. In particular, cases with physical evidence and cooperative witnesses are more likely to result in a conviction than cases without such evidence (Chen, 1991; Forst et al., 1977, 1982).

Given the conclusion that lack of evidence leads to the rejection and dismissal of cases, an important question becomes, Why isn't the evidence to support a conviction present in any given case? It is with this question that there is disagreement. One argument suggests that evidence is not recognized because police are uncertain with regard to what they are looking for, or evidence is lost because of other inadequate police practices. For instance, witnesses are not available because the police are unable to locate them or witnesses do not wish to cooperate because of the officers' actions toward them (Forst et al., 1982). Police officers may not collect (or recognize) physical evidence, at least in part, because of the lack of feedback from prosecutors on the necessity of such evidence in obtaining convictions (McDonald et al., 1982). However, research that has examined the effectiveness of programs designed to increase communication between the police and the prosecutor has found that such efforts do little in reducing the amount of case attrition (for example, see Garofalo [1991]).

The opposing argument suggests that the evidence needed to secure a conviction is just simply often not available. Factors inherent within the offense, and beyond the control of the police, largely determine the amount and nature of the evidence available. Research has consistently shown, for example, that a prior relationship between the victim and defendant is strongly related to lower conviction rates (see Chen [1991], Garofalo [1991], and Schmidt and Steury [1989]). The primary reason for this is that victims in such cases are often uncooperative during the prosecution process, if they wish to pursue the case at all. Another reason is that crimes that occur between friends may be viewed by the prosecutor (and the police) as not being as serious as crimes that occur between strangers. When there is a relationship between the parties, the crime may be viewed more as a private matter than a criminal matter. It follows then, completely independent of police action, that in crimes with certain circumstances (like personal crimes, which often occur between friends, acquaintances, or relatives), convictions are inherently more difficult to attain than in others. In this regard, it is interesting to note that personal crimes are more likely to be solved than property crimes but are less likely to result in a conviction.

Satisfying Crime Victims

The use of victim satisfaction as a standard on which to judge the performance of investigators is a relatively new concept. The satisfaction outcome emerged from the citizen attitudes studies conducted since the turbulent 1960s and has taken on new importance during the last few decades with the movement toward community policing. The satisfaction outcome is essentially an extension of the consumer perspective into the public sector.

Typically, through interviews or self-administered questionnaires, crime victims who recently reported their victimization to the police are asked about their degree of satisfaction with the police response or certain aspects of it. For example, Brandl and Horvath (1991) asked a sample of crime victims to describe specific aspects of the police response (expectations of response time, officer demeanor, officers' crime scene activities, and existence of recontacts) and to express their overall satisfaction with the police with regard to the incident. These data not only provide insight into the effectiveness of the process in relation to victim satisfaction but may also provide a means to identify policies and practices that need adjustment or change.

Several arguments can be offered in support of victim satisfaction as a standard on which to judge the effectiveness of the criminal investigation process. First, and most basically, satisfying victims (or citizens, more generally) is thought to represent a legitimate goal in itself—a "good" end to be pursued for its own sake. This reasoning is congruent with notions of "community policing" (Goldstein, 1987).

A second argument in support of victim satisfaction as an investigative outcome is that victim satisfaction is a prerequisite for victim *cooperation* with the police—a means by which victims/citizens and the police can become coproducers of crime prevention—again, a cornerstone of the community policing concept. In this light, ensuring satisfaction may be of utmost importance because, as discussed earlier, the police are dependent on victims to report incidents and to provide information necessary to identify, apprehend, and convict offenders.

One frequently offered argument against the use of the victim satisfaction standard is that it distracts from efforts at attaining more important outcomes like solving crimes. Significant resources can be applied toward satisfying victims, but, as the argument goes, they are essentially wasted resources because they often have little to do with solving crimes.

Also potentially problematic is that using victim satisfaction as an indicator of investigative effectiveness assumes that the performance of the police can substantially affect the victims' degree of satisfaction. If other factors such as prior experiences with the police and background characteristics (such as race, age, and income) exert a substantial independent impact on satisfaction, the use of satisfaction as an indicator of investigative effectiveness would be inappropriate. Recent research suggests that this is, in fact, the case (Brandl et al., 1994; Parks, 1984).

Studies show that most crime victims are quite satisfied with the performance of the police in handling their victimization incident (Brandl and Horvath, 1991; Percy, 1980; Shapland, 1983). Studies also show that many factors influence victim satisfaction with police performance. Specifically, research shows that the demeanor of the patrol officer during the initial investigation is one of the most important factors in determining victim satisfaction. According to Shapland (1983), "the major determinant of satisfaction was . . . [the police officer's] attitude toward the victim. Those police officers who appeared to be interested in what the victim said, took the time to listen to them and seemed to take them seriously, promoted feelings of satisfaction in the victims" (p. 253). In the study by Brandl and Horvath (1991), the officers' demeanor was the most powerful predictor of satisfaction. The importance of the officers' conduct during the initial investigation was highlighted by some of the comments provided by victims on the returned questionnaires. For example, "The police officers who came to the scene were unfriendly, rude, and very uncaring. They treated me like I was the criminal. I would never call them for help again." "I felt that the officers had a poor attitude." "I felt as if the officer didn't believe me, because of the way he was talking to the other officer who showed up." "The officer had a very bored attitude. It seemed that he felt dissatisfied by having to 'stoop' so low as to write down anything about a 'minor burglary.'"

Investigative activities performed by the patrol officer during the initial investigation have also been found to be strongly related to victim satisfaction (Brandl and Horvath, 1991; Percy, 1980; Poister and McDavid, 1978). For example, Percy (1980) found that when the officer made an arrest, comforted someone, or provided crime prevention information, victims were more likely to be satisfied. According to Brandl and Horvath (1991), investigative effort was positively related to victim satisfaction in property crimes but not

The behavior of police officers during the initial investigation is one of the most important factors in determining victim satisfaction.

personal crimes. In particular, the importance of looking for fingerprints was evident by the frequency of related comments provided on the returned questionnaires. A few quotes from dissatisfied victims speak to the issue:

> They could have taken fingerprints but did not until two days later and only because I complained to the department . . .

> My children asked why the police didn't take fingerprints . . . I explained to them that we were not important enough . . .

> I felt that a more thorough investigation including taking fingerprints would possibly have helped solve the crime.

> The police officer who responded to the call was very nice and courteous. However, when asked if they could take fingerprints, I was told no . . .

> I figured the window used to gain entry should have been dusted for fingerprints . . .

> There were fingerprints all over the dashboard and nothing was done about that either.

Response time is another dimension of the police response that has been found to affect victim satisfaction. Poister and McDavid (1978) found that victims who perceived the police to take more time to respond (in minutes) were more likely to be dissatisfied. According to Percy (1980), victim *expectation* of police response time was a better predictor of satisfaction than actual response time. Victims who perceived the police to respond faster than expected were more likely to be satisfied than victims who perceived the police to respond slower than expected. Brandl and Horvath (1991) found the same general relationship, but that expectation of response time was more important in determining the satisfaction of personal crime victims than property crime victims.

Conclusion

Several observations concerning the effectiveness of the reactive criminal investigation process can be offered. It appears that none of the investigative outcomes are within complete control of the police. Because circumstances outside the control of the police affect the probability of crimes being solved, convictions being obtained, and crime victims being satisfied, structural changes in the investigative process may have relatively little effect on apprehension or conviction success (Greenwood et al., 1976). It is important to note, however, that other types of changes, especially those of a technological nature, may likely have a significant and direct impact on apprehension and conviction success. For example, AFIS technology may enhance the usefulness of fingerprints in identifying suspects. DNA printing can provide a positive link between human cells recovered from a crime scene and a particular identified individual, and thus can greatly enhance the usefulness of such physical evidence in obtaining convictions.

The police may be most able to affect victim satisfaction through procedural changes. For example, given the importance of expectations of response time in satisfying victims, police telephone operators could, as a matter of policy, provide crime victims with an estimate of police arrival time (Percy, 1980) and thus make expectations congruent with the services actually received. With regard to officer demeanor, it does not seem unreasonable, at the very least, to stress among officers the importance of sensitivity in interpersonal interaction with victims. As for investigative effort, at a minimum, victims could be made aware of the tasks that were, or will be, performed during the investigation.

In addition, to establish the utility of certain investigative practices, it is necessary that the three outcomes be considered simultaneously because what is important for achieving one outcome may not be important in achieving another. For instance, research has shown that fingerprints have traditionally not been very useful in solving crimes (but see Chapter 6). On this basis, one might be tempted to conclude that obtaining fingerprints is not an important aspect of investigative operations. However, it has also been shown that victims (especially victims of serious property crimes) often expect the police to exert effort investigating the crime, including "dusting for prints," and are dissatisfied if they do not. Now, whether the police should routinely collect fingerprints to promote feelings of satisfaction is debatable. On one hand, this activity appears to influence victim satisfaction, which is arguably an important outcome of the investigative process. On the other hand, such an activity may unjustifiably support and promote the medialike image of the police and, as a consequence, create unrealistic expectations that the police should be able to solve the crime if fingerprints are recovered. The solution appears to be one of balancing efficiency with education and satisfaction (Brandl and Horvath, 1991).

Moreover, research also indicates that the presence of physical evidence—especially fingerprints—substantially improves the probability of obtaining convictions. Given this broader perspective, it would be an error to conclude that obtaining or looking for fingerprints is an insignificant aspect of investigative operations. In short, it seems appropriate to broaden the conceptualization of the desired outcomes of the criminal investigation process when judging the success of it.

Undercover Investigations

Covert, or undercover, investigations are often controversial but potentially powerful strategies to combat crime problems. Undercover investigations, which involve a variety of strategies such as stings and decoys, are powerful and controversial because of their structure. The police become involved in the investigation before a crime actually occurs, or are in position to take action immediately after the crime occurs. In a sense, it is fair to say that the police, in operating in undercover mode, *instigate* crime.

Undercover strategies are also increasing in popularity among law enforcement agencies (Marx, 1988). Several reasons can be offered to help explain why undercover strategies are more frequently used now than just thirty years ago. First, it is reasonable to expect that as crimes change, so too must the investigative response. As Marx (1988) explains, "as crime becomes more organized, devious, specialized, and complex, so too does law enforcement" (p. 38). Clearly, if the police are to combat crimes such as public corruption, sale of drugs, vice, fraud, or the trafficking of child pornography, they need to be in a position to detect the crime as it occurs. Undercover strategies provide such an opportunity.

Second, there are currently resources available to fund such operations. In particular, the "war on drugs" and the funding that goes with it has allowed for the development and operation of such strategies. In addition, laws have also provided for the necessary resources to operate such strategies. In particular, asset forfeiture laws allow the police to seize property and cash that is believed to be directly related to illegal activities such as drug trafficking and sales. The goods confiscated can be used by the police to fund undercover operations. In this respect, undercover strategies are financially self-sustaining.

Third, other legislative and judicial supports have encouraged the development and operation of undercover strategies. For example, restrictions on interrogation while in custody, and limitations on searches and seizures have indirectly encouraged undercover work. As Marx (1988) notes, "the greater the restriction on police in overt investigations, the greater will be their use of covert investigations" (p. 47). He continues, "restrict police use of coercion, and the use of deception increases. Restrict investigative behavior after an offense, and increased attention will be placed on anticipating an offense" (p. 47).

A final factor that may help explain the increased use of undercover investigations is that these strategies allow investigators to get maximum benefit from the use of technology. For example, if the police are in a position to record secretly on videotape a criminal transaction, this evidence may be quite powerful evidence in court. Clearly, a defense attorney may find it rather difficult to assert the innocence of her client if the evidence against him includes a videotape showing the defendant's illegal behavior. Undercover investigations allow the police to be in a position to use such technology effectively.

There are many different types of covert investigative strategies. Perhaps the most well-known and most common type is the *sting*, which usually involves an investigator posing as someone who wishes to buy (or sell) some illicit goods (such as drugs or sex), or to execute some other sort of illicit transaction. Once a "seller" (or "buyer") is identified and the particulars of the illicit transaction are determined, police officers waiting nearby can execute an arrest. Sting operations come in a multitude of varieties, and over the years the police have used such strategies in rather imaginative ways. For example, a recent sting operation in Las Vegas involved police officers posing as wealthy Middle Eastern men who desired the services of a local "call girl" service. With initial arrangements made over the telephone, the two women came to the hotel for the "transaction." With the Arabic men knowing little English, the women did most of the talking in setting the terms of the deal. Once the particulars were determined, officers in an adjacent room, who were watching the transaction being negotiated on closed-circuit television, entered the room and arrested the women. As another example, the Denver Police wished to apprehend individuals who were wanted on warrants but evaded apprehension by the police. The police decided on a rather creative sting operation. Using official-looking but bogus sweepstakes letterhead, prize award letters were sent to the last known address of the individuals on the warrants list. The letter indicated that the named recipient was the winner of two Denver Bronco football game tickets.

All that needed to be done to claim the prize was to show up at a particular office at a particular time with valid identification. As the individuals arrived, police checked their identifications and made arrests.

Another common strategy involves undercover police officers acting as *decoys*, during which an attempt is made to attract street crime by presenting an opportunity to an offender to commit such a crime. Once a crime has been attempted, nearby officers who are standing by can make an arrest of the would-be perpetrator. As an example of such an operation, during the course of several years, the police in a college town received numerous reports from college-age women that they were "flashed" by a man while walking on campus at night, usually on their way home from class. The man reportedly appeared between houses and always hollered "Hey!" to get the attention of the victim. By the time the police were notified and responded to the area, the man could never be found. After numerous incidents, the police decided to conduct a decoy operation. A female police officer acted as the decoy; she dressed like a typical college student, wore a backpack over her shoulder, and walked around at night in the areas in which the flasher was known to operate. The undercover officer had a two-radio attached to her backpack so she could quickly notify the two officers who were waiting nearby in an unmarked squad car. After six weeks into the operation, and the perpetrator nowhere to be seen, the operation ended, but so too did the incidents. It is suspected that the man either moved out of the city or was arrested on another charge. As another example, the FBI is currently conducting an ongoing investigation known as *Innocent Images*. This investigation targets people who use computers to receive or distribute child pornography and to recruit minors into illicit sexual relationships. In the latter case, agents log on to computers and pose as minors in various chat rooms on the Internet. Sometimes sexually oriented conversations are developed and these sometimes lead to arrangements being made by the offender to meet with the minor for purposes of sexual relations. As actual face-to-face meetings are to occur, agents make arrests. According to the FBI, hundreds of convictions have been obtained during the past ten years for such offenses (FBI, 2002).

Undercover fencing operations are another type of undercover investigative strategy. A *fence* is a business that buys and sells property that is known to be stolen. When the police go undercover and establish a fencing operation, they let it be known on the streets that there is someone who is willing to buy stolen goods. The police make purchases, track the origin of the merchandise, and then make arrests. An example of a fencing operation was the first stage of the ABSCAM operation, as described in the introduction to this chapter. Undercover agents made it known that there was someone in town who was willing to buy artwork known to be stolen. As individuals brought artwork to the undercover officers to be sold, agents could make arrests for theft of the work or, at the very least, for being in possession of stolen property.

Other covert methods include surveillance and stakeouts. Surveillance usually involves watching a person or persons to monitor their activities. Stakeouts most often involve watching a place and monitoring activities at that place. As an example of a surveillance-type operation, private companies on occasion hire investigators from private security firms to act as "spies." The "spy" goes to work and performs the same functions as a regular employee but also has the job of secretly reporting to management the illegal at-work behaviors of other employees (for example, stealing company property, drug use). When the assignment is complete, the operative quits the job so no one learns his true identity or purpose. As an example of a stakeout, the police in Michigan were investigating a series of brutal, sexually motivated homicides of young college-age women from the University of Michigan and Eastern Michigan University (EMU). After six victims, the police had no good leads. With the body of the seventh victim discovered in a remote rural area, the police secretly removed the body and replaced it with a store mannequin and set up a stakeout of the area believing that the killer might return at some point to view the dead body. As the stakeout was in progress, the culprit returned to the area and was seen by the police, but he saw the police first and fled before the police could apprehend him (see the introduction to Chapter 4 to learn the details—and outcome—of this investigation).

Undercover investigations are controversial for several reasons, all of which relate directly or indirectly to entrapment. Entrapment is defined as "the act of government officers or agents in inducing a person to commit a crime that is not contemplated by the person, for the purpose of instituting a criminal prosecution against him or her" (del Carmen, 1995; p. 166). In essence, the police can provide an opportunity for a person to commit a crime but cannot compel a person to commit a crime. There is often a fine line between providing an opportunity to commit a crime and compelling a person to commit a crime. Such a determination is made on a case-by-case basis.

There are two basic tests to determine whether entrapment took place: the subjective test and the objective test (del Carmen, 1995). The subjective test focuses most directly on the predisposition of the offender in committing the offense. Here, entrapment exists if the accused had no predisposition to commit the offense but committed the crime because of inducement by the police. If the accused was predisposed to committing the offense, then there is no entrapment, regardless of the actions of the government agent. The objective test focuses directly on the actions of the government agent. Here the question is, Did the conduct of the law enforcement agent induce the person to commit the crime? The culprit's previous criminal activity or disposition to committing the current offense is irrelevant; the focus is on the conduct of the agent.

Beside these two approaches to deciding the existence of entrapment, there are several other issues that are relevant. First, how are targets of the undercover investigation selected? Does the undercover operation resemble a wild-goose chase trying to entice anyone into committing a crime, or is it focused on a particular person or place known to be criminally inclined. The more focused the operation and the more reason to believe that the individuals involved are already criminally motivated, the more legally defensible the operation. A second question relates to who initiates the illegal action. This issue relates directly to the conduct of the undercover officers. The most legally defensible position is when agents are passive in setting the terms of the deal, the nature of the agreement, or in setting the trap. For all practical and legal purposes, agents should not set the terms of the deal (recall the Las Vegas prostitution sting operation discussed earlier during which the undercover officers acted as though they could not speak English—they could only say "yes" . . . "yes" . . .). The third issue has to do with the nature of the temptation. If the rewards of the criminal behavior are extraordinary, the defense of entrapment may be more salient. These issues are inherent in the operation and defense of undercover strategies.

Outcomes of Undercover Investigations

The ultimate goal of undercover investigations is to reduce crime through either deterrence or incapacitation. Why might undercover strategies lead to deterrence or incapacitation? With deterrence, the logic is that if would-be offenders realize that undercover investigations are being conducted, they would also perceive the chances of detection and arrest to have increased. Overall, then, criminal behavior may be viewed by offenders as being more risky with undercover operations in place. With the threat of punishment more significant, one might expect that criminal behaviors will be avoided. As for a crime reduction through incapacitation, one might expect that with more offenders arrested as a result of undercover investigations, more offenders would be incarcerated, reducing the number of people able to commit additional crimes.

So, do undercover investigations reduce crime? No question, some undercover operations have been effective at identifying and apprehending offenders, and thereby producing a decline in crime through either incapacitation or deterrence. One can be equally sure, however, that some undercover operations have not been effective in this regard. Overall, there is little research evidence to suggest that these strategies actually deter individuals from engaging in crime on a long-term basis or that they lead to a meaningful crime reduction through incapacitation (Marx, 1988).

In fact, some research shows that such strategies actually increase crime. In particular, with undercover fencing operations, if it becomes known on the street that someone is willing to buy stolen property, then a market, or a larger market, may be created for such property. This in itself may lead to more burglaries and robberies, at least among those who are already so criminally inclined. In addition, with sting operations, like drug buy–bust strategies, it is not uncommon for undercover officers to be willing to purchase drugs for prices that are beyond the current market price. If someone is willing to purchase a quantity of drugs for, as an example, twice its normal market value, it may create considerable additional interest in dealing such drugs. Decoys may also provide considerable opportunity for crime and thus decoys may actually increase the frequency of crime.

Furthermore, undercover investigative strategies may have other unexpected and undesirable outcomes. First is the issue of displacement. Arrests are often viewed as an indicator of success in undercover investigations, whereas a lack of arrests is often viewed as a sign of deterrence. This logic, however, is not necessarily valid. It is possible that the lack of arrests means that the crime has been displaced. Crime may be displaced, or moved, across time or space. For example, if offenders realize that certain enforcement operations are in place at a particular time or place, offenders can simply wait to commit their crimes at some other time or can commit crimes in some other place at that time. If crime is displaced, it is not accurate to say it has been successfully prevented or deterred; it has just been pushed around.

Second, through undercover investigations, the police may be most likely to identify and apprehend inexperienced or less knowledgeable offenders. Experienced criminals may be able to identify decoys, undercover agents, and other traps quickly, whereas inexperienced offenders may not yet have acquired these skills and knowledge. There is empirical evidence to suggest that this, in fact, is the case (Marx, 1988).

Third, undercover investigations may pose additional safety concerns for all those involved. For example, they may be unsafe for police officers and citizens, as illustrated in the Detroit Police Department's now defunct STRESS project (Stop The Robberies—Enjoy Safe Streets). During a three-year period, this decoy operation resulted in three officer deaths, 100 officers injured, sixteen suspect deaths, and fifty-eight suspects injured (Marx, 1988). Such operations may also pose safety risks to officers as a result of "friendly fire" incidents. Undercover officers may not be easily identifiable to other (undercover) officers and, as a result, tragic confusion may result.

Fourth, undercover operations may pose significant management and coordination challenges. This is particularly true in the supervision of officers acting in undercover roles and in coordinating undercover investigations that are conducted in the same geographical areas (Miller, 1987). It is possible that investigations may overlap, and undercover officers in one operation may interfere with another investigation in the area. In such cases, officers may unwittingly jeopardize the success of other investigations.

Finally, there may be other hazards associated with undercover work. Officers in such jobs may experience role conflict and moral misgivings about their work. Undercover officers may come to overidentify with the suspect group and, in the process, lose their own identity. The conclusion of many undercover operations involves the betrayal of the suspect group, which may bring its own psychological problems. Undercover officers may also face a variety of temptations while working in their covert roles. Using drugs and profiting from the sale of drugs are two such possibilities. In addition, officers working in undercover operations may also face dangers associated with being discovered and may experience associated anxieties (Miller, 1987).

Other Proactive Police Strategies

Along with undercover investigative strategies, there are also other proactive strategies that may allow the police to be in a better position to deal with crime as it occurs. Three such strategies are discussed here: crackdowns, hot-spot patrol, and selective apprehension.

Crackdowns

Simply defined, a *crackdown* is a strategy in which the police abruptly enforce laws at a higher than normal level (Sherman, 1990; Worden et al., 1994). The increased enforcement activity associated with crackdowns can be focused on particular geographical areas (such as a downtown business district or university campus) or on particular types of crime (for example, jaywalking, drug selling, prostitution, driving while intoxicated). Crackdowns can also be designed to place the police in an overt (uniformed police presence—such as speeding enforcement) or covert (undercover—such as drug trafficking) mode of operation. Crackdowns consist of (1) an increase in police presence in a particular area or against a particular type of crime, (2) increased use of sanctions by police officers (e.g., arrests, citations), and (3) media coverage of the increased enforcement to make potential offenders aware of the police presence and sanctions.

Crackdowns are designed to be short term in nature because they are expensive to operate. After the crackdown is well advertised and is fully implemented for a period of time, the crackdown is then suddenly or gradually withdrawn (i.e., the "back-off"), but the back-off is not advertised. As a result of this process, the crackdown strategy is not only supposed to result in an initial deterrent effect while the crackdown is in full operation, but also results in a residual, or continuing, deterrent effect after enforcement activities have stopped. The expected residual decline in crime is also known as a *hangover effect*, when the impact of previous activities lingers after those activities have concluded. It is this potential "free" benefit that makes the crackdown strategy particularly attractive to the police as a crime control strategy (Sherman, 1990).

Crackdowns are supposed to increase the actual or perceived risk of apprehension and punishment for committing offenses in question. According to deterrence theory, with the increased certainty of punishment comes the likelihood that criminal behavior will be deterred, that potential offenders will choose not to commit risky behaviors. As for the residual deterrent effect in particular, if one perceives a higher than normal level of risk to be present, and has no evidence to suggest otherwise, the deterrent effect may continue without interruption.

Do crackdowns work? Several conclusions can be drawn regarding the effectiveness of crackdowns in reducing crime (see Sherman [1990]). First, there have been relatively few systematic empirical studies that have examined the effects of crackdowns. Second, most of these studies show that crackdowns usually result in an initial deterrent effect. In addition, these initial deterrent effects are more likely with certain types of crime (e.g., driving while intoxicated) than with others (e.g., street-level drug dealing). Third, relatively few studies show that crackdowns actually produce a residual deterrent effect. Finally, several studies show a displacement effect, indicating that the targeted crime was not really deterred, just moved to a different place or to a different time. Many studies that did not report a displacement effect did not even consider such a possibility.

Hot-Spot Patrol

Hot-spot patrol strategies are similar to crackdowns in that they involve an increase in police presence in a particular area, but they are different from crackdowns in that they do not necessarily involve media publicity, increased use of sanctions, or undercover officers. In addition, hot-spot patrol is always geographically based in relatively small high-crime areas. Hot-spot patrol is also sometimes referred to as *directed patrol* or *saturation patrol*. The patrol is directed, as opposed to random, because it focuses on particular places and may require that officers engage in particular activities (e.g., traffic stops, field interrogations). The patrol is saturated because many more officers than usual are assigned to patrol these identified high-crime areas. Hot-spot patrol can involve merely increasing police patrol presence in an area or it can involve officers performing more proactive activities in the area (e.g., vehicle stops, field interrogations).

For the most part, crime is not a random event; rather, it is highly concentrated in particular places and at particular times. In a study conducted by Sherman et al. (1989) in Minneapolis, it was found that during a one-year period of time, all robberies reported to the police occurred at only 2.2 percent of all places in the city, all auto thefts occurred at only 2.7 percent of all places, and all rapes occurred at only 1.2 percent of all places. It was also determined that ninety-five percent of the places in the city were free of any of these types of crimes during the one-year period. As such, one could reasonably conclude that if the police are to have an effect on crime, it may be most likely in the areas where crime is concentrated. It is on this theoretical basis that hot-spot patrol rests.

Once again, relatively few studies have examined the effects of hot-spot patrol. Sherman and Weisburd (1995) found that in Minneapolis, where the police increased their patrol presence in identified hot spots, the patrols led to a significant decline in crime and an even more pronounced decline in disorder (e.g., prostitution, loud music). Research conducted by Sherman and Rogan (1995) in Kansas City, Missouri, examined not only the impact of increased police presence in identified hot spots but also the effects of efforts aimed at confiscating illegal guns being carried by individuals in vehicles and on the street. This study showed that patrol focused on "getting guns" led to significant declines in gun-related crimes in the particular areas.

Selective Apprehension

Selective apprehension involves the allocation of police resources to identifying, monitoring, and arresting repeat or high-rate offenders. As described by Martin and Sherman (1986), the Repeat Offender Project (ROP) in Washington, DC, represents an example of the selective apprehension concept. The ROP consisted of a specially created unit of officers that used intelligence, surveillance, stings, decoys, and other traps to apprehend people who were wanted on warrants and people who were believed to be very active in criminal activity. So, whereas crackdowns and especially hot-spot patrols are geographically focused and rely on geographical crime analysis, selective apprehension is person focused and relies on person-based crime analysis.

The theory supporting the selective apprehension strategy is that a relatively small proportion of people are responsible for a relatively large proportion of crime. With this realization, it makes sense that the police would have the largest impact on crime by identifying and incapacitating this relatively small group of people. The limited research on the strategy (Martin and Sherman, 1986) shows that such an initiative can lead to a substantial increase in arrests of repeat offenders.

Questions for Discussion and Review

1. What are the four types of police action according to Marx (1988)?

2. What are the three primary sets of tasks that comprise preliminary investigations?

3. What are the two major factors on which case screening decisions are usually made?

4. Briefly, what does the research say about how detectives spend their working time?

5. Why do some cases receive more investigative attention from detectives than others?

6. What are solvability factors?

7. What are the differences and similarities between cold-case squads and task forces?

8. What are the problems associated with using clearance and arrest data to measure the success of criminal investigations?

9. What determines whether crimes are solved, circumstances of the crime, or efforts of the investigators?

10. What conditions are necessary for a fast police response to have an impact on whether the police make an on-scene arrest?

11. What are the major arguments in favor and in opposition to "convicting suspects" and "satisfying victims" as indicators of investigative success?

12. What are the major reasons for case attrition?

13. What are the factors most closely associated with victim satisfaction with police investigative performance?

14. Why have undercover investigations become more common during the last few decades?

15. What are the major types of undercover investigations?

16. What is entrapment and what are the issues relating to it?

17. Do undercover investigations reduce crime?

18. What are crackdowns? How are they supposed to work? How effective are they?

19. What is hot-spot patrol? What is the theory on which it rests? How effective is the strategy? Explain.

20. What is selective apprehension? What is the theory on which it rests? How effective is the strategy? Explain.

Related Internet Sites

www.findlaw.com

This is a comprehensive legal resource site. Click on "US Sup Ct" and check out the U.S. Supreme Court case *Jacobson* v. *United States* (1992) for a landmark decision regarding entrapment in a child pornography case.

www.businesscontrols.com

This is the web site for Business Controls, Inc., a firm that offers undercover investigative services to corporate customers. Particularly useful is the newsletter located under the "news and articles" link.

www.washingtonpost.com/wp-srv/local/longterm/tours/scandal/lescaze.htm

This is a link to a *Washington Post* article written by a reporter who was the landlord of the house the FBI rented during their ABSCAM investigation.

THE ROLE OF EVIDENCE IN CRIMINAL INVESTIGATIONS

OBJECTIVES

After reading this chapter you will be able to

- Differentiate between judicial evidence and extrajudicial evidence
- Differentiate between exculpatory evidence and inculpatory evidence
- Discuss the nature of proof and its various levels or standards
- Discuss probable cause as a standard of proof
- Compare direct evidence with indirect evidence and give an example of each
- Identify the types or forms of circumstantial evidence
- Discuss the meaning and nature of testimonial evidence, real evidence, and demonstrative evidence
- Compare the function and role of lay witnesses with expert witnesses
- Discuss the major exceptions to the hearsay rule

- Discuss and give an example of corpus delicti evidence
- Discuss and give an example of corroborative evidence
- Discuss and give an example of cumulative evidence
- Discuss and give an example of associative evidence
- Discuss and give an example of identification evidence
- Discuss and give an example of behavioral evidence
- Based on the Michigan Coed Killer case, discuss how proof was established that the killer murdered Karen Beineman

IMPORTANT TERMS

Criminal evidence

Judicial evidence

Admissible evidence

Extrajudicial evidence

Inadmissible evidence

Exculpatory evidence

Inculpatory evidence

Proof

Standards of proof

Probable cause

Beyond a reasonable doubt

Reasonable suspicion

Preponderance of the evidence

Direct evidence

Indirect/circumstantial evidence

Testimonial evidence

Lay witnesses

Expert witnesses

Hearsay evidence

Hearsay rule

Real evidence

Demonstrative evidence

Corpus delicti evidence

Corroborative evidence

Cumulative evidence

Associative evidence

Identification evidence

Behavioral evidence

INTRODUCTION

The nightmare began on the evening of July 10, 1967, when nineteen-year-old Mary Fleszar did not return to her apartment located just a few blocks from the Eastern Michigan University campus in Ypsilanti, Michigan, where she was a student. As is the case in most missing person investigations, the first investigative task was to determine when and where the individual was last seen. In reconstructing the last known whereabouts of Mary, an EMU police officer recalled seeing a girl matching her description walking near campus at about 8:45 PM the night before she was reported missing. She was by herself. Another witness reported that he saw the girl at about 9:00 PM that same night in the same area walking on the sidewalk. The witness reported that at about this time a car drove up next to her and stopped. According to the witness, the only occupant of the vehicle was "a young man" and the vehicle was "bluish gray in color, possibly a Chevy." The witness stated that the young man inside the car apparently said something to Mary, she shook her head, and the car drove off. Shortly thereafter, the same car passed the witness' house again, and pulled into a driveway in front of Mary, blocking her path. Mary walked around the back of the car and continued down the sidewalk. The car pulled out of the driveway and, with a squeal of the tires, drove down the street. At this point, the witness lost site of Mary and the vehicle. Mary Fleszar was never again seen alive.

On August 7, 1967, a heavily decomposed nude body was found on farm land two miles north of Ypsilanti. Through dental records, the body was identified as Mary Fleszar. It appeared to investigators that given the area in which the body was found (an open field) and the circumstances of her disappearance, that the cause of death was not natural or accidental. In addition, given the area in which the body was found and that no clothes were found in the vicinity, in all probability she was not killed where she was found. Her body was probably dumped there. With the crime established as a homicide, the next question for investigators became: Where was she killed? It also appeared that because of matted grass around the body and the positioning of the body, that the corpse had been moved several times. But by whom or by what? Did the killer return to the scene or was the body moved by animals? The autopsy conducted on the body of Mary Fleszer revealed that she had been stabbed approximately thirty times, and that she had been severely beaten. It could not be determined if she had been sexually assaulted. Most puzzling was that the girl's feet were missing and her lower leg bones had been apparently smashed. Wild animals may have been able to carry away the feet, but only the killer could have crushed her leg bones.

Two days before the funeral for Mary, it was reported by one of the maintenance men at the funeral home that an individual in a bluish gray Chevy came to the funeral home and asked to take pictures of the corpse, but this person was not carrying a camera. Certainly of extraordinary interest to investigators, the worker could only describe this man as "sort of young, sort of ordinary looking." Investigators had no good leads into who caused the death of Mary Fleszar. The description of the vehicle possibly involved in the crime was the most promising lead, but even that was nearly worthless.

To the relief of residents, students, parents, and the police, through the spring of 1968 there were no more murders. It appeared that the murder of Mary was an isolated event. Then on Monday, July 1, 1968, a second EMU student, twenty-year-old Joan Schell, was reported missing. Police determined from several eyewitnesses, one of whom was her friend, that she was last seen at a bus stop when a car with three men stopped and talked to her. The car was described as a late-model two-door with a red body and a black vinyl top. One of the men in the car was described as being in his twenties, about six feet tall, clean-cut, good-looking, with dark hair and a green T-shirt. After what appeared to be a brief conversation between Joan and the men, Joan got into the car and the car drove off. One of the witnesses told the police that he saw one of the men in the car in the EMU Union at about 11:00 PM that evening, after the building was closed. In checking this possible lead, the police found no signs of forced entry into the Union, indicating that whoever this was must have had a key.

The disappearance was, not surprisingly, front-page news. Joan's boyfriend, Dickie Shantz, who was absent-without-leave from his Army base at the time of Joan's disappearance, was questioned but eventually cleared. Other friends and acquaintances of Joan were also questioned but quickly dismissed as possible suspects. On Friday, four days after she was reported missing, the body of Joan Schell was found at a nearby construction site. The body was nude and covered with dried blood, although no blood was found in the area near her body. Most unusual about the body was that the top one-third was in an advanced state of decomposition but the bottom two-thirds of the body was well preserved. In addition, the grass around the corpse was trampled, perhaps indicating that the body was just disposed of. Once again, the question was: Where was she killed? And where was the body kept until it was disposed of? The autopsy provided few answers. It revealed that Joan Schell was stabbed twenty-five times, including once into the side of her head, with a knife about four inches long. With the presence of seminal fluid and related injuries, it was determined that she had been sexually assaulted.

At this point, a task force was created to coordinate the activities of the five police agencies involved in the investigation, and a reward for information relating to the arrest of the killer was established. With few good leads to pursue, the major activity on the part of investigators was to find where the body of Joan Schell was kept prior to being dumped at the construction site. Investigators needed a crime scene, and hoped to find valuable evidence at the crime scene. A sketch of the individual with whom Joan was last seen was prepared and disseminated through the media. Two EMU students came forward to the police and told them that they saw Joan with an individual by the name of John Collins the night she disappeared. Interestingly, John was a student at EMU and held a part-time job at the Union (Joan also worked part-time at the Union). The information provided by these witnesses did not match the information provided by the other witnesses, but, not to leave any stone unturned, police found and interviewed him. Throughout this interview it was learned that John drove an old De Soto, and it was neither red nor black. He told the detectives that he was not in the city when Jill disappeared, and that he was the nephew of a Michigan State Police officer. Another apparent dead end.

On the morning of March 21, 1969, the body of a young woman was found in a cemetery located about four miles outside Ypsilanti. The woman who discovered the body lived near the cemetery and she told the police that she saw a white station wagon leave the cemetery at about midnight the previous night. Another witness reported that he saw a late-model green station wagon cruising around the cemetery the night before the discovery of the body. Through items contained in an overnight case found near the body, the victim was identified as Jane Mixer, a twenty-three-year-old law student at the University of Michigan. The victim was fully clothed and appeared to be deliberately and carefully placed in line with a grave marker. One of her shoes rested on her lower abdomen. The victim had two gunshot wounds to her head and a tightly bound noose from a nylon stocking around her neck. Was there any significance to the shoe on her abdomen? Why was she placed at this particular grave site? And where was she killed? The autopsy revealed that she died from the gunshot wounds to her head; the noose was placed around her neck after she was already dead. It was also determined that the victim was currently in her menstrual period and that she had not been sexually assaulted.

In tracking the last activities of Jane, the police learned that she posted a note requesting a ride home on the ride board at the University of Michigan Student Union. In searching her apartment, the police discovered on her desk a note that read "David Hanson Lvg. 6:30 PM" and a checkmark by "David Hanson" in the phonebook. The police thought they had a big break. They quickly found David Hanson but he told investigators that he was in theater practice at 6:30 the night Jane disappeared, that he had no knowledge of her or her attempt to find a ride home, and that he drove a green Volkswagen. Another apparent dead end. The police determined that the killer probably saw the ride request posted by Jane, called her, said he was David Hanson, would give her a ride home, and would pick her up at 6:30 PM. He was late, so she looked in the phone book, called David Hanson, and found that he was not at home.

Probably just minutes later, the killer, believed to be David Hanson by Jane, showed up at her apartment, and Jane left with him never to be seen alive again. Once again, the police had few leads to pursue in the investigation. And they still did not even have a crime scene. Investigators spoke with Jane's boyfriend and other acquaintances but they were all cleared of any wrongdoing. They checked and interviewed all the David Hansons in the area, but to no avail.

The nightmare was only to get worse. On March 25, 1969, the nude and beaten body of Maralynn Skelton, age sixteen, was found. The body was found in a remote rural area one-quarter mile from where Joan Schell's body was found the previous summer. The victim was severely beaten to death, with numerous welts covering her body, as if she had been flogged by a belt with a large buckle. She sustained massive head injuries. Other marks on her hands and feet indicated that she had been bound, probably during the beating. A piece of dark-blue cloth was found deep in her throat. But most atrocious was a tree branch that protruded from her vagina. All her clothes were piled neatly nearby except for her underwear. In searching for witnesses in the area, the police found one witness who heard someone scream a few nights prior to the discovery of the body, another witness saw a red car in the area, another saw a small white two-door car in the area. The police determined that the last place she was known to be alive was a nearby shopping center. Maralynn called a friend from the shopping center to see if she could pick her up. No other witnesses saw or heard anything of Maralynn after that phone call.

Little progress seemed to be made in the investigation of the four homicides, which now many believed were related. The media began to refer to the case as the "coed murders." Indeed, the similarities between the cases were striking. Only the murder of Jane Mixer appeared substantially different (death as a result of a gunshot). The major and fundamental problem in the investigation was a lack of *good* information. At this point, six jurisdictions were involved in the investigation and twenty persons were assigned to the investigative task force. The task force received and considered a substantial amount of information, including the possible relevance of other unsolved homicides in other jurisdictions in the state and across the country. One promising suspect that came to the attention of the police was a man by the name of David Parker. He was a suspect in the Boston Strangler homicides and was, strangely enough, at the time of the murders, a graduate student at the University of Michigan. He even had a connection with a David Hansen (with an "e"). But after much investigation, it was determined that he was not in the area when some of the murders occurred. Things were not going well for investigators. They still did not even have a crime scene.

A month after the murder of Maralynn Skelton, on April 16, 1969, the body of thirteen-year-old Dawn Basom was discovered in a remote residential area outside Ypsilanti. The girl had been reported missing the night before and was determined to have disappeared within one-half mile of her home as she was walking on the sidewalk near her home. When found, the victim was clad only in her bra and blouse. It was determined that she was dead for less then twelve hours. She had been strangled with a black electrical cord which was still tightly knotted around her neck. It also appeared that she had been repeatedly slashed across her torso, gagged, and raped. Later, the police found some of her clothes in the area as if they had been tossed from a moving vehicle.

Then the police finally got a break, but it did not turn out to be a very big one. In searching for witnesses to the murder of Dawn Basom and for a place where she, or any of the other women, may have been murdered, a police officer came across an abandoned farmhouse. The farmhouse was just outside Ypsilanti and close to where some of the bodies had been found. In searching the farmhouse, the officer discovered some women's clothes, jewelry, and, in the basement, found blood and a black electrical cord—a black electrical cord that matched the one used to strangle Dawn Basom! A crime scene at last. The basement of the house, it was reasoned, could also have been a naturally cool place in which to preserve a human body (the body of Joan Schell). The police set up a stakeout operation at the farmhouse and hoped that the killer would return, maybe even with another victim. The police had difficulties in keeping the discovery and stakeout of the farmhouse a secret, but they hoped for the best. After a week of watching the farmhouse, nothing unusual was observed. Investigators went into the farmhouse once again and discovered, to their great surprise, another earring in the basement (later determined to belong to Maralynn Skelton) and a piece of a blouse (that belonged to Dawn Basom). This meant four things: (1) the killer returned to the farmhouse, (2) at least some of the murders were probably committed by the same person, (3) the stakeout did not work very well, and (4) the killer was keeping personal items from the victims as souvenirs. A few days later, a fire broke out at the barn and destroyed it, but the house was undamaged. Police quickly made an arrest of the arsonist, Robert Gross, but after questioning and a polygraph it was determined by investigators that he was not involved in the homicides. Shortly after the fire and the arrest of Robert Gross, a reporter from the *Ypsilanti Press*, John Cobb, found five plump lilacs on the driveway of the farmhouse. Cobb brought the discovery to the attention of the police, and the police found it strange that only he noticed these flowers, even though many police officers were in the area. The police wondered, did the five lilacs represent the five dead girls? Did the killer return again? Was Cobb the killer? The police found a crime scene but they still had more questions than answers.

There seemed to be no end. On June 9, 1969, a body of a woman was discovered in a rarely used driveway of another deserted farm in the area. The body was partially clad in a torn blouse and skirt. On the ground next to the body were torn underwear and pantyhose, the pantyhose slashed through the crotch. She had been stabbed multiple times, as though her killer was in a frenzy, but a single gunshot to her head caused her death. Her throat was cut but it appeared that this occurred after her death. She had been sexually assaulted. Once again, it did not appear that she was killed where her body was found. In canvassing the area, investigators found shoes, buttons to a coat, and blood in the same general area where several of the other bodies were found. All these items were matched to the unidentified body. After several days with the body still not identified, the police placed a photograph of the dead woman's face in the newspaper to determine her identity. In recognizing the picture, the victim's roommate came forward and identified her as Alice Kalom, a twenty-three-year-old University of Michigan student. At about this same time, Alice's parents were reading the account in the newspaper; they identified Alice's body later that same day. The police were unable to track the last activities of Alice. Understandably, investigators were extremely frustrated. They had six homicides and no suspects. They had some evidence to believe that most, if not all, the crimes were related (MO) and they had numerous incomplete descriptions of vehicles that could have been involved. They did not have much.

After this sixth homicide, a *Detroit Free Press* reporter contacted Peter Harkos, a well-known psychic (the same psychic who identified the wrong person as the culprit in the Boston Strangler case, and who worked weekends at a Lake Tahoe nightclub) and asked if he could provide a telepathic composite of the killer. The reporter met with Harkos in California and he provided a description. Among other details, he said the killer was five foot seven, brilliant, maybe a student, loved cars, drove a motorcycle, had one eye bigger than the other, had a knife, worked in gardens, and that there would be more victims. Reluctantly, the police later met with Harkos in Michigan and he provided to the police accurate descriptions of some of the crime scenes, including details not previously released, but none of the information provided new leads for the police to pursue.

At 11:15 PM on Wednesday July 23, 1969, Karen Beineman, a nineteen-year-old EMU student, was reported missing past curfew at her dorm. Her roommates were the last to see her. She left school to go to downtown Ypsilanti to a wig shop—Wigs by Joan—that Wednesday afternoon. The police went to the wig shop with a picture of Karen, and two ladies who worked at the shop remembered that Karen was at the wig shop and left with a guy on a motorcycle. They described this man as "nice looking, clean cut, short dark hair, early twenties, nice build, about six feet tall, and he was wearing a green and yellow striped shirt." The bike was "big, loud, and shiny—dark blue, possibly a Honda." The police put out an all-points bulletin for the missing girl, had a composite sketch drawn of the man last seen with Karen, and got a list of registrations for all motorcycles in the Ypsilanti area. The police located another witness who saw the girl on the motorcycle and she said the bike was definitely a Triumph.

Meanwhile, a young City of Ypsilanti police officer who just graduated from EMU received a briefing on the missing girl and remembered that he saw a guy in a striped shirt on a motorcycle talking to a girl on the street on the afternoon in question. He did not remember his name but knew that he was associated with the Theta Chi Fraternity. He decided to go to the fraternity house and ask some questions. He learned from the other guys at the house that a person by the name of John Collins matched the description, but that he did not live at the house anymore. The officer went to where John was said to live and he found John working on one of four motorcycles in the garage. The officer asked John if he saw anyone that looked like him driving around picking up girls that Wednesday afternoon. John said that he saw nothing of the sort. Before leaving, the officer wrote down the license plate numbers of each of John's motorcycles and John got angry: "What the hell are you doing that for? Bug off and play policeman somewhere else" (Keyes, 1976; p. 204). Then the officer found a girl that he knew was a friend of John's and the officer asked if she had a picture of John that he could borrow. She gave him a picture of John and he took it to the wig shop. One of the ladies said that the man in the picture was definitely the guy seen on the motorcycle with the missing girl; the other lady said that it was "pretty close." With the positive identification, John Collins became a prime suspect in the disappearance of Karen Beineman.

Within minutes of when John Collins was identified as a suspect, the body of Karen Beineman was found. The nude body was discovered in a residential area of Ypsilanti, approximately twenty feet down a gully embankment. The discovery was to be top secret. Based on previous crimes, the police believed that the killer often returned to see the dead bodies and they hoped that he would do so again. The police removed the body, replaced it with a store mannequin, and set up "Operation Stakeout." They hoped for better luck than the last time they used a stakeout. As it grew dark on that hot rainy night, the police hid in the nearby bushes and waited for the killer to return. After a few hours of waiting and watching, an individual was observed by the police running from the area, but before the police could notify each other as to what was seen and the direction in which the man was running, the person had vanished. Thinking that maybe the person had been able to get close enough to touch the body, the police checked for fingerprints on the mannequin, but the only ones recovered were those of the district attorney who had set the mannequin in place.

The autopsy on the body revealed that she had been dead for about three days or so, probably killed at about 3:00 PM (she was seen riding away on the motorcycle at about 1:00 PM). She had been strangled, severely beaten, and semen was present. Her chest and breasts had been severely mutilated as if they had been burned with some type of a liquid or acid. It appeared that she also had been bound, as evidenced by ligature marks on her wrists and ankles. Burlap material was found in her throat. Recovered from the victim's vagina were her underwear. On closer examination of the underwear, a most interesting discovery was made. In the underwear were tiny head/hair particles, hair clippings. Where did they come from? Was Karen Beineman killed in a barber shop?

Meanwhile, the police maintained surveillance on their prime suspect, John Collins. Other young women came forward to the police and said that the man pictured in the composite had tried to get them to go for a ride. Another said that Collins offered her $50 if he could take pictures of her. With the evidence mounting against Collins, two young Ypsilanti police officers took it upon themselves to question him. They accused him of the murder, and in the process, told him what they knew about the crime. John provided an alibi to the officers, and told them that his uncle, David Leik, a Michigan State Police officer, would not be happy that they were making such accusations of him. This premature questioning of Collins turned out to be another big mistake, one of many in the investigation.

During the next several days, the police spent time verifying Collins' alibi for the date and time of the disappearance and murder of Karen, and it seemed to hold up. Why? Was it true? Or did he have the time and forewarning to create an alibi? The police continued to uncover evidence that at least indirectly suggested that Collins was the coed killer. The task force, however, was in turmoil, and it was believed by many that the investigation was being poorly managed. As a result, just as the case was to break wide open, the governor of Michigan assigned responsibility of the investigation to the Michigan State Police. The *Detroit Free Press* headline read: "The Keystone Kops Get Help."

At about this same time, Mrs. Leik went to the basement of her Ypsilanti home to do the laundry after a twelve-day vacation away from home. She noticed something quite strange—dried black paint across the basement floor and also on a ladder. On a shirt hanging in the basement were several small brownish spots. She also noticed other items either missing or out of place. She wondered if John, her nephew, had any knowledge about the condition of the basement as he was the only one with access to the house while the Leiks were on vacation. She called David at his State Police office and told him about the basement. Shortly thereafter, David was told by his supervisor at the State Police post that John was a suspect in the murder of Karen Beineman. Although nearly impossible to believe, David then told his supervisor about what was found in his basement. They agreed that the crime lab should examine the basement just to be sure. At the basement, investigators carefully scraped the black paint off the floor, expecting that under this paint was going to be blood. An initial test was immediately conducted on the drops visible under the paint and it was determined to be . . . varnish! Then, while on his hands and knees on the basement floor, one of the investigators looked under the washing machine and found several blonde head hair clippings; clippings that were similar, it seemed, to those found in Karen's underwear recovered from her body. Then three drops of blood were found, including blood recovered from the shirt hanging in the basement. The police finally had what they believed was a good crime scene, and John Collins was the only one who had access to it. Evidence was falling into place. The hair clippings were in the basement because that is where Mrs. Leik always trimmed her children's hair. The police reasoned that Karen was in the basement, and while she was probably being tortured and killed, the hair got in her underwear. Collins then put the underwear in her vagina. In addition, when cleaning the basement after he killed Karen, John noticed what he thought was a stubborn stain of blood and, not being able to remove it, he decided to paint over it. John made a mistake; it was varnish and it had always been there. When John was questioned and confronted with his mistake, he "drew a sharp breath that caught in his throat, and then, as though a plug had been dislodged, the tears spilled out and ran down his cheeks" (Keyes, 1976; p. 283).

John Collins was arrested and a search warrant was issued for his apartment and car. Recovered from his apartment was a black paint spray can, .22 caliber shells, and several knives; but the police did not find what they were really hoping to find. All along, the police believed that the killer was taking and keeping souvenirs from his victims, but the police found nothing of the sort in his apartment. Later it was learned from one of John's roommates that after being prematurely questioned by the two officers, John carried out of the apartment a box of things that could have contained items that belonged to the victims. In addition, the police conducted a lineup for the purpose of having the wig shop workers identify John as the man seen with Karen. The police interrogated Donald Baker, a friend of John's, and Baker provided information that destroyed John's alibi, portrayed him as a thief who committed burglaries and stole motorcycle parts, and that he often carried a knife on his motorcycle.

The trial of John Collins for the murder of Karen Beineman began June 2, 1970. The prosecution had three primary objectives, three points to prove. First, the prosecution sought to prove that Karen was last seen with John Collins near the wig shop on his motorcycle. The eyewitnesses were used to establish this point. Second, prosecutors needed to establish that Karen was in the basement of the Leik house and was probably killed there. The primary evidence used to establish this link was the hair found in the basement and the hair in the victim's underwear found in her vagina. Third, it needed to be established that John was the only one who had access to the home at the time the crime occurred there. (See Figure 4–1.)

The defense offered three counterpoints. First, they questioned the procedures used by the police to identify John as the man last seen with the victim. It was argued that the lineup identification of John was invalid because the witnesses were earlier

The Leik house, where Karen Beineman was murdered

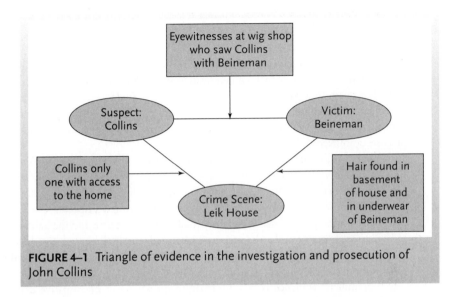

FIGURE 4–1 Triangle of evidence in the investigation and prosecution of John Collins

shown a single picture of John as the perpetrator. It was argued that this biased the witnesses' beliefs and perceptions. Second, the defense raised questions about the actual whereabouts of John during the critical time period in question and argued, through witnesses, that John had a valid alibi. As a result, it was argued, he could not have possibly committed the crime. Finally, the defense questioned the methods used to confirm that the victim was in fact in the basement. They questioned the results of the hair and blood comparison analysis (remember, this case took place before the discovery of DNA analysis; see Chapter 6). The trial lasted seventeen days and, in all, fifty-seven witnesses provided testimony. Collins did not testify. After five days of deliberation, the jury found John Collins guilty of the murder of Karen Beineman. John Collins was sentenced to life in prison (see Keyes [1976]).

Some people question why Collins was never tried for any of the other homicides that were believed to be part of the series. The probable and most likely reason was that the prosecutors did not believe that they had enough evidence to prove beyond a reasonable doubt that Collins was responsible for these crimes. There was little physical evidence that associated Collins with these other crimes. It has also been reported that the prosecutor held back some evidence and did not pursue the other homicide charges in the event that Collins was found not guilty of the crime charged or if Collins successfully petitioned for a new trial, which he requested in 1988 (James, 1991).

John Collins has never publically confessed to any of the suspected crimes for which he is believed responsible. By all available accounts, Collins is not a model prisoner; he even tried to escape by tunneling out of prison. He remains incarcerated in Michigan.

The Meaning of Criminal Evidence

Broadly defined, criminal evidence is any crime-related information on which an investigator can base a decision or make a determination. It consists of supposed facts and knowledge that relate to a particular crime or perpetrator. Evidence is the intended product of investigative activities; investigative activities are performed to discover and collect evidence. Evidence is used to establish proof that a crime was committed or that a particular person committed that crime.

A basic and fundamental distinction can be made between judicial evidence and extrajudicial evidence. Judicial evidence is evidence that is admissible in court and meets the rules of evidence (Chapter 5). As such, it is often referred to as *admissible evidence*. An example of judicial evidence would be hair recovered from a suspected crime scene where investigators used proper legal procedures in obtaining that hair, and the hair may be related to the crime in question. In the case just presented, the statements from the eyewitnesses who saw Collins with the victim, the hair recovered from the underwear, and the hair and blood found in the basement were all examples of judicial evidence.

Extrajudicial evidence is *any* information on which an investigative decision can be based but is not allowed in court proceedings. It is often referred to as *inadmissible evidence*. An example of extrajudicial evidence may be the results of a polygraph examination taken by a suspect. It is certainly not unreasonable that investigators would consider the results of a polygraph examination when judging whether a particular person perpetrated the crime in question. At the same time, however, it is often the case that this "evidence" would not be allowed by a judge to be introduced into court proceedings; it would likely not meet the rules of evidence. In this sense, evidence can be quite useful, even though it may not be admissible in court.

Another basic distinction can be made between *exculpatory evidence* and *inculpatory evidence*. Exculpatory evidence is evidence that tends to exclude or eliminate someone from consideration as a suspect. If a witness described the perpetrator as being six feet tall and having black hair, that would tend to exclude a suspect who was five feet tall with blonde hair. Inculpatory evidence is evidence that tends to include or incriminate a person as the perpetrator. For example, a lack of an alibi for a suspect may be inculpatory, as would a suspect's description that matched the perpetrator's description. Through the course of an investigation, investigators may uncover both inculpatory and exculpatory evidence. It is a legal requirement that the police and prosecutor share not only the inculpatory evidence but also the exculpatory evidence with the defendant's attorney through the discovery process.

Standards of Proof

Evidence is used to establish proof that a crime was committed or that a particular person committed that crime. To prove something (e.g., that John Collins killed Karen Beineman and killed her in the basement of Collins' uncle's house) is to eliminate uncertainty, or to

TABLE 4–1 Standards of Proof in Criminal Matters

Standard	Critical Question	Situations of Relevance
Probable cause	Is it more likely than not that a particular circumstance exists?	To make an arrest, to conduct a search
Beyond a reasonable doubt	Is the doubt about the defendant's guilt meaningful or significant?	To obtain a conviction
Reasonable suspicion	Is there reason to believe that particular circumstances exist?	To stop and frisk

eliminate some degree of uncertainty, regarding the truthfulness of the conclusion. Proof is not a one-dimensional phenomenon; there are various levels, or standards, of proof. For example, as discussed in more detail later, the police usually need enough evidence to establish *probable cause* to justify a search or an arrest. Probable cause, then, is a standard of proof. Probable cause exists when it is more likely than not that a particular circumstance exists; the degree of certainty is greater than fifty percent. Probable cause is the standard of proof of most direct concern and relevance to investigators in investigating crimes.

Another standard of proof is *beyond a reasonable doubt*. Beyond a reasonable doubt is the standard of proof needed in a trial to conclude that a defendant is guilty of the crime. With this level of proof, a jury (or a judge in a bench trial) may have a doubt about the defendant's guilt but this doubt cannot be meaningful or significant. Beyond a reasonable doubt is the level of proof of most direct consequence to prosecutors, who have as their responsibility to present evidence in court to obtain a conviction. A third level of proof is *reasonable suspicion*. In order for police to stop and frisk an individual legally on the street, the police have to have a reasonable suspicion about that person's involvement in or association with a criminal act. A fourth major level of proof is *preponderance of the evidence*. Preponderance of the evidence is the degree of certainty needed to prove and win a civil case. It is the functional equivalent of probable cause but applies only to civil matters.

It is important to understand that all levels of proof are subjective in nature. The determination of what constitutes "proof" depends on the judgments of individuals. As a result, what constitutes probable cause for one judge may not constitute probable cause for another judge. One jury may find guilt beyond a reasonable doubt, and another may find reasonable doubt. The weight and value of evidence in establishing proof is an individual determination.

The Meaning and Nature of Probable Cause

Probable cause stems directly from the Fourth Amendment to the U.S. Constitution and it constitutes a critical ingredient needed to justify a legal search, seizure, or arrest. In general, if probable cause does not exist to conduct a search or to make an arrest, any evidence collected as a result of that search is not admissible in court, nor is that arrest considered valid (see Chapter 5). Probable cause is critical indeed.

Probable cause exists when "the facts and circumstances within the officers' knowledge and of which they had reasonably trustworthy information are sufficient in themselves to warrant a man of reasonable caution in the belief that an offense has been or is being committed" (*Brinegar* v. *United States*, 1949). This definition highlights the subjective nature of probable cause. Like pornography, probable cause may be difficult to define but one may know it when one sees it. Police officers may determine probable cause and act on it, but their judgment and actions may be subject to review at trial. Alternatively, police officers can bring evidence to a judge or magistrate who would consider the evidence, make a determination regarding the presence of probable cause, and then issue a warrant. There are two primary advantages for the police to obtain a warrant: (1) officers will know that the search will be considered valid and (2) having a warrant is a valid defense in civil cases for damages brought against the police officers for alleged violations of defendants' rights.

Throughout the years, several U.S. Supreme Court decisions have given meaning to the probable cause requirement. For example, as noted earlier, the court has articulated what is known as the "man of reasonable caution" or the "reasonable person" standard (*Brinegar* v. *United States*, 1949). On the basis of this standard, one would ask, What would a reasonable person have thought or done under these circumstances? In the *United States* v. *Ortiz* (1975) the court ruled that police officers could legitimately draw on their experience and training in determining whether probable cause existed in a particular situation. As a result, what may look like innocent activity to the "reasonable person" may indeed be sufficient to establish probable cause for a police officer.

In *Aguilar* v. *Texas* (1964), the court established a two-pronged test to determine probable cause when information is given to the police by an informant. The two prongs were (1) the reliability of the informant and (2) the reliability of the informant's information. This is particularly relevant when the police obtain information from a person who has been engaged in criminal activity and has low credibility.

The Aguilar two-pronged test was abandoned with *Illinois* v. *Gates* (1983) when the court ruled that the "totality of the circumstances" must be considered in establishing probable cause. As stated by the court, "[t]he elements under the two pronged test concerning the informants 'veracity,' 'reliability,' and 'basis of knowledge' should be understood simply as closely intertwined issues that may usefully illuminate common sense." In addition, "this flexible, easily applied standard will better achieve the accommodation of public and private interests that the Fourth Amendment requires than does the approach that developed from Aguilar. . . ." So, with specific reference to this case, not only should the informant's tip be considered in determining probable cause, so too should the corroborating information from other independent police sources.

As a practical matter, establishing probable cause can be viewed as a process by which some evidence can lead to other evidence, which can lead to still more evidence. The accumulation of this evidence may eventually provide a basis on which probable cause can be established. Consider the case of the kidnaping and murder of seven-year-old Danielle van Dam of San Diego in February 2002. During the early morning hours of February 2,

Danielle was taken from her home while she slept in her bed by David Westerfield, (age, 50)—a neighbor of the van Dams. On notification of the missing girl, the police, using police dogs, launched a massive door-to-door search of more than 200 homes in the neighborhood, and interviewed each of the residents of the neighborhood. Westerfield was the only neighbor the police were unable to contact because he was not at home.

Westerfield returned home on February 4 and was then questioned by the police. He told the police that at about 3:30 AM February 2, he began a meandering 550-mile motor home trip to various places in and around San Diego and Imperial counties. The nature and

A San Diego County Sheriff's Department search and rescue team searches for evidence in the disappearance of Danielle van Dam.

timing of this trip was suspicious to the police. In addition, police found it unusual that a garden hose used to equip his motor home with water that was in front of his house appeared hastily placed there, as though he had been in a hurry before he left, but everything else appeared to be in perfect order. On checking his story about this trip, the police discovered that Westerfield got stuck in the sand in the desert and had to call a tow truck to get him out. According to the tow truck driver, Westerfield was in such a hurry to leave after getting pulled out of the sand, that he left some of his equipment behind. The more investigators heard, the more suspicious they became. The police asked Westerfield to take a polygraph examination. He agreed but reportedly failed it badly, raising additional suspicions about his involvement in the disappearance of the little girl. All this information was used by the police to establish probable cause to justify a search warrant of Westerfield's property. In conducting the search, the police seized his sport utility vehicle, boxes of personal property, several computers (some of which contained images of child pornography), and his motor home. Further examination of Westerfield's motor home revealed blood that matched Danielle's, along with her fingerprints and hair. Blood on Westerfield's jacket recovered from a dry cleaner also matched Danielle's (Dillon and Perez, 2002; Roth, 2002a, b). Based on all this evidence, probable cause was established to justify an arrest warrant for kidnaping and possession of child pornography. While in custody, Westerfield was charged with homicide after the badly decomposed body of the missing girl was found along a roadside west of San Diego. In August 2002, David Westerfield was found guilty of kidnaping, murder, and possession of child pornography, and was sentenced to death. He is now on death row at San Quentin State Prison awaiting execution (Chapter 5 provides additional details about this investigation).

Types of Evidence

Various types of evidence can be used to establish proof. All evidence can be classified as being either direct or indirect, and all evidence can be classified as either testimonial, real, or demonstrative. Each of these types of evidence are discussed next.

Direct versus Indirect Evidence

Direct evidence refers to crime-related information that immediately demonstrates the existence of a fact in question. As such, no inferences or presumptions are needed to draw the associated conclusion. On the other hand, *indirect evidence*, which is also known as *circumstantial evidence*, consists of crime-related information in which inferences and probabilities *are* needed to draw an associated conclusion. Of course, from the prosecutor's perspective, the ultimate "conclusion" that needs to be drawn is that the defendant committed the crime; however, there may be other conclusions that would be useful to establish before concluding that the defendant committed the crime. In determining whether evidence is direct or circumstantial in nature, one needs to consider the conclusion that is trying to be established. For example, in the Michigan coed killer case, the fact that witnesses saw Karen Beineman with John Collins on a motorcycle is circumstantial evidence that John Collins killed the victim, although it is direct evidence that she was with him on the motorcycle. If a witness saw Collins stab the victim, that information would be direct evidence that he killed the victim, because no inferences would be needed to draw the conclusion. Consider a case in which a knife, identified as the likely murder weapon, has the defendant's fingerprints on it. Are the fingerprints direct evidence or circumstantial evidence? Again, it depends on the conclusion trying to be established. The fingerprints on the knife would be best considered direct evidence that the defendant touched or held the knife but circumstantial evidence that the defendant murdered the victim with the knife.

Circumstantial evidence is often viewed as less valuable than direct evidence in establishing proof. This is generally just not the case. In fact, circumstantial evidence can be quite powerful in establishing proof, perhaps even more influential than direct evidence, especially if there is much circumstantial evidence that can be presented. It is true that one can be convicted of a crime on circumstantial evidence alone. Case in point is, once again, the Michigan coed killer case. Investigators had three critical pieces of circumstantial evidence to prove that John Collins murdered Karen Beineman. First, recall that witnesses at the wig shop saw Collins with the victim on the motorcycle. Because she was not seen alive after that time, one could *infer* that Collins was responsible for her death. Second, physical evidence (hair in her underwear and in the basement) allows one to conclude that Karen Beineman was in the basement of the Leiks' house, and, with an inference, one could conclude that she was probably killed there. Third, John Collins was shown to have exclusive access to the house while the owners were gone. There was no evidence of forced or otherwise illegal entry into the house. This suggests that only Collins could have been with the victim in the house, and the only one who could have killed her in the house (see Figure 4–1). These three pieces of circumstantial evidence are much stronger when combined and considered together than when they are considered separately. If one of these "angles" was not present, do you think a jury would have found Collins guilty beyond a reasonable doubt?

With regard to circumstantial evidence, many factors may be used to infer guilt or innocence. First, one's physical ability to commit the crime can be introduced as circumstantial evidence of guilt or innocence. For example, consider the trial of O.J. Simpson for the murder of his ex-wife, Nicole Brown Simpson, and her friend Ron Goldman. On June 12, 1994, at approximately 11:00 PM, the two victims were found slashed and stabbed to death on the front walkway of Nicole's home in Brentwood, a wealthy section of Los Angeles. With substantial physical evidence associating Simpson with the homicides (see the introduction to Chapter 6 for a detailed discussion of the investigation), he was arrested and charged with the crimes. During the trial, the prosecution provided evidence to the jury about the nature of the crime and the nature of the wounds inflicted on the victims. In turn, the defense provided testimony about the poor physical condition of Simpson, resulting from the effects of arthritis caused by a career of playing professional football. The defense argued that whoever committed these homicides had to be of superior physical strength and abilities, and, as a result, it could not have been Simpson. The prosecution countered this testimony by introducing a recently produced commercial exercise videotape showing a physically capable Simpson engaged in an aerobic exercise routine. With this evidence, the prosecution argued that Simpson was capable of committing the crime, thereby allowing one to *infer* that he committed the crime.

Second, MO, or the method in which the crime was committed, may be introduced as circumstantial evidence. In particular, if a series of crimes are committed in a particular manner, and a defendant has been linked to one of these crimes through other evidence, one could infer that the defendant committed the other similar crimes as well. The reasonableness of the inference may depend strongly on the uniqueness of the MO. Consider in the Michigan coed killer case that most of the girls were college age, most were abducted off a street, most were beaten or stabbed to death, most were raped, and most of the bodies were disposed of in the same general area. The similarities of the homicides would allow one to infer that whoever committed one of the crimes also committed at least several of the others.

Third, the existence of an identifiable motive (or lack thereof) may represent circumstantial evidence of guilt or innocence. Motive, a reason why the crime was committed, is an important dimension of identifying a perpetrator. If a motive (e.g., anger, revenge, greed, jealousy) on the part of the perpetrator can be established, one may reasonably infer that the defendant is responsible for the crime. During the trial of David Westerfield, his possession of and interest in violent child pornography was presented by prosecutors as evidence of motive for the murder of Danielle van Dam.

Fourth, the existence of prior threats made by or similar behaviors of an individual relating to the crime may be introduced as circumstantial evidence of that person's guilt in the crime. According to Keyes (1976), if John Collins was to take the stand in his own defense, the state was going to introduce a witness who was going to testify that Collins brought her to the Leik house and made advances toward her the weekend before Karen Beineman was killed there. This testimony could have been used to infer the guilt of John Collins in the homicide for which he was charged.

Fifth, evidence concerning an individual's attempts to avoid apprehension after the crime occurred can be used to infer guilt. For example, if Collins would have tried to escape after he realized the police considered him a prime suspect, this could have been used as circumstantial evidence of his guilt.

Sixth, if an individual is found to be in possession of the fruits of the crime, this evidence could be used to infer that that person is guilty of the associated crime. Consider once again the Michigan coed killer case. It was suspected early on in the homicides that the perpetrator was keeping souvenirs from the girls he murdered (e.g., earrings, clothing). It was determined that Collins disposed of a box of things shortly after being prematurely interrogated by the inexperienced police officers. If the police could have conducted a search of Collins' apartment prior to his disposing of the belongings of his victims, and if the police would have seized this evidence, it would have been powerful circumstantial evidence that he was responsible for the other murders as well. How else could he explain why he had in his possession jewelry and other items that belonged to the victims?

Finally, character witnesses can be introduced to help establish the innocence of the defendant. Character witnesses are used by the defense to bring evidence to court that the defendant is incapable of committing a crime like the one in question. In the Michigan coed killer case, the defense considered but chose not to call character witnesses, including Collins' high school football coach, his favorite teacher in high school, a nun, and even his aunt, Mrs. Leik. The good things they may have said about Collins could have served as circumstantial evidence that Collins was not guilty of the murder in question.

Testimonial versus Real versus Demonstrative Evidence

Just as all evidence can be considered either direct or indirect in nature, all evidence can be classified as either testimonial, real, or demonstrative. Each is discussed next.

TESTIMONIAL EVIDENCE

Testimonial evidence is evidence that is presented in court through witnesses speaking under oath, when the witnesses would commit perjury if they did not state what they believed to be the truth. Witnesses can be considered either lay witnesses or expert witnesses. Lay witnesses are individuals whose testimony is limited to the facts as personally observed. In limited situations, lay witnesses may also offer judgments as they relate to the particular case at hand (e.g., "in my best judgment, the person I saw running through my backyard was about six feet tall"). The individuals who testified that they saw Karen Beineman with an individual determined to be John Collins on a motorcycle were lay witnesses.

Expert witnesses are persons who possess special knowledge about a particular issue or phenomenon under examination (e.g., battered women's syndrome, DNA analysis, accuracy of eyewitness identifications). Expert witnesses often hold academic positions and conduct research on the issue at hand. Expert witnesses are able to express their opinions about the issue in court and speak about hypothetical cases. Ideally, the function of expert witnesses is to help the jury (or judge) understand the complex issue under consideration.

Associated with the admissibility of expert testimony are the Frye and Daubert standards. Briefly, the Frye standard holds that in order for the results of a scientific technique (and corresponding testimony) to be admissible, it must have gained general acceptance in its particular field. With the Daubert standard, the trial judge must screen the scientific evidence and testimony to ensure that it is relevant and reliable. The meaning and implications of the Frye and Daubert standards are discussed in more detail in Chapter 5. In addition to issues regarding the admissibility of expert testimony, the use of expert witnesses in court is quite controversial from an ethical perspective (see Chapter 13).

One form of testimonial evidence is *hearsay*. Hearsay is "an oral or written assertion . . . made or carried on by someone other than a witness who is testifying at a trial or hearing, which is offered in evidence to establish the truth of the matter asserted" (Waltz, 1997; p. 73). In other words, when someone repeats information that someone else said, that is hearsay. Hearsay is most often excluded from consideration in court proceedings because it is considered unreliable. The serious concerns about the reliability of hearsay relate to (1) the fact that the person who made the original statement was not under oath and therefore was not obligated to tell the truth, and (2) that the person who originally made the statement cannot be cross-examined to test his/her perception, memory, veracity, and ability to be articulate (Waltz, 1997). Simply stated, "criminal cases cannot be made on gossip and secondhand accounts of what happened" (Waltz, 1997; p. 82). To avoid the complications of hearsay, investigators need to get information "from the horse's mouth." To understand the importance of these factors, consider the following (see Waltz [1997]). Suppose a lawyer has a witness who has critical information about the crime but this witness would not likely leave a favorable impression on the jury, and probably would not be believed by the jury. The witness is sloppy, not very articulate, is intoxicated most of the time, and is of questionable mental competence. Without the hearsay rule that excludes most hearsay evidence, the lawyer could have this witness meet with another individual who would have a much more favorable impression on a jury. This witness is bright, articulate, and attractive. The sloppy witness could tell the articulate witness the relevant points of the testimony and then the lawyer could call the articulate witness to testify. Obviously, this hearsay testimony could raise all sorts of questions about fairness and the discovery of the "truth."

As with just about every rule, there are exceptions. So too it is with the hearsay rule. There are instances when hearsay is admissible as testimony in court. Several of the most important exceptions to the exclusionary rule are discussed here. First, previously recorded testimony that was provided under oath and was subject to cross-examination is admissible as hearsay as long as the witness is no longer available. For example, if a witness testified in court but subsequently died, that witness' testimony could be read in court if a new trial was ordered for the defendant. Second, under certain conditions, dying declarations of a victim may be admissible in court through hearsay. The statement must be stated as fact, not as a guess or opinion. For example, the statement "I think James shot me" probably would not be admissible, but "James shot me" probably would be. In addition, the victim's statement must be related to the cause of the impending death, not to matters unrelated to the victim's death, and the victim must have believed that death was near and certain. Third, a defendant's previous admission and confession can be admitted into court as hearsay. An admission involves acknowledging some aspect of involvement in the crime (e.g., "I was at the gas station at about midnight"), whereas a confession involves acknowledging the actual involvement in the crime (e.g., "I robbed the gas station at about midnight"). In this case, a defendant's claim that the statements were not subject to cross-examination would be rather strange. With such hearsay, the defendant is limited to denying that such statements were made or explaining what was actually meant by the statements.

A fourth exception to the hearsay rule is that statements that relate to a witness' state of mind may be admissible as hearsay evidence as long as there is a question at hand about the person's state of mind at a particular time and the statements made were made in an apparently sincere manner. As an example, in a rape trial, an alleged culprit's out-of-court statement such as "Amy [the victim] is hot and I need some of her" may be admissible as hearsay. Fifth, excited utterances or spontaneous exclamations may be admissible as hearsay as long as the utterance relates to a question at hand and as long as the statement was made in close proximity to when the crime occurred or to when the observation that prompted the statement was observed. The spontaneity of such statements is supposed to ensure the reliability of the statements. Finally, statements regarding one's physical condition are often admitted as hearsay evidence. For example, a defendant's statement "I am so drunk" could be admitted through hearsay to refute the defendant's current claim that he was totally sober at the time of the crime and his memory of the incident is crystal clear. There are several other, rarely encountered exceptions to the hearsay rule that are not discussed here. For an additional discussion of this issue see Waltz (1997).

REAL EVIDENCE

Real evidence is also known as *physical evidence, scientific evidence*, or *forensic evidence*. Real evidence refers to tangible objects that can be held or seen and are produced as a direct result of the commission of the crime. Examples of real evidence would include blood splatters on a wall, semen recovered from the victim, and the knife used to kill the victim. In the Michigan coed killer case, the blood and hair recovered from the victim and the basement were types of real evidence. All real evidence that is introduced in court must be accompanied by testimony that demonstrates compliance with the rules of evidence.

DEMONSTRATIVE EVIDENCE

Demonstrative evidence refers to tangible objects that relate to the crime or the perpetrator that are produced indirectly from the crime. For example, diagrams of the crime scene may

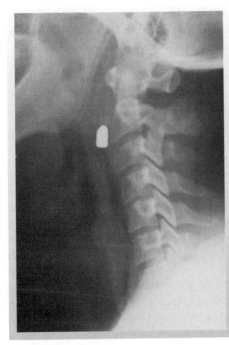

Medical X rays are a type of demonstrative evidence and may be valuable in documenting the nature of injuries sustained by a victim.

be produced by investigators for evidentiary reasons and may be used in court, photographs of the victims (or victims' injuries) may be produced as a result of the crime and used in court, and radiographs showing injuries to the victim may be produced for medical reasons and introduced in court. Photographs, diagrams, and medical records are all common forms of demonstrative evidence.

The Functions of Evidence

Evidence, be it testimonial, real, or demonstrative, or circumstantial or direct, may serve various purposes or functions in establishing proof. In this sense, evidence can be classified as either corpus delicti evidence, corroborative evidence, cumulative evidence, associative evidence, identification evidence, or behavioral evidence. Each function of evidence is discussed next.

Corpus Delicti Evidence

Corpus delicti evidence refers to evidence that establishes that a crime actually occurred. For example, a dead body with an electrical cord tied around the neck is best considered corpus delicti evidence that a homicide occurred. The presence of semen recovered from a victim *may* help establish that a rape occurred (of course, the presence of semen does not prove that a rape occurred, just as the absence of semen does not prove that a rape did not occur). A victim's statement that property is missing from his house and that no one had permission to take it serves to establish that a burglary occurred. In such cases, the dead body, the semen, and the victim's statement constitute corpus delicti evidence.

Corroborative Evidence

Corroborative evidence is evidence that is supplementary to the evidence already available, and strengthens or confirms it. For example, a suspect is apprehended near a burglary scene and his fingerprints are collected from the scene. The fingerprints would corroborate the statements of a witness who saw the suspect running from the house with a television. In the Michigan case, the eyewitness statements about seeing Collins with the victim on the motorcycle corroborated the evidence found in the basement as well as the evidence that Collins had exclusive access to the basement in establishing that Collins killed the victim.

Cumulative Evidence

Cumulative evidence is evidence that duplicates but does not necessarily strengthen already existing evidence. For example, cumulative evidence would be when investigators find five witnesses (as opposed to just one) who can provide the same details about the same incident.

Associative Evidence

Associative evidence is evidence that can be used to make links between crimes, crime scenes, victims, suspects, and tools or instruments. Evidence may also prove to be disassociative, showing a lack of association between crime scenes, victims, and so forth. Most evidence in criminal investigations is used to establish associations. For example, in the Michigan case, the basement of Collins' uncle's house (a crime scene) was associated with the last victim, Karen Beineman, via the hair found at the crime scene and with the victim, Collins was associated with Beineman through eyewitness statements, and many of the homicides were linked as a result of the common MO. In other cases, the suspect has been linked to the victim as a result of bite marks either caused by the victim biting the suspect or the suspect biting the victim. As another example, tools, and the marks they leave, can be linked to pry marks left on doors and windows as a result of burglaries.

Identification Evidence

Evidence that leads to the identification of the perpetrator is considered *identification evidence*. Fingerprints most commonly serve this purpose. Fingerprints may be recovered from a crime scene and, through the use of an automated computerized search, the perpetrator may be identified (see Chapter 6). Dental evidence can also be used to make identifications, usually of dead bodies.

Behavioral Evidence

Behavioral evidence provides a basis on which to identify the type of person who may be responsible for a particular crime and considers directly the nature of the crime and how it was committed. Behavioral evidence constitutes the building blocks on which a psychological or geographical profile may be built or on which linguistic analysis may be conducted (see Chapter 9). Behavioral evidence and psychological profiles are discussed most often in relation to serial crimes—particularly homicides, rapes, and, to a lesser extent, arson. However, such evidence may be available in other crimes as well. For example, in a burglary, what could be inferred from the fact that the only property missing from a residence was a Sony PlayStation? This "evidence" might suggest that whoever broke into the house knew that the game was there (perhaps a neighbor, a friend), it may also suggest that the culprit was a teenager or young adult, and that he was probably male.

In an apparent sexually motivated serial homicide (most serial homicides are sexually motivated to some identifiable degree), the behavioral evidence may be more elaborate. Experts sometimes differentiate between MO and the "signature" of the criminal (Douglas, 2000); both represent behavioral evidence. The *MO* refers to the mechanics of the crime: What were the circumstances under which it occurred? Generally speaking, what was the manner in which the crime was committed? *Signature* refers to that part of the crime that provides emotional satisfaction to the perpetrator. For example, consider the Michigan coed killer case. The MO that was reflected in most of the homicides was that the primarily college-age women were often apparently abducted from a street with an offer to go for a ride (in a car or motorcycle), and some were apparently killed at an abandoned farmhouse. The signature appeared to be the beating and rape of the victims, along with the keeping of some of the victims' personal effects (jewelry, clothing). In this sense, if grocery shopping was akin to committing a homicide, the store where one chooses to shop would be the MO and the actual items one purchases would be the signature. This and other types of behavioral evidence are discussed in more detail in Chapter 9.

Questions for Discussion and Review

1. What is the fundamental difference between judicial evidence and extrajudicial evidence?

2. What is the difference between exculpatory evidence and inculpatory evidence? Give an example of each.

3. What is the standard of proof necessary for the police to make an arrest? To stop and frisk an individual? To obtain a conviction in court?

4. What is the fundamental difference between direct evidence and indirect evidence? Is one more powerful than the other? Why or why not?

5. What are the various types or forms of circumstantial evidence?

6. What is testimonial evidence? Real evidence? Demonstrative evidence?

7. Give examples of how real evidence can be either direct evidence or circumstantial evidence.

8. What is the role of the expert witness in court? What is the role of the lay witness in court?

9. What is the hearsay rule? What is the reason for it? What are the primary exceptions to the hearsay rule?

10. What are the various functions of evidence? Define and give an example of each.

11. What is behavioral evidence? How might behavioral evidence be useful to investigators in an investigation?

12. Based on the Michigan coed killer case described in the introduction to this chapter, answer the following questions:

    a. How was John Collins first identified as a prime suspect in the murder of Karen Beineman? How was his name developed and how was he linked to the missing girl?

b. Identify and discuss the most significant mistakes that detectives made in investigating this case.

c. What do you think was the biggest mistake that John Collins made? Why?

d. During the investigation, the police discovered what they thought to be two crime scenes. Identify these two places. One of these crime scenes was more useful than the other. Explain why.

e. During the trial, two forms (or pieces) of forensic evidence were introduced to help establish a fact in question. What were these two types of evidence? Where were they found? What was the specific fact trying to be established with this evidence? To infer that John Collins killed Karen Beineman, what other specific fact needed to be established?

Related Internet Sites

www.theiai.org

This is the address for the International Association for Identification, a professional association for those engaged in the forensic identification, investigation, and scientific examination of physical evidence. Many useful resources are provided here.

www.crimeandclues.com

This site provides articles on the art and science of criminal investigation and covers numerous types of evidence including physical, testimonial, and behavioral.

www.certmedillustrations.com

This site is of a graphic arts company that provides illustrations (demonstrative evidence) for legal and medical purposes.

THE LAW AND CRIMINAL INVESTIGATION

OBJECTIVES

After reading this chapter you will be able to

- Discuss the qualities evidence must have in order for it to be admissible in court
- Discuss the Frye test and the Daubert standard
- Discuss the chain of custody and its importance in obtaining convictions in court
- Discuss the role of arrest warrants and search warrants in the criminal investigative process
- Discuss the meaning of the Fourth Amendment to the U.S. Constitution
- Identify and discuss the situations in which the police do not need a search warrant to conduct a search
- Discuss the major U.S. Supreme Court decisions that relate to and define the exceptions to the search warrant requirement
- Discuss the exclusionary rule, its intended

purpose, and the major exceptions to the exclusionary rule
- Discuss the impact of the exclusionary rule on criminal investigations and the reasons for the (lack of) impact
- Discuss the ways the police may "get around the Fourth"
- Discuss the meanings of the Fifth and Sixth Amendments to the U.S. Constitution
- Identify the Miranda warnings and the circumstances under which the police must notify suspects of their Miranda rights
- Discuss the major U.S. Supreme Court decisions that relate to and define the parameters of the Miranda decision
- Discuss the impact of the Miranda decision on criminal investigations, and the criminal justice process in general

IMPORTANT TERMS

Relevant evidence	Probable cause, reasonable suspicion	Search incident to arrest exception	Purged taint exception
Material evidence			Independent source exception
Competent evidence	Exigent circumstances exception	Stop and frisk exception	
Frye test		Plain-view exception	Miranda warnings
Daubert standard	Vehicle exception	Consent exception	Custodial interrogation
Necessary evidence	Inventory search	Exclusionary rule	Subtle compulsion
Chain of custody	Other places exception	Good-faith exception	Christian burial speech
Arrest, arrest warrant	Hot-pursuit exception	Inevitable discovery exception	Public safety exception
Search, search warrant			

IMPORTANT U.S. SUPREME COURT CASES

Arizona v. *Fulminante* 499 U.S. 279 (1991)

Brewer v. *Williams* 430 U.S. 387 (1977)

California v. *Prysock* 453 U.S. 355 (1981)

Chambers v. *Maroney* 399 U.S. 42 (1970)

Chimel v. *California* 395 U.S. 752 (1969)

Daubert v. *Merrell Dow Pharmaceuticals* 509 U.S. 579 (1993)

Edwards v. *Arizona* 451 U.S. 477 (1981)

Escobedo v. *Illinois* 378 U.S. 478 (1964)

Frye v. *United States* 293 F. 1013 (1923)

Gideon v. *Wainright* 372 U.S. 335 (1963)

Katz v. *United States* 389 U.S. 347 (1967)

Knowles v. *Iowa* 525 U.S.113 (1998)

Mapp v. *Ohio* 367 U.S. 643 (1961)

Maryland v. *Buie* 494 U.S. 325 (1990)

Massiah v. *United States* 377 U.S. 201 (1964)

Michigan v. *DeFillipo* 443 U.S. 31 (1979)

Michigan v. *Long* 463 U.S. 1032 (1983)

Miranda v. *Arizona* 384 U.S. 436 (1966)

Moran v. *Burbine* 475 U.S. 412 (1986)

New York v. *Quarles* 467 U.S. 649 (1984)

Nix v. *Williams* 467 U.S. 431 (1984)

Oliver v. *United States* 466 U.S. 170 (1984)

Payton v. *New York* 445 U.S. 573 (1980)

Rhode Island v. *Innis* 446 U.S. 291 (1980)

Schneckloth v. *Bustamonte* 412 U.S. 218 (1973)

Schrember v. *California* 384 U.S. 757 (1966)

Smith v. *Illinois* 469 U.S. 91 (1984)

South Dakota v. *Opperman* 428 U.S. 364 (1976)

Terry v. *Ohio* 392 U.S. 1 (1968)

Texas v. *Brown* 460 U.S. 730 (1983)

United States v. *Crews* 455 U.S. 463 (1980)

United States v. *Leon* 468 U.S. 897 (1984)

United States v. *Santana* 427 U.S. 38 (1976)

Warden v. *Hayden* 387 U.S. 294 (1967)

Wong Sun v. *United States* 371 U.S. 471 (1963)

INTRODUCTION

During the early morning hours of March 3, 1963, in Phoenix, Arizona, eighteen-year-old Kathy Midare (not her real name) was on her way home after working the evening shift at a local movie theater. It was about 12:10 AM when she got off the bus to walk the remaining short distance to her home in the northeast section of the city. As Kathy was walking down the sidewalk, a car stopped about a block in front of her, a man got out of the car, and walked toward her. As he approached her, he grabbed Kathy, put his hand over her mouth, and dragged her to his car. Once in the backseat of the car, the man tied her hands behind her back and then tied her ankles. He drove for about twenty minutes to the desert and then raped her in the back seat of the vehicle. He took $4 from her, then drove her back to the city, and let her out of his car a half mile from her house. He then drove off.

The police were notified of the incident by Kathy's sister who was home when Kathy arrived. Kathy told the police that the man appeared to be in his late twenties, was Mexican, had a scant mustache, was about six feet tall, and weighed about 175 pounds. He had short black curly hair, was wearing blue jeans, a white shirt, and glasses. She described the car as either a Ford or a Chevy and that it was light green with brown upholstery. She noted that in the car there was a loop of rope hanging from the back of the front seat. Police initially had concerns about the truthfulness of the often confusing and conflicting statement provided by Kathy, but these concerns were mitigated when they learned from her family that Kathy was mentally disabled, having the intelligence of a twelve- or thirteen-year-old. Nevertheless, the police administered a polygraph to Kathy to verify the truthfulness of her statements; the results of the polygraph were inconclusive.

On March 11, as the police were looking for the man who attacked Kathy Midare, a brother-in-law of Kathy notified the police that two days earlier, when he was giving Kathy a ride home, they saw a green car in the neighborhood that Kathy said looked like the one driven by the attacker. He told the police that the license plate number of the vehicle was DLF-312 and the make of the vehicle was a Packard. The police discovered that the license plate number DLF-312 was registered to an Oldsmobile that could not have been the vehicle involved. On searching further, they found that license plate DLF-317 was registered to a green Packard and the owner was a woman who lived in Phoenix, her name was Twila N. Hoffman. On checking at the address of the woman, it was learned that she and her live-in boyfriend had just recently moved out of the house. On March 13, the police tracked down the woman at her new address and found the green Packard in the driveway. In looking inside the car, an officer saw a loop of rope hanging from the back of the front seat, just as described by Kathy.

The police found Ernest Miranda asleep in the house. Miranda was twenty-three years old and, it was quickly learned, had a long history of delinquent and criminal behavior, including arrests for burglary, armed robbery, sex offenses, and motor vehicle theft. The police arrested Miranda, transported him to police headquarters, and placed him in a lineup with three other Mexican Americans to be viewed by the victim. Although Kathy thought that Miranda had similar features and build as her attacker, she could not positively identify him as the perpetrator. In the interrogation room, police told Ernest that he had been identified by the victim. After two hours of questioning, he confessed to the kidnaping and rape of Kathy Midare as well as two other recent crimes—a robbery of a woman and an attempted rape of another young woman. Police then provided a sheet of paper to Miranda on which to provide a handwritten confession. The following disclaimer was at the top of the paper: "I, (Ernest A. Miranda), do hereby swear that I make this statement voluntarily and of my own free will, with no threats, coercion, or promises of immunity, and with full knowledge of my legal rights, understanding that any statement may be used against me" (Thomas, 1998). The confession provided by Miranda was similar to the account provided by his victim.

At the trial, which took place June 20, 1963, the prosecutor presented Miranda's written confession along with testimony from the victim, her sister, and the two police officers who found and questioned Miranda. The defense did not present any witnesses or evidence. The confession was admitted in court despite the objections of Miranda's court-appointed attorney who argued to the judge that the confession was coerced and therefore inadmissible. The judge ruled that the case of *Gideon* v. *Wainright* (1963) offered the benefit of defense counsel at trial, not the arrest, and therefore that the confession was legally obtained and admissible. The jury found Ernesto Miranda guilty of rape and kidnaping, and he was subsequently sentenced to a term of twenty to thirty years in prison.

Miranda's attorney appealed the conviction to the Arizona Supreme Court with the argument that the confession was not voluntarily offered. Meanwhile, during this time and while Miranda was serving his sentence in prison, the U.S. Supreme Court ruled in the case *Escobedo* v. *Illinois* (1964). In this case, the court held that defendants have the right to an attorney at the interrogation stage of criminal proceedings.

Ernest Miranda

However, because Miranda had not requested an attorney at the time he was questioned by the police, the Arizona Supreme Court ruled that the Escobedo decision did not apply to Miranda. The court upheld the conviction.

In June 1965, a request for review of the case by the U.S. Supreme Court was made by Miranda's new defense counsel, attorneys from one of the largest law firms in Phoenix who were hired by the American Civil Liberties Union but worked pro bono. In writing the appeal, the attorneys framed the legal issue of the case as being whether a suspect needs to be explicitly informed of his right to counsel by the police or if suspects should simply know those rights without being advised of them. Arguments were made in front of the U.S. Supreme Court for three days beginning February 28, 1966. The court issued its decision on June 13, 1966. Chief Justice Earl Warren wrote the sixty-page opinion for the five-member majority. The court held that:

> [t]he prosecution may not use statements, whether exculpatory or inculpatory, stemming from questioning initiated by law enforcement officers after a person has been taken into custody or otherwise deprived of his freedom of action in any significant way, unless it demonstrates the use of procedural safeguards effective to secure the Fifth Amendment's privilege against self-incrimination.

As for the procedural safeguards to be used,

> the person in custody must, prior to interrogation, be clearly informed that he has the right to remain silent, and that anything he says will be used against him in court; he must be clearly informed that he has the right to consult with a lawyer and to have the lawyer with him during interrogation, and that, if he is indigent, a lawyer will be appointed to represent him.

As a result of this decision, the conviction of Ernest Miranda was overturned, but Miranda did not go free. Prosecutors who won the original case against Miranda decided to retry Miranda on the rape and kidnaping without the original confession as evidence. At the new trial, held on February 15, 1967, Miranda's common-law wife, Twila Hoffman, provided testimony that Miranda had earlier confessed to her about the rape. Ernest Miranda was convicted again and received a sentence of twenty to thirty years. Miranda was released on parole in 1972 after serving a total of nine years for the crimes committed against Kathy Midare. During the following years, Miranda was cited on several occasions for driving and traffic violations, and once for being in possession of a firearm. For this arrest (and violation of parole) he was sent back to prison for a year. In January 1976, after being released from prison, Miranda got into a fight in a bar, apparently over $5, and was stabbed to death. Ernest Miranda was thirty-six years old. No arrests for his murder have been made (Baker, 1983).

Basic Legal Terminology

Before proceeding to a discussion of the qualities of evidence and the legal procedures involved in collecting evidence, it is necessary first to understand some basic legal terminology. The concepts of arrest, arrest warrant, search, and search warrant are discussed here.

First, an *arrest* occurs when the police take a person into custody for the purposes of criminal prosecution and interrogation (*Dunaway* v. *New York* 1979). Most simply stated, when a person is under arrest, the police deprive that person of freedom, if only the freedom to leave. The person that is arrested must understand that he or she is under arrest, either by police words or actions. Generally, if a person is free to leave, that person is not under arrest. All arrests must be based on probable cause that a crime occurred and the person under arrest committed it.

Second, *Black's Law Dictionary* (2000) defines an *arrest warrant* as "a writ or precept issued by a magistrate, justice, or other competent authority addressed to a sheriff, constable, or other officer, requiring him to arrest the body of a person therein named, and bring him before the magistrate or court to answer, or to be examined, concerning some offense which he is charged with having committed" (p. 1756). The overwhelming majority of arrests made by the police are made without an arrest warrant. Although the courts recommend that warrants be obtained before making arrests, an arrest warrant is generally required only when the police must enter a home to make an arrest, and in some cases a warrant is not required here either (e.g., domestic violence). By matter of policy, some police departments require that investigators obtain arrest warrants prior to making arrests in criminal investigative situations, when time is less of an issue than when an officer is confronted with a criminal incident and suspect on the street. In any case, arrest warrants must be based on probable cause that a crime occurred and that the person to be arrested committed that crime. The arrest warrant must be issued by a neutral and detached magistrate. The arrest warrant must name the accused or provide a description of the person so that his or her identity is not in question.

Third, a *search* can be defined as a governmental infringement into a person's reasonable expectation of privacy for the purpose of discovering things that could be used as evidence in a criminal prosecution (*Katz* v. *United States* 1967). A reasonable expectation of privacy exists when a person believes that his activity will be private, and that belief is reasonable (*Katz* v. *United* States 1967). A *seizure* is an act of the police in taking control over a person or thing because of a violation of a law. What is seized may constitute evidence and could include items such as contraband (e.g., drugs), fruits of the crime (e.g., stolen goods), instruments of the crime (e.g., weapons), and mere evidence of the crime (e.g., blood-stained clothing). Nearly all searches must be based on probable cause, although, as discussed later, some limited searches can be based on a lesser standard of reasonable suspicion.

Lastly a *search warrant* is similar to an arrest warrant except that it specifies the person, place, or vehicle to be searched, and the types of items to be seized by the law enforcement authority. Similar to arrests, most searches are conducted without a search warrant. In obtaining a valid search warrant, several requirements must be satisfied:

In The Superior Court Of California, County of San Diego
Central Division
Search Warrant
No. 27830

The People of the State of California, to any sheriff, constable, marshal, police officer, or any other peace officer in the County of San Diego:

Proof, by affidavit, having been this day made before me by James Hergenroeather, a peace officer employed by the San Diego Police Department, that there is substantial probable cause for the issuance of the search warrant pursuant to Penal Code section 1524, you are therefore, commanded to make search at any time of day, good cause being shown therefore, the premises and all parts therein, including all rooms, attics, basements, cellars, crawl spaces, safes, mail receptacles, storage areas, containers, surrounding grounds, trash areas, garages and outbuildings assigned to or part of the residence located at 11995 Mountain Pass Drive, City of San Diego, County of San Diego; the residence is contained in a two story single family style house having a primarily light stucco exterior with white trim and a red tile roof, having the numbers "11995" attached to an east pillar by the front door and visible from the public street; for the following property, to wit: to seize and take "adhesive trace lifts" also known as "tape lifts" from all footwear on the premises, to include all boots, shoes, slippers and sandals; binding materials, including tape, rope, leather or rope necklaces or collars; and to seize and view all videotapes whether commercially made or homemade, as well as all CDs, electronic recordings and recording devices, cameras and associated equipment, undeveloped film, negatives, prints or other images, drawings, depicting nudity and/or sexual activities, whether real or simulated, involving juveniles, juveniles with juveniles, and juveniles with adults, and papers, documents and effects which tend to show domination and control over said premises, including fingerprints, clothing, photographs, photographic negatives, undeveloped film, handwritings, documents and effects which bear a form of identification such as a person's name, photograph, Social Security number or diver's license number, keys; and to intercept incoming phone calls during execution of the warrant; and, if you find the same, or any part thereof, to bring it forthwith before me at the Superior Court of the State of California, County of San Diego, Central Division, or to any other court in which the offense in respect to which the property or things is triable, or retain such property in your custody, subject to the order of this Court, pursuant to section 1536 of the Penal Code.

Given under my hand and dated this 13th day of February, 2002

Judge of the Superior Court
Central Division

- The search warrant must be based on probable cause (*Franks* v. *Delaware* 1978).
- The facts must be truthful (*Illinois* v. *Gates* 1983).
- Probable cause cannot be based on stale information (*United States* v. *Leon* 1984).
- Probable cause must be determined by a neutral and detached magistrate (*Coolidge* v. *New Hampshire* 1971).
- The search warrant must be served immediately.
- The search warrant must identify what is to be seized and what is to be searched (*Maryland* v. *Garrison* 1987; *United States* v. *Leon* 1984).

In a search warrant application, there are generally three documents. First is the search warrant itself. Second is the affidavit that provides facts to establish the probable cause needed to support the warrant. Third is the search warrant "return," which is a document completed after the search warrant has been executed that identifies the items seized. The return is usually filed with the court that issued the warrant.

An example of a search warrant is provided in Exhibit 5–1. This is one of several warrants issued for the search and seizure of evidence associated with the kidnaping and murder of Danielle van Dam by David Westerfield (as described in Chapter 4). The forty-page affidavit associated with this warrant can be found at www.signonsandiego.com/news/metro/danielle/transcripts/westerfield_001.pdf. An example of a search warrant "return" is shown in Exhibit 5–2.

EXHIBIT 5–2 Search warrant return

CIRCUIT COURT   )

                                                                    ss.

COUNTY OF MILWAUKEE   )

Dated at _____ Wis., _____, 20___
I hereby certify that by virtue of the within writ I searched the within named premises and found the following:

_____

_____

_____

_____

_____ and have same now in my possession subject to the disposition of the Circuit Court.

_____

                                                                    Police Officer

The Rules and Admissibility of Evidence

All evidence admitted into court for consideration by a judge or jury must have certain qualities. First, all evidence must be relevant. If evidence is relevant, then the evidence has some bearing on the case or some fact that is trying to be established. For example, in the O.J. Simpson case, the judge ruled that prior statements of Detective Mark Fuhrman, relating to his use of the "n-word," were relevant to the case (and the defense argument that Simpson was framed by a racist cop). Accordingly, the judge allowed evidence relating to this issue to be introduced at trial and to be considered by the jury. In the Westerfield trial, homemade videotapes confiscated from the home of Westerfield (two of which showed female neighbors in their homes being secretly videotaped) were ruled by the judge to be irrelevant to the murder charge and, as a result, were not admissible at trial (Roth, 2003).

Second, all evidence must be material. Evidence is material if it is significant. Evidence is material if it makes the existence of a fact more probable than it appeared prior to the introduction of the evidence. If evidence is material, then it may influence the issue at hand. In extending the previous example, the questions would be, Is the prior use of the "n-word" by Detective Fuhrman significant that Fuhrman is racist? Is evidence of racism significant in establishing that evidence was planted and Simpson was framed? These determinations are made by judges, and depend heavily on the particular facts of the case. In practice, the distinction between relevancy and materiality is often blurry at best.

Third, all evidence must be competent. Incompetent evidence is of questionable value. It is considered invalid or untruthful. There are three categories of incompetent evidence: (1) evidence wrongfully obtained (e.g., as a result of an illegal search or an involuntary confession), (2) statutory incompetency (e.g., when federal or state law prohibits the introduction of certain forms of evidence, such as a polygraph), and (3) court-established rule (e.g., hearsay evidence). If evidence is ruled incompetent, it is not admissible even if it is relevant and material. With regard to statutory incompetence in particular, the rulings from two court cases are of importance. First, the *Frye test* relates to *Frye* v. *United States* (1923) when the U.S. Court of Appeals refused to admit novel evidence in court that was not generally accepted in the scientific community. The court stated the following:

> Just when a scientific principle or discovery crosses the line between the experimental and the demonstrable stages is difficult to define. Somewhere in this twilight zone the evidential force of the principle must be recognized, and while courts will go a long way in admitting expert testimony deduced from a well-recognized scientific principle or discovery, the thing from which the deduction is made must be sufficiently established to have gained general acceptance in the particular field in which it belongs. (*Frye* v. *United States* 1923)

The Frye test dominated the admissibility of scientific evidence for the next seventy years. In 1993, in the case of *Daubert* v. *Merrell Dow Pharmaceuticals* (1993), the U.S. Supreme Court replaced the Frye test for determining the admissibility of scientific evidence. The Frye approach was ruled too restrictive. The fundamental question for Daubert is: Is the evidence and corresponding testimony based on scientific knowledge? Daubert provided some factors that should be considered by judges in making this determination:

- Whether the theory or technique on which the testimony is based is capable of being tested
- Whether the technique has a known rate of error in its application
- Whether the theory or technique has been subjected to peer review and publication
- The level of acceptance in the relevant scientific community of the theory or technique
- The extent to which there are standards to determine acceptable use of the technique

Beyond Daubert, another basis on which to exclude scientific evidence is Federal Rule 403 and its state court equivalents that allow a trial judge to exclude evidence that is relatively weak or may cause confusion, consume too much time, or cause unnecessary prejudice to a party (Daniels, 2002).

Fourth, as mentioned earlier, the introduction of all evidence at trial must be necessary. Evidence must be introduced to establish a point. If the only purpose of presenting evidence is to arouse feelings or to be dramatic, the introduction of the evidence is not necessary. It may only prejudice a jury. Arguments regarding the necessity of evidence are often raised by defense attorneys with regard to the introduction of particularly gruesome crime scene photographs.

Finally, with regard to physical evidence specifically, the chain of custody must be maintained. The *chain of custody* refers to the record of individuals who maintained control (custody) over the evidence from the time it was obtained by the police to when it was introduced in court. The chain of custody is to ensure the security and corresponding integrity of physical evidence. If a chain of custody is not established, or if the chain of custody can be questioned, the value of the evidence itself may be questioned. Consider once again the case of Simpson. As discussed in more detail in Chapter 6, a blood sample was taken from Simpson at police headquarters prior to his arrest, and then that vial was taken back to the crime scene (as captured on news film) and placed under the control of the crime scene technician at the scene. Although the appropriateness of this procedure may be questioned in its own right, what compounded the chain-of-custody problem for the police was that later, when examined, it appeared that some of the blood was missing from the vial (based on what the nurse recorded as having been drawn from Simpson compared with what was produced later in court). The "loose" procedures regarding the custody of the blood evidence provided an opportunity for Simpson's defense attorneys to argue that Simpson's blood was planted at the crime scene and in his Bronco sport utility vehicle by a racist cop.

Constitutional Constraints on the Collection of Evidence

In order for evidence to be admissible in court, not only does the evidence have to have certain qualities, but the police also have to follow certain legal rules in collecting it. These laws are intended to protect citizens from unwarranted governmental intrusion into their lives. These rules represent the civil liberties of citizens and, as far as criminal investigation is concerned, relate to the protections offered by the Fourth, Fifth, and Sixth Amendments of the U.S. Constitution. The procedures associated with arrests, searches, and seizures relate to the Fourth Amendment and courts' interpretation of it.

Fourth Amendment

The Fourth Amendment reads as follows:

> The right of the people to be secure in their persons, houses, papers, and effects, against unreasonable searches and seizures, shall not be violated, and no warrants shall issue but upon probable cause, supported by oath or affirmation, and particularly describing the place to be searched, and the person or things to be seized.

In essence, the intent of the Fourth Amendment is to protect individuals' privacy and protect against arbitrary intrusions into that privacy by government officials. As such, as interpreted by the courts, the Fourth Amendment offers protection in a variety of situations. For instance, as stated in *Katz* v. *United States* (1967), searches are restricted wherever individuals have a reasonable expectation of privacy. In the case of Katz, it was during phone conversations in a public telephone booth. In this case, the Supreme Court ruled that the Fourth Amendment protects people not places, so the fact that the eavesdropping took place at a public phone booth was not an issue. Other cases have further defined the parameters of the Fourth Amendment protections. For example, in the case of *O'Conner* v. *Ortega* (1987) it was ruled that a reasonable expectation of privacy exists in a defendant's desk and file cabinets. A defendant has a reasonable expectation of privacy in his home even if a murder occurred there (*Thompson* v. *Louisiana* 1984; *Mincey* v. *Arizona* 1978). Surgery constitutes a search and seizure (*Winston* v. *Lee* 1985). As ruled in *Ybarra* v. *Illinois* (1978), patrons in a tavern have a reasonable expectation of privacy even if the police have a warrant to search the tavern and the bartender.

The Search Warrant Requirement and Its Exceptions

The general rule is that the police need a search warrant to conduct a legal and valid search. However, there are exceptions to this rule. In fact, as noted earlier, most searches conducted by the police are conducted without a warrant, just as most arrests made by the police are without a warrant (del Carmen, 2001). Probable cause (or reasonable suspicion, in some cases) is required in all searches, regardless if conducted with or without a warrant. When a search is conducted without a warrant, the burden is on the police to establish a valid and lawful reason for the search. Specifically, when a search is conducted without a warrant, police actions must relate to one of the exceptions to the search warrant requirement. These exceptions can be classified into several categories:

- Exigent circumstances
- Vehicles
- Other places/things not covered by the Fourth Amendment
- Hot pursuit
- Incident to arrest
- Stop and frisk
- Plain view
- Consent

EXIGENT CIRCUMSTANCES EXCEPTION

Exigent circumstances, or emergency situations, may require that the police conduct a search without first obtaining a warrant. In general, the rationale for the exigent circumstances exception is that without immediate police action, the suspect may escape, may destroy evidence, or may pose a threat of danger to the police or the public (see Hendrie [1998]). Consider the case of *Schrember* v. *California* (1966). Schrember was hospitalized as a result of an automobile accident during which he had apparently been driving. A police officer smelled alcohol on his breath and noticed symptoms of intoxication at the scene of the accident as well as at the hospital. Schrember was placed under arrest and informed of his rights. On the officer's direction, and despite Schrember's refusal, hospital medical staff took a blood sample. A chemical analysis of his blood indicated intoxication and this evidence was admitted at trial. On appeal, the Supreme Court ruled that exigent circumstances existed in this situation because the alcohol in a person's blood stream may disappear in the time required to obtain a warrant. As a result, obtaining evidence in this manner, under these circumstances, and without a warrant, did not constitute a violation of a defendant's constitutional rights.

In the case of *Payton* v. *New York* (1980), the Supreme Court ruled that there were no exigent circumstances and, correspondingly, that the warrantless search was unconstitutional. After two days of intensive investigation, New York detectives had assembled evidence sufficient to establish probable cause to believe that Payton had murdered the manager of a gas station. The next day officers went to Payton's apartment intending to arrest him. They did not have a warrant. There was no response after they knocked on the door. The police then used crowbars to gain entry into the apartment. No one was there. In plain view was a .30-caliber shell casing that was seized and later admitted into evidence at Payton's murder trial. Payton was convicted and he appealed. The Supreme Court ruled that in the absence of consent or exigent circumstances, the police may not enter a suspect's home to make a routine felony arrest without a warrant. As a result, the evidence seized from the search was not admissible.

Vehicle Exception

Vehicles (including motor homes; see *California* v. *Carney* 1985) are not treated in the same manner as homes and other places in affording rights to privacy. The rationale is that vehicles are mobile and, as such, it is more difficult for the police to collect evidence contained in vehicles. Several cases have defined this exception to the search warrant requirement. Consider the case of *Chambers* v. *Maroney* (1970). Shortly after an armed robbery of a gas station, the police stopped the car of Chambers and three other men. The stop was based on information (including a description of the getaway car used by the perpetrators) supplied by the service station attendant and bystanders. The occupants of the car were arrested and the car was driven to the police station. During the course of the search of the car at the police station, the police found concealed in a compartment under the dashboard two .38-caliber revolvers, a glove containing change, and certain cards bearing the name of another service station attendant who had been robbed a week earlier. In conducting a warrant-authorized search of the petitioner's home the day after the arrest, police found and seized .38-caliber ammunition. At the trial, the materials taken from the car and the bullets seized from the home were introduced as evidence. Chambers was convicted of robbery of both service stations. On appeal, the Supreme Court held that if probable cause exists that a vehicle contains evidence, and if that vehicle is mobile, an officer may search that vehicle at the scene or at the police station without a warrant. The search was valid and the evidence admissible.

In *South Dakota* v. *Opperman* (1976) the court ruled that when the police tow and impound a vehicle, even for a parking violation, a routine inventory search, without a warrant or without probable cause that the vehicle contains evidence, is reasonable. This procedure protects the owner's property, protects the police against claims that the owner's property was stolen while the car was impounded, and protects the police from potential danger. However, inventory searches conducted solely for the purpose of discovering evidence are illegal regardless of what is discovered during the course of the search. In addition, during an inventory search, it is reasonable for the police to search closed containers (e.g., backpack) without a warrant (*Colorado* v. *Bertine* 1987).

In *Michigan* v. *Long* (1983), the Supreme Court spoke of the dangers associated with roadside encounters with suspects and stated that this can justify searches of vehicles in such situations. While on patrol in a rural area at night, two police officers observed a car traveling erratically and at excessive speed. When the car swerved into a ditch, the officers stopped to investigate and were met by Long, the only occupant of the car, at the rear of the car. The door on the driver's side of the vehicle was left open. Long did not respond to initial requests to produce his license and registration. When he began walking toward the open door of the car, the officers followed him and saw a knife on the floorboard of the driver's side of the car. At that time, the officers subjected him to a pat-down search, but no weapons were found. One of the officers shone a light into the car and saw something protruding from under the armrest of the front seat. On lifting the armrest, the officer saw an open pouch that contained what appeared to be marijuana. Long was then arrested for possession of marijuana. A further search of the car revealed no additional contraband, but the officers decided to impound the vehicle. As a result of the subsequent search, more marijuana was found in the trunk. The marijuana was introduced at trial and Long was convicted of possession of marijuana. On appeal, the Supreme Court held that if an officer has reasonable suspicion that a motorist who has been stopped is dangerous and may be able to gain control of a weapon in the car, the officer may conduct a brief warrantless search of the passenger compartment even if the motorist is no longer inside the car. Such a search should be limited to areas in the passenger compartment where a weapon might be found or hidden. If contraband is discovered in the process of looking for a weapon, the officer is not required to ignore it.

Similar to *Michigan* v. *Long* (1983), in *Knowles* v. *Iowa* (1998) the court ruled that as a result of a traffic stop made to issue a traffic citation, the police may order the occupants out of the vehicle, but to justify a brief search of that vehicle there must be a reasonable suspicion of danger to the officer. Furthermore, to look inside a closed container in a vehicle without a warrant, there must be probable cause to suggest that evidence is contained in the container (*California* v. *Acevedo* 1991). In any case, there must be a reason to stop a vehicle in which a search is executed. As held in *United States* v. *Ortiz* (1975), a search at a fixed checkpoint requires consent, probable cause, or a warrant. Random searches are not legally permissible.

OTHER PLACES AND THINGS EXCEPTION

The third exception to the search warrant requirement applies to other places and things that are not afforded Fourth Amendment protections. For example, consider *Oliver* v. *United States* (1984). Narcotics agents from the Kentucky State Police received information that marijuana was being grown on the farm belonging to Oliver. Arriving at the farm, the agents drove past the house to a locked gate that displayed a No Trespassing sign. A footpath led around the side of the gate. The agents walked around the gate and along the road for several hundred yards. At that point, someone standing in front of a camper on the property shouted, "No hunting is allowed. Come back up here." The officer shouted back that they were the police, but they found no one when they returned to the camper. The officers resumed their search without a warrant and found a field of marijuana approximately a mile from Oliver's house. Oliver was charged with and convicted of manufacturing a controlled substance. On appeal, the Supreme Court ruled that a reasonable expectation of privacy does not apply to open fields. No Trespassing signs around the property do not establish any reasonable expectation of privacy. Consequently, the police can enter the property without a warrant or probable cause. Other decisions of the U.S. Supreme Court have held that there is no reasonable expectation of privacy in garbage left for collection outside a house (*California* v. *Greenwood* 1988), in greenhouses viewed from the sky (*Florida* v. *Riley* 1989), or in bank records obtained via a subpoena from a bank (*United States* v. *Miller* 1976). Firefighters do not need a warrant to enter a building to extinguish a fire, or to conduct an investigation of the cause of a fire (*Michigan* v. *Tyler* 1978).

Hot-Pursuit Exception

Several cases relate to the hot-pursuit exception to the search warrant requirement. Consider the decision rendered in *Warden* v. *Hayden* (1967). Early one morning an armed robber entered a taxicab company, took $363, and ran. Two taxicab drivers in the area followed the man, and a dispatcher relayed the information to the police who were on their way to the scene of the robbery. Within minutes, the police arrived at the house where they believed the suspect had entered. An officer knocked and announced his presence, he asked for permission to search the house, and Mrs. Hayden offered no objection. The officers found Hayden upstairs pretending to be asleep. He was arrested. Another officer discovered a shotgun and a pistol. The pistol, a clip of ammunition for the pistol, and a cap, jacket, and pants that matched the description of the clothing worn by the perpetrator were all admitted as evidence. Hayden was convicted. On appeal, the Supreme Court ruled that the police may make a warrantless search and seizure when they are in "hot pursuit" of a dangerous suspect. The scope of the search may be as extensive as reasonably necessary to prevent the suspect from resisting or escaping. Officers do not need to delay an arrest if doing so would endanger their lives or the lives of others.

Another case that relates to hot pursuit is *United States* v. *Santana* (1976). In this case Santana was standing in the doorway of her house as the police arrived. The police had probable cause to believe that the paper bag she was holding contained heroin. The police did not have a warrant to enter her house. As the police officers approached, she retreated into her house. The police followed her into the house and arrested her. The Supreme Court held that there is no reasonable expectation of privacy outside one's home. If a suspect enters her house to avoid arrest, the police may enter the house without a warrant and conduct a search accordingly.

Search Incident to Arrest Exception

This exception to the search warrant requirement applies to situations in which the police conduct searches of individuals as a result of their arrest. Over the years, there have been numerous cases that have addressed this exception to the search warrant requirement. In the case of *Chimel* v. *California* (1969), police officers with an arrest warrant, but not a search warrant, were admitted into Chimel's home by his wife. On arriving home, Chimel was served with the arrest warrant. Although he denied the officers' request to "look around," they conducted a search of the entire house, including the attic, garage, and workshop. At his trial on burglary charges, items seized from Chimel's home were admitted over objection that they had been unconstitutionally seized. The Supreme Court agreed. The Supreme Court held that the search of Chimel's home went far beyond his person and the area within which he might have harbored either a weapon or something that could have been used as evidence against him. There was no justification for extending the search beyond the area within his immediate control—the area covered by the spread of the suspect's arms and hands.

In *Maryland* v. *Buie* (1990) the Supreme Court ruled that a larger search was justified because of the potential for danger to officers. In this case, police officers obtained and executed arrest warrants for Buie and an accomplice in connection with an armed robbery. On arrival at the house, officers "fanned out" through the first and second floors. One of the officers watched the basement so that nobody could surprise the officers. This officer shouted into the basement ordering anyone down there to come out. The officer stated that he was the police. Eventually, Buie emerged from the basement and was arrested, searched, and handcuffed. Another officer then entered the basement to determine whether anyone else was there. In plain view he noticed a red running suit similar to the one worn by a suspect in the robbery. The running suit was admitted into trial. Buie was convicted of robbery. On appeal, the Supreme Court held that "the Fourth Amendment permits a properly limited protective sweep in conjunction with an in-home arrest when the searching officer possesses a reasonable belief based on specific and articulable facts that the area to be swept harbors an individual posing a danger to those on the arrest scene." The officer went into the basement not to search for evidence but to look for the accomplice or anyone else who might have posed a threat to the officers. This was acceptable. However, a protective sweep by the police is not allowed every time an arrest is made, and it must be limited in scope.

If an arrest occurs outside a house, the police may not search a house as a search incident to lawful arrest (*Vale* v. *Louisiana* 1970). However, the police may monitor the movements of a person who has been arrested. If the person who has been arrested proceeds into a private place (e.g., dorm room), the police may accompany him. If evidence is then observed in plain view, it may be seized (*Washington* v. *Chrisman* 1982). In addition, any lawful arrest justifies the police to conduct a full-scale search of that person even without officer fear for safety or belief that evidence would be found (*Gustafson* v. *Florida* 1973).

STOP AND FRISK EXCEPTION

The police may conduct a *search* of a person even though an *arrest* of that person may not be justified. Many court decisions have clarified and defined the intricacies of this exception to the search warrant requirement. Most of the decisions note the importance of ensuring officers' safety in justifying stop and frisk or "pat-down" searches. The most famous of these cases was the landmark case of *Terry* v. *Ohio* (1968). The facts of the case are as follows: While patrolling a downtown beat that he had been patrolling for many years, Cleveland police officer McFadden observed two strangers on a street corner. It appeared to the officer that the two men were casing a store. Each of the men walked up and down the street, peering into the store window, then both returned to the corner to confer. At one point they were joined by a third man, who left abruptly. Officer McFadden followed them a couple blocks away where the two men were joined by the third. He approached them, identified himself, and asked for their identification. The men "mumbled something," whereupon McFadden frisked all three men. Terry and one other man were carrying handguns. Both were tried and convicted of carrying concealed weapons. On appeal, the Supreme Court held that "where a police officer observes unusual conduct which leads him to reasonably conclude in light of his experience that criminal activity may be afoot and that the persons with whom he is dealing may be armed and presently dangerous" and he identifies himself as a police officer, "he is entitled for the protection of himself and others in the area to conduct a carefully limited search of the outer clothing of such persons in an attempt to discover weapons which might be used to assault him." The practice of stop and frisk is valid.

Many cases relate to the question of what constitutes "reasonable suspicion" that criminal activity is afoot—the prerequisite for a legal stop and frisk. In *Illinois* v. *Wardlow* (2000), reasonable suspicion was determined to have been present when the suspect fled from the police once the suspect saw the police, and that this occurred in a high narcotics trafficking area. However, in *Brown* v. *Texas* (1979) the Supreme Court ruled that just because an individual looked suspicious and that he was never seen in the area before, the police did not have reasonable suspicion that criminal activity was afoot. Vague suspicion is not enough to justify a stop and frisk of an individual or to require that the person give the police his name. Furthermore, a stop and frisk based on an anonymous tip is not legally permissible (*Florida* v. *J.L.* 2002). Similarly, police may not stop a vehicle to check the motorist's driver's license and car registration without reasonable suspicion that the driver does not have a license, that the vehicle is not registered, or that the law is somehow being violated (*Delaware* v. *Prouse* 1979) or without consideration of the totality of the circumstances that illegal actions are afoot (*United States* v. *Arvizu* 2002).

When a motorist is stopped for a traffic violation, the officer may order the motorist out of the car (*Maryland* v. *Wilson* 1997); however, a pat-down search for weapons requires reasonable suspicion that the person is armed (*Pennsylvania* v. *Mimms* 1977). When conducting a pat-down search under any circumstances, non-threatening contraband (e.g., drugs) may be seized only if it is immediately apparent and it is not found as a result of squeezing, sliding, or otherwise manipulating the contents of the defendant's pockets (*Minnesota* v. *Dickerson* 1993).

Beyond the stop and frisk, the Supreme Court has ruled that other actions of the police must be limited in nature. For example, in *Hayes v. Florida* (1985), the police interviewed the defendant (Hayes) along with about thirty other men who fit the general description of the suspect in a series of burglary/rapes. Later the police decided to go to Hayes' home to obtain his fingerprints and to arrest him if he did not cooperate. No warrant was sought to authorize their actions. At his house, Hayes was approached by the police and asked to accompany them to the station. He replied that he would reluctantly go rather than being arrested. He was later arrested after it was determined that his prints matched those at the scene. The Supreme Court ruled that "where there is no probable cause to arrest, no consent to journey to the police station, and no prior judicial authorization for detaining him, the investigative detention at the police station for fingerprinting purposes violated Fourth Amendment rights." Reasonable suspicion alone does not justify detention to obtain fingerprints; police must have probable cause. In the same manner, without probable cause, a suspect cannot be detained and transported to a police station for purposes of interrogation (*Dunaway v. New York* 1979).

PLAIN-VIEW EXCEPTION

When the police conduct a search with a warrant or when the police are legally present at a particular place and evidence is observed, that evidence may be seized under the provisions of the plain-view exception to the search warrant requirement. Consider the case of *Texas* v. *Brown* (1983). In Fort Worth, Texas, Brown's car was stopped at a routine checkpoint at night by a police officer. The officer asked to see Brown's driver's license, shone his flashlight into the car, and saw a green opaque party balloon, knotted near the tip, fall from Brown's hand to the rear seat. Based on the officer's experience in drug offense arrests, he was aware that narcotics are often stored in these types of balloons. He then shifted his position to obtain a better view and noticed small plastic vials, loose white powder, and an open bag of party balloons in the glove compartment. After a failure to produce a driver's license, Brown was asked to exit the car and he was placed under arrest. At trial, Brown was convicted of narcotics offenses. The Supreme Court held that the officer's initial stop of the car was valid and by shining his flashlight into the car and changing position, Brown's Fourth Amendment rights were not violated. The officer had probable cause to believe that the balloon contained narcotics, so the seizure was also justified.

In the case of *Horton* v. *California* (1990), the police were conducting a warrant search for the proceeds of a robbery and in the process of looking for the proceeds, the police inadvertently discovered weapons in plain view. The Supreme Court ruled that the seizure of items not listed in the warrant is permissible, as long as those items were in plain view. In other cases, however, additional actions with regard to the items found in plain view have been ruled by the Supreme Court not to be acceptable. For example, in *Arizona* v. *Hicks* (1987) the Supreme Court held that moving a stereo in plain view to record its serial number constituted a search and was not permissible without a warrant.

CONSENT SEARCH EXCEPTION

The most common exception to the search warrant requirement is search after a waiver of constitutional rights, also known as a consent search. Sutton (1986) estimates that ninety-eight percent of searches conducted by the police are as a result of consent being obtained. Consider *Schneckloth* v. *Bustamonte* (1973). A car containing six men was stopped for a traffic violation by a California police officer. The driver of the car was not able to produce a license. The officer asked the driver if he could search the car. The driver gave consent and helped the officer open the trunk and glove compartment. Under the rear seat the officer found several checks that had previously been stolen from a car wash. The checks were admitted as evidence in trial. Bustamonte was convicted. The Supreme Court held that after validly stopping a car, an officer may ask the person in control of the car for permission to search it. Even if there is not probable cause or reasonable suspicion, the officer may conduct a search if consent is given. The voluntariness of the consent is to be determined by the totality of the circumstances. Consent need not be in writing. The police do not have to inform subjects of their Fourth Amendment rights prior to receiving valid consent; however, the burden lies on the officer to prove that the consent was valid.

In other related cases, the Supreme Court ruled that consent was valid if it was received from a third person who was believed at the time to have common authority over the premises (*Illinois* v. *Rodriguez* 1990) or if consent was received to search a bedroom of a common-law spouse of the defendant. A search of a hotel room was not valid, however, when consent was received from the hotel night clerk (*Stoner* v. *California* 1964). In *Florida* v. *Jimeno* (1991) the Supreme Court held that a consent to search a vehicle included the search of closed containers unless restrictions were provided to the police on the scope of the search when consent was given.

The Exclusionary Rule and Its Exceptions

If a search is determined to be unreasonable, the evidence obtained must be excluded from trial; it is considered incompetent evidence. This basic principle is known as the *exclusionary rule*. The exclusionary rule relates specifically to unreasonable searches and seizures. As discussed later, however, evidence that is collected in violation of other constitutional rights is also excluded from trial although not technically as a result of the exclusionary rule (del Carmen, 2001). The exclusionary rule took some time to evolve. In 1914, in *Weeks* v. *United States,* the Supreme Court ruled that evidence obtained by federal officers in violation of the Fourth Amendment could not be used in federal prosecutions. Evidence that was collected illegally by state officers, however, could be used in federal prosecutions. This practice was known as the *silver platter doctrine.* It was not until 1961, in the case of *Mapp* v. *Ohio,* that the Supreme Court extended the exclusionary rule to the states. As a result, evidence seized in violation of the Fourth Amendment cannot be used in federal prosecutions or in state prosecutions.

In the case of *Mapp* v. *Ohio* (1961), three Cleveland police officers arrived at the Mapp residence as a result of information that they received that "a person [was] hiding out in the home, who was wanted for questioning in connection with a recent bombing." The officers knocked on the door and demanded entrance. Mapp telephoned her attorney and refused to let the officers in without a warrant. Three hours later, additional officers arrived at the scene. Miss Mapp's attorney also arrived but the police would not allow him in the house or to see Mapp. She demanded to see a search warrant. A paper, claimed by the officers to be a warrant, was held up by one of the officers. She grabbed the warrant and a struggle ensued. Mapp was handcuffed and the police searched her entire house including dresser drawers, suitcases, and closets. In the basement a trunk was searched and inside obscene materials were discovered. She was charged and convicted of possession of these materials. At the trial, no search warrant was produced. On appeal, in a five-to-four decision, the Supreme Court ruled that the exclusionary rule prohibits, in state criminal proceedings, the use of evidence that results from unreasonable searches and seizures. The evidence was not admissible.

As another example of the exclusionary rule in action, consider the case of *Davis* v. *Mississippi* (1969). During a rape investigation, the police collected finger and palm prints on the windowsill through which the assailant entered the home. The victim, however, could not provide the police with any details regarding the assailant aside from the fact that he was an African-American juvenile. The police, without warrants, took twenty-four African-American juveniles to police headquarters to be questioned and fingerprinted. Davis was questioned and released. Later, without a warrant or probable cause, the police took Davis into custody and held him in jail overnight. During this time, his fingerprints were found to match those collected from the crime scene. Davis was tried and convicted of the rape. On appeal, the Supreme Court held that "[f]ingerprint evidence is no exception to the rule that all evidence obtained by searches and seizures in violation of the Constitution is inadmissible in state court. The Fourth Amendment applies to involuntary detention occurring at the investigatory stage as well as at the accusatory stage."

There are exceptions to the exclusionary rule. The exceptions identify circumstances when something may have made the search and seizure technically illegal but the evidence is still admissible in court. First, the courts have ruled that when the police make an unintentional error, or an honest mistake, in conducting a search with or without a warrant, the resulting evidence should not be excluded from trial. This is known as the good-faith exception and it is the most common and significant exception to the exclusionary rule. For example, in *Michigan* v. *DeFillipo* (1979), Detroit police officers were called to investigate two persons who appeared to be intoxicated in an alley. On arriving, the police discovered DeFillipo and a young woman in the alley. The police subsequently arrested DeFillipo for the violation of a Detroit ordinance. During the search after the arrest, the police discovered drugs, and he was charged and eventually convicted of a drug offense. The Supreme Court ruled that although the ordinance was unconstitutionally vague, the officers were acting in good faith in making the arrest and conducting the search. As a result, the drugs found during the search were admissible.

As another example, in *Arizona* v. *Evans* (1995), Evans was arrested by Phoenix police during a routine traffic stop when the police computer indicated that Evans was wanted on an outstanding warrant. While being handcuffed, Evans dropped a marijuana cigarette. A subsequent search of Evans' vehicle revealed more marijuana. Later, it was determined that the warrant was no longer valid. This information had not been entered into the computer because of a clerical error. At the trial, Evans moved to suppress the marijuana as the fruit of an unlawful arrest. The Supreme Court ruled that the police acted in good faith in making the arrest and conducting the search. The error was not the fault of the police and, therefore, the police should not be punished. The marijuana was admissible.

In *United States* v. *Leon* (1984), Burbank, California, police officers obtained from a state Superior Court judge a seemingly valid warrant based on probable cause to conduct a search of Leon's automobiles and three residences. The search led to the seizure of a large quantity of drugs. Later, the search warrant was found to be unsupported by probable cause. The Supreme Court ruled that the officers acted in good faith with reasonable reliance that the search warrant was valid and, therefore, the evidence was admissible.

A second exception to the exclusionary rule is known as the *inevitable discovery exception*, and it has usually been applied when the evidence in question is either a dead body or a weapon. This exception holds that if the police were reasonably expected to discover the evidence through lawful means and without the information produced from the illegal actions taken, then that evidence may still be admitted despite the exclusionary rule. For example, in the case of *Nix* v. *Williams* (1984), Williams was arrested for the kidnaping of a ten-year-old girl who had disappeared from a YMCA in Des Moines, Iowa. The arrest was based on probable cause. On the instruction of Williams' attorney, the police were not to question Williams during the drive back to Des Moines. However, while on the trip, one of the officers began a conversation with Williams that led to Williams revealing where the child's body was located. The officers, knowing that Williams was deeply religious, and that it was near Christmas, informed him that it would be nice to give the girl a Christian burial. They asked Williams to "think it over." The statements Williams then made led to the discovery of the body. Williams' statements were admitted into trial and he was convicted of the crime. The verdict was appealed on this basis. The U.S. Supreme Court held that the evidence of the victim's body was properly admitted on the grounds that the body would inevitably have been discovered even if no constitutional violation had taken place. The burden is on the prosecution to show "inevitable discovery." (Although the victim's body was admissible, the Supreme Court ruled that the suspect's statements were not; see *Brewer v. Williams* 1977 later in this chapter).

Third, the *purged taint exception* holds that the illegal actions of the police may be overcome by the voluntary actions of the suspect. In essence, the voluntary actions of the suspect can eliminate the tainted nature of the evidence and allow it to be admitted. For example, in *Wong Sun* v. *United States* (1963), federal agents in San Francisco conducted a search and arrest of Wong Sun without a warrant and without probable cause. Wong Sun was then released. Several days later, Wong Sun was interrogated. After the interrogation, the agent read back to Wong Sun the statement made by him. Wong Sun refused to sign the statement, although he admitted to the accuracy of it. A few days later, Wong Sun voluntarily went back to the police station and signed the confession. The Supreme Court ruled that Wong Sun's act manifested free will and therefore purged the taint of the illegal arrest. The act of free will broke the causal chain between the taint of the evidence and the illegal police conduct, so the evidence became admissible.

Finally, the *independent source exception* to the exclusionary rule states that evidence obtained from an independent source not directly related to an illegal search or seizure should be admissible into court. For example, consider *United States* v. *Crews* (1980). In the women's restroom at the Washington Monument, a woman was accosted and robbed at gunpoint by a young man. The victim immediately reported the incident to the police. Several days later a boy who matched the description of the suspect was seen by the police in the area by the monument. He was briefly taken into custody, questioned, photographed, and then released. Later the victim identified the person in the photograph as her assailant. The suspect was then again taken into custody. During a lineup, the boy was identified by the victim. Crews was indicted for armed robbery and other offenses. The Supreme Court ruled that the initial arrest of the suspect, the identification of the suspect via the photo, and the identification of the suspect in the lineup, were all illegal. However, the in-court identification of the defendant was legal. The initial illegal detention of the suspect could not deprive the prosecutors of the opportunity to prove the defendant's guilt through the introduction of evidence wholly untainted by police misconduct.

The Impact of the Exclusionary Rule on Criminal Investigations

The discussion of the exclusionary rule and its exceptions raises a fundamentally important question: What is the purpose of the exclusionary rule? The answer is that the exclusionary rule is supposed to deter unlawful police conduct in search and seizure cases. The reasoning is that if the police know that illegally seized evidence cannot be used in court to prove the suspect's guilt, then the police will not seize the evidence illegally—they will follow the law in collecting the evidence. As a result, the police will not violate citizens' rights, the fundamental aim of the constitutional protections in the first place. But does the exclusionary rule really deter police misconduct in conducting searches and seizures? The answer to this question is no, at least not as much as what many would hope or expect. The reason why the exclusionary rule does not necessarily deter police misconduct is that there are ways, as Sutton (1986) puts it, of "getting around the Fourth Amendment." According to the research conducted by Sutton (1986), the police can use several strategies to circumvent the rule. If these strategies do not break the law, they at least bend it. For example, one strategy involves the extensive use of the "consent" exception. As discussed earlier, if the police receive a voluntary waiver from a citizen allowing for a search, then the police can conduct a valid search. The issue becomes, however, what is "voluntary"? Consider a situation in which the police wish to conduct a search of a house that they have a suspicion contains illegal guns but they do not have a warrant for the search. The police may say to the homeowner, "If you let us come in and take a look at your guns we won't take any of them. But, if we have to go get a search warrant we're going to come back and pack up your whole house. So . . . do you mind if we come in?" If the citizen gives consent to the police to conduct a search under these circumstances, is it voluntary? Probably not. But if the police officer tells a judge that the citizen said, "Be my guest, come on in," how is voluntariness to be determined? A judge is the final arbiter of this question, but it may be an issue of he said/she said between the officer and the citizen. It may be difficult to determine who is really telling the truth and, correspondingly, it may be difficult for a judge to strike down the evidence gathered from a consent search.

As a second strategy of "getting around the Fourth," the police may conduct an illegal search with full knowledge that any evidence seized would not be admissible and that the case will not be prosecuted. For instance, the police could obtain evidence illegally to pressure a particular person to provide information about a particular crime or criminal (e.g., Tell us what you know about T-bone and that old man getting killed or you are going to be arrested for possession of marijuana). Or, the police could conduct an illegal search and seize evidence just to harass a suspect. Does this really happen? In a survey of Illinois police officers conducted by Martin (1994), it was found that twenty-five percent of officers stated that they witnessed at least one illegal search of a subject during the past year.

Third, Sutton (1986) reported that police officers sometimes engage in "judge-shopping," when "officers seek out magistrates who appear favorably disposed to warrant requests" (p. 439). Some judges may examine requests for warrants more closely than others and some judges may be more likely to find probable cause than others. The police may use this to their advantage in requesting warrants and executing searches. Knowing this, it is interesting to note that warrant applications are rarely rejected by judges or magistrates (Uchida and Bynum, 1991).

Finally, sometimes some police officers simply lie. For a variety of reasons, police officers may misrepresent the facts of a case to a judge or a jury and, as a result, the "fruits" of an otherwise illegal search may be admitted into trial and may be considered in determining the guilt or innocence of the accused. The fact that the police sometimes lie is well understood by other police officers, judges, and attorneys (see Dershowitz [1982]). Police officers sometimes refer to it as *testilying* (Cunningham, 1999). In the research conducted by Martin (1994), it was found that four percent of officers knew of other officers who provided false testimony in traffic cases, three percent knew of false testimony in criminal cases, and seven percent of officers knew of arrest reports written in a false manner. Given the sensitive nature of this area of inquiry, one might expect that these illegal behaviors are greatly underreported by officers. Although deception by the police in these types of situations is certainly troubling, the issue is complicated by the fact that in other situations it is legal for the police to lie. For instance, in interrogation settings, the police can legally deceive suspects in a variety of ways. For example, the statement "your partner in the crime just confessed so you might as well too" would be legally acceptable even if the partner did not really confess. If the police feel that the law is simply a barrier to effective performance, deception in many situations may be understandable (but in many situations is still not acceptable). Indeed, the most common reason for police lying is that the police view it as a necessary means to achieve the desired ends (Cunningham, 1999; Martin, 1994). In any case, it represents a strategy of the police to get around the exclusionary rule. Clearly, the exclusionary rule does not prevent the police from engaging in any of these questionable or illegal actions.

Does the exclusionary rule result in the loss of cases? Are potentially guilty suspects freed because of search and seizure problems? Numerous studies have attempted to address these questions. When the landmark decision of *Mapp* v. *Ohio* (1961) was rendered, the police believed that their actions were going to be constrained in a way that was detrimental to solving crimes and obtaining convictions. The research on the issue is mixed, although the prevailing conclusion appears to be that the exclusionary rule does not result in the loss of a significant number of cases.

For example, in a study conducted by the General Accounting Office (1979) in which more than 2,800 cases in 1977 and 1978 were analyzed, it was found that of all cases that were accepted for prosecution, in sixteen percent there was some type of suppression motion filed (to exclude evidence based on illegal police action). In eleven percent of these cases the Fourth Amendment was cited. In only 0.4 percent of the defendants' cases were charges dropped or not made as a result of Fourth Amendment search and seizure problems. In addition, successful motions were made in only 1.3 percent of prosecuted cases.

In an analysis of 7,500 cases in nine counties in Illinois, Michigan, and Pennsylvania, Nardulli (1983) found that motions to suppress physical evidence were filed in less than five percent of all felony cases and only 0.69 percent of such motions were successful. Even when the motion to suppress evidence was successful, many defendants were still convicted based on the other evidence in the case. Less than 0.6 percent of cases were lost because of the suppression of physical evidence.

Uchida and Bynum (1991) examined 2,115 court cases in seven cities in 1984 and 1985. They found that in thirteen percent of cases there was a motion to suppress physical evidence but in less than one percent of the cases was this motion successful. In total, 1.4 percent of all defendants in the sample of cases were allowed to "go free" because of an exclusionary rule problem.

Although these studies suggest that the exclusionary rule has little impact, it is important to realize that these studies did not examine the impact of the exclusionary rule on crimes being solved. In addition, the focus on "lost cases" at the court stage during the process draws attention away from the possibility that some of the cases when the police intentionally and obviously violate the provisions of the exclusionary rule are not even brought to the attention of prosecutors for further action, and therefore could not be "lost" at the prosecutorial stage. In these cases, the exclusionary rule did not deter police misconduct or lead to the case being lost; it simply deterred the police from formally processing the case.

Fifth and Sixth Amendments

The Fifth Amendment to the U.S. Constitution protects citizens against self-incrimination. It reads in part: "[n]o person shall be compelled in any criminal case to be a witness against himself, nor be deprived of life, liberty or property, without due process of law."

The Sixth Amendment identifies several rights, the most important of which from the perspective of criminal investigation is the right of individuals to be represented by an attorney in legal proceedings. The Sixth Amendment states, in part, "[i]n all criminal prosecutions the accused shall enjoy the right to . . . have the assistance of counsel for his defense."

The protections offered in the Fifth and Sixth Amendments are relevant when determining the admissibility of incriminating statements obtained from suspects. If information is obtained from suspects illegally, then that information is inadmissible in court, because it violates the due process rights of the accused. In criminal investigations, extremely valuable information can come from suspects, but this information is only useful in establishing proof in court if the police follow the legal procedures in collecting that evidence. The fundamental question is: When are incriminating statements made by a suspect admissible in court and when are they not? Most of the remainder of this chapter is devoted to addressing this important question.

The most famous and widely applied case associated with the Fifth (and, to a lesser extent, the Sixth) Amendment protection against self-incrimination is *Miranda* v. *Arizona* (1966), as described in the introduction to this chapter. The decision in Miranda requires the police to read suspects their "Miranda warnings" when a suspect is in "custody" and prior to "interrogation." The Miranda warning consists of the following:

- You have the right to remain silent.
- Anything you say can be used in a court of law against you.
- You have a right to have an attorney with you during the interrogation.
- If you are unable to afford an attorney, one will be provided for you without cost.

If these rights are waived by a suspect, the waiver is to be done voluntarily and intelligently. (See Exhibit 5–3.)

The Miranda decision extended the earlier decisions made by the U.S. Supreme Court in *Gideon* v. *Wainright* (1963) and *Escobedo* v. *Illinois* (1964). In *Gideon* v. *Wainright*

EXHIBIT 5–3 Example Miranda waiver form

Incident Number: _____

Defendant: _____

Address: _____

Charge: _____

Constitutional Rights
Miranda Warnings

_____ You have the right to remain silent. Anything you say can and will be used against you in a court of law.

_____ You have the right to talk to a lawyer and have him/her present with you while you are being questioned.

_____ You can decide at any time to exercise these rights and not answer any questions or make any statements.

_____ At this time, I, _____, wish to waive my constitutional rights and agree to voluntarily provide a written statement to the Glendale Police Department. This statement is given voluntarily of my own free will and there have been no promises or threats made to me.

Signature _____ Date _____ Time _____

Witness _____ Date _____ Time _____

Title _____

Statement:

Signature _____ Page ___ of ___

To verify that Miranda warnings were given and waived, police departments often require investigators to complete a form similar to the one illustrated here prior to the interrogation of a suspect. REPRINTED WITH PERMISSION OF GLENDALE POLICE DEPARTMENT.

(1963), Gideon was arrested and charged with breaking and entering—a felony. Gideon appeared in court without an attorney because he could not afford one. He asked that the court appoint counsel for him. His request was denied because the law provided a right to counsel only in capital cases. He conducted his own defense. He was convicted and sentenced to five years in prison. On appeal, the Supreme Court ruled "the right of an indigent defendant in a criminal trial to have the assistance of counsel is a fundamental right essential to a fair trial, and petitioner's trial and conviction without the assistance of counsel violated the Fourteenth Amendment." In the Escobedo case, Escobedo was arrested by the police, taken to police headquarters, and questioned about the fatal shooting of his brother-in-law. Escobedo was not advised by the police of his right to remain silent. During the police interrogation, Escobedo confessed to the murder. During the interrogation, he also requested to see his lawyer who was present in the building. The police refused. His confession was admitted in trial and he was convicted. On appeal, the Supreme Court ruled that the confession was inadmissible because of the circumstances of the interrogation; namely, that Escobedo was denied the right to counsel and was not notified of his right to remain silent. The Escobedo decision extended the right to counsel to the interrogation stage. *Gideon* v. *Wainright* (1963) and *Escobedo* v. *Illinois* (1964) set the stage for the Miranda decision that explicitly outlined the rights of the accused and the procedures to be used by the police to protect those rights.

Several decisions of the Supreme Court relate to the more technical and definitional aspects of the Miranda rights and the waiver of those rights. For example, how must the Miranda warnings be read? In *California* v. *Prysock* (1981) the police informed a juvenile murder suspect of his Miranda rights but they were not read from a standard script. The suspect was told that he had "the right to talk to a lawyer before you are questioned, have him present with you while you are being questioned, and all during the questioning." He was told that he could have his parents present, and then was informed that he had "the right to have a lawyer appointed to represent you at no cost to yourself." After Prysock waived these rights, he made incriminating statements and these were admitted into trial. The boy was convicted of first-degree murder. On appeal, the Supreme Court ruled that these warnings were adequate. The police do not have to give verbatim warnings as long as the suspect is advised of his rights and no limitations are placed on those rights. The order in which the warnings are read does not determine their validity. The Supreme Court ruled that the incriminating statements were admissible.

In *Smith* v. *Illinois* (1984) the waiver of some of the Miranda rights by the suspect were clear, although some were rather ambiguous. When asked if he understood his right to consult with a lawyer and to have a lawyer present, Smith replied, "Uh, yeah. I'd like to do that." In reading the rest of the warnings, and asking for his understanding of them, Smith stated, "Yeah and no, uh. I don't know what's that, really." The police continued, asked Smith questions, and Smith eventually made incriminating statements. The Supreme Court ruled that the defendant's request for counsel was not ambiguous and that all questioning should have stopped at that point. The statements made by Smith were not admissible.

For what offenses and under what circumstances must the Miranda warnings be read? In *Berkemer* v. *McCarty* (1984) the police arrested McCarty for suspicion of intoxicated driving and he was interrogated at the police station. At no point was he informed of his Miranda rights. During questioning, McCarty made incriminating statements including that he was "barely" under the influence of alcohol. He was later charged with and convicted of operating a motor vehicle under the influence of alcohol and drugs. On appeal, the Supreme Court held that the police do not have to provide Miranda warnings prior to the roadside questioning of a motorist, because this does not constitute a custodial interrogation. However, any person who is subjected to custodial interrogation must be given Miranda warnings, regardless of the severity of the offense. As a result, the Supreme Court ruled that the incriminating statements made during the custodial interrogation at the police station were not admissible.

What is an interrogation? In *Rhode Island* v. *Innis* (1980) the Providence, Rhode Island, police arrested Innis as a suspect in a murder of a taxicab driver based on an eyewitness identification. Innis was advised of his Miranda rights. He said that he understood his rights and wanted to speak with an attorney. He was then placed in a car and driven to the station. During the drive one of the officers commented that there were "a lot of handicapped children in the area" because a school for such children was nearby. He further stated how horrible it would be if one of the children found the gun (used in the murder) and something happened. Innis then proceeded to tell where the gun could be found. The Supreme Court ruled that the respondent was not interrogated in violation of his rights. The statements the officer made did not constitute express questioning or its functional equivalent. The officers had no reason to believe that their statements would have led to a self-incriminating response of the suspect. Subtle compulsion does not constitute an interrogation.

In the case of *Brewer* v. *Williams* (1977) the police explicitly sought to obtain incriminating evidence from Williams with regard to his involvement in a kidnaping/murder. Knowing that he was a former mental patient and deeply religious, the officer called Williams "Reverend" and referred to the fact that the missing girl's parents should be entitled to a Christian burial for their daughter who was taken from them on Christmas Eve. Williams then showed the police where to find the dead body. The Supreme Court held that the "Christian burial speech" was the functional equivalent of an interrogation. The statements were not admissible as evidence but the body of the girl was admissible (under the "inevitable discovery" exception to the exclusionary rule; see *Nix* v. *Williams* 1984).

Other decisions have been rendered that establish parameters under which Miranda warnings must be provided. In the case of *Massiah* v. *United States* (1964), Massiah was arrested on drug trafficking charges, he retained an attorney, pled not guilty to the charges, and was released on bail. A few days later, a coconspirator of Massiah decided to cooperate with government agents in their continuing investigation of Massiah. Through the use of a radio transmitter, conversations between Massiah and his partner were recorded and were incriminating. These statements were later used in court to obtain a conviction of Massiah. The Supreme Court held that Massiah's Fifth and Sixth Amendment rights were violated in that incriminating statements were deliberately obtained from him after he had been indicted and in the absence of retained counsel. The Supreme Court ruled that once a suspect has been indicted and has engaged an attorney, the police can no longer question him.

In a related case, *Edwards* v. *Arizona* (1981), Edwards was arrested on charges of robbery, burglary, and first-degree murder. At the police station he was informed of his Miranda rights and he declined to talk to the police without an attorney present. The next day, Edwards was once again given his Miranda warnings and he then implicated himself in the crimes. At his trial these statements were used and Edwards was convicted. The Supreme Court ruled that a suspect cannot be questioned again for the same offense after invoking his right to remain silent unless the suspect has consulted with a lawyer or the suspect initiates further communication, exchanges, or conversations with the police. In *Arizona* v. *Robertson* (1988), the Edwards decision was extended to questioning about the same or different offenses and to questioning conducted by the same or different law enforcement authorities. The bottom line seems to have been established with *Minnick* v. *Mississippi* (1990): Questioning of a suspect may not resume without an attorney present if the suspect has been given the Miranda warnings and if he has invoked the right to counsel.

Does silence on the part of a suspect constitute evidence? It depends on the meaning and form of "silence." In *Griffin* v. *California* (1965) the court ruled that a prosecutor cannot comment to the jury that the defendant not testifying constitutes evidence (of guilt). However, in *South Dakota* v. *Neville* (1983) it was ruled that the fact that a defendant refused to submit to a blood alcohol test is admissible in court as evidence.

There are several other situations when statements made by a defendant may be admissible without the Miranda warnings having been given or having been waived. These decisions may be thought of as exceptions to the Miranda requirement. For example, in *New York* v. *Quarles* (1984), a woman approached two police officers who were on patrol and told them that she had just been raped. She described her assailant as a black man and told the police that he was carrying a gun and had just entered the nearby supermarket. One officer entered the store and spotted Quarles, who matched the description given by the woman. On seeing the officer, Quarles turned and ran down an aisle. Once he was seen again, he was ordered to stop and was subdued. Quarles was frisked and the officer discovered that he was wearing an empty shoulder holster. After handcuffing him, the officer asked where the gun was located. Quarles nodded in the direction of some empty cartons, where the gun was then found. The suspect was given Miranda warnings only after the gun was found. The gun was admitted as evidence and Quarles was convicted. On appeal, the Supreme Court said that the gun was admissible as evidence under a public safety exception. The gun posed a possible immediate danger to the public; the potential danger justified the officer's failure to provide immediately the Miranda warnings.

When a suspect is not aware that he is speaking to a law enforcement officer (e.g., during undercover operations), the police are not required to provide the Miranda warnings to the suspect. Any voluntary statements made by the suspect in this circumstance are admissible (*Illinois* v. *Perkins* 1990). However, as ruled in *Arizona* v. *Fulminante* (1991), statements obtained as a result of implied duress, and without the benefit of the Miranda warnings, are not admissible. In this case, a paid police prison informant promised Fulminante that he would protect him from the other prisoners if Fulminante would tell him the truth about the abduction/murder of a child victim. Fulminante then confessed to the crime. He was convicted of murder, partially on the basis of this confession. The Supreme Court ruled that Fulminante's confession was involuntary because it was motivated by fear of physical violence if he did not receive protection. As a result, the confession was not admissible at trial.

Voluntary statements obtained as a result of police questioning, but without the full protection of Miranda, may be used in court for impeachment purposes (*Oregon* v. *Haas* 1975). Specifically, in this case the Supreme Court stated that "when a suspect in police custody has been given and accepts the full warnings prescribed by Miranda and later states that he would like to telephone a lawyer, but is told he cannot do so until reaching the station, and he then provides inculpatory information, such information is admissible as evidence at the suspect's trial solely for impeachment purposes after he has taken the stand and testifies to the contrary." Similarly, even an illegally obtained confession may be used by a prosecutor in court to prove that a defendant who testifies in court is lying (*Harris* v. *New York* 1971). In any case, if the arrest is illegal, but Miranda warnings are provided and waived, incriminating statements may not be used against this individual. The Miranda warnings do not purge the taint of the illegal actions of the police (*Brown* v. *Illinois* 1975). However, when an arrest is legal and Miranda warnings are provided to a suspect, and the suspect invokes those rights, and the police stop questioning but the suspect subsequently provides information voluntarily, then that information is admissible at trial (*Michigan* v. *Mosley* 1975).

What if the suspect does not invoke his Miranda rights, but a third party does on his behalf? Are incriminating statements provided by the suspect then admissible? Consider the case of *Moran* v. *Burbine* (1986). In this case, Burbine was arrested for a murder and was held by the police. Burbine's sister made arrangements for an attorney to represent Burbine while he was in custody, but Burbine was not aware of his sister's actions. The attorney then contacted the police and she stated that she would act as his counsel. She was informed by the police that they would not question him until the next day. Again, all actions were unknown to Burbine. The police subsequently informed Burbine of his Miranda rights and he waived them. The police then questioned him about the murder. At no time did he request an attorney. Burbine confessed to the murder. The Supreme Court ruled that neither the conduct of the police nor the respondent's ignorance of the attorney's efforts taints the validity of the waiver of rights. The Supreme Court held that the confession should not be excluded.

The Impact of Fifth Amendment Legislation on Criminal Investigations

The reaction to the Miranda decision was intense. A self-confessed and convicted rapist was given another chance at freedom because the police did not tell him about his right to remain silent. The police were outraged. Certain members of the U.S. Congress called for the impeachment of Chief Justice Earl Warren (Malone, 1998). The assumption was that if suspects are told that they do not have to talk to the police, and that what they say may be used against them, then suspects just will not talk. Confessions, it was believed, will be a thing of the past. This was the conventional wisdom. Most of the research that has been conducted to examine the impact of Miranda on police ability to obtain confessions has shown that the Miranda decision has had minimal impact; at the least, less impact than what was believed at the time of the Supreme Court decision.

To understand the impact of Miranda, at least two issues need to be considered. First, to what extent are confessions that have been obtained by the police subsequently ruled to be inadmissible? Second, to what extent are confessions not obtained by the police because of Miranda? And what impact does the lack of confession evidence have on prosecutors' ability to obtain convictions? The second question is more complicated than the first because it must be understood that perhaps no confession was obtained because there was no confession to give (i.e., the person being interrogated did not commit the crime), and just because there was no confession does not mean that the case was lost; other evidence may have been available to obtain a conviction.

With regard to the first question, Nardulli (1983) examined more than 7,000 cases in Illinois, Michigan, and Pennsylvania, and found that only five convictions were lost as a result of confessions being ruled as illegally obtained and therefore inadmissible. Not surprisingly, this study concludes that Miranda has had a relatively small impact on police effectiveness.

With regard to the second question, Leo (1998a) analyzed 182 investigations in three police departments and found that in seventy-eight percent of the cases, suspects waived their Miranda rights and answered the questions of the police. In the remaining twenty-two percent of cases, suspects invoked their rights and did not talk. Cassell and Hayman (1998) examined more than 200 cases and found that of the 129 cases for which the police provided suspects with their Miranda rights, approximately eighty-four percent waived them and agreed to answer the questions of the police. As demonstrated in both of these studies, because a large majority of suspects still decide to speak with the police even after they are informed of their rights, it appears that Miranda has not kept suspects from talking with the police. Some have even suggested that the Miranda warnings may increase the likelihood that suspects will make incriminating statements. The Miranda warnings make it clear that the police believe that the subject is guilty. It may be believed by suspects that a willingness to answer questions will help clear them of responsibility (e.g., If I answer your questions because I have nothing to hide, may I then go home?) (Thomas, 1998a, 1998b). It is interesting to note that in a study by Leo (1998a), suspects with a felony record were more likely to invoke their rights than suspects without a felony record, and suspects who waived their rights (i.e., answered the questions of the police) were more likely to be convicted than those who did not invoke their rights.

According to Cassell (1998), studies have shown that after the Miranda decision, the confession rate dropped between two to thirty-five percent. Cassell (1998) claims that the best estimate is that Miranda results in a lost confession in roughly one of every six criminal cases (sixteen percent). Furthermore, he estimates that in twenty-four percent of cases a confession is necessary to obtain a conviction. As a result, he concludes that Miranda results in a lost conviction in 3.8 percent (16% ¥ 24%) of all serious criminal cases. Cassell (1998) argues that although this is a relatively small percentage, it translates into a large number of cases. Schulhofer (1998) noted many of the deficiencies of Cassell's analyses and calculated the attrition rate at 0.78 percent, not 3.8 percent. In any case, regardless of the study, it appears that the impact of Miranda on lost cases is relatively small (Thomas, 1998a, 1998b).

Questions for Discussion and Review

1. What qualities must evidence have in order for it to be admissible in court?

2. What is the rationale of the Frye test and the Daubert standard for the admission of scientific evidence and testimony?

3. What is the chain of custody and why is it important? To what form of evidence does it apply?

4. What is an arrest? What is a search?

5. Arrest and search warrants must have certain features. Identify these features.

6. What is a reasonable expectation of privacy?

7. What is the search warrant requirement and what are the exceptions to the requirement?

8. What is the rationale for each of the exceptions to the search warrant requirement?

9. What is an inventory search of an automobile?

10. When is reasonable suspicion a standard of proof necessary to warrant a search?

11. What is the proper scope of a stop and frisk search? Search incident to lawful arrest? Vehicle search?

12. What is the exclusionary rule? What is its intended purpose?

13. How did the Supreme Court case of *Mapp* v. *Ohio* (1961) shape the exclusionary rule?

14. What are the four main exceptions to the exclusionary rule? Give a case example of each.

15. Does the exclusionary rule deter police misconduct in conducting searches and seizures? Explain.

16. What are the primary ways the police have been found to "get around the Fourth" according to the research conducted by Sutton (1986)?

17. Why is deception by the police a "tricky" issue in criminal investigations?

18. Does the exclusionary rule lead to the loss of a significant number of cases? Explain.

19. What are the Miranda warnings and under what circumstances must they be given to a person?

20. What is a custodial interrogation?

21. Under what circumstances must a suspect not be questioned by the police?

22. Under what circumstances can statements of a suspect be admissible even when the Miranda warnings have not been provided?

23. Based on the research, how often are confessions that have been obtained by the police subsequently ruled to be inadmissible?

24. Based on the research, how often are confessions not obtained by the police because of the Miranda warnings?

25. To what extent has the Miranda decision affected the police and the effectiveness of the criminal investigation process? Explain.

Related Internet Sites

www.signonsandiego.com/news/metro/danielle/index.html
This is the address for the *San Diego Union Tribune* newspaper section that contains coverage of the murder of Danielle van Dam and the trial of David Westerfield.

www.nolo.com
This is an excellent legal "self-help" web site. It provides information on virtually every legal issue one could think of, from taxes, to trademarks, to traffic tickets.

www.findlaw.com
This web site was also listed in Chapter 3, but it is so good that it is highlighted again. It is a comprehensive legal resource site for legal professionals, students, businesses, and the public. Good information about seeking employment in the legal profession can also be found here.

www.supremecourtus.gov
This is the official web site of the U.S. Supreme Court. It provides useful information on the court, its history, and its operation.

PHYSICAL EVIDENCE

OBJECTIVES

After reading this chapter you will be able to

- Discuss the three roles or functions of physical evidence in the criminal investigation process
- Discuss how physical evidence can serve as direct evidence or circumstantial evidence in criminal investigations
- Discuss the role of physical evidence in the larger criminal justice process
- Identify the most important guidelines that should be followed in recovering and preserving physical evidence from major crime scenes
- Discuss Locard's Exchange Principle
- Compare and contrast class characteristic evidence with individual characteristic evidence
- Identify types of class characteristic evidence and individual characteristic evidence
- Identify the crimes at which different types of physical evidence are most likely to be found
- Discuss the evidentiary value of the different types of physical evidence

- Identify the various uses of DNA in criminal investigations
- Differentiate between nuclear DNA and mitochondrial DNA (MtDNA)
- Compare the value and contribution of DNA evidence with fingerprint evidence in criminal investigations
- Explain how DNA and AFIS technology differentially affect criminal investigations
- Discuss the Combined DNA Index System (CODIS) and how it may make DNA analysis even more powerful in criminal investigations
- Discuss the most significant characteristics of cases in which DNA results were used to overturn the convictions
- Discuss forensic science and its subspecialities
- Discuss the location and primary workload of crime laboratories
- Discuss the most significant aspects of the investigation of the murders of Nicole Brown Simpson and Ronald Goldman

IMPORTANT TERMS

Physical evidence

Corpus delicti evidence

Associative evidence

Corroborative evidence

Direct and circumstantial evidence

Crime scene

Secondary crime scene

Crime scene procedures

Locard's Exchange Principle

Types of physical evidence

Class characteristic evidence

Individual characteristic evidence

DNA

DNA printing

Restriction fragment length polymorphism (RFLP)

Polymerase chain reaction (PCR)

MtDNA and nuclear DNA

CODIS

DNA databank

Forensic science

Criminalistics, forensic pathology, forensic anthropology, forensic odontology, forensic entomology

INTRODUCTION

On Sunday, June 12, 1994, just before 11:00 PM Steven Schwab was walking his dog in the Brentwood section of northwest Los Angeles when he was confronted by an excited and agitated dog, an Akita. As the dog followed Steven home, he noticed what appeared to be blood on the dog's paws and belly. When Steven arrived home, the dog still behaved in an unusual manner. Steven alerted his neighbor, Sukru Boztepe, and asked if he could keep the dog until the morning when Steven would search for the dog's owner. Boztepe initially agreed but then decided to take the dog for a walk and see if he could find its owner. He proceeded to follow the dog and it took him to the front walkway of 875 South Bundy Drive. As Boztepe looked up the dark walkway, he saw what appeared to be a lifeless human body surrounded by a massive amount of blood.

At 12:13 AM the first police officers arrived at the scene. Officers found the body of a woman clad in a short black dress. She was barefoot and lying face down with wounds to her throat and neck area. Next to her was the body of a man. He was lying on his side and his clothes were also saturated with blood. The woman was quickly identified by the police as the owner of the house, Nicole Brown Simpson, thirty-five years old and the ex-wife of the pro football player and sportscaster O.J. Simpson. The dead body of the man next to her was identified through identification in his wallet, still in his back pants pocket, as Ronald Goldman, age twenty-five, a waiter at a restaurant that Nicole and her family had visited earlier in the evening. Police also discovered the two children of Nicole and Simpson, ages nine and six, asleep in their beds in the house.

At 2:10 AM Detective Supervisor Phillips and Detectives Fuhrman and Roberts had arrived at the scene. Shortly thereafter, Phillips was notified that Detectives Tom Lange and Phil Vannatter from the Homicide Special Section of the Los Angeles Police Department's (LAPD's) Robbery Homicide Division were assigned as the lead investigators in the case; these detectives were on the scene by 4:30 AM.

In examining the area in which the bodies lay, the detectives noticed several items: a set of keys (determined to belong to Goldman), a dark blue knit cap (believed to be the perpetrator's), a beeper (Goldman's), a blood-splattered white envelope (that contained the eyeglasses of Nicole's mother, who left them at the restaurant earlier that night; Goldman was at Nicole's house to return those glasses), and a blood-soaked left-hand leather glove (also believed to be the perpetrator's). Leading away from the bodies toward the back of the property were shoe prints transferred to the concrete surface from blood on the shoes. Alongside the shoe print trail were drops of blood. The shoe prints and the blood drops appeared to be from the perpetrator.

Detectives decided to try to make contact with Simpson to notify him of the murder of his ex-wife and to arrange for him to collect his children, who were still at the house. It was a five-minute drive from the South Bundy address to Simpson's estate on Rockingham Avenue. It was now about 5:00 AM. Once at Simpson's property, detectives observed a white Ford Bronco, front wheels on the curb, with the back of the vehicle sticking out into the street. It was determined to be a vehicle that belonged to Simpson. On closer examination of the vehicle, Detective Furhman noticed what appeared to be a blood spot inside the vehicle near the door handle. Detectives called the phone number of the house to gain entry over the five-foot-high stone wall that surrounded the property, but no one responded. With no response, Fuhrman climbed the wall and let the other detectives in by unlatching the lock of the gate. (According to the detectives, this action was taken because of the belief that someone in the house may have been bleeding and in grave danger; however, defense attorneys later argued that this action constituted an illegal search and hence, any evidence collected as a result of the search should be excluded from the trial.) The detectives knocked on the front door of the main house, but there was no answer. They proceeded to the small guest houses located on the property. After they knocked on the door of the first house, a man by the name of Kato Kaelin, a friend and house guest of Simpson's, answered the door. At the next house they found Arnelle Simpson, Simpson's daughter. Fuhrman stayed with Kaelin while the other detectives accompanied Arnelle to the main house to confirm that no one else was home or in any sort of danger. The detectives returned to Kaelin and interviewed him. He told the detectives that before Simpson caught a late flight to Chicago that previous night, he went with him to a McDonald's and then returned home. Kaelin said that when they returned Simpson went into the house and he, Kaelin, went to his bungalow. At about 10:45 PM Kaelin heard several loud banging noises outside near the bungalow's air-conditioning unit. He said he thought it was an earthquake. He then went outside to investigate and saw a limousine parked at the gate to take Simpson to the airport. A few minutes later, according to Kaelin, Simpson was off to the airport in the limousine. While talking to Arnelle, police were able to determine that Simpson was staying at the Chicago O'Hare Plaza Hotel. While Fuhrman checked the area around the air-conditioning unit, Detective Phillips called Simpson in Chicago and notified him of the homicide. According to Phillips, Simpson appeared very concerned about what Phillips told him, but Simpson never asked for any details about what happened, nor did he even ask which ex-wife had been killed (Simpson had two ex-wives). Simpson told Phillips that he would return to Los Angeles on the next available flight.

Shortly after this phone call, Detective Fuhrman returned to the house and told Vannatter of his discovery along the side of the house near the air-conditioning unit in the back of the bungalow occupied by Kaelin. There, lying on the ground among some leaves, was a blood-stained leather glove. (The defense later argued that not only was this "search" conducted without a warrant, this glove was actually "planted" there by Fuhrman, a racist cop. Their claim was that both gloves were found at the crime scene, and Fuhrman took one of them with him to Simpson's.) It appeared to be the right-hand match of the one found at the crime scene on Bundy. All of the detectives except for Vannatter then left to notify investigators at the Bundy address of another possible crime scene, or an extension of the Bundy crime scene. Still at Rockingham, Vannatter discovered what appeared to be blood drops in the driveway. They led to the Ford Bronco. Inside the Bronco, he saw other red spots on the driver's side door and on the console between the two front seats. He discovered more blood leading to the front door of the main house. (The defense later argued that this blood was also planted and that it actually came from the sample that was drawn from Simpson at the police department after the initial interrogation by Vannatter and Lang. Interestingly, the nurse who drew the blood from Simpson testified he drew 8 cc of blood. The LAPD could only account for 6.5 cc.) All this evidence was later photographed, the glove was seized, the Bronco was impounded, and the entire area was secured. Fuhrman returned to the Rockingham scene to supervise, and Vannatter proceeded back to Bundy, and then, with his partner, went to the West Los Angeles Police Station to prepare a warrant to search Simpson's house and vehicle.

With search warrant in hand, the detectives returned to the Rockingham property. While they were conducting their search of the premises, Simpson arrived home. Simpson and his attorneys agreed that it would be okay for Simpson to talk with Detectives Lang and Vannatter about what he knew about these crimes and to do so without his attorneys present. At 1:35 PM, June 13, the "interrogation" of Simpson by Detectives Lang and Vannatter began. After the interrogation was over, Simpson was fingerprinted, wounds on his left hand were photographed, and a sample of his blood was drawn. The vial of blood was labeled and was placed in an evidence envelope. Vannatter then took the sealed envelope back to Simpson's home and gave it to Dennis Fung, the criminalist who was responsible for collecting and recording the evidence at the Bundy and Rockingham scenes. To maintain the chain of custody, Fung checked the contents of the envelope and, according to procedure, wrote on the outside, "Received from Vannatter on 6-13-94 at 1720 hours." It was then placed in the LAPD's crime scene truck. This whole sequence of events was done in full view of the numerous media film crews who were at the scene. (As far as the defense was concerned, this showed that Simpson's blood was taken back to the scene where his blood was said to have been discovered by the police.)

Meanwhile, back at Rockingham, the search of Simpson's residence revealed additional evidence of interest including blood-stained black socks and additional blood drops inside the house (more planted evidence according to the defense). In all, forty-one items of evidence were collected from Simpson's Bronco, his house, and the Bundy crime scene. Through scientific analysis, numerous links could be drawn from this evidence. Specifically, as outlined by Fuhrman (1997; pp. 156–164), evidence recovered from the glove found at the Bundy crime scene consisted of

- One hair from Nicole
- Fibers consistent with Goldman's shirt
- Fibers consistent with Goldman's jeans
- Dog hair from the Akita

By itself, this single glove was not that useful. One would suppose from the discovery of the glove that the murderer wore gloves while committing the homicides.

On the glove found at Simpson's Rockingham estate were

- Several hairs from Nicole
- Several pulled hairs from Goldman
- Fibers consistent with Goldman's shirt
- Dog hair from the Akita
- One fiber from the Bronco's carpet
- Several blue-black cotton fibers consistent with fibers found on Goldman's shirt

Given the blood and fibers found on the glove, the fact that it was found on Simpson's property, and that the identical matching glove was found at the crime scene, the glove linked all the key individuals and places together: Simpson, Nicole, Goldman, and the crime scene. As such, this glove was an extremely valuable piece of evidence. If Simpson did not commit the murders, how else could this discovery be explained?

On the socks found in Simpson's bedroom at Rockingham were

- Blue-black cotton fibers
- Blood from Simpson and Nicole

If the socks were Simpson's (a reasonable conclusion given that they were found in his bedroom), and if the blood was not planted on them, then the socks served as corroborative evidence that, at the least, Simpson was near Nicole when she was bleeding.

On Goldman's shirt were

- One hair consistent with Simpson's
- Twenty-five hairs from Nicole
- Several hairs from the Akita
- Four torn fibers from Nicole's dress
- Several fibers from the knit cap

- One fiber consistent with the lining of both gloves
- Many blue-black fibers

This evidence associated Goldman with Simpson, Nicole, the gloves and cap of the perpetrator, and probably the clothes of the perpetrator (blue-black fibers).

On Ron Goldman's pants were

- Several hairs consistent with Nicole's
- Several hairs from the Akita

This hair linked Nicole with Goldman, and Goldman with the dog. This was relatively insignificant evidence in establishing who was responsible for the homicides, but was perhaps useful for other purposes, such as for reconstructing the crime.

On the blue knit cap found at the Bundy crime scene were

- Several hairs from the Akita
- Twelve hairs matching Simpson's, not pulled or torn
- Several fibers consistent with Goldman's shirt
- One fiber consistent with the lining of both gloves
- One fiber consistent with the Bronco's carpet

Once again, this was evidence that provided additional strength to the conclusion that Simpson was at the crime scene and was wearing, at least temporarily, the cap. One could reasonably conclude from this evidence alone that Simpson was the likely perpetrator. But there was even more physical evidence.

Among the blood evidence found at the Bundy crime scene were

- Blood drops near the victims that matched Simpson's
- Four blood drops on walkway that matched Simpson's
- Two shoe prints of size twelve Bruno Magli shoes in blood that matched Nicole's
- Blood stains from Goldman's boot matched Goldman's and Nicole's

Through DNA analysis, the blood found at the crime scene that was not Nicole's or Goldman's was confirmed to be Simpson's. This evidence positively linked Simpson to the scene of the crime (plus Simpson had an unexplained cut to his hand). In order for Goldman's boot to leave a print in Nicole's blood, she had to be bleeding before Goldman fell. It is reasonable to conclude that Nicole was attacked first, then Goldman. The Bruno Magli shoe prints were probably left by the perpetrator. (In the trial, the prosecution introduced a photograph of Simpson reporting from the sidelines of a National Football League football game and wearing the shoes in question, but his lawyers argued that the photograph was a fraud.)

Among the blood evidence found in and on the Bronco were

- Blood matching Simpson's found on driver's door interior and on the instrument panel
- Blood on the center console that matched Simpson's
- Blood on the steering wheel that matched Simpson's and Nicole's
- Blood on the center console that matched Simpson's and Goldman's
- Blood on the driver's side wall that matched Simpson's
- Blood on the carpet that matched Nicole's
- Blood on the center console that matched Simpson's, Nicole's, and Goldman's

More evidence linked Simpson with the dead victims and the crime scene.
Among the blood evidence at Rockingham were

- Blood on the glove that matched Goldman's
- Of the four blood samples on a sock, two that matched Nicole's and two that matched Simpson's
- Blood drops in the foyer that matched Simpson's
- Blood trail on the driveway that matched Simpson's

More blood linked Simpson to the homicides. As Fuhrman (1997) explained, there was not just a mountain of evidence showing that Simpson killed his ex-wife and Ron Goldman, there was a Mt. Everest of evidence, but it was explained away by the defense by arguing that Simpson was framed.

In addition to the physical evidence, there were the interesting facts that Simpson had seven abrasions and three cuts to his *left* hand (and that the *left*-hand glove was found at the crime scene) and Simpson did not have a reasonable explanation for these injuries or his whereabouts during the time the homicides occurred (see Chapter 8).

On Friday June 17, 1994, an arrest warrant for O.J. Simpson was prepared. Simpson's new attorney, Robert Shapiro, was instructed by the police to accompany Simpson to police headquarters. He was to surrender at 11:00 AM. Simpson was nowhere to be found. Police later discovered that he was with his friend Al Cowling driving around Orange County, near Los Angeles, in Simpson's Bronco. The police followed them and the convoy became the then-famous slow-speed chase. It ended hours later at Simpson's residence at Rockingham. Simpson was arrested and taken into custody for the murder of Nicole Brown Simpson and Ronald Goldman. The investigation that led to his arrest was only the first part of the story. The jury trial began on January 23, 1995. The case took many twists and turns before Simpson was found not guilty on October 2, 1995. The jury deliberated for less than five hours.

L.A.P.D. Detective Mark Fuhrman is seen pointing to a piece of evidence near the body of Nicole Brown Simpson.

The Role of Physical Evidence in the Criminal Investigative Process

Physical evidence, also known as *forensic evidence* or *real evidence*, can serve several important roles during the criminal investigative process, many of which are illustrated in the Simpson investigation. First, physical evidence can help establish the elements of a crime, and thus function as corpus delicti evidence. For example, pry or tool marks on a window can help establish that a burglary occurred. Semen recovered from a victim can help establish that a rape occurred. The presence of flammable liquids or combustibles can help establish that arson occurred. Of course, the lack of pry marks, the lack of semen, or the lack of combustibles does not necessarily indicate that a crime did not occur. A burglary can occur without evidence of forced entry, a rape can occur without semen being present (or a rape may not have occurred even if semen is present), and arson can be committed without flammable liquids. It is in this manner that physical evidence can *help* establish the elements of a crime, or assist investigators in determining whether a crime actually occurred.

Even though the presence of forensic evidence may not conclusively establish that a crime occurred, it can make establishing proof much less difficult. Consider the case of Mark Chmura, the former pro-bowl tight end of the Green Bay Packers. Chmura was accused of sexually assaulting a sixteen-year-old girl and former babysitter of his children at an early morning after-prom party in April 1999. The assault allegedly took place in a bathroom of the house where the party was being held—the house of one of the victim's friends and a neighbor of Chmura's. According to the victim's statement to the police and corresponding court testimony, Chmura was in the bathroom about to change his clothes after being in an outside hot tub with the victim and several of her friends when he motioned to the intoxicated victim for her to enter the bathroom. Chmura then closed the door, placed the victim on the floor, removed her pants, and penetrated her vagina in an unknown manner. Subsequent to this event, the victim underwent a sexual assault examination. The exam revealed minor injuries to the victim but no semen was present. The defense argued that no such encounter occurred in the bathroom. There was no sexual assault. There was no semen because there was no rape. It was argued that the injuries to the victim occurred in an unknown manner (possibly from an ill-fitting swimsuit, according to one of the defendant's expert witnesses). It was argued that Chmura was set up by the victim because she did not like him (during the trial, the defense provided testimony from witnesses that when talking to some of her friends at the party earlier that night the victim referred to Chmura as "a sick fuck") and wanted to get money from him. These issues could be raised because there was no semen. If semen was found, sexual intercourse would have been established and, because the victim was sixteen, consent would not have been an issue. The jury found Mark Chmura not guilty.

A second important role of physical evidence in the criminal investigation process is that it can be used to make associations between crime scenes, offenders, victims, and instruments (e.g., tools). In fact, forensic evidence collected during criminal investigations is used most often to establish associations. Consider the case of Simpson: The glove found on Simpson's property that contained Nicole's hair and Goldman's hair and blood associated, at the least, Simpson's property with the homicide scene. Simpson's blood found at the crime scene and at his house further strengthened the association between Simpson and the homicides.

Finally, in helping to establish the elements of a crime or in making associations between offenders, victims, and so forth, physical evidence can function as corroborative evidence and thereby support other evidence that establishes an issue in question. For example, physical evidence (e.g., pry marks) can support a victim's statement about a burglary having occurred, or physical evidence (e.g., semen) can support the victim's statement about the identity of the assailant.

It is also worthwhile to note that physical evidence can act as direct *or* circumstantial evidence. For example, as direct evidence, physical evidence (blood) can be used to address questions such as, Was Simpson at the crime scene? Was Karen Beineman (the last victim in the Michigan coed killer case; see Chapter 4) in the basement of John Collins' uncle's house? Physical evidence can also be used to *infer* conclusions such as that Simpson killed Nicole Brown Simpson and Ron Goldman, and that Collins killed Karen Beineman. In this sense, physical evidence serves as circumstantial evidence.

Although physical evidence is useful at helping to establish the elements of a crime, making associations between offenders, victims, crime scenes, and so forth, and serving a corroborative function with other evidence, physical evidence is not very effective at identifying a culprit when one is not already known. The presence of physical evidence alone rarely leads to a culprit being identified or the crime being solved. Consider once again the case of O.J. Simpson. If Simpson had not been identified as a suspect through other means (e.g., being the exspouse of Nicole, having a shaky alibi, having a cut finger without a clear explanation), the blood that was found at the crime scene (but that did not belong to either of the victims) may not have been very useful in the investigation. It was only after Simpson was identified as a suspect that the blood was useful for investigative purposes: The blood at the crime scene could be positively matched to Simpson. As such, Simpson could be associated with the crime scene, and the blood corroborated other factors that led to Simpson being considered the culprit.

To illustrate this point further, consider the following examples (adapted from Peterson et al., 1984).

> The nude body of (an adolescent) female was discovered in a county park adjacent to a river. The scene revealed little but the body and a trail of blood, which covered more than one hundred feet through a gravel parking lot. A large clump of long blond hairs matted in the blood in the parking lot were later matched to the victim.
>
> After the scene had been documented, the body was wrapped in a sheet and transported to the county morgue. Examination of the body revealed some sixteen stab wounds, in addition to a deep cut across the throat ending at the right ear. The body had suffered numerous abrasions and it was apparent that large quantities of both head and pubic hair had been pulled from the victim.
>
> A further search of the park revealed several items of clothing—a pair of jeans, blouse, scarf, and socks. Some 175 pulled pubic hairs were recovered from these items, all of which matched the victim. Seven black polypropylene fibers, four green nylon 6-6 fibers, and one Caucasian body hair, foreign to the victim, were recovered. In addition, a pink material, probably vomit, was present on the jeans and formed a three inch wide ribbed pattern.
>
> After about one week the investigation focused on a distant relative of the victim. His truck was searched and several blond pubic hairs were observed between the seat belt retractor and the seat. In addition, black polypropylene fiber floor mats over green nylon carpeting were noted.
>
> A ribbed three inch pattern was observed in the seat design and a pink material was present in the seams of the seat. Small splotches of red material, later shown to be blood, were present on the headlights.
>
> During the course of the laboratory examination the pulled pubic hairs found in the suspect's truck were matched to the victim's pubic hair . . . The black and green fibers from the victim's clothing were matched to the mats and carpeting in the suspect's truck. The body hair from the victim's blouse was matched to the suspect's chest hair. The pink material from the victim's jeans was shown to be consistent with that from the truck seat in color and composition. In addition, the pattern of the vomitus material on the victim's jeans was shown to be indistinguishable from the pattern on the truck seat.
>
> Two witnesses were identified who were able to state that a truck similar to the one owned by the suspect was in the park shortly before the body was found.
>
> The suspect was convicted of murder (pp. 83–84).

Clearly, in this example, the physical evidence (hair, fibers) associated the victim with the defendant and the defendant's truck. But what was the most significant development the investigation, without which the physical evidence would have been of minimal use? The fact that *"After about one week the investigation focused on a distant relative of the victim."* Without the identification of this individual (through unspecified means), the physical evidence would not have been nearly as useful.

In a study of homicide investigations, 100 solved and unsolved cases were analyzed (Brandl, unpublished manuscript). Of the eighty-nine solved cases, in only three did the presence of physical evidence contribute significantly to the case being *solved*. Consider these three representative cases:

1. Relatives found an elderly man dead in the basement of his house with his skull crushed by a barbell that was still resting on his head. The victim's daughter told the police at the time of the discovery that a woman by the name of "Jan," who was a drunken, violent prostitute, often lived with the victim. She said that her father and Jan often visited a neighborhood tavern. Investigators went to the tavern, asked about Jan and obtained her last name and an address where she was known to sometimes sleep. In looking for Jan, they first found Jan's sister. She told police that Jan confessed to her that she killed the old man because he was going to kick her out of his house. She then told the police where Jan could be found. The police found Jan and they told her that her sister said she confessed to her. Jan then confessed to the police that she killed the old man. She was arrested and charged with the homicide.

2. An individual was arrested as a "suspicious person" in Chicago. He was discovered driving a vehicle that he did not own; the vehicle was registered to a person with a Milwaukee address. Chicago police contacted the Milwaukee police about their discovery. Police in Milwaukee tried to contact the owner at the address listed, but with no success. Milwaukee police officers went to his house and found it locked. The police broke into the house and discovered a person dead, identified as the owner of the house and the owner of the vehicle (through a driver's license in his pocket). He had been stabbed to death. Chicago police were notified of the homicide. On checking the vehicle further, the police found many other items belonging to the victim. On questioning the suspect, he confessed to the murder and theft. The suspect was arrested and charged with murder.

3. A brother and sister, both adults, were arguing about him moving out of the sister's house. A physical altercation resulted and the sister was stabbed once in the leg. The police were notified of the argument and screaming by a neighbor. The police arrived, and, in a dying declaration, the victim stated that her brother stabbed her. He was still at the scene. When questioned, the brother confessed to killing his sister. He was arrested and charged with the crime.

So, what was the impact of physical evidence in the investigation and arrest of these perpetrators? If you said none, you would be correct! Why is this the case? In homicides as well as in rapes, assaults, and some robberies, there is often powerful evidence in the form of an eyewitness identification of the suspect, and the suspect and victim (or witnesses) are often known to each other. For example, in the homicide study conducted by Brandl (unpublished manuscript), the victim and the suspect were known to each other in fifty-seven of the eighty-three solved cases (sixty-nine percent), and a witness was able to provide the name (or partial name) of the perpetrator in fifty-five of the solved cases (sixty-six percent). Clearly, these "circumstances" and the associated evidence are much more useful to investigators than any physical evidence that may be available. Indeed, forensic evidence has the greatest impact in investigations when the chances of solving the crime are the smallest—when suspects are neither named nor identified quickly after the crime (Peterson, 1987).

The Role of Physical Evidence in the Criminal Justice Process

In general, it is fair to say that physical evidence has more of an impact on convicting a suspect (i.e., proving beyond a reasonable doubt that a defendant is guilty) than on solving the crime (i.e., determining who committed the crime on the basis of probable cause and then apprehending the perpetrator). Indeed, research has shown that cases with physical evidence result in higher rates of conviction than cases without such evidence (Peterson, 1987). In addition, research has also shown that if forensic evidence strongly associates the defendant with the crime, prosecutors are less likely to offer a plea bargain (Peterson, 1987).

It is important to note that physical evidence is becoming more important and more influential in the criminal investigation and criminal justice processes. With increased analysis capabilities (especially DNA printing, discussed later in this chapter) and increased storage and processing capabilities (such as automated fingerprint identification systems and DNA banks, also discussed later), certain types of physical evidence are able to break the general rule that physical evidence is not very effective at identifying a culprit when one is not already known.

The Crime Scene and Associated Procedures

A crime scene is the area within the immediate vicinity in which the criminal incident occurred or was believed to have occurred. The area where significant evidence relating to a crime is (or could be) found is also sometimes considered a crime scene, commonly referred to as a *secondary crime scene*. For example, in a homicide, several places may be related to the crime and may contain evidence associated with the crime: the place where the victim was encountered, the place where the victim was first attacked, the place where the murder occurred, the place where the body was dumped, and the place where property was dropped. The more sites identified by the police, the more likely the crime is to be solved (Rossmo, 2000). Not all crime scenes are equal in their value to investigators. Some crime scenes may be more valuable than others because only certain people may have access to particular places (for example, recall that in the Michigan coed killer case, Collins was the only one with access to his uncle's house). In addition, some crime scenes contain little evidence whereas some contain a wealth of evidence. Accordingly, appropriate and necessary crime scene procedures vary considerably from crime to crime. In addition, resources and the policies of particular police departments may also dictate the proper course of action in crime scene investigations. Searching for and collecting physical evidence from crime scenes is not an inexpensive endeavor; it takes time. As a result, although relatively little time may be spent processing burglary crime scenes in most jurisdictions, much time may be reasonably spent on homicide scenes. This reflects a triage system of sorts in prioritizing crime scenes.

With these understandings as a backdrop, it is important to realize that there are basic guidelines that should be followed by investigative personnel in preserving and recovering physical evidence from major crime scenes. The guidelines discussed here are typically ones that should be followed in major crime investigations such as homicides (see National Institute of Justice [NIJ; 2000a]).

Arriving at the Scene: Initial Response/Prioritization of Efforts

The first and one of the most important steps in a crime scene operation is securing the crime scene to minimize contamination by external factors (e.g., bystanders, witnesses) that could lead to the destruction of evidence. The initial responding officer should approach the crime scene cautiously and should be aware of any persons or vehicles in the area, or leaving the area, that may be related to the crime. The officer should make sure that it is safe to enter the crime scene to take further action. It is important that the officer remain alert and attentive when approaching and processing the scene.

Second, a top priority in and around the crime scene is officer safety. Officers should look for possible threats to safety including hazardous materials, chemical threats, and dangerous persons. If such threats are apparent, appropriate personnel/backup should be immediately notified.

Third, after neutralizing dangerous persons or other threats, the officers' next responsibility is to provide or summon necessary medical attention for injured parties. Officers should ensure that medical personnel do not unnecessarily disturb the crime scene. If resources allow or if the victim is in grave danger of death, an officer should accompany the victim to the medical facility to document any comments made (e.g., a dying declaration) and to preserve evidence.

Fourth, the crime scene must constantly be protected from persons at or near the scene. Individuals must be prevented from entering and altering the crime scene and the physical evidence located there. In addition, suspects and witnesses must be identified and separated. Critical information can be quickly compromised when witnesses are allowed to share with each other their version of events.

Fifth, officers must establish and protect the boundaries of the crime scene. The boundaries include where the crime actually occurred, paths of entry and exit of the suspects, and places where the victim/evidence may have been moved or discarded. No person should be allowed to alter the crime scene through such actions as smoking, eating or drinking, moving any items, opening windows, or littering.

Sixth, when appropriate, the initial responding officers should brief the investigators taking charge of the investigation. This action provides critical continuity during the initial phases of the investigation.

Seventh, all activities and observations of the responding officers should be recorded in the required reports as soon as possible. This documentation must include descriptive information about the crime, the crime scene, and information obtained from witnesses, victims, suspects, and other individuals at the scene.

Preliminary Documentation and Evaluation of the Scene

With investigators now in charge of the crime scene, it is their responsibility to review the activities of the initial responding officers. The first step then is once again to assess the crime scene. Safety should be reevaluated and crime scene boundaries should be confirmed. Investigators should make sure that suspects, witnesses, and victims continue to be separated and monitored. Personnel should be assigned to interview these individuals as soon as practical. A determination should be made about the necessity of obtaining a search warrant or obtaining consent to search. A path of entry and movement for authorized personnel should be established. The need for additional investigative resources (e.g., equipment, legal consultation) should be determined and requested if necessary. Efforts should be made to search for and locate other witnesses not present at the immediate crime scene (e.g., a neighborhood canvass).

Processing the Scene

The first step in processing the crime scene is determining who is responsible for what, and establishing the composition of the investigative team. The responsibilities should be divided and the performance of activities supervised. Second, the investigator in charge must require that all personnel follow procedures to ensure safety and the integrity of the evidence being documented and collected. Security of the evidence and the crime scene must be continually maintained. Third, the investigator in charge must be responsible for or supervise the taking of photographs, video, sketches, measurements, and notes. Photographs and sketches are the primary means by which the crime scene is documented, and both serve as the official record of the condition and nature of the crime scene (See Exhibit 6–1 and Exhibit 6–2 for examples of crime scene sketches.) Specific guidelines regarding these tasks can be found in the *Handbook of Forensic Services* (FBI, 1999c).

Fourth, the investigator in charge should determine the order in which physical evidence is collected, focusing first on evidence that is subject to easy alteration or destruction. If appropriate and necessary, other methods of evidence collection should be considered and used (e.g., blood pattern documentation, blood illumination techniques, projectile trajectory analysis). Fifth, the team members should ensure the proper collection, preservation, packaging, and transportation of evidence. Evidence must be collected and handled

EXHIBIT 6–1 Apartment crime scene sketch

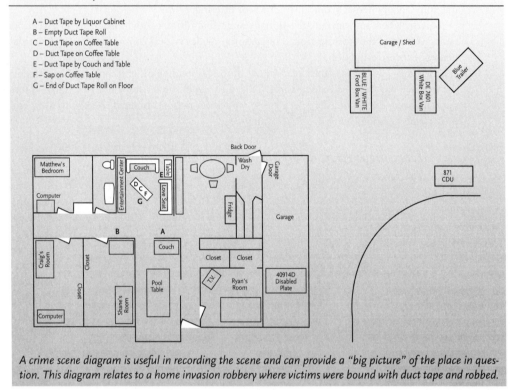

A – Duct Tape by Liquor Cabinet
B – Empty Duct Tape Roll
C – Duct Tape on Coffee Table
D – Duct Tape on Coffee Table
E – Duct Tape by Couch and Table
F – Sap on Coffee Table
G – End of Duct Tape Roll on Floor

A crime scene diagram is useful in recording the scene and can provide a "big picture" of the place in question. This diagram relates to a home invasion robbery where victims were bound with duct tape and robbed.

properly for it to be of use in an investigation and prosecution. The chain of custody is critical and must be maintained.

In conducting a search for evidence at a crime scene, various methods can be used. These methods include the grid, strip, and spiral search (see Exhibit 6–3). The basic idea for each of these approaches is to be thorough and systematic, and not to overlook or miss any area or any item within the boundaries of the crime scene. The search should be approached with "Locard's Exchange Principle" in mind. This principle holds that any time a person comes into contact with a place or another person, something of that individual is left behind and something of that place is taken with the individual. Although this principle is often valid, it is not *necessarily* valid. It is, nevertheless, a useful approach to take when conducting a search. The bottom line is to expect to find evidence. The *Handbook of Forensic Services* published by the FBI (1999c), provides additional guidelines for an effective crime scene search:

- Search from the general to the specific for evidence.
- Be alert for all evidence.
- Search entrances and exits of the crime scene.

EXHIBIT 6–2 Blockbuster video store crime scene diagram

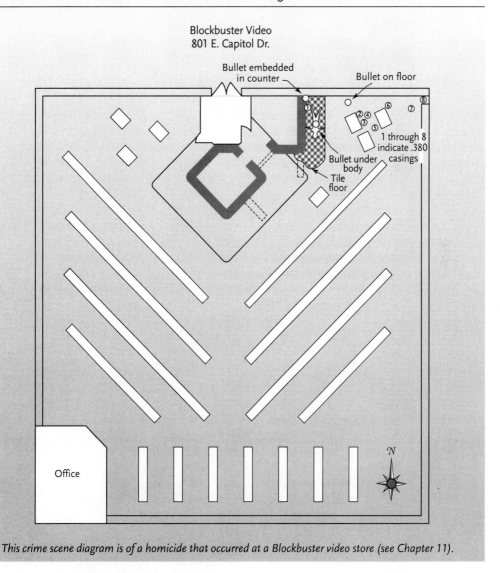

Blockbuster Video
801 E. Capitol Dr.

Bullet embedded in counter

Bullet on floor

Bullet under body

Tile floor

1 through 8 indicate .380 casings

Office

N

This crime scene diagram is of a homicide that occurred at a Blockbuster video store (see Chapter 11).

- Mark evidence locations on the sketch.
- Wear gloves to avoid leaving fingerprints.
- Do not excessively handle the evidence after recovery.
- Take steps to avoid inadvertently transferring evidence (e.g., carpet fibers on shoes) to a crime scene or between crime scenes.
- Make a complete evaluation of the crime scene.

Photograph #1

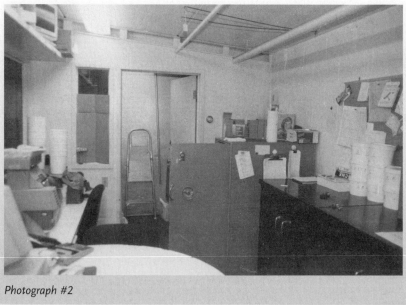

Photograph #2

Crime scene photographs should tell a story, or should be able to be used to construct a story. In this case, two robbers entered a restaurant at closing time, ordered the manager and another employee down the steps into the basement (photo #1) and to the office where the safe was located (#2). At gunpoint , they demanded that the manager open the safe. Unknown to the robbers, another employee was upstairs in the restaurant and

Photograph #3

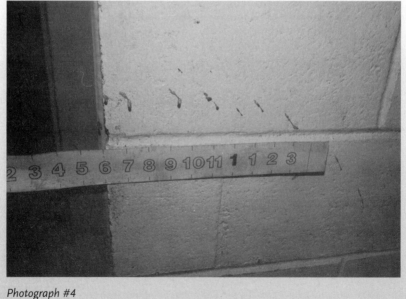

Photograph #4

heard the commotion. He realized a robbery was taking place. He armed himself with a metal churning rod (as seen laying on the floor in photo #3) and as the robbers were coming up the steps with bags of money, the employee hit one of the robbers with rod causing injury to the robber (#4). The robber dropped the bag of cash

Photograph #5

Photograph #6

(#5). The other robber pulled a gun and pointed it at the employee. The employee then moved away and both of the robbers fled through the back door without any money (#6). One of the suspects dropped his cap on the way out (#7). Note that the blood splatters shown in photo #4 reveal that the direction from which the blow was struck was from left to right, similar to the angle of each blood drop and the entire blood splatter.

Photograph #7

EXHIBIT 6–3 Crime scene search patterns

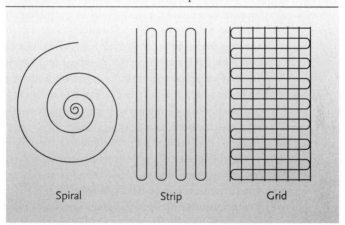

Spiral   Strip   Grid

Completing and Recording the Crime Scene Investigation

To complete the crime scene investigation, the investigator in charge should first establish a crime scene debriefing team. This team will discuss and determine the need for any remaining activities prior to releasing the scene, and will discuss immediate steps that need to be taken during the follow-up investigation. Crime scene findings can be reviewed at this time and a summary of the evidence collected can be offered. Second, a final survey of the crime scene should be made to make sure that the crime scene investigation is complete and that no materials or evidence are left behind.

Finally, the investigator in charge should ensure that all necessary reports and other documentation are completed. This includes reports completed by the initial responding officers, emergency personnel documentation, entry/exit documentation, photographs/ video, crime scene sketches and diagrams, and search warrant or other search documentation. These reports and other documentation can serve as a basis to direct further investigative activities and to provide continuity during the investigation across investigators.

An investigator only has one shot at a crime scene. It should be treated carefully and processed thoroughly. The value of critical evidence can be quickly destroyed through inappropriate or hasty crime scene procedures.

Types of Physical Evidence

The most common types of forensic evidence collected and analyzed for investigative purposes are drugs and fingerprints followed by firearm evidence, blood and blood stains, and semen (Peterson, 1987). During homicide investigations specifically, shells or casings from a gun, weapons, blood, and fingerprints are the most common types of physical evidence recovered from crime scenes (Brandl, unpublished manuscript). Although the media often place much emphasis on more esoteric forms of forensic evidence, research shows that this evidence is rarely present or analyzed during criminal cases (Brandl, unpublished manuscript; Peterson, 1987).

Physical evidence can be broadly classified as being either class characteristic evidence or individual characteristic evidence. Class characteristic evidence has characteristics that are common to a group of objects or persons. A positive association or link *cannot* be made on the basis of class characteristic evidence. Individual characteristic evidence has characteristics that can be identified as originating with a particular person or source. A positive association *can* be made on the basis of individual characteristic evidence. Although this classification may seem relatively simple and straightforward, it is best considered a conceptual distinction. As such, it is sometimes difficult to categorize evidence as either class or individual characteristic evidence. For example, blood has been traditionally considered class characteristic evidence; however, with the use of DNA analysis, blood is now best considered individual characteristic evidence. Shoe prints are usually considered class characteristic evidence; however, as explained later, there are circumstances when shoe prints could best be considered individual characteristic evidence. Depending on the condition of a recovered bullet, that bullet might best be considered class or individual characteristic evidence. In any case, for physical evidence to be of any value, it must be treated carefully and collected in accordance with the law and the chain of custody.

The discussion offered here provides information on the nature of the evidence, its potential usefulness in establishing proof, and basic guidelines for collecting and handling such evidence. More detailed and technical information about the collection of the evidence can be found in other sources (e.g., FBI [1999c]).

Soil

Soil consists of organic natural materials such as rock, minerals, and decomposing plants, and may also contain man-made materials such as brick, concrete, glass, or paint. Examination of the color, texture, and composition of soils may allow for an assessment of whether the soils share a common origin (FBI, 1999c). One of the most common scientific techniques of analyzing soil is the density gradient tube. With this procedure, the densities of soil samples are analyzed via chemicals that separate the particles that comprise the soil. If the pattern of separation is similar in two or more samples, it indicates a match (Owen, 2000). Soil evidence is most likely to be found on the bottom of shoes, places where soil on shoes may be left (e.g., floor of vehicles, hard-surface walkways), clothing, and on the tires, fenders, and body of vehicles. It is recommended that if soil samples are to be collected, that samples be taken as soon as possible because soil can change quickly and dramatically. In addition, if available, soil should be collected from the immediate crime scene area as well as from the apparent entrances and exits of the crime scene. Samples should be collected from wherever there is a noticeable change in the color or composition of the soil. It is often necessary to collect numerous soil samples from a scene. A map should be drawn showing where soil samples were taken. Investigators should not remove soil from recovered shoes, clothing, or tools. Paper bags should be used to package materials containing soil, and soil samples should be placed in plastic film-type canisters (FBI, 1999c).

Paint

Paint is a pigmented polymer that is applied and adheres to various surfaces. It is possible to compare microscopically the color and shape of paint chips or other samples, as well as to determine through the use of gas chromatography the chemical properties of paint to determine whether samples match. Some forensic laboratories (such as the FBI crime laboratory) maintain a database of vehicle paint samples with which the color, year, make, and model of an automobile can be determined by analyzing recovered vehicle paint samples. Paint evidence may be found when paint has been transferred from one surface to another, either as wet paint or chips from dried paint. Paint is often present as evidence in hit-and-run cases when it may be transferred from one vehicle to another or from a vehicle to a person who has been struck. It is also sometimes present in burglaries during which paint may be transferred from a building to the perpetrator or when it may be transferred from a building to tools used to gain entry. Paint chips tend to be located in pant pockets and pant cuffs. If paint samples are to be collected, it is necessary that the paint be chipped off the surface, as opposed to scraped off, to preserve the layer structure of the paint. With hit-and-run victims, the victim's clothing should normally be submitted for laboratory analysis as should entire vehicle components (e.g., bumper) that contain paint evidence. Paint particles should be packaged in pillboxes or sealed envelopes without any additional packing materials (FBI, 1999c).

Glass

Through microscopic examination of glass particles, and their density and refractive properties, it can be determined whether a particular glass sample likely originated from a particular (broken) source of glass. In addition, large pieces of glass may be able to be fit into a broken source of glass (e.g., a window) to make a match. Glass fracture examinations can determine the direction of breaking glass. The location of broken glass may also be of evidentiary value. Like paint, glass is most often found at hit-and-run and burglary crime scenes. Glass particles should be packaged in plastic containers. Larger pieces of glass should be packaged in solid packing containers with cotton packing material (FBI, 1999c).

Fibers

Any type of fabric or textile material contains fibers. Natural fibers include wool, cotton, glass, fur, and others. Synthetic, or man-made, fibers include nylon and polyester, among others. Fibers from one source are easily transferred to other surfaces such as fiber to fiber (e.g., clothing to clothing), fiber to skin, fiber to shoes, or fiber to vehicle. Examination of fiber evidence can vary in its sophistication. For example, a match may be made between two fibers based on a relatively simple microscopic examination of the color, diameter, and other distinguishing characteristics of the fibers. A more precise match may be made between fibers based on color through the use of microspectrophotometry. This procedure involves essentially shining light on a fiber and recording the absorption of that light. Chromatography can also be used to identify the chemicals used to make the dye of the fiber and to make a match on this basis. In any case, the more rare the fiber, the more significant the match. Fiber evidence is most often found in homicides, assaults, and hit-and-run offenses and may be found on clothing, skin, shoes, and carpeting, among other places. Fibers should be packaged in paper envelopes with sealed corners. When possible, the entire garment or textile should be submitted for analysis (FBI, 1999c).

Hair

Hair consists of the outer core of overlapping cells known as the cuticle, the cortex (which contains the pigment of the hair), and sometimes there is the medulla (an inner layer of cells). Hair also contains a root, which can be of great use in the scientific analysis of the hair. There is often significant variation in hair structure within the same individual, particularly hair from different places on the body (e.g., head, face, pubic). As a result, a range of comparison samples must be analyzed to make a match to an individual. Through relatively simple microscopic examination of a hair shaft, numerous conclusions about the hair can be drawn: whether it is from a human or an animal (and if it is from an animal, what type of animal), the race of the individual, the body area from which it came, the method of removal, and whether the hair was damaged or altered (e.g., dyed or bleached). Chemical examination of the hair may reveal the presence of contaminants in the hair, as well as identify drugs ingested and how long ago the drugs were ingested. Neutron activation analysis may be used to analyze and measure with extreme precision the presence of various trace elements in a hair sample. On the basis of the presence of the trace elements, a match between hair samples may be made (Owen, 2000). The most powerful of all is DNA analysis (discussed later in this chapter), which can be performed with the root of a hair (advances in DNA technology also allow for shafts of hair to be subject to such DNA typing). Hair is most likely to be found in homicides and assaults, especially when there was some struggle between the victim and the perpetrator. Hair may also be found on the perpetrator's clothing, vehicle, and personal items. Hair played an important role in the investigation of the kidnaping and murder of Danielle van Dam by David Westerfield. In this case, the victim's hair was found in the lint trap of the clothes dryer in Westerfield's house and in the sink drain of his motor home. Hair samples should be packaged in the same manner as fibers—in an envelope with sealed corners. In collecting comparison samples, at least twenty-five hairs from different parts of the head (or pubic area) should be obtained. Hairs should be combed and pulled out (FBI, 1999c).

Firearms

There are various types of evidence associated with firearms and various examinations can be done on such evidence. The gun itself can be examined to determine its general condition and whether it is functional. Alterations in the functioning of the weapon can be determined (altered to fire in automatic mode). The trigger-pull can be tested to determine the amount of pressure necessary to fire the weapon (particularly useful if a perpetrator claims that the trigger was pulled accidentally). Usually the most useful examination involves the test firing of the firearm to determine whether a recovered bullet matches the test-fired bullet and, hence, if a recovered bullet was in fact fired from the gun. This examination is done through the microscopic examination of the striations on the bullet caused by the bullet moving through the barrel of the gun. Although the striations are unique for each weapon, if a recovered bullet is deformed, a valid comparison is difficult, if not impossible, to make. Recovered bullets may also be analyzed for other purposes. It is possible to determine from a bullet its caliber and its manufacturer. The most common firearm evidence available at crime scenes where a shooting occurred is spent cartridge cases (or shotgun shell casings) and unfired cartridges and shells. From this evidence one is able to determine the caliber or gauge and the manufacturer of the weapon. Microscopic examination of spent casings can provide information about whether they were fired from a specific firearm.

Also common and useful evidence in crimes during which a weapon was fired is gunshot residue. Residue patterns may be found on a victim, and from this evidence the distance of the muzzle from the victim may be estimated. In addition, gunshot residue may be found on the individual (e.g., hands, clothing) who fired the weapon. Residue tests are commonly performed on individuals at or near the crime scene, near the time of the shooting, who are believed to have possibly fired the weapon.

When collecting firearm evidence, it first should be photographed and, if possible, fingerprinted (weapons and unfired cartridges). Firearms should be handled with great care and with the use of a ring that passes through the trigger guard. The ring device prevents contact with the firearm and preserves fingerprints or other evidence on the weapon itself. Weapons and casings should be collected and packaged separately. Clothing submitted for gunshot residue examination should also be packaged separately in paper envelopes.

Tool Marks

A tool mark is any mark that is created when an instrument (e.g., pry bar, screwdriver) has contact with another surface (e.g., wood on a windowsill). The marks left by a tool may indicate the type of tool, the size of the tool, and even the skill of the perpetrator (usually, the fewer the marks/damage, the greater the skill of the perpetrator). Through microscopic examination of the marks and a tool, a match may be made. Tool marks are most commonly found in burglaries around windows and doors. Tool marks can be photographed and casts can be made of the impressions.

Shoe Prints, Impressions, and Tire Tracks

Shoe prints are created when material from the bottom of shoes (e.g., blood) is transferred to another surface, leaving an outline of the bottom of the shoe. Shoe impressions and tire

EXHIBIT 6–4 Individualistic shoe prints

Notice how the shoe on the left is somehow altered and different from the right shoe. Such a pattern may make these prints and shoes individualistic evidence.

tracks are most often left in soft material such as mud or snow, and reveal the outline of the shoe or tire. Shoe prints and impressions may reveal the perpetrator's entrance to and exit from the crime scene, as well as the movements around the crime scene. It is also possible to determine from an analysis of the shoe print or impression the size of the shoe and the make and brand of the shoe (as was the case in the O.J. Simpson investigation). In some instances, shoe prints and impressions reveal individual characteristics (see Exhibit 6–4).

With regard to tire racks, they may reveal the direction of travel, the size and manufacturer of the tires, and possibly the make and model of the vehicle. Prints, impressions, and tracks first should be photographed and then, if possible, a cast of the impression or track should be made. If the impression or print is left in soil or mud, the recovery procedure involves pouring dental stone (a variant of the type of gypsum used to make dentures) into the impression. When the stone hardens, the mold reveals the outline of the impression. If the track or impression is in snow, then the snow is first sprayed with a special wax to harden the impression, and then dental stone is used to recover the impression.

Computer and Other Electronic Evidence

Computers, cellular phones, and personal digital assistants may provide a wealth of information regarding communications, schedules, and criminal behaviors, and therefore are potentially valuable sources of evidence in criminal investigations. Through the examination of a computer hard drive and disks, the content of e-mail, Internet activity, and other communications, valuable information may be obtained. The time and sequence that the files were created can be determined, and files that have been deleted from the computer can be recovered. Examinations of electronic hardware are quite technical in nature and, if not properly performed, can result in lost evidence (FBI, 1999c). Cellular phone records (as well as other telephone records) can be used to establish the time and length of phone calls, and the phone numbers associated with the calls. Such information is often useful in establishing the last activities of a missing or dead victim, and in examining alibis. Electronic evidence may also likely be relevant to investigations during which the crime involved a high degree of planning, coordination, communication with others, or occurred as a result of or in conjunction with Internet activity.

Videotape Evidence

Video is a potentially extremely powerful form of evidence. If a crime is captured on video, there may be little doubt about who committed the crime. Videotape may be enhanced to maximize the clarity of the images captured on the tape. In addition, still photographs can be obtained from videographic images. Videotapes can be repaired for playback if the damage is not too extensive (FBI, 1999c). Videotape images are most often available as evidence in robberies, during which video surveillance is provided in a particular place (e.g., automated teller machines, convenience stores).

Blood

Blood consists of red and white blood cells, which are located in plasma—a nearly clear, watery liquid. An adult has about ten pints of blood. In liquid form blood is red, but when dried it can take on several different hues such as brown, black, gray, or even green depending largely on the nature and color of the surface on which the blood is located. Blood can be a potentially powerful type of forensic evidence. The scientific analysis of blood can reveal, at the simplest level, the blood type of the individual or the type of antigens in the red blood cells. There are four blood groups: type A (forty-two percent of the U.S. population has type A blood), type B (nine percent), type O (forty-six percent), and type AB (three percent). In addition, the Rhesus factor (or Rh factor), is another test that is used to classify blood groupings further. When the Rhesus antigen is present, the blood is said to be Rh positive; if it is not present, then it is said to be Rh negative. Rh positive is most common. Obviously, the ability to include or exclude an individual as the possible source of the blood depends greatly on the type of blood recovered. Type AB blood can eliminate ninety-seven percent of individuals from consideration whereas type O blood can only eliminate fifty-four percent of the population. Other enzyme analyses conducted on blood can further narrow the scope of the donor pool.

Blood is also an excellent source of DNA and, as such, blood is often subjected to DNA analysis. DNA analysis can produce virtually certain results that two blood samples are a match. Blood can also be useful for evidentiary purposes through an analysis of splatters, drips, and the location in which blood is found. For example, the crime scene investigation into the murder of Nicole Brown Simpson and Ron Goldman revealed that the perpetrator was bleeding, and showed where the perpetrator exited the crime scene (blood drops present along the back walkway). The fact that blood was found on O.J. Simpson's vehicle and property immediately pointed to him as a possible suspect. The shape and size of blood drops may show how far and how fast the blood traveled before hitting the surface on which it is located. As noted in the photo array presented earlier, blood splatters may also reveal the amount of force used and even the manner in which the force was delivered—factors that may be useful to know when reconstructing the crime.

Blood is often very visible to perpetrators and investigators and, as a result, perpetrators may take precautions to minimize the presence of blood by cleaning the crime scene, or cleaning or disposing of articles stained with blood. Such precautions may not be effective. Consider once again the Michigan coed killer case when Collins painted over what he thought was blood, only to draw attention to the basement. Several techniques can be used to locate blood when it may not be visible to the naked eye. For example, a powerful light held at various angles may reveal traces of blood that were not otherwise visible. In addition, application of the chemical luminol to surfaces that possibly at one time contained blood can reveal bloodstains even if they are diluted by a factor of 10,000 (Owen, 2000). Blood stains treated with luminol are visible as a faint blue glow. Luminol, however, often destroys the properties of blood so it is to be used primarily to detect the presence of blood that might otherwise go undetected. Finally, the procedure used to confirm that a substance is in fact blood involves mixing the substance with phenolphthalein and hydrogen peroxide. If a deep-pink color is produced, the substance is blood.

Blood is one of the more common forms of evidence found at scenes of serious crimes such as homicides and assaults. Blood may be found in a variety of places—on or near the victim; at entrances and especially exits of crime scenes; in sinks, wash basins, and towels at the crime scene; on weapons found at the crime scene or in other places; or on the perpetrator's clothing. Even if attempts have been made to remove blood, it can still be located under vinyl flooring, under furniture, and in cracks and crevices.

Depending on the nature and condition of the blood evidence, various methods can be used to collect and package the evidence. In liquid form, blood can be absorbed with a cotton cloth, air-dried, and then packaged in a paper bag. For DNA analysis, blood should be collected in a plastic tube and treated with the preservative ethylenediaminetetraacetic acid. Blood—either in dried or liquid form—should be refrigerated prior to submission to the forensic laboratory.

Semen

Semen consists of sperm suspended in seminal fluid. One milliliter of semen from a healthy adult man contains approximately 60 to 100 million sperm cells. In liquid form, semen is grayish white and has a chlorine-type odor. When dry, it is clear and starchlike. Several tests can be performed to identify the presence of semen: the microscopic identification of spermatozoa, the acid phosphatase test (which tests for the presence of the enzyme acid phosphatase found in seminal fluid), and Choline and p30 (which test for the presence of proteins in seminal fluid) (White, 1998). Semen, and spermatozoa, is a rich source of DNA, and is often the subject of DNA printing procedures. Seminal fluid is most often found as a result of sexual crimes such as rape and can be found with the victim, on the victim's clothing, or in places where the assault may have taken place (e.g., bed sheets, carpeting). With regard to the collection and packaging of materials that may contain semen, it should be dried naturally, placed in a paper bag, and kept frozen until submitted to the crime laboratory.

Dental Evidence

Dental evidence can take two primary forms: dental identification and bite marks. In both instances, the fact that each individual has a unique set of teeth in terms of form, arrangement, dental work, and bite, makes dental evidence a powerful form of criminal evidence. The physical characteristics of bite marks and dental identification may consist of the distance between teeth, the shape of the mouth/bite, teeth alignment, teeth shape, missing teeth, and wear patterns of the teeth. A primary means of identifying decomposed dead bodies is dental identification during which dental radiographs of the individual are compared with those of the dead body. On the basis of a comparison, a match may be made. Of

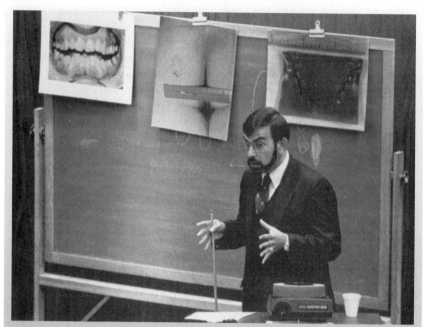

Bite marks can be very powerful evidence in an investigation. Here an expert witness provides testimony in the trial of Ted Bundy, who bit one of his victims.

A forensic artist constructs a forensic model from a recovered human skull.

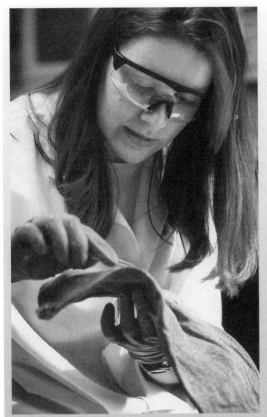

Police dust for fingerprints at a homicide crime scene.

A forensic scientist examines a suspect's clothing for potential evidence.

course, this manner of identification is only possible if a dead body is suspected to be a particular individual, and if X-ray records are available from the decedent's dentist.

Bite marks can be either offensive or defensive. Offensive bite marks would be left on a victim by a perpetrator; defensive bite marks would be left on a perpetrator by the victim. It is also possible that bite marks, or tooth impressions, would be left on food or chewing gum that could be recovered from a crime scene. In any case, clear marks can reveal individual characteristics of the biter's teeth and, as such, can be used to make associations between the perpetrator and the victim. A potentially rich source of DNA, saliva may also be recovered from the area in which bite marks are located. Bite marks should be photographed under ultraviolet light (West and Barsley, 1992). The bite mark impressions can then be compared with test impressions taken from a suspect. Suspects should not be told in advance of the desire to collect a test bite impression or mold because they could attempt to alter their teeth impressions.

Fingerprints

The early foundation of forensic science rested on the principle that each person has a unique pattern on his or her fingers. This principle is still valid and fingerprints are still potentially powerful evidence in criminal investigations. Fingerprints consist of ridges, depressions (i.e., hills and valleys), and separations (where ridge lines end or split). Fingerprints remain unchanged and consistent throughout one's lifetime. Each fingerprint on each finger is unique. Fingerprints can be broadly classified on the basis of the pattern of ridges that comprise the print. These patterns are classified as loops (ulnar loop, radial loop), whorls (plain whorls, double loops, central pocket loops, accidental loops), and arches (plain arch, tented arch); see Exhibit 6–5. The most common type of fingerprint is loops (approximately sixty-six percent of the population have loop prints), followed by whorls (approximately thirty-three percent). Only about one person in twenty has any prints that resemble arches.

Fingerprints taken as a the result of the fingerprinting process (i.e., "being fingerprinted") are most often recorded on a ten-print fingerprint card, often with the use of ink. (More sophisticated technology involves the digital capture of prints and no ink is involved.) On the card, the prints are arranged as a double row in a particular sequence. (See Exhibit 6–6.)

Fingerprints recovered from a crime scene can generally be of three types: visible transferred prints, such as when ink, blood, or some other visible liquid material is transferred from the fingerprint to some other surface; visible impression prints, when the print is left in a soft or sticky material such as wet paint, clay, or putty; and latent prints, the most common type, which are made when the oil and perspiration naturally present on fingertips are transferred to another surface but are invisible until developed through various techniques. The most common techniques used to recover latent prints consist of the application of powders, chemicals, and glue fumes (FBI, 1999c). "Dusting" for prints involves the application of a fine powder with a fine brush to surfaces that are believed potentially to contain latent prints. The powder adheres to the oil and perspiration transferred from fingers and makes the prints visible. This technique is most likely to reveal prints when the surface is hard, smooth, and nonabsorbent such as glass, painted wood, or metal. Different-color powder can be applied to provide contrast with the surface being dusted. Fluorescent powder can also be used in a similar manner to enhance the visibility of latent prints. Chemical methods can be used to recover prints from soft or more porous surfaces such as paper or clothing. Various types of chemicals can be applied either by spraying the surface, through a process of fuming, or by dipping the object containing prints into a chemical solution. Another technique involves glue (or cyanoacrylate) fuming. With this method, the object examined for prints is either placed in a sealed tank and is then exposed to the vaporized cyanoacrylate, which adheres to the print and makes it visible, or the fumes are applied via a fuming "wand." In addition to these methods of making latent prints visible, laser technology has been used for highlighting prints on difficult surfaces. Regardless of the method used to recover prints, the visible prints first should be photographed and then "lifted" by placing adhesive tape over the print where the powder adheres to the tape. The tape is then placed on a card that provides contrast with the lifted

EXHIBIT 6–5 Types of fingerprint patterns

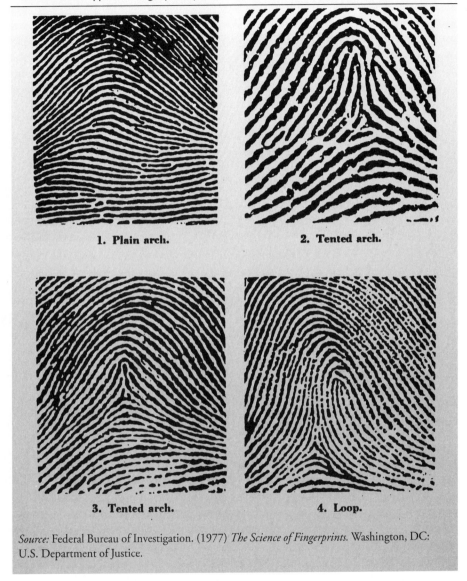

Source: Federal Bureau of Investigation. (1977) *The Science of Fingerprints.* Washington, DC: U.S. Department of Justice.

print, thereby preserving the print and making it visible for further analyses and comparison.

Locating quality latent prints is not an easy task and it depends on the crime scene. Obvious places such as door handles, drinking cups, and weapons, as well as less obvious places such as the telephone and toilet handle should be examined

EXHIBIT 6–5 *(continued)*

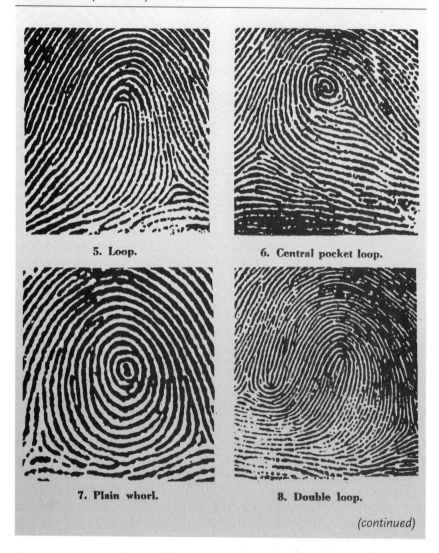

5. Loop.

6. Central pocket loop.

7. Plain whorl.

8. Double loop.

(continued)

for prints. Many recovered prints are of poor quality, making them nearly worthless as evidence. Fingerprints can be smeared, they can become dirty, or fingers could have been dirty—all of which would obscure the individual characteristics of the fingerprints.

If fingerprints are recovered from a crime scene, then elimination prints need to be taken. Elimination prints are fingerprints of all persons who are known to have had legal access to the scene. These prints must then be compared with the other recovered prints, and the ones that do not match may belong to the perpetrator.

EXHIBIT 6–5 *(continued)*

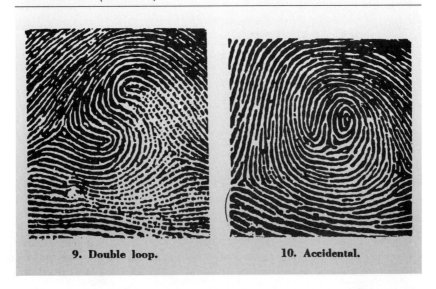

9. Double loop.   10. Accidental.

AFIS has made fingerprints more useful in identifying perpetrators. With AFIS in place, whenever a person is fingerprinted by the police in that jurisdiction as a result of being arrested, applying for particular jobs, or for some other reason, those fingerprints are entered and stored in AFIS. Then, after a fingerprint is collected from a crime scene, it is scanned into AFIS and the computer searches the system, looking for a match. The newest and most powerful systems on the market today can search hundreds of thousands of prints within minutes; older systems require hours to search the same number. As a result of the computerized search, the system may identify several prints that are the most similar in their pattern and unique characteristics. The print in question must then be manually compared with the "hit" print by a fingerprint examiner. It is in this manner that fingerprints recovered from a crime scene may lead to the identity of a perpetrator.

Prior to AFIS technology, fingerprints were used in several different ways. First, when a fingerprint was recovered from a crime scene, it was simply filed away until a suspect was identified through some other means and then a comparison of that suspect's prints and the recovered prints was made. Second, if a suspect was already identified, a comparison could have been conducted immediately. Third, a manual search could have been made through the fingerprints on file in that particular jurisdiction, or on file with the FBI. No question, this process resembled trying to find a needle in a haystack and rarely did it have a positive outcome. Consider this exceptional example (Peterson et al., 1984):

A night clerk was robbed and killed during a Christmas Eve holdup at a local motel. The crime scene unit was called to the scene and latent fingerprints were found on a metal cash box and on various papers that had been removed from the cabinet file safe.

EXHIBIT 6–6 Example of completed ten-print fingerprint card

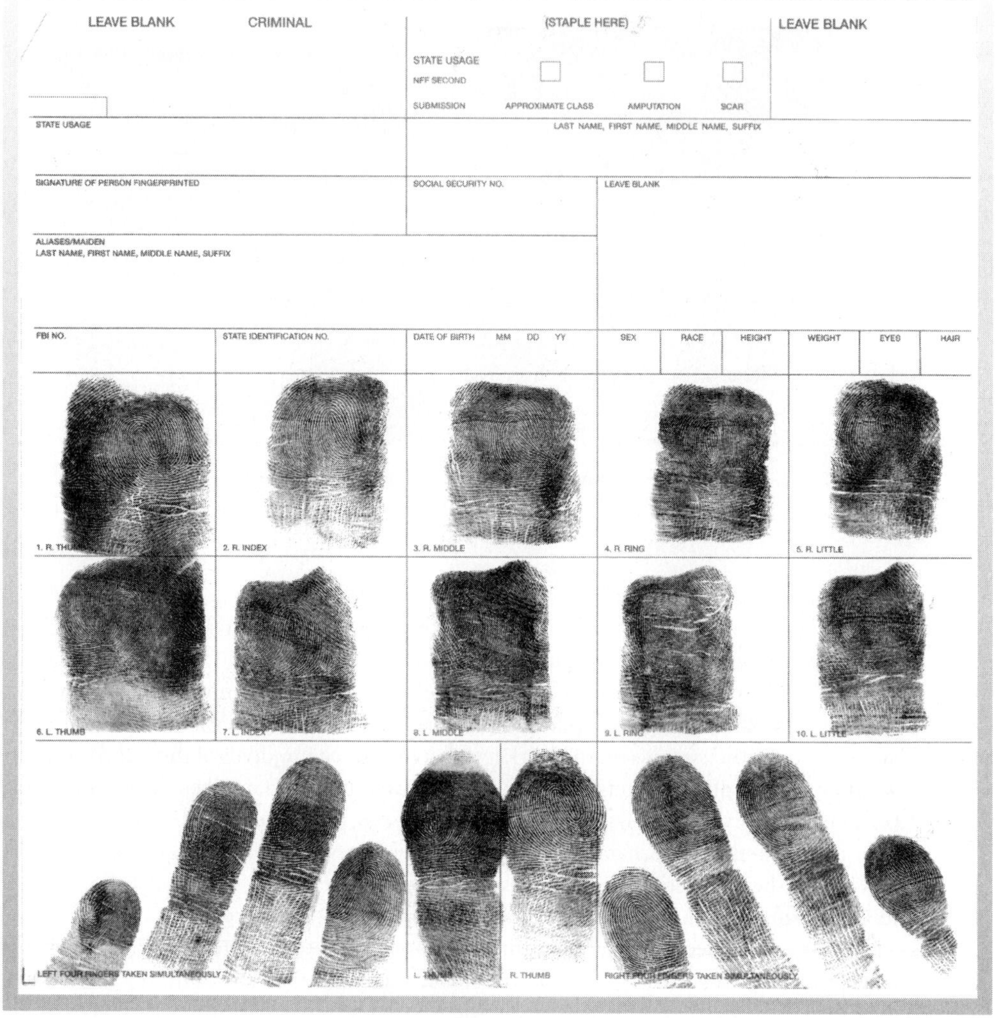

The latent prints on the metal surface appeared to be fresh. A latent fingerprint matching the one taken from the metal cash box was found on an envelope next to the body. There were no witnesses to the crime and the detectives had no good suspects.

With these latent prints a search was made of the crime scene unit's approximately 10,000 active suspect/known fingerprint cards. This search proved fruitless. A second general search was then begun of the department's main fingerprint records of over

140,000 individuals. This search paid off when the latent prints were found to match those of a prior criminal offender.

Armed with this information, investigators determined the suspect's current address and searched his room. Several packs of rolled coins reported stolen in the robbery were found in the suspect's bedroom, inside a wool cap. Several dog hairs were found in this same wool cap which were similar to dog hair found on the victim's trousers. Based largely on this physical evidence, the suspect was charged and convicted of first degree murder.

Although AFIS provides great promise and certainly makes the processing of fingerprints much more efficient, there are several drawbacks to the technology. First, it must be realized that there is potentially considerable expense associated with collecting fingerprints from crime scenes and analyzing them via AFIS. Although at first glance it sounds easy—collect fingerprints from a crime scene, enter them into AFIS, get a match, and make an arrest—the process is much more complicated and time-consuming. Fingerprints are most likely to be available for recovery from burglary crime scenes, stolen autos, and certain types of robberies (Peterson, 1987). To have the most impact on crime solving, then, AFIS should have the most relevance to the investigation of these crimes. However, given the sheer volume of these types of crimes in many jurisdictions, the routine collection and AFIS analysis of fingerprints may simply not be feasible. For example, in Chicago there are approximately 40,000 burglaries, 25,000 robberies, and 30,000 motor vehicle thefts annually (FBI, 2002). Considering just burglaries, figure that in approximately three-fourths of these cases, it would be reasonable to search for fingerprints at the crime scenes. Also figure that it would take at least one hour of police time to dust or otherwise search for prints at these scenes. If fingerprints are collected from the scene, then elimination prints must be collected and analyzed, taking at least one more hour of time. Then one must consider the labor involved in entering the prints into the AFIS system. Just to this point in time, the fingerprinting process will have consumed at least three additional hours of time per case. With 30,000 cases, this amounts to an additional 90,000 hours of time. Figure 90,000 hours at a minimum hourly rate of $30 and it amounts to a cost of $2.7 million. Expensive indeed.

A second limitation is that a multimillion-dollar AFIS can be foiled by a pair of $0.59 latex gloves. That is, even if the perpetrator's prints are in the system because of a previous arrest, but the perpetrator is careful enough to not leave fingerprints, AFIS will not be of any use.

Third, the system can only be of use if the suspect's prints are already contained in the system. Of course, even if a perfectly clear fingerprint is collected from a crime scene, a valid match will not be obtained if the suspect's prints were not previously entered into the system. Making this problem more salient is that many of the larger police departments in the country own and operate their own systems. Recently, with newer and less expensive models on the market, even smaller police departments have purchased and operate such systems. Most states also operate AFIS (operated out of the state police or department of law enforcement agencies). Once again, however, the downfall with this arrangement is that these systems are most often self-contained; only the fingerprints collected in that jurisdiction are contained in that system. As a result, if a suspect's prints are held in one AFIS but his prints are recovered by a police department in another jurisdiction, a match would not be obtained. A reasonable question becomes: Even if considerable resources are spent searching, collecting, and submitting fingerprints for AFIS analysis, what are the chances of obtaining a valid "hit?"

To improve, potentially, the effectiveness of AFIS technology, the FBI has developed and implemented the Integrated Automated Fingerprint Identification System (IAFIS). According to the FBI (2000), "the primary purpose of the IAFIS is to provide a national repository of criminals' fingerprints for maintaining a criminal history record for each arrested individual. The IAFIS repository contains approximately 40 million ten print fingerprint records and provides an excellent source for searching unidentified latent fingerprints from unsolved crimes in an effort to identify perpetrators" (p. 3). The IAFIS allows other federal, state, and local law enforcement agencies to connect electronically with IAFIS to expand dramatically the number of fingerprints available to be searched to identify perpetrators. Several agencies have established direct connections with IAFIS and have made identifications of individuals who were not in their local AFIS repository (FBI, 2000).

DNA Analysis and Its Impact on the Usefulness of Physical Evidence

Arguably, the most significant advance in the technology of criminal investigation *ever* is the science of DNA analysis (Berger, 2002). DNA, or deoxyribonucleic acid, is the genetic building block of all living organisms. It is found in virtually every cell in the human body and its structure is the same in every cell. The DNA in a person's blood is the same as the DNA in his hair, skin cells, saliva, semen, and perspiration. Except for identical twins, no two people have the same DNA. Because of its absolute uniqueness and individual characteristics, human cells and the DNA obtained from these cells can be a powerful form of evidence in criminal investigations (NIJ, 2001).

There are two types of DNA: MtDNA and nuclear DNA. MtDNA is found in the mitochondrion in each cell of the body; nuclear DNA is found in the nucleus of a cell. MtDNA is more limited in function than nuclear DNA. MtDNA is inherited from one's mother only. It is limited compared with nuclear DNA in that it cannot differentiate between individuals who have the same maternal lineage (i.e., between offspring with the same mother). MtDNA is available for analysis when the biological evidence is degraded or small in quantity. Hair shafts, bone, and teeth are common substances on which MtDNA analysis is conducted (Isenberg and Moore, 1999; NIJ, 2001).

DNA analysis, or *printing* as it is sometimes known, was first used in a criminal investigation in 1987 by Dr. Alec J. Jeffreys to corroborate a suspect's confession that he was responsible for two rape/murders in England. Tests proved that the suspect was not the perpetrator. Police then obtained DNA samples from several thousand men who lived in the

EXHIBIT 6–7 Identifying DNA evidence

Identifying DNA Evidence

Since only a few cells can be sufficient to obtain useful DNA information to help your case, the list below identifies some common items of evidence that you may need to collect, the possible location of the DNA on the evidence, and the biological source containing the cells. Remember that just because you cannot see a stain does not mean there are not enough cells for DNA typing. Further, DNA does more than just identify the source of the sample; it can place a known individual at a crime scene, in a home, or in a room where the suspect claimed not to have been. It can refute a claim of self-defense and put a weapon in the suspect's hand. It can change a story from an alibi to one of consent. The more officers know how to use DNA, the more powerful a tool it becomes.

Evidence	Possible Location of DNA on the Evidence	Source of DNA
baseball bat or similar weapon	handle, end	sweat, skin, blood, tissue
hat, bandanna, or mask	inside	sweat, hair, dandruff
eyeglasses	nose or ear pieces, lens	sweat, skin
facial tissue, cotton swab	surface area	mucus, blood, sweat, semen, ear wax
dirty laundry	surface area	blood, sweat, semen
toothpick	tips	saliva
used cigarette	cigarette butt	saliva
stamp or envelope	licked area	saliva
tape or ligature	inside/outside surface	skin, sweat
bottle, can, or glass	sides, mouthpiece	saliva, sweat
used condom	inside/outside surface	semen, vaginal or rectal cells
blanket, pillow, sheet	surface area	sweat, hair, semen, urine, saliva
"through and through" bullet	outside surface	blood, tissue
bite mark	person's skin or clothing	saliva
fingernail, partial fingernail	scrapings	blood, sweat, tissue

Source: National Institute of Justice. (1999) *What Every Law Enforcement Officer Should Know About DNA Evidence.* Washington, DC: U.S. Department of Justice.

area to identify the true perpetrator. Although the perpetrator attempted to avoid providing a DNA sample, he was eventually identified and charged with the crimes. DNA printing was first used in the United States in a criminal case in 1987, during which a Florida jury convicted Tommy Lee Andrews of rape (NIJ, 1996).

DNA analysis may be used to associate positively and absolutely a perpetrator to a crime scene, to the victim, or to tools used in the crime. Similarly, DNA analysis can be used to eliminate positively and absolutely a person from consideration as a suspect. In each of these instances, the DNA recovered from a crime scene or victim would be compared with a DNA sample taken from a specific person. In this sense, DNA is similar to fingerprints, but fingerprints left by a perpetrator at a crime scene may be of poor quality (smudged or smeared), may be left on surfaces from which the prints cannot be recovered (e.g., rough wood), or perpetrators can take relatively simple precautions to avoid leaving fingerprints at a crime scene in the first place.

DNA can also be used to confirm the identity of victims, or the remains of victims when no body can be found. In such cases, a DNA sample may be taken from hair recovered from the victim's hairbrush or from skin cells recovered from the victim's toothbrush, and then compared with the victim or the victim's remains. Another possibility is to compare the DNA from relatives with the DNA of the body or remains (NIJ, 1999b). DNA analysis was used in this manner to confirm the identity of many of the victims of the World Trade Center attack in September 2001. DNA was also sought from Osama bin Laden's relatives to use for the possible identification of human remains recovered from various bombing sites in and near Afghanistan (Lumpkin, 2002).

Extraordinary caution needs to be exercised when collecting DNA analyzable evidence for at least two reasons: first, because the biological material may contain hazardous pathogens (e.g., human immunodeficiency virus, hepatitis) that can cause lethal diseases; and second, because samples containing DNA can be contaminated quite easily. As for con-

EXHIBIT 6–8 Ways to avoid contaminating DNA evidence

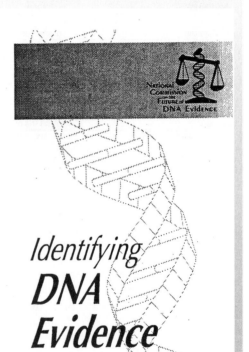

To avoid contamination of evidence that may contain DNA, always take the following precautions:

- Wear gloves. Change them often.
- Use disposable instruments or clean them thoroughly before and after handling each sample.
- Avoid touching the area where you believe DNA may exist.
- Avoid talking, sneezing, and coughing over evidence.
- Avoid touching your face, nose, and mouth when collecting and packaging evidence.
- Air-dry evidence thoroughly before packaging.
- Put evidence into new paper bags or envelopes, not into plastic bags. Do not use staples.

Identifying DNA Evidence

Source: National Institute of Justice. (1999) *What Every Law Enforcement Officer Should Know About DNA Evidence.* Washington, DC: U.S. Department of Justice.

tamination, this could happen when someone sneezes or coughs over the evidence, or when one simply touches the evidence without taking sterile precautions (NIJ, 1999b).

When transporting or storing evidence that may contain DNA, the evidence must be kept dry and at room temperature. The evidence should be stored in paper bags or envelopes and, of course, the chain of custody must be maintained. Evidence that may contain DNA should never be placed or otherwise stored in plastic bags because plastic will retain moisture that may damage the DNA. Direct sunlight and warmer conditions can also damage DNA evidence (NIJ, 1999b).

Just like fingerprints, elimination samples may need to be taken to eliminate from consideration those individuals who have legitimate reason to be at the crime scene or in contact with the victim. For example, when investigating a rape, it may be necessary to collect the DNA from the victim's recent consensual partners, if any, to eliminate them as suspects in the crime. In addition, DNA should be taken from the victim to compare it with other DNA found at the crime scene. For example, consider the investigation of the murder of Nicole Brown Simpson and Ron Goldman. The recovery and analysis of the blood found at the crime scene revealed three unique DNA sequences. They were determined to be from Nicole, Goldman, and someone else—that "someone else" was believed to be the perpetrator.

There are two primary methods available to analyze DNA samples: RFLP and PCR. RFLP was the first type of DNA test to be widely used by crime laboratories. Briefly, the RFLP method involves extracting the DNA from sample cells. The DNA is then cut by an enzyme into restriction fragments, which are suspended in a gel, divided by size, and then these fragments are transferred onto a membrane. To see the fragments, they are identified by radioactive-labeled probes, and then the membrane is placed over X-ray film. The radiation from the probe produces an image of the DNA fragments. This image is known as an *autoradiogram*. A match is confirmed when the pattern of the DNA evidence matches the DNA pattern of the suspect. A statistical probability that the evidence is from the suspect is then calculated. RFLP is a scientifically valid methodology but it has disadvantages: It cannot be used on degraded specimens, it is time-consuming, and working with radioactive material requires extra precautions.

Another method of analyzing DNA is known as PCR. PCR can be used if a sample is too small for RFLP or if the sample is too degraded. With the PCR technique, the DNA is copied many times ("amplified"). Two DNA molecules are produced from the original molecule and are repeated many times until millions of copies of the DNA sequence are produced. From these copies, a DNA print can be generated and compared with the DNA print from a suspect. A statistic is then calculated to show how often one would expect this particular DNA profile to appear in the general population (NIJ, 1998). For example, in the case of the murder of Danielle van Dam, forensic scientists were able to determine through DNA analysis that the chances the blood found in Westerfield's motor home belonged to someone other than Danielle was one in 4.9 billion and that the chances that blood found on Westerfield's jacket belonged to someone other than Danielle was one in 25 quadrillion (Roth, 2002a).

On the basis of DNA testing, three types of results may be found. First, the suspect may be *included* as the possible source of the evidence; however, the certainty of the inclusion will depend on the number of locations on the DNA strand that are examined and how common or rare the resulting DNA print is in the general population (as noted earlier). Second, in the same manner that an individual can be included as a suspect, an individual can also be *excluded* as a suspect. Third, the results of the analysis may be *inconclusive*—a person cannot be included or excluded as the source of the evidence. Inconclusive results may occur for a variety of reasons: the poor quality of the DNA sample may not allow for interpretable results or the evidentiary sample may contain a mixture of DNA from several individuals (e.g., a sample recovered from a victim of a gang rape).

Both methods, and DNA testing properly applied in general, are accepted as admissible under Frye and Daubert standards. The courts have ruled that there should be extensive discovery requirements in the admission of the results of DNA analysis. For instance, in *Schwartz* v. *State* (1989), the court stated that "ideally, a defendant should be provided with the actual DNA sample(s) in order to reproduce the results. As a practical matter, this may not be possible because forensic samples are often so small that the entire sample is used in testing. Consequently, access to the data, methodology, and actual results is critical . . . for an independent expert review." The National Research Counsel concluded most directly: "The state of profiling technology and the methods for estimating frequencies and related statistics have progressed to the point where the admissibility of properly collected and analyzed DNA should not be in doubt" (NIJ, 1996; p. 214). Although the science of DNA analysis may be quite difficult to attack, the procedures used in collecting the evidence in the first place may be more easily called into question. During the trial of O.J. Simpson, for example, the defense attorneys did not attack the science of DNA analysis but they did attack the collection of the evidence on which DNA analysis was performed. All the science and precision of DNA analysis can be foiled if the evidence is collected incorrectly or if claims can be made about the overall integrity of the evidence.

Until recently, DNA evidence has been limited in the same manner that physical evidence is limited; it was generally not well suited to identify a perpetrator when one was not already known. Only when a suspect was identified through some other means could the recovered DNA evidence be compared with the DNA taken from the identified suspect. However, recent technological advances are making DNA more powerful and useful in investigations. Specifically, CODIS is an electronic database that allows federal, state, and local crime laboratories to exchange and share DNA profiles electronically (FBI, 2000). Today, all states participate in CODIS (BJS, 2000). As of the year 2000, CODIS contained DNA profiles of nearly 500,000 individuals who have been convicted of certain crimes such as homicide, rape, and child abuse as well as more than 21,000 DNA profiles collected as a result of other investigations (FBI, 2000; NIJ, 1998). In addition to CODIS, some states operate their own independent DNA banks and some require that DNA from all convicted felons be entered into the system. In many respects, these systems are to DNA what AFIS is to fingerprints. With such systems, investigators can enter into the system the DNA prints obtained from evidence recovered from crime scenes, and the computer will scan the stored prints for a match. As with AFIS, however, if the perpetrator's print is not in the system, a match will not be obtained. In that case, the culprit will still have to be identified through other more traditional means.

It would be inaccurate to consider DNA analysis only a tool of the prosecution used to convict suspects. DNA analysis is a powerful tool of justice—a tool that can be used to identify and convict the guilty *and* to free the innocent. A National Institute of Justice study published in 1996 (NIJ, 1996) identified and summarized twenty-eight cases in which DNA test results proved that the person convicted of the crime could not have committed the crime. As seen in Table 6–1, these cases had numerous characteristics in common: Most of the cases occurred during the 1980s, a time when DNA analysis was available but not widely used. All of the cases involved some type of sexual assault, some involved a homicide along with a sexual assault; all of the perpetrators were male, all of the victims were female. All but one case involved a jury trial, and in most of the cases a verdict was returned in less than one day. The twenty-eight defendants served a total of 197 years in prison before their convictions were overturned on the basis of DNA evidence. Most defendants appealed their convictions at least once; many appealed more than once before being exonerated. Police knew fifteen of the defendants prior to their arrests for the crime primarily because of prior arrests. All the cases, except for the six homicides, involved the victim identifying the suspect prior to the trial and at the trial. Many cases also had other eyewitness identifications to support the conviction of the defendant (in one case, five witnesses testified that they saw the defendant with the victim on the day of the murder). Many of the defendants provided an alibi but, obviously, they were not believed by the juries. A majority of the cases had non-DNA physical evidence admitted into trial that supported the conviction of the defendant. Finally, eight of the cases involved allegations of police or prosecutor misconduct, including officers who provided perjured testimony, and prosecutors who kept exculpatory evidence from the defense and who intentionally and knowingly admitted erroneous laboratory results.

There have been a few attempts to try to fool the science of DNA analysis. Perhaps the most well-known case is that of Anthony Turner, a convicted and incarcerated serial rapist from Milwaukee. While serving time for three rape convictions, convictions obtained in part through DNA analysis of semen recovered from his victims, Anthony devised a plan to try to fool investigators and to make authorities question the validity of DNA analysis results. The plan unfolded with an apparent fourth sexual assault in the same neighborhood where Turner committed his rapes years before. The victim contacted the police, told them she had been raped, and then underwent a sexual assault examination. The recovered semen was analyzed, a DNA print was created, and that print was compared with the DNA prints on file in the State of Wisconsin DNA bank, a file that contains DNA samples of all convicted felons in the state. A match was made to Anthony Turner. On hearing of this match, Turner argued that he obviously did not commit this crime and he reasserted his claim that he did not commit any of the other rapes either. Initially, this was rather puzzling. Could two people—Anthony Turner and the real rapist—have the same DNA profile? As investigators began to ask questions of Turner's associates in prison and the "victim" of the latest rape, Turner's scheme began to unravel. It was determined that about one month prior to the last "rape," Turner told his mother that she should expect an envelope in the mail from him in the next few weeks and that she should give this envelope to one of Turner's female friends who lived in the neighborhood. Furthermore, it was learned that in this envelope

TABLE 6–1 Overview of Selected Evidence and DNA Testing

Defendant	Selected Evidence	DNA Testing
Alejandro, Gilbert	DNA evidence testimony; victim ID	Restriction Fragment Length Polymorphism (RFLP) tests of semen stain on victim's nightgown excluded Alejandro.
Bloodsworth, Kirk	Five witness IDs; self-incriminating statements	Polymerase Chain Reaction (PCR) test of panties excluded Bloodsworth.
Bravo, Mark Diaz	Victim ID; blood analysis; misrepresentation	RFLP test of blanket, sheet, and victim's panties excluded Bravo.
Brison, Dale	Victim ID; hair analysis; weak alibi	RFLP test of semen-stained panties excluded Brison.
Bullock, Ronnie	Two victims IDs; police ID; proximity of residence	PCR test of semen-stained panties excluded Bullock. DNA test on vaginal and anal swabs were inconclusive.
Callace, Leonard	Victim ID; blood analysis; weak abili	RFLP test of semen-stained jeans excluded Callace.
Chalmers, Terry Leon	Victim ID; weak alibi	PCR test of two vaginal swabs excluded Chalmers.
Cotton, Ronald	Victim ID; similarity of shoes and flashlight	PCR test of vaginal swab and underwear excluded Cotton.
Cruz, Rolando	Alleged "dream visions" of the murder; inculpatory witness statements	PCR test of semen-stained underwear excluded Cruz and included Brian Dugan.
Dabbs, Charles	Victim ID; blood analysis	RFLP test of semen-stained panties excluded Dabbs.
Davis, Gerald Wayne	Victim ID; semen analysis	PCR test of the victim's underwear excluded Davis. No DNA found matching the victim from DNA tests done on Davis' bedsheets and underwear.
Daye, Frederick Rene	Victim ID; witness ID; blood analysis; misrepresentation	PCR test of semen-stained jeans excluded Daye.
Dotson, Gary	Victim ID; semen analysis; hair analysis	RFLP test of panties was inconclusive. PCR test of panties excluded Dotson and included victim's boyfriend.

Defendant	Selected Evidence	DNA Testing
Green, Edward	Victim ID; blood analysis	RFLP test of the victim's clothing excluded Green.
Hammond, Ricky	Victim ID; victim ID of car; hair analysis; weak alibi	RFLP and blood tests excluded Hammond.
Harris, William O'Dell	Victim ID; semen analysis	PCR test of evidence slide excluded Harris.
Hernandez, Alejandro	Self-incriminating and inculpatory statements; inculpatory witness statements	PCR test of semen-stained underwear excluded Hernandez and included Brian Dugan.
Honaker, Edward	Victim ID; witness ID; hair analysis; similarity of clothing	PCR test of vaginal swab excluded Honaker and both of victim's boyfriends.
Jones, Joe C.	Victim ID; proximity to crime scene; similarity of pants; 2 witness IDs	PCR test of partial vaginal swab excluded Jones.
Kotler, Kerry	Victim ID; non-DNA genetic analysis	PCR test of panties excluded Kotler and victim's husband.
Linscott, Steven	Blood analysis; hair analysis; "dream confession"	Pretrial DNA tests were inconclusive. PCR test excluded Linscott.
Nelson, Bruce	Testimony of codefendant, self-incriminating statement	RFLP test excluded Nelson.
Piszczek, Brian	Victim ID; weak alibi	PCR test of vaginal and anal swabs and nightgown excluded Piszczek.
Scruggs, Dwayne	Victim ID; similarity of boots	PCR test of vaginal swab and bloodstain excluded Scruggs.
Shephard, David	Victim ID; blood analysis; weak alibi	DNA test of panty liner excluded Shephard.
Snyder, Walter (Tony)	Victim ID; similarity of clothing; blood analysis; weak alibi	PCR test of vaginal swab excluded Snyder.
Vasquez, David	Witness ID; no alibi; confession; hair analysis	PCR test of evidence matched Timothy Spencer. Attempts to compare hair with blood samples were inconclusive.
Woodall, Glen	Blood analysis; hair analysis; victim ID; similarity of clothing	PCR and RFLP tests of vaginal swabs and clothing excluded Woodall.

Source: National Institute of Justice. (1996) *Convicted by Juries, Exonerated by Science: Case Studies in the Use of DNA Evidence to Establish Innocence After Trial.* Washington, DC: U.S. Department of Justice.

was a ketchup packet that contained Anthony's own semen. Anthony smuggled his semen out of prison! Anthony's female associate used this semen to stage the rape. An ambitious and imaginative plan, but it did not work.

Other instances have also been reported when perpetrators have left DNA evidence (e.g., hair, fingernails, blood) from other sources at crime scenes in an attempt to foil police efforts at identifying the real culprit. Investigative personnel should be aware of this possibility in collecting such evidence.

The Role of Crime Laboratories in Criminal Investigations

As discussed in this chapter, physical evidence is made most useful through scientific analysis. Most of the scientific procedures and tests discussed in this chapter are conducted in the controlled environment of crime laboratories. The fundamental role of the crime laboratory is to assist the police in conducting investigations to determine, first, whether a crime has been committed and, second, who committed it. Crime labs in the United States are predominantly publicly funded organizations that operate at several different levels. For instance, laboratories exist in many hospitals and at medical examiner's offices. These laboratories are primarily for use by medical personnel. Every state operates at least one crime laboratory to which state and local agencies can submit evidence for analysis. Several federal agencies operate forensic laboratories for their own use (e.g., U.S. Customs Service, DEA). The FBI operates the largest and most well-funded laboratory in the world (FBI, 1999b), and it handles requests made by the FBI as well as military, state, and local agencies across the country. All FBI laboratory services and associated expert testimony are provided free of charge; however, the FBI will not reexamine evidence that has already been subjected to the same test, and no request will be granted from an agency that has the capability of performing the same test. In addition, the FBI laboratory only accepts evidence relating to violent crimes; it does not normally accept evidence relating to property crimes (FBI, 1999c). Because local agencies most often are able to submit evidence to their state crime laboratory for analysis, services are usually not requested from the FBI laboratory. State laboratories also usually do not accept evidence from police agencies that relate to misdemeanors. Finally, there are numerous privately run facilities that provide forensic evidence examinations. Most often these laboratories are used by defense attorneys to verify the validity of the results provided by the government facility.

With regard to workload, drug cases, firearms, and trace evidence examinations account for the majority of total crime laboratory case loads (BJS, 2000). Violent and property crimes constitute usually less than thirty percent of case loads, although there is variation across different laboratories (Peterson, et al., 1985).

The analysis of forensic evidence relates to the field of forensic science. Forensic science broadly refers to the field of science that addresses legal questions. Specialized fields in the area of forensic science include criminalistics, forensic pathology, forensic anthropology, forensic odontology, and forensic entomology. Criminalistics refers specifically to the science of physical evidence, which includes the scientific analysis of trace evidence (e.g., blood, semen, fibers), fingerprints, firearms, DNA analysis, and tool marks. Much of the work of crime laboratories relates to criminalistics.

Forensic pathology is the science of dead bodies and autopsies. Through the analysis of dead bodies by forensic pathologists (e.g., medical examiners), the body may yield information about identity and the nature and cause of death. In homicides in particular, an autopsy may reveal the type of weapon used, the nature of the injuries, and time of death (see Chapter 11).

Forensic anthropology is a branch of physical anthropology that relates to the identification of skeletal remains of humans. Analysis of human remains may provide information about the gender, age, race, and height of the individual as well as sometimes the cause of death (e.g., skull fracture). Also included in this area of study is facial reconstruction. Based on an understanding of the characteristics and variation in cranial and facial structure, faces may be developed on the basis of a skull.

Forensic odontology refers to the application of dentistry to legal matters. It involves the scientific analysis of teeth and bite marks for the purposes of identification. The specialty areas of forensic odontology and forensic anthropology provide some overlap. Analysis of teeth (in a dead body) may assist in the determination of the subject's age, facial characteristics (teeth and jaw structure), race, socioeconomic status (through dental work), and even habits or occupation.

Finally, forensic entomology relates to the science of insects in answering legal questions. Of particular focus is estimating the time of death based on the insect activity on the body of the deceased (see Chapter 11).

Questions for Discussion and Review

1. How can physical evidence help establish that a crime occurred?

2. What is the most common function of physical evidence in criminal investigations? Explain.

3. What is the most significant limitation of physical evidence in criminal investigations? Why?

4. What is Locard's Exchange Principle?

5. What is the difference between class characteristic and individual characteristic evidence? Why is this distinction sometimes rather blurry?

6. Identify three specific types of class characteristic and individual characteristic evidence and explain their potential value in a criminal investigation.

7. What is DNA and how is it useful in criminal investigations?

8. What is the difference between MtDNA and nuclear DNA?

9. Why does extraordinary care need to be taken in collecting physical evidence for DNA analysis?

10. What are elimination DNA samples and elimination fingerprints, and why are they important?

11. What are the two primary methods used to analyze DNA samples?

12. What is CODIS and what impact may it have on criminal investigations?

13. What are some ways that perpetrators may attempt to fool the science of DNA analysis?

14. Where are crime laboratories operated?

15. What is forensic science and what are the primary specialized areas of practice within the field of forensic science?

16. With regard to the investigation into the murder of Nicole Brown Simpson and Ronald Goldman, answer the following questions:

   a. What do you think was the most powerful physical evidence that suggested that Simpson was responsible for the murders?
   b. What do you think was the most powerful evidence that suggested that Simpson was not responsible for the murders?
   c. Identify the most important mistakes that the police made in collecting the physical evidence in the investigation.
   d. What do you think were the biggest lessons learned by the police as a result of the investigation?

Related Internet Sites

www.crime-scene-investigator.net/index.html
This site contains information on a variety of issues related to crime scenes and physical evidence.

www.pbs.org/wgbh/pages/frontline/shows/dna
This site examines the case of Ronald Cotton, who was exonerated of a rape conviction as a result of DNA analysis after serving more than ten years in prison. The Cotton case is one of the twenty-eight cases cited in an NIJ (1996) report. The site also provides useful information on the validity and reliability of eyewitness identifications (Chapter 7).

www.fbi.gov/hq/lab/labhome.htm
This link brings you to the web site of the FBI crime laboratory. A wealth of useful information about the collection of physical evidence and crime scene procedures is provided here.

INTERVIEWS

- Identify the difference between primary and secondary witnesses and give an example of each

- Identify and discuss the methods by which witnesses may provide eyewitness identifications

- Discuss the advantages and disadvantages associated with FACES, the Identikit system, and police sketch artists

- Discuss the value of eyewitness identifications in establishing proof

- Identify the three phases of human memory and discuss how factors during each phase may affect the accuracy of eyewitness accounts

- Discuss how the wording of questions may affect the retrieval of information from witnesses

- Identify and discuss the rationale of the four recommended lineup procedures

- Discuss the role of hypnosis in criminal investigations and identify the three

- approaches that may be used to obtain hypnotically elicited testimony

- Discuss the research that has been conducted on the accuracy of hypnotically elicited testimony

- Discuss the guidelines for the collection of hypnotically elicited testimony

- Discuss the cognitive interview approach and identify the techniques used to facilitate memory recall

- Compare and contrast the cognitive interview approach with standard police interviews

- Discuss the contribution of cognitive interviewing in enhancing memory recall

- Identify the evidence collected by investigators in the Super America gas station robbery and discuss its role in the identification and apprehension of the perpetrator

Investigative interview	FACES	Acquisition, retention, and retrieval phases of memory	Sequential lineups
Primary witness	Mug shots		Hypnosis
Secondary witness	Show-up identifications	Relative judgment memory process	Confabulation
Eyewitness	Photo lineups		Cognitive interview
Identikit	Physical lineups	Mock witness test	

INTRODUCTION

The Introduction to this chapter consists of a police report that documents an investigation into an armed robbery of a Super America Gas Station that occurred on September 30, 1993, in Germantown, Wisconsin (a suburb of Milwaukee). The report serves as an example of a criminal investigation case report and also highlights issues that are discussed in this chapter, including the construction and use of a composite sketch of the perpetrator, lineup procedures, and the reliability of eyewitness identifications. Issues that are discussed in other chapters, including the value of physical evidence, tip lines, and interrogations, are also discussed in this case report.

Report 93–020572

On Thursday, September 30, 1993, at 10:43 PM, the Germantown Communications Center received a holdup alarm at the Super America convenience store. Officers Stieve, German, and Gardner responded.

On arrival Officer Stieve met with Super America attendant Nathan L. Wascol (M/W, date of birth [DOB]12–25–75).Wascol informed Officer Stieve of the following:

At approximately 10:40 PM a subject wearing a gray-hooded jacket/sweatshirt and black scarf covering his face entered the Super America store. The subject approached the front of the counter, at which time the attendant was checking out witness Forrest S. Mathews (M/W/07–03–57). The subject, who was carrying a sawed-off double-barrel shotgun, pushed the gun into the back of witness Mathews' head and instructed Mathews to give him his wallet. After removing approximately $100 in cash from Mathews, he instructed Mathews to remove his wristwatch, at which time Mathews did so. The subject then instructed Wascol to remove all the money from the cash register. The subject instructed Mathews to lie on the floor, at which time he did. The subject then aimed the gun in the direction of Wascol and instructed him to place the money from the cash register into a bag. After handing the subject the bag full of money, the subject instructed Wascol to give him his money. Wascol removed approximately $80 to $90 from his wallet and gave the subject the money. The subject then ran around behind the counter and instructed Was-

GERMANTOWN POLICE DEPARTMENT

INCIDENT/OFFENSE REPORT

Date/Time Reported:	09/30/93 22:43 THU	Incident 93-020572
Nature of Incident:	Robbery	
Location of Incident:	W178 N9653 Riversbend Lane	
Time/Incident From:	09/30/93 22:43 THU	
Time/Incident To:		
Cpl/Victim Information:	Super America Gas Station	
	W178 N9653 Riversbend Lane	
	Germantown, WI 53022	
Reporting Person:	Same	
Stolen Property $:	165.58	
Reporting Officer:	Jeffrey G. Stieve	
Remarks:	Super America reports being robbed by an armed subject.	

Closed:__X__

Persons Information:

Type V　　　　　　　Name: Wascol, Nathan L.　　　　DOB 12/25/75　Sex M　Race W

Eyes_____Hair_____Wgt_____Hgt_____

3407 E. Friess Lake Road
Hubertus, WI 53033

Type W　　　　　　　Name: Joiner, Wayne K.　　　　DOB 8/26/49 Sex M Race W

Eyes_____Hair_____Wgt_____Hgt_____

W163 N10157 Tomahawk Ct.
Germantown, WI 53022

Type S　　　　　　　Name: Unknown Suspect　　　　DOB / /　Sex M　Race B

Eyes BLK　Hair BLK　Wgt 160　Hgt 506

Type S　　　　　　　Name Branigan/Amos/NMI　　　DOB 04/30/69 Sex M Race B

Eyes BLK Hair BLK Wgt 150 Hgt 506

8245 N. 17th Street

col to lie on the ground. The subject then pointed the gun at Wascol's head and asked him if he thought that this was a joke. Wascol did not respond. The subject then struck Wascol in the head with the sawed-off shotgun, and repeatedly kicked him in the head and arms. Wascol did feel severe pain on being struck.

Wascol stated that neither he nor any employee of Super America gave the suspect permission to remove the $165.58 from the cash register.

SUSPECT DESCRIPTION Male, black, five foot six inches tall, medium build, approximately 170 lb, wearing a black scarf over his face, a gray-hooded sweatshirt pulled over his head, faded blue jeans, and a pair of tennis shoes.

Supplement by Officer German

Officer German responded with other on-duty Germantown police units to a report of an armed robbery at the Super America gas station on County Line Road. While at the Super America, officers received a report of another armed robbery at the Mobil gas station also on County Line Road. All officers involved had previously been briefed about a suspect vehicle that had been used in a previous armed robbery of the Germantown Mobil station on Tuesday, September 28, 1993. The vehicle was described as a 1990 red Pontiac Firebird two-door, and it displayed Wisconsin registration plates LIL-BRD. The vehicle had been taken in a carjacking in Wauwatosa on September 21, 1993. Officer Stieve, in his preliminary investigation of the Super America station robbery, received information that the suspect had left in a red Pontiac Firebird. The suspect was described as a black man with a physical description that matched the earlier Mobil station robber.

Officers Gardner and Johnson spotted the stolen red Firebird on the north side of the Germantown Super 8 Motel. The vehicle was occupied by a black man who matched the description of the suspect in the Super America and the two Mobil rob-

These are two still photographs obtained from the video surveillance camera inside the gas station that showed the robbery as it occurred.

beries. They immediately broadcast the description of the vehicle and that it was fleeing the lot onto Emmer Drive. Several police units, including Sgt. Steitz, Officer German, officers from the Washington County Sheriff's Department, and Menomonee Falls Police Department, attempted to close all exits from the Super 8 Motel but were not successful. The red Firebird exited Emmer Road through the one-way entrance and crossed County Line Road, then proceeded southbound onto Richfield Way.

Sgt. Steitz initiated pursuit of the vehicle and observed the operator of the vehicle point a double-barrel shotgun at him. Shortly thereafter Sgt. Steitz yielded to Officer German in preference to a marked police squad car maintaining the chase. Officer German continued the pursuit in his fully marked police car. At the time of the pursuit, Officer German was displaying red and blue emergency roof-top lighting visible for 360 degrees and he was also sounding the police squad car siren.

The red Firebird continued to accelerate and was operating in a reckless manner, as evidenced by a high rate of speed in a residential area. At times, speeds reached eighty to ninety miles per hour and the red Firebird was observed on several occasions to lose rear wheel traction during cornering. Officer German was able to observe the vehicle clearly, was directly behind it, and had it in view during the entire pursuit.

Officer German continued the pursuit, noting the absence of any vehicular or pedestrian traffic, although Officer German had a difficult time matching the speed of the red Firebird. As the red Firebird turned south onto the ramp to U.S. Highway 41, the rear wheels again broke traction. The vehicle slid into the center divider and went out of control. The left rear tire blew as the car crossed the center divider and, still out of control, the red Firebird crossed back onto the ramp to southbound Highway 41 and then went down into a deep ditch along the west side of the ramp. Officer German pulled up his squad car overlooking the red Firebird and illuminated it with his spotlight. He drew his firearm and shouted several commands to the operator of the vehicle, identifying himself as a police officer and ordering the suspect to halt and not to move. The red Firebird was up against the freeway fence and the driver of the car was observed exiting through the passenger's front side window. The passenger side was up against the fence and the window had broken on impact with the fence. The operator of the Firebird appeared to have something in his hands, which looked to Officer German to be a brown paper bag. The operator was a black man in his twenties, short, stocky, with a round face, wearing a hooded sweatshirt that could have been described as gray in color.

After the suspect exited the vehicle, he crawled onto the top of the Firebird and jumped over the fence. Officer German continued his pursuit on foot across the property at 4614 Fond Avenue on the west side of the freeway fence. The suspect then crossed Fond Avenue, jumped a second fence into the backyard at 8688 Keith Circle, and rounded the corner of the garage at that residence. At that point Officer German terminated the pursuit. Several Menomonee Falls Police Department units flooded the area and set up a containment perimeter. An all-out search of the area had begun.

Officer German later retraced the foot pursuit and recovered rolls of coins, loose change, and single dollar bills along that route. A brown paper sack covered with blood was also recovered at the point where the suspect jumped the fence into the

The gun as it was discovered in the vehicle after it had crashed (left); gun at the police station (right). Could the unusual nature of the weapon be of any assistance in the investigation?

backyard on Keith Circle. The bag was torn and empty, and the blood on the bag was very fresh and probably came from wounds the suspect had received to his hands as he crawled over the freeway fence.

Officer German photographed the red Firebird at the point of impact. Officer German, Detective Piotrowski, and Sgt. Steitz inventoried the vehicle at the Germantown Police Department garage. Other items recovered by Officer German were also inventoried. Additional photos of the vehicle were taken by Officer Stieve at the Germantown Police Department garage.

Supplement by Detective Piotrowski

On September 30, 1993, at 11:00 PM Detective Piotrowski was notified at his residence and requested to respond and investigate as a result of two armed robberies that had occurred at Super America and Germantown Mobil. On September 30, 1993, at 11:30 PM Detective Piotrowski arrived at the police department and at this time proceeded to take statements from the various victims and witnesses pertaining to both robberies. In addition, items were processed for latent prints from within the recovered vehicle, the 1990 Firebird. Items that were found inside and processed for prints included

1. (1) Double-barrel shotgun, 12 gauge, make and model unknown
2. (2) Cassette tapes: "Ghetto Boys" "Little Texas Big Time"
3. (1) Can of Classic Coke (12 oz.)
4. (1) Bottle of 24-count Nuprin
5. (1) Emergency service card
6. (1) Clorets package
7. (1) Package of Newport cigarettes
8. (1) 40-oz. bottle of Olde English 800 malt liquor
9. (1) Red 1990 Pontiac Firebird two-door; VIN, 1G2FS23E511209672; Plate, LIL-BRD

The only print of good quality appeared to be on the emergency road service card.

On October 1, 1993, at 9:10 AM Officer Rick Simons of the Wauwatosa Police Department called and spoke to Detective Piotrowski regarding the recovered auto. He was advised regarding what had transpired the previous evening and stated he would contact the car owner, Evonne Y. Waeltz, and advise her of the recovery of the vehicle.

On October 1, 1993, at 9:30 AM Evonne Y. Waeltz called to speak to Detective Piotrowski and stated that when the car was taken from her she had just over 40,000 miles on the odometer and that the items that were in the car at the time of the theft included an umbrella, a navy-blue blanket that was in the trunk, two tapes (one of Alabama and another of Little Texas), and some groceries. She stated the only other driver for that particular car was her daughter Tiffany Waeltz. She was advised that when she came to the Germantown Police Department that she should bring her daughter Tiffany with her to obtain comparison fingerprints. She was asked whether the emergency road service card that was found in the pocket of the passenger door was hers and she replied that it was not.

On October 1, 1993, at 10:30 AM Captain Jack Petroff of the Menomonee Falls Police Department called and stated that he had received a call from Officer Gallagher of the Oak Creek Police Department advising him that he (Gallagher) had arrested a black man matching the description of the robber. He stated that the person arrested in Oak Creek driving a stolen white Corsica was a Lafayette L. Dixit (M/B, DOB 11–03–71) who was described as five foot six inches and 156 lb. A faxed copy of the composite picture that was produced as a result of witness descriptions at the earlier Mobil robbery was sent to Officer Gallagher for comparison purposes.

On October 1, 1993, at 1:30 PM Detective Michael Jankowski (Milwaukee Police Department) came into the station and spoke to Detective Piotrowski. At this time he provided Detective Piotrowski with a copy of the Milwaukee Police Department report of the robbery at the Open Pantry store located at 8632 North 107th Street in Milwaukee that occurred on September 30, 1993, at 10:40 PM. In their robbery, an unknown black man entered the store armed with a sawed-off shotgun and mask, demanded and obtained money from the cashier and customers, and was last seen on foot southbound from the scene. In addition, a witness had seen a red Pontiac Firebird fleeing the area of the robbery.

Supplement by Detective Culver

On October 2, 1993, at 11:40 AM Detective Culver received a phone call from the previously mentioned Super America employee Nathan Wascol. Wascol provided the following information. He recalled that it was possible that the robbery suspect had been in Super America earlier during the afternoon on the date of this robbery (September 30, 1993). He recalled that two black men had come into the station sometime before it got

EXHIBIT 7–1 Composite sketch of robber

WANTED
For
ROBBERY

SEP. 2 8 1993
Germantown Police Dept.
Officer Brian Henning
Police Composite Artist

ANY INFORMATION CONTACT: GERMANTOWN POLICE DEPARTMENT

1-414-251-1710

N112 W16877 MEQUON
GERMANTOWN, WI 5302

DESCRIPTION

CASE NO: 93-20425
OFFENSE: ROBBERY
LOCATION: GERMANTOWN MOBIL STATION
N96W17500 HWY Q
DATE: 09-28-93
TIME: 11:16 PM

RACE: BLACK
SEX: MALE
AGE: 20-25YRS
EYES: BROWN
HAIR: BLACK

HEIGHT:505"
WEIGHT:170
BUILD:MEDIUM
SUSP VEH:PONT FIREBIRD
LIC# LILBRD WI 94

NARR:SUSPECT ENTERED WEARING A BLACK SILK SCARF
DEMANDED MONEY AFTER THREATENING ATTENDANT.ATTENDANT WAS
ORDERED TO LAY ON THE FLOOR WHILE SUSPECT FLED WITH
.SUSPECT VEH PONTIAC FIREBIRD RED LIC# LIL BRD WI 94
VEH WAS ENTERED STOLEN BY WAUWATOSA PD

This composite picture was developed by a police artist on the basis of witnesses' descriptions of the robber in a robbery that occurred two days prior to the Super America robbery. In this earlier robbery, the perpetrator did not disguise his identity.

dark, probably between 3:00 PM and 6:30 PM. He was not sure what, if anything, either of these people may have purchased at the time they were in the station. He recalled that one of the black men was a larger person and the second black man was a smaller person who was similar in physical appearance to the robbery suspect. Those two people should be on the same surveillance videotape that included the actual robbery.

On October 2, 1993, at 12:50 PM Detective Piotrowski, in processing evidence found within the suspect vehicle, acquired a good latent print from an emergency service card. The owner of that card was a victim of an armed robbery that occurred in the city of Milwaukee. It appeared that the person who committed that robbery was the same person involved in the Super America robbery. The owner of that emergency service card appeared at the Germantown Police Department at this time to be fingerprinted for comparison purposes. The card owner was Donna M. Roe–Basile (F/W, DOB 10–08–43). Detective Culver took Roe–Basile's fingerprints, and it appeared that the latent print obtained by Detective Piotrowski from the emergency service card did not belong to her.

On October 2, 1993, at 1:00 PM Anne E. Schneider, a reporter for WISN TV appeared at the Germantown Police Department and met with Detective Culver. Detective Culver had spoken to Schneider earlier, requesting that she consider profiling the armed robbery cases on the WISN TV Channel 12 Crime Line news segment. Detective Culver turned over to Schneider the two videotapes from both Super America and the Mobil station. Detective Culver also gave Schneider a copy of the composite drawing of the suspect. Detective Culver also had Schneider and her assistant videotape the vehicle used in the robbery, including showing the personalized plate on the vehicle. Schneider advised Culver that a segment profiling the two armed robberies would be shown on the 6:00 PM and 10:00 PM news on Channel 12 that evening, October 2, 1993.

On October 2, 1993, at 2:45 PM Detective Culver took the previously mentioned emergency service card with the latent print to the Milwaukee Police Department, Bureau of Identification. Identification technician David Groth would process that latent print through the Milwaukee Police Department AFIS hopefully the next day (October 3, 1993) or Monday, October 4, 1993.

On October 2, 1993, at 4:00 PM the owner of the vehicle used by the suspect in the robberies, Yvonne M. Waeltz, and her daughter Tiffany M. Waeltz appeared at the Germantown Police Department to be fingerprinted for comparison purposes in regard to the latent print on the emergency service card. The latent print recovered from the card did not match either subject.

On October 2, 1993, at 6:00 PM and 10:00 PM Channel 12 WISN TV news showed the previously mentioned surveillance videotapes of the robberies at Super America and Mobil, the videotape of the vehicle used by the suspect, and the suspect composite drawing on the Crime Line segment of the news, which included the We Tip information.

On October 2, 1993, at 10:49 PM the Germantown Police Department received information from We Tip that they had received information that a person matching the description of the robbery suspect was someone named "Al," a black man, thirty years old, five foot nine inches tall, 200 lb. who worked as a janitor at the Belle Elementary School in Germantown. This witness further stated that they saw the vehicle with the plate LIL-BRD in the lot at that location.

On October 3, 1993, at 8:40 AM Mark A. Amadon (M/W, DOB 02–16–54) appeared at the Germantown Police Department and met with Detective Culver.

Amadon provided the following information. His residence is the Vintage Insurance Building on Holy Hill Road. While outside his residence that past week on a number of occasions he saw what may have been the suspect vehicle being driven by a black man. The last time he saw that vehicle was on Monday or Tuesday, September 27 or 28. The vehicle was being driven recklessly and the tires were squealing on the road, but had slowed down in front of his house, at which time he got a good look at the driver of the vehicle. He saw this vehicle driven by the same black man another two or three days prior to Monday or Tuesday. The vehicle went past his residence at about the same time, 5:00 PM, on all those occasions. He had seen the Channel 12 Crime Line profile of these robberies, including the composite drawing of the suspect, and thought the drawing looked similar to the person he saw driving the red Firebird. He did not see the license plate on the Firebird when it had driven past his residence.

On October 3, 1993, at 10:05 AM Detective Culver received a phone call from Glen G. Gerstner (M/W, DOB 12–22–62) who provided the following information. He had seen the Channel 12 Crime Line profile of the robbery suspect and he had recently seen a person that matched that description. On Tuesday, September 28, 1993, at about 10:00 AM he observed a black man, five feet nine inches to five foot ten inches tall, about twenty years old, medium build, wearing a jean jacket with sweats under it in the strip mall on Mequon Road. He observed this person looking into the Serv-U Pharmacy a number of times, and from the way he was acting, he (Gerstner) felt that that person was getting ready to rob the pharmacy. Gerstner continued to observe this person for a time and subsequently saw the person go into the Schulz Delicatessen in that same strip mall. The person he observed was alone and he did not observe a vehicle to be associated with him.

On October 3, 1993, at 12:55 PM Detective Culver determined that the Belle School employee was Alfonso Govin of 4344 North 51st Street, Milwaukee. The state criminal history record check run on that person disclosed Alfonso H. Govin, M/B, DOB 09–16–59, five foot nine inches tall, 195 lb. with a single arrest by the Cedarburg Police Department in 1980 for a traffic offense. Based on the physical description of Govin it appeared that he was not a match for the robbery.

On October 6, 1993, at 4:45 PM Detective Culver planted in the area of the Vintage Building on Holy Hill Road until 5:20 PM in an effort to see whether the suspect routinely traveled through the area, as reported by Amadon. The suspect was not observed by Detective Culver.

On October 6, 1993, at 7:00 PM Detective Culver went to the Milwaukee Police Department, Bureau of Identification, and picked up the emergency service card with the latent print that had been run through AFIS. No identification had been made via AFIS regarding the owner of the latent print.

On October 7, 1993, at 3:35 PM Detective Culver received a phone call from Marie A. Korkos (F/W, DOB 06–30–65), who provided the following information. She was in the parking lot of the Pick N' Save on Mequon Road in Germantown that day (October 7, 1993) at 2:30 PM when she saw a person walking from the direction of the Pick

N' Save to his car. She had seen the composite drawing of the robbery suspect in the newspaper and on seeing this person felt he closely resembled the composite of the robber. This person was a black man, five foot five inches to five foot six inches tall, 160 to 170 lb. (medium build/muscular), twenty-five to thirty years old with short close-cropped hair, dark complexion, wearing a red T-shirt and tan pants. She watched him get into a vehicle. The vehicle was large, dull, black, was old, and she thought the license plate number was KJK–987.

Detective Culver asked Korkos if she would appear at the Germantown Police Department to discuss her observations further. Korkos advised Culver she would come to the police station immediately.

On October 7, 1993, at 3:55 PM Marie Korkos appeared at the Germantown Police Department and met with Detective Culver. Culver had found that the license number KJK–987 was listed to a 1987 Buick belonging to a person in Green Bay. Culver inquired of Korkos regarding whether she was positive of the license plate number on the vehicle she had observed. Korkos advised Culver that she was not positive and thought that the license plate could also have been KFK–987. Culver ran that number and found that it belonged to a 1975 Oldsmobile Regency two-door registered to Michael A. Will of 3347 North 13th Street, Milwaukee. Culver showed Korkos a photo of all the 1975 Regency Oldsmobiles in the 1975 auto mug book. Korkos stated that the 1975 Oldsmobile 98 Regency looked very much like the vehicle she had observed at the Pick N' Save. Culver also showed Korkos a copy of a composite drawing of the robbery suspect. When Korkos viewed it she stated that the composite appeared to be an exact match of the person she had seen at the Pick N' Save. Culver also showed Korkos one of the black-and-white photos taken at the Mobil station of the robbery suspect when he was unmasked, which was of poor quality. Korkos stated that despite the fuzziness of the photo, the suspect shown in that photo appeared to be the same person she saw at the Pick N' Save.

Culver obtained a DOB on Michael A. Will of 3347 N. 13th Street, Milwaukee, the listed owner of the 1975 Oldsmobile with license number KFK–987. The DOB was June 3, 1965. Record checks run on that person with that DOB disclosed no record in the Wisconsin criminal history record identification files and also no record in the NCIC file. That person was neither wanted nor on probation or parole. The physical description given for Michael A. Will was male, black, five foot seven inches, 180 lb.

On October 7, 1993, at 4:50 PM Detective Culver once again parked in the vicinity of the Vintage Building on Holy Hill Road until 5:20 PM and did not observe anyone passing through that area that resembled the robbery suspect.

On October 7, 1993, at 6:48 PM Detective Culver received a phone call from Carolyn M. Lucke (F/W, DOB 04–24–42), who provided the following information. She had seen the composite drawing of the robbery suspect in the newspaper. She worked at the Bradley Convalescent Center on Bradley Road in Milwaukee. She observed that an employee of the Bradley Convalescent Center who mops floors during the day closely resembles the composite of the robbery suspect. She described that person as a black man about thirty years old, five foot four inches to five foot five inches with a stocky build. She did not know his name or anything else about him.

On October 7, 1993, at 6:55 PM Detective Culver phoned the Bradley Convalescent Center and spoke to Barb Melzer. Melzer identified the person mentioned by Carolyn Lucke as Elijah Sanidas (M/B, DOB 06–15–56, five foot five inches and heavy set). She personally knew Sanidas and knew him to be a good employee, and someone she would not suspect as being involved in the robberies. Record checks were run on Elijah Sanidas and, based on his age, physical description, and arrest history background, Sanidas appeared to be an unlikely candidate as a suspect in the robberies.

On October 8, 1993, the Wauwatosa Police Department advised they had arrested four black men after robbing a woman of her purse at 11:20 PM, September 11, 1993. The MO involved in that robbery was very similar to the MO of the robbery suspect who stole the red Firebird in Wauwatosa and stole the emergency service card in Milwaukee. The four people arrested by the Wauwatosa Police Department on September 11, 1993, were (1) Roberson, Curtis Bernard, M/B, DOB 01–27–65, six feet, 175 lb., medium complexion; (2) Kennedy, Alvernest Floyd, M/B, DOB 02–07–70, five foot six inches tall, 177 lb.; (3) Lester, Robert Leslie, M/B, DOB 02–01–69, five foot seven inches tall, 185 lb.; and (4) Bridges, Earnest, M/B, DOB 02–21–68, five foot nine inches tall, 195 lb.

Culver faxed a copy of the robbery suspect composite drawing to Wauwatosa Police Department Detective Tom Simons. Culver also ordered a copy of the mug photos of the four Wauwatosa Police Department arrestees.

Supplement by Detective Piotrowski

On October 7, 1993, at 8:50 AM Detective Piotrowski took the double-barrel shotgun and the latent print that had been developed on the emergency road service card to the regional crime lab in Milwaukee. Identification technician John Neilson was requested to check the electricians tape on the sticky side for latent prints. He also asked to have the firearms unit check the weapon to see whether it was operational. In addition, Neilson was requested to run the latent print that had been obtained on the card through AFIS of the State of Wisconsin to determine whether the identity of the person could be ascertained.

Supplement by Detective Culver

On October 12, 1993, at 9:20 PM Detective Culver returned a phone call to Bridgette Burkert who is an employee of the Channel 12 news room. Burkert provided the following information. After learning of the description of the suspect in the robbery and the red Firebird with the personalized plate LIL-BRD, she recalled having seen that vehicle on the east side of Milwaukee near the University of Wisconsin–Milwaukee sometime between one and two weeks ago. She had no other information.

On October 13, 1993, the Milwaukee Police Department contacted Detective Culver and informed him that they had in custody a suspect who matched the description of the robber of the Super America, Mobil, and other Milwaukee robberies. He was apprehended while fleeing a robbery scene. That suspect was Branigan, Amos, B/M, DOB 04–30–69. The Milwaukee Police Department had scheduled a lineup in the detective bureau for 7:00 PM October 13, 1993. Branigan would be standing in that lineup.

On October 13, 1993, at 7:00 PM, Detectives Culver and Piotrowski took the following victims/witnesses from the robberies in Germantown to the Milwaukee Police Department to view the lineup: Officer Bruce Gardner, Forrest, Mathews, David Pellegrini, Wayne Joiner, Joy Brooks, Nathan Wascol, Mark Sadowski, and Byron Adams. At 7:40 PM on October 13, 1993, the lineup was conducted at the Milwaukee Police Department by Lieutenant Robert Schroeder. The lineup consisted of five black men ranging in age from twenty-two to thirty-two years, from five foot six inches to five foot nine inches in height, and from 150 to 190 lb. Amos Branigan (suspect) was placed in position two.

Each of the witnesses was given a "special identification show-up" card that bore the name of the witness, their address, and the numbers one through six, corresponding to the persons standing in the lineup (in this case, one through five; see Exhibit 7–2). The witnesses were instructed to circle the number of anybody standing in the lineup that they thought was the suspect they observed involved in either of the robberies at Super America or the companion Mobil armed robbery cases.

During the course of the conduct of the lineup, each of the five persons standing in the lineup stepped forward individually and was viewed from different sides, and was also told to make certain statements. Those statements included, "This is no joke," "Get

How well does the suspect match the composite picture?

EXHIBIT 7–2 Blank copy of a special identification show-up card

Date: _____

Time: _____

Offense: _____

Complainant: _____

Name of Witness:_____

Address of Witness:_____

Suspect Identified   1   2   3   4   5   6   -unable
(circle one)

on the floor," and "This is a holdup." The results of the witness identifications are as follows: Joiner and Mathews were unable to make an identification. Officer Gardner and Brooks picked out the person bearing number five. Pellegrini picked out the person bearing number four. Adams, Wascol, and Sadowski all picked out the person bearing number two, suspect Amos Branigan. After the witnesses left the lineup room, Detectives Culver and Piotrowski had an identification technician from the Milwaukee Police Department take photographs of the suspect Branigan's hands (palms only). Branigan had numerous cuts and puncture-type wounds to the palms of both his hands. These wounds were still in the healing process.

Following the lineup, Milwaukee Police Department Detective Dan Phillips questioned Branigan regarding the robberies committed in Milwaukee. After Detective Phillips concluded questioning Branigan, Detective Culver then met with Branigan in a holding cell in the detective bureau and, after reading Branigan his Miranda warning at 11:45 PM on October 13, 1993, Detective Culver questioned him regarding the robberies in Germantown. Branigan waived his Miranda rights, signed the Miranda waiver form, and agreed to answer questions concerning the robberies. During the course of Detective Culver's interrogation of Branigan, Detective Culver had gone over the details of the robbery with the suspect. When Detective Culver went through the details of the suspect exiting the vehicle through a broken window on the passenger side of the vehicle after it had crashed, climbing over a cyclone fence and injuring his hands doing so, and subsequently dropping a bloody paper bag on the ground, Branigan questioned Detective Culver twice regarding whether Detective Culver was sure about the suspect dropping the bloody paper bag on the side of the fence opposite where the car was located. Branigan asked, "If the guy didn't cut his hands on the fence, how could you have blood on the bag on the other side of the fence?" Detective

Culver responded to Branigan by saying, "If you're saying that the person who fled the car cut his hands on something else, such as a broken window glass when he came out of the vehicle and dropped the bag on the same side of the fence as the car, that wouldn't make any difference. The blood still would have come from the suspect, that being you." Branigan then agreed with Detective Culver that it would not make any difference as far as the identity of the suspect, especially because Officer German had observed the suspect drop the bag. The detail that the paper bag was in fact dropped on the same side of the cyclone fence as the car is important because only the person who actually dropped the bag would know this detail (other than Officer German). Detective Culver concluded his questioning of Branigan at 1:15 AM on October 14, 1993.

On October 14, 1993, at 3:15 PM Detective Piotrowski received a phone call from Milwaukee Police Department Detective Lieutenant Larry Godager. Godager provided the following information. Milwaukee Police Department Detectives Jankowski and Phillips questioned the suspect Branigan and Branigan confessed to them that he had committed the armed robbery at the Mobil station in Germantown on September 28, 1993, and the armed robberies of that same Mobil station and the Super America station on September 30, 1993.

On October 14, 1993, at 3:45 PM Detective Culver went to the Washington County District Attorney's office and met with Assistant District Attorney Todd Martens for the purpose of obtaining a search warrant to obtain blood from the suspect, Amos Branigan. Martens prepared the search warrant affidavit and indicated that he would present it to a judge the following day. He would contact the Germantown Police Department with the results.

On October 15, 1993, at 1:47 PM Washington County Circuit Court Judge James B. Schwalbach issued a search warrant compelling the suspect Amos Branigan to provide a sample of his blood. Detective Piotrowski received two copies of that search warrant signed by Judge Schwalbach and brought those search warrants back to the Germantown Police Department.

On October 15, 1993, at 3:29 PM Milwaukee Police Department Detective Thomas Meyer faxed eleven pages of Milwaukee Police Department Detective Jankowski and Phillips' interview of the suspect, Amos Branigan. Branigan gave them a statement in which he admitted committing the Mobil station armed robbery in Germantown on September 29, 1993; admitted committing the robbery at that same Mobil station in Germantown on September 30, 1993; as well as the robbery of the Super America station in Germantown on September 30, 1993. Branigan signed the original statement forms.

On October 15, 1993, at 6:00 PM Detectives Culver and Piotrowski went to the Milwaukee County Jail for the purpose of executing the search warrant for blood on the suspect Amos Branigan.

At 7:00 PM Detective Piotrowski once again spoke with Branigan about the robberies in question. Branigan was informed of his Miranda warnings and Branigan indicated he did not care to answer any more questions at that time. Branigan did sign the Miranda waiver form. At that time Branigan did agree to view the copies that Culver had of the eleven-page Milwaukee Police Department report that contained Branigan's confession to Milwaukee Police Department detectives. The last four of those pages contained the confession by Branigan to the Germantown armed robberies. Branigan reviewed those pages, acknowledged that it was the confession he had given to the Milwaukee detective at that time, that the statement was true and accurate, and that he signed, dated, and put the time on each of those four pages of the Milwaukee Police Department report.

Branigan further stated that he would attempt to locate and return the watch that he stole from the victim Forrest Mathews at the Super America station in Germantown on September 30, 1993. Following this meeting with Branigan, Culver and Piotrowski returned to Germantown.

NOTE: These reports were edited for length and clarity, the names and addresses of witnesses and other citizens were changed, and all telephone numbers were deleted from the reports.

Amos Branigan was convicted of five counts of armed robbery and one count of taking and driving a motor vehicle without the owner's consent, and was sentenced to fifty-four years in prison. In 1999, while in prison, Branigan was linked, through DNA, to three sexual assaults that occurred in Milwaukee in 1993. He was found guilty of these crimes and was sentenced to an additional sixty years in prison. His release date is scheduled for 2107.

Interviews Defined

An investigative interview can be defined as any questioning or other interaction that is intended to produce information regarding a particular crime or regarding a person believed responsible for a crime. Interviews are usually nonaccusatory and have the goal of developing information to move a criminal investigation forward. As seen in the Super America robbery investigation, the police had reason to interview numerous individuals in an attempt to develop leads in the investigation. Several witnesses were eventually able to confirm the identity of the robber in a lineup.

Depending on the information obtained from a subject, an interview can easily turn into an interrogation during which accusations may be made and incriminating statements may be sought. For example, consider the case of the murder of Danielle van Dam discussed in previous chapters. On being notified of the missing girl by her parents, the police immediately began to contact the neighbors of the van Dams. They sought information from these individuals regarding anything that they may have seen or heard the previous evening or during the early morning. David Westerfield, fifty years old, who lived two houses away from the van Dams, was the only neighbor who was not at home the time the police first contacted individuals in the neighborhood. Two days later, the police were able to contact and interview Westerfield. They asked him where he was the past two days and whether he saw anything unusual or heard anything suspicious. Westerfield walked the police through his house and explained to them that he was traveling around San Diego County and the desert in his motor home. The more the police heard, the more suspicious they became. Westerfield was eventually taken into custody and questioned about the crime. As evidence accumulated, Westerfield was arrested and charged with the kidnaping and murder of Danielle van Dam.

Types of Witnesses

Witnesses can be classified as either primary or secondary, depending on the information they are able to provide to the police. Primary witnesses are individuals who have direct knowledge of the crime in question or of the suspected perpetrator of the crime. Primary witnesses can be further classified as either eyewitnesses or noneyewitnesses. Eyewitnesses are individuals who saw the crime occur or saw related events that occurred just prior to or just after the crime. Non-eyewitnesses are individuals who heard the crime occur or heard events just before or after the crime.

Secondary witnesses are individuals who possess information about related events before or after the crime. For example, an individual who heard someone bragging about the crime, or an individual who reported seeing someone with property that was believed to be stolen would be considered a secondary witness. Crime victims, individuals who are either directly or indirectly the focus of the criminal act, could be primary or secondary witnesses depending on their involvement in the crime and the information they are able to provide. Confidential informants, or "street sources," are most likely to be secondary witnesses. As illustrated in the Super America gas station robbery investigation, for a variety of reasons, the information developed through interviews of witnesses may not be accurate or relevant to the investigation. Investigators must be aware of this possibility throughout the process of collecting and assembling information from witnesses.

Types of Information Obtained from Witnesses

There is a multitude of information that may be obtained from eyewitnesses and witnesses in general. The most important and potentially valuable information that can be provided are the actions of the perpetrator, the description of the perpetrator, and, most useful, the identification (or name) of the perpetrator.

Understanding the actions of the perpetrator is particularly useful in establishing his MO. In turn, this can assist the police in linking crimes and may also represent important behavioral evidence. For example, the robber of the Super America station was believed to have committed other robberies as well. The robberies were committed at similar times of the day, most were of convenience stores and gas stations, he stole cash from the cash register as well as from the attendants and other customers, and during the robberies he often used similar language (e.g., "This is no joke," "Do you think that this is a joke?"). In another example, in one city that experienced hundreds of robberies a year, there was a series of robberies committed during which the perpetrator, after taking the victims' money, ordered the victims to remove their pants. This unique MO, which was established through the statements of victims, allowed the police to link the crimes, look for similarities in the descriptions of the perpetrator provided by victims, and develop information about the geographical area in which he was committing the crimes. When the culprit was eventually identified and arrested, the police were able to clear all the crimes that were believed to have been committed by this individual.

Furthermore, a description may provide a basis for the development of a composite picture or sketch of the offender. In addition, once a suspect has been located by the police, an eyewitness may identify the suspect through a show-up, photo lineup, or physical lineup.

Methods of Eyewitness Identification

There are several methods by which an eyewitness may identify a perpetrator. These methods consist of (1) the witness providing information for the development of a picture of the perpetrator, (2) the witness viewing mug shot books (collections of photographs of previously arrested or detained persons), (3) the witness viewing the suspect in a show-up situation during which the suspect is detained by the police at the scene of the crime or at another place, (4) the witness viewing photographs of the suspect and others in a photo lineup or photo array, and (5) the witness actually viewing the suspect and others in a physical, or live, lineup.

Development of a Picture

Pictures of suspects can be created either through a witness providing descriptive details of the suspect's face to a police artist who then draws the portrait, or through composite systems, such as Identikit or FACES. As described by Laughery and Fowler (1980):

> Identikit is a set of transparent celluloid sheets, each containing a line drawing of a facial feature. There are a large number of sheets for each feature (i.e., many types of noses, eyes, etc.). A trained technician constructs a composite face by interacting with a witness to select appropriate features that are then superimposed to make a face. A special marking pencil is available for the technician to make additional modifications or to add detail. (p. 308)

FACES composite picture software is similar to Identikit but it is computer based. With FACES, the technician who constructs the perpetrator's face can select from nearly 4,000 different facial features to create a realistic-looking picture.

EXHIBIT 7–3 FACES composite picture

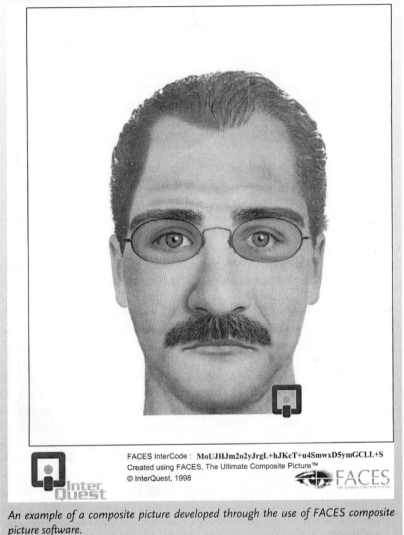

FACES InterCode : **MoUJHJm2o2yJrgL+hJKcT+u4SmwxD5ymGCLL+S**
Created using FACES, The Ultimate Composite Picture™
© InterQuest, 1998

InterQuest

FACES

An example of a composite picture developed through the use of FACES composite picture software.

Each method of constructing a composite picture has advantages and disadvantages. A potential disadvantage of all methods is that witnesses who provide information for the creation of a composite picture of a suspect often perform more poorly in subsequent lineup identifications than those who have not provided such information (see Lindsay [1994]). The composite construction exercise may influence memory in a negative way. With regard to unique advantages, police artist drawings and FACES pictures score high on realism and therefore are potentially more recognizable. Artists have a virtually unlimited number of features to incorporate into a picture. Identikit and FACES are more available to the police than are capable artists. In addition, there is generally more variation in artists' pictures than in those developed through Identikit or FACES. Some artists are more skilled than others, and it shows in their sketches (Laughery and Fowler, 1980). Some studies (e.g., Laughery and Fowler [1980]) have shown that sketch artists are more likely to produce more accurate facial images than Identikit or FACES technicians, but others show that accuracy varies little across the various methods (e.g., Ellis [1984]). This may have more to do with the complexity of the task than the method used. Wells (1993) explains:

> Faces are processed not just as sets of separate features but as interactive systems of features that include interfeatural properties such as distance between features, relative sizes, and other topographical types of information. . . . The same nose on two different faces can appear to be a quite different nose; changes in the hair style can make chin lines or lips appear to change; and a simple featural change (e.g., loss of a moustache) can lead a person to notice that a face now looks different, but the person cannot necessarily specify what feature has changed. (p. 558)

Because of the likelihood that a composite sketch may be inaccurate, some police departments are reluctant to use or disseminate composite pictures of suspects except under extraordinary circumstances. If it turns out that the composite picture does not resemble the suspect/defendant, it may work to the detriment of the police and prosecutor. The inaccurate picture may create a legitimate doubt in the minds of jurors about the responsibility of the suspect for the crime, despite other evidence in the case. As seen in the Super America robbery investigation, another potential problem is that pictures may generate numerous false leads and contribute to an unproductive investigation even if they resemble the suspect.

Along with the Super America robbery, another example of the use of a police sketch drawing of a culprit based on a witness' description is the case of the kidnaping and murder of five-year-old Samantha Runnion in Stanton, California. On July 15, 2002, Samantha was playing with a friend, also five years old, outside the apartment where she lived. At about 6:45 PM an individual drove up and asked Samantha and her friend if they saw his lost dog. The man then proceeded to grab Samantha as she was kicking and screaming, and put her in his car. He then drove off. The police arrived immediately and began an intensive search for the girl and her abductor. They learned that the only witness was Samantha's five-year-old friend. She provided a description of the man along with a description of his car. She described him as Hispanic, between the ages of twenty-five and forty, with black hair and a moustache. She described the car he was driving as a light-green two-door. Police determined from her description that the car was possibly a Honda or an Acura. The police began working with the little girl to develop a sketch of the suspect. The next day, July 16, Samantha's nude and sexually abused body was found on the side of a nearby road. With the description of the perpetrator and his vehicle disseminated to the public, on July 17 a tip (one of more than 2,000) was received by the police naming Alejandro Avila as a possible suspect in the case. By July 19 the artist's sketch of the suspect was completed and widely disseminated. The sketch looked remarkably similar to Avila. That same day Avila was arrested for the murder of Samantha Runnion (McDonald, 2002). Even though the sketch closely resembled the perpetrator, it probably was of limited value in the investigation because the police had the suspect identified even before the sketch of him was completed. In the Super America robbery investigation, what was the value and contribution of the composite sketch of the perpetrator?

Mug Shot Books

When the police have not yet identified a suspect, and when there are few other leads to pursue, the police may request that the witness view mug shot books that contain photographs of previously arrested or detained subjects to identify the perpetrator. These photographs may be organized in ways to limit the number of photographs to be reviewed. For example, a robbery victim may be shown only pictures of individuals who are believed to commit robberies in the area of the city in which the crime occurred. Most often the viewing of mug shot photographs is a rather unproductive activity, akin to some investigators to finding a needle in a haystack.

Show-Up Identifications

Show-up identifications, or curbside identifications, involve bringing the suspect back to the scene or to the location of the witness, or bringing the witness to the location of the suspect to determine whether the witness can identify the suspect as the perpetrator of the crime. Show-ups are most often conducted when the suspect flees the scene but is quickly apprehended by the police. They are much more common than lineup procedures (Gonzalez et al., 1993). Logistically, it is a simple procedure; however, show-ups are quite suggestive and, as a result, may lead to false identifications. Show-ups are suggestive because the single person available to be identified has already been detained by the police under suspicion of being a suspect in the crime. Certainly it is possible that the police could detain a wrong person as a possible suspect. As explained by Yarmey et al. (1996), research shows that "identifications from one-person lineups are less accurate, and put innocent suspects at more risk, than identifications from six person lineups" (p. 468). Misidentification is most likely if the detained subject is wearing clothing similar to that worn by the culprit (Yarmey et al., 1996).

On the other hand, show-ups may actually offer several advantages. First, with a show-up, an identification is usually made quickly after the crime has occurred so the witness' memory may be fresh. Second, the police are probably less sure that the suspect is the culprit in a show-up situation than in a lineup, during which the police are often looking for confirmation rather than information. As a result, there may be less pressure placed on the witness by the police in a show-up than in a lineup. The relative lack of pressure may be more likely to lead to an accurate identification in the show-up situation. Finally, research has shown that witnesses are more cautious in making identifications in show-ups than in lineups: "they are more reluctant to say that the person they see is the perpetrator, even when he or she is" (Gonzalez et al., 1993; p. 536). Considering these issues, the courts have generally supported the practice of show-ups and have ruled that a suspect does not have the right to counsel at a show-up.

Photo Lineups

Photo lineups are useful when investigators have a reason to believe that a particular individual is the culprit in a particular crime. With a photo lineup, a picture of the person who investigators believe is the culprit is often placed in a 8.5 3 11-inch frame with usually five others who generally match the initial description provided by the witness. The witness is typically asked to take a good look at each of the pictures and to indicate whether any individual included in the lineup is the person who committed the crime. If a picture is selected, then the witness is asked how confident he or she is that the person identified is actually the culprit. The procedures used in conducting a photo lineup can greatly affect the accuracy of the results. Similar to show-ups, a suspect does not have the right to counsel at a photo lineup procedure.

Example of a six-person photo lineup

Physical Lineups

Physical, or "live," lineups involve witnesses viewing the suspect and other subjects in a controlled setting, most often at a police station or jail. Usually the witness views the individuals through one-way glass. Each individual may be asked to speak or to say a certain phrase (e.g., "This is no joke"). Physical lineups usually consist of six people, the person the police believe is the perpetrator of the crime and five others (i.e., "foils" or "distractors"). The foils are usually individuals who are detained in jail at the time the lineup is conducted. As with showups and photo lineups, the procedures used in conducting a physical lineup can greatly affect the accuracy of the results. As a rule, the foils should be selected on the basis of the initial description provided by the witness. At a minimum, the race and gender of the foils must be the same as the suspect. All of the participants in the lineup should be similarly dressed, especially if the suspect was described by the witness as wearing certain clothing (e.g., a black baseball cap). These and other factors are considered by the courts in determining the fairness of the procedure and the potential suggestive nature of the identification. Suspects have the right to have counsel present at a physical lineup but suspects cannot refuse to participate, even though their participation may be incriminating.

The robbery suspect in this case was described as approximately 6'0", 200 lbs., with a medium build. Who do you think was the perpetrator? It was subject #2. Also notice his body language and the similarities between subjects #4 and #5.

Value of Eyewitness Identifications in Establishing Proof

Eyewitness identification is among the least reliable types of evidence yet is extremely persuasive in establishing proof. As explained by Wells et al. (1998), "false eyewitness identification is the primary cause of the conviction of innocent people" (p. 603). Wells et al. (1998) identified forty recent cases in which innocent people were convicted of crimes and served time in prison, until DNA analysis was used to establish their innocence. These cases consisted of the twenty-eight listed in the NIJ (1996) report (see Chapter 6) and an additional twelve identified by Wells et al. (1998). Of the forty cases, thirty-six (ninety percent) involved inaccurate eyewitness identification evidence. Furthermore, Wells (1993), in citing other research on the issue, explains that "analyses of what went wrong in producing more than 1,000 convictions of innocent people have revealed that the single largest factor leading to these false convictions was eyewitness error" (p. 554). More than 100 cases of false convictions are profiled on the web site of the Innocence Project, and these too reveal the prominence of eyewitness error (see www.innocenceproject.org). Other accounts of inaccurate eyewitness identification leading to false arrests and jail time have also been reported (e.g., Ferkenoff [2002]). In addition, the same accuracy problem has been revealed in experimental studies during which eyewitness identification errors have occurred at a rate of a few percent to more than ninety percent (Wells, 1993). Compounding the accuracy problem is that despite the error-prone nature of the evidence, witnesses often express high confidence in their judgments and in the accuracy of their identification. Hence, eyewitnesses may be confident and persuasive in their inaccurate testimony (Wells, 1993), and this confidence may be quite influential on jurors and their verdicts (Rattner, 1988).

The Memory Process and the Identification Task

The human memory and its associated processes have been the subject of countless theories and empirical analyses. At the simplest level, memory consists of three phases: encoding, storage, and retrieval (Fisher and Geiselman, 1992). Others have identified equivalent stages: acquisition, retention, and retrieval (Loftus et al., 1989). The encoding or acquisition stage is when the event or other stimulus is perceived and represented in the individual's mind. The storage or retention stage involves the activation of a mental record of the event and the "filing" of the information. The retrieval stage occurs when the mental record of the event or stimulus is activated and the "file" is opened. Retrieval brings about recollection. During the encoding–storage–retrieval process, many things may happen to inhibit or distort accurate memory. For example, when a crime is witnessed, it is impossible to *encode* every single detail of the incident. Rather, only certain dimensions of the situation, those deemed most significant, may be encoded (e.g., he has a big gun, he is pointing it in my face, he is telling me to give him all my money). If minimal attention is given to a particular dimension of the situation, it is likely that that dimension will be encoded inaccurately. During the *retention* stage, details of the event may be forgotten. Or, details may be distorted by postevent information in the form of other witness accounts or investigator statements. During the *retrieval* stage, a witness searches his or her memory and tries to recall what happened or who committed the crime. Retrieval may take the form of reporting to the police, viewing lineups, or testifying in court. At this stage, the circumstances under which the retrieval occurs may affect the accuracy of the information recalled. Clearly, errors and distortions can occur at each stage of memory; human memory is not a video recorder and recall is not a matter of viewing the videotape (Sanders and Simmons, 1983).

As noted, in some instances, a retrieval task may involve a witness identifying the perpetrator through a lineup. According to Wells (1993), this retrieval task most often involves a relative-judgment memory process. "A relative-judgment process is one in which the eyewitness chooses the lineup member who most resembles the culprit *relative to the other members of the lineup*" (p. 560). This process is not necessarily problematic as long as the actual culprit is in the lineup. If the actual culprit is not in the lineup, a natural tendency may be for the witness to select an individual who most resembles the mental image of the observed perpetrator. Furthermore, just because an investigator may believe that the actual culprit is included in the lineup, it does not necessarily mean that the culprit is actually included in the lineup. In such a situation, if a person is identified it would be the wrong person. Even if the wrong person is selected, the witness may still express high confidence that the person selected was actually the culprit. Variation in eyewitness identification confidence does not vary with eyewitness identification accuracy. As such, "the relative-judgment process is seductive yet dangerous" (Wells, 1993; p. 560).

Why Is Eyewitness Identification Evidence Often Inaccurate?

Factors at each stage of the memory process—acquisition, retention, retrieval—may affect the accuracy of an eyewitness account or identification (see Loftus et al. [1989]). First, during the *acquisition* stage, factors that relate to the circumstances and nature of the event, as well as the characteristics of the witness, may affect the resulting information. For instance, with regard to the circumstances of the event, it is reasonable to expect that factors such as lighting conditions, distance, and obstructed views would have an affect. The duration of the event and the amount of time spent actually observing the event may affect accuracy. "The longer a person looks at something the better the memory of it will be" (Loftus et al., 1989). However, some estimates—particularly of how long certain events lasted—are frequently inaccurate regardless of the surrounding circumstances of the observation. The nature of the event may also impact the accuracy of memory. Events perceived as insignificant at the time of acquisition are less likely to be recalled accurately. In addition, some research suggests that acts of violence are more difficult to recall accurately. Witnesses also often experience difficulties recalling events that occurred immediately prior to their observations of violent actions (Loftus et al., 1989).

Characteristics of witnesses may also have an effect on accuracy of recall. For instance, the psychological condition of the witness may be an important consideration. Research has demonstrated that fear and stress improve physical performance, including eyewitness performance, up to a certain point, but then it becomes counterproductive (known as the Yerkes–Dodson law) (Goodman and Hahn, 1987). In addition, people who experience general chronic levels of stress or stress associated with life changes (e.g., death of a spouse, job change) show reduced memory performance, presumably because the stress causes preoccupation and distraction. Of course, the physical condition of the observer (e.g., intoxication, eyesight) may influence accuracy. A witness' expectations may also affect the ultimate accuracy of statements. That is, the way one recalls events is often the way one would expect events to occur or to be. Interestingly, in one study, subjects were asked to estimate a person's weight after being told some information about that person. Subjects' estimates of the person's weight were less when subjects were told that the person was a dancer than when they were told that the person was a truck driver (Christiaansen et al., 1983). Furthermore, the knowledge that a witness possesses regarding a particular object that is observed may also affect accuracy. For instance, an eyewitness of a robbery who knows little about guns might describe the gun held by the perpetrator as "big and shiny." An individual who is knowledgeable about guns may describe the weapon as "a blue metal .357 Glock semi-automatic." With regard to the demographic characteristics of witnesses and accuracy of their statements, age has been shown to be of most importance. Research shows that young children and the elderly generally have the poorest perception and memory performance. Young children have also been shown to be more suggestible than older children or adults. The research on the influence of gender on perception and memory is mixed. Generally it has been shown that men and women focus on different aspects of events, people, and situations. Men and women tend to focus on things of interest to them, which are oftentimes different.

Second, several factors may affect the *retention* of information. As noted, the most significant factor that may distort memory at this stage is misleading or inaccurate information obtained at or near the time of the event. The source of this information may be statements made by other witnesses, questions asked by authorities, or information contained in newspaper accounts or even television coverage. As an example of how the questions asked of a witness may affect the information retained in memory, Loftus et al. (1989) report a study during which subjects viewed a film and then were asked questions about it. When asked "How fast was the car going when it passed the barn?" many subjects responded as though they saw the car pass a barn when in fact a barn was not even shown in the film.

Third, with regard to the *retrieval* stage, several factors may serve to distort the accuracy of the eyewitness account. Of most significance is the manner in which the retrieval of information occurs. For example, the wording of questions used to elicit memory details may be influential. Loftus and Palmer (1974) conducted an experiment during which subjects viewed films of automobile accidents and then were asked questions about the events depicted in the films. When subjects were asked "About how fast were the cars going when they *smashed* into each other?" higher estimates of speed were provided than when questions that contained the words "collided," "bumped," "contacted," or "hit" instead of "smashed" were asked. Subjects who were asked about the cars "smashing" were also more likely to state that they saw broken glass, when actually there was no broken glass. Other studies have noted differences in asking questions with more subtle wording differences such as "Did you see a gun?" versus "Was there a gun?" (the former question suggests that there may have been a gun but that it may not have been seen), or "Did you see a broken headlight?" versus "Did you see the broken headlight?" In essence, leading questions may distort the information retrieved from a witness' memory (Loftus et al., 1989).

Guidelines for the Collection of Eyewitness Evidence

Given the multitude of factors that may affect the accuracy of eyewitness statements, and given that the courts are generally concerned about quality of evidence—to the point of not admitting it (e.g., hearsay)—one might expect that there would be a number of barriers to the admission of eyewitness evidence in court. This, however, is generally not the case, although the courts have recognized the potential problems associated with eyewitness testimony. In the case of *Neil* v. *Biggers* (1972), when a rape victim identified her attacker on the basis of a show-up that took place seven months after the crime, the Supreme Court let the conviction stand and identified five criteria to be considered in determining the accuracy of an eyewitness identification of a suspect. They are as follows:

- The eyewitness' opportunity to view
- The attention paid by the eyewitness
- The accuracy of the witness' preliminary description of the culprit
- The certainty of the eyewitness
- The amount of time between the event and the attempt to identify

These factors have been criticized as an inadequate basis on which to judge the accuracy of eyewitness identifications. Among the criticisms are that four of the five factors rely on the memory of the eyewitness, which is exactly what is questioned in an eyewitness identification.

There are other safeguards in place that may, ideally, prevent false eyewitness identifications from leading to miscarriages of justice. For example, defendants have the right to counsel at lineups, motions can be made by the defense to suppress eyewitness evidence, eyewitnesses may be cross-examined, and experts can be called to testify on the problems associated with accurate eyewitness identifications. In many respects, however, these safeguards are incomplete and inadequate (Wells et al., 1998). The right to counsel exists only at lineups, not photo arrays or show-ups, and most identifications of suspects are from show-ups and photos, not physical lineups. Motions to suppress eyewitness evidence are rarely successful. Cross-examination of eyewitnesses may not be helpful when witnesses are trying to be truthful but are simply mistaken. Eyewitness expert testimony may not overcome the influential nature of eyewitness evidence, it may not be allowed by the judge, and it may be prohibitively expensive (Wells et al., 1998).

Given the potential inaccuracy of eyewitness identifications and the current safeguards in place, Wells et al. (1998) identify several guidelines for the collection of eyewitness identification evidence (these guidelines are also outlined in the NIJ document *Eyewitness Evidence: A Guide for Law Enforcement* [1999a]). These guidelines are based on theories about human memory, research findings of eyewitness identification studies, and the science of testing. The aim of the guidelines is to improve the quality of the evidence and, accordingly, to reduce the risk of mistaken identifications. The authors note that just as there are procedures and rules that must be followed in collecting and presenting physical evidence such as fingerprints and DNA, there should be rules and procedures in collecting and presenting eyewitness identification evidence through lineups and photo spreads.

First, "the person who conducts the lineup or photo-spread should not; be aware of which member of the lineup or photo-spread is the suspect" (Wells et al. 1998; p. 627). This recommendation relates to the possibility that an investigator may explicitly or, more likely, unknowingly lead a witness to select a particular lineup member. The process of identification may be one filled with anxiety and uncertainty for the witness, and hence the witness may be quite interested and responsive to the cues of the investigator. Wells et al. (1998) cite research that shows that subtle cues such as smiling and other nonverbal actions can call attention to a particular photograph and can lead to false identification. Also, previous research has shown that feedback given to the witness about the selection (e.g., "Good, you identified the right guy") can have dramatic effects on the witness' confidence about the accuracy of the selection and the witness' confidence about his or her ability to identify the suspect (Wells and Bradfield, 1998). This false confidence may translate into increased but unwarranted credibility of the witness in the minds of jurors. In addition, it is not out of the realm of possibility that investigators may knowingly say something to highlight or reinforce a particular person as the suspect/culprit. Consider the case of *South Carolina* v. *Washington* (1997). In this case, a detective investigating a robbery believed that a person by the name of James Washington was responsible for committing the crime. The detective obtained a picture of a person who he believed was James Washington and placed this picture along with pictures of five other "foils" in a photo lineup. He then showed it to the eyewitness and the eyewitness identified "James *Washington*" as the robber. Subsequent to this identification, it was determined that the picture thought to be of James Washington was, in fact, not James Washington; it was of a person who could not have had anything to do with the robbery. In addition, the person in the picture had no resemblance to the real James Washington. In examining the validity of this photo lineup, Wells et al. (1998) provided an actual picture of Washington to fifty people and asked them to select the person most similar to him from the original photo spread. Not one person identified the picture of the subject who was originally believed to be James Washington. What happened during the photo spread process? The detective who assembled and administered the photo spread probably facilitated, in some way, the identification of the wrong suspect.

If the person who administers the lineup does not know who the suspect is, then that person would not be able to provide any cues or other information to influence the selection, nor would that person be able to provide any feedback to the witness that might distort the witness' certainty or confidence in the selection. This precaution should allow eyewitness identification to be based on the eyewitness' memory, not external information. Hence, it should provide for a more valid lineup procedure.

Second, "eyewitnesses should be told explicitly that the person in question might not be in the lineup or photo-spread and therefore should not feel that they must make an identification. They should also be told that the person administering the lineup does not know which person is the suspect in the case" (Wells et al. 1998; p. 629). The first part of this recommendation relates to the research that shows that eyewitnesses are less likely to identify an innocent suspect if they are told that the actual culprit may not be in the lineup. The tendency to identify the person that most resembles the culprit, even if it is not the culprit, reflects the relative-judgment process discussed earlier. Research has shown that although this "warning" reduces the rate of incorrect selections in lineups in which the culprit is not present, it does not reduce the rate of correct selections when the culprit is present in the lineup. Of course, if all lineups included the actual culprit, this recommendation would be needless; however, one should not assume that this is, in fact, the case. If the investigator is certain that the culprit is included in the lineup, what is the purpose of the lineup? According to Wells et al. (1998), the actual perpetrator was not included in the lineups for all of the forty cases of false eyewitness identifications referenced earlier.

The second part of the recommendation, that witnesses "should be told that the person administering the lineup does not know which person is the suspect in the case," is related to the first recommendation. Simply, not only should the administrator of the lineup not know who the suspect is in the case, but the witness should be *told* that the administrator does not know who the suspect is in the case. This may prevent the eyewitness from trying to look to the administrator of the lineup for cues about which person to select.

Third, "the suspect should not stand out in the lineup or photo-spread as being different from the distractors based on the eyewitness' previous description of the culprit or based on other factors that would draw attention to the suspect" (Wells et al., 1998; p. 630). If the suspect stands out in some way from the others in the lineup, it may be difficult to determine whether the selection was based on true recognition or whether it was based on a unique factor (see www.uni.edu/psych/eyewitness.html for several examples of questionable photo lineups). With this reasoning, Wells et al. (1998) explain that they have "grave concerns about the use of show-ups" as a method of identification. Show-ups are clearly suggestive to the witness that a particular person is the suspect. In addition, "there is clear evidence that show-ups are more likely to yield false identifications than are properly constructed lineups" (Wells et al., 1998; p. 631). The Supreme Court has acknowledged the potential suggestive nature of show-ups but has generally ruled them to be acceptable police procedure.

Wells et al. (1998) explain that the validity of lineups can be tested through a mock witness procedure, although they do not actually recommend the use of such procedures in the field setting, presumably because of the logistic issues involved in such a "test." Wells (1993) describes the procedure in the following way:

Mock witnesses are people who are given the eyewitness's description of the culprit, shown the lineup, and asked to choose the person that they think the police suspect of the offense. If mock witnesses can use this limited information to infer which lineup member is suspected by the police, then one cannot assume that the eyewitness himself

EXHIBIT 7–4

THE FAR SIDE® BY GARY LARSON

"*That's* him! *That's* the one! ... I'd recognize that silly little hat anywhere!"

or herself used nothing beyond such scanty information to make an identification of the suspect. (p. 563)

In essence, if a mock witness can determine who the suspect is with limited information, then there may be a concern about whether the eyewitness' identification of the suspect was based on memory or the same deductive process apparently used by the mock witness. Therefore, the bottom line is that the distractors or "foils" included in the lineup should not necessarily look similar to the suspect; *they should be selected on the basis of the description provided to the investigators by the witness.* At the extreme, if foils are included so that they look like the suspect, one could conceivably have the suspect and his clones included in the lineup. Clearly the chances of a false identification may be high in such a circumstance. On the other hand, verbal descriptions of perpetrators provided by witnesses tend to be quite general, and inclusion of individuals on this basis may allow people with different appearances to be included in the lineup.

There are several potential problems with this approach to constructing lineups. First, what if the description provided by the witness does not actually match the description of the suspect? In such a situation, it is recommended that a blend of the description of the culprit and the features of the suspect be considered when selecting foils in the lineup (Wells et al., 1998). Second, what if the suspect has a unique feature (e.g., a facial scar) that the eyewitness did not mention? If the witness did not mention a unique feature, then it may not be necessary to replicate that feature across the members of the lineup. If the unique feature is recognized by the witness, memory recall may be the reason. Third, what if the witness describes the perpetrator as having a unique feature (e.g., a particular tattoo)? In this case, it may not be necessary to conduct a lineup. With a specific and unique description, there may be little doubt about the identity of the suspect. Lineups are useful when the witness' description of the perpetrator is vague and when the identity of the perpetrator is uncertain. Finally, what if there is more than one witness and they provide conflicting descriptions of the perpetrator? In this situation, it is recommended by Wells et al. (1998) that separate lineups be constructed for each witness, based on the description of the perpetrator provided by each witness.

The final recommendation offered by Wells et al. (1998) is that "a clear statement should be taken from the eyewitness at the time of the identification and prior to any feedback as to his or her confidence that the identified person is the actual culprit" (p. 635). This statement may take the form of a response to the question: On a scale of one to ten, with ten being absolute certainty and one being absolute uncertainty, how confident are you that the person you identified is the actual culprit? The confidence expressed by the witness at the time of the identification may be the single most important factor in judging the credibility of the eyewitness and the accuracy of the identification in further proceedings (e.g., at trial). However, as noted earlier, confidence of a witness about an identification can be affected substantially by events that occur after the identification that have nothing to do with the witness' memory. Simply stated, confidence should be based on memory, not outside forces. A clear statement from the witness along with the administrator not knowing who the suspect is in the lineup, should help provide a valid representation of confidence in the selection.

It is explained by Wells et al. (1998) that the cost of implementing these four guidelines would be minimal, although the benefits could be substantial. Most important, according to Wells et al. (1998), these procedures do not reduce the probability of identifying the guilty party but they do serve to protect innocent suspects.

The authors also comment on two other issues in the identification process: the use of sequential lineups and the practice of videotaping lineups. Wells et al. (1998) support the use of both practices but do not consider them as significant as their four primary recommendations. The use of sequential lineups involves the eyewitness viewing one lineup member at a time and determining whether that person is the perpetrator. Research shows that this procedure produces fewer mistaken identifications but does not reduce the rate of accurate identifications. The recommendations presented earlier, however, overcome most of the problems of traditional lineup procedures so that sequential lineups would not be necessary with the recommendations implemented. Videotaping lineups may also offer numerous benefits; however, videotaping by itself would not lessen the chance of false eyewitness identification. In addition, it is unclear how videotaping may affect the behavior of witnesses.

Videotaping may raise anxiety and actually lessen the chances of accurate eyewitness identification (Wells et al., 1998).

Investigative Tools in Interviewing

Hypnosis

Hypnosis is most often simply viewed as an altered state of consciousness that is characterized by increased responsiveness to suggestion (Orne et al., 1984). A more elaborate definition is provided by Goldenson (1984):

> [Hypnosis is] a superficial or deep trance state resembling sleep, induced by suggestions of relaxation and concentrated attention to a single object. The subject becomes highly suggestible and responsive to the hypnotist's influence, and can be induced to recall forgotten events, become insensitive to pain, control vasomotor changes and, in the hands of an experienced hypnotherapist, gain relief from tensions, anxieties and other psychological symptoms. (p. 358)

Hypnosis can be used in the therapeutic setting as well as in the criminal investigative setting. The practice is used in the therapeutic context most often to identify and deal with conflict experienced by the subject through age regression. For purposes of criminal investigation, hypnosis focuses on enhancing memory recall of a witness with regard to an actual criminal event (Council on Scientific Affairs, 1985; Reiser, 1989). For investigative purposes, there are three approaches to obtaining hypnotically elicited testimony: free recall, during which the hypnotized witness is asked for a complete and unstructured account of everything observed; structured recall, during which the witness is asked specific questions about observations; and recognition, during which the witness is asked to recognize or identify certain aspects of a situation or event (e.g., clothing worn by the perpetrator) (Sanders and Simmons, 1983).

The theory of hypnosis is that memory occurs at the conscious and subconscious levels. Details about observations are recorded and stored at both levels at the same time. However, a person may not know what has been encoded in the subconscious memory—or, as a defensive mechanism, conscious memories may be pushed to the subconscious level. Hypnosis is a method of retrieving subconscious observations (Reiser, 1989).

Various techniques may be used to induce hypnosis. Most of these include "instructing the individual to focus attention, to concentrate on the hypnotist's voice, to relax, and eventually to close the eyes and imagine what the hypnotist is suggesting" (Orne et al., 1984; p. 175). When under hypnosis, "the subject's attention is intensely focused on the hypnotist, and there is an increased tendency to please the hypnotist and to comply with both explicit and implicit demands in the hypnotic context" (Orne et al., 1984; p. 175). As for investigative hypnosis specifically, the most widely practiced method is the television technique (Scheflin and Sapiro, 1989). As described by the Council on Scientific Affairs (1985):

Once hypnotized, the subject is told to imagine a television screen in his mind and that he will soon begin to see a documentary of the to-be remembered event. As in a sporting event on television, he will be able to stop motion, go fast forward or backward, and "zoom in" in order to see any detail that might otherwise not be clear. Finally, it is explained that, while he may see himself in this documentary and accurately observe what happens, he need not experience any of the troublesome feelings of pain that may have occurred at the time, but rather will see in an objective manner the events that transpired. (p. 1919)

This technique is controversial because it encourages the hypnotized subject to imagine and fantasize, which may in turn lead to the subject providing inaccurate information.

How accurate is hypnotically elicited information? Most research has come to the conclusion that hypnotically elicited testimony is deficient, especially when leading or even specific questions are asked of the subject (Sanders and Simmons, 1983; Steblay and Bothwell, 1994). The reason for this is that hypnotized subjects are, by definition, more susceptible to suggestion. As Orne et al. (1984) explain, "subjects in the hypnotic situation feel relaxed and less responsible for what they say because they believe that the hypnotist is an expert and somehow in control. The hypnotist in turn makes certain that subjects cannot fail" (p. 176). Furthermore, subjects wish to please the hypnotist—to receive reassurance—so information may be provided by the subject until such feedback is received. This process can readily result in fabrications or false information, often referred to as *confabulation*. For example,

> [i]f during hypnosis, an individual is asked to "look at" an event 100 yards away using hallucinated binoculars, he or she may describe in detail the pattern on the necktie of a participant in that event, despite the fact that such a "perception" exceeds the limits of visual acuity. Needless to say, the pattern may have nothing to do with the individual's necktie unless the hypnotized person had an opportunity to see it previously. Without prior information of such details, the hypnotized subject will nonetheless respond to the suggestion to observe with binoculars by hallucinating or imagining details of the event. (Orne et al., 1984; p. 177)

Reiser (1989), an advocate of the use of hypnosis for investigative purposes, explains that in most cases when investigative hypnosis is used there are no suspects. Hence, "it is impossible to suggest to a witness what is not known by the investigator" (p. 158). Clearly, as illustrated in the binoculars example, suggestions may be more subtle than the provision of specific case information to a witness.

Steblay and Bothwell (1994) conducted a meta-analysis of sixteen studies that examined the effectiveness of hypnosis in criminal investigations. Based on their analyses, the researchers concluded the following:

- Hypnotized subjects performed better (i.e., provided more accurate information) than control subjects in free recall situations, but the difference was minimal.

- In structured recall situations during which leading questions were asked, hypnotized subjects provided less accurate information than control subjects.
- In recognition (i.e., lineup) situations, hypnotized subjects were not more likely to make accurate identifications than control subjects. In fact, several of the studies showed that hypnotized subjects were significantly less likely than control subjects to respond correctly.
- Despite the fact that hypnotized subjects usually provided more inaccurate information than control subjects, hypnotized subjects were more often more confident about the accuracy of their recall.

On the basis of their study, Steblay and Bothwell (1994) conclude that "hypnosis is not necessarily a source of inaccurate information; at worst it may be a source of inaccurate information provided with confident testimony" (p. 649).

Others are more negative on the use of hypnosis for investigative purposes. For example, consider the findings of the Council on Scientific Affairs (1985) of the American Medical Association. "[W]hen hypnosis is used to refresh recollection, one of the following outcomes occurs: (1) hypnosis produces recollections that are not substantially different from non-hypnotic recollections; (2) it yields recollections that are more inaccurate than non-hypnotic memory; or, most frequently, (3) it results in more information being reported, but these recollections contain both accurate and inaccurate details" (p. 1921). Accordingly, the Council on Scientific Affairs (1985) concluded that "[t]he use of hypnosis with witnesses and victims may have serious consequences for the legal process when testimony is based on material that is elicited from a witness who has been hypnotized for purposes of refreshing recollection" (p. 1918).

With regard to the admissibility of hypnotically elicited testimony, there is variation in how the courts treat hypnotized witnesses and the resulting evidence. The most common rule is that previously hypnotized witnesses may testify regarding their recollections prior to hypnosis, but the hypnotically elicited testimony itself is not admissible in court. As such, it is necessary for the police to record the witness' account of the event prior to hypnosis because only this testimony is admissible. In some states, any testimony from witnesses who have been hypnotized is inadmissible in court. In other states, hypnotically elicited testimony is admissible, and virtually no particular requirements for collecting or introducing such testimony are necessary. Finally, some states allow hypnotically elicited testimony in court as long as certain safeguards and procedures are used in obtaining and presenting it. Federal courts also vary in their treatment of hypnotically elicited testimony, although these courts have most often adopted rulings that are consistent with the particular corresponding state court position.

Given the potential value of and problems with hypnotically elicited testimony, as well as the rules of the state and federal courts, there have been numerous recommendations offered to guide properly the collection of hypnotically elicited evidence (see Council on Scientific Affairs [1985]). First, before being hypnotized, recollections of the witness should be obtained and recorded. As discussed later, other techniques of enhancing memory recall (e.g., cognitive interview) should first be attempted. As explained by Sanders and Simmons

(1983), "it is recommended that the use of hypnosis in criminal investigations be limited to eliciting testimony from witnesses with mind blocks and be used only as a last resort" (p. 70). Second, hypnosis should be conducted by a psychiatrist or psychologist skilled in the use of the method. Third, great caution needs to be taken to ensure that suggestions not be made to the hypnotized subject. It must be understood that hypnotized subjects are quite susceptible to suggestion, even in subtle ways. Fourth, a complete record of the session should be made, preferably on videotape. Fifth, only the psychiatrist or psychologist who is conducting the hypnosis should be present when the subject is hypnotized. This is a further attempt to protect the hypnotized subject from external cues that may influence the testimony provided. Finally, the hypnotist should first obtain unpressured free recall from the subject (e.g., "Go on . . ." "Continue . . ." "Yes . . .") and then, if necessary, specific but nonleading questions may be asked. When asking questions, it should be made clear to the hypnotized subject that the response "I don't know" is acceptable. It is suggested that these guidelines will provide for the collection of more valid hypnotically elicited testimony. As such, this evidence may be more useful in the criminal investigation and judicial process.

Cognitive Interview

Another method of enhancing witness recall is cognitive interviewing. The cognitive interview is an approach that encourages the witness to reinstate the context in which the observed event took place and to search through memory systematically and methodologically for details of the event. It is the interviewer's responsibility to guide the witness through this process and to assist in the retrieval of information (Fisher and Geiselman, 1992).

As part of the cognitive interview approach, several techniques are used to facilitate memory recall. First, as noted, the witness is encouraged to recreate the context of the original event. The context consists not only of the event itself but also the physical and psychological characteristics of the environments in which it occurred. An interviewer can assist in the recreation of the context through instructions. For example, the interviewer can tell the witness, "Try to put yourself back into the same situation as when the crime was committed. Think about where you were standing at the time, what you were thinking about, what you were feeling, and what the room looked like" (Fisher and Geiselman, 1992; p. 100). The witness may be asked to think about his activities prior to, during, and after the event, even about activities that took place hours or days before or after the event. Again, the attempt is to get the witness fully immersed in the situation about which details are to be recalled.

Second, the witness is encouraged to concentrate deeply in a focused manner. Concentration is critical when searching through memory for details. As suggested by Fisher and Geiselman (1992), the following statement may serve this end:

> I realize that this is a difficult task, to remember the details of the crime. All of the details are stored in your mind, but you will have to concentrate very hard to recall them. You have all the information, so I'm going to expect you to do most of the work

here. I understand that this may be difficult, but try to concentrate as hard as you can. (p. 103)

Beyond encouragement, another important factor that is necessary to facilitate concentration is avoiding interruptions. Interruptions on the part of the interviewer break the concentration of witnesses and inhibit recall of information. Fisher and Geiselman (1992) identify the avoidance of interruptions as "the single most important skill" in interviewing. Focused concentration can also be encouraged through open-ended questions and by maintaining eye contact with the witness.

Third, the witness should be encouraged to search memory thoroughly—to keep looking. If you lose your car keys and after a couple of minutes of searching you cannot find them, you do not just give up, right? So it is with witnesses searching for details of the crime in a cognitive interview. A thorough search of memory can be encouraged by avoiding certain behaviors such as (see Fisher and Geiselman [1992, pp. 107–108]):

- Opening the interview with a request for factual details, instead of a more personal introduction
- Indicating at the outset that the interview will take only a short time
- Constantly checking the time
- Leaving the radio on and interrupting frequently to listen to incoming calls
- Attending to issues related to other cases
- Fidgeting while sitting
- Standing during the interview (especially by an exit door) when it would be more appropriate to sit
- Speaking quickly
- Asking questions immediately after the [witness] stops responding
- Interrupting in the middle of the [witness'] response

Fourth, varied retrieval of the event should be encouraged. Most common and most natural is for a witness to recall the event in chronological order. However, describing events in reverse order requires more concentration and more thought (similar to reciting the alphabet in reverse order) but additional details may be recalled. Reverse order may also reduce extraneous or even deceptive information (Bennett and Hess, 1991). Another varied retrieval method is to ask the witness to slice the event into "frames"—like pictures—and then ask the witness to describe each of the frames. Yet another method is to ask the witness to provide a description of events from the perspective or location of someone else in the area in which the crime occurred. The interviewer may ask the witness to describe the event like viewing a film that was taken from an angle different from that of the witness (Bennett and Hess, 1991). This technique may provide additional details about the event and may also reduce the trauma associated with the crime. However, this technique may also encourage the witness to fabricate information or to provide inaccurate information. Accordingly, the interviewer must remind the witness to report only the events and details actually observed.

Finally, during a cognitive interview, other techniques may be used to enhance the recollection of specific pieces of information (e.g., faces, clothing, vehicles, license plate numbers). Even though a witness may not be able to recall certain specific information, the witness may have some partial memory about the information. Focused questions may be used to help retrieve this potentially useful information. For example, in recalling a license plate of a car involved in a crime, the witness may be asked about the features of the characters on the plate, such as: Was the sequence composed mainly of digits or numbers? Were the letters consonants? Did two letters occur twice? What shape did the first or any other letter have? Was the digit pattern familiar in any way (similar to a friend's phone number)? What color were the characters and the background? And so forth (Fisher and Geiselman, 1992). This sort of probing may help stimulate the witness' memory.

The cognitive interviewing approach is quite different from the approach taken during standard police interviews. Whereas cognitive interviewing encourages the witness to explore deep memory and is open ended in nature, the standard interviewing approach encourages only superficial exploration and is more closed ended in nature. Fisher et al. (1987) analyzed numerous police interviews with robbery victims and witnesses and found numerous problems that inhibited memory recall on the part of the subjects. First, interviewers frequently interrupted witnesses' descriptions and accounts of the event. This led to witnesses providing short, quick answers and encouraged witnesses to be less focused. Second, interviewers asked too many short-answer, closed-ended questions. On average, interviewers asked three open-ended questions (e.g., Can you describe the subject's clothing?) and twenty-six short-answer questions (e.g., What color was the subject's shirt?). The short-answer questions may help keep the interview on track but require less concentration on the part of the witness and encourage short, incomplete answers. In addition, because the witness is placed in a passive role with such questions, if the interviewer does not think to ask a particular question, the witness may not provide the information. Missed information may be the likely result. The third common and significant problem with traditional police interviews is the inappropriate, arbitrary, or rigid sequencing of questions. The researchers found that interviewers often used a sequence of questions that was not congruent with the witness' memory of the event. The researchers explain that on one occasion, a witness began describing the suspect by providing an estimate of the subject's height. She was interrupted by the investigator and asked to begin instead with an estimate of the subject's age. When the researchers asked the investigator about this, the investigator responded that there was really no reason why he interrupted the witness, other than that age was asked about first on the report that he was required to complete. Again, the rigid sequencing of questions may inhibit accurate memory recall.

Numerous other problems, although less common, were also evident during the interviews. First, interviewers sometimes used negative phrasing (e.g., "You don't remember, do you, if . . . ?"), suggesting to the witness that interviewer does not believe the witness can recall or remember the details. This sort of questioning also makes it easy for the witness to respond "I don't know," and discourages a thorough search of memory. Second, investigators sometimes used nonneutral or leading questions (e.g., Was the gun silver?), which may suggest to the witness that the investigator's description is correct, and may also bias the witness' later recollection of the event. Third, the researchers observed interviewers using inappropriate language—wording that was too formal ("Did you have occasion earlier today to witness . . .), too stylized ("Calling your attention to the incident . . ."), or too intelligent ("So you were in a *supine* position?") (Fisher et al., 1987; p. 182). A fourth problem was the rapid rate of questioning. On average, there was one second between the end of the witness' answer and the interviewer's next question. This clearly inhibited witnesses from elaborating or clarifying previous statements. Fifth, on occasion, the researchers observed interviewers making judgmental, rude, or insensitive comments to the witnesses (e.g., "They [previous investigators] thought that it was funny that you had all of your clothes on and [the suspect] didn't have all his clothes on") (Fisher et al., 1987; p. 183). Rapport and trust can be quickly destroyed with such comments. Finally, there was at times a lack of follow-up on potential leads. For instance, on one occasion a witness stated that the suspect "looked like a librarian," but there was no follow-up questioning to explore the meaning of this descriptive statement.

As discussed by Fisher et al. (1987) the structure of a traditional police interview is conducive to note taking and report writing. Traditional police interviews also take relatively little time to complete. With cognitive interviews, on the other hand, it is more difficult for an interviewer to record the potential multitude of details provided and, in general, cognitive interviews take considerably more time to conduct. In addition, the cognitive interview approach takes more mental concentration on the part of the interviewer and requires more flexibility. However, cognitive interview techniques can be easily learned, cognitive interviewing requires little training, the method is easily administered, witnesses should have few reservations about participating in such an interview, and it raises few legal issues compared with hypnosis.

The most significant benefit of the cognitive interviewing approach is that it has been shown to be an effective tool in enhancing memory recall. In a study that examined the amount and accuracy of information obtained by detectives in standard police interviews and cognitive interviews, it was demonstrated that after being trained in the cognitive interview approach, detectives were able to obtain forty-seven percent more information from witnesses and this information was deemed highly accurate (corroborated with other independent information produced in the investigation) (Fisher et al., 1989). In another study, subjects viewed a film of a simulated crime and were interviewed forty-eight hours later by law enforcement personnel. Those subjects who were interviewed about the crime through the cognitive interview approach recalled twenty to thirty-five percent more (correct) information than the subjects who underwent a standard police interview (Fisher et al., 1987). In short, as stated by Geiselman and Fisher (1989), the research confirms "that cognitive interviewing reliably enhances the completeness of a witness's recollection, without increasing the number of incorrect or confabulated bits of information generated" (p. 213).

Besides the method used to elicit information from a witness, there are other principles and basic rules associated with conducting effective police interviews. First, witnesses should be interviewed one at a time so that independent accounts from each witness can be received, compared, and evaluated. Reasonable precautions should be taken to prevent witnesses from sharing information with each other. Second, interviews should be conducted in places that are away from distractions. The witness' work location is generally a poor place to conduct an investigative interview; the police station or even the witness' home are generally better places. Third, interviews should be conducted as soon as possible after the event except under extraordinary circumstances (e.g., health problems). This should allow information about the event to be more easily recalled (Geiselman and Fisher [1989]). Finally, it is important for investigators to build a rapport with witnesses. Sandoval and Adams (2001) suggest that interviewers engage in matching or mirroring techniques in an effort to build rapport. That is, interviewers should match or mirror the witness' kinesics (e.g., display the same sort of body language and posture as the witness), language (e.g., use similar words, phrases, and expressions), and paralanguage (e.g., use a similar rate, volume, and pitch of speech). In addition, in building rapport, it is important for the interviewer to provide feedback to the witness that suggests an understanding of what the witness has experienced and shows concern for the witness. The interviewer can share similar personal experiences, and the interviewer and witness can discuss other things they have in common. Although the witness and the interviewer may have different immediate goals, emphasis should be placed on identifying common goals and team building. Information that comes from witnesses is potentially extremely valuable for investigators and prosecutors in proving guilt. Such information is similar to physical evidence and confessions in terms of its influence.

Questions for Discussion and Review

1. What is an investigative interview? What is the goal of an interview?

2. What is the difference between a primary and a secondary witness?

3. What are the primary methods of establishing an eyewitness identification?

4. What are the relative advantages and disadvantages of the use of Identikit and sketch artist drawings in identifying suspects?

5. What is a relative-judgment process and how does it relate to the lineup identification task?

6. What are some of the factors during the acquisition stage that may affect the accuracy of eyewitness accounts? During the retention stage? During the retrieval stage?

7. How might the wording of questions asked of witnesses affect the accuracy of responses?

8. What are the five criteria to be considered in determining the accuracy of eyewitness identifications according to *Neil* v. *Biggers* (1972)? What is the problem with these criteria as a basis on which to judge eyewitness accuracy?

9. What are the four recommended procedures for conducting lineups? What is the rationale of each?

10. How may hypnosis be used in criminal investigations?

11. How accurate is hypnotically elicited information? Explain.

12. What is a cognitive interview and how does it differ from a standard police interview?

13. What are the primary costs and benefits of the cognitive interview approach?

Related Internet Sites

www.uni.edu/psych/eyewitness.html
This is the address of the eyewitness identification laboratory at the University of Northern Iowa. Much information about eyewitness identifications is provided at the site, including examples of photographic lineups, a library with research reports and articles on eyewitness identification, and related links.

www.psychology.iastate.edu/faculty/gwells/homepage.htm
This link takes you to the homepage of Dr. Garry Wells, a recognized expert on issues relating to eyewitness identification. Numerous news articles, research reports, and other informative sources are provided at this site.

www.innocenceproject.org
The Innocence Project is a nonprofit legal clinic located at the Benjamin N. Cardozo School of Law. The project handles cases when postconviction DNA testing may lead to the overturning of guilty verdicts. Information on more than 100 cases of false convictions is provided. Other information on legislation and other related links are also provided.

www.hypnosis.org
This is the link to the American Board of Hypnotherapy. It includes a discussion board and links to other hypnosis-related web sites.

INTERROGATIONS

OBJECTIVES

After reading this chapter you will be able to

- Differentiate between a "successful" and an "unsuccessful" interrogation

- Explain how an interrogation is essentially a task of persuasion

- Identify and discuss the various forms of police deception in interrogations

- Identify and discuss the ingredients of a successful interrogation

- Discuss why adequate time needs to be spent in an interrogation

- Discuss rationalization, projection, and minimization (RPM) in interrogations

- Differentiate between the sledgehammer and feather approach in interrogations

- Identify the nine steps in an interrogation, according to Inbau et al. (1986)

- Identify the difference between emotional and nonemotional offenders, and the significance of the distinction

- Identify the themes most effectively used with emotional offenders and with nonemotional offenders according to Inbau et al. (1986)

- Discuss the reasons why a person may falsely confess

- Discuss the relationship between false confessions and Miranda

- Discuss the general theory underlying the detection of deception

- Identify and discuss nonverbal behaviors commonly indicative of deception

- Identify and discuss verbal behaviors commonly indicative of deception

- Describe the stages of the polygraph examination process

- Compare the relevant–irrelevant test (RIT) polygraph methodology with the control question technique (CQT) polygraph methodology

- Discuss the accuracy and "usefulness" of the polygraph

- Differentiate between false-positive errors and false-negative errors in polygraph examinations

- Discuss the difficulties in establishing the accuracy of the polygraph

- Identify the factors that may affect the outcome of polygraph examinations

- Discuss the admissibility of polygraph results in court

- Discuss voice stress analysis and its accuracy as a method of detecting deception

IMPORTANT TERMS

Custodial interrogation

Confession

"Successful" interrogation

Interrogation plan

Interrogation themes and tactics

RPM

Feather and sledgehammer approach in interrogations

Emotional and nonemotional offenders

Denials and objections in interrogations

False confession

"Fight-or-flight" syndrome

Kinesics as a tool to recognize deception

Emblems

Illustrators

Congruence

Incongruence

"Created jobs"

Verbal behavior as a tool to recognize deception

Polygraph

RIT

CQT

Relevant and control questions in a polygraph examination

False-positive and false-negative errors in polygraph examinations

Voice stress analysis

INTRODUCTION

The following are excerpts from the interrogation of O.J. Simpson by Los Angeles Police Department Detectives Tom Lange and Philip Vannatter during the early afternoon of June 13, 1994. Recall from Chapter 6, Simpson's ex-wife, Nicole Brown Simpson, and her friend Ronald Goldman were murdered outside her home in Brentwood, Los Angeles, at approximately 10:30 PM on June 12, 1994. The initial investigation suggested that Simpson could have been the perpetrator (e.g., blood drops found at the crime scene indicated that the perpetrator was bleeding, blood was found on Simpson's Bronco and at his house, and a bloody glove that was found at the crime scene matched the one found on Simpson's property). Detectives Lange and Vannatter spent thirty-two minutes questioning Simpson about his possible role in the double homicide. This transcript provides a good example of, by most accounts, a poorly conducted interrogation, and is illustrative for this purpose. The interrogation transcript presented here has been edited for length. It begins after Simpson has been read his Miranda warnings and he agrees to waive them. The asterisks indicate a break in the sequencing of questions.

> **VANNATTER:** Okay. All right, what we're gonna do is, we want to . . . We're investigating, obviously, the death of your ex-wife and another man.
> **LANGE:** Someone told us that.
> ***** Questions about Simpson and his relationship with Nicole Brown Simpson, their divorce, and their attempts at reconciliation
> ***** Questions about a previous domestic violence incident between Simpson and Nicole
> ***** Questions about Nicole's maid who lived at her house
> **LANGE:** Phil, what do you think? Maybe we can just recount last night . . .

VANNATTER: Yeah. When was the last time you saw Nicole?

SIMPSON: We were leaving a dance recital. She took off and I was talking to her parents.

VANNATTER: Where was the dance recital?

SIMPSON: Paul Revere High School.

VANNATTER: And was that for one of your children?

SIMPSON: Yeah, for my daughter Sydney.

VANNATTER: And what time was that yesterday?

SIMPSON: It ended about six-thirty, quarter to seven, something like that, you know, in the ballpark, right in that area. And they took off.

VANNATTER: They?

SIMPSON: Her and her family, her mother and father, sisters, my kids, you know.

VANNATTER: And then you went your separate way?

SIMPSON: Yeah, actually she left, and then they came back and her mother got in a car with her, and the kids all piled into her sister's car, and they . . .

VANNATTER: Was Nicole driving?

SIMPSON: Yeah.

VANNATTER: What kind of car was she driving?

SIMPSON: Her black car, a Cherokee, a Jeep Cherokee.

VANNATTER: What were you driving?

SIMPSON: My Rolls-Royce, my Bentley.

VANNATTER: Do you own that Ford Bronco that sits outside?

SIMPSON: Hertz owns it, and Hertz lets me use it.

VANNATTER: So that's your vehicle, the one that was parked there on the street?

SIMPSON: Mm hmm.

VANNATTER: And it's actually owned by Hertz?

SIMPSON: Hertz, yeah.

VANNATTER: Who's the primary driver on that? You?

SIMPSON: I drive it, the housekeeper drives it, you know, it's kind of a . . .

VANNATTER: All-purpose-type vehicle?

SIMPSON: All purpose, yeah. It's the only one that my insurance will allow me to let anyone else drive.

VANNATTER: Okay.

LANGE: When you drive it, where do you park it at home? Where it is now, it was in the street or something?

SIMPSON: I always park in the street.

LANGE: You never take it in the . . . ?

SIMPSON: Oh, rarely. I mean, I'll bring it in and switch the stuff, you know, and stuff like that. I did that yesterday, you know.

LANGE: When did you last drive it?

SIMPSON: Yesterday.

VANNATTER: What time yesterday?

SIMPSON: In the morning, in the afternoon.

VANNATTER: Okay, you left her, you're saying, about six-thirty or seven, or she left the recital?

SIMPSON: Yeah.

VANNATTER: And you spoke with her parents?

SIMPSON: Yeah.

VANNATTER: Okay, what time did you leave the recital?

SIMPSON: Right about that time. We were all leaving. We were all leaving then. Her mother said something about me joining them for dinner, and I said no thanks.

VANNATTER: Where did you go from there, O.J.?

SIMPSON: Ah, home, home for a while, got my car for a while, tried to find my girlfriend for a while, came back to the house.

VANNATTER: Who was home when you got home?

SIMPSON: Kato.

VANNATTER: Kato? Anybody else? Was your daughter there, Arnelle?

SIMPSON: Arnelle, yeah.

VANNATTER: So what time do you think you got back home, actually physically got home?

SIMPSON: Seven-something.

VANNATTER: Seven-something? And then you left, and . . .

SIMPSON: Yeah, I'm trying to think, did I leave? You know I'm always . . . I had to run and get my daughter some flowers. I was actually doing the recital, so I rushed and got her some flowers, and I came home, and then I called Paula as I was going to her house, and Paula wasn't home.

VANNATTER: Paula is your girlfriend?

SIMPSON: Girlfriend, yeah.

***** Questions about Paula, the spelling of her name, and her address; the reason why he was supposed to be in Chicago that morning (to play in a charity golf tournament)

VANNATTER: Oh, okay. What time did you leave last night, leave the house?

SIMPSON: To go to the airport?

VANNATTER: Mmm hmm.

SIMPSON: About . . . the limo was supposed to be there at ten forty-five. Normally, they get there a little earlier. I was rushing around, somewhere between there and eleven.

VANNATTER: So approximately ten forty-five to eleven.

SIMPSON: Eleven o'clock, yeah, somewhere in that area.

VANNATTER: And you went by limo?

SIMPSON: Yeah.

VANNATTER: Who's the limo service?

SIMPSON: Ah, you have to ask my office.

VANNATTER: Did you converse with the driver at all? Did you talk to him?

SIMPSON: No, he was a new driver. Normally, I have a regular driver I drive with and converse. No, just about rushing to the airport, about how I live my life on airplanes, and hotels, that type of thing.

***** Questions about his flight to Chicago

LANGE: So yesterday you did drive the white Bronco?

SIMPSON: Mmm hmm.

LANGE: And where did you park it when you brought it home?

SIMPSON: Ah, the first time probably by the mailbox. I'm trying to think, or did I bring it in the driveway? Normally, I park it by the mailbox, sometimes . . .

LANGE: On Ashford or Ashland?

SIMPSON: On Ashford, yeah.

LANGE: Where did you park yesterday for the last time, do you remember?

SIMPSON: Right where it is.

LANGE: Where is it now?

SIMPSON: Yeah.

LANGE: Where, on . . . ?

SIMPSON: Right on the street there.

LANGE: On Ashford?

SIMPSON: No, on Rockingham.

LANGE: You parked it there?

SIMPSON: Yes.

LANGE: About what time was that?

SIMPSON: Eight-something, seven . . . eight, nine o'clock, I don't know, right in that area.

LANGE: Did you take it to the recital?

SIMPSON: No.

LANGE: What time was the recital?

SIMPSON: Over at about six-thirty. Like I said, I came home, I got my car, I was going to see my girlfriend. I was calling her, and she wasn't around.

LANGE: So you drove the . . . you came home in the Rolls and then you got in the Bronco?

SIMPSON: In the Bronco 'cause my phone was in the Bronco. And because it's a Bronco. It's a Bronco, it's what I drive, you know. I'd rather drive it than any other car. And, you know, as I was going over there, I called her a couple of times, and she wasn't there, and I left a message, and then I checked my messages, and there were no messages. She wasn't there, and she may have to leave town. Then I came back and ended up sitting with Kato.

LANGE: Okay. What time was this again that you parked the Bronco?

SIMPSON: Eight-something, maybe. He hadn't done a Jacuzzi, we had . . . went and got a burger, and I'd come home and kind of leisurely got ready to go. I mean, we'd done a few things . . .

LANGE: You weren't in a hurry when you came back with the Bronco?

SIMPSON: No.

LANGE: The reason I ask you, the car was parked kind of at a funny angle, stuck out in the street.

SIMPSON: Well, it's parked because . . . I don't know if it's a funny angle or what. It's parked because when I was hustling at the end of the day to get all my stuff, and I was getting my phone and everything off it, when I just pulled it out of the gate there, it's like, it's a tight turn.

LANGE: So you had it inside the compound, then?

SIMPSON: Yeah.

LANGE: Oh, okay.

SIMPSON: I brought it inside the compound to get my stuff out of it, and then I put it out, and I'd run back inside the gate before the gate closes.

**** Questions about the telephone number for O.J.'s office

VANNATTER: How did you get the injury on your hand?

SIMPSON: I don't know. The first time, when I was in Chicago and all, but at the house I was just running around.

VANNATTER: How did you do it in Chicago?

SIMPSON: I broke a glass. One of you guys had just called me, and I was in the bathroom, and I just went bonkers for a little bit.

LANGE: Is that how you cut it?

SIMPSON: Mmm, it was cut before, but I think I just opened it again. I'm not sure.

LANGE: Do you recall bleeding at all in your truck, in the Bronco?

SIMPSON: I recall bleeding at my house, and then I went to the Bronco. The last thing I did before I left, when I was rushing, was went and got my phone out of the Bronco.

LANGE: Mmm hmm. Where's the phone now?

SIMPSON: In my bag.

LANGE: You have it?

SIMPSON: In that black bag.

LANGE: You brought a bag with you here?

SIMPSON: Yeah, it's . . .

LANGE: So do you recall bleeding at all?

SIMPSON: Yeah, I mean, I knew I was bleeding, but it was no big deal. I bleed all the time. I play golf and stuff, so there's always something, nicks and stuff, here and there.

LANGE: So did you do anything? When did you put the Band-Aid on it?

SIMPSON: Actually, I asked the girl this morning for it.

LANGE: And she got it?

SIMPSON: Yeah, 'cause last night with Kato, when I was leaving, he was saying something to me, and I was rushing to get my phone, and I put a little thing on it, and it stopped.

***** Questions about who has keys to the Bronco and who was the last person to drive it

***** Questions about the last time Simpson was at Nicole's house

***** Questions about whether he had a conversation with Nicole last night and the nature of that conversation

VANNATTER: What were you wearing last night, O.J.?

SIMPSON: What did I wear on the golf course yesterday? Some of these kind of pants, some of these kind of pants, I mean I changed different for whatever it was. I just had on some . . .

VANNATTER: Just these black pants?

SIMPSON: Just these . . . They're called Bugle Boy.

VANNATTER: These aren't the pants?

SIMPSON: No.

VANNATTER: Where are the pants that you wore?

SIMPSON: They're hanging in my closet.

***** More questions about his pants and shoes

***** Questions about the expected length of his trip to Chicago

VANNATTER: O.J., we've got sort of a problem.

SIMPSON: Mmm hmm.

VANNATTER: We've got some blood on and in your car, we've got some blood at your house, and sort of a problem.

SIMPSON: Well, take my blood test.

LANGE: Well, we'd like to do that. We've got, of course, the cut on your finger that you aren't real clear on. Do [you] recall having that cut on your finger the last time you were at Nicole's house?

SIMPSON: A week ago?

LANGE: Yeah.

SIMPSON: No. It was last night.

LANGE: Okay, so last night you cut it?

VANNATTER: Somewhere after the recital?

SIMPSON: Somewhere when I was rushing to get out of my house.

VANNATTER: Okay, after the recital?

SIMPSON: Yeah.

VANNATTER: What do you think happened? Do you have any idea?

SIMPSON: I have no idea, man. You guys haven't told me anything. I have no idea. When you said to my daughter, who said something to me today that somebody else might have been involved, I have absolutely no idea what happened. I don't know how, why, or what. But you guys haven't told me anything. Every time I ask you guys, you say you're going to tell me in a bit.

VANNATTER: Well, we don't know a lot of the answers to these questions yet ourselves, O.J., okay?

SIMPSON: I've got a bunch of guns, guns all over the place. You can take them, they're all there, I mean, you can see them. I keep them in my car for an incident that happened a month ago that my in-laws, my wife, and everybody knows about that.

VANNATTER: What was that?

SIMPSON: Going down to . . . And cops down there know about it because I've told two marshals about it. At a mall, I was going down for a christening, and I had just left and it was like three-thirty in the morning and I'm in a lane, and also the car in front of me is going real slow, and I'm slowing down 'cause I figure he sees a cop, 'cause we were all going pretty fast and I'm going to change lanes, but there's a car next to me, and I can't change lanes. Then that goes for a while, and I'm going to slow down and go around him, but the car butts up to me, and I'm like caught between three cars. They were Oriental guys, and they were not letting me go anywhere. And finally I went on the shoulder, and I sped up, and then I held my phone up so they could see the light part of it, you know, 'cause I have tinted windows, and they kind of scattered, and I chased one of them for a while to make him think I was chasing him before I took off.

LANGE: Were you in the Bronco?

SIMPSON: No.

LANGE: What were you driving?

SIMPSON: My Bentley. It has tinted windows and all, so I figured they thought they had a nice little touch.

LANGE: Did you think they were trying to rip you off?

SIMPSON: Definitely, they were. And then the next thing, you know, Nicole and I went home. At four in the morning I got there to Laguna, and when we woke up, I told her about it, and told her parents about it, told everybody about it, you know? And when I saw two marshals at a mall, I walked up and told them about it.

VANNATTER: What did they do, make a report on it?

SIMPSON: They didn't know nothing. I mean, they'll remember me and remember I told them.

VANNATTER: Did Nicole mention that she'd been getting any threats lately to you? Anything she was concerned about or the kids' safety?

SIMPSON: To her?

VANNATTER: Yes.

SIMPSON: From?

VANNATTER: From anybody?

SIMPSON: No, not at all.

VANNATTER: Was she very security conscious? Did she keep that house locked up?

SIMPSON: Very.

VANNATTER: The intercom didn't work, apparently, right?

SIMPSON: I thought it worked.

VANNATTER: Oh, okay. Does the electronic buzzer work?

SIMPSON: The electronic buzzer works to let people in.

VANNATTER: Did you ever park in the rear when you go over there?

SIMPSON: Most of the time.

VANNATTER: You do park in the rear?

SIMPSON: Most time when I'm taking the kids there, I come right into the driveway, blow the horn, and she, or a lot of times the housekeeper, either the housekeeper opens or they'll keep a garage door open up on the top of the thing, you know, but that's when I'm dropping the kids off, and I'm not going in, and sometimes I go to the front because the kids have to hit the buzzer and stuff.

***** Questions about continuing attempts at reconciliation between him and Nicole

VANNATTER: How long were you together?

SIMPSON: Seventeen years.

VANNATTER: Seventeen years. Did you ever hit her, O.J.?

SIMPSON: Ah, one night we had a fight. We had a fight, and she hit me. And they never took my statement, they never wanted to hear my side, and they never wanted to hear the housekeeper's side. Nicole was drunk. She did her thing, she started tearing up my house, you know? And I didn't punch her or anything, but I . . .

VANNATTER: Slapped her a couple times?

SIMPSON: No, no, I wrestled her, is what I did. I didn't slap her at all. I mean, Nicole's a strong girl. She's a . . . one of the most conditioned women. Since that period of time, she's hit me a few times, but I've never touched her after that, and I'm telling you, it's five, six years ago.

VANNATTER: What's her birth date?

SIMPSON: May 19th.

VANNATTER: Did you get together with her on her birthday?

SIMPSON: Yeah, her and I and the kids, I believe.

VANNATTER: Did you give her a gift?

SIMPSON: I gave her a gift.

***** Questions about the gift, when he gave it to her, and that she gave it back to him

LANGE: Did Mr. Weitzman, your attorney, talk to you anything about this polygraph we brought up before? What are your thoughts on that?

SIMPSON: Should I talk about my thoughts on that? I'm sure eventually I'll do it, but it's like I've got some weird thoughts now. I've had weird thoughts . . . You know, when you've been with a person for seventeen years, you think everything. I've got to understand what this thing is. If it's true blue, I don't mind doing it.

LANGE: Well, you're not compelled at all to take this, number one, and number two, I don't know if Mr. Weitzman explained it to you—this goes to the exclusion of someone as much as to the inclusion so we can eliminate people. And just to get things straight.

SIMPSON: But does it work for elimination?

LANGE: Oh, yes. We use it for elimination more than anything.

Simpson: Well, I'll talk to him about it.

Lange: Understand, the reason we're talking to you is because you're the ex-husband.

Simpson: I know I'm the number one target, and now you tell me I've got blood all over the place.

Lange: Well, there's blood in your house and in the driveway, and we've got a search warrant and we're going to go get the blood. We found some in your house. Is that your blood that's there?

Simpson: If it's dripped, it's what I dripped running around trying to leave.

Lange: Last night?

Simpson: Yeah, and I wasn't aware that it was . . . I was aware that I . . . You know, I was trying to get out of the house. I didn't even pay any attention to it. I saw it when I was in the kitchen and I grabbed a napkin or something, and that was it. I didn't think about it after that.

Vannatter: That was last night after you got home from the recital when you were rushing?

Simpson: That was last night when I was . . . I don't know what I was, I was in the car getting my junk out of the car. I was in the house throwing hangers and stuff in my suitcase. I was doing my little crazy what I do, I mean, I do it everywhere. Anybody who has ever picked me up says that Simpson's a whirlwind. He's running, he's grabbing things, and that's what I was doing.

Vannatter: Well, I'm going to step out and I'm going to get a photographer to come down and photograph your hand there. And then here pretty soon we're going to take you downstairs and get some blood from you. Okay? I'll be right back.

Lange: So it was about five days ago you last saw Nicole? Was it at the house?

Simpson: Okay, the last time I saw Nicole, physically saw Nicole, I saw her obviously last night. The time before, I'm trying to think. I went to Washington, DC, so I didn't see her, so I'm trying to think. I haven't seen her since I went to Washington. I went to Washington, what's the date today?

Lange: Today's Monday, the 13th of June.

Simpson: Okay, I went to Washington on maybe Wednesday. Thursday I think I was in . . . Thursday I was in Connecticut, then Long Island Thursday afternoon and all of Friday. I got home Friday night, Friday afternoon, I played, you know . . . Paula picked me up at the airport. I played golf Saturday, and when I came home I think my son was there. So I did something with my son. I don't think I saw Nicole at all then. And then I went to a big affair with Paula Saturday night, and I got up and played golf Sunday, which pissed Paula off, and I saw her at the . . .

Lange: Okay, the last time you saw Nicole, was that at her house?

Simpson: I don't remember. I wasn't in her house, so it couldn't have been at her house, so it was, you know, I don't even physically remember the last time I saw her. I may have seen her even jogging one day.

LANGE: Let me get this straight. You've never physically been inside the house?
SIMPSON: Not in the last week.
***** Additional questions about when he last saw Nicole and when he was last at her house
LANGE: We're ready to terminate this at 14:07.

By most accounts, this interrogation was a failure. The detectives learned very little as a result of the questioning of their prime suspect. They came nowhere even close to obtaining a confession or even getting a firm account of his activities the previous night. As discussed in this chapter, many of the general rules of how to conduct an interrogation of a suspect were not followed by the detectives. Also instructive for purposes of this chapter is that many of the answers provided by Simpson in response to the critical questions asked by detectives appeared to be classic examples of deception. These issues, and others, are discussed in this chapter.

Interrogations Defined

An interrogation can be defined as any questioning or other action that is intended to elicit incriminating information from a suspect when this information is intended to be used in a criminal prosecution. Interrogations of subjects are usually conducted when the subject is in the custody of the police (i.e., custodial interrogation). "Custody" exists when the suspect is under the physical control of the police and when the suspect is not free to leave. The police may also conduct noncustodial interrogations of a suspect. This occurs when the suspect voluntarily accompanies the police and when the suspect is told that he is not under arrest and is free to leave at any time (*California* v. *Beheler* 1983). Although Miranda only applies to custodial interrogations, as a matter of practice, police are often trained to advise all subjects who may provide incriminating statements of their constitutional rights prior to questioning (Cassell and Hayman, 1998). In contrast to interviews, interrogations are usually more of a process of testing already developed information than of actually developing information. For example, in the homicide investigation of Nicole Brown Simpson and Ron Goldman, the police had evidence that led them to believe that O.J. Simpson was possibly (or probably) responsible for the murders. In the interrogation of Simpson, the detectives attempted to test this evidence by asking him questions about when he last drove the Bronco (and where he parked it), how and when he injured his hand, and his activities the night of the murders.

The ultimate objective of an interrogation is to obtain a confession; however, the police must walk a fine line in this regard. It is possible that the individual who is believed to be responsible for the crime may not have actually committed it. As a result, of course, a confession would not be a desirable or appropriate outcome of the interrogation. Short of obtaining a confession, an interrogation may be successful if the subject provides admissions to investigators (e.g., "I was at Nicole's house last night but I didn't kill her"), or even if investigators can obtain from the subject a firm and detailed account of actions that may be related to the crime (e.g., "I cut my hand on my cell phone last night") (Zulawski and Wicklander, 1992). If the alibis and explanations offered by the subject are checked and tested against other known facts of the crime, and the story is consistent with those facts and constitutes a reasonable explanation, then the subject's account may be truthful. If the subject's story is inconsistent with other facts developed in the investigation, if the subject provides contradictory or conflicting details, or if the story just does not make sense, then the subject's lies may be evidence of guilt. The attempt to deceive may suggest that the subject is hiding involvement in the crime, or some aspect of it. Further questioning may then highlight the inconsistencies of the subject's story and how it conflicts with the other facts of the investigation. This line of questioning may elicit incriminating statements from the subject. As discussed in more detail later in the chapter, it is important to note here that statements indicative of deception may not necessarily suggest involvement in the crime in question. Subjects may attempt to deceive investigators for reasons unrelated to the crime under investigation (e.g., to hide other illegal actions). This possibility can make interrogations more complicated.

The Psychology of Persuasion

Interrogation is basically a task of persuasion—of getting someone to do what he really does not want to do. A salesperson may persuade a person to buy a car for more money than he wants to spend, a wife may persuade her husband to go somewhere he really does not want to go, or an investigator may persuade a suspect to confess to a crime despite that fact that the confession may lead to significant sanctions being imposed on the suspect (e.g., shame, imprisonment). As explained by Simon (1998), "[the detective] becomes a salesman, a huckster as thieving and silver-tongued as any man who ever moved used cars or aluminum siding—more so, in fact, when you consider that he's selling long prison terms to consumers who have no genuine need for the product" (p. 57).

For sake of illustration, it may be instructive to consider the persuasion that occurs when a salesperson is trying to sell someone a car. Specifically, why do some people end up purchasing a car for more money than they really wanted to spend? The basic answer is that for some reason, the person believes that there was some benefit in doing so. Perhaps the buyer fell in love with the car. Perhaps the buyer just wanted to get the sale over with so that he could drive the car home and show it to his friends. Perhaps the final price was not really that much different than the intended price. Perhaps the buyer came to believe that the amount that he was intending to pay was unreasonably low. Perhaps the financing terms made the cost of the car less of an issue. Perhaps the buyer really liked the salesperson. There are many different reasons, many of which may have been influenced by the salesperson and the tactics he used in the "negotiations."

So why do *suspects* confess? Again, for some reason, the suspect comes to believe that there is some benefit in doing so. According to Gudjonsson (1992) there are basically three reasons why suspects confess. The first is to relieve feelings of guilt. One's conscience, the part of the mind where guilt resides, can make one's life tortured. Confession, often viewed as a "good" thing to do, may be seen as a way of purging those troubling feelings of guilt. A second reason why suspects confess is because of persuasive police actions. The police may wear down the suspect; they may make him tired. He may just want the accusations to stop; he may just want to go home. The police may convince him that confessing is the best thing, the easiest thing, or even the only thing, to do. The third, and most common, reason for confessing is that the suspect *believes* that there is no point in denying the crime because the police have proof of his involvement in the crime. The suspect's *belief* is critical. This belief may be largely influenced by the actions and tactics of the interrogator. In most confessions, each of these three reasons may be present to some extent; a combination of factors may bring suspects to confess. In any case, the extraction of a confession is a process of persuasion, and persuasion takes time.

The Role of Police Deception in Interrogations

Leo (1992) argues convincingly that the nature of interrogations in the United States has changed dramatically over the years. Although interrogations used to rely most heavily on physical violence and coercion (i.e., the third degree), interrogations today rely most heavily on psychological techniques of persuasion and deceit. As noted by Marx (1988), "restrict police use of coercion, and the use of deception increases" (p. 47). Indeed, deception is central to modern interrogation methods. As Simon (1998) explains, "what occurs in an interrogation room is indeed little more than a carefully staged drama, a choreographed performance that allows a detective and his subject to find common ground where none exists" (p. 54). For example, one of the fundamental objectives of an investigator conducting an interrogation is to project a sympathetic and understanding image to develop the suspect's trust, which may in turn make it easier for the suspect to confess. This foundation by itself may be fundamentally deceptive. There is nothing legally wrong with "being nice" during an interrogation, even if this portrayal is deceptive; however, this deception combined with other forms of deception may lead to problematic outcomes.

Consider the case of the murder of Stephanie Crowe. Stephanie was stabbed to death during the early morning hours of January 21, 1998, at her home while she slept in her bed. Believing the crime was committed by someone who was already in the house, San Diego County detectives immediately turned their attention to Michael Crowe, Stephanie's fourteen-year-old brother. After several hours of questioning over a period of several days, without his parents or an attorney present, Michael confessed and implicated two of his friends in the murder. In February 1999, on the eve of the trial, charges against Michael and his two friends were dropped when it was determined that neither Michael nor his friends had anything to do with the murder. On the basis of DNA evidence, a drifter with a long history of arrests and severe mental illness was arrested for the homicide (but as of 2003 he has yet to be tried for the crime). Portions of the interrogation excerpt that show how the detectives developed and portrayed an image of sympathy and understanding to Michael are provided here:

DETECTIVE CLAYTOR: We're really trying to believe what you say. We want to believe what you say. Would you have any problems with taking a truth verification exam?

MICHAEL: No.

DETECTIVE CLAYTOR: You act like you are disgusted.

MICHAEL: I, I've told you before, I wouldn't mind.

DETECTIVE CLAYTOR: What's the problem, Mike?

MICHAEL: I've spent all day away from my family. Couldn't see them. I feel like I'm being treated like I killed my sister, but I didn't. It feels horrible.

*****

DETECTIVE MARTIN: You know I'm a pretty good guy. You can obviously sense that. I mean, I'm not hitting you with a rubber hose, am I? I'm here to verify what you are saying. Okay?

MICHAEL: Okay.

DETECTIVE MARTIN: We're going to work through this together. Okay?

MICHAEL: Okay.

*****

DETECTIVE MARTIN: Maybe there's something we need to understand about Michael and about your sister that we didn't understand, and maybe somebody could have helped. It's okay. It's okay to feel the way you feel.

*****

DETECTIVE CLAYTOR: You're a child. You're 14 years old. Nobody's going to hold you to the same standards that they would some criminal on the street. You're gonna need some help through this.

Beyond the portrayal of false sympathy, another common dimension on which the police commonly deceive is the nature of the evidence in the case (Leo, 1992). Even if there is no evidence that the suspect committed the offense, the police may legally deceive the suspect into believing that such evidence exists. This deception is limited to verbalization; it is not legally permissible to fabricate evidence even if just used in the interrogation setting. Telling the suspect that his fingerprints were found on the murder weapon, that he has been identified by eyewitnesses, or that the victim stated that he was the killer in a dying declaration are common ploys. In general, this sort of deception is legally permissible as long as it would not induce an innocent person to confess. Consider the following exchange between Michael, Detective Claytor, and Detective Martin, when Michael is confronted with the (false) evidence of his hair being found in Stephanie's hand and her blood being found in his bedroom:

DETECTIVE MARTIN: I'm looking at you right now, okay, and inside you're about ready to burst. We can't bring her back. She's gone, okay? You're fighting it. You're, you're, you're . . .

MICHAEL: I don't know what to do anymore.

DETECTIVE MARTIN: I understand.

MICHAEL: Now I'm being told that I'm lying and I know that I'm not.

DETECTIVE MARTIN: Michael, I'm not saying that. Have you heard me say that? What if they come back and say to you, "Michael, we have your hair." They say, "Michael, we have your hair in her hand." And all of a sudden you go, now what? I mean what are you going to do at that point? I mean . . .

MICHAEL: At that point, I would do a complete breakdown . . . of knowing it, because I don't know.

DETECTIVE MARTIN: Hypothetically, could this have happened?

MICHAEL: No, not that I know of.

DETECTIVE MARTIN: Not that you know of?

MICHAEL: Like I said, I would have to be completely unaware of it.

DETECTIVE MARTIN: Okay. Have you ever blacked out before?

MICHAEL: No, never. If I knew who did it then you would know. Everyone would know it now.

DETECTIVE MARTIN: Okay, why?

MICHAEL: Because whoever did it, I, if I ever find out I would hate them forever. I loved her. I loved her deeply.

*****

DETECTIVE CLAYTOR: We found blood in your room already.

MICHAEL: God. Where did you find the blood?

DETECTIVE CLAYTOR: I'm sure you know.

MICHAEL: Why God? No I don't know. I didn't do it. I'll swear to that.

DETECTIVE CLAYTOR: Does that mean you can't tell me about the knife?

MICHAEL: I don't know what you are talking about.

DETECTIVE CLAYTOR: You're 14?

MICHAEL: Yes.

DETECTIVE CLAYTOR: You've got your whole life ahead of you, don't you?

MICHAEL: Yeah, God. Oh God. God why?

DETECTIVE CLAYTOR: You tell me.

MICHAEL: Why are you doing this to me? If I did this I don't remember it. I don't remember a thing.

DETECTIVE CLAYTOR: And you know what? That's possible.

The use of deception in this case appears tragic because, as noted, Michael eventually confessed but it was determined later that he had nothing to do with the murder. A less troubling example of the strategic use of deception in the interrogation setting is the case of Susan Smith, the woman who, on October 25, 1994, buckled two young children in her car and let the car roll into John D. Long Lake near Union, South Carolina. Her children drowned. Susan summoned the police and told them that a black man around forty years of age, wearing a dark knit cap, a dark shirt, jeans, and a plaid shirt had carjacked her car while her kids were in the back seat. In the national media spotlight, she pleaded for the safe return of her children. Susan told the police that when her car was carjacked, she was stopped at a red light at a particular intersection and no other cars were at the intersection. Investigators found this suspicious because that particular light was set always to be green unless a car on the cross street triggered the light to switch. In order for the light to be red, another car had to be at the intersection. Additional questioning revealed other inconsistencies in her story. Susan agreed to a polygraph exam and the results indicated deception. Additional interrogations of Susan ensued. At one point, Susan was confronted with her lie about where the carjacking actually occurred. The police told her that it could not have possibly occurred there because of the triggered light. Susan then changed her story, claiming that the carjacking actually occurred at a different intersection in a different city (fifteen miles away). The police then told Susan that this intersection was under police surveillance for a drug investigation at the time she said the carjacking supposedly occurred (which was not true) and that the police officers who were there did not see any carjacking. After the officer told Susan this, she reportedly began to cry and said, "You don't understand . . . My children are not alright." Susan then confessed. It was the ninth day after she reported that her children were taken.

Along the same line as presenting fictitious evidence to the suspect is another tactic that was used in the interrogation of Michael Crowe—the use of technology (in this case a computer voice stress analyzer) to detect deception and overstating the technology's capability. As discussed later in this chapter, most research has come to the conclusion that the voice stress analyzer produces completely unreliable and invalid results. However, consider this exchange in the interrogation:

> **DETECTIVE MARTIN:** I can tell you this instrument here. Okay it is what they call a Computer Voice Stress Analyzer. Now you will appreciate this, being into computers. *Its accuracy rate is phenomenal, okay?* And that's what makes it such a great tool [emphasis added].
>
> **DETECTIVE MARTIN:** What are some things we want to learn here do you think?
>
> **MICHAEL:** If I know who did it, if I did it.
>
> **DETECTIVE MARTIN:** Okay, well let's do that then. Do you know who, let's say, took Stephanie's life?
>
> **MICHAEL:** No.
>
> **DETECTIVE MARTIN:** Okay, would that be a good, fair question?
>
> **MICHAEL:** Yes.
>
> **DETECTIVE MARTIN:** Do you know who took . . . Do you know how she died?
>
> **MICHAEL:** No.
>
> **DETECTIVE MARTIN:** Are you sitting down?
>
> **MICHAEL:** Yes.
>
> **DETECTIVE MARTIN:** Do you know who took Stephanie's life?
>
> **MICHAEL:** No.
>
> **DETECTIVE MARTIN:** Is today Thursday?
>
> **MICHAEL:** Yes.
>
> **DETECTIVE MARTIN:** Did you take Stephanie's life?
>
> **MICHAEL:** No.
>
> **DETECTIVE MARTIN:** Let me go over these charts and I'll be back here in a couple of minutes, okay?
>
> **MICHAEL:** Okay.

Detective Martin then returned to the interrogation room and told Michael that he failed the test, indicating that he was lying in answering the critical questions.

Along the same line, Simon (1998) presents a case in which Detroit detectives were said to have used a photocopy machine as a lie detector. The detectives loaded three pieces of paper in the Xerox machine. The first one read "truth," the second one read "truth," and the third one read "lie." The suspect was led into the room and told to put his hand on the side of the machine. He was first asked his name. After he answered, the copy button was pushed. The paper with "truth" was printed. He was asked where he lived. "Truth." He was asked if he shot the victim. "Lie." "You flunked," he was told, "you might as well confess."

Another common form of deception in interrogations is misrepresentation of the seriousness of the crime (Leo, 1992). For instance, the police may tell the suspect that the murder victim is still alive, that he is in good condition, and that he doesn't want to press charges, so that the suspect can confess with few perceived implications. Along the same line, the police may offer the suspect psychological excuses or moral justifications for his actions—again, in an attempt to make confessing psychologically easier (e.g., the rape was an act of love, or the victim may have come on to you). As discussed later, whatever form the deception takes, the strategic use of deception by the police in interrogation settings is a powerful and oftentimes necessary, but controversial, tool in persuading suspects to confess.

The Ingredients of a Successful Interrogation

In order for an interrogation to occur, the suspect must first waive his Miranda rights and be willing to answer the questions of the investigators. If the suspect invokes his Miranda rights, interrogation is irrelevant. Persuasion has an extremely limited role at this stage. Legally, the police may not try to "convince" a suspect to waive his rights; however, in most cases it is not necessary. In a study by Cassell and Hayman (1998), it was found that eighty-four percent of felony suspects who the police wished to question voluntarily waived their Miranda rights and submitted to questioning. In a study by Leo (1996), seventy-five percent of suspects waived their Miranda rights and twenty-one percent invoked their rights (four percent of suspects did not receive Miranda warnings because they were not considered by the police to be "in custody" at the time of the interrogation). The findings of these studies are generally in line with other research that has shown, on average, that approximately twenty percent of suspects invoke their Miranda rights prior to questioning by the police (see Cassell and Hayman [1998]). Most suspects talk to the police because, as explained by Simon (1998), "every last [suspect] envisions himself parrying questions with the right combination of alibi and excuse; every last one sees himself coming up with the right words, then crawling out the window to go home and sleep in his own bed" (p. 54).

According to Cassell and Hayman (1998), of those suspects who waived their Miranda rights, approximately forty-four percent provided a verbal or written confession, and an additional twenty-four percent of suspects provided some type of incriminating statement to investigators. As such, sixty-eight percent of interrogations were considered successful. The bottom line is that if suspects agree to talk, they will probably say something incriminating.

It is interesting to note that those individuals who invoked their Miranda warnings (i.e., who would not talk to the police) were more likely to have a previous criminal history and were slightly less likely to be convicted of the current offense. On the other hand, suspects who provided incriminating information as a result of the interrogation were, not surprisingly, more likely to be charged by prosecutors, less likely to have their cases dismissed, more likely to be found guilty and convicted, and more likely to receive more severe sentences following their conviction. No question, incriminating statements from suspects serves as very powerful evidence in the criminal investigative and criminal justice processes.

Provided that the suspect waives his rights and agrees to answer the questions of the police, what are the ingredients necessary to produce a successful interrogation? The basic ingredients consist of:

- A plan
- Adequate time
- Control of the interrogation
- An understanding of the facts of the case
- Familiarity with the suspect's background
- A good relationship with the suspect (see Vessel [1998], Simon [1998], Napier and Adams [1998], and Leo [1996, 1998a])

First, with regard to a plan, prior to beginning the interrogation it must be determined what information is to be obtained. What dimensions of the crime and of the evidence need to be tested with the suspect? It appears from the transcript provided in the introduction to this chapter that the detectives who interrogated O.J. Simpson were not prepared for the interrogation. The most critical questions to be asked and answered were the following: (1) When did Simpson last drive the Bronco? (2) What were his actions and activities last night (the night of the murders) and (3) How did he cut his hand? These are basic but fundamentally important questions in the investigation but there was no concerted effort on the part of the detectives to obtain a clear statement from Simpson regarding any of these issues. The questions were asked but Simpson was allowed to give confusing, vague, and contradictory answers. As one of many examples, consider this exchange:

VANNATTER: How did you get the injury on your hand?
SIMPSON: I don't know. The first time, when I was in Chicago and all, but at the house I was just running around.

Inexplicably, there was no follow-up to press for a clear answer. At the conclusion of the interrogation, the detectives had no clear explanation as to how Simpson cut his hand.

Consider the exchange regarding when he last drove the Bronco:

LANGE: When did you last drive it?
SIMPSON: Yesterday.
VANNATTER: What time yesterday?
SIMPSON: In the morning, in the afternoon.

Again, there was no attempt to get a straight answer from the suspect on this important issue. At the conclusion of the interrogation the detectives had no clear idea as to when Simpson last drove the Bronco.

Regarding his activities the previous night, consider this exchange:

VANNATTER: That was last night after you got home from the recital when you were rushing?

SIMPSON: That was last night when I was . . . I don't know what I was, I was in the car getting my junk out of the car. I was in the house throwing hangers and stuff in my suitcase. I was doing my little crazy what I do, I mean, I do it everywhere. Anybody who has ever picked me up says that Simpson's a whirlwind. He's running, he's grabbing things, and that's what I was doing.

Again, his answer to the question makes no sense, but little effort was made to try to pin down his activities or a time line for those activities. In addition, it is clear that some of Simpson's answers were completely contradictory. At times he said that he "kind of leisurely got ready to go" and at another time he said that he was in a "whirlwind." This was a contradiction that Simpson was never pressed to clarify or explain.

Also, with regard to a plan, if more than one investigator is to be involved in the questioning, the respective role of each investigator must be determined. Most fundamentally, who is to be in charge and lead the questioning? It appears from the Simpson transcript that neither detective was in charge. A review of the transcript shows numerous instances when one of the detectives interrupted the other, and when one changed the line of questioning that the other was pursuing. Having two detectives involved in the interrogation should work to the advantage of the police, but in the interrogation of Simpson it did not.

Second, adequate time needs to be spent in an interrogation to persuade a suspect to confess or, at the least, to get the suspect to commit to a certain version of events and to get the details necessary to develop contradictions in statements. Time is also needed to allow for a relationship with the suspect to be developed. Indeed, Leo (1996) found that successful interrogations were six times more likely than unsuccessful ones to have lasted more than an hour. Nearly thirty percent of interrogations lasted for more than one hour, thirty-five percent lasted for less than one-half hour (including those during which the suspect immediately invoked the Miranda warnings). The length of the interrogation is one of the most important factors in differentiating successful from unsuccessful interrogations. The interrogation of Simpson lasted just more than thirty minutes. The crime being investigated was a double homicide. Simpson was the prime suspect and he agreed to waive his Miranda rights. Given these circumstances, a thirty-minute interrogation is difficult to understand.

Third, control is fundamentally important in an interrogation setting. Investigators must control the topics of discussion during the interrogation. If investigators are determined to elicit or test certain information during an interrogation, investigators must direct the nature of the questioning. During the Simpson interrogation it was sometimes difficult to determine who was questioning who. Simpson was allowed to take the questioning off course. For instance, consider this exchange:

VANNATTER: What do you think happened? Do you have any idea?

SIMPSON: I have no idea, man. You guys haven't told me anything. I have no idea. When you said to my daughter, who said something to me today that somebody else might have been involved, I have absolutely no idea what happened. I don't know how, why, or what. But you guys haven't told me anything. Every time I ask you guys, you say you're going to tell me in a bit.

VANNATTER: Well, we don't know a lot of the answers to these questions yet ourselves, O.J., okay?

Following this exchange, Simpson told the detectives about an incident during which two "Oriental guys" harassed him on the highway, and the detectives proceeded to ask questions about this completely irrelevant incident. In short, it did not appear that the detectives had control over the interrogation.

Another dimension of control in the interrogation setting is the physical environment in which the questioning takes place. As explained by Inbau et al. (1986), the room should be quiet with no visual distractions. There should not be a telephone in the room nor should telephones be audible from the room. For safety reasons, locks should be removed from the door. The room should have proper lighting—not too dark or too bright. There should be two chairs in the room about four to five feet apart and they should face each other with nothing placed between them. The chairs should have straight backs and be of the same size so that the questioner and the suspect are at the same eye level. Ideally, the room should be equipped with an adjacent observation room, and a two-way mirror should separate these rooms. This arrangement would allow other investigators to observe the interrogation and to observe the suspect when he is alone in the room. The aim is to control every aspect of the interrogation session. In this sense, the suspect is placed under additional stress, albeit rather subtle.

Fourth, investigators involved in the interrogation must have a good understanding of the facts of the case to ask the right questions and to understand when an answer is conflicting with the other facts of the case. Information about the case is also important in establishing a plan for the interrogation. During the interrogation of Simpson, the detectives knew about the blood in the Bronco, the blood at Simpson's house, and the bloody glove found at Simpson's house that matched the one at the crime scene. They asked many of the right questions but failed at getting straight answers.

Fifth, interrogators should have a familiarity with the suspect's background. In the questioning of Simpson, the detectives knew that he was not an experienced criminal and he certainly was not a professional killer. They knew that Simpson and Nicole had a turbulent relationship. They knew that the police were, on at least one earlier occasion, summoned to intervene in a domestic incident between Simpson and Nicole. All this knowledge could have been used by the detectives in developing a plan on how best to interrogate their prime (and only) suspect.

Sixth, investigators should build a good relationship with the suspect. The suspect has to feel like he can trust the investigators, that the investigators are there to help. Building a relationship in an interrogation setting takes time. In the Simpson case, detectives simply did not spend the time necessary to establish a rapport with him.

Finally, investigators should be familiar with and comfortable using a variety of persuasive themes, approaches, and tactics. Vessel (1998) identifies various "themes" such as minimizing the seriousness of the crime (e.g., "the homeowner says $1,000 was taken, but I wouldn't be surprised if it was only $100"), blaming the victim (e.g., "I agree with you. One has to ask why she was going for a walk by herself so late at night . . ."), decreasing the shamefulness of the act (e.g., "Tell me about the missing girl . . ." without asking about the details of the suspected sexual assault of the girl), increasing guilt feelings (e.g., "If you tell me what happened, I'm sure that the guilt that is eating you alive will go away."), and appealing to the subject's hope for a positive outcome as a result of cooperation (e.g., "I'll tell the prosecutor that you were helpful . . ."). The logic behind the use of these "themes" is that they lower the psychological hurdles necessary for one to confess to actions for which there may be significant negative consequences.

According to Napier and Adams (1998) there are certain "magic" words and phrases that make it easier for suspects to confess. These words and phrases relate to three commonly used defense mechanisms: rationalization, projection, and minimization or RPM. In particular, rationalization "offers plausible explanations for suspects' actions that reflect favorably on them by presenting their actions in a positive light" (p. 12). It is intended that through the use of rationalizations, the suspect will believe that the investigator sees the suspect's behavior as rational in nature, thereby making it easier to confess. For example, in a child abuse case, the investigator may speak to the suspect about the importance of "discipline" to control the "misbehavior" of a child (e.g., "Discipline is necessary when a child misbehaves . . ."). With projection, responsibility for the criminal behavior is given to someone else, in an attempt to convince the suspect that the action was really not his fault. Again, as a result, it may then be easier for the suspect to confess to his role in the event. For example, again in a child abuse case, the investigator could state that if the *child* would have behaved, she would not have been disciplined. Or, that if the *child's mother* would be more responsible for taking care of the child, this would not have happened. With minimization, the investigator reduces the suspect's role in the crime or the seriousness of the crime. The investigator may speak of the act as an "accident" or as a "mistake," but not as a "murder" or a "beating." Soft word are chosen over harsh words. Again, the point is that this may make it easier for the suspect to acknowledge his role in the crime.

Along with the effective use of RPM, Napier and Adams (1998) also suggest that investigators provide the suspect with reasons to confess. These reasons may vary by individual, by motivation, and by the nature of the crime. In some cases, a good reason to confess from the perspective of the suspect might be finally to get help for the problem, to ease feelings of guilt, or to tell the other side of the story. According to Napier and Adams (1998), to be most effective, the RPM and the reasons to confess should be delivered via a "feather" approach versus a "sledgehammer" approach. Consider the following illustrations (from Napier and Adams [1998]):

Sledgehammer: Brad, you have lied to me from the beginning. You're not fooling me with the story, and I'm going to shove it down your throat. You'll be sorry.

Feather: Brad, I have some problems understanding your story. I've seen this happen before and realize you are uncertain about what you can tell me. That's natural, but

I'm really concerned with how you got into this mess. Let's keep it simple and honest. Let's not make this any worse than it is.

Sledgehammer: You strangled Valerie. Why don't you just say you did it?

Feather: Brad, my experience in similar cases is that the person sitting in your chair has a lot on his mind. He is asking himself, 'What is going to happen to me? Who is going to know that I did this thing? Am I better off telling the entire story and my version of how this thing started?' Let's handle these questions one at a time, keeping each concern in its proper perspective and not letting it run wild (pp. 14–15).

The "feather" approach shows warmth, sincerity, and a commitment to get the truth—all of which may go a long way in persuading a suspect to do what he really does not want to do. As such, in most cases, the feather approach leads to a more productive interrogation.

Leo (1996) found that some tactics were more likely than others to elicit incriminating information from suspects. In particular, the most successful interrogation tactics were to appeal to the suspect's conscience (ninety-seven percent of the time that this tactic was used it led to incriminating information being produced), identify contradictions in the suspect's story (ninety-one percent), use praise or flattery (ninety-one percent), and offer moral justifications and psychological excuses (ninety percent). The more interrogation tactics used by investigators, the more likely the interrogation was to result in a confession or other incriminating information being produced. This factor (along with the length of the interrogation) was most important in differentiating successful from unsuccessful interrogations.

Besides these general rules that should be followed to increase the chances of a successful interrogation, Inbau et al. (1986) provide additional recommendations regarding the conduct of interrogations. These recommendations include the investigator not using paper or pencil in the interrogation setting, the investigator should not be dressed in a uniform nor should the investigator be armed, the investigator and suspect should remain seated throughout the questioning, there generally should not be any smoking allowed, language easily understood by the suspect should be used, the status of a low-status subject should be elevated (e.g., referring to the suspect as Mr.) whereas the status of a high-status person should be lowered (e.g., referring to the subject by his first name), the suspect should be treated with respect and should not be handcuffed or shackled during the interrogation, and, finally, reactions to the suspect's lies should be concealed. It is expected that these factors will further create an environment in which suspects will find it easier to confess.

Steps in the Interrogation of Suspects

Inbau et al. (1986), the definitive source on the conduct of interrogations, outline nine steps that should be followed in conducting interrogations. These steps are outlined in this section.

The first step is to confront the suspect directly with a statement that he committed the crime (e.g. "O.J., the results of our investigation indicate that you are responsible for the death of Nicole and Ron") and then wait for a reaction. The nature of the denial may be revealing. What would be a reasonable reaction to such an accusation? "You're wrong! You are frickin' crazy if you think I killed Nicole" or "Why do you think I did it? Honestly, I didn't do it." The second denial is certainly more curious than the first. During the investigation of the kidnaping and murder of Danielle van Dam, David Westerfield's repeated denial was "As far as I'm concerned, I didn't do it." Not exactly a strong or convincing claim of innocence. Certainly, the nature of the initial denial may give additional insight into the guilt of the suspect. After the initial denial is made by the suspect, then the investigator should repeat the accusation. A statement should then be made showing the commitment to determining what really happened and who is responsible (e.g., "Okay, work with me O.J. and we're going to get this straightened out.").

Second, the suspect should be classified by the investigator as either an emotional offender or a nonemotional offender. An emotional offender is one who is likely to experience considerable feelings of remorse regarding the crime. This judgment may be informed by an understanding of the crime, the suspect's background, the suspect's previous experience or involvement in similar crimes, and his body language. It is instructive to note that most suspects who waive their Miranda rights are best classified as emotional offenders. A nonemotional offender, on the other hand, does not experience a troubled conscience, is perhaps more sophisticated, and does not feel a need to answer the questions of the police. According to Inbau et al. (1986), this classification is important in determining which themes to use in the interrogation. The following themes are most effectively used with emotional offenders:

■ Sympathize with the suspect, saying that anyone else under similar circumstances would have done the same thing. Tell the suspect that you (the interrogator) have done or have been tempted to do the same thing.

■ Reduce the suspect's feelings of guilt by minimizing the seriousness of the offense (e.g., "this is really pretty normal, it happens all the time, a lot of people do this").

■ Suggest to the suspect a less revolting and more acceptable motivation for the offense (e.g., "it was an accident," "it was due to having a few too many beers," "it was due to the use of drugs," "it was not planned").

■ Sympathize with the suspect by condemning others (e.g., blame the victim, an accomplice, or anyone else).

■ Appeal to the suspect's pride through flattery (e.g., the guts and skill it took to commit the crime, the good deeds the suspect has done in the past).

■ Acknowledge that the accuser may have exaggerated the nature and seriousness of the crime (e.g., "I believe you had intercourse with her but I don't believe that it was rape.").

■ Highlight the grave consequences of continued criminal behavior on the part of the suspect (e.g., "In the long run it is good that you got caught because now you can get the help that you really deserve.").

Inbau et al. (1986) identify the following themes as being most effective with nonemotional offenders. It is reasonable to expect that these themes would be effective with emotional offenders as well.

■ Attempt to obtain an admission about some incidental aspect of the crime (e.g., of being in the store at about the time of the robbery). Such a statement may be facilitated through the use of false evidence (e.g., "We have witnesses who saw you in the store that day."). Once this admission is made, further steps can be taken to elicit a confession.

■ Point out the futility of denials. Convince the suspect that his guilt has been established and that there is no point in denying involvement in the crime (e.g., "The only reason I'm talking to you is so that you can explain the circumstances that may make a difference.").

■ When the individual's suspected partner in the crime has also been arrested, one offender can be played against the other offender (e.g., "Your buddy in the next room is blabbing away, saying you planned the whole thing. You may as well be straight with me.").

The third step according to Inbau et al. (1986) is to deal with continued denials. Denials beyond the initial one should be cut off. The suspect should not be allowed to reiterate denials. It should be pointed out, once again, that denials are pointless. Guilt has already been proved.

Fourth, a suspect who moves from denials to objections (e.g., "I couldn't have done that, I don't own a gun.") is likely moving toward a confession but is not there yet. Objections may provide useful information for the development of themes. For instance, a suspect who says, "I couldn't have hurt that little girl, I love kids; I work with kids" might be susceptible to well-placed flattery or to the theme that the "thing" that happened was "an accident." In any case, the interrogator should avoid getting into an argument with the suspect. The interrogator must move forward (e.g., "You don't own a gun? That tells me that this thing was not your idea . . . that your buddy got you involved in this.").

Fifth, it must be continually clear to the suspect that the interrogator is interested in getting the truth, that the interrogator is not wearing out, and that the interrogator will not stop until the truth is obtained. Eye contact should be maintained. The interrogator should move his chair closer to the suspect.

Sixth, theme development should continue. Statements should be made to convince the suspect that confessing is the best course of action. At this point, the need for repeated questioning is minimal.

The seventh step is to present an alternative question to the suspect (e.g., "Did you plan this or did it just happen by accident?"). The intent is to get the suspect to make a statement. Again, denials should be immediately cut off. A confession may be close at hand. A question that allows for a one-word confession should then be offered (e.g., "All you wanted was to scare her. You didn't mean to hurt her, right?").

The eighth step is to have the suspect orally relate the details of his involvement in the crime. Questions should be neutral (e.g., "Then what happened? What happened next? Good. That's what I thought."). As the confession is in full gear, an inquiry into the details of the crime and the suspect's involvement in it should be made.

The final step is to turn the oral confession into a written one either in the form of responses to open-ended questions or a narrative written by the suspect.

This process is really one of guiding the suspect, step by step, to a confession. Reasons are provided to make the suspect believe that a confession is the best course of action. The reasons and rationales basically pave the way toward a confession. The suspect becomes convinced that denials and objections are pointless. Resistance is futile. A confession is the only way out.

Getting someone to confess is a good thing; unless, of course, that person is not responsible for the crime to which he confessed. Under deep psychological stress, it is possible that certain individuals may falsely confess. It is to this troubling issue that our attention now turns.

The Issue of False Confessions

There are two types of false confessions: those in which the individual is totally innocent but confesses to the crime, and those in which the individual was involved in the offense but he overstates his involvement in the crime (Gudjonsson, 1992). Why would anyone confess to a crime they did not commit? Several related explanations have been offered. The first is referred to as *stress compliant false confession*. With this type of false confession, a confession is offered "to escape the punishing experience caused by the adverse—but not legally coercive—stressors typically present in all accusatory interrogations" (Leo, 1998b; p. 277). In this instance, the zealousness on the part of the police elicits the confession from the individual. The confession is an attempt on the part of the individual simply to end the misery of the interrogation.

The second explanation for false confessions is referred to as a *persuaded false confession*. In this instance, the suspect has "been persuaded (by legally non-coercive techniques) that it is more likely than not that he committed the offense despite no memory of having done so" (Leo, 1998b; p. 277). In essence, the police are so convincing that the subject believes his guilt even though he has no memory of committing the crime. Numerous factors have been identified that increase the likelihood of a persuaded false confession (Ofshe [1989] as reported in Gudjonsson [1992]):

- The interrogator repeatedly states his belief in the suspect's guilt.
- The suspect is isolated from anyone who may contradict the claims of the interrogator and is not told of other information that may lead one to believe that he did not commit the crime.
- The interrogation is lengthy and emotionally charged.
- The interrogator repeatedly claims that there is scientific proof of the suspect's guilt.
- The suspect is repeatedly reminded of previous instances of memory problems or blackouts. If these do not exist, then other factors are identified by the interrogator that could account for lack of memory of the incident.
- The interrogator demands that the suspect accept his version of events and explanations for the crime.
- The interrogator induces fear in the suspect's mind about the consequences of repeated denials.

It is interesting to note that many of these factors are present in the interrogation protocol presented by Inbau et al. (1986). It is also noteworthy that *all* of these factors were apparently present in the interrogation of Michael Crowe discussed earlier. Of course, not everyone is equally susceptible to the influence of these tactics. Research has shown that the individuals most likely to provide such false confessions most often have several characteristics in common: an extraordinary trust of people in authority, lack of self-confidence, and heightened suggestibility (e.g., because of young age, mental handicap) (Gudjonsson, 1992). Research has shown that the one factor that stress compliant and persuaded false confessions have in common is that they are elicited after extremely long interrogation sessions, many times more than ten hours. Sometimes these interrogation sessions occurred over the course of several days (Leo and Ofshe, 1998).

A third explanation for false confessions is known as *voluntary false confession*. In this instance, an individual comes forward to the police and confesses to a crime, a crime that may not have even occurred (Gudjonsson, 1992). There may be several reasons why an individual would take such an action: a morbid desire for fame, guilt about some other crime that was committed, mental illness (especially when the individual cannot differentiate what is real from what is not, such as schizophrenia), or to protect the person who actually committed the offense.

False confessions, for whatever reason they are given, are an important issue because confessions are extremely powerful evidence in the criminal investigation and criminal justice process. In fact, confessions are *the* most powerful evidence of guilt in a criminal trial (Gudjonsson, 1992; Leo and Ofshe, 1998). In addition, once a confession is made, it is extremely difficult to recant it convincingly. Accordingly, given a confession, the influence of the confession, and the defendant's possible inducements to plea bargain, one is able to understand how a (false) confession can lead to a plea bargain and, tragically then, a minimal testing of the other evidence in the case. It is difficult to understand why individuals may confess to crimes they did not commit because the police do not use physical force or duress when obtaining confessions (except under scandalous circumstances). The bottom line is that psychological methods of interrogation and persuasion may cause innocent suspects to confess. Leo and Ofshe (1998) identify sixty high-profile cases in which the police obtained, in all probability, false confessions. They identify these cases as the tip of the iceberg. The consequences of false confessions can be devastating.

Unfortunately, the most significant legal procedure that relates to confessions, the Miranda warnings, has little impact on the issue of false confessions. Miranda focuses more on the process of interrogations than on the outcomes. Did the police inform the suspect of his rights? Were those rights voluntarily and knowingly waived by the subject? If these questions can be answered in the affirmative, then the process requirements of Miranda are generally satisfied (Leo, 1998b). Hence, Miranda is largely irrelevant to the issue of false confessions. In addition, if the methods used to elicit confessions are not deemed coercive, then false confessions are legally not problematic (Leo, 1998b).

So what can be done about the issue? First, and most fundamental, the police must be mindful that, for a variety of reasons, some people may falsely confess. In fact, the people who are most likely to waive their Miranda rights are the most likely to confess falsely (Malone, 1998). Persuasion can simply go too far (e.g., the interrogation of Michael Crowe).

Second, the police must realize that a person who appears deceptive, and therefore guilty and warranting of a more pressing interrogation, may be deceptive not to cover involvement in the crime in question but to cover some other action. An example, as discussed in the introduction to Chapter 2, was the maid at the Lindbergh estate who lied to the police about her whereabouts the night of the kidnaping, not to cover her role in the kidnaping but to cover the fact that she was having a secret affair. Police pressure did not lead her to confess, it led her to suicide.

Third, the police should, as a matter of policy, videotape (or at least audiorecord) the entirety of all interrogations. A 1990 survey of police departments found that approximately one third of all agencies serving populations of more than 50,000 people videotaped at least some interrogations, most often those relating to homicides (Geller, 1998). Besides verifying the accuracy of statements made during interrogations, and overcoming objections to the voluntary nature of the interrogations, agencies also noted that videotaping has led to improvements in how interrogations are conducted (e.g., investigators are better prepared for interrogations, videotapes can be used for training purposes). In short, videotaped interrogations may benefit the police, prosecutors, and even defense attorneys.

Finally, the police and prosecutors should systematically evaluate the credibility of the confessions obtained. Is there independent evidence of the suspect's guilt? Is there internal corroboration for the confession? As recommended by Leo and Ofshe (1998), until there is, an arrest should not be made. Specifically, did the confession lead to the discovery of other evidence that indicates guilt (e.g., location of the murder weapon)? Did the confession include detailed information that was not known to the public (e.g., the nature of the wounds to the victim, how the victim was clothed)? These questions can allow for a judgment of the credibility of the confession and take the necessary precautions to prevent against the receipt and use of false confessions.

Investigative Tools in Recognizing Deception

Deception is a critical survival skill, especially for criminals and card players. For obvious reasons, offenders have a great incentive to deceive investigators. Other people too, like victims and witnesses, may also wish to deceive the police to cover their own illegal actions. Understanding this, the ability to detect deception is an important skill for investigators when obtaining information from people. There are several methods used to differentiate truthful from deceptive information. These methods can be generally classified as either nonmechanical (e.g., recognizing verbal and nonverbal cues) or mechanical (e.g., polygraph, voice stress analysis).

The basic theory underlying each of these methods relates to the *fight-or-flight syndrome*. When confronted with a threat, such as being asked threatening questions and having to lie when answering them to avoid arrest, the human body prepares either to fight the threat or to flee from it. In preparing for this action, the body changes in physiological ways. The body increases the secretion of hormones, including adrenaline, which in turn causes an increase in blood pressure, heart rate, rapid breathing, and increased blood flow to the arms and legs, among other reactions. In an interrogation setting, physically fighting the threat (the investigator asking the questions) or fleeing the threat are not feasible or wise. As a result, the individual must try to repress the fight-or-flight response. When a person tries to repress this response, physiological changes become apparent through body movement, posture, verbal behavior, heart rate, and so forth.

Verbal and Nonverbal Detection of Deception

At the outset, it must be realized that detecting deception from verbal and nonverbal cues is a difficult task and is subject to a high degree of error. Most studies show accuracy rates of judgments of deception based on such cues in the range of forty-five to sixty percent (whereas fifty-percent accuracy would be expected by chance) (Porter and Yuille, 1996; Zuckerman et al., 1984). This is at least in part because of the variation that exists among people in their behaviors. In particular, in evaluating the meaning of various nonverbal and verbal behaviors, various factors need to be considered (Zulawski and Wicklander, 1992). First, no single behavior is always indicative of deception. Second, individual differences need to be considered. Individuals may differ in their verbal and nonverbal behaviors, their degree of nervousness, their ability to cope with the nervousness, their intelligence, their medical condition, and so forth. Actions that appear to signal deception for one person may not for another. Third, group differences need to be considered. For example, women tend to behave and speak differently than men. Women generally sit differently than men, women tend to use "hedges" more commonly when speaking (e.g., "kind of," "sort of," "I feel"), and women tend to use more modal verbs (e.g., may, might, could, should) (Ainsworth, 1998). There are also culturally based behavioral differences in individuals. Fourth, because verbal and nonverbal behaviors are largely situational, the situation and environment need to be considered when evaluating behaviors (e.g., amount of visible perspiration needs to be considered in relation to temperature and activities immediately preceding the questioning). Fifth, although single behaviors may not be meaningful, behavioral clusters may be. Several behavioral or verbal cues displayed at the same time are more indicative of deception than a single cue. Finally, the timing of the verbal and nonverbal cues needs to be considered. When was the cue displayed in relation to the questions asked? Timing may be an important consideration when inferring meaning from displayed behavioral cues.

KINESICS

Kinesics relates to the study of body movement and posture to convey meaning (Walters, 1996). Information derived from an understanding and interpretation of "body language" can be quite useful during an investigation. Again, the fundamental theory behind the study of nonverbal behavior to recognize deception is that lying is stressful and individuals try to cope with this stress through body positioning and movement. In addition, individuals try to cope with the threat posed by the questions and the stress of the deception by engaging in self-protection-type behaviors. In this sense, the deception "leaks" from the person in the form of recognizable nonverbal behaviors.

Some nonverbal behaviors are meant to convey direct meaning. For example, "emblems" are gestures that are the equivalent of words (e.g., shaking the head no, shrugging the shoulders, pointing thumbs up). "Illustrators" are hand and arm displays that are used to illustrate what is being said (e.g., "the fish was this big"). Other nonverbal behaviors are more subtle. Although no single behavior is always indicative of deception, there are patterns (Zulawski and Wicklander, 1992). Generally, one looks for congruence and incongruence. Congruence is when there is a match between truthful verbal behavior and truthful physical behavior. Incongruence is when the words being stated do not correspond to the nonverbal behaviors (Zulawski and Wicklander, 1992).

What are the most common deceptive nonverbal behaviors? With regard to facial expressions, an individual's eyes are the most revealing. In normal conversation with most people, eye contact is usually in the range of forty to sixty percent, although there is significant variation across ethnic and social groups, individuals, and situations. "Any break in the normal level of eye contact, which is a timely response, is a sign of stress" and possible deception (Zulawski and Wicklander, 1992; p. 91). Dry mouth, and other actions involving the mouth (e.g., biting fingernails) and nose (e.g., rubbing the nose) are also often indicative of deception (Zulawski and Wicklander, 1992).

Regarding body positioning and posture, one should be most aware of protective or defensive sorts of actions taken by a subject when asked and when answering threatening questions. These behaviors include moving the chair farther away from the questioner, sitting sideways in the chair, sitting in a straddle position on the chair with the back of the chair as a barrier of separation, sitting so as to protect the abdominal region (e.g., slumping, extending feet and legs to provide distance between himself and the questioner, crossing arms, sitting with knee over leg with the knee protecting the abdomen), bouncing of legs while in a sitting position, and use of hands to cover mouth either to muffle a (deceptive) answer or as an unconscious attempt to keep the mouth from making deceptive statements. Deceptive subjects also tend to put their head back or forward out of the plane of the shoulders. The timing of these actions is critical when inferring that a subject is being deceptive.

Gestures may also be revealing of attempts to deceive. Particularly significant are the use of manipulators, or "created jobs," as an attempt to divert attention from the threatening questions being asked, and the deceptive answers being provided. These created jobs are

EXHIBIT 8–1 "The best way to unsettle a suspect. . . ."

It has been suggested that the best way to unsettle a suspect is to post signs in interrogation rooms that read: "Behavior patterns that indicate deception: Uncooperative, Too Cooperative, Talks too Much, Talks too little, Gets his Story Perfectly Straight, Fucks his Story Up, Blinks too Much, Avoids Eye Contact, Doesn't Blink, Stares." (Simon, 1998; pp. 63–64)

What indicators of deception is this individual displaying?

basically busywork for the hands (Walters, 1996) and include such actions as picking lint from clothing, checking jewelry, cleaning fingernails, and smoothing hair. As Walters (1996) explains, "deceptive subjects generally tend to have a greater number of touches to the head than do truthful subjects" especially to the nose (p. 81). Other potentially revealing gestures include coughing, yawning, throat clearing, sighing, and frequent swallowing (dry mouth and throat). Once again, the timing of these gestures in relation to the threatening questions being asked of the subject is critical and most meaningful.

Verbal Behavior

Verbal behaviors are generally easier to control than nonverbal behaviors. As a result, particular care needs to be taken when inferring meaning from verbal behavior. Verbal behavior on the extremes is most indicative of deception.

There are numerous verbal cues of deception (see Walters [1996], Inbau et al. [1986], and Rabon [1994]). In general, deceptive subjects often offer vague and confusing answers. They tend to use more generalized statements. As Rabon (1994) explains, "some deceptive individuals will relate events vaguely, with a series of actions or blocks of time summed up in such phrases as 'messed around,' 'talked for a while,' or 'got my stuff together' " (p. 50). Truthful subjects usually provide details because it is their desire to *convey* meaning to the questioner. Deceptive subjects, however, only wish to *convince*. For example, consider the following exchanges in the interrogation of O.J. Simpson:

LANGE: About what time was that (that you last parked your Bronco)?

SIMPSON: Eight-something, seven . . . eight . . . nine o'clock, I don't know, right in that area.

*****

VANNATTER: Where did you go from there, O.J.?

SIMPSON: Ah, home, home for a while, got my car for a while, tried to find my girl-friend for a while, came back to the house.

*****

VANNATTER: How did you get the injury on your hand?

SIMPSON: I don't know. The first time, when I was in Chicago and all, but at the house I was just running around.

Deceptive subjects also often provide conflicting statements. For example, Simpson alternated between stating that he was in a hurry when he was getting ready to leave for the airport and that he was leisurely getting ready to go.

SIMPSON: I'd come home and kind of leisurely got ready to go.

SIMPSON: I was hustling at the end of the day.

SIMPSON: I was rushing to get out of my house.

Or consider this exchange, and how it compares with the answer regarding when he last parked the Bronco:

LANGE: When did you last drive it (the Bronco)?

SIMPSON: Yesterday.

VANNATTER: What time yesterday?

SIMPSON: In the morning, in the afternoon.

Deceptive subjects also have a tendency to provide explanations that do not make sense. For example, apparently Simpson had a hard time remembering how and when he cut his hand. As noted, he first stated that he cut his hand in Chicago earlier that day, then he stated that he cut it the previous night at his house when he was running around getting ready to leave for the airport. This cut was significant enough to drip blood. One could reasonably expect that a person would remember the circumstances of such an injury, especially if it just occurred within the last twenty-four hours. When Simpson realized that the police discovered drips of blood at his house and in his Bronco, he stated that he cut himself when he was rushing to get his cell phone. Is a cell phone a likely place from which to receive a laceration? Consider this exchange:

SIMPSON: I know I'm the number one target, and now you tell me I've got blood all over the place.

LANGE: Well, there's blood in your house and in the driveway, and we've got a search warrant and we're going to go get the blood. We found some in your house. Is that your blood that's there?

SIMPSON: If it's dripped, it's what I dripped running around trying to leave.

LANGE: Last night?

SIMPSON: Yeah, and I wasn't aware that it was . . . I was aware that I . . . you know, I was trying to get out of the house. I didn't even pay any attention to it. I saw it when I was in the kitchen and I grabbed a napkin or something, and that was it. I didn't think about it after that.

Also with regard to the words used by subjects, deceptive individuals often use the present tense when describing a past occurrence (e.g., "he then goes to the store and buys some beer"). Deceptive subjects also tend to use modifiers in their speech (e.g., "sort of," "usually," "most of the time") more often than truthful subjects and, as such, deceptive subjects generally lack conviction about their own assertions. Deceptive subjects tend to reduce or eliminate self-references (e.g., use of the word I) whereas second-person references (i.e., you) are more likely to be used. Sentences indicative of deception are more likely to begin with verbs or with descriptions.

Deceptive subjects also often use sentences that are unusually short, unusually long, or unusually complicated. Deceptive subjects also tend to provide incomplete sentences in answering incriminating questions. The incomplete sentences are not only a result of mental confusion about the lies and how they may overlap, but also an attempt to avoid giving answers to threatening questions. The transcript of the Simpson interrogation shows repeated instances of Simpson providing incomplete sentences.

Deceptive subjects often complain (e.g., about the weather, their health, their treatment) especially early during the interrogation. This can most often be interpreted as an attempt on the part of the subject to gain the investigator's sympathy. Deceptive subjects tend to offer premature excuses or explanations. They tend to focus on irrelevant points. Consider the following exchange between Simpson and Detective Vannatter:

VANNATTER: Well, we don't know a lot of the answers to these questions yet ourselves, O.J., okay?

SIMPSON: I've got a bunch of guns; guns all over the place. You can take them. They're all there, I mean, you can see them. I keep them in my car for an incident that happened a month ago that my in-laws, my wife, and everybody knows about that.

VANNATTER: What was that?

SIMPSON: Going down to . . . And cops down there know about it because I've told two marshals about it. At a mall, I was going down for a christening, and I had just left and it was like three-thirty in the morning and I'm in a lane, and also the car in front of me is going real slow . . .

The discussion about guns and the incident on the roadway were irrelevant to the crime in question. Deceptive subjects tend to focus on irrelevant points because they are likely to be true and, as a result, easier to talk about.

There is a tendency among deceptive subjects to delay in answering even basic questions (e.g., Did you drive to work this morning?), because subjects who intend to be deceptive must determine what they need to lie about and what they do not need to lie about. Deceptive subjects often make verbal filler in thinking of a response to questions ("Uhmmmm . . ."). Deceptive subjects may have a tendency to repeat the question that has been asked or to respond to a question with a question. All these are strategies to create additional time to think about the possible incriminating nature of the question and a deceptive response to it. Consider the following exchanges in the Simpson interrogation:

> **VANNATTER:** So what time do you think you got back home, actually physically got home?
> **SIMPSON:** Seven-something.
> **VANNATTER:** Seven-something? And then you left, and . . .
> **SIMPSON:** Yeah, I'm trying to think, did I leave? You know I'm always . . . I had to run and get my daughter some flowers . . .
> *****
> **LANGE:** Did Mr. Weitzman, your attorney, talk to you anything about this polygraph we brought up before? What are your thoughts on that?
> **SIMPSON:** Should I talk about my thoughts on that? I'm sure eventually I'll do it, but it's like I've got some weird thoughts now. I've had weird thoughts . . .

Similarly, deceptive subjects may attempt to avoid answering the question posed. For example:

> **VANNATTER:** What were you wearing last night, O.J.?
> **SIMPSON:** What did I wear on the golf course yesterday? Some of these kind of pants, some of these kind of pants, I mean I changed different for whatever it was. I just had on some . . .

Deceptive subjects may also be overly helpful, excessively polite, or extremely respectful. They may talk softly, mumble, or talk through their hands. Deceptive subjects may place extra and repeated emphasis on claims of truthfulness (e.g., "Really," "Honestly," "To tell you the truth") and may invoke religious statements to that affect (e.g., "Honest to God," "I swear on a stack of Bibles"). These actions are usually in an attempt to be extra convincing when the subject knows that he may not be convincing at all.

Deceptive subjects often claim to experience memory problems. They often have a selectively good memory or an extraordinary memory. It is clear from the interrogation of Simpson that he did not have a very clear memory of his activities the previous evening. As Walters (1996) explains, "when discussing critical areas, deceptive subjects experience more frequent occurrences of memory failure than do truthful subjects" (p. 29). In other instances, a subject may offer an immediate response to a question that would normally require some thought or even clarification. For example, if a subject immediately answered "I was working on my car" to the question "What were you doing last week Tuesday?" it would certainly be odd and rather suspicious because the question is quite broad and the time referent is rather distant. A more reasonable response might be "Gee, that was six days ago. Let me think. Okay. What time on Tuesday are you talking about?"

Guilty, and of course innocent, subjects often deny their involvement in the crime in question; however, innocent subjects most often present stronger denials as the questioning continues whereas guilty subjects most often begin with strong denials regarding their involvement in the crime (Walters, 1996). Finally, deceptive subjects sometimes use "buy-out" statements (Walters, 1996). These are used to try to get out of the situation without having to admit to the crime (e.g., "I didn't steal it but I'd be willing to pay the victim for it anyway."). Truthful subjects simply are unlikely to try to engage in such a negotiation.

Mechanical Means of Detecting Deception

The polygraph and voice stress analysis are the primary mechanical methods of detecting deception.

POLYGRAPH

A polygraph is a machine that records physiological responses to psychological phenomena. Like verbal and nonverbal indicators of deception, the premise of the polygraph is that lying is stressful and that this stress can be detected in physiological ways. Specifically, the theory holds that the polygraph can detect this stress through the recording of variations in a person's respiration rate (recorded through pneumographs, tubes filled with air, placed around the subject's chest and abdomen), blood pressure (recorded by a blood pressure cuff placed around the subject's upper arm), and galvanic skin response (a measure of sweat on the subject's fingertips and recorded through the use of galvanometers attached to the subject's fin-

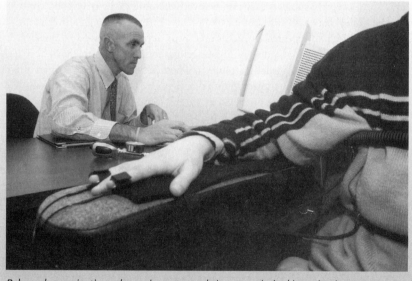

Polygraph examinations play an important role in some criminal investigations.

gers). However, as noted by Ney (1988) and as discussed here, "the correlations between what people feel and how they physiologically express what they feel are not at all straightforward or simple" (p. 66).

Throughout the years there have been several methods of conducting polygraph examinations. The first widely used methodology was referred to as the *general question test* or the *relevant–irrelevant test*. The RIT consisted of a series of ten to fifteen questions, some of which were relevant to the crime (e.g., Did you kill Jake Koplin last night?) and some that were irrelevant to the crime and neutral in their content (e.g., Are you sitting down?). It was presumed that a guilty person would answer the relevant questions deceptively and the irrelevant questions truthfully. The physiological reactions to the truthfully answered (irrelevant) questions could then be compared with the subject's physiological reactions to the deceptively answered (relevant) questions (Raskin and Honts, 2002). As such, it was expected that the deceptive subjects would react substantially more strongly to the relevant than the irrelevant questions. These expectations were shown to be naive because relevant questions proved to be arousing, and to cause a greater reaction, for truthful and deceptive subjects. A truthful denial can be as arousing as a deceptive denial. Research has shown this methodology to produce a substantial number of false-positive errors (identifying innocent subjects as guilty) and, as such, is strongly biased against truthful subjects (Lykken, 1981; Raskin and Honts, 2002). This polygraph method is now used infrequently.

The primary and most generally accepted methodology for conducting polygraph examinations today is known as the *Control Question Technique*. There are several variations in the CQT methodology, the most common of which is the use of "probable lie" questions (Raskin and Honts, 2002). With the CQT methodology, responses to relevant questions (Did you take the gold watch?) are compared with responses to emotionally arousing "control" questions (e.g., Did you ever tell a lie? Did you ever take anything of value that was not yours?). These control questions are broad, vague, and refer to behaviors the subject has likely engaged in, at least at some point in the past. It is believed that in this approach, a subject who is truthful concerning the relevant questions will be more concerned with and will react more strongly to the control questions (i.e., an innocent subject would not be worried about telling the truth on the relevant questions but would be more worried about the control questions). Alternatively, a subject who is deceptive on the relevant questions (a guilty subject) will be more concerned with and have a greater reaction to the relevant questions than the control questions. In essence, the control questions threaten the innocent (truthful), whereas the relevant questions threaten the guilty (deceptive) (Elaad and Kleiner, 1990; Raskin and Honts, 2002). An example of the questions that could comprise a CQT polygraph examination is as follows (from Raskin and Honts [2002]):

> Do you live in the United States?
> During the first 27 years of your life, did you ever tell even one lie?
> Did you rob the Quickmart at Fourth and Main last night?
> Prior to 1987, did you ever break even one rule or regulation?
> Did you take the money from the cash register at the Quickmart last night?
> Did you participate in any way in the robbery of the Quickmart last night?

Before age 27, did you ever even make one mistake?
Were you born in the month of November? (p. 23)

The questions are usually presented twice in mixed order. Again, it is presumed that a person who is guilty will have the greatest physiological reaction to the relevant questions, a person who is innocent will have the greatest reaction to the control questions.

Polygraph tests normally begin with an extensive pretest interview that usually takes between forty-five to ninety minutes (Raskin and Honts, 2002). During this interview, consent to administer the exam is obtained from the subject, biographical data are obtained from the subject, the crime in question is discussed, as is the subject's version of the event. A description of the polygraph, how it works, and how "well" it works are discussed. The issues under examination and the exact questions to be asked of the subject are identified and discussed by the investigator administering the exam. The transducers are then attached to the subject. After the questioning is done, a postexam interview is usually conducted. At this time, the subject may be told that he was determined to be deceptive (e.g., You flunked the test.) and this may lead to a more formal interrogation being conducted, including accusations of responsibility for the crime. The entire polygraph process usually lasts between two and three hours.

Estimates regarding the accuracy rates of the polygraph vary. Some studies estimate the CQT technique as producing accuracy rates of near eighty to ninety percent (see Carroll [1988] and Raskin and Honts [2002]). Others claim the accuracy rate as closer to sixty to seventy percent (Lykken, 1981). As stated by Raskin and Honts (2002), "the voluminous scientific literature indicates that [polygraph examinations] can be highly accurate when properly employed in appropriate circumstances, but they are also subject to abuse and misinterpretation" (p. 38). At the opposite extreme, Blinkhorn (1988) simply states "there are no good reasons for placing credence in the results [the polygraph] produces" (p. 39). The research debate on the validity of polygraph testing is continuing. The one aspect that virtually all research agrees on is that the CQT technique is more prone to false-positive errors (identifying innocent subjects as guilty) than false-negative errors (identifying guilty subjects as innocent) (Lykken, 1981; Raskin and Honts, 2002).

The usefulness of the polygraph may not rest entirely on its accuracy. The polygraph has proved useful in eliciting confessions regardless of its accuracy. If a confession is obtained before, during, or after a polygraph test has been conducted, the confession is usually admissible (Raskin and Honts, 2002). Furthermore, the polygraph may be useful as a threat by which detectives can judge the reaction of a subject when asked the feared question: Would you be willing to take a lie detector test? Indeed, a polygraph test is probably only administered once for every 100 times it is threatened (Brandl, 1993).

Several factors have been identified that can affect the outcome of polygraph examinations. First, research has found that some personality characteristics and disorders may be related to polygraph errors. In particular, psychopaths—as well as others with a low "anxiety IQ"—may be better able to mask deception than others. These individuals may be less aroused, less worried, and feel less anxiety regarding the relevant questions in a polygraph examination (Lykken, 1981).

Second, continuing research is examining the influence of drugs on the accuracy of polygraph results. Some research shows that subjects under the influence of alcohol or other drugs may be more likely to produce false-positive results (Raskin and Honts, 2002).

Third, the skill and experience of the polygraph examiner is a factor shown to be consistently important in the accuracy of polygraph results. The equipment must be properly used, test questions must be properly worded, and the results must be properly interpreted. Examiner error is the most common and consistent problem in the administration of polygraph examinations (Elaad and Kleiner, 1990; Raskin and Honts, 2002). Interpretation of polygraph results can be a difficult task (Carroll, 1998). In addition, there is some debate regarding the accuracy of "friendly" polygraph examiners—examiners hired by the defense to perform polygraphs on defendants. Although there is no evidence that "friendly" polygraph examiners consistently identify guilty defendants as truthful (Gudjonsson, 1992), this issue highlights the possibility that the test procedure may be unstructured enough so that an unethical examiner could easily bias the results (Lykken, 1981).

There is much discussion and debate about whether, or to what degree, the polygraph can be "beat" (i.e., when a deceptive subject could take actions so as to be judged truthful). Gudjonsson (1992) states "under certain circumstances, the accuracy of the polygraph in detecting deception can be seriously undermined by the use of countermeasures" (p. 187). These countermeasures are meant to enhance one's reaction to the control questions, so that the physiological response to the control and relevant questions are more similar. Most common are the use of physical manipulations such as inducing physical pain or muscle tension (e.g., biting one's tongue, pressing toes against the floor, temporarily stopping breathing, tightening leg or buttocks muscles, placing a thumbtack in one's sock, and stepping on the thumbtack when the control questions are asked) (Gudjonsson, 1988; Lykkens, 1981). Other attempted manipulations are mental countermeasures—thinking emotionally, arousing thoughts as questions are asked. Mental countermeasures are generally less effective than physical ones but they are impossible to detect. According to Gudjonsson (1988), the use of several countermeasures at the same time appears to increase the likelihood of defeating the polygraph. If any countermeasures have an effect, they most often lead to "inconclusive" results (Gudjonsson, 1988). If any countermeasures are discovered by the polygraph examiner, such actions would be viewed as a failure to cooperate. These actions may clearly be interpreted as attempted deception.

Polygraph results are infrequently admissible in court. The courts' primary objections to the introduction of polygraph results are that they are unreliable, that the polygraph invades the responsibility and task of the jury (to determine guilt or innocence), and that polygraph results, because of their scientific nature, may overwhelmingly influence the jury. Although each of these objections may be subject to debate, this is the prevailing wisdom of courts today (Raskin and Honts, 2002). Some states have absolute bans on the introduction of polygraph evidence in court whereas other states require a stipulation prior to admittance. In states requiring a stipulation, usually the defense and prosecution must agree to introduce the polygraph results. As one would reasonably expect, this is an infrequent occurrence. At the federal level, different circuits have different rules governing the admission of polygraph results. Without specific rules regarding what must be done for

EXHIBIT 8–2 Voice stress analysis patterns

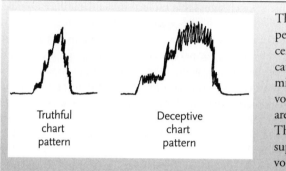

Truthful chart pattern   Deceptive chart pattern

The theory is that when a person is lying, the central nervous system causes an increase in microtremors in the voice. These microtremors are detected and displayed. The research does not support the validity of voice stress analysis.

polygraph results to be admitted, the Daubert standard applies, leaving the decision to judicial discretion.

Voice Stress Analysis

The psychological stress evaluator (PSE) is a machine that is supposed to detect stress in one's voice. The theory is that deception causes stress, and that this stress can be detected in one's speaking voice. Similar to the polygraph, a subject's known, truthful verbal response to a control question (e.g., Are you sitting down?) is compared with a subject's verbal response to a relevant question (e.g., Did you steal the gold watch?). Differences in the voice print patterns in the questions are interpreted as a reflection of deception (see Exhibit 8-2). There has been no verifiable scientific research that has demonstrated that stress in one's voice is indicative of deception, nor has any research shown that stress can be measured through voice stress analysis. In short, the PSE has about zero validity (Horvath, 1982; Lykken, 1981). However, despite its lack of accuracy, and as demonstrated by the Michael Crowe interrogation discussed earlier in the chapter, the PSE may still be "useful" in eliciting confessions from subjects.

Questions for Discussion and Review

1. What is an interrogation? What is a custodial interrogation? What makes an interrogation "successful"? How does an interrogation differ from an interview?

2. Why do suspects confess?

3. Is police deception in interrogations necessary? Why?

4. Give two examples of the use of police deception in interrogations.

5. What are the ingredients necessary for a successful interrogation?

6. Why do you think most suspects waive their Miranda rights and talk to the police?

7. Why is it so important to spend adequate time in an interrogation? Why is it important that the police maintain control of the interrogation?

8. Give an example of the use of RPM during an interrogation.

9. What is the feather approach and the sledgehammer approach to interrogations?

10. What are the nine steps that should be followed in conducting an interrogation, according to Inbau et al. (1986)?

11. According to Inbau et al. (1986), what are the most effective themes to be used with emotional suspects? With nonemotional suspects?

12. Why would anyone confess to a crime they did not commit?

13. What is the relationship between Miranda and false confessions? Explain.

14. What can be done about false confessions?

15. How does the fight-or-flight syndrome relate to the detection of deception?

16. Why is recognizing deception through verbal and nonverbal cues difficult?

17. What nonverbal behaviors are often indicative of deception?

18. What verbal behaviors are often indicative of deception?

19. What is a polygraph and what is it supposed to do?

20. What are the primary differences between the RIT and CQT methods of conducting a polygraph examination?

21. How accurate is the polygraph as a tool to recognize deception?

22. What factors may influence the results of a polygraph examination?

23. What countermeasures may be taken to try to "beat" the polygraph?

24. Are polygraph results usually admissible in court? Why or why not?

25. What is voice stress analysis and how accurate is it as a tool in recognizing deception?

26. Why is the interrogation of O.J. Simpson a good example of a poor interrogation?

Related Internet Sites

www.signonsandiego.com/news/reports/crowe/crowe2.html
This is the page of the *San Diego Union Tribune* newspaper that contains the complete story of the crime and investigation of the murder of Stephanie Crowe.

www.reid.com
This is the web site for John E. Reid and Associates, recognized experts in interrogation and lie detection issues.

www.howstuffworks.com/lie-detector.htm
This site provides an overview of how polygraphs work. Links to many other interesting and relevant topics are also provided here.

www.cvsa1.com
This is the official site of the National Institute for Truth Verification—the manufacturer of the Computer Voice Stress Analyzer, the instrument used during the interrogation of Michael Crowe.

BEHAVIORAL EVIDENCE

OBJECTIVES

After reading this chapter you will be able to

- Discuss the process of psychological profiling, including the types of crimes for which psychological profiling is most suitable, the basic theory underlying the process, and the goals associated with psychological profiling

- Differentiate between psychological profiling, crime scene profiling, and offender profiling

- Discuss the history of psychological profiling

- Identify the steps in the process of constructing a psychological profile

- Discuss the importance and usefulness of the distinction between organized and disorganized crime scenes

- Identify the important features of the crime presented in the introduction for purposes of constructing a psychological profile of the perpetrator

- Discuss the meaning of various perpetrator actions and crime characteristics

- Differentiate between MO and signature

- Discuss how information about the victim may reveal information about the offender

- Discuss staging, its meaning, and its drawbacks as an investigative clue

- Discuss the utility and accuracy of psychological profiles

- Define geographical profiling and its role in criminal investigations

- Identify and discuss the fundamental premise of geographical profiling

- Discuss the role of psycholinguistics as an investigative methodology

- Discuss what is involved in the linguistic analysis of statements and the goals associated with the method

- Discuss how psycholinguistics was applied to the Lindbergh baby kidnaping, the Unabomber investigation, the investigation into the anthrax letters, and the ransom note in the Ramsey murder investigation

INTRODUCTION

The Crime

The New York City Police Department requested the assistance of the FBI after police detectives were at an apparent dead end in their investigation of the murder and mutilation of a twenty-six-year-old woman whose body was found on the roof of a Bronx public housing apartment building where she had lived with her parents. An investigative task force of twenty-six detectives and supervisors had interviewed more than 2,000 individuals, many of whom lived or worked in the apartment building. Record checks of known sex offenders in the area was of no assistance. The police had twenty-two suspects, but nothing conclusive.

A fifteen-year-old boy discovered the victim's wallet in the stairwell as he was leaving the building on his way to school. On returning home from school for lunch that afternoon, the boy gave the wallet to his father, who in turn went to the victim's apartment to return it. The victim's mother then called the day care center where the victim worked to notify her daughter that her wallet was found. At that time, the victim's mother was told that her daughter had not shown up for work that morning. The mother, the victim's sister, and a neighbor then proceeded to search the building and discovered the body. The body was located at 3:00 PM; the victim had left her apartment at approximately 6:15 AM.

The victim was found nude. She had been beaten about the face and strangled with the strap of her purse. The cause of death was determined to be strangulation—first manual and then ligature. The victim's jaw and nose were broken, and several of her teeth were loosened. She sustained several other facial fractures. Her nipples had been cut off after death and were placed on her chest. There were bite marks, which were determined to have occurred after death, on her thighs. Numerous contusions and lacerations were present on her body. The words "You can't stop me" were written in ink on the inside of her thigh, and "fuck you" was written on her abdomen. A necklace pendant that she usually wore was missing and presumed taken by the killer. Her underpants were placed on her head and pulled over her face. Her nylons were removed and were loosely tied around her wrists and ankles. Her earrings were removed and placed symmetrically on each side of her head. An umbrella and writing pen had been forced into her vagina and a hair comb was placed in her pubic hair. Semen was recovered from the victim's body; it appeared that the killer stood over the victim and masturbated. Human feces was discovered on the roof landing and it was covered with the victim's clothing.

Key Crime Scene Characteristics

The crime did not appear to be planned. All the instruments used to perpetrate the crime were the victim's (e.g., purse strap, umbrella, pen), except for the knife used to remove the victim's nipples. This knife was probably small enough to have been routinely carried by the killer. He probably first hit her with his fist to render her unconscious and then used his hands and the purse strap to strangle her. These are weapons of opportunity. He did not have a gun, rope, tape, or gag. If the perpetrator had such "tools," it would indicate a degree of planning. Rather, this crime appeared to be a spontaneous event. In addition, the victim did not appear to have been threatened by the perpetrator's presence. She did not attempt to flee or scream prior to being rendered unconscious by the offender. The initial violence to the victim was sudden.

Although the crime was unplanned, it did appear to be well rehearsed and thought-out. The positioning of the victim, the mutilation of the victim, the placement of the umbrella and pen, the removal and placement of her earrings, the writing on the body, and the bite marks indicated that the perpetrator was acting out something that he had seen before. The crime may have been based on sexual fantasies that may have been rooted in sadistic and violent pornography.

The offender was best classified as disorganized (see a later discussion for details and the importance of this classification). The crime appeared to be a spontaneous event. The victim was not stalked, but confronted. The victim appeared to have been immediately overcome with sudden violence and rendered unconscious. The victim was not moved from the general crime scene. The dead body was left in view at the location in which she was probably killed. There were sexual acts performed on the body after death. Evidence and the tools used to commit the crime were left at the scene. All of these crime scene characteristics are reflective of a disorganized offender.

The crime was high risk. It was committed in daylight. Considerable time was spent by the offender in perpetrating the crime (e.g., removing earrings, masturbating, defecating). The victim was at low risk of becoming a victim. She was a quiet woman, small in stature (four feet eleven inches, ninety pounds). She was plain looking and did not date. She lived with her parents. Her lifestyle did not expose her to much risk for victimization. The area in which the crime occurred was a low violent crime area, further reducing the likelihood of victimization.

The Resulting Criminal Profile

The profile indicated that the offender is a white man, between twenty-five and thirty-five years of age, and of average appearance. The methodical organization of the crime scene (positioning of the body, placement of earrings, etc.) is unusual for an impulsive teenager or someone in his early twenties. It is not likely that the perpetrator is in his late thirties or forties because someone of this age would have probably committed other earlier murders and it would be difficult for a person to commit such crimes over the span of years without being apprehended. He is of average intelligence and is a high school or college dropout. He is unemployed; if employed, it is in a blue-collar or unskilled job. Alcohol or drugs does not play a role in the crime. The suspect is socially inadequate and is not married. He lives or works near the crime scene. All these characteristics are typical of disorganized murderers.

The fact that the crime was a spontaneous event further increases the probability that the offender lives or works near the scene of the crime. He had reason to be there at 6:15 AM. If he was not planning to commit the crime at that time, he had to have some other reason for being there—probably because of employment or because he lived in the apartment building.

The sexual acts performed on the victim show sadistic tendencies. He has obvious mental problems. He likely has a collection of pornography. A rage or hatred of women is present in the crime. That he inflicted these acts on a dead or unconscious victim indicates an inability to interact with a live or conscious person, and reinforces his social inadequacy.

The fact that the crime is high risk (e.g., committed in daylight, in a public place, and that it took considerable time) and the victim was at a low risk for victimization suggests, once again, that the killer feels comfortable in the area. He has been there before and believes no one will interrupt the crime. He is familiar with the area and likely lives or works there.

The Outcome

On receiving the profile of the killer, the police reviewed their list of twenty-two suspects. One person seemed to match the profile more closely than the others. The suspect's father lived on the same floor of the apartment building as the victim. The suspect's father initially told the police that his son was a patient at a local psychiatric hospital. On investigating further, the police learned that the son had been missing from the hospital the day and evening prior to the murder. Investigators discovered that he was unemployed and that he dropped out of school. He was thirty years old and was never married. He had no girlfriends. He suffered from depression and was receiving treatment at the psychiatric hospital. He had attempted suicide before and after the offense. A collection of pornography was discovered during a search of the suspect's father's apartment.

The suspect was arrested, tried, and found guilty of the homicide. He never confessed to the crime but it was proved that security was lax at the hospital in which he was staying; he could come and go as he wished. The most influential evidence against the suspect at trial were the bite marks that he inflicted on the victim. Several forensic odontologists testified that the suspect's teeth impressions matched the bite marks found on the victim's body. He was sentenced to twenty-five years to life for the crime (see Douglas et al. [1986], Porter [1983], and Geberth [1996]). (Note: This crime occurred before the era of DNA printing. Of course, with such technology, the conduct of this investigation may have differed in significant ways.)

Psychological Profiling

Psychological Profiling Defined

Psychological profiling (also known as *crime scene profiling;* see Homant and Kennedy [1998]) "is a technique for identifying the major personality and behavioral characteristics of an individual based upon an analysis of the crimes he or she has committed" (Douglas et al., 1986; p. 413). Information and details about the crimes committed represent the major input into the profiling process. Previous similar crimes for which the offenders have been apprehended are used as a basis on which to identify the characteristics of the person who committed the current crime. As such, psychological profiles are based on probabilities and inferences. As a simple example, it is known that "the serial rapist more often than not comes from an average or advantaged home, and as an adult, is a well-groomed, intelligent, employed individual who is living with others in a family context" (Hazelwood and Warren [1989, p. 25]; also see Rossmo [2000]). Accordingly, a profile developed on a serial rapist based on the crimes he committed may include this baseline description and then additional details may be added depending on uniqueness of his offenses.

Psychological, or crime scene, profiling is different from the practice often referred to as *offender profiling*. Offender profiling consists of the identification of the type of person believed to be most commonly involved in a particular type of crime (e.g., carrying drugs), and the targeting of individuals by the police who match this description. Offender profiling is criticized because one of the primary descriptive features of suspected offenders is often race, hence the familiar but controversial practice of "racial profiling." Psychological profiling is also different from the profiling that occurs when psychologists and psychiatrists attempt to understand the life histories and current motivations of criminals. As an example of such an effort, it has been reported that behavioral scientists from the FBI have interviewed suspected al-Qaida members imprisoned at the Naval Base in Guantanamo Bay, Cuba, to understand better the motivations of terrorists (Newton, 2002). Clearly this process is different than crime scene profiling, as illustrated in the introductory case example.

Psychological profiling is most suitable for crimes for which the perpetrator has shown indications of psychopathy, such as lust and mutilation murders, murders that involve postmortem slashing and cutting, evisceration, rape, sadistic torture in sexual assaults, pedophilia, "motiveless" fire setting, and satanic and ritualistic crime (Holmes and Holmes, 1996). In simple terms, as far as psychological profiling is concerned, the more bizarre the crime the better.

Although most suitable when psychopathy is exhibited in the crime, basic elements of the psychological profiling process may be applied to other crimes as well. For example, consider a case in which a house was burglarized and a Sony Playstation video game unit was the only property taken. Nothing else was disturbed. Based on this limited information about the crime, one may be able to make inferences about the characteristics of the person who was responsible for the crime. A reasonable guess may be that the perpetrator entered the house for the specific purpose of taking the unit, which is why nothing else was taken or disturbed. If this is the case, this person must have known that a Playstation was in the house, perhaps because he was in the house previously and he saw it or even played it. Perhaps the perpetrator is a friend (or neighbor) of the individual who owned and played the Playstation. Furthermore, it may be inferred that the perpetrator is about the same age, or in the same age range, as the individual in the house who was the primary player of the Playstation. Chances are that the perpetrator is male, because men/boys seem to have more of an attraction to video games (or at least to certain types of video games), and are overrepresented as burglary offenders. In sum, based on a simple analyses of a not-very-complicated crime, it would be reasonable to suggest that the perpetrator of the crime is male, probably in his teens, who is a friend of the primary player of the Playstation, and he may live in the neighborhood, perhaps even next door. Might this profile be correct? Might certain aspects of it be correct? Certainly. Again, a profile is a probabilistic statement based on an understanding of the current crime as well as previous similar crimes.

The basic theory underlying the psychological profiling process is that the crime reflects the characteristics and personality of the offender. As stated by Douglas et al. (1986), "behavior reflects personality, and by examining behavior the investigator may be able to determine what type of person is responsible for the offense" (p. 403). This concept is similar to the idea that one's personality is reflected, to some extent, in the clothes the person wears, the car the person drives, and the decorations in the person's home. This is especially true if the clothing, car, or decorations are unusual or even bizarre. For example, one might be more confident (and accurate) in "profiling" a person who drives a 2003 red BMW convertible than a person who drives a 1997 white Honda Accord. As discussed in more detail later, the manner in which the victim was killed, the amount of planning apparently involved in the crime, and how the victim was selected may all give important clues about the characteristics of the offender.

Goals of the Profiling Process

Several goals have been associated with the profiling process. The first and perhaps most important goal is to provide a social and psychological assessment of the offender. In particular, as shown in the profile presented in the introduction to the chapter, psychological profiles often include information about the offender's race, age (or age range), employment status, type of employment, marital status, level of education, and location of residence (Holmes and Holmes, 1996). This information is most useful in focusing the investigation, in reducing the number of suspects considered by the police. Of course, psychological profiles are not capable of identifying a suspect when one is not already known. In this sense, psychological profiles are limited in the same manner as much physical evidence is limited. In addition, it is clear that the psychological profiling process is oriented toward answering questions about the *type* of person who committed the particular offense, not *why* the person committed the offense.

A second goal of psychological profiling is to provide information about the belongings that may be in the possession of the offender (e.g., news clippings about the crime, pornography). This information may be particularly useful in the development and execution of search warrants related to the crime. In the example presented in the introduction, the role of fantasy in the crime was clearly evident, which led to the inference that the perpetrator had access to or was in possession of a collection of pornography. This expectation proved to be correct.

A final goal of profiling is to provide suggestions and strategies to investigators about how to interrogate the suspect when he is apprehended. Insight into the perpetrator's personality and psyche may assist in the identification of "themes" and other tactics that may be most effectively used during the interrogation process (Holmes and Holmes, 1996).

It is worthwhile to note here that psychological profiles are most often used when all leads have been exhausted in an investigation, which may happen relatively quickly in some crimes, particularly crimes without an apparent traditional motive (e.g., passion, hatred, revenge, jealousy, fear) (Douglas, 1996). Motive often casts light on possible suspects. For example, investigators can attempt to determine who was jealous of the victim, who hated the victim, and so forth. Because psychological profiles are often used in cases without a traditional motive, they are often used in the most difficult of investigations. The crimes of most relevance for psychological profiling are ones that are sexually motivated. In any case, if a profile can generate a lead, focus an investigation, assist in the search warrant process, or facilitate an interrogation, a profile may be a beneficial investigative tool.

The History of Psychological Profiling

Psychological profiling is not a new phenomenon, even though it has become a widely known investigative technique only during the past twenty years. One of the first written accounts of the practice of psychological profiling was in Edgar Allan Poe's 1841 classic *Murders in the Rue Morgue*, when, based on an analysis of how the murders were committed, investigators concluded that only an ape could have perpetrated the crime. Attempts were made to construct a profile of Jack the Ripper based on the mutilation murders of several women in the late 1800s in England. A crime scene profile was developed on the crimes of New York City's Mad Bomber in the 1950s and the Boston Strangler in the 1960s. It was not until the late 1970s, however, with the creation of the Behavioral Science Unit in Quantico, Virginia, that the FBI got involved in the practice of psychological profiling.

Today, psychological profiling is primarily the expertise of a select group of agents of the FBI along with a number of other independent psychologists, psychiatrists, and behavioral scientists (Holmes and Holmes, 1996). In 1996, it was reported that the FBI employed twelve full-time profilers and was involved in profiling approximately 1,000 cases per year (Wikin, 1996).

The Construction of Psychological Profiles

The construction of psychological profiles is often seen as a mysterious process during which it is unclear how seemingly miniscule bits of information about a crime, or series of crimes, is turned into specific clues about the identity of the perpetrator. The mystery is perpetuated when profilers do not explain the basis for their predictions (Homant and Kennedy, 1998). As a famous and often-used example, consider the profile developed for New York City's Mad Bomber in the 1950s. The profile developed by Dr. James A. Brussel, a New York psychiatrist, read simply as follows (Geberth, 1996; p. 708):

> Look for a heavy man. Middle aged. Foreign born. Roman Catholic. Single. Lives with a brother or sister. When you find him, chances are he'll be wearing a double-breasted suit. Buttoned.

When the man believed to be the Mad Bomber, George Metesky, was apprehended, he matched the profile exactly, including the buttoned double-breasted suit (Geberth, 1996). Psychological profiling is not a mystery. It involves a process of mapping the characteristics of offenders of previous crimes onto offenders of currently unsolved crimes. The details about an offender that are provided in a profile are simply a result of an educated guess based on an understanding of the crime and the sort of person who would commit it.

Specifically, there are several steps in the process of constructing a psychological profile (see Pinizzotto and Finkel [1990], O'Toole [1999], and Holmes and Holmes [1996]). The first step is to develop an understanding and classification of the current crime. This involves the examination and review of police reports, the crime scene, crime scene photographs, witness statements, forensic laboratory reports, autopsy photographs, as well as other materials that may be available. The second step is to examine the background and activities of the victim. Information about the victim's physical traits, marital status, lifestyle, occupation, and so forth, represent important input in the profiling process. Third, a motivation for the crime is determined. The fourth step is to develop an understanding of the characteristics of individuals who have committed this type of offense in the past. This understanding may be based on experience or research that has examined similar previous offenders/crimes. Finally, a description of the overt characteristics of the perpetrator is provided.

In constructing a profile of a murderer, a fundamental and important classification is made between organized and disorganized crime scenes (see Geberth [1996] and Ressler and Burgess [1985]) (see Table 9–1). An organized crime scene is likely to be orderly and reflects a high degree of control. The scene tends to be neat, even clean. There is most often little or no evidence present at the scene, nor is a weapon likely to be found there. The condition of the scene suggests that the offense was planned. The victim is likely to be a targeted stranger. Restraints are likely to have been used on the victim. Aggressive acts are likely to have occurred on the victim prior to death. The victim's body is likely to have been moved or transported and is likely to be hidden.

A disorganized crime scene, on the other hand, is likely to be sloppy and disorderly. There is most often evidence present at the scene, as is a weapon. The weapon is likely to be something that the offender either did not carry with him to the crime scene (e.g., a telephone cord used to strangle the victim) or was easily carried with him to the scene (e.g., a small knife). The condition of the scene suggests that the offense was not planned. The victim or the location of the murder is likely to be familiar to the offender. The victim is likely to have been overcome by a sudden and overwhelming attack. Restraints are not likely to have been used on the victim. Sexual acts are likely to have occurred with the victim after death. The victim's body is likely to be left at the death/murder scene.

This classification scheme has been developed as a result of research conducted by the FBI (FBI, 1985) and has been shown to be valid (see Homant and Kennedy [1998]). The value of the organized/disorganized classification is that various characteristics have been associated with offenders who produce the different types of crime scenes (see Table 9–2). In particular, a typical offender who leaves a disorganized crime scene (i.e., a disorganized murderer), usually ranges in age from sixteen to his late thirties. He is usually the same race as the victim, is single, and lives alone. He is usually of below-average intelligence, often a high school dropout, or at least a marginal student. He may have a history of mental illness. A disorganized murderer usually has a thin build and has some form of physical or verbal impediment (Geberth, 1996). He tends to live or work near the crime scene. He may not own a vehicle. If he does, it is often an older model that is "junky" in appearance. If he is

TABLE 9–1 Crime Scene Differences Between Organized and Disorganized Murderers

Organized	Disorganized
Planned offense	Spontaneous offense
Victim a targeted stranger	Victim/location known
Personalizes victim	Depersonalizes victim
Controlled conversation	Minimal conversation
Crime scene reflects overall control	Crime scene random and sloppy
Demands submissive victim	Sudden death to victim
Restraints used	Minimal use of restraints
Aggressive acts prior to death	Sexual acts after death
Body hidden	Body left in view
Weapon/evidence absent	Evidence/weapon often present
Transports victim or body	Body left at death scene

Reprinted from Ressler and Burgess, the *FBI Law Enforcement Bulletin*, August 1985.

employed, it is usually in unskilled work (e.g., dishwasher, maintenance man, etc.). He usually does not have any prior military history. Previous arrests for offenses such as voyeurism, burglary, or exhibitionism are common. He is often a loner and might be considered by others as "weird" or "odd" (Geberth, 1996). He is sexually incompetent and may never have had a sexual experience with someone of the opposite sex. Interpersonal relationships are difficult for the disorganized offender.

A typical organized murder offender is usually approximately the same age as the victim. The mean age for this type of offender is younger than thirty-five years. He is usually the same race as the victim. He is usually married or living with a partner. He is usually of average or above-average intelligence and may have attended or graduated college. He is not likely to have a history of mental illness. He is likely to be well built, even athletic (Geberth, 1996). He most often lives away from the crime scene, and has a clean and well-maintained car. He is likely to be employed in a skilled profession. He may have a military history. He may have previous arrests for offenses such as driving while intoxicated, interpersonal violence, or sex offenses (Geberth, 1996). He is usually an outgoing, socially competent person. He may be described as a "good talker" and a "lady's man" (Geberth, 1996). In short, as explained by Douglas et al. (1986):

Motivation is more easily determined in the organized offender who premeditates, plans, and has the ability to carry out a plan of action that is logical and complete. On the other hand, the disorganized offender carries out his crimes by motivations

TABLE 9–2 Profile Characteristics of Organized and Disorganized Murderers

Organized	Disorganized
Average to above-average intelligence	Below-average intelligence
Socially competent	Socially inadequate
Skilled work preferred	Unskilled work
Sexually competent	Sexually incompetent
High birth order status	Low birth order status
Father's work/stable	Father's work/unstable
Inconsistent childhood discipline	Harsh discipline as child
Controlled mood during crime	Anxious mood during crime
Use of alcohol with crime	Minimal use of alcohol
Precipitating situational stress	Minimal situational stress
Living with partner	Living alone
Mobility with car in good condition	Lives/works near crime scene
Follows crime in news media	Minimal interest in news media
May change jobs or leave town	Significant behavior change (drug/alcohol abuse, religion, etc.)

Reprinted from Ressler and Burgess, the *FBI Law Enforcement Bulletin*, August 1985.

that frequently are derived from mental illness and accompanied distorted thinking. (p. 414)

The organized/disorganized classification and corresponding characteristics are ideal types. In the real world, "pure" organized crime scenes and offenders, and "pure" disorganized crime scenes and offenders may not be frequently encountered. In such cases, the most important dimensions of the crime must be determined and analyzed. Exactly what is "most important" is yet to be clearly articulated (Homant and Kennedy, 1998). In other cases that reflect a mix of organization and disorganization, it may be because more than one offender was involved in the crime (e.g., one offender was disorganized, one was organized; see Geberth [1996, pp. 742–748]). Note that the murder described in the introduction to this chapter fits nicely into the disorganized category, as did the offender. Similarly, the crimes of John Collins, the coed killer described in Chapter 4, resembled those of an organized offender, as did Collins.

The Meaning of Perpetrator Actions and Crime Characteristics

Beyond the primary classification of a crime scene as being "organized" or "disorganized" and the associated link to offender characteristics, there are other inputs to the crime scene profiling process. First, for example, the crime may reveal whether the offender has likely struck before or whether he may strike again. For a murder, such evidence consists of post-mortem mutilation or cannibalism, particular positioning of the corpse, sexual assault, overkill, torture, souvenir and trophy collection, and necrophilia (Kocsis and Irwin, 1998). Souvenirs provide the culprit with a memory of the victim and the crime (e.g., an earring taken from the victim). Trophies are something of intrinsic value to the offender; a reward for committing the crime (e.g., a body part) (Holmes and Holmes, 1996). In a rape, evidence that the perpetrator committed previous crimes or will likely commit future crimes consists of manifestation of sadistic or violent behavior, certain verbal scripts demanded from the victim, the offender's inability to penetrate the victim or to climax, and a souvenir or trophy collection (Kocsis and Irwin, 1998). With arson, such evidence consists of sexual activity at the crime scene, presence of signature (e.g., graffiti, described later), destruction of property in addition to the fire damage, and particular behaviors used in the setting of the fire (Kocsis and Irwin, 1998).

Second, crimes may reveal if they were committed by the same person, and this information may be included in a profile. Individuals' preferences tend to remain relatively stable. Personalities do not change or, if they do, they change gradually. Human beings are creatures of habit. As such, an offender's behavior at a crime scene may indicate whether the offender has committed other crimes as well. An understanding of the offender's MO and "signature" may be significant in this regard. MO refers to the actions taken to commit the crime. It may include, for example, the manner in which entry was gained into a residence, the method used to abduct the victim, or the way the victim was restrained. MO can serve as a basis on which to link crimes, but not necessarily. MO may be quite stable or it can change. MO may change when the offender determines a better way to commit the crime, or it may change as a result of the offender's understanding of the police investigation and the clues collected (Douglas and Munn, 1992). "Signature" is what is done by the offender to derive emotional satisfaction from the crime. It is fantasy based. It is a unique and personal expression of the offender (Douglas and Munn, 1992). Signature may include, for example, the type and nature of injuries inflicted on the victim, or specific forms of torture administered on the victim (Hazelwood et al., 1992). It may include souvenir and trophy collection. Whereas MO is more dynamic, signature is more static (Douglas and Munn, 1992, 1997). As such, signature may be a more reliable means by which to link crimes.

Although the distinction between MO and signature may initially appear clear, there are problems with the distinction. First, signature too may change. It may evolve; it may become more developed and more clear over time. Second, signature may not be present at every crime scene. The offender may be interrupted or he may not have received the expected or desired victim response. Third, signature may not be obvious or even identifiable because of its subtle nature or even because of factors such as decomposition of the body. Finally, it may not be discernible as to what is MO and what is signature. For example, it is possible that a particular method used by an offender to abduct a victim may actually be emotionally satisfying to the offender, to be signature and not just MO. Or, as an example discussed earlier in the book, consider the robber who demanded that victims remove their pants after they gave the robber their money. Was this action part of his MO or was it signature? It is difficult to determine. In any case, even if MO is not differentiated from signature, behavioral patterns evident in a crime or crime scene may serve to establish a link between crimes, and this may be determined through the process of psychological profiling.

Third, information about the victim may reveal characteristics of the offender. As noted by Rossmo (2000), "victim choice may provide insights to the nature of the offender, and detailed victimology is one of the key information requirements in the criminal profiling process" (p. 27). Particularly informative is an assessment of how prone the victim was to criminal attack. According to Hazelwood (1995), a low-risk victim is one whose activities would not normally expose the victim to risk of criminal victimization. A murderer or rapist who victimizes this type of individual is likely to know the victim and is likely to seek out the victim (O'Toole, 1999). A moderate-risk victim is one whose victimization risk is elevated because of employment (e.g., nature of employment, working hours), lifestyle (e.g., dating), or personal habits (e.g., going for long walks at night). A high-risk victim is one whose lifestyle (e.g., drug dealing) or employment (e.g., prostitution) consistently exposes the victim to the risk of victimization. The probability of constructing an accurate profile with high-risk victims is small, simply because the number of potential offenders is extremely large (O'Toole, 1999). Information about the victim may also be helpful for other investigative purposes. In particular, information about the victim's lifestyle, occupation, last-known activities, and so forth may bring to light the victim's associates, friends, enemies, and other possible suspects (Holmes and Holmes, 1996).

Fourth, an assessment of the risk associated with the crime itself is an important input in the profiling process. The risk associated with a crime is determined by the circumstances of that crime (e.g., the place that it occurred, the time of day at which it occurred, the type of victim involved). Crimes that are high risk to the offender usually indicate either that the offender targeted that particular victim (and that there was some type of relationship between the victim and the offender), or that the offender needed an element of high risk or thrill to be satisfied by the crime (i.e., signature) (O'Toole, 1999).

Fifth, the offender's method of approach or attack may provide clues regarding his characteristics. A surprise or blitz-style attack during which the victim was immediately rendered unconscious may indicate a lack of social abilities on the part of the offender. Low self-esteem or a verbal or physical impediment of some sort may prevent a conversation to be used to lure the victim away (Geberth, 1996). In addition, a blitz-style attack often indicates a younger killer and, as noted, a disorganized offender (Porter, 1983). A victim who was killed slowly and methodically indicates a more sadistic personality, and a man in his twenties or thirties. Defensive injuries (e.g., knife wounds to hands) are an indication that the attack was not blitz style. The presence of defensive injuries on the victim often indicates that the interaction began as a verbal exchange or altercation and was followed by physical assault, during which the victim had time and warning to react (O'Toole, 1999).

Sixth, evidence of depersonalization may be indicative of the characteristics of the offender. For example, trauma to the face usually indicates a relationship between a victim and an offender. The more severe the attack, the closer the relationship. The use of blindfolds on the victim and covering the victim's face may or may not be indicative of a relationship between the offender and the victim (Holmes and Holmes, 1996). Holmes and Holmes (1996) note that forced oral sex with a blindfold on the victim usually indicates a stranger-perpetrated crime; no blindfold usually indicates an acquaintance-perpetrated crime. In general, acts of depersonalization are often associated with disorganized murderers.

Finally, the presence of staging may reveal information about the identity of the culprit. Staging "occurs when someone purposely alters the crime scene prior to the arrival of the police" (Douglas and Munn, 1992; p. 7). Staging consists of the introduction of false clues designed to throw the police investigation off course. An example of staging was present in the kidnaping of fourteen-year-old Elizabeth Smart, who was abducted from her Salt Lake City home during the early morning hours of June 5, 2002. Reportedly, the police found that a window screen in the house was cut, presumably by the offender, in an attempt to disguise the way in which entry was gained into the house. It was initially suspected by investigators that the cut screen was staged because it was not large enough for an individual to gain entry. Later it was determined that the cut screen may not have been staged. Most often, a crime scene is staged by an offender who knows or is familiar with the victim. The staging is done in an attempt to distract the police from discovering such a relationship. Another reason why scenes may be staged is to protect the victim or the victim's family from embarrassment. For example, in rape/murder cases or autoerotic deaths, the family member who discovers the body may dress the victim or make it look like a suicide (sometimes even write a suicide note) (Douglas and Munn, 1992). Although the presence of staging may allow one to infer information about the identity of the perpetrator, the difficulty is that it may be difficult to determine whether a particular crime scene dimension is staged or whether it is legitimate. For example, in the Carol Stuart murder investigation, discussed in Chapter 3, the gunshot sustained by Charles Stuart was staged, but the police initially believed it to be legitimate. In the unsolved murder of JonBenet Ramsey (discussed later in this chapter) it is unclear whether the ransom note left at the scene was staged or whether it was legitimate. In short, the recognition of staging at the crime scene may provide useful clues, but staging is not always easily identifiable.

The Effectiveness of Psychological Profiles

Few studies have systematically examined the overall usefulness of psychological profiles in the criminal investigative process. In 1981, the FBI conducted an internal study on the value of psychological profiles to the agencies that requested one (reported in Pinizzotto [1984]). Of the 192 total requests for a profile, a suspect was identified in eighty-eight cases (forty-six percent). Of these solved cases, it was reported that in fifteen (seventeen percent), the profile helped in the identification of the suspect. In another fifteen cases (seventeen percent), the profile was deemed by investigators to be of no assistance. In the remaining solved cases, the most commonly cited benefit of the profile was that it helped focus the investigation (see also Homant and Kennedy [1998]).

In a study by Trager and Brewster (2001), representatives from primarily large police departments in the United States were surveyed and asked about their experiences with psychological profiles in criminal investigations. Twenty-five departments (sixty-three percent) stated that they had used psychological profiles in the past. Of these departments, ten (thirty-eight percent) indicated that psychological profiles had helped identify a suspect, but six (twenty-five percent) indicated that psychological profiles actually hindered the identification of a suspect. Few methodological details or other findings were provided in the study.

One study examined the accuracy of psychological profiles. In this study, experienced profilers reviewed case documentation on two actual cases, a murder and a rape. Profilers then constructed profiles of the perpetrators based on this information. It was determined that approximately one half the information provided by the experienced profilers was correct, although there was considerable variation among the profilers. For the students who reviewed the case materials and constructed the profiles, it was found that approximately forty percent of the resulting details were correct (Pinizzotto and Finkel, 1990). Other literature that makes claims about the accuracy of profiles provides primarily anecdotal accounts of profiles that have been "right on the mark."

Given the paucity of research on the topic, it is hazardous to draw conclusions about the impact and accuracy of psychological profiles in criminal investigations. According to Homant and Kennedy (1998):

> [o]ur take on the evidence at this point is that it is important to expect that a significant number of mistakes will occur with profiling. Where the mistakes can be guarded against, there is no reason not to use it. For example, in the area of criminal investigation, certainly no significant leads should be overlooked simply because someone does not fit a profile, and no particular suspect should be focused on without supporting evidence. (p. 339)

To be more confident and certain about the utility and accuracy of psychological profiles in criminal investigations, additional research is clearly needed. In particular, the research needs to be conducted by neutral researchers, researchers who do not have a vested interest in the success of psychological profiles. In addition, the studies should not be published for only a limited (e.g., agency-based) audience. Finally, the studies need to include a representative sample and provide systematic analyses of the data. Each of the studies reported here that has examined the utility of psychological profiles has at least one or more of these deficiencies. Although there is clearly room for improvement, it should also be noted that it may be difficult to assess empirically the accuracy of psychological profiles if the suspect is never apprehended. "It is possible that accurate profiles may be more likely to result in solved cases; thus inaccurate profiles may be less likely to come to light (Homant and Kennedy, 1998; p. 340).

Geographical Profiling

Geographical profiling "is an investigative methodology that uses locations of a connected series of crime to determine the most probable area of offender residence" (Rossmo, 2000; p. 1). The methodology is useful in serial crimes as well as "single crimes that involve multiple scenes or other significant geographic characteristics" (Rossmo, 2000; p. 1). According to the letter sent by the Vancouver (British Columbia) Police Department to agencies that request a geographical profile, a geographical profile:

> . . . is an investigative support technique for serial violent crime investigations. The process analyzes the locations connected to a series of crimes to determine the most probable area of offender residence. It should be regarded as an information management system designed to help focus an investigation, prioritize tips and suspects, and suggest new strategies to complement traditional methods. (Rossmo, 2000; p. 216)

The process of developing a geographical profile normally follows the following steps:

- Thorough review of the case file, including investigative reports, witness statements, autopsy reports, and criminal profile (if any)
- Detailed examination of the crime scene and area photographs
- Interviews with lead investigators and crime analysts
- Visits to each of the crime sites, when possible
- Review of neighborhood and demographic information
- Study of street, land use, and transit maps
- Analysis
- Report preparation (Rossmo, 2000; p. 219)

Just as the case with the construction of psychological profiles of offenders, certain actions of the perpetrator may provide probabilistic clues regarding the characteristics of the perpetrator. For example, a crime scene (e.g., a place where the victim's body was disposed of) on or close to a major road may indicate that the murderer is not from the area or is not intimately familiar with the area. A crime scene a mile or more from a major road suggests the killer is from the area (Rossmo, 2000). The more remote the area of the crime scene (e.g., location of the encounter, attack, crime, body disposal, etc.), the more likely the culprit is well acquainted with the area.

The fundamental premise of geographical profiling is that human beings do not move randomly throughout their environment. People spend time in areas in which they are most familiar—they spend most of their time in their "comfort zone." Within this comfort zone there are anchor points and familiar routes to and from these points. Anchor points consist of the most important places in the zone and most often include an individual's residence as well as work site, friends' homes, places of entertainment, and so forth. The familiar routes to and from these places comprise an individual's cognitive map of an area, which is likely much less detailed and complete than an actual map of the area.

For the sake of a simple illustration, consider the task of grocery shopping. Chances are that when you go grocery shopping, you shop at a particular store more often than you shop at any other store, even though there may be numerous stores from which you could choose where to do your shopping. This store is likely to be in relative close proximity to where you live, or on a street that you travel regularly (e.g., the route that you take from your home to your place of work). The fact that this store is located in a familiar area and that you visit this particular store more often than any other store, provides a certain comfort level—with everything from how to get to the store, where to park when at the store, the layout of the store, to the products sold by the store. This familiarity makes the task of shopping relatively easy. Have you ever, just for the fun of it, randomly picked a store on the other side of town, or in a different city, in which to go grocery shopping? Maybe, but probably not. It would be relatively difficult to shop at this place. You might need a map to get there, you might feel uncomfortable there, you might simply feel lost. The desire to exist and live in familiar areas is a powerful force on human behavior. The same logic can be applied to criminal behavior. For example,

> in investigating a murder, it is important to ask why the killer decided to search that particular area for a victim, why he chose a particular area to dump the body, and why he picked the particular travel route that he did. What were the geographic characteristics that made the victim selection area, body disposal location, and route of travel so attractive? These choices of the particular offender should not be considered to be mere accident (Holmes and Holmes, 1996; p. 154).

The assumptions of geographical profiling—namely, that most activity occurs in one's comfort zone and that travel is nonrandom—is well supported by the research that has examined spacial issues in the distribution of criminal behaviors. Among the most significant and consistent findings is that offenders most often commit crimes relatively close to their homes. This is especially true for juvenile offenders, for those who commit violent crimes, and for the initial crimes of serial offenders (see Holmes and Holmes [1996]). Indeed, based on a review of the literature conducted by McIver (1981), it was concluded that "[w]hile criminals are mobile, they don't seem to go very far in committing a crime. A majority of crimes appear to take place within a mile of the criminal's residence. This conclusion seems true for all types of crime" (p. 22).

The ultimate objective of geographical profiling is to identify the area in which a suspect lives. Indeed, although stated with few supporting details and little empirical support, Rossmo (2000) claims that "geographic profiling determines the location of offender residence within five percent of the total hunting area" (Rossmo, 2000; p. 242).

Psycholinguistics

Psycholinguistics involves the analysis of spoken or written words to (1) develop information about the person responsible for the statement, (2) associate crimes based on the similarities of communication, and (3) identify deception and other hidden meanings of the statement (Adams, 1996; Gudjonsson, 1992; Miron and Douglas, 1979). The "theory" that underlies the methodology of psycholinguistics is that the words and patterns evident in written statements are potentially unique to the writer and may reveal the characteristics of the writer. As explained by Douglas et al. (1986):

> Psycholinguistic techniques have been used to compose a "threat dictionary," whereby every word in a message is assigned, by computer, to a specific category. Words as they are used in a threat message are then compared with those words as they are used in ordinary speech or writings. The vocabulary usage in the message may yield "signature" words unique to the offender. In this way, police may not only be able to determine that several letters were written by the same individual, but also to learn about the background and psychology of the offender. (p. 402)

Psycholinguistics is also often referred to as *statement analysis* or *stylometry*—"the branch of psycholinguistics and literary studies that attempts to quantitatively identify the ways in which the writings, or spoken words, of one individual differ from those of another" (Adams, 1996; Gudjonsson, 1992). In each approach, the language structure of the statement or document is analyzed for clues about the individual who wrote or spoke the words. This analysis may include an examination of grammar, the use of certain words, syntax, spelling, word frequency, sentence length, sentence structure, number of syllables used per 100 words, and other linguistic characteristics (Gudjonsson, 1992; Miron and Douglas, 1979).

With regard to the linguistic analysis of statements, the identification of particular pronouns, nouns, and verbs, and how they may be used in statements, may be revealing. This approach is most useful in identifying deception and other hidden meanings of statements. For example, with regard to the use of pronouns, most people use "I" to refer to their own behaviors and actions. If another pronoun (or no pronoun) is used, it may signal an attempt to hide or minimize involvement in some action. Consider this statement:

> *I* got up at 7:00 when my alarm clock went off. *I* took a shower and got dressed. *I* decided to go out for breakfast. *I* went to the McDonald's on the corner. Met a man who lives nearby. Talked to him for a few minutes. *I* finished breakfast and drove to work. (Adams, 1996; p. 14)

The first four sentences show normal use of the pronoun "I", but the next two statements are odd in that "I" is not included. On the face of it, it is not clear why the speaker changed his pattern of speech; however, it is potentially significant and worthy of additional exploration. Perhaps meeting this man was incriminating in some way and the speaker wished to minimize his involvement with this individual.

Along the same line, most people use the pronoun "we" to indicate more than one person, and to show a togetherness or relationship of some sort between people. The use of "we" is appropriate and normal in some instances but not in others. Consider a statement from a rape victim that "We then went into the woods." It is unusual that a rape victim, or any victim for that matter, would use the word "we" to indicate herself and the perpetrator. More likely would be a statement such as "*He* forced *me* into the woods." At the least, the use of the pronoun "we" indicates a relationship between the victim and the offender, and this possibility should be explored during the investigation (Adams, 1996).

The use of possessive pronouns (e.g., my, his, their) may also be revealing. Possessive pronouns indicate attachment toward a person or object. Changes in the use of possessive pronouns may be an attempt to hide attachment. Consider this statement from a person whose home burned to the ground (Adams, 1996):

> I left *my* house right after breakfast to join my friends at the track for the day . . . I drove back to *my* house, made a few phone calls, then went out to dinner with Stan Thompson . . . Stan dropped me off at *my* house around 10:00. After I changed my clothes I left *the* house to spend the night at my cousin Tom's. Around midnight we heard fire engines and got up to see what was going on. (p. 16)

What is most curious about the statement is the last reference to his house as "the" house. Prior to the mention of "the" house, "my" house was used consistently. Was that because he gave up possession of the house before it was set on fire? Again, this unusual word usage may be worthy of further exploration and questioning by investigators.

Another potentially important dimension of statement analysis is an examination of the use of nouns (words used to indicate persons, places, or things). Once again, changes in the use of nouns in a statement may be a red flag and worthy of additional attention. For example, a husband was a suspect in the fatal shooting of his wife. The statement that he provided to the police made consistent reference to "my wife" seven times and then the noun use changed abruptly as he described the actual shooting:

> . . . I lost control of the gun. I sensed that the barrel was pointing in *Louise's* direction and I reacted by grabbing at the gun to get it back under control. When I did this the

gun discharged. It went off once and I looked over and saw blood on *Louise's* face (Adams, 1996; p. 16).

The question is, Why did the noun referent change? Perhaps it would have been more difficult to admit to killing his "wife" than it was to shoot this person named "Louise" accidentally. Perhaps even more significant and revealing is if he would have simply used the pronoun "her" instead of "Louise." In addition, in his statement there was no introduction to "Louise." The suspect went from speaking about his "wife" to speaking about "Louise." "The norm for healthy relationships is a proper, clear introduction. But in tumultuous relationships, introductions often are confusing or missing completely. The lack of a proper introduction most likely indicates a poor relationship between the husband and his wife" (Adams, 1996; p. 17). In any case, examination of the use of nouns in communications may provide some insight into the truth.

Finally, the verbs one uses in expressing meaning may be revealing. Verbs are action words and can be expressed in the past, present, or future tense. The norm is past tense because when the event is recalled, it has already occurred. Consider this unusual statement:

It happened Saturday night. I *went* out on my back deck to water the plants. It was almost dark. A man *runs* out of the bushes. He *comes* onto the deck, *grabs* me and *knocks* me down (Adams, 1996; p. 18).

The change to the present tense beginning in the fourth sentence reveals a certain awkwardness in recalling the story and may be indicative of deception. Although past tense is normal in recounting past events, use of the present tense is normal in referring to missing persons. For example, one of the statements made by Susan Smith to the media in speaking about her missing children was "They *needed* me" (Adams, 1996). This was an unusual statement because at the time it was reasonable to believe, especially from the children's mother, that the children were alive and that they were still in *need* of her. As it was later revealed, they did not need her at the time she made the statement because they were already dead, and she knew it.

As an example of how psycholinguistics may be used to develop information about a culprit, consider the investigation of the anthrax letters sent to the editor of the *New York Post*, Senate Majority Leader Tom Daschle, and NBC news anchor Tom Brokaw in September and October 2001. Each letter contained deadly weapons-grade anthrax. The letters contaminated several U.S. Post Office facilities as well as other places, led to the deaths of five people, injured eighteen others, and required 35,000 people to take antibiotics as a precautionary measure (BBC News, 2002). As of 2003, the persons responsible for sending the letters have not been identified.

The first determination made by linguistic experts was that the three letters were written by the same individual. As noted by Gideon Epstein, former chief forensic document examiner for the U.S. Army and the INS, the letters sent to the *Post* and to Tom Brokaw were identical in form and content. The letter to Daschle was similar to the other two in

EXHIBIT 9–1 Three Anthrax letters

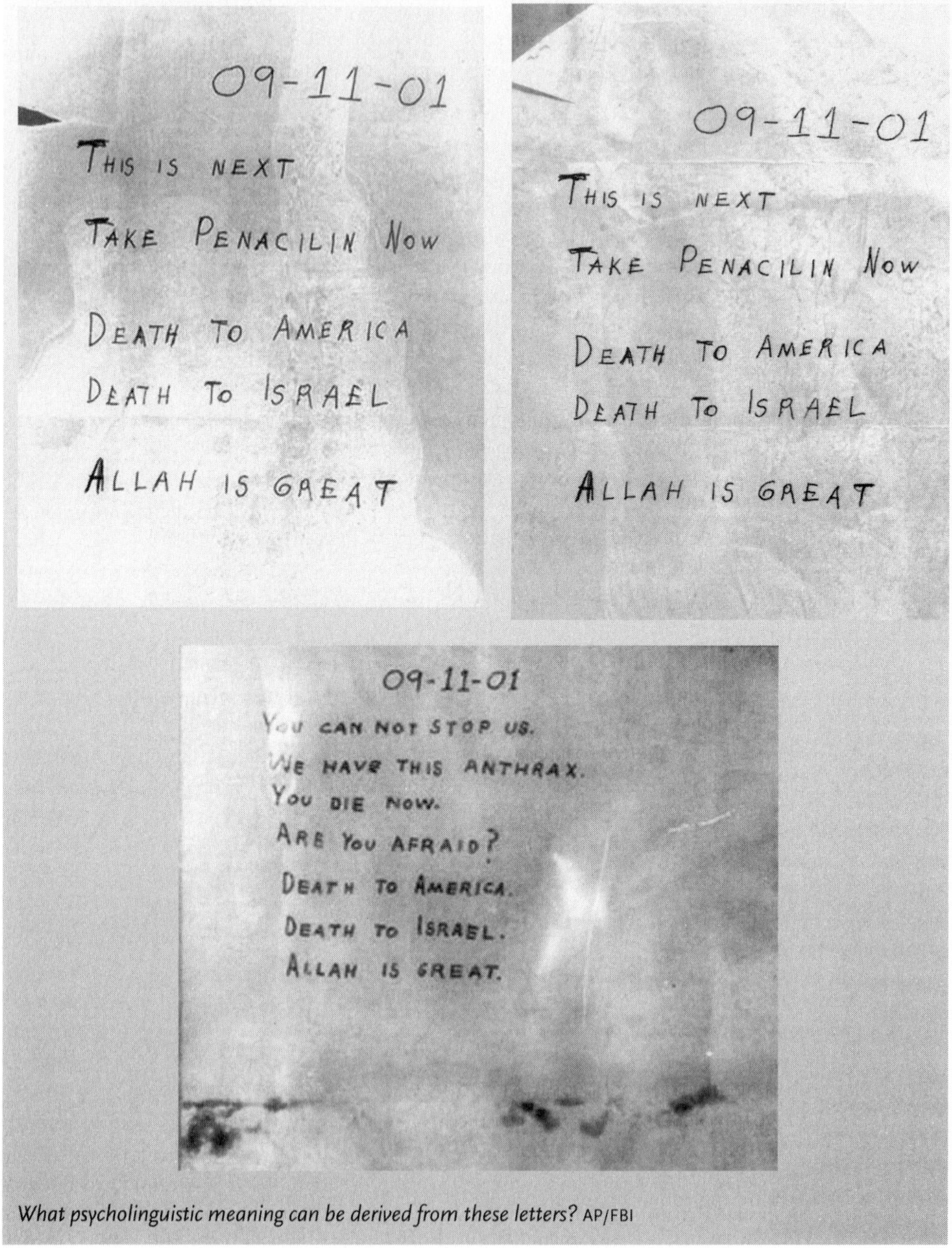

09-11-01
THIS IS NEXT
TAKE PENACILIN NOW
DEATH TO AMERICA
DEATH TO ISRAEL
ALLAH IS GREAT

09-11-01
THIS IS NEXT
TAKE PENACILIN NOW
DEATH TO AMERICA
DEATH TO ISRAEL
ALLAH IS GREAT

09-11-01
YOU CAN NOT STOP US.
WE HAVE THIS ANTHRAX.
YOU DIE NOW.
ARE YOU AFRAID?
DEATH TO AMERICA.
DEATH TO ISRAEL.
ALLAH IS GREAT.

What psycholinguistic meaning can be derived from these letters? AP/FBI

content, although it was more threatening (i.e., "you die now"). The spacing between words, letters, and lines was consistent across the notes, as were the margins. Each note contained letters that were very similar in structure (e.g., Gs that look like 6s) (Peterson and Jackson, 2001). As for clues about the writer, the phrase "Allah is great" was potentially most revealing. The simplistic and obvious stereotypical slogan might point to someone who was a theologically conservative Muslim or, more likely, one who was trying to disguise the letters as being written by a Muslim terrorist. A more common Arabic phrase, "Allahu Akbar," would more likely be used by Muslims in such a context (Peterson and Jackson, 2001). In addition, all of the notes had childlike, simple letters, which may indicate that the writer was someone unfamiliar with the English language or, perhaps more likely, was trying to disguise his handwriting deliberately. The misspelling of "penicillin" might also be meaningful. It could suggest a foreigner or, more likely, someone who was trying to make the notes look like the work of a foreigner. In addition, as noted by Professor Don Foster, a well-respected forensic linguist, the advice provided in the two letters to "take penicillin now" is curious because penicillin is the wrong antibiotic to take. Whoever was dealing with this sophisticated form of anthrax probably knew that penicillin was not the medication to take; this was probably an attempt to throw off investigators—"Hey, don't think that I'm a scientist, don't think that I know anything about antibiotics" (BBC News, 2002). Recently, the FBI has begun investigating the possible role of several U.S. government scientists in the deadly anthrax mailings. As with psychological profiling and geographical profiling, statement analysis may be most useful in focusing an investigation; although, as noted in this case, little solid information that actually points to the identity of the perpetrator can be derived from the notes.

As another example of the application of psycholinguistics, consider the investigation into the murder of six-year-old JonBenet Ramsey on December 25, 1996. At approximately 5:00 AM on December 26, Patsy Ramsey, the mother of JonBenet, woke and proceeded down the steps of their exclusive home in Boulder, Colorado. At the foot of the staircase, she found a two and one-half page ransom note that stated that JonBenet had been kidnaped. She then went to JonBenet's bedroom, opened the door, and found that she was not in her bed. The police were notified and arrived minutes later. After searching the home several times, John Ramsey, JonBenet's father, discovered JonBenet's dead body in a closet in the basement of the house. It was determined that she had died as a result of a blow to the head and was strangled (via ligature). Investigative attention immediately focused on the ransom note. The note was hand written with a pen and written on a tablet of paper from the house. It read as follows:

Mr. Ramsey:

Listen carefully! We are a group of individuals that represent a small foreign faction. We [cross-out] respect your bussiness but not the country that it serves. At this time we have your daughter in our posession. She is safe and un harmed and if you want her to see 1997, you must follow our instructions to the letter.

You will withdraw $118,000.00 from your account. $100,000 will be in $100 bills and the remaining $18,000 in $20 bills. Make sure that you bring an adequate size attache to the bank. When you get home you will put the money in a brown paper bag. I will call you between 8 and 10 am tomorrow to instruct you on delivery. The delivery will be exhausting so I advise you to be rested. If we monitor you getting the money early, we might call you early to arrange an earlier delivery of the [page 2] money and hence a earlier [delivery crossed-out] pick-up of your daughter.

Any deviation of my instructions will result in the immediate execution of your daughter. You will also be denied her remains for proper burial. The two gentlemen watching over your daughter do not particularly like you so I advise you not to provoke them. Speaking to anyone about your situation, such as Police, F.B.I., etc., will result in your daughter being beheaded. If we catch you talking to a stray dog, she dies. If you alert bank authorities, she dies. If the money is in any way marked or tampered with, she dies. You will be scanned for electronic devices and if any are found, she dies. You can try to deceive us but be warned that we are familiar with Law enforcement countermeasures and tactics. You stand a 99% chance of killing your daughter if you try to out smart us. Follow our instructions [page 3] and you stand a 100% chance of getting her back. You and your family are under constant scrutiny as well as the authorities. Don't try to grow a brain John. You are not the only fat cat around so don't think that killing will be difficult. Don't underestimate us John. Use that good southern common sense of yours. It is up to you now John!

Victory!
S.B.T.C.
(Douglas, 2000)

The Ramsey House. The ransom note left in the scene of the JonBennet Ramsey homicide raised more questions than answers about who was responsible for her death.

No doubt, much was made (and continues to be made) of the ransom note. It was odd for several reasons not the least of which was that JonBenet was not taken from her house. When a ransom note is present, there is rarely a body; when a body is present there is rarely a ransom note. The note did not seem to fit. But was the note staging? Over the years, a multitude of theories have been developed to explain the still unsolved homicide. Many include John or Patsy as being responsible for the note and the murder. All the theories include some explanation of the ransom note. John Douglas, the famed and now retired FBI profiler, was hired by the Ramsey's to assist in the investigation. In his book *The Cases That Haunt Us* (2000), he provides his thoughts on the ransom note and who was responsible for writing it. Among his conclusions:

■ The note was written with block letters, not a common style of printing. This suggested someone who was either very nervous or someone who was trying to disguise his or her handwriting.

■ Given the length and the rambling nature of the note, it had to have been written prior to the murder. No one would have the ability to compose such a letter after killing the little girl and with her body lying in the basement. As such, it could not have been part of a "staged" crime scene. "Anyone trying to make up a ransom note as staging would write something as short and to the point as possible. You'd be careful not to give any unnecessary clues" (p. 322).

■ Except for a few instances, the spelling is correct and syntax is proper, indicating that an educated individual wrote the note.

■ The ransom amount is curious. It is a small amount, given the wealth of the Ramsey's, and it is specific—$118,000. This amount of money had been recently deposited into John Ramsey's bank account. The writer was not a sophisticated or professional criminal (or the amount would have been much larger). The writer of the note was likely in the house before and had seen some documentation regarding this amount of money. This "inside" information is more reason that the Ramsey's were not responsible than it is that they were responsible. Why would they point the finger at themselves with this information?

■ Some sentences are awkward and rather silly (e.g., "Listen carefully!" "We are a group of individuals that represent a small foreign faction.") This is the sort of line one might expect to hear in a Hollywood movie. These sorts of phrases may indicate a teenager or young adult who is familiar with movies. Other phrases in the note also parallel movie lines (e.g., "Don't try to grow a brain") (see Douglas, 2000; p. 323 for other examples).

■ The reference to "execution" and "beheaded" is also unusual, especially from parents who may have been involved in the death of their child. The thought of being "denied her remains for proper burial" is also unheard of coming from parents of a dead child.

Douglas (2000) concludes:

> I can't be certain from the note who wrote it and who killed JonBenet, but from the psycholinguistic analysis, it does not appear to have been written by a forty-year-old woman panic-stricken over having just accidentally killed her daughter. (p. 324)

Other experts have also analyzed the note and have come to a different conclusion (see www.statementanalysis.com listed in Related Internet Sites at the conclusion of this chapter). Particularly significant is that the note does not make sense as a true ransom note, the peculiar use of the word "hence" and the corresponding sentence structure, and the odd use of several other words. For example, the word "hence" is unusual and the sentence in which it is used is noteworthy: "we might call you early to arrange an earlier delivery of the money and hence a earlier (delivery crossed-out) pick-up of your daug hter." The word "delivery" was used before and after the word "hence" (although the second "delivery" was crossed out), and the word "and" was placed before "hence," which is not necessary or usual. In December 1997, almost a year after the murder, a church service was held in Boulder for JonBenet. In the program there was a written message from the Ramsey's. It read: "Had there been no birth of Christ, there would be no hope of eternal life, and hence, no hope of ever being with our loved ones again." Does the sentence structure look familiar? A coincidence? The case remains unsolved.

As additional examples, consider the Lindbergh baby kidnaping discussed in the introduction to Chapter 2. Several of the words used, and the spelling of those words (e.g., "mony," "anyding," "gut"), suggested that the author was German speaking with a German accent. In the Unabomber investigation, discussed in Chapter 1, consider the significance of the phrase "You can't eat your cake and have it too." Recall, this phrase was included in the Unabomber's manifesto, which was published in *The Washington Post* and was recognized by David Kaczynski, Ted Kaczynski's brother, as a unique phrase used by Ted. These signature words, and later a more thorough comparison of the manifesto with other writings of Ted, led to the identification of Ted Kaczynski as the Unabomber.

In sum, behavioral evidence, analyzed through the methods of psychological profiling, geographical profiling, or psycholinguistics is potentially useful evidence in the criminal investigative process. It is by its nature, however, probabilistic and subject to error, as is other evidence available to investigators.

Questions for Discussion and Review

1. What is a psychological profile?

2. What is the difference between psychological profiling, crime scene profiling, and offender profiling? What are the similarities?

3. What is the basic theory underlying the psychological profiling process?

4. What are the goals of the psychological profiling process? How is a psychological profile similar to physical evidence?

5. What are the steps in the process of constructing a psychological profile?

6. What is the importance of the distinction between organized and disorganized crime scenes and offenders? What are the characteristics of each?

7. What is the difference between MO and signature? Why is it potentially important? What are the problems with the distinction?

8. How does victim risk relate to the construction of a psychological profile?

9. How does the risk associated with the crime itself relate to the construction of a psychological profile?

10. What is staging? Why is it done? What is the problem associated with the identification of staging at a crime scene?

11. Based on the research that has been conducted on the issue, what can one conclude about the effectiveness of psychological profiling?

12. What is geographical profiling? What is the primary goal of geographical profiling?

13. What is a comfort zone? What are anchor points? What is a cognitive map? How do they relate to the process of geographical profiling?

14. What is psycholinguistics? What are the goals associated with the methodology?

15. What might the peculiar use of pronouns, nouns, and verbs reveal about a person who provides a particular statement?

16. What meanings could be revealed from the psycholinguistic analysis of the anthrax letters? The ransom note in the JonBenet Ramsey murder case? The Unabomber's manifesto? The Lindbergh baby ransom note?

Related Internet Sites

www.statementanalysis.com
As the name of this link suggests, this site is devoted to the issue of investigative statement analysis. Much valuable and interesting information is provided here. It applies linguistic analysis to several famous cases, including the murder of JonBenet Ramsey.

www.crimemagazine.com/jonbenet.htm
This site provides a comprehensive review of the investigation into the murder of JonBenet Ramsey. Various investigative theories are presented and discussed.

www.casebook.org
This site offers everything you ever wanted to know about Jack the Ripper but were afraid to ask.

OTHER SOURCES OF INFORMATION

OBJECTIVES

After reading this chapter you will be able to

- Summarize the investigation of the sniper case that occurred during October 2002, and discuss how the suspected perpetrators were identified and apprehended
- Discuss the role of the media and tip lines in the sniper investigation
- Discuss the use of computer databases during the sniper investigation and how this investigation highlighted some of the limitations of such databases
- Discuss how tip lines, television shows, and alerts may assist in criminal investigations
- Discuss the potential problems associated with the use of tip lines, the public, and the media for crime information
- Discuss the role of confidential informants in criminal investigations
- Describe the various forms of crime analysis and how it can be used as a tool in criminal investigations

- Discuss the purpose of the Violent Criminal Apprehension Program (VICAP), explain how it works, and identify its limitations
- Discuss the role and limitations of computer databases and information networks in criminal investigations
- Discuss the NCIC, what information it contains, and how it works
- Discuss the National Law Enforcement Telecommunications System (NLETS), what information it contains, and how it works
- Identify other databases that could be of assistance in conducting criminal investigations
- Discuss the role and usefulness of psychics in criminal investigations

IMPORTANT TERMS

The public as a source of information in criminal investigations

Crime Stoppers, Crime Solvers, and We Tip programs

America's Most Wanted television show

AMBER plan/alert

Confidential informants

Crime analysis

Computerized Crime Statistics (COMPSTAT)

VICAP

Intra- and interdepartmental databases

NCIC

NLETS

Psychics

INTRODUCTION

The manhunt began the night of October 2, 2002, when James Martin, age fifty-five, was shot dead in a parking lot of a grocery store in Wheaton, Maryland. It ended eleven victims and twenty-one days later when two suspects, John Allen Muhammad, age forty-one, and John Lee Malvo, age seventeen, were arrested while they slept in their car at a rest stop off Interstate 70, approximately fifty miles northwest of Washington, DC. During the course of the deadly rampage, thirteen individuals were shot, each with a single bullet fired from a distance with a high-powered rifle; ten of the victims were killed, three were critically injured. The deadliest day was October 3, when five people were shot. All the victims were going about their usual activities at the time they were gunned down—mowing the grass, cleaning the car, leaving a restaurant, getting off a bus, going to school, shopping. The victims varied in age; the youngest was thirteen, the oldest was fifty-five. The victims were white, African American, and Latino. The shootings occurred at night, during the day, weekdays, and weekends. Seven of the shootings took place in Maryland, five in Virginia, and one in Washington, DC. The millions of people who lived and worked in the area were in the firm grip of fear. A sniper, or snipers, were on the loose.

Through the first seven shootings, which occurred October 2 through 4, the police had few clues, few good leads. What seemed to be most significant was that the police had witnesses. No one actually saw the shooter, but witnesses reported seeing a white van in the area after several of the shootings. In other incidents, witnesses reported seeing a white box truck in the vicinity. In one incident, a witness told the police that he saw a dark-colored Chevrolet Caprice driving away from the scene with its lights off. The importance of the Caprice, however, got drowned out by the continued sightings of the white van and white truck. By October 12, the police and FBI had obtained enough information from witnesses to develop a composite picture of the van and the truck believed to be involved in the shootings. The pictures of these vehicles were then released to the public through the media. The police checked out and searched hundreds of white vans and trucks, looking for anything suspicious and anything that was linked to the shootings. They found nothing.

Along with the witness reports of the white van and truck, the police also had some idea regarding the sniper's MO. In particular, all the victims were shot with the same ammunition—a .223-caliber bullet, popular with hunters, competitive shooters, and the military. Given the distance at which many of the victims were believed to have been shot, the police also suspected that the sniper had some skill and training as a marksman, maybe a military background. Most of the shootings were concentrated in the Montgomery County area, suggesting that the killer lived in that area. There was also a hint that the killer was watching developments in the investigation on television, and altering his activities based on investigative developments. For example, when officials appeared on television and discussed how geographical profiling was going to be used in the investigation, and what it could reveal about the killer, the shooting moved to Virginia. When Montgomery County Police Chief

Charles Moose appeared on television and reassured parents that their children were safe, the sniper's next victim was a thirteen-year-old boy who was critically wounded after arriving at school. It was after this shooting on October 7 that the police obtained an important piece of evidence, and it was believed to have come directly from the killer. In searching the area around the school where the shooting occurred, the police discovered a tarot "death" card along with a spent shell casing in some matted grass. On the back of the card was a message that read, "Dear Policeman, I am God." Along with the card was a note that stated that the police should not reveal the message to the media. The discovery of the card and its message was "leaked" to the media and, for reasons that became clear later, this may have actually helped the investigation.

The police devised a plan to shut down Interstate 95, the shooter's suspected escape route after previous shootings, and set up roadblocks and checkpoints in response to any additional shootings. It was hoped that after a shooting, the sniper would get ensnared in the roadblock on his way back to his home territory of Montgomery County. The police did not have to wait long to try it out. On October 14, a woman was gunned down in the parking lot of a Home Depot store in Falls Church, Virginia. The police immediately obtained information from several witnesses that, again, a white van was seen driving away from the scene after the gunshots were heard. One witness in particular provided what seemed to be a good lead, the most specific information yet—the shooter was driving a cream-colored Chevrolet Astro van with a burned-out left taillight and a chrome ladder rack on its roof. Better yet, the witness also told the police that he saw the shooter and his gun. The gun was described as an AK-47 and the shooter had dark skin. Another witness reported seeing a dark-colored Chevy or Chrysler leaving the store parking lot after the shooting. The police focused on the more specific white van. The plan to shut down traffic was quickly implemented. Traffic around the Washington, DC, area was backed up for miles as the police searched dozens upon dozens of white vans as they moved through the roadblocks. Again, the police found nothing. (The roadblock tactic was used two more times, on the evening of October 19 after a man was fatally shot in a Ponderosa restaurant parking lot in Ashland, Virginia, and on the morning of October 22 after a bus driver was fatally shot in Silver Spring, Maryland. None of the roadblocks were helpful in the investigation. It was believed at the time that the shooter was familiar enough with the area to evade the police by using side roads.) After additional questioning of the witness who provided the information about the van and the shooter, the police concluded that it was impossible for him to see what he said he saw. Security surveillance video from inside the Home Depot store showed that he was inside the store the entire time. The "witness" fabricated the information. He was subsequently charged with providing false information to the police. More frustration and still not even close to solving the case.

On October 17, an operator at the police tip line that was established to receive tips from the public about the shootings received a telephone call from an individual who stated that he was the sniper, and he was angry because he was unable to get through to the police earlier. (The sniper had earlier called the general police number in Rockville, Maryland, and spoke with a police operator. He tried to prove that he was the sniper by providing certain information including the intended secret words written on the tarot card [i.e., "I am God"]. The police telephone operator told him that her agency was not involved in the investigation and referred him to the Montgomery County tip line. On at least one occasion, the sniper called the tip line and was disconnected. It was reported that the police tip line received hundreds of apparently bogus calls during which the caller claimed to be God.) To try to get the police to take him seriously, the sniper provided a clue, a big clue. The caller reportedly told the police that they should "look to Montgomery" and that they would realize then that he was not joking. The police were initially unsure as to what the message meant. Montgomery? The only thing that was clear was that the caller spoke broken English and had a strong but unidentifiable accent.

The next day, October 18, the sniper was back at work in Ashland, Virginia. At 8:00 PM a man was fatally shot in a Ponderosa restaurant parking lot. In searching the area around the restaurant after the shooting, the police found a note tacked to a tree in a nearby woods. It was handwritten and was four pages long, including a cover page on which five stars were neatly drawn. The letter contained threats and made demands. In the note, the sniper railed about his previous attempts to communicate unsuccessfully with the police. It identified the phone numbers that he called and the names of the persons with whom he spoke on the six previous calls to the police. It also made reference to a phone call he made to a "Priest in ashland." The note read in part:

> . . . These people took of calls for a Hoax or Joke, so your failure to respond has cost you five lives. If stopping the killing is more important than catching us now, then you will accept our demand which are non-negotiable.
> You will place ten million dollar in Bank of America account no. [ ]
> Pin no. [ ]
> Activation date [ ]
> Exp date [ ]
> Name [ ]
> member since [ ]
> Platinum Visa Account
> We will have unlimited withdrawl at any atm worldwide.
> You will activate the bank account, credit card, and Pin number. . . .
> You have until 9:00 AM Monday morning to complete transaction.
> Try to catch us withdrawing at least you will have less body bags. . . .
> If we give you our word that is what takes place. "Word is Bond."
> P.S. Your children are not safe anywhere at any time.
> (Kovaleski and Horwitz, 2002)

The note contained a wealth of clues. First, the Bank of America bank information. In tracing the credit card identified in the note, it was discovered that it was reported stolen by a Greyhound bus driver in Flagstaff, Arizona, on March 25, 2002. She did not realize that it was taken from her until April 11, when the bank contacted her about a gasoline purchase in Tacoma, Washington. That purchase was determined by the bank to be fraudulent and the account was closed. The writing style of the note was also of significance. It appeared to match the speaking style of the individual who made the earlier phone call to the police. The reference to the phone call that was made to the "Priest in ashland" was also intriguing. Further investigation into this phone call led investigators to the Reverend William Sullivan, a priest at St. Ann's Roman Catholic Church in Ashland. When questioned by investigators, he told them that on the prior day, October 18, he received a phone call from someone who stated that he was God and that he was the sniper. The caller said that he was calling because he was not able to get through to the police. The priest also told the police that the caller made reference to a crime that occurred recently in Montgomery, Alabama. The priest said that he dismissed the call as a hoax, and as a result did not report it earlier to authorities. With this information, particularly the reference to the shooting in Montgomery, Alabama, the earlier phone call reference to "Montgomery" made sense. The FBI immediately contacted the Montgomery, Alabama, Police Department and learned about a robbery/homicide that occurred there on September 21. The police in Montgomery explained to the FBI agents that two clerks who worked at the ABC Liquor Store were shot by a black man, approximately twenty years old. One of the clerks was killed; the other injured. The suspect fled the scene on foot and was chased by responding officers. Although the killer was not apprehended, a composite sketch of the suspect was developed and a fingerprint was recovered from a gun catalog that the suspect was believed to have been looking at just prior to the robbery. The Montgomery police explained that they ran the print through their AFIS but were unable to match the print to a suspect.

On October 20, the fingerprint recovered from the crime scene in Montgomery, Alabama, was examined through the use of the FBI IAFIS (see Chapter 6) that also includes fingerprints obtained from the INS. This time there was a hit—the fingerprint was of an individual by the name of John Lee Malvo. His fingerprint was in the INS file because he was known to be a Jamaican citizen who was in the United States illegally. The pieces were beginning to come together. Investigators speculated that the five stars drawn on the cover page of the note left at the Ponderosa shooting scene were related to the Jamaican band "Five Stars." "Word is Bond" were lyrics to a song sung by the band. The possible Jamaican connection also fit with the heavy accent noted in the previous October 17 phone call to the police and with the poor English used in the note. The information on John Lee Malvo that was contained in the fingerprint file led investigators to Washington state, the same place where the stolen credit card identified in the note was used to purchase gasoline. At about this same time, the police tip line received a telephone call from a resident of Tacoma who reported that a person named "Muhammad" and another person with a nickname "Sniper" used to live at a specified address in Tacoma and had, on occasion, used a tree stump in their backyard for shooting practice. Once investigators were in

Tacoma, the link between John Malvo and an individual by the name of John Muhammad was confirmed, and information was received that Muhammad was possibly Malvo's stepfather. It was also learned that Muhammad was previously in the military and was a Gulf War Veteran. The investigation finally seemed to be coming together but the perpetrators were still not in custody. No one could relax until they were. The media and public were unaware of the progress being made in the investigation.

On the morning of Monday, October 21, the sniper called the police to reiterate his demands. The police were ready, or so they thought. The phone call made by the suspect was traced to a public telephone at a gas station near Richmond, Virginia. Shortly after the telephone call was received by the police, the police converged on the telephone and found a white van parked next to it. Two Hispanic men were pulled from the van and arrested. Headlines immediately followed: "Two Men in Custody in Sniper Hunt" (Breed, 2002). There was only one problem: They were not Malvo and Muhammad. The two individuals in the van happened to be in the wrong place at the wrong time. They had nothing to do with the shootings. And as coincidence would have it, they were driving a *white* van. The killers had gotten away. If the snipers had used that phone to contact the police, they got away before the police arrived. That afternoon Chief Moose provided a message to the sniper through the media: "The person you called could not hear everything you said. The audio was unclear and we want to get it right. Call us back so that we can clearly understand."

From the images on television, the police were looking rather silly. On the morning of October 22, the snipers claimed their thirteenth victim. Conrad Johnson, age thirty-five, a city bus driver, had parked his bus on the side of a street in Silver Spring, Maryland. As he stood up and began to walk down the steps of his bus, he was shot once in the abdomen. He died hours later. A note found in a nearby park reiterated the demand for $10 million.

As the police were investigating this latest shooting, investigators were busy developing information in Washington state. Additional information was received by investigators to confirm that Malvo and Muhammad used to live in the same house in Tacoma and that on several occasions while they lived there, there were gunshots heard from the house. It was reported by a neighbor that a tree stump in the backyard served as a target stop for what sounded like a high-powered rifle. Police conducted a search of the home and cut and carried away a large stump that reportedly contained bullet fragments. The search of the outside of the house and the removal of the tree stump by investigators was broadcast live on national television. Investigators also visited Bellingham High School, seeking information on John Malvo, who used to attend the school. Handwriting samples of Malvo were collected.

Reasonably certain now that Malvo and Muhammad were connected to the sniper shootings, investigators requested that police from area departments query their databases for any noted police contact with either of these suspects. It was discovered that on the night of October 8, the day after the thirteen-year-old boy was shot outside his school, Baltimore police had contact with John Muhammad when they found him asleep in his car in a parking lot outside a Subway sandwich shop.

The police woke him and told him to be on his way. It was noted in the police computer that he was driving a blue 1990 Chevrolet Caprice with a New Jersey license plate, number NDA21Z. (After the license plate number was discovered, police from area departments were asked once again to query their databases for any recorded check of the plates. It was found that between October 2 and October 23 the police had seen the Caprice and checked the license plate number at least twelve times. After finding that the car was not stolen and the occupants were not known to be wanted for any crimes, no additional investigations of the vehicle or its occupants were conducted.)

With this information in hand, at approximately 9:00 PM Wednesday, October 23, Chief Moose revealed on national television that one John Muhammad, age forty-one, and John Malvo, age seventeen, were wanted in connection with the sniper shootings. He stated that these individuals were last seen driving a blue 1990 Chevrolet Caprice, and he provided the license plate number. Approximately four hours later, the police received a telephone call from a truck driver who said that he was currently at a rest stop off I-70 near Frederick, Maryland, and that the car they were looking for was parked there. The police instructed him to block the exit with his truck, and for him and the others in the area to stay in their vehicles with their doors locked. A police tactical unit arrived shortly thereafter and found Malvo and Muhammad asleep in the car. They were arrested without incident. Reportedly, a Bushmaster XM15 rifle was found in the car along with a global positioning satellite system, a pair

Based on a tip, the police in Tacoma searched the backyard of the former residence of Muhammad and Malvo.

of two-way radios, two handguns, two shooting mittens, a Sony laptop computer, a single .223-caliber cartridge, a pair of bolt cutters, and a wallet containing several driver's licenses with Muhammad's photograph but with different names. It was also reported that there was a hole cut in the back of the trunk of the car, from which the shots were probably fired. The police had the snipers. Malvo and Muhammad appeared to have been living out of their vehicle. Further investigation has revealed that Malvo and Muhammad are also believed to be responsible for at least seven other shootings in the Washington, DC, area; Washington state; Arizona; and Louisiana. As of late 2003, both suspects are awaiting trial on multiple counts of murder, attempted murder, and robbery.

The Role of the Public and Media in Criminal Investigations

The public consists of people who may have information relating to a particular crime or criminal but who are not able to be identified by investigators as "witnesses" through traditional methods, such as neighborhood canvasses. During the sniper investigation, several members of the public provided critical information to investigators; in particular, the priest, the resident in Tacoma, and the truck driver. Most of this information was provided to the police through a tip line that was established especially for the investigation. The most important information in the investigation was probably provided by John Malvo, also through the tip line. No doubt, the public is a potentially extremely valuable source of information in criminal investigations, and tip lines allow for the easy transmission of such information to the police.

Some people may have knowledge about a crime simply because they may have seen or heard something relating to a crime during the course of their normal living activities, even though at the time they may not have realized that their observations actually related to a crime. In these cases, the task for the police is to get these people to realize that they may have information that relates to a crime and to report the information that they possess. In other cases, citizens may already realize that they possess information that relates to a crime and may need only minimal encouragement to report the information. As discussed in more detail later, the problem is that members of the public may think that their information may relate to the crime in question when actually it does not. During the sniper investigation, residents called the police to report sightings of hundreds upon hundreds of white vans and white box trucks. As it turned out, none of this information was useful or relevant. Recall that in the Super America robbery (Chapter 7), a media alert generated numerous apparently false leads in the investigation. No question, through the use of the media and tip lines, the police can get easily overwhelmed with leads that are eventually determined to be false. In any case, newspaper and television coverage, and press releases can be used by the police to make citizens aware of particular criminal incidents and to encourage them to call the police with information that may relate to the investigation. Dedicated phone lines within police departments can be established to receive the incoming calls, or citizens can be asked to call the telephone number of a local tip line program such as Crime Stoppers, Crime Solvers, or We Tip.

Crime Stoppers represents a formal strategy that brings together the police, media, and citizens in an effort to solve crimes. Crime Stoppers is a non-profit corporation and was established in 1976. As of 2003, Crime Stoppers had 1,148 programs in operation (see www.c-s-i.org). Crime Stoppers offers cash rewards (up to $1,000) to anonymous persons who contact the tip line and provide information that leads to the arrest of persons responsible for crimes. Law enforcement personnel staff the phone lines (which are most often located in police dispatch centers) and draft press releases on crimes in the community.

According to the Crime Stoppers web site, information provided to Crime Stoppers programs has led to more than a half million crimes being solved and more than $3 billion worth of stolen property and narcotics being recovered. Although these are impressive statistics, it may actually be quite difficult to determine precisely the role of the information received through the tip line in solving crimes. Of course, information in an investigation may come from various sources (e.g., physical evidence, other witness statements) beside the tip line, and each of these sources of information/evidence may contribute to the crime being solved. There is no research that has examined the actual impact of tip line information on the likelihood of crimes being solved (Rosenbaum et al., 1989).

EXHIBIT 10–1 Crime Solvers media release

ALEXANDRIA CRIME SOLVERS, INC.

Alexandria Crime Solvers are looking for the person, or persons, who killed Mary Ellen Gray, age 40, of the 4700 block of Kenmore Avenue. Mrs. Gray was found lying in the hallway of her apartment building at 7:00 AM on Tuesday, October 21st, of this year.

She was unconscious and appeared to have been severely beaten. She was transported to Alexandria Hospital, where she later died. Investigators have been unable to establish a motive in this brutal murder.

If you know the person, or persons, responsible for Mrs. Gray's death, call Crime Solvers at 838-4858. If your tip leads to an arrest and indictment, you will receive a $1000 cash reward.

In some instances, tip lines have been established on the Internet. For example, in the wake of September 11, 2001, the FBI established an online tip line as a way of receiving information from the public concerning suspected terrorist activity. In addition, The National Center for Missing and Exploited Children (NCMEC) has in place a "cyber tip line" to receive information about sex offenders and children who are at risk of sexual abuse. Consider the following case described at the home page of the NCMEC (www.ncmec.org):

> On September 26, 2000, NCMEC's CyberTipline received a lead from a lawyer representing the owner/operator of an adult-oriented fantasy telephone service. One of the workers was continually receiving calls from a New York City resident who told her he had been previously convicted for child rape in California and was now routinely stalking and abducting young women in New York. After confirming the information they had received, staffers from NCMEC's Exploited Child Unit performed multiple database searches in an attempt to locate the man within the city. Analysts contacted the California Department of Justice and found that the suspect was a registered sex offender with a twenty-two page "rap sheet," whose crimes ranged from sexual offenses to bomb threats. He had also served a prison term for sexually abusing a minor, indecent exposure, and aggravated harassment. This information was immediately forwarded to the New York Police Department's Computer Investigations and Technology Unit. [The detective assigned to the case] learned that he was teaching elementary and middle schoolers at a Brooklyn School as well as posing as the head of an online modeling agency. When the police arrested the perpetrator, they searched his residence and recovered child pornography in the form of movies, photographs, and digital images—many in which he was shown molesting young girls. . . . The suspect was arrested on charges of disseminating indecent materials to minors and failure to register with the state as a sex offender. . . . The case is still under investigation. (See home page for the National Center for Missing and Exploited Children, www.ncmec.org)

Television shows such as *America's Most Wanted* are another method of disseminating information about unsolved crimes and encouraging citizens to contact authorities with related information. *America's Most Wanted* has been described as a "nationwide neighborhood watch" and an extension of the FBI's Ten Most Wanted List first used in the 1950s to enlist the assistance of the public in solving crimes (Nelson, 1989). *American's Most Wanted* premiered in 1988 and is hosted by John Walsh, whose own son was abducted and murdered by a serial killer in 1981. As of November 2002, more than 700 shows have aired and more than 2,000 cases have been profiled (www2.amw.com/amw.html). The show consists of reenacted crimes with actors. After the case is presented, viewers who believe they have information about the perpetrator are asked to contact authorities through the show's toll-free telephone tip line. The tip line center is staffed by investigators from the agencies responsible for the cases profiled. Nearly all the cases profiled on the show involve serious violent crimes (e.g., murders, rapes, missing persons) for which the police have a good idea regarding the identity of the perpetrator. The suspect's name is often known, a photograph is often shown, and details about the person are often provided (e.g., he likes to drink Pepsi, he is a soccer fan, he is a skilled carpenter). According to the producers of the show, as of 2003, information developed as a result of the show has resulted in the apprehension of more than 700 suspects (www2.amw.com/amw.html). Throughout the years, other "crime-time" television shows (Nelson, 1989) have also aired that focus on particular unsolved crimes, including the 1988 special *Manhunt Live!*, a show about the Green River, Washington serial homicide case; and *Unsolved Mysteries*, a television series that premiered in 1987 and includes unsolved crime stories as well as other "mysteries."

Another method of mobilizing the public in providing crime information to the police is the "AMBER plan" (some states have similar programs with different names). The AMBER plan was created in 1996 after nine-year-old Amber Hagerman was abducted and murdered while riding her bicycle in Arlington, Texas. With the AMBER plan, when a law enforcement agency is notified that a child abduction has taken place or is suspected of having taken place, an alert that includes a description and picture of the missing child, the suspected perpetrator, the suspected vehicle, a tip line phone number, and any other information that may assist in locating the child is faxed to area radio and television stations for immediate broadcast. In some situations, information relating to the abduction is placed on electronic freeway emergency signs. The AMBER plan and alert system is modeled after the alerts that are used to notify people of impending severe weather. Prior to an alert being activated, it has been suggested that three criteria be satisfied (see www.ncmec.org):

1. Law enforcement officials confirm a child has been abducted.
2. Law enforcement officials believe that the circumstances surrounding the abduction indicate that the child is in danger of harm or death.
3. There is enough reliable information about the child, the suspect, or the suspect's vehicle to believe that an immediate alert will be of help.

According to the NCMEC, as of 2003 twenty-one children have been recovered as a result of information received from an AMBER alert.

Along with tip lines, television shows, and special alerts, other methods have also been used to obtain information from the public. For example, the city of Atlanta, Georgia, has experimented with making available to citizens standardized forms by which citizens can anonymously inform on drug dealers and other criminals. The NCMEC regularly sends "Have you seen me?" mailings via the U.S. Postal Service.

Representatives from numerous local, state, and federal agencies have assembled their own "most wanted" lists and have publicized them in newspapers and on the Internet. Finally, some police departments regularly disseminate "crime alerts" to notify citizens of particular criminal incidents and to put them on the lookout for related suspicious activity.

Along with the obvious benefits, there are also several potential problems associated with the use of tip lines, the public, and the media for crime information. First and most fundamental, with this approach, investigators may quickly become overwhelmed with information—and much of this information may prove to be irrelevant to the investigation. In fact, most of the tips received by the police through tip lines are often completely unrelated to the case at hand, even if the information seems potentially useful at the time it is

EXHIBIT 10–2 "Have You Seen Me?" mailer distributed by NCMEC

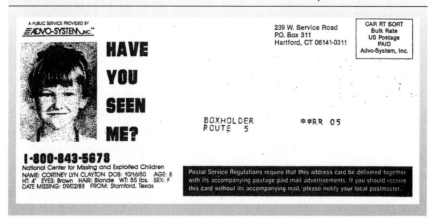

received. Consider several examples: In the sniper case, 60,000 calls were received by authorities (Potter, 2002), and only a few proved to be instrumental in arresting the perpetrators. In the Unabomber investigation (Chapter 1), the police received more than 20,000 calls to their tip line, but none of them turned out to be useful in the investigation. Within a month after the September 11, 2001, terrorist acts in New York and Washington, DC, authorities had received nearly 500,000 tips on suspected terrorists and terrorist activity (Davis et al., 2002). After the anthrax letters case was profiled on *America's Most Wanted*, more than 700 tips were received by authorities. As of 2003, the case remains unsolved.

The false information received through tip lines may bring to police attention innocent "suspects." Accordingly, questions may be raised about how subjects may be affected when the police take action against them as a result of anonymous information. It is certainly possible that in some instances individuals may call to report falsely the conduct of friends or associates (or husbands or wives for that matter) as a way of getting revenge. The police can be used by citizens in this regard and the consequences may be unpleasant for everyone.

Another potential problem is determining how reward money should be fairly allocated among the people who provided useful information. In the sniper case for example, the reward fund was $500,000, and would have likely been more if it had not been not capped (Schulte and Moreno, 2002). Who should get this money and how should these decisions be made? Should the priest get it? The caller from Washington state who reported that Malvo and Muhammad used a high-powered gun in their backyard? The individual who noticed the suspects' car at the rest stop? These are difficult decisions and there is no precise way of making them.

Other potential problems associated with the use of the public as a source of information include questions about (1) the credibility and motivation of citizens who inform for purposes of money, (2) how the publicity on the case may affect the perceptions of others with information on the case (e.g., the repeated sightings of a white van in the sniper investigation), (3) how publicity may affect other dimensions of the case (e.g., pretrial publicity

EXHIBIT 10–3 Personal safety update

Middle Ridge Police Department
PERSONAL SAFETY UPDATE

There have been several incidents of first degree sexual assault which have occurred on the east side of Middle Ridge over the last several weeks. The description of the suspect and his methodology are sufficiently similar in all three reported cases to strongly support the belief that these attacks are the actions of one individual. What follows is a brief description of those attacks and the suspect reported in each case.

Date:	Sunday December 1, 2002
Time:	10:00 p.m.
Location:	1700 Block of N. Arlington
Victim:	21 year old female
Suspect:	Black male, late 20s to early 30s, 5¢8≤ to 5¢9≤ 160 lbs., medium build, mustache, short natural hair

While leaving the rear of her residence, the victim was attacked by the suspect who placed a handgun to her head, demanded and received money, and forced the victim to perform multiple sexual acts at gun point. The suspect fled when a neighbor arrived at the scene.

Date:	Thursday December 5, 2002
Time:	5:35 a.m.
Location:	3400 Block of N. Cramer
Victim:	20 year old female
Suspect:	Black male, 20s to 30s, 5¢8≤ to 5¢10≤, medium build

While walking to work, the victim was attacked from behind by the suspect who knocked her to the ground and told her that he had a gun and she should cooperate. The suspect then fondled the victim but fled when the victim kneed the suspect in the groin.

Date:	Thursday December 12, 2002
Time:	2:35 a.m.
Location:	2800 N. Murray
Victim:	25 year old female
Suspect:	Black male, late teens to early 20s, 5¢9≤, slim build

Victim returned home when she observed a figure in the shadows. When she called out asking who it was, the suspect ran toward her, grabbed her, and as she turned to flee he dragged her to an open garage where he told her not to scream. He also told her that he had a gun and would kill her. He then fondled her and threw her to the ground. He then searched her bag but took nothing. He then fled the area.

Police departments may use notices like the one here to call attention to particular crimes.

and ability to receive a fair trial), and (4) whether money should be paid for actions that are arguably one's civic responsibility. These are difficult questions to address, but investigators should at least be aware of them when considering information from the public.

Associated with the public as a source of information in criminal investigations is the use of confidential informants. Confidential informants are most often used by the police in ongoing undercover investigations (see Chapter 3), typically those that are drug related. As Marx (1988) explains, "a majority of undercover operations must rely to some degree on persons in the criminal milieu for information, technical advice, "clients," contacts, and introductions" (p. 152). Informants are often associated with the criminal underworld; they are in a position to have the information that the police need to "make"cases, and the knowledge about the inner workings of criminal groups (i.e., who, what, where, when, and why). Informants may have several different motivations to reveal their secrets. They may be recruited by the police with the lure of money, they may come to the police as a result of a desire for revenge on an associate, they may have a desire to "go straight" or to "come clean," or the police may pressure them to reveal information (e.g., Tell me what you know about T-Bone or you are going to jail.). Although the use of informants is often viewed as necessary during certain investigations, the practice is certainly not without controversy. In particular, is it ethical for the police to pay criminals for information? Other controversies arise from the sometimes close working relationship between the police and informants. In any case, it is certainly an area that needs to be managed closely (see Mount [1990]). "The problems created by informers can be lessened by awareness and constant vigilance and by appropriate policies and procedures, which include written guidelines, criteria for selection and evaluation, centralized informant records, and explicit instructions" (Marx, 1988; p. 158).

Crime Analysis and Mapping

"Crime analysis involves the collection and analysis of data pertaining to a criminal incident, offender, and target" (Canter, 2000; p. 4). Crime analysis often serves as a basis on which police managers develop strategies to confront and investigate particular crimes or patterns of crimes. Crime analysis can provide the necessary information to make informed patrol allocation decisions, to make predictions about future targets of offenders, and to track offender movements. Maps are a commonly used and useful tool in the task of crime analysis.

Methods of crime analysis vary considerably in their sophistication. At the most basic level are maps with color-coded pins that are used to illustrate visually where various crimes have occurred in a particular jurisdiction over a particular period of time. Through a quick inspection of such a map, a basic understanding of the distribution of crime across space can be developed. More elaborate crime analysis methodologies include the use of geographical information systems (GISs) that allow for the automated recording and plotting of criminal incidents on detailed computerized maps. Many of these systems also allow for the manipulation of the corresponding crime data to reveal patterns of crime (or certain types of crime) across time (time of day, week, month, year) and space (e.g., crime that occurs in and around schools, public transportation stops and stations, etc.).

EXHIBIT 10—4 City of Detroit raids map

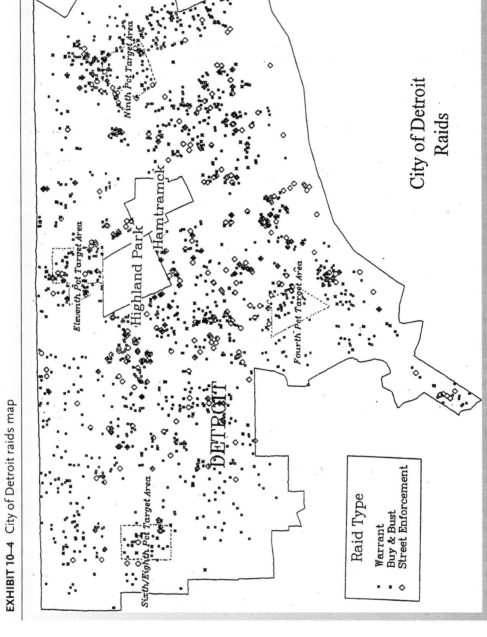

City of Detroit
Raids

Raid Type
- Warrant
× Buy & Bust
◇ Street Enforcement

Ninth Pct Target Area

Eleventh Pct Target Area

Highland Park

Hamtramck

Fourth Pct Target Area

Sixth/Eighth Pct Target Area

DETROIT

Crime maps are able to provide a quick visualization of criminal activity in a particular area. BYNUM AND WORDEN (1998)

Some crime analysis systems operated by police departments include automated crime report information. These systems allow investigators to extract specific subsets of data records (e.g., all robberies that occurred between 1 AM and 3 AM on Fridays when the perpetrator was described as a white man, approximately twenty years of age) to identify more clearly patterns of crimes (Maltz et al., 1991). Some police departments have made the crime analysis function central to the management of the organization. Such is the case with COMPSTAT in the New York City Police Department and other departments. This system has been used to identify crime patterns and to manage, monitor, and assess the impact of various crime control strategies. Critical to the COMPSTAT system are the meetings that take place during which precinct commanders brief department executives on the results of crime control initiatives that have been undertaken to deal with the identified crime problems (McGuire, 2000). Rightfully or not, the dramatic crime decline in crime in New York City during the 1990s has been largely attributed to the use of COMPSTAT (McGuire, 2000).

Another example of a sophisticated crime analysis system is VICAP. VICAP is a nationwide computerized database system maintained and operated by the FBI. It has been in operation since 1985. The system is designed to collect, collate, and analyze specific crimes of violence to identify similar MO or signature aspects of the crime. If crimes can be linked in this manner, if the crimes were committed by the same offender, then representatives from the various agencies can come together and work cooperatively in investigating the crimes. In this regard, VICAP officials can assist in conducting a multiagency investigative conference. VICAP is a tool that can be used to overcome what has been referred to as *linkage blindness*—the tendency of law enforcement agencies to be unable to identify serial crimes that occur across jurisdictional boundaries (Egger, 1998). Similar crime databases are operated in several states (e.g., the Homicide Investigation and Tracking System, or HITS, in Washington state; the Florida Violent Crime Investigation System, or ViCIS; and the New Jersey Homicide Evaluation and Assessment Tracking, or HEAT) that are integrated with the VICAP system (Keppel and Weiss, 1993; Rossmo, 2000).

VICAP is focused on three primary types of crimes: (1) solved or unsolved homicides or attempts (especially those that involve an abduction, appear sexually motivated, or are suspected of being part of a series), (2) missing persons in which foul play is suspected, and (3) unidentified dead bodies in which the cause of death was believed to be as a result of a homicide. When law enforcement authorities are confronted with such a crime, they may submit specific information on the case to the FBI for VICAP analysis. When a case is entered into the VICAP database, it is compared with all other cases on the basis of potentially unique aspects of the crime. The specific case information on the crime is collected via a standardized thirteen-page, 186-item questionnaire. The questionnaire is divided into nine sections: administration, victim information, offender information, identified offender information, vehicle description, offense MO, condition of victim when found, cause of death or trauma, and forensic evidence (Howlett et al., 1986).

There are many success stories associated with the operation of the VICAP system. Two such examples are provided here (see FBI, National Center for the Analysis of Violent Crime, 2003, www.fbi.gov/hq/isd/cirg/ncavc.htm):

VICAP became involved in the investigation of [Rafael] Ramirez who would eventually be the suspect in various crimes in Texas and Kentucky. When Texas authorities first learned that two Texas cases were possibly linked by a common offender, VICAP was contacted. Based on certain behaviors and methodology of the offender in their two cases, VICAP was able to tell them of a similar case in Kentucky that had occurred two years before. Investigators followed up with a DNA analysis which matched the cases, and this became the catalyst for authorities to realize that they had a national serial offender on the loose. VICAP assisted the investigation by providing the Texas authorities with other possibly related cases occurring elsewhere in the United States.

VICAP continues to be used to solve crimes from the past. In 1989 investigators from Pennsylvania entered a case from 1951 into the VICAP database. In this case a man was found guilty of murdering a young girl. Not long after, investigators from Illinois entered an unsolved case from 1957, in which an approximately eight-year-old girl was murdered. Analysis in VICAP noticed similarities in the two cases. Due to these similarities and other related evidence, detectives in Illinois were able to solve a crime that occurred almost forty years ago.

Clearly, VICAP has the potential to be a powerful tool in linking the crimes of serial offenders; however, it also has limitations. Most important, if the MO used by the offender across crimes is not similar, or if signature aspects of the crime are missing, not recognized, or change across crimes, the VICAP system will be of limited use. In addition, by its design, VICAP may do little in actually solving crimes—that is, identifying and apprehending perpetrators. As noted, the system is designed to identify crimes committed by the same offender, not necessarily to identify that offender. As illustrated in the second example provided earlier, only in select instances may VICAP *directly* contribute to the solving of crimes. Finally, to link crimes, crimes have to be contained in the database. Investigators must voluntarily submit their case data to the FBI VICAP, and this involves additional work on the part of investigators. Up until the last few years, the system contained information on only 15,000 cases. Recently, improvements have been made in streamlining the data collection and submission process (including electronic submissions). The system now reportedly contains more than 80,000 cases (Vuong, 2002).

A different but somewhat related form of crime analysis involves the empirical analysis of previous crimes in an effort to respond more effectively to such crimes in the future. For example, it is known that if a child is abducted by a stranger, the victim is killed within the first hour in forty-four percent of cases, within three hours in seventy-four percent of cases, and within twenty-four hours in ninety-one percent of cases. In only forty-two percent of cases were the victims still alive when they were reported missing (see Rossmo [2000]). This finding clearly highlights the need for a quick law enforcement response in responding to child abduction cases (e.g., AMBER alert). In cases in which a victim was killed and when the victim was not believed to have been transported by vehicle, ninety-eight percent of the bodies were found within fifty yards of a footpath. In cases that did involve victim transportation, eighty-eight percent of bodies were located within fifty yards of a road or vehicular path (see Rossmo [2000]). This type of information may be useful in directing search efforts for missing (abducted) persons. Other analyses conducted on offender characteristics may provide assistance in the construction of psychological profiles.

Computer Databases and Information Networks

There is a multitude of electronic databases that investigators may use to obtain critical information needed during a criminal investigation. These databases can be classified as either intradepartmental or interdepartmental.

Intradepartmental Databases

Intradepartmental databases are ones that are operated and maintained by individual law enforcement agencies. Depending on the resources available and the size of the agency, there may be many such systems available to investigators or there may be relatively few. For example, investigators may have access to pawn shop records. In many jurisdictions, pawn shop operators are required to submit to their local police department a record of all merchandise received and information about from whom merchandise was purchased. Depending on the organization of the system and how current the information is kept, such records could be particularly useful in burglary and robbery investigations. As another example, some police departments keep computerized files on all individuals with whom the police have had contact (e.g., as victims, complainants, witnesses, suspects, etc.). This information may be useful in developing a police contact history of individuals. As a final example, databases are being used in some departments to record and to provide easy access to information on suspected offenders, especially those believed to be involved in gangs and narcotics trafficking. One such computer program is known as GRIP (or Gang/Narcotics Relational Intelligence Program). GRIP provides a computerized way to compile, store, categorize, and retrieve information on suspected offenders. The database stores various types of information on subjects including demographic data, physical characteristics, gang affiliation, criminal history, aliases, vehicles, and addresses and phone numbers associated with the subject. Pictures of subjects are also included in the database. Searches of the database can be made on any of these dimensions. Electronic photo lineups can also be created through the use of the system.

Interdepartmental Databases

The two largest and most used interdepartmental databases are the NCIC and NLETS. These and several other databases are discussed next.

National Crime Information Center

The NCIC is the largest and most well-known crime information network system in the United States. It is maintained by the FBI at its headquarters in Washington, DC. The NCIC began operations in 1967; by 1971, police agencies in all fifty states were linked to the system. Today, more than 80,000 law enforcement and criminal justice agencies have access to the NCIC database. The system contains more than 34 million records (including criminal history records contained in the Interstate Identification Index). Nearly two million queries are made of the system daily.

The NCIC consists of a centralized database and a network of connecting computer terminals located in criminal justice agencies throughout the country. Representatives of agencies may enter information into the database and make queries of the database. The originating agency also has the responsibility for removing records once the record is no longer valid (e.g., when a missing person is found). The system contains information in various files including (see Duyn [1990] and FBI [1996]):

- Wanted persons (for either questioning or arrest; including name, DOB, offense, date of warrant, whether armed, number of companions, and whether the person is considered dangerous)
- Missing persons (divisions within this file consist of missing disabled persons, endangered missing persons, involuntary missing persons, and missing juvenile persons)
- Unidentified persons (descriptions of unidentified dead persons)
- Criminal history and fingerprint classification (details on individuals who have been arrested for felony, murder, and other serious crimes, as well as a description of their fingerprint patterns)
- Stolen and felony vehicles (contains information on vehicles that have been reported stolen as well as those vehicles known to have been used in the commission of a crime)
- Recovered vehicles (contains information on vehicles that have been recovered by law enforcement authorities)
- Stolen and recovered firearms (includes information on the type and description of the firearm, serial number, date of theft/recovery, and persons apprehended during the course of recovering the firearm)
- Stolen and recovered heavy equipment (contains information on stolen farm and construction equipment)
- Stolen and recovered boats and marine equipment (includes date of theft/recovery, description of boat, type of boat, registration number, and hull identification number)
- Stolen license plates (includes date of theft, license number, state, year, and number of plates stolen)
- Stolen and recovered securities (includes serial numbers and other details about stolen U.S. Treasury notes, bonds, and bills; municipal and corporate bonds, and stocks)

- Stolen and recovered identifiable articles (includes identifying details about stolen and recovered auto parts, avionic equipment, computers, cameras, tools, musical instruments, and office equipment)
- Canadian warrants (includes information on individuals that are wanted on warrants issued by the Royal Canadian Mounted Police and who may be in the United States)
- U.S. Secret Service protective file (a classified data file that contains information on individuals considered of danger to the president, former presidents, high officials, and visiting heads of state)
- Interstate identification index (provides criminal history information on individuals who are either wanted or missing)
- Foreign fugitive file (provides information on foreign individuals who are wanted on warrants)
- Violent gang/terrorist file (provides information on individuals believed to be terrorists or members of violent gangs)

The NCIC has the capability of quickly putting vast and critical information in the hands of police and investigators. As such, the NCIC can be a powerful investigative tool. The list of instances when the NCIC information led to the apprehension of offenders, the discovery of missing persons, and the recovery of property is a long one. As just one example, consider the apprehension of Timothy McVeigh, who was responsible for the bombing of the federal building in Oklahoma City. Once investigators had developed the name of Timothy McVeigh as a suspect in the bombing, they entered his name in the NCIC database and learned that an Oklahoma state trooper had just run an NCIC search on McVeigh. A telephone call to this agency revealed that McVeigh was stopped on the highway and was currently in custody of the police. Only as a result of the NCIC was such a quick apprehension possible.

NATIONAL LAW ENFORCEMENT TELECOMMUNICATIONS SYSTEM

NLETS is a network that links law enforcement agencies, other criminal justice agencies in the United States, and motor vehicle and licensing departments. The information available through the system includes

- Vehicle registrations by license or VIN
- Driver's license and driving record by name and birth date or driver's license number
- Criminal history records by name and birth date
- Boat registration information
- Snowmobile registration information
- Hazardous material file data
- Private aircraft data including registration information
- Index to parole/probation and corrections information
- Sex offender registration information.

INTERPOL Case Tracking System (ICTS)

The ICTS contains information about persons, property, and organizations involved in international criminal activity (see Chapter 1).

Central Index System (CIS) and Related Databases

The CIS is operated and maintained by the INS. It contains information on legal immigrants, naturalized citizens, and aliens who have been formally deported or excluded from the United States. The Nonimmigrant Information System of the INS contains information on the entry and departure of nonimmigrants (aliens) in the United States for a temporary stay. The Law Enforcement Support Center is also operated by the INS and provides information to local, state, and federal law enforcement agencies about aliens who have been arrested. The National Alien Information Lookout System consists of an INS index of names of individuals who may be excludable from the United States. The Consular Lookout and Support System is a related database operated by the U.S. Department of State. It contains information on several million individuals who have been determined to be ineligible for visas, those who need additional investigation prior to issuance of a visa, and those who would be ineligible for visas should they apply for one.

El Paso Intelligence Center (EPIC)

EPIC is designed to collect, process, and disseminate information concerning illegal drug use, alien smuggling, weapons trafficking, and related criminal activity. EPIC was established to facilitate the exchange of information across agencies that are responsible for the enforcement of drug and related laws.

Sentry

Sentry is operated by the Federal Bureau of Prisons and contains information on all federal prisoners incarcerated since 1980. The available information includes the inmate's physical description, location, release information, custody classification, and sentencing information, among other items.

Equifax

Equifax is a company that provides credit information on individuals. Databases within its operation may be used to collect various information on people including recent addresses and demographic information. Trans Union is another consumer credit information company that offers background information, spending activity, and employment information on individuals.

OTHER DATABASES

Beyond these databases, numerous other sources of public information may be useful to investigators in investigating crimes. These sources are diverse and their particular usefulness depends heavily on the issue at hand. These sources include motor vehicle registrations (e.g., useful when constructing a list of all vehicles registered in a particular area that match a particular description), credit card receipts and information (e.g., to document purchases and travel), bank records (e.g., to verify unusual deposits and withdrawals), attendance records at school or work (e.g., to verify a suspect's alibi or to help verify when a victim was last seen), reverse telephone directories (e.g., to determine a phone number from a known address), other telephone records (e.g., to verify phone calls made and received, and the timing of those calls), and sex offender registries and related Department of Corrections information (e.g., to determine the whereabouts of particular offenders or to identify offenders who live in a particular area).

LIMITATIONS

The primary limitation of information databases is that the database is only as good as the information that it contains. Of course, if information is not entered into the system (e.g., in the case of the NCIC, if a gun is not reported as stolen or a missing person is not entered as missing), the database will be of little use to the police in this regard. Similarly, if a person has not been identified as "wanted" in a particular crime, the information contained in the database will not provide the information necessary to make an apprehension. Consider the Washington, DC, sniper case discussed in the introduction to this chapter. As noted, at various times during the course of the shootings, police in the Washington, DC, area performed numerous NCIC and NLETS queries on the vehicle that was eventually linked to the shooters. On at least one occasion, the name of the driver of the vehicle—John Muhammad—was run through the system. None of the checks revealed that the vehicle or the driver was wanted or connected to any crime. Indeed, the vehicle was not stolen nor was the driver wanted for previous offenses. It was only after the suspects were identified by name through other means that the NCIC and NLETS were useful in identifying the make and model of the car that the suspects were believed to be driving.

Psychics

When all else fails, when there is nowhere else to turn, when the police are at a loss regarding what to do next, the police may turn to a psychic for assistance in an investigation. In such a situation, investigators may be trapped between the embarrassment of an unsolved high-profile case and the embarrassment of enlisting the help of a psychic.

Psychic phenomena are related to the science of parapsychology, or extrasensory perception (ESP). There are several forms of ESP, including telepathy (the ability to read minds and transmit thoughts, or *thought transference*), clairvoyance (the ability to see objects and events beyond the range of physical vision), precognition (the ability to perceive future events), and retrocognition (the ability to see into the past). These phenomena have been studied at length; in fact, there is even a scholarly journal devoted to the study of such phenomena (*Journal of Parapsychology*). Although there is a paucity of scientific research that documents and verifies the existence of ESP, there is much anecdotal evidence that some people have such abilities. Indeed, you may believe that you have experienced ESP at some time. If this is the case, you are not alone. Sixty-seven percent of adult Americans have said that they have experienced ESP on at least one occasion (Constable, 1987).

During the past several decades there has been a number of stories about psychics assisting in criminal investigations. As an example, consider the case of Dorothy Allison, who assisted the police in finding a missing boy in New Jersey in 1967. She told the police that she had a dream:

> The boy was dead . . . and his body was caught in the drainpipe of a pond; his shoes were on the wrong feet, and he wore a green snowsuit with a religious medal pinned to it. In the background, she saw a gray wall, a building with gold lettering, and the number eight. Two months later, the boy's body was discovered in a drainpipe in Clifton, New Jersey. He was wearing a green snowsuit, and when the police removed his rubber boots, they found that his sneakers were on the wrong feet. Nearby were a gray concrete building, a factory with gold lettering on the front door, and an elementary school—P.S. 8. (Constable, 1987; p. 42)

Also consider the work of Peter Hurkos, a well-known psychic who used to be an advisor to several movie stars and was a sometimes-advisor to the police. In the early 1960s, Hurkos was asked to assist in the Boston Strangler investigation. During the course of several weeks, Hurkos "psychometrized" numerous items that belonged to the victims and provided amazingly accurate details about the wrong man. He said that the killer lived in the Boston College area, was a small man with a French accent, thin hair, and he had a pointed nose. Hurkos said the killer slept on bed springs, that he heard voices from God, and that he was a shoe salesman. The police later identified an individual who lived in the area and matched the description provided by Hurkos. In his possession, the police found drawings of women in various positions along with men's scarves with knots in them (like those used to tie up the victims in the strangling crimes). The man had a history of mental illness and, subsequent to his identification by the police, he committed himself to a mental hospital. He never confessed to the crimes, nor was he ever charged with the murders. About a month later, the police identified Albert DeSalvo as a suspect in the killings, and he confessed to the crimes. DeSalvo had a history of sexual assaults on women and previously admitted to his wife and to the police about breaking into homes and raping women. DeSalvo was charged and convicted of the crimes.

As described in Chapter 4, Peter Hurkos also was brought in to assist in the Michigan coed killer case. As described by Keyes (1976), Hurkos provided numerous details to the police about the killer, a few of which turned out to be accurate, but none of them were useful to the police in identifying and apprehending the killer. Browning (1970) described Hurkos as having played a much larger role in the investigation than was described by Keyes (1976). For example, she states, "It was Peter who led the police to the wig shop and to the sales girl who had sold Karen Sue the wig" (Browning, 1970; p. 250). There is no mention of police activities that led to the witnesses nor was there mention of the blood and hair found in the basement where the last murder occurred.

Only one study has examined the usefulness of psychics in criminal investigations. Reiser et al. (1979) had twelve self-proclaimed professional and nonprofessional psychics evaluate evidence in four rape and homicide cases and make predictions about the case based on their extrasensory abilities. In none of the cases did the psychics offer consistently accurate facts. The highest degree of accuracy in the information provided was the gender of the victim and the perpetrator, and this was just above chance levels. Reiser et al. (1979) concluded: "The research data [do] not support the contention that psychics can provide significant additional information leading to the solution of major crimes" (p. 21–22).

Although it is possible that certain people may have psychic abilities at certain times and under certain circumstances, there are undoubtedly a nearly countless number of pretenders. Many of these individuals have 1–900 numbers and charge a per-minute fee. With regard to the value of psychics in criminal investigations in particular, one must consider the number of details provided by the psychic in relation to the number of accurate details *and* the usefulness of those details in advancing the investigation. The problem is that numerous details may be provided and, at best, only a few (if any) may be accurate. Even the information that is accurate may not provide leads for the police to pursue (e.g., the victim is female).

Questions for Discussion and Review

1. Explain how the sniper case was solved. From where did the most critical information in the case come? Describe the role of the public and the media in the investigation.

2. What are crime tip lines and what is their potential contribution in solving crimes?

3. Why is it difficult to determine the actual impact of tip lines in solving particular crimes?

4. What is the potential contribution of television shows such as *America's Most Wanted* on criminal investigations? What are the common features of most cases profiled on the show?

5. What is the AMBER plan?

6. What are the potential problems associated with the use of tip lines, the public, and the media for crime information?

7. How are confidential informants most commonly used in criminal investigations? How do confidential informants differ from the public as a source of criminal information?

8. What is crime mapping? How can it be used in criminal investigations?

9. What is VICAP? What problem is it designed to address? What are the most significant limitations of VICAP?

10. Identify three examples of intradepartmental databases and five examples of interdepartmental databases.

11. What is the NCIC? What information does it include? How could the NCIC be used in an investigation?

12. What is NLETS? What information does it include? How could NLETS be used in an investigation?

13. What are the most significant limitations of criminal information databases?

14. What are psychics? What is the demonstrated role and usefulness of psychics in criminal investigations?

Related Internet Sites

www.c-s-i.org

This is the address for Crime Stoppers International, a non-profit corporation that provides monetary awards for information leading to the arrest of criminals. Also see www.crime-stoppers.org for the Crime Stoppers Program of Houston, Texas; www.mccrimesolvers.com for the Crime Solvers Program of Montgomery County, Maryland; and www.wetip.com for the web site of We Tip, another non-profit tip line program.

www2.amw.com/amw.html

This address brings you to the web site of *America's Most Wanted* television show. The site contains many interesting links and a listing of criminals profiled on the last 700 shows that have been aired.

www.crimetime.com/online.htm

This is the address for the web site "Black Book online." The site provides a variety of public record information from sex offender registries to reverse telephone directories.

www.virtualgumshoe.com

Investigative resources galore! This site can help you find just about anything.

ISSUES IN THE INVESTIGATION OF VIOLENT CRIME

CHAPTER

11

OBJECTIVES

After reading this chapter you will be able to

- Explain how the murder of the Blockbuster Video store security guard was solved
- Discuss the major trends and characteristics of murder
- Discuss how the circumstances in which murder often occur contribute to the relatively high clearance rate for murders
- Discuss the major trends and characteristics of aggravated and simple assault
- Discuss how these trends and characteristics differ from those of murder
- Discuss how a decedent's manner of death is established and identify three major considerations in this determination
- Discuss the importance of establishing motive in murder investigations
- Discuss the importance of physical evidence in murder investigations
- Identify and discuss the various methods of determining postmortem interval (PMI)
- Identify the reasons why establishing PMI may be of importance in an investigation
- Identify what may be determined through an analysis of insect activity on a dead body beside PMI
- Discuss the major trends and characteristics of forcible rape and other sexual assaults

- Discuss the importance of compassion and understanding in interacting with victims in sexual assault investigations
- Discuss the information that may be produced from an investigative interview with a sexual assault victim and the potential importance of this information in an investigation
- Discuss the importance of physical evidence in sexual assault investigations
- Discuss the evidence that may be obtained from a forensic examination of the victim
- Discuss how an interrogation of a rape suspect may be assisted by an understanding of his motive in committing the crime
- Discuss the major trends and characteristics of robbery
- Explain why robbery tends to have a lower clearance rate than murder or rape
- Discuss the potential value of eyewitness evidence in robbery investigations
- Discuss the potential value and limitations of security camera video evidence in robbery investigations
- Discuss the importance of establishing the robber's MO in robbery investigations
- Discuss the potential value of physical evidence in robbery investigations

- Discuss proper police procedure in responding to robbery scenes

- Discuss the interrogation strategies most likely to be most effective in robbery investigations

IMPORTANT TERMS

Murder

Felony murder

Aggravated assault

Simple assault

Manner of death

Cause of death

Staging

Defense wounds

PMI

Livor mortis

Rigor mortis

Forensic entomology

Postmortem, antemortem, perimortem

Decomposition

Forcible rape

Other sexual assaults

Sexual assault nurse examiner (SANE)

Specimen samples

Reference samples

Sexual assault evidence kit

Contact and sexual aggressor rapists

Robbery

Armed robbery

Strong-arm robbery

Dye pack

Holdup alarm

INTRODUCTION

On Friday December 29, 1995, at approximately 7:15 PM an individual entered a crowded Blockbuster Video store in Milwaukee, Wisconsin, looked at movies on the shelves for several minutes, and then proceeded to the store exit. Just prior to exiting the store, he confronted the store's security guard, thirty-two-year-old Anthony Porter (not his real name), who was sitting near the front doors of the store. The subject proceeded to shoot Porter seven times in the chest, killing him instantly. The subject then removed Porter's gun, a Smith and Wesson .357 magnum, from his holster belt and fled the store with Porter's gun and the murder weapon in hand.

The police were on the scene by 7:30 PM. At the scene, the police recovered the security guard's weapon belt without the gun, three copper-jacketed bullets, eight .38-caliber chrome casings, books and binders of the victim, a black Nike baseball cap found outside the store, and the video surveillance tape of the inside of the video store.

The police officers and detectives interviewed twenty-two individuals who were in or near the store at the time of the shooting. Of the eighteen customers and employees inside the store, no one actually saw the shooting occur, although three individuals (two employees and a customer) told the police that they saw a young black man, approximately twenty years of age, run from the store immediately after the shooting stopped. One witness who was just outside the video store at the time of the shooting told police that he saw a black man run out of the store and toward the adjacent parking lot of a large grocery store. Another witness who was sitting in his car that was parked outside the exit of the video store told police that after he heard the gunshots he saw a black man run from the store to the grocery store parking lot and then he saw him enter the grocery store. While witnesses were being interviewed, several

EXHIBIT 11–1 Blockbuster store and crime scene diagram

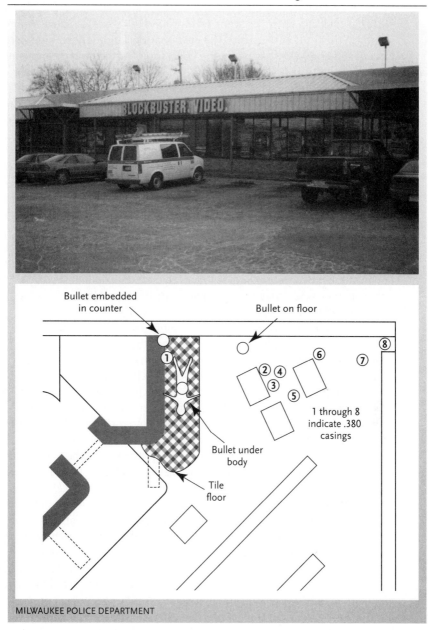

MILWAUKEE POLICE DEPARTMENT

detectives examined the video surveillance tape. Among other activities in the store, the black-and-white and rather grainy videotape showed a young black man wearing a black baseball cap enter the store, walk around the store for a few minutes, and then approach the front of the store. The next images caught on the tape were of the customers and employees laying on the floor, some on their hands and knees. The tape did not show the actual shooting.

With the witness statements and the video surveillance tape, the police felt confident that the perpetrator was a young black man and that the baseball cap found outside the store was his. They were also confident that the perpetrator fled the video store in the direction of the grocery store parking lot, and may have actually entered the grocery store. Accordingly, the police proceeded to enter and secure the grocery store. The police immediately talked to the manager and informed him of the shooting that just took place at the nearby Blockbuster Video store. The grocery store was then closed and the exits were locked. All customers and employees in the store were asked to assemble near the front of the store. At this time, the police identified eight of the customers in the store as roughly matching the description of the perpetrator. Two employees working at the store at the time also appeared to match the perpetrator's description. The police had ten suspects. Each of these individuals was questioned at the grocery store and, for each, a gunshot residue test was performed. Each gunshot residue test was negative and none of the subjects immediately raised the suspicions of the investigators.

At this point in the investigation, the biggest question was motive. Why would someone enter a crowded video store, shoot the security guard to death, and then take his gun? It did not seem to make much sense. The perpetrator made no attempt to rob the store. The victim appeared to be targeted and, shooting him seven times, it appeared that the perpetrator definitely wanted him dead. One shot could have killed him; seven appeared to be overkill. Perhaps the shooting was an act of revenge. But revenge for what? Maybe Porter sold bad drugs to the killer. Maybe Porter never paid back a debt. Maybe he had a girlfriend or a boyfriend who wanted him dead. Maybe the murder was a "hit." Maybe Porter had a girlfriend and the perpetrator was an ex-boyfriend. So many possibilities. So few answers. Little did the police know, they were not even close.

Into the second day of the investigation, with more than ten homicide detectives working on the case, the investigation was going in several different directions. First, extensive investigation was being conducted on the victim and his background. Who were his friends? Who were his enemies? Who could have wanted him dead? The police talked to Porter's family members, they talked to his supervisor and to his coworkers. They interviewed numerous friends of Porter, including his current girlfriend and a previous girlfriend. The police talked to the current boyfriend of the victim's ex-girlfriend. From these interviews it was learned that Porter was an honest, hard-working employee who had a good relationship with his girlfriend with whom he was planning a not-too-distant wedding. Porter was not a gang member, he did not use drugs, and he did not sell drugs. Porter's girlfriend said that she did not have any jealous previous boyfriends. Porter's previous girlfriend had had no contact with him for years. No good leads.

Second, more information was sought from the individuals who were located in the grocery store. Did their alibis hold up? Did any of them have a link to the victim or to any associates or friends of the victim? One of the employees of the store came under increased police scrutiny because he was very uncooperative with the police and he had an extensive criminal background, although not for any violent offenses. His whereabouts at the time of the shooting were also not confirmed. Several of the subjects agreed to take polygraph exams; the suspicious employee refused. A further investigation was conducted on this individual, as well as the others. They were the best leads for the police to pursue.

Third, tips were provided to the police by other citizens who came forward during the investigation. Among the potentially most valuable information, one witness told the police that while she was in the parking lot of the grocery store on the night of the homicide, a black man described as "being in his twenties" asked for a ride but she did not give him one. Another citizen came forward and told the police the name of an individual who she thought might have committed the murder. On a previous occasion, she told the police, the victim flirted with the girlfriend of the cousin of this named person. She thought that this person might have gotten back at Porter by killing him. The police checked out these leads. More dead ends.

Fourth, the police wanted to find Porter's gun—the gun that was taken from him just after or just prior to when he was shot. The serial number of the gun along with its description was entered into the NCIC database (see Chapter 10), and officers in the department were made aware of the significance of this gun. Investigators figured that if they could find the gun, they would find the killer.

Finally, additional analysis and enhancements were conducted on the images captured on the video surveillance tape. If the image of the suspected perpetrator was obtained from the tape, it could be shown on television, and perhaps this would produce additional leads. Given the quality of the images on the tape, however, it proved to be of little value.

On January 2, 1996, at approximately 10:30 AM, a bank in Milwaukee was robbed at gunpoint. As the two perpetrators were fleeing the bank, crossing the street, and running down the sidewalk, dye packs in one of the bags of money taken from the bank exploded. The suspect carrying the bag dropped it and paper bills began blowing around in the wind. One of the robbers continued to run but the other stopped and attempted to pick up the money. As he was doing this, the police arrived at the scene, apprehended this suspect, and took him into custody. In discreetly searching the area around the bank, the police located a suspiciously parked vehicle with one person sitting in it. It was the getaway car. This person was also taken into custody. On searching the car, the police discovered a gun. It was a Smith and Wesson .357 magnum handgun. It was registered to Anthony Porter.

On interrogating the would-be driver of the getaway car, Marteze Harris, he confessed to his involvement in many prior robberies (including several bank and store robberies) and the video store homicide. He also implicated his two friends, Willie Dortch and Myron Edwards, in these crimes and identified Edwards as the triggerman in the video store homicide. Harris also led the police to several other vehicles used by the suspects. The search of these cars revealed evidence of previous bank robberies, including papers with bank addresses on them, shell casings, a holster, a face mask, and other clothing. The police then searched Harris' apartment, with his consent, and found even more evidence—numerous guns and ammunition (including .357 magnum cartridges), pagers, cell phones, a mask, and a large quantity of cocaine.

Edwards, the suspected perpetrator of the video store homicide, was a nineteen-year-old African American man who was identified by the police as a gang member and a drug dealer. He had numerous prior arrests for property and violent offenses. He had a history of drug abuse. Edwards was placed in a lineup for the video store witnesses and he was identified as the man who ran from the store. On interrogating Edwards, he confessed to killing the security guard. He also confessed to a recent robbery and homicide at a liquor store, where an employee and a patron were murdered, as well as previous bank robberies. He told police that he did not go into the grocery store after he fled Blockbuster Video and he did not ask anyone in the parking lot for a ride (see Exhibit 11–2 for Edward's statement to investigators).

Edwards and his accomplices were charged with two other homicides and four other armed robberies in Milwaukee. In total, each was convicted of three counts of party to the crime of first-degree intentional homicide, five counts of armed robbery, and one count of attempted armed robbery. Edwards was sentenced to two life sentences without the possibility of parole plus 260 years. He is currently serving time in the "supermax" prison in Wisconsin.

The police are often portrayed as being engaged in a "war" on crime. This metaphor highlights the importance of strategy in combating crime and conducting criminal investigations. As in any war, it is critical that one understands the tactics and motivations of the enemy. It is only by knowing this information that effective countermeasures may be developed to neutralize the enemy. The intent of this chapter as well as Chapter 12 is to familiarize readers with the major types of crimes investigated by the police, examine the motivations and tactics of perpetrators in committing these crimes, and discuss the evidence most likely to be present in these investigations. This discussion calls attention to the importance of various tasks in investigating particular crimes. The information provided in this chapter, as well as the next, relates to the investigation of specific types of crimes. Details provided in other chapters that relate to other more general principles of evidence and investigation (e.g., legal issues, evidence collection, crime scene searches, physical evidence, interviews, interrogations, etc.) are not repeated here.

EXHIBIT 11–2 Excerpt of statement of Myron Edwards as recorded by Milwaukee homicide detectives

Regarding the homicide of the black guard at the Blockbuster video store on E. Capital Drive about 2–3 days before New Years. Said he had problems with his girlfriend and had no place to go. Marteze was always trying to get guns. Said the day before the shooting, Marteze and his girlfriend told Myron that they were at Blockbuster video and there was a white security guard there who was carrying a "Glock." They were talking about getting the guard's gun. Myron was asked how they were going to get the gun and he said "every time we do something illegal, I'm the one who has to do it." Stated the next night they used the white Tempo and Willie was driving and Marteze was in the front seat and Myron was in the back. They drove by Blockbuster on E. Capital and saw through the window a black security guard but they decided to get the gun anyway. Myron said he did it because he didn't want them to think he was scared. Before at the house Myron stated he smoked two marijuana cigarettes. Said Marteze gave him a silver gun with black inlay panels on the grips. Myron said he felt high as he went into Blockbuster. Once inside he was walking around and had no intention of killing anyone. Stated he was just walking around but felt "like everyone was staring at him." He said he "felt paranoid." He saw that the guard had a big gun in his holster. He said he "thought he could just run up and snatch the gun out of the guard's holster." Said the guard was talking to a black girl. He said he took out his gun and pointed it at the guard and the girl looked at him. He said he was going to yell "freeze" but the gun went off. Said he saw a lot of blood on the guard's shoulder. Said the guard was sitting on a stool or chair and once he was shot he turned around toward Myron. The guard was sliding off the chair and was also going for his gun. Said "I got real nervous, the guard was going for his gun in his right holster and I wasn't really trying to pull the trigger, it seemed like a hair trigger and it just kept going off." He said it went off "6–7 times." "The guard was on the ground so I reached down and pulled the gun out." "I don't know if I unsnapped the holster or not." "The gun barrel was not long and I knew it was a revolver." Myron said he walked out of the store with "the revolver in my coat pocket." Stated outside he walked then ran to the Ford Tempo. Said he either took off the hat he was wearing or he lost it. Said the car was on Humboldt Avenue. By the car he saw a white guy looking at him and Marteze said to Myron "look at that guy, you might have to shoot him." Myron said he pulled back the slide of the .380 but it was already back. He yelled at Willie "go go." He gave the .380 to Marteze and kept the .357 he got from the guard.

Said he couldn't believe he did it. Later he saw the news and knew the security guard was fatally shot.

Stated he hasn't had a good night's sleep since the shooting. Said "I know what I did was wrong." Said "I thought I'd always be there for my son not like other black men." Myron was cooperative with us during the entire interview.

Homicide and Battery

Varieties, Trends, and Characteristics of Homicide

Murder, as defined by the FBI *Uniform Crime Reports*, refers to the "willful (non-negligent) killing of one human being by another" (FBI, 2002; p. 44). To establish that a murder has occurred, there must be evidence of a dead body (or that death has occurred if a dead body is not recovered) and that another person willfully caused that person's death. As discussed in more detail later, a basic task of investigators is to determine whether the death was a result of foul play or whether it resulted from natural causes, accident, or suicide. In this respect, a murder investigation is similar to an arson investigation (Chapter 12), for which it must be determined whether the fire was caused by arson, accident, or other means. Fortunately, there is often much evidence available to homicide investigators to assist in accurately determining the manner of death.

Murder is a relatively infrequent crime. In 2001, 15,980 persons were murdered in the United States (not including the deaths that resulted from the events of September 11, 2001) (FBI, 2002). There are typically more murders and a higher murder rate (i.e., the number of murders per 100,000 persons) in large urban areas than in smaller cities, suburbs, or rural areas (see Table 11–1). Given the extraordinarily serious nature of the crime, police departments that regularly investigate murders devote a large proportion of resources to them. In addition, unlike other most other crimes, homicide cases are likely to be assigned to numerous investigators (Wellford and Cronin, 1999). Nationwide, year 2000 and 2001 murder rates have trended higher than the immediately preceding years although the longer trend is downward. Murder is down approximately twelve percent from 1997, and down about thirty-two percent since 1992. This national trend, however, may not represent the experience of individual jurisdictions.

With regard to the characteristics of homicide victims, the largest proportion of victims (thirty-four percent) are between the ages of twenty and twenty-nine. Nearly seventy-

TABLE 11–1 Violent Crimes Known to the Police for Select Cities, 2001

City	Population	Murder	Rape	Robbery	Aggravated Assault
Palm Springs (FL)	12,002	0	5	19	30
Sanger (CA)	19,283	1	8	31	121
Saginaw (MI)	62,125	5	75	190	980
Pittsburgh (PA)	341,414	55	134	1,384	1,391
Denver (CO)	569,653	45	317	1,250	1,462
Houston (TX)	1,997,965	267	945	9,921	12,286

Source: FBI (2002)

two percent of victims are between seventeen and forty-four. More than seventy-six percent of homicide victims are male; just under twenty-four percent are female (FBI, 2002).

The most common circumstance in which homicides occur is an argument between the victim and the offender (thirty percent). The second most common circumstance in which homicides occur is in conjunction with other felonies, particularly robberies (7.6 percent) and drug transactions (4.1 percent). These homicides are often referred to as *felony murders*. Juvenile gang killings account for just more than six percent of homicides, and other circumstances account for approximately sixteen percent of homicides. In just more than thirty-two percent of homicides, the circumstances associated with the incident are unknown (many of the unsolved cases) (FBI, 2002).

With regard to the relationship between the victim and the offender, approximately forty-two percent of victims knew their assailant (approximately twenty-nine percent were acquainted with the killer, thirteen percent were related to the assailant). Thirteen percent of murder victims were known to have been murdered by a stranger. In the remainder of cases, the relationship between the victim and offender is unknown. The most striking pattern concerning relationships between victims and offenders is that, in 2001, nearly thirty-three percent of *female* homicide victims were killed by a husband or boyfriend. In contrast, of all *male* homicide victims, less than three percent were killed by a wife or girlfriend (FBI, 2002).

Several methods are used most commonly to kill others. Without question, firearms are the most common weapon used in homicides. In 2001, 63.4 percent of all homicides involved the use of a firearm, and most of these were handguns. Other weapons used in homicides were knives (13.1 percent), personal weapons (6.7 percent; e.g., hands, fists, feet), and blunt objects (4.8 percent; e.g., clubs, hammers, etc.). Only two percent of murders were caused by poison, drowning, strangulation, or asphyxiation (FBI, 2002).

The circumstances in which the homicide took place, the relationship between the victim and the offender, and the nature of the weapon used in the offense may represent important and useful information during an investigation. Partly because of the circumstances of the crime, murder has the highest clearance rate of any index offense: 62.4 percent (FBI, 2002). There is, however, considerable variation in homicide clearance rates across police departments. In general, as in many other crimes, smaller departments tend to have a higher clearance rate for murder than larger departments. Even among large agencies, however, there may be considerable variation. For instance, in recent years, Baltimore, Maryland, has experienced about 250 homicides a year and has a clearance rate of approximately eighty percent for these crimes. Detroit, Michigan, on the other hand, has usually about 450 homicides a year and has a clearance rate of just more than forty percent. These differences are probably best explained by the nature and circumstances of homicides in each jurisdiction and the investigative response of each agency (Wellford and Cronin, 1999).

Of the murders that are cleared nationally, nearly ninety percent of individuals arrested were adults, and just more than eighty-seven percent were male. By race, the percentage of arrestees was nearly even: 48.7 percent of arrestees were black, 48.4 percent were white, and other races accounted for less than two percent (see Table 11–2). Based on arrest statistics, it is noteworthy that of all index crimes, juveniles have the lowest proportional involvement in homicides (FBI, 2002).

TABLE 11–2   Violent Crime Arrests by Age, Sex, and Race

Offense	Percent by Age		Percent by Sex		Percent by Race		
	<15	<25	Male	Female	White	Black	Other
Murder	10.2	51.3	87.5	12.5	48.4	48.7	1.9
Rape	16.8	45.4	98.8	1.2	62.7	34.8	2.5
Robbery	23.6	62.0	89.9	10.1	44.5	53.8	1.7
Aggravated Assault	25.0	39.8	79.9	20.1	64.0	33.7	2.3

Source: FBI (2002)

Varieties, Trends, and Characteristics of Battery

The crime of aggravated battery, or assault, is very similar in its characteristics to murder except, of course, the victim does not die as a result of the attack. As such, the investigation is similar to that of murder except that instead of a dead body there is a live victim who may be able to provide information to the police about the crime and the perpetrator. As defined by the FBI (2002), aggravated assault "is an unlawful attack by one person upon another for the purpose of inflicting severe or aggravated bodily injury" (p. 37). The crime usually involves the use of a weapon or other means that would likely cause death or great bodily harm. Attempted murder is included in this definition. The most significant legal difference between aggravated assault and nonaggravated (simple) assault is the amount of injury sustained by the victim. Simple assaults result in minor injuries. Not being an index crime, few details are provided by the FBI *Uniform Crime Reports* (FBI, 2002) about simple assaults.

In most jurisdictions—large, medium, or small—aggravated assault is usually the most common violent index crime (see Table 11–1). Nationally, there were approximately 900,000 aggravated assault offenses in 2001—the lowest number since 1987. Nationally, the rate of aggravated assault offenses (number of offenses per 100,000 persons) has declined nearly seventeen percent since 1997 and approximately thirty percent since 1992 (FBI, 2002).

Compared with homicide victims, a greater proportion of aggravated assault victims are female (although most aggravated assault victims are still male). In addition, aggravated assault victims tend to be younger and they are more likely to be African American. Victims of simple assaults tend to be even younger than victims of aggravated assault and are even more likely to be female (many instances of domestic violence are included as simple assaults) (BJS, 2002a). As with homicide, the circumstance most likely to lead to an assault is an argument (BJS, 2002a).

With regard to the relationship between the victim and the offender, it is more likely that there is a relationship between the victim and the offender in aggravated assaults than in homicides. Approximately half of aggravated assault victims reported that they knew their attacker. Furthermore, simple assaults are even more likely than aggravated assaults to occur among victims and offenders who know each other (BJS, 2002a). Again, this may be largely a function of the large proportion of domestic violence incidents in this category. As with homicides, it is much more likely that there is a relationship between the victim and the offender when the victim is female than when the victim is male (BJS, 2002a).

Weapons are less likely to be used in aggravated and simple assaults than in homicides. In only approximately thirty percent of such incidents was a weapon used. Of course, this may help account for the lesser injuries sustained by victims in assaults compared with homicides. When weapons are used, they are usually hands, fists, or feet (FBI, 2002), not guns or knives (BJS, 2002a).

As with homicides, the circumstances during which aggravated (and simple) assault typically take place contribute to the relatively high clearance rate for the crime. Particularly important is that there is face-to-face contact between the victim and the offender, and that the offender is often known to the victim. Overall, 56.1 percent of aggravated assaults reported to the police were cleared by the police in 2001, a slightly lower rate than that of homicide (FBI, 2002). Once again, smaller departments tend to have a higher clearance rate for aggravated assaults than larger departments. Aggravated assaults that involved a knife or other cutting instrument were the most likely to be cleared, and those that involved a firearm were the least likely to be cleared. Compared with homicide, those arrested for aggravated assault are more likely to be younger than the age of eighteen but about equally likely to be younger than the age of twenty-five. Those arrested for aggravated assault are also more likely to be female and to be white (see Table 11–2; FBI, 2002). Based on arrest statistics for all the violent index crimes, juveniles have the highest proportional involvement in aggravated assaults (FBI, 2002).

Investigative Considerations With Homicide and Battery

Homicide and related crimes often provide a wealth of clues for investigators to pursue. As noted, aggravated assault is usually investigated in the same manner as murder except that instead of a dead body there is a live witness. If the crime occurred in a private place (e.g., a residence), most often there is a relationship between the victim and the offender, and the identity of the offender is relatively easy to discern. If the crime occurred in a public place (e.g., on a street, in a tavern) there may be witnesses who may be able to provide critical information to investigators regarding the identity of the assailant. In either case, battery victims are likely to be able to provide critical information about the incident and the identity of the offender.

Homicide investigations usually begin with a focus on the dead body and the place in which the body was found. This place is usually where the crime occurred. As noted earlier in the text, crime scenes are potentially valuable because of the evidence (e.g., physical evidence, witnesses) that may be found there. They may also be valuable because of who had access to the scene. Nowhere is this more true than with homicides. The procedures for processing, searching, and documenting crime scenes outlined in Chapter 6 are most relevant in homicide investigations.

Homicide investigations are generally guided by several basic questions:

- Who is the decedent?
- What was the manner in which the person died?
- If the victim died as a result of a homicide, who is the offender?

Each question is discussed in turn.

WHO IS THE DECEDENT?

Usually, it is relatively easy for investigators to determine the identity of the decedent. Witnesses, friends, neighbors, or family members may be at the scene and may be able to provide this information to the police. In other instances, the police may be able to make a tentative identification through items in the possession of the person (e.g., identification card in a billfold or purse), and then a positive identification may be made by a family member or friend at the hospital or the medical examiner's office. In some instances, because of injuries or decomposition, the body may not be recognizable. In these cases, identification may be made through personal characteristics (e.g., a unique and visible tattoo) or through scientific methods such as fingerprints, dental records, DNA comparisons, or other means. With the discovery of an unidentified dead body when it is believed that death occurred quite some time prior to the discovery, it may first be necessary to compare the circumstances of the discovery and characteristics of the found body with missing persons reports and the reported circumstances of those disappearances. In rare instances, there

The necklace known to be worn by Danielle van Dam the night she disappeared. Jewelry and other personal effects help in the tentative identification of a dead body, as was the case in the identification of Danielle van Dam.

may be a need for anthropological facial reconstruction to recreate the face of the decedent for recognition purposes. In such cases, media coverage may assist investigators in developing necessary information to determine the identify of the decedent.

What Was the Manner in Which the Person Died?

All deaths can be explained in one of four ways: deaths are either the result of natural causes (e.g., heart attack or illness), accident (e.g., vehicle crash), suicide (e.g., willfully jumping from a tall building), or homicide. Most deaths, sixty to seventy percent, are the result of natural causes, followed in frequency by accidents, suicides, and homicides (Castleman, 2000). In most cases, the manner of death is a straightforward determination. However, because this is not necessarily the case, police investigators are often summoned to all death scenes to conduct death investigations. In such instances, the manner of death should be assumed to be homicide until homicide is ruled out (Castleman, 2000). It is also important for investigators to remember that, in rare instances, deliberate efforts may be made by others to disguise the true manner of death through the process of staging (recall Chapter 9). When staging occurs, it is most common that a murder is made to look like an accident or a suicide. Other instances of staging may involve making a suicide look like an accident or making a murder that occurred between intimates appear as one that occurred between strangers (and having a sexual motive) (Geberth, 1996).

To determine manner of death, at least three considerations are paramount: investigators must consider the nature of the injuries sustained by the decedent (the cause of death), the characteristics of the decedent, and the circumstances of the death. This information may come from an examination of the body, an examination of the scene, and from witnesses. For instance, if there are no visible injuries to the body, the body was found at home in bed, there were no signs of forced entry into the home, and it was learned from relatives that the victim lived alone, had a history of poor health, and was eighty years old, then the most reasonable conclusion would be that the person died of natural causes. If a person was discovered facedown on the sidewalk with a knife protruding from his back, and witnesses stated that they heard arguing and screaming before seeing the person lying there, homicide would be a reasonable conclusion. Of course, establishing the manner of death is not always quite so clear. When there is uncertainty regarding the manner of death, it usually involves differentiating between suicide and homicide, and suicide and accident. Again, information from witnesses may be of most assistance in this determination. In particular, the person who last saw the decedent alive may possess particularly important information about the manner of death. This information may include the decedent's state of mind (e.g., he seemed very depressed), his last activities (e.g., he was arguing with another person), or his state of physical well-being (e.g., he was complaining of chest pain).

It may also be instructive to consider directly and carefully the nature of the injuries and whether the decedent could have inflicted the injuries on himself, in determining the manner of death and when differentiating between suicide and homicide in particular. Deaths that are caused by different actions will leave different wounds on the body (see

EXHIBIT 11–3 Information developed from the autopsy of the victim is the definitive word on the nature of the injuries and the cause of death.

Autopsy Protocol of Anthony Porter, Blockbuster Video store guard and homicide victim

---

Final Anatomic Findings

1. Exsanguination, secondary to multiple gunshot wounds to the chest and abdomen.
   a. Lacerations of the left subclavian and left internal jugular veins.
   b. Lacerations to bilateral lungs, liver, and ascending colon.
   c. Bilateral hemothorax.
   d. Seven entrance wounds to chest and upper extremities.
   e. Two exit wounds to right and left upper extremities.
2. Laceration of trachea with aspiration of blood to distal airways.

Evidence of Internal Injury:

The bullet entering through **WOUND #1**, passed through the right apex of the chest cavity and ended in the musculature just anterior to the scapula. There was a fracture in the scapula near where the bullet was recovered. This bullet is a deformed 5.7 gm copper jacketed projectile with visible lateral rifling. The angle of the bullet was mostly left to right at 45 degrees off of horizontal, anterior to posterior very slightly and downward at 60 degrees off of sagittal. The left internal jugular vein was also lacerated by this bullet.

The bullet entering through **WOUND #2** passed between the left first and second ribs, then through soft tissue surrounding the thoracic aorta to lodge posterior to T4. The bullet recovered from this site was a mushroomed 5.7 gm copper jacketed projectile with visible lateral rifling. This bullet was angled from left to right at 60 degrees off of horizontal, from anterior to posterior just slightly off of the coronal plane, and downward at 45 degrees off of the sagittal plane. The left subclavian vein was lacerated by this bullet.

The bullet that entered through **WOUND #3** passed through the soft tissues in the right anterior shoulder to exit though **WOUND #11**. This bullet angled from left to right at approximately 5 degrees off of horizontal, from anterior to posterior at 5 degrees off of the coronal plane, and downward at 5 degrees off of horizontal.

The bullet that entered through **WOUND #4** passed between the right first and second ribs laterally and then between the first and second ribs medially to be embedded in T2. The bullet recovered from this site was a 5.7

continued

EXHIBIT 11–3 continued

gm mushroomed copper jacketed projectile with visible lateral rifling. The bullet angled anterior to posterior at 5 degrees off of coronal, right to left at 5 degrees off of coronal and upward at 5 degrees off of horizontal.

The bullet that entered through **WOUND #5** passed between the left fifth and sixth ribs then through the left upper lobe and the apex of the left lower lobe, through the inferior pericardium and then through the left diaphragm, through the left and caudate lobes of the liver, through the ascending colon, and then through the lateral aspect of the right lobe of the liver to come to rest in the peritoneal cavity just deep to the liver. The bullet causing **WOUND #10** first passed through the clothing (an intermediate target) in the left lateral seam of the outer shirt and causing **WOUND #10**, passing through the soft tissue of the abdomen at **WOUND #6** where it lay embedded in the subcutaneous tissue just deep to the skin. This bullet was a 5.7 gm mushroomed copper jacketed projectile with visible lateral rifling. This bullet had moved from left to right at a 45 degree angulation off the coronal plane. It moved in a downward direction at 5 degrees off of horizontal and from posterior to anterior at 60 degrees off of sagittal.

The bullet that passed though **WOUND #7** exited the left arm at **WOUND #8** and then impacted the skin of the left lateral chest at **WOUND #9** causing an abrasion. From here, it bounced off of the body. The angulation of this bullet was mostly left to right with a 30 degree angulation off of horizontal, slightly posterior to anterior at 5 degrees off of coronal, and downward at approximately 30 degrees off of horizontal.

The left pleural cavity contained 650 cc of blood and the right pleural cavity contained 400 cc of blood.

Geberth [1996] and Castleman [2000] for a detailed discussion of this issue). For example, death by asphyxiation, ligature strangulation in particular, will leave an imprint of the ligature on the victim's neck. There may also be scratch marks from the victim's fingers in the same general area as a result of the victim's attempt to loosen the ligature. Manual strangulation will likely leave bruising and hand or finger marks on the victim's neck. Blunt-force injuries are evidenced by lacerations, bruising, and possibly broken bones in the area of impact. Cutting wounds will show a slicing of tissue. Death by poison will usually not produce any obvious indicators, but this depends on the nature of the poison.

Toxicology tests on the body conducted during an autopsy may confirm the presence of poison in the body. On first examination, gunshot wounds and stab wounds may look similar (as holes in the body), although with gunshot wounds there may be soot stains or burns around the hole and there may be exit wounds that are generally much larger than the wounds where the bullet entered (see Geberth [1996] for numerous photographic examples of such wounds).

An immediate clue as to the cause of death or injury is the presence of shell casings at the scene. Shell casings are a frequently retrieved form of physical evidence. MILWAUKEE POLICE DEPARTMENT

Clearly, stab wounds or gunshot wounds in the back are unlikely to be a result of suicide, as is a fatal gunshot wound with no gun found near the victim (unless the gun was removed as an attempt at staging the scene). The presence of defense wounds (i.e., injuries that appeared to have been sustained by the victim in an attempt to protect himself, such as cuts to the hands from grasping a knife) are usually indicative of homicide. Despite all the evidentiary considerations, in some instances it may not be possible to determine conclusively the manner of death. In these instances, judgments are made by investigators and forensic pathologists based on the best evidence available.

IF THE VICTIM DIED AS A RESULT OF A HOMICIDE, WHO IS THE OFFENDER?

Once again, information about the circumstances of death and the characteristics of the victim are critical in answering this question, and this information is most likely to come from witnesses or other individuals with relevant information. In many instances, witnesses will be able to identify the offender and provide information to the police about the relationship between the victim and the offender. Often, the most critical and difficult task for investigators is locating witnesses who have this information. Tip lines and media publicity serve important purposes in this regard. A parallel consideration is the motive for committing the crime. Who would want to kill this person? Who would benefit from this person being dead? As seen in the Blockbuster Video store security guard homicide discussed in the introduction to this chapter, the police were at a loss in the investigation because no reasonable motive was apparent nor was there an apparent relationship between the victim and the offender. Without these circumstances or without this information, investigators have a definite handicap. Diaries, letters, e-mail, appointment books, and recent telephone calls of the victim may provide insight into activities of the victim and clues about the identity of the killer.

Depending on the circumstances of the murder, physical evidence on the victim's body or at the crime scene may also provide information about the identity of the killer. For example, once again consider the scene of the murder of Ron Goldman and Nicole Brown Simpson (Chapter 6). The physical evidence present at the scene (e.g., blood drips, shoe prints, cap with hairs in it, glove with blood on it) did not lead to the initial identification of O.J. Simpson as the perpetrator but tended to confirm that he was responsible for the crimes once he had been identified as a suspect through other means. For this same reason, a routine procedure associated with homicide investigations involves "bagging" the victim's hands to preserve evidence that may be present under the fingernails of the victim (e.g., where the victim scratched or struggled with the perpetrator and where the perpetrator's DNA may then be recovered). In addition, as shown in the Blockbuster investigation, the weapon used in a homicide (or battery for that matter) may also be valuable evidence in identifying the culprit. If the instrument or gun used in the crime can be suggested based on an analysis of the wounds sustained, or on an analysis of the bullets recovered, and if police are able to find the weapon used to cause these wounds, it may assist in finding the culprit.

In some homicide investigations, the time at which the victim died is unknown but it may be a critical piece of the evidence puzzle, particularly as it relates to the alibi of the suspect. Approximate time of death, or the approximate time the crime occurred, may be estimated by the condition of the dead body or by other circumstances of the crime, as established by witnesses. For instance, with regard to the murder of Nicole Brown Simpson and Ron Goldman, and the prosecution of O.J. Simpson for these crimes, the time at which the crimes occurred was critical. Simpson was known to be on his way to the Los Angeles airport shortly after 11:00 PM the night of the murders. As a result, the closer the murders occurred to 11:00, the less likely that Simpson could have been the killer. The approximate time at which the crime occurred—approximately 10:00 PM—was established through various witness statements about related events the night of the crime (e.g., witnesses hearing a barking dog that was later determined to belong to Nicole, another witness discovering the dog outside Nicole's property). In the case of the kidnaping of Danielle van Dam by David Westerfield, Westerfield's attorneys argued that his client could not have killed the girl because at the time of her death, he was considered a suspect and was under constant surveillance by the police and the media. In support of this argument, a forensic entomologist testified at the trial about the condition of the little girl's body and how long she had been dead at the time her body was discovered.

With regard to estimating time of death from the condition of the dead body, it is necessary to consider what happens to a body upon death. When a person dies, when the heart stops beating, a series of relatively predictable changes begin to occur in the body. These changes may provide a basis on which to make an *estimate* regarding the time of death or, as it is sometimes called, the *postmortem interval* (or PMI). Many factors can influence the changes and the rate of the changes that occur in the body after death. As a result, it is important to realize that the estimates are, at best, approximations of PMI.

The first indicator of PMI is the temperature of the body. Normal body temperature is 98.6 degrees Fahrenheit. On death, internal body temperature falls at a rate of approximately one and one-half to two degrees per hour depending on the build of the victim, amount of clothing on the body, and the surrounding environmental temperature (Owen, 2000).

Within two hours of death, livor mortis becomes evident. When the heart stops beating, blood begins to pool in the body in accordance with gravity. The blood settles and shows as a bruising purplish type of discoloration on the body. After eight to twelve hours, the blood becomes fixed and the areas of discoloration will not move, even if the body is moved. Accordingly, if there is a question about whether the body has been moved after death (e.g., because of an attempt to stage the scene or for some other reason) and if livor mortis is present, an examination of the pattern of livor mortis may reveal the answer.

Shortly after death, as a result of chemical changes in the dead body, the muscles of the body begin to become stiff. This process is referred to as *rigor mortis*. It is usually fully established after about twelve hours of death and will be present for at least twelve more hours. It will begin to disappear after another twelve hours and usually will be be gone within sixty hours of death (Castleman, 2000). Again, this process is greatly affected by individual (e.g., weight) and environmental (e.g., temperature) factors.

Another potential method of determining PMI involves measurement of potassium levels in the vitreous humor, the fluid that fills the inside of the eyeball. As blood cells break down through the process of livor mortis, potassium is released at a predictable rate. Measurement of the potassium can provide an estimate regarding the time of death (Owen, 2000).

The degree of decomposition of the body can also serve as an indicator of the time of death; although, once again, decomposition is greatly affected by environmental conditions. Within two days after death, skin discoloration becomes evident. This process begins with a green staining of the abdomen and progresses to purplish lines ("marbling") on the body. After three to four days, the staining spreads to the extremities of the body and the body begins to swell from the production of gases inside the body that are unable to escape. After seven days, skin blisters are evident, fluids seep from the body, and the body has a putrid odor (Castleman, 2000; Goff, 2000; Owen, 2000). If the state of decomposition is not congruent with the environmental conditions in which the body was located, then one may be led to believe that the body had been moved after death from one environment to another.

During the process of decomposition, visible insect activity is also likely to be present. Insects are most likely first to invade open wounds and areas of bleeding. After these areas are attacked, then the eyes, mouth, nose, and ears are attacked. Next to be invaded are the genitals and anus, if exposed. Usually the pelvic area is not attacked by insects for as long as twelve to thirty-six hours after death unless there was trauma and bleeding in those areas (Haskell and Haskell, 2002). With bleeding, insects will be present much sooner. Accordingly, if insects (larva) found on the face are at the same stage of development as those in the pelvic region, it may be concluded that these areas were invaded at about the same time and, hence, that there was pelvic trauma (Haskell and Haskell, 2002). In addition, wounds inflicted after death (postmortem) are generally less attractive to insects than wounds before death (antemortem) or at the time of death (perimortem) because of the lack of blood at the site of the wound. It is also interesting to note that it is possible to detect chemicals or poisons that are in a decomposing body through an analysis of the contents of the gut of maggots recovered from the body. In addition, if there is a question about whether the recovered maggots were actually feeding on a particular corpse, it is possible to extract human DNA from the maggot and associate it with a particular body (Wells et al., 2001).

Along with the presence of insects, their stage of development, and the contents of their gut, also informative is the type of insects that are present on the body. Certain types of insects are most likely to be the first to lay eggs on the body; others are more likely to be present later. Blow flies (green bottle and blue bottle flies) are generally the first to arrive and may lay eggs on a dead body within minutes of death. Eggs hatch between eight and fourteen hours later, depending on environmental (temperature and humidity) conditions. Maggots then develop and proceed through three developmental stages, reaching maturity ten to twelve days after the eggs were laid (Owen, 2002). Dump flies (a relative of the housefly) may be present on the body several days to several weeks after the time of death. False stable flies (another relative of the housefly) usually appear after the dump flies (Haskell and Haskell, 2002). By this time, beetle activity is most prominent on the body. After all insect activity has stopped, only bones and hair remain.

The last method of estimating time of death involves an analysis of the contents of the victim's stomach or gastrointestinal tract. If the time of the last meal is known, and the body is not in a state of advanced decomposition, it may be possible to estimate the time of death based on the degree to which food has been digested. Generally, the stomach empties in two to six hours after consumption of food (Castleman, 2000).

Homicide investigations in which there is no apparent relationship between the victim and the offender pose a unique challenge to the police. The ultimate investigative challenge, however, is investigating homicides that are suspected of being part of a series, that are suspected of being the responsibility of a serial killer. These crimes often appear as "random" and without a traditional motive. Serial murders may be mobile, further complicating the task of identifying the perpetrator. These crimes are often well planned and lack witnesses and other evidence. As seen in the Michigan coed killer case discussed in Chapter 4, there may not be a crime scene, or even a body. The difficulty in investigating such crimes is apparent in the nature of the crime. The killer is able to be a *serial* killer because he is not caught. If he was caught after the first homicide, he would not have a chance to continue his crimes. Fortunately, serial homicides are relatively uncommon. Given the lack of favorable investigative circumstances in investigating homicides suspected of being part of a series, investigators often have to rely on nontraditional investigative techniques in such investigations. Primary among them, as discussed in previous chapters, are psychological profiling, crime analysis networks (e.g., VICAP), media alerts (e.g., AMBER alerts), and even psychics.

Forcible Rape and Other Sexual Assaults

Varieties, Trends, and Characteristics of Rape

Forcible rape refers to the "carnal knowledge of a female forcibly and against her will" (FBI, 2002; p. 29). Interpreted, this means forced sexual intercourse. In most jurisdictions, the

FBI definition has been expanded to include male victims. Forcible rape also includes sexual relations with a person who is unconscious, under the influence of drugs or alcohol, or is feebleminded. There are numerous other forms of sexual assault besides forcible rape. For instance, statutory rape involves sexual intercourse with a minor without force. Minors younger than the age of consent legally cannot give consent for sexual relations. For minors older than the age of consent, enforcement of the law is more discretionary and may depend on the circumstances associated with the behavior. Many states do not provide a crime of "rape" in their criminal codes; the behavior is criminally defined as sexual assault, sexual battery, sexual abuse, criminal sexual conduct, indecent assault, or sexual assault of a child. In addition, various degrees of the crime may be provided depending on the nature of the sexual contact. In the FBI *Unified Crime Reports*, (2002), other forms of sexual contact beside forcible rape are classified as "other sex crimes."

Only murder occurs more infrequently than rape. In 2001 there was a total of 90,491 rapes reported to the police (FBI, 2002). However, estimates indicate that less than forty percent of rapes/sexual assaults were reported to the police in 2001 (BJS, 2002a). Based on FBI statistics, 62.2 of every 100,000 females were victims of forcible rape in 2001 (FBI, 2002). Like most other forms of predatory crime, rape is primarily an urban phenomenon (see Table 11–1). Nationwide, rates of rape have been on the decline since 1992. This national trend, however, may not represent the experience of individual jurisdictions. Given the serious nature of the crime, police departments that regularly investigate rapes devote a large proportion of investigative resources to the investigation of such crimes. In addition, additional demands are placed on investigators because of the sensitive nature of such crimes. In fact, in many larger departments, these crimes are handled by investigators who are assigned to a "sensitive crimes" unit.

With regard to the characteristics of rape victims, most are young. The highest victimization rate is for females between the ages of sixteen and twenty. Individuals between the ages of twelve and fifteen and between twenty and twenty-four have about equal chances of sexual assault/rape victimization. Most victims were not married at the time of the incident. The largest proportion of sexual assault/rape victims had annual family incomes of less than $7,500. Clearly, marital status and income of victims may be a function of their age (BJS, 2001a). In addition to the rape, other injuries are common in such incidents but are not the norm. Thirty-eight percent of victims reported additional injuries, which ranged from bruises to chipped teeth to broken bones to gunshot wounds (BJS, 2002b).

With regard to the relationship between the victim and the offender, of all rapes/sexual assaults, approximately sixty-six percent of victims knew their attacker (approximately forty-eight percent were friends or acquaintances with the perpetrator, sixteen percent of victims were in an intimate relationship with the perpetrator, and two percent were related in some other way to the perpetrator). In thirty percent of the cases, the perpetrator was a stranger to the victim, and in four percent the relationship was unknown (BJS, 2002a). However, in those crimes reported to the police, a smaller proportion of cases involve victims and offenders who know each other. The closer the relationship between the victim and the offender, the less likely the crime was reported to the police (BJS, 2002b). Rapes/sexual assaults are usually committed without the use of a weapon. In the seven percent of cases during which a weapon was used, most common was the use of a knife (four percent) (BJS, 2002a).

As with homicides, the circumstances (face-to-face contact between the victim and the offender, and the presence of a relationship between the victim and the offender) in which rape often occurs significantly contributes to its relatively high clearance rate. Nationally, just more than forty-four percent of rapes were cleared in 2001. Of the rapes that are cleared, approximately eighty-three percent of individuals arrested were adult and nearly all were male. Only homicides involved juveniles as arrestees to a lesser extent than rapes (FBI, 2002). By race, nearly sixty-three percent of those individuals who were arrested were white, thirty-five percent were black, and the remaining arrestees were of other races (see Table 11–2).

Investigative Considerations With Rape and Other Sexual Assaults

The most important source of information in a rape investigation is the victim. In particular, critical information about the crime is often obtained from the investigator's interview of the victim and from a physician's forensic examination of the victim.

INFORMATION FROM THE INTERVIEW OF THE VICTIM

Sexual assault is one of the most traumatic types of criminal victimization. In most instances, the emotional trauma caused by the crime is much greater than the physical trauma. As a result, it is critical that investigators be mindful of victims' experiences and be sensitive to their needs. Investigators who are compassionate, sincere, and comforting in their interactions with victims may create a positive atmosphere in which victims may regain a sense of control and desire to be of assistance in the investigation. This is true in all investigations, but especially in sexual assaults.

Considerable attention has been devoted to how the police and other criminal justice personnel can best respond to crime victims in their time of need. A U.S. Department of Justice (2001) report titled *First Response to Victims of Crime* offers several suggestions for investigators about how they should respond to victims of sexual assault. These include the following:

- Be unconditionally supportive and permit victims to express their emotions.
- Approach victims calmly. Showing your outrage at the crime may cause victims even more trauma.
- Interview victims with extreme sensitivity. Minimize the number of times victims must recount details of the crime to strangers.
- Ask the victims whether they would prefer talking with a male or a female officer.
- If possible, only one investigator should be assigned to the initial interview and subsequent investigation.
- Remember that it is normal for victims to want to forget, or actually to forget, details of the crime that are difficult for them to accept.
- Encourage victims to get medical attention. Explain to the victim why medical attention and a forensic examination is important.

- Encourage victims to obtain counseling. Identify and refer them to support services for assistance.
- Victims should be interviewed in a private place. Often, victims proceed to a hospital before the police are even contacted. In such cases, police interviews with victims may be best conducted in a private room at a hospital. (p. 1)

From an evidentiary perspective, the interview of the victim is extremely important because the victim is usually the only witness to the crime. Simply stated, if information is to be produced about the offender, it is most likely to come from the victim. Most useful, of course, is whether the victim can provide details that would lead to the identification and apprehension of the perpetrator. In many cases when the perpetrator is known to the victim, the victim may be able to provide investigators with his name. If this information is obtained, then the investigation into the crime may be relatively straightforward. Most often, the most problematic issue in these types of cases is establishing lack of consent for the act (corpus delicti). Interestingly, the issue of consent is unique in rape cases; it rarely, if ever, emerges as an issue in other type of crimes.

If the assault was not committed by someone the victim knew or was acquainted with, and the victim is not able to provide a name of the suspect, then the task of identifying and apprehending the perpetrator is likely to be much more difficult for the police. In these types of cases, details from the victim regarding the characteristics and the actions of the perpetrator may be most useful. Besides basic descriptive information about the offender (e.g., his approximate height, weight, hair color, build), other details may also be helpful. For instance, given the close contact between the offender and the victim during the assault, the victim may have noticed tattoos, unusual or distinctive body marks (e.g., moles), a unique smell of the perpetrator, or other distinctive characteristics or mannerisms (e.g., his style of walking, speech impediments).

Along with obtaining a description of the offender, it is important that investigators ask other questions as well. Answers to questions about the nature and circumstances of the attack may provide investigators with insight into the type of person who committed the crime, his MO, other clues about his identity, and interrogation strategies that may be most effectively used when the perpetrator is apprehended. Hazelwood and Burgess (1995) suggest the following line of questioning be conducted:

- What method of approach was used by the offender? Did he "con" or trick the victim into gaining his trust? Did he use immediate and overwhelming physical force? Did he attack the victim by surprise?
- How did the offender maintain control during the incident? Did he use verbal threats, display a weapon, use a weapon, use other force?
- What amount of physical force was used by the attacker?
- Did the victim resist and, if so, how? Did the victim's actions cause injury to the attacker? If the perpetrator is identified, would one be able to see these injuries?
- If resistance occurred, what was the offender's reaction? Did he change his demand, compromise, use threats, use force?

- During the attack, did the assailant experience a sexual dysfunction such as erectile insufficiency, premature ejaculation, retarded ejaculation, or conditional ejaculation? It is worthwhile to note that these conditions may also be experienced by the offender when he is with his consensual partner. If a suspect is identified, this information may be verified.

- What type and sequence of sexual acts occurred during the assault? This information may provide insight into the motivation, preferences, and experiences of the offender. Interestingly, as noted by Hazelwood and Burgess (1995), anal assault may indicate that the offender spent time in prison.

- What was the verbal activity of the attacker? Did he use particular unusual words or phrases? An understanding of the language used by the offender may help establish MO and the motivation for the attack. Verbal activity of the attacker may also reveal clues about his identity.

- Was the victim forced to say anything? What were these words or phrases? Again, this information may reveal motivation and signature aspects of the crime.

- Was there a sudden change in the offender's attitude/behavior during the attack? Is there any speculation on the part of the victim about what may have prompted this change?

- What precautionary actions were taken by the offender? For example, did he wear a mask? Disguise his voice? Order the victim to shower? The degree of sophistication in the precautionary actions of the offender may serve as an indicator of the experience level of the offender.

- Was anything taken by the offender? Were these items of evidentiary value (e.g., clothing with biological stains on them), personal value (e.g., photographs of the victim), or monetary value (e.g., jewelry)?

- Does the victim have any reason to believe that she was targeted as a victim? For example, does she have any knowledge of peeping tom activity or prowlers at her house or in her neighborhood? Did she recently receive any unusual phone calls or notes? If the victim was targeted, there is a good chance that the perpetrator may have previous arrests for burglary, prowling, or voyeurism.

Effectively interviewing adult sexual assault victims may be a challenge for investigators but, no question, interviewing child sexual assault victims poses even greater challenges. Successful interviews with child victims requires investigators to have special communication skills, an expertise in child psychology, and training in the use of various supplementary interviewing methodologies, such as the use of artwork and sketches, and anatomically correct dolls (see Morgan [1995]). Regardless of the age or other characteristics of victims, compassion and understanding on the part of investigators during the interview is absolutely necessary.

INFORMATION FROM THE FORENSIC EXAMINATION OF THE VICTIM

In perhaps no other type of criminal investigation does physical evidence play such a potentially large role as it does in the crime of rape. With rape, the victim's body is the primary crime scene. It is important for investigators to keep perspective and to remember that the victim is a person who has undergone a horrific experience. A sense of sensitivity is just as critical in seeking physical evidence as it is in conducting an interview.

Forensic examinations of victims are conducted at hospitals and are performed by either a physician or a nurse who has received special training in forensic matters. Nurses with such training are often referred to as sexual assault nurse examiners (or SANEs). The primary objectives of forensic examinations of sexual assault victims are to document injuries caused by the assault, recover biological evidence present as a result of the assault, and to provide treatment for injuries sustained as a result of the assault (see Crowley [1999] for an excellent and detailed discussion of forensic issues in sexual assault cases; also see Moreau and Bigbee [1995] and Grispino [1990] for a discussion of related issues. The following discussion was drawn from these sources).

Although it depends on the specific nature and circumstances of the assault, the physical examination of the victim usually involves a number of procedures, including the collection of oral, nasal mucous, vaginal, and rectal specimen samples; the victim's clothing that was worn at the time of the assault; fingernail scrapings from the victim; any foreign material or debris on the victim's body (e.g., dirt); other substances that may be in the form of stains on the victim's body; pubic hair combings (which may include hair from the attacker); swabs and photographs of bite marks (for documentation purposes and possible traces of saliva); and blood and urine samples for toxicology screening. Toxicology screens may be conducted to test for the presence of alcohol, drugs, and, if suspected, Rohypnol or GHP, the so-called "date rape drug." Tests may also be conducted for pregnancy and sexually transmitted diseases.

In addition, reference standards may be collected from victims and their recent consensual partners. Reference standards are specimens collected to determine whether other recovered evidence (e.g., evidence collected from the victim's body, clothing, or actual crime scene) is from the victim, the victim's consensual partners, or if it is from someone else, such as the perpetrator. Reference samples typically include blood, pulled head hairs, pulled pubic hairs, a saliva sample, and other body hair samples (male victims). The collection of specimen samples and reference standards may be facilitated through the use of a sexual assault evidence kit, a preassembled package of prelabeled containers that are used to collect and store the physical evidence collected from a particular victim. A "sexual assault evidence kit" should not be confused with a "rape kit," which is a collection of tools (e.g., rope, gloves, tape) that may be used by a rapist to facilitate an attack and that may be found in possession of the perpetrator.

On occasion, rapists use condoms in an attempt either to limit the biological evidence available for recovery and analysis or to protect against sexually transmitted diseases. When perpetrators use condoms, other valuable evidence may be left behind (see Blackledge [1996]). For instance, trace amounts of particulates (e.g., the powder in condoms that prevents them from sticking to themselves), lubricants, and spermicide may be recovered during the forensic examination of the victim. If such evidence is recovered, it may be possible to link the condom to its manufacturer and to determine the brand. In addition, such evidence may provide corpus delicti of the crime, link crimes of a serial rapist, be a source of other physical evidence (e.g., fingerprints on the condom package found at the scene), or may be of other value (e.g., condoms of a particular brand indicated by the trace evidence may be subsequently found in possession of the perpetrator during the execution of a search warrant).

Beyond the victim as a source of physical evidence, it is important for investigators also to search for and collect evidence from crime scenes, usually the victim's home. It is in such a search that the crime scene procedures outlined in Chapter 6 are of most relevance.

INFORMATION FROM SUSPECTS

If a suspect can be named by the victim, then the physical evidence recovered from the rape victim or from the crime scene may be of immediate use. In addition, when a suspect is identified, a search of the suspect's home or automobile may be conducted (based on probable cause) to seize evidence related to the crime. Furthermore, based on court order, the suspect may be required to undergo a forensic examination. Depending on the nature of the assault, the acts committed, and the time that elapsed from the time of the crime to the time of the examination, the examination of the suspect may involve the documentation of the wounds inflicted by the victim (e.g., bite marks, scratches); the collection of saliva, blood, and hair (e.g., head, facial, body, pubic) specimens; the seizure of the suspect's clothing worn at the time of the attack or that contained suspected evidence; and the collection of penile swabs for evidence that may link the suspect to the victim.

In addition, interrogation of the suspect may produce information that leads to the suspect being identified as the perpetrator. As discussed in detail in Chapter 8, identification of the most productive tactics to be used during an interrogation of a suspected rapist, or a suspect in any type of crime for that matter, often depends on an understanding of the motivations of that individual for committing the crime. This information may relate directly to the motivations and MO of the offender. For instance, Merrill (1995) makes the distinction between "contact" rapists and "sexual aggressor" rapists. Contact rapists are those perpetrators whose primary motivation is sexual pleasure and their victims are most often their "friends" or acquaintances. Contact rapists are most likely to respond to emotional themes during the interrogation whereby the investigator blames the victim or reduces the moral seriousness of the offense to encourage a confession. As explained by Merrill (1995), investigators "should emphasize that the suspect, a healthy man with normal needs and desires, simply allowed the situation to escalate beyond his control" (p. 10). Ideally, this will allow the suspect to confess without embarrassment and to place some of the blame for what happened on the victim.

Sexual aggressor rapists, on the other hand, usually do not know their victims. The act of rape is an expression of anger or control. Merrill (1995) draws on the work of Hazelwood and Burgess (1995) in further differentiating between these types of rapists. Briefly, for the power reassurance type of rapist, rape is an expression of power. He may apologize to the victim, ask for forgiveness, he may recontact the victim; he is a "gentleman rapist" who lacks a social and sexual capability to interact with women. According to Merrill (1995), this rapist is most likely to confess when the moral seriousness of the crime is minimized and his "nice guy" image, based on how "nicely" he treated the victim, is emphasized. The power assertive type of rapist commits the crime to dominate the victim. He shows no concern for the well-being of the victim. He is likely to use a moderate to excessive amount of force on the victim. This type of rapist is a "man's man"—he has no doubts about his masculinity. He will rape when he needs a woman. This type of rapist is most likely to respond favorably during an interrogation when investigators flatter him, allow him to brag about himself and his prowess, and to condemn his victim. The anger retaliatory rapist, who commits rape for the purposes of revenge and anger and who often uses excessive force on the victim, and the anger excitation rapist, whose primary motive is to inflict pain and suffering on the victim and who most often uses brutal force on the victim, are most likely to respond to *unemotional* themes in an interrogation setting. Most productive, according to Merrill (1995), is to convince the suspect that his guilt has been proved and that he has no choice but to admit it (see Hazelwood and Burgess [1995] for a more detailed discussion of this typology of rapists).

Similar to homicides, rapes committed by offenders who are strangers to victims pose a serious challenge for the police. It is likely that any rapist who attacks a stranger is, or could become, a serial rapist. According to statistics provided by Rossmo (2000), eighty-four percent of serial rapists are strangers to their victims. In these instances, the information provided by a victim about the assailant may be of limited value in actually identifying the culprit. Once again, with these crimes, and as discussed in previous chapters, it is imperative that the police use all the means at their disposal for identifying and apprehending these perpetrators including DNA banks, tip lines, media alerts, crime analysis, computer databanks, and psychological profiles.

A final comment with regard to rape investigations relates to the issue of *false* rape allegations. Extraordinary accounts are sometimes told about "victims" who deliberately make up stories of rape that did not occur. For example, in one jurisdiction, during the course of two weeks, the police were informed by a woman that she had been raped sixty-eight times . . . by Elvis Presley. The woman had a history of severe mental illness and there was no other evidence to substantiate her claim. The police had good reason to believe that these allegations were not true. Of course, not all false allegations are quite so obvious. The fact of the matter is that a small percentage of rape allegations are suspected and substantiated as being false. Crowley (1999) estimates this percentage to be approximately eight percent of all reported rapes; other estimates are closer to two percent (U.S. Department of Justice, 2001). False rape allegations are probably less common than false burglary or robbery allegations. In any crime, investigators must be aware of accounts provided by victims that just do not seem to make sense and that appear suspicious. Aiken et al. (1995) identify numerous "red flags" of false rape allegations. The more of these circumstances that are present, the more likely the allegation is false. These include

- History of mental or emotional problems
- Previous similar allegations
- Delayed report
- No description of assailant
- Involvement of more than one assailant
- Inability to tell investigators where the crime occurred

- Inability to provide details regarding the sexual acts involved
- Extensive injuries but indifferent and lack of concern about them
- No injuries to sensitive areas
- Injuries made by fingernails
- Injuries claimed to be defense wounds although the nature of the injuries do not indicate that they are defense wounds
- Condition of clothing worn at the time of the attack does not fit with the injuries sustained

As noted by Aiken et al. (1995), however, "[i]t must be remembered that even those who are emotionally prone to make a false allegation can be raped. Basic principles of police professionalism require that officers who investigate rapes remain objective and compassionate" (p. 238).

Robbery

Varieties, Trends, and Characteristics of Robbery

Robbery refers to "the taking or attempting to take anything of value from the care, custody, or control of a person or persons by force, threat of force, violence, and/or by putting the victim in fear" (FBI, 2002; p. 32). To establish that a robbery has occurred, the victim must state that property was taken by force and without permission.

In most jurisdictions, robbery is the second most common violent crime; only aggravated assault usually occurs more frequently. Similar to murder, there are typically more robberies and a higher robbery rate (i.e., the number of robberies per 100,000 persons) in large urban areas than in smaller cities, suburbs, or rural areas (see Table 11–1). Nationwide, the 2001 robbery rate increased slightly from the year 2000, but since 1992 the robbery rate has declined nearly forty-four percent. Despite the national trend, not all jurisdictions have experienced a similar decline (FBI, 2002). Because robbery is a serious and relatively frequent crime, and the circumstances of the crime are such that a suspect is rarely immediately identifiable (compared with other violent crimes), police departments that experience robberies at a high rate typically allocate a large proportion of investigative resources to such investigations.

Robberies of persons in public places accounted for the largest proportion (44.3 percent) of robberies in 2001. Robberies of commercial establishments (e.g., gas stations, banks, convenience stories) accounted for just more than twenty-six percent of the total robbery offenses reported. Robberies of persons in residences comprised approximately thirteen percent of the total (FBI, 2002). In 2001, the average loss that resulted from each robbery was $1,258. Bank robberies involved the greatest average loss at $4,587 per incident. Convenience store robberies averaged the smallest average loss at $618 per incident (FBI, 2002).

With regard to the characteristics of robbery victims, the largest proportion of robbery victims (twenty-seven percent) are between the ages of sixteen and nineteen. Nearly sixty-six percent are between twelve and twenty-four. More than sixty-nine percent of robbery victims are male, and just less than thirty-one percent are female (BJS, 2002a). Among all violent crimes, robbery is least likely to involve victims and offenders who know each other. In only twenty-nine percent of robberies is there a relationship between the victim and the offender. Robberies that occur between people who know each other often involve illicit goods (e.g., drug-related robberies) and are the least likely to be reported to the police (BJS, 2002a).

Robberies are usually committed with a weapon (armed robbery). In 2001, fifty-five percent of robberies involved the use (or display) of a weapon, most common of which was a firearm (thirty-one percent) (BJS, 2002a). The next most common method involved strong-arming the victim (i.e., taking property by force but without the use of a weapon) (FBI, 2002).

The circumstances in which robberies usually occur are not favorable for their solution. Usually little physical evidence is left behind at robbery scenes. In addition, even though there is often face-to-face contact between the victim and the offender, the victim may not be able to provide the information necessary for the police to identify and apprehend the perpetrator (e.g., the perpetrator's name) because there is usually not a relationship between the victim and the offender. Indeed, of all violent crimes, robberies have the lowest clearance rate. Nationally, in 2001, approximately twenty-five percent of robberies were cleared. In general, as in many other crimes, smaller departments in rural areas tend to have the highest clearance rate for robberies and large departments tend to have the lowest clearance rate (FBI, 2002). Of the robberies that were cleared in the United States in 2001, nearly seventy-six percent of arrestees were adults, and just less than eighty percent were male. By race, nearly fifty-four percent of arrestees were black, approximately forty-five percent were white, and other races accounted for less than two percent (see Table 11–2).

Investigative Considerations With Robbery

As noted, there is often little evidence available in robbery investigations that will directly lead to the perpetrator. Typically, the best evidence available in robberies is eyewitness descriptions of the perpetrator. This evidence is certainly not foolproof. Depending on the victim and the circumstances of the crime, it may be possible for the victim or witnesses to provide details in order for investigators to develop a composite picture of the perpetrator. In addition, the victim or witnesses may be able to provide a description of the getaway car, if there was one. The composite picture or a description of the car may then be advertised via the media, and information relating to the crime may be obtained by the police via a tip line. Recall, this was the primary investigative approach used by the police in the robbery investigation discussed in the introduction to Chapter 7. In the robbery/homicide of the Blockbuster Video store security guard discussed in the introduction to this chapter, investigators had even less; they had a vague description of the perpetrator and (inaccurate) information about him going into a nearby grocery store. In some cases, the victim or witnesses may also be able to provide other details about people loitering in the area prior to the robbery or unusual phone calls received prior to the robbery. This information may also provide leads for investigators to pursue.

If the perpetrator was caught on security camera video while committing the crime, which is common with robberies of banks and other commercial establishments but rare in other types of robberies, then those images may also be shown in media alerts with the hope of generating useful leads from citizens. However, there are at least two problems with surveillance video. First, most robbers of commercial establishments are aware that security cameras are present and, as a result, wear a disguise to hide their identity (Wright and Decker, 1997). Second, most security camera video images are of relatively poor quality. In the Blockbuster case, the images of the gunman were just too grainy to be of any help, even though he did not wear a disguise. Despite these common problems, video images may still be useful. Although facial characteristics of the perpetrator may not be evident, distinctive clothing and other characteristics may be, and this may be enough to generate useful leads.

In addition, perpetrators frequently visit (i.e., "case") the business establishment as a "customer" prior to robbing the place. It is in this manner that perpetrators become more familiar with the place and more comfortable being there prior to the time of the actual robbery. A review of earlier security camera video footage by the victim or witnesses may lead to a particular "customer" being recognized as the perpetrator, and the perpetrator may not be in disguise.

As with rapes, victims and witnesses may also be able to provide information to the police to substantiate the offender's MO. In particular, it may be useful to know how the robber approached the target, what was said by the robber, and what was done by the robber. Distinctive behaviors and language use may help link crimes and provide evidence to indicate that several similar crimes were committed by the same perpetrator. For example, consider a street robber that demands that victims surrender their money and then take off their pants. This is a rather strange demand among robbers and, along with a similar description of the perpetrator, provides investigators a good basis to conclude that the robberies were committed by the same perpetrator. Certain unique or signature phrases such as "Give me the money. Do you think this is a joke?" (see introduction to Chapter 7) spoken by a robber may also provide a basis on which crimes may be linked.

The woman in the white hat is a bank robber. Although it is impossible to see her facial characteristics, if the photograph was released to the media, the white hat might generate leads from the public.
GLENDALE POLICE DEPARTMENT

STILL

10:17:23 06-22-95 120HR

Security camera video can also help establish the offender's MO. Here the perpetrators of a bank robbery set off smoke bombs in the bank prior to their departure.
GLENDALE POLICE DEPARTMENT

MO may also provide a clue regarding the offender's level of experience and knowledge. Specifically, as with many other crimes, robberies that appear to have been well planned are usually perpetrated by older and more experienced (i.e., serial) offenders (Feeney, 1999; Wright and Decker, 1997). Well-planned robberies usually involve more than one person, are committed with a weapon, with a disguise, and involve a getaway car. Younger offenders, who usually are the least likely to engage in preoffense planning, are the most likely to talk about their crimes with one another and with others. If others report these overheard conversations to the police, good leads may result.

Another valuable aspect of an understanding of the offender's MO relates to the degree of knowledge the robber appeared to have about the place being robbed. Robberies of businesses, particularly restaurants, are often committed by former disgruntled employees who were fired from their employment, or by the associates of these former employees. These individuals may have feelings of anger and a desire for revenge, and also have the knowledge of the inner workings of the business (e.g., closing procedures, location of the safe, amount of money in the safe, knowledge of who has the combination to the safe, etc.) to commit a successful robbery. Accordingly, it is prudent to consider as suspects employees and recently fired employees, especially when it appears that the perpetrator had "inside" knowledge about how best to commit the crime.

If an arrest can be made of a suspect for a robbery, and if this person had a distinctive physical description or MO, then it may be possible to link this person to other robberies that he may have committed. The suspect who has been arrested and who is believed to have committed other robberies can then be placed in a photographic or live lineup for possible identification by the previous robbery victims. It is in this way that investigators may be able to solve previous robberies by making an apprehension for a current robbery. The suspect's responsibility for the crimes can be made more certain if investigators are able to obtain a confession from him. Recall from the introduction to Chapter 7 that it was this sequence of events that led to the identification of Amos Branigan as the perpetrator of the gas station robberies.

Another potential valuable lead in robbery investigations may be the identification and discovery of the weapon used to commit the crime. In particular, if a gun is used in the crime and can be described by the victim or witnesses, or if the gun was fired by the robber at the scene and ballistics tests reveal information about the gun, and if that gun is eventually seized by the police for some unrelated reason, then investigators may be able to link the robbery to the person in possession of the gun. Recall from the introduction to this chapter, it was in a similar manner that the police solved the robbery/homicide of the Blockbuster security guard.

It is also possible for leads to be developed in a robbery investigation through physical evidence recovered from the scene. Of course, physical evidence is usually not very good at identifying a suspect when one is not already known. Physical evidence is usually best at confirming the identity of a suspect who has previously been identified by some other means. In addition, robbery crime scenes are usually not very extensive, and usually little physical evidence is available.

However, despite the fact that little physical evidence may be produced as a result of the crime, it is still critical that investigators search for such evidence. Fingerprints may be recovered from cash registers, countertops, entrance/exit doors, dropped cash, or from other items touched by the perpetrator. Demand notes may be recovered. In addition, in a surprising number of cases, the perpetrator leaves other valuable evidence behind (e.g., bill-fold, identification card, car keys, clothing) or these items are lost along the escape route. As a result, it is important that investigators conduct thorough searches of robbery crime scenes and suspected escape routes. Recall, from Chapter 10 how the Washington, DC, snipers were identified. In a robbery/homicide at a Montgomery, Alabama, liquor store

Robbery crime scenes typically do not leave much physical evidence for investigators to recover. GLENDALE POLICE DEPARTMENT

committed several weeks prior to the shootings in DC, police recovered a fingerprint from a gun catalog at which the perpetrator was reportedly looking prior to the robbery. With a tip from the sniper himself, this fingerprint was eventually used to identify John Malvo as the perpetrator of the robbery/homicide in Montgomery as well as the sniper shootings in Washington, DC. Even though it is rare at robbery scenes, physical evidence can definitely make a difference.

Yet a another source of leads in a robbery investigation may come from the money or property taken. If the items taken in a robbery can be found, the perpetrator may be identified. The primary motivation for robbery is money, and money is what is most often taken (Wright and Decker, 1997). Most often the money is used to buy drugs and alcohol, to gamble, and to buy clothes (Wright and Decker, 1997). This direct and quick "payoff" is often identified as part of the attractiveness of the crime to robbers. As stated by one robber:

> Robbery is the quickest money. Robbery is the most money you gonna get fast. . . . Burglary you gonna have to sell the merchandise and get the money. Drugs, you gonna have to deal with too many people, [a] bunch of people. You gonna sell a fifty-dollar or hundred-dollar bag to him, a fifty-dollar or hundred-dollar bag to him, it takes too long. But if you find where the cash money is and just go take it, you get it on all one wad. No problem. I've tried burglary, I've tried drug selling . . . the money is too slow. (Wright and Decker, 1997; pp. 51–52)

In general, stolen items—taken as a result of robberies, burglaries, or other thefts—are usually difficult to find. This is because, as discussed in more detail in Chapter 12, the process of converting property into cash is usually not very visible to the police. Finding stolen cash is probably the most difficult. It is possible, but quite unlikely, that robbers would deposit stolen money into a bank account. Of course, if they did, and if this was recognized by investigators, it could be a big break. More likely, but still not common, sudden access to a large amount of money may be noticeable to the perpetrator's friends, associates, or family members and this may prompt a tip to the police. Along the same line, offenders may show off jewelry or other items taken in a robbery and this too might prompt a tip to the police. Another possibility is that the police may discover suspected stolen property in the possession of an individual, and this property could then be linked to a particular victim and robber. Yet another possibility is for the police to recover cash that has been stained as a result of an exploding dye pack. Usually associated with bank robberies, dye packs are contained in certain designated packs of bills and are placed into a bag by a teller along with the other cash taken in a robbery. As the robber exits the building, a radio transmitter in the stack of bills is activated and within seconds the dye pack explodes. Red dye is released and the package often burns. The dye may also stain the clothing and hands of the perpetrator. Finding cash stained in this manner, or finding a person stained in this manner, may lead to the identification of a robber.

The police have the best chance of apprehending robbers when they are notified of the crime while it is happening and they respond quickly to the scene, thereby allowing for an on-scene apprehension. This fact highlights the importance of holdup alarms that are present in most banks and in some commercial establishments. Compared with burglar alarms (see Chapter 12), holdup alarms are much less likely to be false. The importance of quick police responses to robbery scenes also calls attention to related police procedures (see Rice [1998]). Robberies have often been identified as one of the most dangerous situations for the police. As a result, a top priority in responding to such calls must be the protection of officers' and victims' safety at the scene. Squad arrivals should not be visible or audible from inside the scene. As officers arrive, the entire area around the scene should be monitored and officers should be aware of persons and vehicles leaving the area, and other suspicious vehicles in the area. Officers should watch for robbery lookouts and getaway cars. Robbers are just as likely to walk from a robbery scene as they are to run, because running is likely to draw more attention (Wright and Decker, 1997). On securing the scene, victims and witnesses should be separated and questioned regarding the description of the perpetrators. Officers should be aware that descriptions of clothing worn by the perpetrator can be misleading because clothing can be quickly changed and discarded. Also relating to the importance of the police being in the right place at the right time, various strategies are available to the police for proactively dealing with robberies. Based on crime analysis, the police may establish decoy or stakeout operations, or increased police presence in those areas most likely to experience robberies. It is in these ways that the police may be better able to respond quickly to robberies when they occur.

Finally, with regard to the most productive interrogation strategies used with robbers, it is important to realize that most robbers are generally angry, hostile, and desperate, and generally have a strong attachment to the street culture (Wright and Decker, 1997). They are unlikely to have feelings of guilt about their crimes. Accordingly, the most effective interrogation approach with robbery suspects is the nonemotional approach. Minimizing the seriousness of the crime and convincing the suspect that his guilt has been, or will be, proved is likely to be most productive in obtaining useful information from the suspect during the interrogation.

Questions for Discussion and Review

1. What is murder? What are the major trends and characteristics of murder?

2. How may the circumstances in which many murders occur contribute to murders being solved?

3. What is aggravated assault? What are the major trends and characteristics of aggravated assault? How do the typical circumstances of aggravated assault differ from simple assault? How do they differ from murders?

4. What are the three basic questions that guide homicide investigations?

5. How are victims most often identified?

6. How is the manner in which a person died best determined? What are the three primary considerations in this determination?

7. Identify various causes of death and the wounds that are likely to be present as a result.

8. What is the value of establishing motive in a murder investigation?

9. What is the importance of physical evidence in murder investigations?

10. What are the various methods of determining PMI?

11. Besides establishing an estimate of PMI, what may insect activity on a dead body reveal about that person's death?

12. Why are serial homicides a major challenge for police investigators?

13. What is forcible rape? What are the major trends and characteristics of forcible rape and other sexual assaults?

14. How may the circumstances of sexual assault contribute to these crimes being solved?

15. Why is compassion and understanding so important in investigators' interactions with sexual assault victims?

16. Why is the interview of the victim so important in sexual assault investigations?

17. What information should an investigator try to obtain from a victim in sexual assault investigations? What may be the value of this information?

18. What is the purpose and importance of a forensic examination of the sexual assault victim?

19. What evidence is typically collected during such an examination? What are specimen samples and reference samples?

20. What is the importance of knowing the suspect's motive when conducting an interrogation of him?

21. Why are serial rapes a major challenge for police investigators?

22. What are false rape allegations? What circumstances signal such an allegation? How frequent are such allegations?

23. What is robbery? What are the major trends and characteristics of robbery?

24. "The circumstances in which robberies occur are usually not favorable for their solution." Explain.

25. What types of information may be obtained from victims and witnesses of robberies? Why is this information potentially important?

26. What is the potential contribution of security camera video images of robbery suspects? How might this evidence be used?

27. What types of information may be gleaned from an understanding of a robber's MO?

28. What is the potential contribution of physical evidence in robbery investigations?

29. What is the value of a quick police response to robbery scenes? What factors should be considered by officers as they approach the scene of a robbery?

Related Internet Sites

www.lawresearch.com/practice/ctcrime.htm
This site provides links to state criminal codes. You can see how criminal behaviors are defined in various states.

www.lapdonline.org
This is the site of the LAPD. It contains a wealth of information on the LAPD and crime in the city. The site also provides access to departmental newsletters, magazines, and other reports.

www.ojp.usdoj.gov/bjs/
This link brings you to the web site of the U.S. Department of Justice, BJS, which features information on crime and victims, criminal offenders, and the criminal justice system.

www.forensic-entomology.com
This is a site devoted to the science of forensic entomology.

ISSUES IN THE INVESTIGATION OF PROPERTY CRIME

OBJECTIVES

After reading this chapter you will be able to

- Explain how the burglary of the Foot Locker store was solved
- Discuss the major trends and characteristics of burglary
- Discuss the difficulties associated with the investigation of burglaries
- Identify the ways in which burglars may become familiar with burglary targets
- Discuss what the actions and MO of burglars may reveal
- Discuss the methods that burglars may use to convert stolen property to cash
- Discuss the major trends and characteristics of motor vehicle theft
- Discuss the difficulties associated with the investigation of vehicle theft
- Identify some of the methods used to steal automobiles

- Identify the indicators of a stolen vehicle
- Discuss the Regional Auto Theft Task Force (RATT) and the South Texas Auto Theft Enforcement Task Force (STATETF) as strategies to combat auto theft
- Discuss the major trends and characteristics of arson
- Discuss the difficulties associated with the investigation of arson
- Identify the various causes (types) of fires
- Discuss the importance of the "point of origin" of fires
- Discuss the possible motivations for fire setting
- Discuss the major trends, types, and characteristics of larceny and fraud
- Discuss the difficulties associated with the investigation of larceny and fraud

IMPORTANT TERMS

Burglary	Chop shop	Incendiary	Larceny
Fence	Arson	Point of origin	Fraud
Motor vehicle theft	Accelerant	Pyromania	Types of fraud
"Peeling"			

INTRODUCTION

The Introduction to this chapter consists of a police report that documents an investigation into a burglary of a Foot Locker shoe store that occurred January 22, 2001 in Glendale, Wisconsin (a suburb of Milwaukee). The report serves as an example of a criminal investigation case report and also highlights the attention investigators place on the stolen property in a burglary investigation. Issues that are discussed in other chapters, including the role of witnesses, tip lines, interviews, and interrogations are also discussed in this case report.

Incident Report	GLENDALE POLICE DEPARTMENT		2001–003434-B

Incident Number: 2001–003434-B
Complainant/Victim Name: Foot Locker
Complainant/Victim Address: 5900 N. Port Washington / Lakeside Mall
Date and Time Reported: 1/22/2001 MON 20:16
Occurred From: 1/20/2001 18:00   Occurred To: 1/21/2001 10:30
Offense Description: Burglary Business – Unlawful Entry

Current Disposition: CLEARED by Arrest

Officer Assigned: 0718 Eichhorn, Chris
Investigating Officer: 0704 Hoppa, James

Persons Involved:

Involvement	Name	Race/Sex	DOB
1) Reported by:	Kuenn, Fleur L.	W/F	01/03/74
2) Arrest:	Blanchard, Bobby L.	B/M	05/03/84
3) Arrest:	Cutter, Christopher	B/M	02/02/85
4) Arrest:	Johnson, Lashion D.	B/M	08/06/80
5) Suspect:	Froll, Michael A.	B/M	05/25/78

Property Taken: Initially reported as 126 pair of athletic shoes. Later determined to be 111 pair of shoes and other clothing and accessories.

M.O.:

Structure Attacked:	Retail
Targets of Criminals:	Entire Bldg/Room
Type of Property Taken:	Clothing/Apparel
Point of Entry:	Front North Door
Point of Exit:	Front North Door
Type of Force Used	Defeated Lock
Suspect Actions:	Unknown

Incident Number: 01–3434; Burglary Incident Report Narrative

On Monday, 01–22–01, at approximately 8:16 PM, I was dispatched to the Foot Locker, 5900 N. Port Washington Rd. for a burglary report. Upon arrival, I spoke to the manager, Fleur L. Kuenn (F/W, DOB 01–03–74). After talking to Kuenn, I discovered there were actually three separate burglaries.

Kuenn said sometime between 01–15–01 at 10:00 PM and 01–21–01 at 10:30 AM someone without permission entered Foot Locker after business hours and stole 126 pairs of shoes. Kuenn said the estimated loss was $12,000.00. Kuenn said the suspect entered and exited through the main entrance. The main entrance has a metal roll down security door that is locked at closing. There is a gap between the bottom of the door and the floor because the floor is not even. The door can be lifted about two inches and a person can reach under the door and unlock the door manually without a key. The door can then be lifted about one foot. The door is not alarmed and there is no security video.

Kuenn said she locked the door Monday, 01–15–01, at approximately 10:00 PM and discovered the door was unlocked when she arrived at work Tuesday, 01–16–01, at approximately 10:00 AM. Kuenn said she did not notice anything missing but thought it was suspicious.

On Wednesday, 01–17–01, Kuenn again locked the door at about 10:00 PM and discovered the door was unlocked on Thursday, 01–18–01, at about 10:00 AM. Kuenn said she noticed a pair of Nike Original Air Jordan shoes missing from her desk. Kuenn said she also noticed whoever took the shoes from her desk took the packing slip out of the shoe box and left it on her desk. Kuenn gave me the packing slip for possible latent prints (GPD Inventory #14809).

On Saturday, 01–20–01, at approximately 10:00 PM, Kuenn closed and locked the front door. On Sunday, 01–21–01, at about 10:30 AM Kuenn found the front door unlocked. Kuenn said the store was ransacked and shoe boxes in the storeroom were moved. Kuenn said she did an inventory and found 126 pairs of shoes missing. Kuenn said this is a very accurate count because they just completed the bi-annual audit in December. Kuenn said she called the police after she conducted her own investigation.

Kuenn said she recently fired an employee. Michael A. Froll (M/W, DOB 05–25–78) was fired on 01–10–01 for giving friends unauthorized discounts. Kuenn said Froll also had some shady friends. Froll has a CIBR (Criminal Investigation Bureau Record) including retail theft, POCS (Possession of a Controlled Substance) and CDTP (Criminal Damage to Property).

At approximately 10:00 PM, I went to Froll's apartment and spoke to him. Froll said he knew nothing about the burglaries and he gave me permission to search his apartment for stolen shoes. I searched the entire apartment and did not find any evidence of the burglaries.

I gave the packing slip (GDP Inv #14809) to Lt. Herlache to look for fingerprints. Lt. Herlache advised there were no comparable fingerprints on the packing slip.

C. K. Eichhorn, Reporting Officer

01–3434 Burglary Supplement

On Tuesday, 01–23–01, PO Dhein advised me of a tip received by Central Dispatch on 01–18–01 at 7:20 AM. The anonymous caller said third shift security guards at Lakeside Mall are stealing merchandise from stores and putting the items in their personal cars.

At approximately 4:00 PM I spoke to Lakeside Mall Manager Laurie Nickels. Nickels said Foot Locker notified her today of the break-ins. Nickels said she was also aware of the anonymous tip about the security guards. Nickels said Merchant Police Supervisor James Durand (M/B, DOB 06–29–53) is investigating the third shift guards.

At approximately 4:30 PM I spoke to Merchant Police Supervisor James Durand by telephone. Durand said security guard Lashion D. Johnson (M/B, DOB 08–06–80) was working third shift on Monday night, 01–15–01 and Wednesday night, 01–17–01. Johnson has been employed by Merchant Police for about six months. Johnson works 10:00 PM to 6:00 AM. Security guard Peter A. Vaden was working third shift on Saturday night, 01–20–01. Durand said Vaden has been working at Lakeside Mall for several years and is very trustworthy. Vaden works Saturdays, 7:00 PM to 7:00 AM. Durand also said the cleaning crew reported a set of Lakeside keys missing. The cleaning crew is employed by Program Cleaning.

A CIB (Criminal Investigation Bureau) check showed Johnson has no prior criminal record but is wanted by MPD for failure to display license plates and OAS (Operating After Suspension).

At approximately 5:30 I spoke to William W. Aston (M/B, DOB 01–19–62) from Program Cleaning. Aston said he has three employees working third shift at Lakeside. Johnny L. Spears (M/B, DOB 05–21–58), Robert L. Herron (M/B, DOB 01–27–53), and Charles J. Ceralo (M/W, DOB 04–25–43). Aston said all three have been employed for a long time and have had no past problems.

C. K. Eichhorn, Reporting Officer

01–3434 Burglary Supplement

Submitted by: Lt. Daniel C. Herlache

Wednesday 01–23–01 at approximately 9:45 PM, suspect Lashion D. Johnson (M/B, DOB 08–06–80), was arrested as he arrived for work at Lakeside Mall. Johnson had two open Municipal warrants with the City of Milwaukee for OAS and failure to display registration plates. Johnson was advised that he was under arrest for the above warrants and on suspicion of Burglary and was transported to GPD by PO Eichhorn for processing.

At 10:25 PM, Johnson was escorted from the lockup to the Det. Bureau for interview. At this time he was read his Miranda warnings. Johnson stated that he understood his rights, waived same, and agreed to answer my questions and give a statement.

Lashion Johnson is a 20 year old male with a high school education. He is currently living in his own home with his girlfriend of three years and their one year old daughter. His girlfriend is also expecting Johnson's second child. Johnson, who is employed by Merchant's Police and assigned 3rd shift security duties, has been assigned to Lakeside Mall for approximately five months.

After obtaining some background information from Johnson, I then began to interview him regarding the burglaries at Foot Locker. Johnson was advised that employee time records show that he was the only person working on the nights and mornings in which two of the burglaries occurred, that being on 01–16–01 and 01–18–01. Johnson was asked directly if he had any involvement in the burglaries. Johnson initially stated that he knew about the burglaries but that he only participated in one of them, that being on Tuesday 01–16–01. Johnson stated that he entered the Foot Locker by opening a metal gate located at the store front by reaching underneath same and opening a latch. Johnson stated that the gate was not locked and that it was common knowledge that one could enter the store without a key. Johnson stated that this occurred at approximately 2 AM and that he took two to three pairs of shoes and placed them in his car. When asked what he did with the shoes, Johnson stated that he sold them on the street for a total of $200.00. When asked if he was the only person involved in the burglary, Johnson stated that he was not, that he allowed a B/M he identified as "Rob" into the mall at approximately 2 AM and let him into the store as well. Johnson stated that "Rob" works as a maintenance/cleaning person for Lakeside Mall, working the second shift. When asked how many shoes "Rob" took out of the store, Johnson stated that "Rob" took four to five pairs of shoes and put same in his (Johnson's) car. When asked if he obtained anything from "Rob" for allowing him to enter the mall and take shoes from Foot Locker, Johnson stated that "Rob" gave him $100.00. I then advised him that I had observed him arrive at work and park his car in the west lot near Sears. He was asked if this is where he normally parks his car when he gets to work, Johnson stated that it was. When asked how he and "Rob" managed to carry approximately ten pairs of shoes from the location of Foot Locker, at the south end of the mall, to his vehicle, Johnson stated that he moved his vehicle to a door near Foot Locker after punching in.

After questioning Johnson about the 01–16–01 burglary, I then asked him about his involvement in a burglary occurring on 01–18–01. Johnson initially denied any involvement in this incident until he was reminded that Boston Store has constant video surveillance at their west doors and that video from 01–18–01 would clearly show anyone entering the Foot Locker. Johnson then admitted that he had also entered Foot Locker on 01–18–01, again at approximately 2 AM, in the same fashion as on 01–16–01. When asked if "Rob" participated in this incident as well, Johnson stated that he took four pairs of shoes and that "Rob" took approximately six pairs of shoes. According to Johnson he and "Rob" later sold the shoes on the street, Johnson getting approximately $300.00 for them. Johnson added that he was supposed to receive $100.00 from "Rob" in return for allowing "Rob" to enter the Mall and participate in this burglary. Johnson stated that he had not received payment from "Rob" as of the time of his arrest.

Johnson was then asked about the burglary on Saturday 01–20–01. Johnson denied any involvement, stating that he did not work that night. Johnson did state that numerous people were aware of the unlocked gate and that he suspected others of taking shoes as well. Johnson could not identify any others as being involved.

My interview of Johnson ended at approximately 10:50 PM. At this time I prepared a written statement for Johnson outlining his verbal statements described above. The statement was read by Johnson and it was read to him by me. Johnson made corrections to the statement by lining out mistakes or misrepresentations and initialing them. Johnson also signed both pages of the documents and dated them 01–23–01 at 11:49 PM.

01–3434 Burglary Supplement

Submitted by: Lt. Daniel C. Herlache
Wednesday 01–24–01 1600 hours I received a telephone call from Merchant Police Supervisor James Durand. Durand advised that the cleaning person involved in the burglaries with Johnson was a Bobbie C. Blanchard (M/B, DOB 05–08–84), and that he was currently working in the Mall.

At approximately 4:30 PM, PO Eichhorn and I met with Security, and Blanchard was later taken into custody. See PO Eichhorn's supplement for details.

01–3434 Burglary Supplement

On Wednesday, 01–24–01, at approximately 5:00 PM Lt. Herlache, PO Harlow and I went to Lakeside Mall, 5900 N. Port Washington Rd. to arrest and question Bobby L. Blanchard (M/B, DOB 05–03–84). When we arrived, Lakeside Mall Security said Blanchard was seen running out the east door wearing a black hat, black jacket, black jeans, a gray sweatshirt and carrying a backpack. PO Bruno saw a subject matching that description getting on a bus at Port Washington Rd. and Silver Spring Dr. The bus was stopped and the subject identified himself to PO Bruno as Bobby Blanchard. Blanchard was placed under arrest, handcuffed, searched, and transported to GPD.

At about 6:30 PM, I read Blanchard his Miranda warnings. Blanchard said he understood his rights and was willing to talk. Blanchard said he works for Program Cleaning at Lakeside Mall M–F 4 PM to 9 PM. Blanchard said while working, he overheard two Foot Locker store managers discussing how the security gate does not completely close and how a person could reach underneath to unlock it.

Blanchard said on Tuesday, 01–16–01, at about 2:00 AM, Security Guard Lashion Johnson let him in the mall. They went to Foot Locker and Blanchard opened the security gate. Blanchard said he took three jogging suits and four T-shirts. Blanchard said he put the merchandise in Foot Locker bags and then put it in Johnson's car. Blanchard said he was supposed to pay Johnson $100.00 for letting him into Foot Locker but he never paid him.

Blanchard said on Thursday, 01–18–01, at about 2:00 AM Johnson let him and his cousin, Christopher Cutter (M/B, DOB 05–02–85), into the Mall. Johnson opened the security gate. Blanchard said he went into Foot Locker with Johnson and Cutter. Blanchard said he took seven pairs of shoes for himself. Blanchard said he did not know what the other people took because it was every person for himself.

Blanchard said on Saturday, 01–20–01, he was at Lakeside Mall with Cutter. Blanchard said they waited inside by the south door until the mall closed at 6:00 PM. Blanchard said at about 7:00 PM he went to Foot Locker and unlocked and lifted the security gate. Blanchard said he and Cutter went inside Foot Locker and put shoes in plastic store bags. Blanchard said he took two pairs of shoes and Cutter took four pairs of shoes. Blanchard said they took the bus to his house. Blanchard said he kept two pairs of shoes for himself and then sold the rest of the shoes and clothes for $150.00. Blanchard said the two pairs of shoes were in plastic Foot Locker bags in his garage.

Blanchard was booked GPD #00–281.

At approximately 7:15 PM, I went to 5522 N. 27th St. and spoke to Bobby Blanchard's mother, Gwen Blanchard. Gwen was notified that Bobby was in custody for burglary. I told Gwen that Bobby said that he put two pairs of shoes in the garage and I asked for consent to search the garage for the shoes. Gwen gave consent to search the garage. Gwen showed me the garage and opened the back door for me. In the garage I found two white and black plastic Foot Locker bags. The bags were inventoried (GPD #14811). I did not find any shoes.

At approximately 7:30 PM Det. Hanaman and I went to 3018 N. 7th St. to arrest Christopher Cutter for burglary. Cutter's mother, Tammy McMillian, met us at the door. Tammy said she heard from Gwen what had happened and she allowed us to enter the house. Tammy said "This is my son Christopher, the one you want. The shoes are in the bedroom." Tammy told Christopher to go get the shoes. I followed Christopher to his bedroom where he showed me four pairs of shoes. The shoes were taken as evidence and inventoried (GPD #14811). Cutter was placed under arrest, handcuffed, searched, and transported to GPD.

At approximately 8:10 PM I read Cutter his Miranda warning. Cutter said he understood his rights and was willing to talk. Cutter said on Saturday, 01–20–01, he was at Lakeside Mall with his cousin, Bobby Blanchard. Cutter said they stayed inside the mall after closing and at about 7:00 PM Blanchard opened the security gate at Foot Locker. Cutter said he took four pairs of shoes out of the boxes and put them in a plastic bag. Cutter said Blanchard took three pairs of shoes. Cutter said they were in the store for about ten minutes. Cutter denied being at Foot Locker on Thursday,

01–18–01. Cutter said he planned to go with Blanchard on Thursday but his mother, Tammy, grounded him and he was not able to go. Tammy confirmed this story.

Cutter was booked (GPD 01–045). At about 9:16 PM Cutter and Blanchard were released and transported to their homes.

At approximately 9:45 PM I received a telephone call from Blanchard. Blanchard said he had two pairs of shoes he wanted to give back. I went to Blanchard's house and he gave me a pair of white Reebok and a pair of white Nike shoes (GPD Inv #14813).

C. K. Eichhorn, Reporting Officer

01–3434 Burglary Supplement

On Monday, 01–29–01, Kuenn gave me a copy of a store inventory that was completed on 01–26–01. The inventory shows 375 items missing from the store including 111 pairs of shoes for a total retail loss of $17,772.55. The other missing items were clothing and accessories.

C. K. Eichhorn, Reporting Officer

NOTES: The report has been slightly edited for length; names and addresses of witnesses, juvenile perpetrators, and other citizens were changed. All telephone numbers were deleted from the report. This report was reprinted with the permission of the Glendale Police Department.

Lashion Johnson was charged and convicted of party to the crime of burglary and sentenced to sixty days in jail and three years of probation. Bobby Blanchard and Christopher Cutter, who were juveniles at the time of the crime, were not charged in the crime.

Burglary

Varieties, Trends, and Characteristics of Burglaries

Burglary refers to "the unlawful entry of a structure to commit a felony or theft. Use of force to gain entry is not required to classify an offense as burglary" (FBI, 2002; p. 44). To establish that a burglary has occurred, there must be evidence of entry, of theft from the structure, or evidence of a felony having occurred there, and a statement from the owner of the structure that entry was obtained without permission.

Burglary is a relatively frequent and serious crime (see Table 12–1). In smaller police departments in particular, a large proportion of investigative resources are spent on the investigation of burglaries. Approximately sixty-five percent of burglaries are residential

TABLE 12–1 Property Crimes Known to the Police for Select Cities, 2001

City	Population	Burglary	Larceny Theft	Motor Vehicle Theft	Arson
Palm Springs (FL)	12,002	143	455	114	0
Sanger (CA)	19,283	147	364	134	12
Saginaw (MI)	62,125	957	1,769	403	110
Pittsburgh (PA)	341,414	3,246	10,766	2,732	173
Denver (CO)	569,653	5,642	14,621	6,935	345
Houston (TX)	1,997,965	25,108	69,371	24,089	1,758

Source: FBI (2002)

(e.g., houses, apartments) and most of these (sixty-one percent) occur during daylight hours when residents are typically not at home. Of the *non*residential burglaries, approximately forty-two percent occur during the daylight hours. In 2001, the average reported loss per burglary was $1,545—slightly less for residential burglaries and slightly more for nonresidential burglaries. The most common items taken in burglaries are things that can be easily converted to cash and that can be easily carried away by perpetrators such as guns, jewelry, small electronics, and, of course, cash (Wright and Decker, 1994).

Nationwide, 2001 burglary rates have increased slightly more than year 2000 rates although the general trend is downward. Burglary is down approximately fourteen percent from 1997, about twenty-nine percent since 1992, and about thirty-nine percent since 1982. This national trend may not represent the experience of individual jurisdictions. Overall, the highest rate of burglary is in August and the lowest is in February.

From the perspective of burglary victims, the crime is often traumatic for at least two reasons: first, their property has been stolen; and second, their personal territory has been invaded. Because of insurance reimbursement, the emotional consequences and fear associated with the intrusion is often viewed as most significant. Victims often view their burglary as a serious crime and, consequently, they may expect the police to investigate the incident to the fullest extent, that the perpetrator will be apprehended, and that the stolen property will be recovered. However, the fact of the matter is that relatively few burglaries are actually solved. In 2001, the clearance rate for burglaries was approximately thirteen percent (FBI, 2002). Like many other crimes, smaller cities tend to have a higher clearance rate for burglaries than larger cities.

Of the burglaries that are cleared, juveniles are disproportionately involved as perpetrators. This is the case in other property crimes as well (see Table 12–2). In 2001, thirty-one percent of the individuals arrested for burglary were younger than the age of eighteen. Nearly sixty-three percent were younger than the age of twenty-five. With regard to gender, more than eighty-six percent of those arrested were male. Finally, nationally, more than sixty-nine percent of individuals arrested for burglary were white, nearly thirty percent were black, and other races accounted for approximately two percent (FBI, 2002).

TABLE 12–2 Property Crime Arrests by Age, Sex, and Race

Offense	Percent by Age		Percent by Sex		Percent by Race		
	<15	<25	Male	Female	White	Black	Other
Burglary	31.0	62.5	86.4	13.6	69.4	28.5	2.1
Larceny Theft	29.6	56.1	63.5	36.5	66.1	31.2	2.7
Motor Vehicle Theft	32.7	65.6	83.6	16.4	57.5	39.8	1.7
Arson	49.5	68.1	84.1	15.9	76.9	20.7	2.4

Source: FBI (2002)

Investigative Considerations With Burglary

As evidenced by the low clearance rate, burglary is a difficult crime to solve. Burglaries are usually discovered only after the crime has occurred and the perpetrator has had ample time to flee. In fact, one of the many problems associated with investigating burglaries is that it is often difficult to determine precisely when the crime actually occurred. As a result, even if a suspect is developed, it may be difficult to associate the suspect with the scene at a particular time. In addition, given the typical lag between when the crime occurred and when it becomes known to the police, offenders are afforded more time to dispose of property. Furthermore, there are usually no eyewitnesses to the crime, no usable physical evidence, and generally few (if any) other good leads for investigators to pursue.

One might expect that burglar intrusion alarms would play an important role in burglary investigations; specifically, that alarms would lead to the quick apprehension of burglars at or near the crime scenes. However, this is not the case for at least three reasons. First, many burglars report that they avoid places with alarms (Wright and Decker, 1994). Overall, this is good but it does not assist in apprehension efforts. Second, some types of alarms can be easily foiled by knowledgeable burglars. Third, most burglar alarms are false. In fact, some estimates are that between ninety-four and ninety-eight percent of alarm calls are false. As a result, many police departments have stopped responding to such alarms (Sampson, 2002). The bottom line is that burglar alarms do not contribute significantly to burglary investigations.

Given the typical lack of evidence available in burglary investigations, the identification of a perpetrator's probable motive and method of target selection may be some of the most valuable information available in the investigation. Research has shown that the selection of a burglary target is rarely a spur-of-the-moment decision. Burglars usually have some knowledge about the contents of a target and the routine of the occupants before actually committing the burglary. According to Wright and Decker (1994), based on their study of burglars in St. Louis, information about a target most commonly comes from the offender's own observations of it (sixty-two percent of burglars stated that this was usually how they learned of the target and its contents). These offenders reported that they watched a specific dwelling for some time before burglarizing it and, most often, these places were discovered during the course of the burglar's normal living activities. As explained by one offender (quoted in Wright and Decker [1994; p. 78]): "[W]e'll pick a house; we'll be just walking around and stuff and we pick a house. . . . You see, it's real simple and easy, you know. It's got to be a house we done watched for awhile."

The second most common way that burglars obtained information about the target was by knowing the occupants (twenty-one percent). Wright and Decker (1994) explain that many burglars spoke of burglarizing neighbors, their drug dealers, or that they had jobs that brought them into potential target homes (e.g., delivery people, cable television installers, cleaning people). For instance, one of Wright and Decker's (1994, p. 68) subjects explained: "When I was reconnecting the cable line, I overheard the lady talking on the telephone and saying that they be out of town for a few days. And when I heard that, I knew what time it was, time to come back and help them out; watch they house for them."

Finally, only a few burglars (six percent) stated that they usually learned of a target on the basis of information ("a tip") provided by someone else. Given the ways that burglars learn of their intended targets, it underscores the importance of investigators questioning victims and potential witnesses about neighbors and their activities around the target, about other people seen in the area, about workers who may have had recent access to the premises, about people making odd or unusual phone calls to the residence, or, in the case of business burglaries, suspicious current employees or recently fired employees. Information about such subjects may turn into productive leads.

The method of gaining entry into the premises may be a good indicator of the perpetrator's skill, experience, and other characteristics. For instance, a burglar who picks a lock or one who does little damage to a window frame when using a crowbar to gain entry into a residence is generally more experienced than a burglar who kicks in a door.

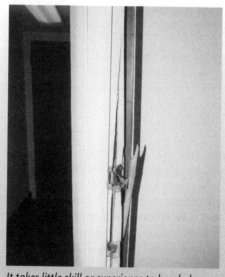

It takes little skill or experience to break down a door to gain entry. GLENDALE POLICE DEPARTMENT

Experienced burglars tend to engage in more preoffense planning than younger, novice offenders. It is also more likely that a more experienced burglar is older. More experienced burglars are also more likely to commit crimes farther away from their homes. On the other hand, the burglaries of juvenile, novice offenders are usually poorly planned. Their crimes are likely to be spontaneous events and are motivated by fun and excitement. Evidence of a poorly planned burglary may be one in which no tools were used to gain entry (to bring tools is to plan) or one in which risk factors did not appear to be considered in committing the crime (e.g., noise was not minimized when gaining entry). Juvenile offenders are most likely to commit crimes near their homes or on walking routes to or from other destinations. Middle-range burglars most often fall between young novice offenders and older more experienced offenders in terms of their methods and motivations.

It is noteworthy that juveniles tend to commit crimes in groups, which often relates to the primary motivation for such crimes. Among some groups of juveniles, status may be enhanced by committing crimes; however, this objective is obtained only if others are told about the crimes that were committed, or the crimes are discussed among the perpetrators themselves. These conversations can be overheard, people can notify the police about these conversations, and good leads may result. Consideration of this possibility calls attention to the importance of tip lines and to the important role of police officers in schools. Police school liaison officers, and other officers in frequent contact with juveniles, are in a good position to develop, receive, or otherwise obtain information about criminal activity from students.

As noted, physical evidence usually plays a relatively small role in burglary investigations. In burglaries, physical evidence most often takes the form of tool marks from screwdrivers or crowbars used to pry open doors and windows, other evidence at the point of entry inside the premises (e.g., footprints), or other items that belong to the perpetrator that are left at the scene. Interestingly, many burglars reported to Wright and Decker (1994) that they often felt a great deal of stress while committing the crime, and tried to commit the crime quickly. As stated by one burglar: "I be shakin' when I'm [doing a burglary] cause, you know, I have a feelin' that I'll be caught. But I'm tryin' not to think about that and have faith in what I'm doin'" (Wright and Decker, 1994; p. 128).

The method used to attack a safe may also be an indicator of the perpetrators' skill. This safe sustained considerable damage and entry to the safe was not obtained quickly. In all probability, the perpetrator(s) were not skilled or experienced burglars.

Most burglars claim that they are typically inside a premises no longer than a few minutes. The burglar's potential haste inside a premises creates the possibility that he will make critical mistakes. This fact underscores the importance of a thorough crime scene search by investigators. In the haste of looking for valuables and fleeing the residence, personal items (e.g., billfold, keys) may be dropped by the perpetrator or otherwise discarded, or other physical evidence may be left behind. Depending on the nature of the evidence, it could be useful in an investigation.

Once inside the premises, burglars try to minimize the amount of time they spend there. This is a simple a risk reduction strategy. As explained by Wright and Decker (1994), most burglars reported that they immediately go to the master bedroom in search of cash, jewelry, and guns. They commonly search dressers, bedside tables, the bed, and the bedroom closet. The second most common place to search for valuables is the kitchen, followed by the bathrooms. As a result, these are also good places for investigators to search for fingerprints and other evidence. The perpetrator's actions in searching for property may also be an indicator of the perpetrator's knowledge of the contents of the premises. For instance, ransacking of a premises is either an act of vandalism (and is most likely committed by juveniles) or it is a result of trying to find property to steal.

If one knows where desired property is located (or hidden), there is little need for ransacking. In one case, a home in an upscale suburb was burglarized and approximately $30,000 of jewelry and other property was taken. The only item in the house that was disturbed was a dresser, specifically the third drawer of a four-drawer dresser, and the property was taken from this drawer. The drawer was pried open with a crowbar-type instrument. Given this MO, it

Useful physical evidence is most likely to be discovered at the point of entry or the point of exit. GLENDALE POLICE DEPARTMENT

This is a basement of a house that was burglarized. Ransacking is usually either an act of vandalism or is done in order to find property to steal. GLENDALE POLICE DEPARTMENT

appeared that the burglar knew exactly where the desired property was located. Investigators eventually arrested the maid who worked at the house along with her son.

Many burglars tend to be rather prolific, committing large numbers of crimes. Wright and Decker (1994) found that thirty-five percent of their sample of burglars committed more than eleven burglaries a year (twenty percent of these committed more than forty-nine burglaries a year). In addition, the burglars in their study were involved in a variety of other crimes as well—including theft, robbery, assault, and murder—although to a lesser extent than burglary. Through the course of an investigation, if a perpetrator is linked to a burglary, the investigative challenge is to determine the other crimes for which he is responsible. In this way, it is possible to clear many crimes, and potentially recover a lot of property, with just one arrest. In addition, criminals tend to know other criminals (Wright and Decker, 1994). As a result, it is little wonder that informants can be a valuable source of information in criminal investigations, even burglary investigations.

Not surprisingly, the primary motive for committing burglaries is money. As described by Wright and Decker (1994), instead of going to a bank to withdraw money when they need it, burglars burglarize. Rarely, however, is cash the only property stolen in burglaries. As a consequence, burglars must convert the stolen property to cash. The process of turning property into cash involves various degrees of risk for offenders and various degrees of opportunity for investigators. The difficulty for the police is that the process is usually not very visible and it occurs quickly after the property is taken. Property is usually converted into cash within hours of the crime (Wright and Decker, 1994). In addition, for even a remote chance of recovering the property, the victim must be able to provide a detailed description of it.

There are at least six ways that offenders can convert property to cash (Wright and Decker, 1994). The first and most common method is to sell the property to a friend, acquaintance, or relative. This is a low-risk option for the burglar who sells the property and, unfortunately for the police, it is not very visible. According to one of Wright and Decker's (1994, p. 185) burglars: "Well, let's just say [I sell what I steal] to friends. . . . I mean I can't sell it to anybody else off the street cause that's basically just publicizing me." The buyer may realize that the property is stolen but the buyer has an incentive to keep the transaction quiet because if the property is discovered by the police, it would be confiscated.

The second option, and a frequently used one, is to trade the property for illicit drugs. Again, this is a low-visibility process but highlights the importance of investigators searching drug houses for stolen property, property that could be traced back to particular burglary victims.

The third option for the burglar involves selling the property to a professional fence, someone who knowingly buys and sells stolen goods. As reported by Wright and Decker (1994), this option is used by more sophisticated burglars. Most burglars did not know a professional fence and would not know how to find one if they had to. The fact that fences are used as frequently as they are, however, highlights the opportunity for the police to recover stolen goods and make arrests through undercover fencing operations.

A fourth option involves selling the stolen property to a pawnshop. The disadvantage of this option for burglars is that pawnshops are highly visible and subject to police scrutiny. In many jurisdictions, pawnshop operators are required by law to take fingerprints or photographs of individuals who sell property. In addition, even if burglars are able to find a pawnshop that is willing to overlook the rules, it is unlikely that easily traceable property (e.g., anything with a serial number) would be accepted. Of course, the disadvantage for burglars is the advantage for the police. If the police routinely monitor the property being purchased by pawnshops in their jurisdiction, useful information may be developed. Unfortunately, disposing of property through pawnshops is usually not a common method for burglars. In addition, for the police, monitoring pawnshop transactions is a rather daunting task. At the extreme, consider the city of Los Angeles. Los Angeles has 117 licensed pawn shops, 3,000 other secondhand dealers, and a nearly countless number of flea markets (swap meets) and antique shows. Of the millions of transactions that occur at these places, only a small percentage likely involve stolen merchandise.

A fifth but rarely used option is selling property to strangers. As noted, this type of transaction is risky for the burglar and could lead to an arrest with relative ease. The final and least common option is that the burglar keeps the stolen property for his own use. This is also risky and in many ways defeats the purpose of committing the burglary in the first place—to get money.

In short, "following the property" offers investigators a chance of finding the perpetrator and recovering the stolen property. However, burglars tend to avoid risk in disposing of property, thus providing limited opportunities for the police. Through the course of an investigation, it is possible that individuals unconnected to the burglary, but with knowledge of the burglary or of the perpetrators, or with knowledge of the property taken in a burglary, would contact the police or would be otherwise found by the police. It is in this manner that investigators may have the greatest chance of solving such crimes. As illustrated in the introduction to this chapter, it was in this way that the burglary of the Foot Locker store was solved.

Vehicle Theft

Varieties, Trends, and Characteristics of Vehicle Theft

Motor vehicle theft refers to "the theft, or attempted theft, of a motor vehicle and includes the stealing of automobiles, trucks, buses, motorcycles, motor scooters, snowmobiles," and so forth (FBI, 2002; p. 53). To establish that a vehicle theft has actually occurred, the police need to determine that the vehicle was taken from the owner without the owner's consent.

In many jurisdictions, vehicle thefts and burglaries occur at about the same rate (see Table 12–1). Accordingly, about equal investigative resources are allocated to vehicle thefts and burglaries. Most vehicle thefts involve automobiles (seventy-five percent) and most of these are for the purpose of joyriding (Fleming, 1999). The average value of motor vehicle reported stolen in 2001 was $6,646 (FBI, 2002).

Vehicle theft trends are also similar to burglary trends. Vehicle theft rates have increased slightly over year 2000 levels, although the longer trend is downward. Vehicle thefts are down approximately nine percent since 1997 and down nearly twenty-four percent from 1992 levels. Once again, given unique conditions and circumstances, these trends may not reflect the experience of particular jurisdictions. In addition, vehicle theft rates are quite varied across jurisdictions. For instance, urban areas generally have a much higher rate of vehicle thefts than rural areas. In addition, cities near ports and international borders typically experience the highest vehicle theft rates in the country. The five cities in the United States with the highest vehicle theft rates in 2001 were Phoenix, Arizona; Miami, Florida; Fresno, Calfornia; Detroit, Michigan; and Sacramento, California (FBI, 2002).

Motor vehicle thefts have one of the highest reporting rates (approximately eighty-two percent of vehicle thefts are reported to the police) but one of the lowest clearance rates. In 2001, the clearance rate for vehicle theft was less than fourteen percent, similar to the clearance rate of burglaries. Of the vehicle thefts in which an arrest is made, the largest proportion of the arrests involves juveniles (see Table 12–2). In 2001, nearly thirty-three percent of the individuals arrested for vehicle theft were younger than the age of eighteen. Nearly sixty-six percent of those arrested were younger than the age of twenty-five. With regard to gender and race of arrestees, nearly eighty-four percent of those arrested were male and nearly fifty-eight percent of arrestees were white, forty percent black, and other races accounted for two percent.

Investigative Considerations With Motor Vehicle Theft

Like burglaries and other property crimes for that matter, vehicle thefts are difficult to solve. Usually they occur very quickly, there are no eyewitnesses to the crime, and there is little or no physical evidence. Even though most stolen vehicles are recovered (seventy percent), many are not intact, and there is usually little information available that will lead to the identification and apprehension of perpetrators. Of the stolen vehicles that are never recovered, many are believed to be shipped overseas or driven across international borders (www.nicb.org/index/shtml).

As with burglaries, the method used to commit the crime may constitute some of the best evidence on which to conduct an investigation. In particular, the perpetrator's MO may reflect the degree of planning involved in the crime and the sophistication of the thief. The least sophisticated methods are generally the most common methods of stealing vehicles. For example, thieves can use the keys left in the ignition, they can find a spare key hidden on the outside of the car, they can commandeer a running but unattended car, they can pay a parking lot attendant for keys to a car, they can steal keys from a parking lot attendant, they can steal keys from a car owner, they can tow the car away, they can do a "bump and run" (when one individual bumps a target vehicle on the road and, when the motorist gets out of the vehicle, the thief enters the car and drives away), or they can "hot wire" a car by breaking open (or "peeling") the steering column and bypassing the ignition to start the car.

Perhaps the most sophisticated (and uncommon) method involves obtaining the ignition code number from the vehicle and making a duplicate key with a portable key maker

It is common to find stolen vehicles with extensive damage to them. GLENDALE POLICE DEPARTMENT

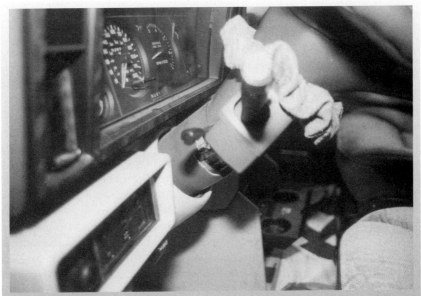

To access the ignition wiring, the steering column must be "peeled." Notice the hair scrunchy used to hide the exposed column. GLENDALE POLICE DEPARTMENT

(see Beekman and Daly [1990]). Depending on the method used, and the location from where the car was taken, there may be eyewitnesses to the crime, but it may be difficult to find them. If there are no eyewitnesses to the actual theft of the vehicle, there may be eyewitnesses to related events (e.g., the theft of the keys that allowed for the theft of the vehicle).

Most vehicle thefts occur when cars are parked on the street or on the owner's property. This fact is not surprising because this is where cars are most often located. However, the risk of theft, per hour parked, is greatest when cars are left unattended in parking lots. Particularly susceptible are cars parked in "park-and-ride" lots, downtown parking lots, shopping mall parking lots, and college parking lots (Clarke, 2002). Once again, these are potentially busy areas where thefts may be witnessed by other parking patrons or where thefts may be captured on parking lot surveillance cameras.

Because of frequent contact with motorists, and their presence on the streets, patrol officers are in a good position to be on the lookout for stolen vehicles. There are several good indicators that a vehicle may have been stolen. These include

- Vehicles being operated without ignition keys, or the use of material to disguise the lack of missing keys
- A broken or otherwise exposed steering column
- Broken window glass
- Dirty license plates/tags on a clean car or clean plates on a dirty car (indicating false or stolen plates)

- Expensive car parts on an inexpensive car or inexpensive parts on an expensive car
- A missing truck lock
- VINs on the same vehicle that do not match

There are at least two primary motivations for stealing vehicles. The first is for the purpose of joyriding, which is most common among younger perpetrators. They are most likely to steal a car when the opportunity presents itself (e.g., keys are found in the car) and for purposes of fun and excitement. As noted, cars used for joyriding are usually recovered, although not necessarily in complete form or in the same condition as when they were taken. As with burglaries committed by juveniles, juveniles are quite likely to talk about their criminal activities and this represents an opportunity for the police. In addition, recovered vehicles may contain property and physical evidence that can be linked to particular suspects. The presence of such evidence may assist in proving their responsibility for the crime.

The other primary motivation for vehicle theft is more instrumental in nature—to make money. Perpetrators can convert stolen autos into cash in a number of ways. Once again, each method reflects differences in the skill and sophistication of the perpetrator. Offenders can attempt to sell the car outright either after slight or major modification to the car, thieves can strip the car and sell its parts, they can transport the vehicle out of the country, or they can use any combination of the three methods (e.g., they can steal cars and then sell them to someone who transports them). Most common among these options involves the stolen vehicle being stripped at a *chop shop*.

The car parts are then sold to salvage yards or dishonest body repair shops. These places can also make money by buying the stolen car parts at a discount and charging consumers full price. A frequent target for these auto thieves are "ordinary" common cars. The more common the car, the larger the market for its parts. Police monitoring of car part and body shop outlets may produce useful leads in auto theft investigations.

Selling cars overseas is probably the most profitable means of converting stolen cars into cash, but is also the most difficult. As explained by Beekman and Daly (1990), "selling stolen cars overseas, where eager buyers will often pay double the original purchase price for a quality automobile, is rapidly changing the domestic auto theft trade" (p. 15). Thieves and exporters are continually deriving devious methods of getting around U.S. Customs procedures (see Beekman and Daly [1990]). One method that is not difficult involves driving the stolen vehicle across the border, usually to Mexico. Once the car is in Mexico, it can either go to a chop shop or be shipped to points beyond. It is estimated that between seventy and eighty percent of vehicles stolen in southern border cities end up in Mexico (Ethridge and Gonzalez, 1996).

Given the magnitude of the auto theft problem in the southern border areas, and the difficulty of investigating such crimes, several agencies have developed and operate comprehensive auto theft task forces, most of which use undercover strategies to identify and apprehend auto thieves. As an example, consider RATT in San Diego County (Casey, 1995). Authorities in San Diego County developed RATT to combat auto theft where individuals were believed to be transporting stolen vehicles through Mexico to Guatemala and El Salvador. RATT was a multifaceted response that included education, crime analysis,

EXHIBIT 12–1 Commonly stolen vehicles

The ten most commonly stolen vehicles in the United States in 2001 were

1. Toyota Camry
2. Honda Accord
3. Honda Civic
4. Oldsmobile Cutlass/Supreme/Ciera
5. Jeep Cherokee/Grand Cherokee
6. Chevrolet Full Size C/K Pickup
7. Toyota Corolla
8. Ford Taurus
9. Chevrolet Caprice
10. Ford F150 Pickup

Source: National Insurance Crime Bureau

This list can be criticized for a number of reasons. First, the cars on the list are not only the most frequently stolen vehicles, they are also the best-selling cars in the United States. The fact that they are so frequently stolen may be a function of the number of these cars that are available to be stolen. Second, the list does not indicate the year of the vehicles that are stolen. Most of the cars on the list are of older models that do not have the factory-installed antitheft systems. Finally, the list does not show variation in the model of cars stolen across states or cities. For example, in Wyoming, the top five stolen vehicles are all American-made trucks. In California, the top five stolen vehicles are all Japanese-made (engineered) vehicles (Hondas and Toyotas).

and law enforcement. Specifically, investigators identified and monitored chop shops in the San Diego area, they developed their own undercover chop shop, and they developed informants by infiltrating car theft rings. Between July 1992 and February 1995, RATT detectives recovered more than 780 stolen vehicles and made more than 100 arrests. A related investigation conducted by federal and state agents in California resulted in the arrest of twenty-eight suspects who ran an auto theft ring that shipped vehicles and parts from the Sacramento area to Russia and Eastern Europe (Organized Crime Digest, 2000).

As another example, STATETF used similar strategies with similar results (Ethridge and Gonzalez, 1996). As in San Diego, the problem in south Texas is that vehicles can be stolen and driven to Mexico even before the owner realizes that the car is missing. Investigators assigned to STATETF conducted surveillance of areas where auto thefts often occurred—parking lots at shopping malls, hospitals, grocery stores, movie theaters, and discount stores—so that they were in a position to take action as the crimes were occurring. They routinely inspected junkyards, vehicle repair shops, and used car lots to identify stolen autos and stolen auto parts. They developed and used informants to obtain information on

Items recovered at a small vehicle chop shop. GLENDALE POLICE DEPARTMENT

auto theft rings. In addition, investigators went undercover as sellers and buyers of stolen vehicles. No question, vehicle theft, particularly organized vehicle theft, is a difficult matter to investigate. RATT and STATETF are examples of "proactive" investigative responses to the problem.

Arson

Varieties, Trends, and Characteristics of Arson

Arson refers to "the willful or malicious burning or attempting to burn, with or without intent to defraud, a dwelling, house, public building, motor vehicle or aircraft, personal property, of another, etc." (FBI, 2002; p. 56). Fires that are simply suspicious or of unknown origin are not considered arson. To establish that arson has occurred, there must be evidence of the fire being deliberately set for the purpose of causing harm. One of the most common ways to establish that arson has occurred is to confirm the use of an accelerant (a flammable liquid such as gasoline, kerosene, or lighter fluid) in setting the fire.

In most jurisdictions, arson is a relatively rare crime (see Table 12–2); however, the consequences of the crime can be serious. Property loss associated with arson can be considerable, and the possibility of the loss of life as a result of the fire is present. In 2001, the average property loss in arson crimes was just more than $11,000 per incident (FBI, 2002). Structural losses averaged $20,128 and losses associated with mobile property (e.g., automobiles) averaged $6,974 per incident. Motor vehicles are the most common type of property burned in arson, followed by single-family homes (see Table 12–3).

Nationwide, 2001 arson rates have increased slightly more than year 2000 rates although, as with other property crimes, the general trend is downward. Larger cities (i.e., those with more than 250,000 inhabitants) generally have a higher rate of arson than smaller cities. This national trend may not represent the experience of individual jurisdictions given their potentially unique conditions and circumstances.

In 2001, the clearance rate for arson was sixteen percent (FBI, 2002), which is slightly higher than the rate for burglaries and auto thefts. As with other property crimes, smaller cities tend to have a higher clearance rate for arson than larger cities. Clearance rates are highest when arson involves industrial or manufacturing structures, and lowest when arson involves motor vehicles (see Table 12–3). Over time, arson clearance rates have remained relatively stable. Of the cases of arson that are cleared, juveniles are involved as perpetrators at a higher rate than in other property crimes (see Table 12–2). In 2001, just less than fifty percent of the individuals arrested for burglary were younger than the age of eighteen. Just more than sixty-eight percent were younger than the age of twenty-five. With regard to gender, more than eighty-four percent of those arrested were male. Finally, nearly seventy-seven percent of individuals arrested for arson were white, approximately twenty-one percent were black, and other races accounted for less than one percent (FBI, 2002). Of all FBI index crime arrests, whites are most highly represented in the crime of arson.

TABLE 12–3 Arson by Type of Property and Clearances

Type of Property	Percent Distribution	Percent Cleared
Total	100.0	16.2
Total Structure	42.2	22.1
Single Residential	17.8	22.9
Other Residential	7.8	21.5
Storage	3.2	18.8
Industrial/Manufacturing	.5	49.9
Other Commercial	4.2	15.8
Community/Public	4.8	28.5
Other Structure	3.9	17.8
Total Mobile	32.5	7.1
Motor Vehicles	30.7	6.7
Other Mobile	1.8	14.3
Other	25.4	18.1

Source: FBI (2002)

Investigative Considerations With Arson

Little question, arson is a difficult crime to solve and it poses unique challenges to investigators. In particular, the investigations associated with the crime are unusual in that considerable time and effort are devoted to determining simply whether a crime was committed. Furthermore, the fire often (but not always) destroys critical physical evidence that could assist in determining whether the fire was maliciously and willfully set, and, if it was, in identifying and apprehending the perpetrator. Fire investigations are also often hindered by the lack of witnesses. In addition, in arson, there is no opportunity to "follow the property," as is the case with burglaries and motor vehicle theft investigations. In short, although determining whether a fire resulted from arson may be difficult, determining who is responsible for the crime is usually even more difficult. Making arson investigations even more complicated is that personnel from several agencies have an interest in fire prevention, control, and investigation. In particular, fire department personnel typically have the expertise at understanding fires and their causes whereas law enforcement personnel have knowledge of the law and criminal investigation procedures. The split responsibility in arson investigations creates the possibility for conflict and turf wars, and may impede progress in investigations.

Once the fire has been extinguished, the first task in investigating the fire is determining its cause. Usually, this is primarily a responsibility of fire department personnel. Ultimately, fires can be classified into several categories based on their cause. Fires can be classified as (Bennett and Hess, 1984):

- Natural (e.g., caused by lightning, heat from the sun)
- Accidental (e.g., stove fires, children playing with matches)
- Suspicious (e.g., not natural or accidental but arson cannot be proved)
- Incendiary (i.e., arson; fires determined to be set deliberately and maliciously)
- Of unknown origin (when the cause of the fire cannot be established)

Legally, the presumption is that all fires have natural or accidental causes. There must be proof that the burning was the result of arson, that the fire was maliciously and willfully set, in order for it to be considered arson. On average, only sixteen percent of all reported fires are determined to be the result of arson (NIJ, 2000b). The cause of a fire is most often established through statements of witnesses and the physical analysis of the fire scene. Arson in particular is most often established with evidence of the use of an accelerent to cause the burning (Bennett and Hess, 1984).

To determine the cause of a fire, it is first necessary to identify *where* the fire started, to identify *the point of origin*. Most basically, for a fire to occur, it needs a source of heat and material to burn. The place that these two ingredients come together is referred to as the *point of origin of the fire*. In addition, items and other materials located at the point of origin may be informative regarding the cause of the fire and whether the fire was a result of arson. For example, items such as a timer (part of an ignition device) or newspaper (material ignited) being found at the point of origin, and where they do not belong, may raise suspicions about the possibility of arson. The identification of the point of origin may be relatively easy or quite difficult depending on the amount of destruction caused by the fire. Generally, the more devastation there is to the property as a result of the fire, the more difficult it is to identify the origin (and cause) of the fire.

The point of origin and the cause of the fire may be established by interviewing witnesses and firefighters, reconstructing and examining the pattern of the fire, examining objects in the structure, and by locating the area of the structure with the most destruction from the fire. Statements of witnesses and firefighters regarding the fire are critical. For instance, investigators may learn about suspicious activity around the scene prior to the discovery of the fire (e.g., that juveniles were seen running from the scene). They may learn the presumed cause of the fire (e.g., that it was caused by careless smoking). From firefighters, investigators may learn about the condition of the fire on their arrival at the scene, the color of the smoke, the color of the flames, the location of the flames, the condition of doors and windows on arrival, whether people were present at the scene, whether there were suspicious persons or vehicles at the scene, the method of entry by fire department personnel, the removal of any property by fire department personnel, any unusual aspects of the fire, and the nature of the fire spread.

An examination of the fire pattern is likely to provide critical clues regarding the cause and origin of the fire and, ultimately, whether the fire was deliberately set. Most fundamental, it is instructive to examine what was burned in relation to what was not burned. For example, in an isolated fire it may be relatively easy to determine the point of origin because it would be what sustained damage from the fire (e.g., a reclining chair). A V-shaped pattern of flame staining and destruction often emanates from items that were on fire (see Bennet and Hess [1984]). In a fire that caused more extensive damage, it may be instructive to examine the layering of material and debris on the floor. If, for example, broken glass from a window is discovered on the floor and is covered by other burned material, it may indicate that the window was broken before the fire started, and before the heat of the fire could have caused the glass to break. Also, in this example, the distance of the glass from the window, the location of the glass in relation to the window, as well as the characteristics of the broken glass, could indicate whether the glass was broken prior to the fire (e.g., as a result of an incendiary device being thrown through the window), because of the fire, or as a result of actions taken by firefighters. In addition, the point of origin of a fire may be identified by tracing the fire from where least damage occurred to where most damage occurred. Areas that sustain the heaviest fire damage tend to indicate the point where the fire started.

An examination of objects in the structure may also provide clues regarding the origin (and cause) of the fire. Again, in general, objects that show the heaviest burning and charring damage tend to be at or near the point of origin. Identification of metal items that have melted can provide a basis for determining the heat of the fire (Bennett and Hess, 1984). Various types of material cause various heat intensities: Flammable liquids produce fires with extraordinary heat. In addition, it is interesting that an examination of furniture springs may be revealing regarding the nature and cause of the fire. Furniture springs are likely to sag as a result of a fire only when the fire originated from inside the cushions or from a fire external to the furniture that was intensified by a fire accelerant (Bennett and Hess, 1984). Examination of lightbulbs may also provide a clue regarding the heat of the fire and the direction from which it originated. Lightbulbs tend to expand on the side that faces the source of the heat. In addition, hot and fast-moving fires (indicated by degree of destruction, white and blue-white flames, black smoke color; see Bennett and Hess [1984]) are usually associated with the presence of accelerents.

With regard to locating the area of the structure with the most destruction from the fire, burn indicators (the impact of fire on material) may be revealing. There are many factors that can influence the amount of char on wood; however, in general, the deeper the char, the longer the material was exposed to the fire. An area characterized by the deepest char may signal the point of origin of the fire. According to Bennett and Hess (1984), "in the majority of fires, the area of most intense burning is the point of origin" (p. 127).

As noted, the clearest indication of arson is the presence of flammable liquid at the point of origin; however, the presence of a flammable liquid does not necessarily mean that the fire was willfully and maliciously set. The associated circumstances are critical considerations. The presence of an accelerent can be positively detected through a variety of means, including human smell, scientific testing devices, and with canines that are trained to detect the odor of accelerants.

It is one thing to determine that a fire was a result of arson, it is quite another to find the persons responsible for the crime. Beside the evidence associated with the fire itself, physical evidence usually plays a rather small role in arson investigations. Investigators should be mindful of the possibility that physical evidence exists, but they should also be aware that the fire and the measures taken to extinguish the fire can easily lead to the loss of such evidence. Because of the lack of evidence regarding who committed the crime, consideration of the motivation of an arsonist becomes an important aspect of the investigation. If it can be determined *why* someone would have wished to burn a structure or other property, it may provide a clue as *who* may have committed the crime. Evidence that associates the person with the scene may then be collected. The motivations for arson are many (see Bennett and Hess [1984] and Douglas et al. [1992]).

Arson may be an expression of anger or revenge. It is critical to determine whether, from the victim's point of view, there is anyone who may have sought revenge by destroying the victim's property as a result of revenge or anger. Did anyone make any prior threats about destroying the property? An ex-boyfriend? An ex-employee? An angry neighbor? When considering revenge as a possible motive, investigators should look to the relationships the owner of the property has with others. It is interesting that when female subjects commit arson it is usually for this reason, and usually the items burned belong to a former boyfriend or husband. When a male subject sets a fire that is motivated by revenge, the target is usually a residence or business.

In addition, arson may be an act of terrorism—an organized effort aimed at creating fear and guided by political beliefs. For example, federal agents believe that several wildfires set in Oregon and Washington in 2001 that caused more than $3 million in damages were the responsibility of the Earth Liberation Front (ELF). The FBI has identified ELF as one of the country's leading domestic terrorist organizations (Crime Control Digest, 2001).

Arson may be an act of vandalism. If this is the case, it would likely point to younger offenders, usually acting in a group, who live in the neighborhood or area where the fire occurred. As discussed earlier with burglaries and vehicle thefts, young offenders are likely to talk about their actions among themselves and with others, and this may offer an opportunity for the police. Young, amateur offenders are also most likely to use flammable liquids to start the fire and do not use a timing device. "Therefore, amateur firesetters are often found either in the fire they set or in the local hospital" (Bennett and Hess, 1984; p. 143). As such, it may be productive for investigators to make inquires regarding treatment for burns at medical facilities after a suspected case of arson is identified. More sophisticated and older arsonists are more likely to use some form of delayed ignition—such as candles, flares, cigarettes, or timers—to start the fire. Remnants of these items may be found at the point of origin (Bennett and Hess, 1984).

Arson may be committed to conceal another crime, to destroy evidence in the other crime, or simply to mislead investigators (i.e., staging). Most often, offenders are unsuccessful at concealing crimes through arson. However, it is essential that investigators are aware of the possibility in searching the arson crime scene. Evidence of other crimes at an arson scene may be quite obvious (e.g., a dead body with gunshot wounds to the back). Large amounts of liquid accelerants are also often present at such scenes (Holmes and Holmes, 1996). It is usually the case that the associated crime reveals more informative leads regarding who was responsible for the crimes than the arson.

Another motivation for arson is profit. The basis for profit in arson is usually insurance fraud. Important but basic questions for investigators to ask are the following: Who would financially benefit if this property was destroyed? Was the property insured? For how long was it insured? Was it overinsured? What is the financial situation of the victim? Answers to these questions may be revealing and may lead investigators to the "victim" as the perpetrator, or to a "hired torch" as the perpetrator—an individual who was hired by the "victim" to set the fire and destroy the property. Other evidence of an "inside job" includes the absence of personal items from the fire scene, the absence of personal records and books, missing tools, pets removed, an empty refrigerator or freezer, or an increase in insurance just prior to the fire (Bennett and Hess, 1984).

Arson may also be committed for the perpetrator's emotional satisfaction. This motivation for fire setting is often referred to as *pyromania*. A pyromaniac is described as having a compulsive need to set fires. In this sense, an outward evidence-based motivation may not be evident to investigators. Offenders with this motivation are the most prolific at fire starting. Targets are often randomly selected. Fires are often made in haste. Fires are most often set at night. In addition, the fire may have been set to allow the arsonist to be a hero, to report the fire, or to save people from the fire. From an investigative standpoint, it is interesting that such offenders have stated that they were the ones who reported the fire, that they stayed at the scene as a spectator, and that they even assisted with first aid or rescuing victims. These offenders are likely to have an arrest record and to have committed the arson by themselves (Rider, 1980a, b). When all the possibilities are considered by investigators, some motives may appear more likely than others and good leads may be developed. Little question, identification of an offender's probable motivation can be a powerful tool in guiding an arson investigation.

Larceny and Fraud

Varieties, Trends, and Characteristics of Larceny

Larceny refers to "the unlawful taking, carrying, leading, or riding away of property from the possession or constructive possession of another. It includes crimes such as shoplifting, pocket-picking, purse snatching, thefts from motor vehicles, thefts of motor vehicle parts and accessories, bicycle thefts, etc." (FBI, 2002; p. 48). To establish that larceny has occurred, there must be evidence of possession of the property by the victim and a statement from the victim that the property was taken without permission.

Larceny is the most common type of property crime (see Table 12–2). The most common form of larceny is theft from motor vehicles (25.8 percent), followed by shoplifting (13.8 percent), theft from buildings (13.3 percent), and all others (31.0 percent; see Figure 12–1). The average dollar value per larceny offense in 2001 was $730, with thefts from buildings involving the highest property loss ($1,037) and shoplifting the lowest ($182).

Nationwide, as with other crimes, 2001 larceny rates have increased slightly more than year 2000 rates, although the general trend is downward. Larceny is down approximately nine percent from 1997 and about eleven percent since 1992. This national trend, however, may not represent the experience of individual jurisdictions. Generally, small communities with large shopping malls show the highest rates of larceny. This is because of the frequency of shoplifting in relation to the number of people who live in the community.

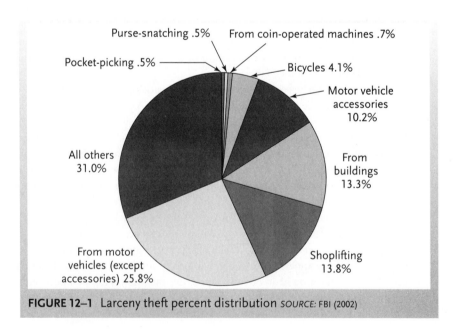

FIGURE 12–1 Larceny theft percent distribution *SOURCE:* FBI (2002)

Overall, just more than seventeen percent of larcenies were cleared in 2001. This figure overstates police success in clearing larcenies because virtually all shoplifting crimes that are known to the police are cleared (the theft is observed and the perpetrator is apprehended at the store), which makes the clearance rate for larcenies close to 100 percent (FBI, 2002). Over time, larceny clearance rates have remained relatively stable.

As with other property crimes, larceny is a difficult crime to solve, as demonstrated by the low clearance rate. Of the larcenies that are cleared, juveniles are disproportionately involved as perpetrators, although to a lesser extent than other property crimes (see Table 12–2). In 2001, less that thirty percent of the individuals arrested for burglary were younger than the age of eighteen. Just more than fifty-six percent were younger than the age of twenty-five. With regard to gender, just more than sixty-three percent of those arrested were male. Of all property crime, female subjects have the greatest representation in larcenies (arrests). Finally, nationally, just more than sixty-six percent of individuals arrested for larceny were white, approximately thirty-one percent were black, and other races accounted for the remaining three percent (FBI, 2002).

Investigative Considerations With Larceny

With larcenies, usually there are few leads for the police to pursue. Larcenies are usually discovered only after the crime has occurred and the perpetrator has had ample time to flee with the property. Furthermore, there are usually no eyewitnesses to the crime, no usable physical evidence, and generally few other good leads for an investigator to pursue. There is little variation in motive; thieves usually steal property that they can use for their own benefit. As a result, it may be more difficult to find and trace property taken during a larceny compared with property taken during a burglary. In addition, the property taken during a larceny may not be remarkable or noticeable to others (as opposed to the perpetrator driving a new car without explanation) or may not be otherwise identifiable (e.g., no serial number). Because such crimes typically involve relatively small losses and provide few leads for investigators to pursue, relatively few investigative resources are allocated to the investigation of larceny offenses. Indeed, in police departments that operate a differential police response strategy (Chapter 3), the majority of larcenies receive a telephone report only. The primary exceptions would be if the property loss was large or if good leads were present that would make it likely that the perpetrator could be identified. In short, larceny poses a tremendous challenge to investigators because little evidence is usually produced during the commission of the crime. It may be necessary for investigators to search for such evidence, but the reality is that usually under the pressure of other more serious cases, larcenies receive low priority.

Varieties, Trends, and Characteristics of Fraud

Fraud is a general and encompassing term that refers to "all the ways one person can falsely represent a fact to another in order to induce that person to surrender something of value"

EXHIBIT 12–2 Crime Solvers press release

Prince William County, Virginia . . . The Prince William County Police Department needs your help in locating suspects involved in a series of larcenies. There has been a recent increase in wallet and purse larcenies throughout the County, although most of the incidents have occurred in eastern Prince William County. There have been 22 reported incidents since May 26th. Detectives believe more than one group of suspects is involved in these cases. The incidents have occurred in grocery stores, restaurants, hardware stores and discount stores. Some victims have had wallets taken from purses left in shopping carts. Some wallets have been taken from purses hanging on chairs in restaurants. Descriptions of suspects were provided after stolen credit cards were used from these incidents.

These are the descriptions of suspects that were provided:

1. Hispanic male, 23–30 years old, 5¢8¢¢, 160 lbs. with a second Hispanic male driving a gray or silver Honda 4 door.
2. Hispanic female, 30–40 years old, 5¢5¢¢, 140 lbs. with a Hispanic male 40–50 years old, 5¢9¢¢, 200 lbs. and a Hispanic male 30–40 years old, 6¢0¢¢, 170 lbs.
3. Black female, 28 years old, 5¢4¢¢, 135 lbs. black and gold framed glasses.
4. White female with a white male, 24–26 years old, 5¢8¢¢, 150 lbs.
5. Black male, 21–33 years old, 5¢11¢¢, 150 lbs. with a black female, 20–30 years old, 5¢5¢¢, 140 lbs with blond hair.
6. White male, 50–60 years old, 6¢0¢¢, 200 lbs.

Citizens should be aware of these incidents and not leave purses unattended at anytime, but especially in restaurants, stores and shopping carts. If anyone knows the identity of the suspects, or has information about these cases, please call Prince William County Crime Solvers at 703–670–3700. You don't have to give your name, just the information. You could earn up to a $1,000 cash reward.

(IRS, 1993). Fraud is treated as a part II crime in the FBI *Uniform Crime Reports* (2002) and, as a result, few details are provided about the nature and extent of the crime. It is safe to say, however, that opportunities for fraud are on the increase and are becoming more devious. Some of the most frequent types of fraud are (see IRS [1993]) the following:

- *Tax evasion* occurs when a person or corporation provides deceptive information to avoid paying taxes.
- *Bribery* occurs when anything of value is offered in exchange for influence in decisions or actions of the taker.
- *Embezzlement* occurs when a person who is entrusted with money of a business uses it for his or her own use and benefit.

EXHIBIT 12–3 Identity Theft

What Identity Thieves Do with Your Information

Identity thieves frequently open new accounts in your name. They often apply for new credit cards using your information, make charges, and leave bills unpaid. It is also common for them to set up telephone or utility service in your name and not pay for it. Some victims have found that identity thieves applied for loans, apartments, and mortgages. Thieves have also been known to print counterfeit checks in a victim's name.

Thieves also often access your existing accounts. They may take money from your bank accounts, make charges on your credit cards, and use your checks and credit to make down payments for cars, furniture, and other expensive items. They may even file for government benefits including unemployment insurance and tax refunds.

Unfortunately, thieves often use a stolen identity again and again. It is very common for victims to learn that thieves have opened and accessed numerous accounts, often over a long span of time.

How Identity Theft Happens

Four out of five victims have no idea how an identity thief obtained their personal information. Among those who think they know what happened, many believe the identity theft occurred when their purse or wallet was stolen or lost. Thieves also steal identities from the trash—this is called "dumpster diving"—and it can occur at home, at work, or at a business. Mail can be stolen from your home mailbox, from a drop-box, at business, and even directly from postal workers. Home computers can be infected with viruses that transmit your data to thieves.

Group identity theft has become a major problem for consumers. A thief gains access to a place that keeps records for many people. Targets have included stores, fitness centers, car dealers, schools, hospitals, and even credit bureaus. Thieves may either use the stolen identities themselves or sell them to other criminals.

"Pretexting" is a method of identity theft that is on the rise. The identity thief poses as a legitimate representative of a survey firm, bank, Internet service provider, employer, landlord, or even a government agency. The thief contacts you to reveal your information, usually by asking you to "verify" some data.

Victims of identity theft often find that someone they know has committed the crime. Roommates, hired help, and landlords all have access to your home, and it is possible for them to access private information. Identity theft within families is also fairly common. This causes particular difficulties, because victims may be reluctant to notify the authorities or press charges. People are especially vulnerable when ending relationships with roommates and spouses.

Identity theft often goes undetected. Within a month of being committed, half of the crimes still remain unnoticed. One in ten stays hidden for two or more years. Identity thieves may change "your" address on an account so that you

(continued)

EXHIBIT 12–3   *(continued)*

won't ever receive bills with the fraudulent charges on them. They will often pay the minimum balances on accounts they have opened, so as to avoid calling attention to the account and having it cut off. They may even use the identities of children or persons who are deceased, so that the crime is less likely to be noticed.

Source: Federal Reserve Bank of Boston

- *Forgery* involves the use of a false document or instrument to defraud the recipient. Types of forgery include counterfeit checks, unauthorized use of credit cards, medical prescriptions, and counterfeit merchandise.
- *Blackmail* involves a demand for money to avoid bodily harm, destruction of property, or the disclosure of secrets.
- *Extortion* occurs when one person obtains property from another as a result of actual or threatened force, fear, or under authority of an official office (e.g., acting as a police officer).
- A *kickback* occurs when a person who sells an item pays the buyer part of the proceeds from that sale.
- *Racketeering* refers to operating an illegal business for personal profit.
- *Insider trading* occurs when a person uses privileged "inside" information to profit through trading of stock in a publicly held corporation.
- *Money laundering* refers to the investment of illegally obtained money (e.g., through drug sales, racketeering) into legitimate businesses so that the original source of the money cannot be established.
- *Investment fraud* occurs when an individual obtains money from another under the false pretext of a legitimate investment.
- *Insurance fraud* refers to when car accidents and injuries are staged, reported property damage is bogus, property damage is self-inflicted (e.g., arson), or even when one's death is fraudulently reported to collect insurance benefits.
- *Welfare and food stamp fraud* involves obtaining or using welfare benefits or food stamps illegally.
- *Identity theft* is when someone illegally obtains personal information about an individual (e.g., social security number) to establish new credit card accounts or new loans, and to obtain access to bank accounts and so forth.
- *Internet fraud* can take a variety of forms, the most common of which is auction fraud, when the property being bid on is misrepresented or when the property is not provided with a winning bid. In addition, the Internet provides opportunities for many other forms of fraud (e.g., credit card fraud, investment fraud, etc.).

Given the wide variety of fraudulent schemes, the authority to investigate fraud is distributed among a multitude of agencies. In many instances, local police departments do not have primary responsibility for such investigations. Rather, the responsibilities are of other local, state, federal, and private agencies including the U.S. Secret Service, the FBI, the IRS, state regulatory agencies, county prosecutor's offices, and private business investigative divisions (e.g., insurance company investigators, bank credit card investigators).

Investigative Considerations With Fraud

With regard to the investigation of fraud, most forms of fraud provide some evidence for investigators to pursue. Given the variety of ways in which fraud can be perpetrated, the appropriate investigative response will vary considerably. In general, nearly all forms of fraud involve the recording of critical information on paper, be it insurance claim forms, credit card applications, or tax forms. Although a simplification, the basic investigative task is to "follow the paper trail" (IRS, 1993) or to "follow the money" (Becker and Rein, 2000). Investigations of fraud rely heavily on records as a source of information. Records may be valuable for the information contained in them (e.g., names, addresses, dates) as well as for forensic purposes (e.g., handwriting analysis to determine whether a signature was forged). A variety of records may contain relevant information depending on the specific nature of the investigation. The possibilities include bank deposit and withdrawal records (e.g., to obtain an example of one's signature, to document or verify the dates of unusual transactions); money transfers and other transactions; real estate records; court records; corporate accounting records; records of the Better Business Bureau; casino records; other public records such as tax returns; welfare agency records; birth, death, marriage, and divorce records; and auto license and sales records. The more complicated the fraud, the greater the knowledge and training required to investigate it. Investigations of fraud are highly specialized and often require knowledge that is not pertinent to other types of criminal investigations (e.g., accounting principles). Personnel who are assigned to such investigations should expect to receive considerable specialized training in such matters. For additional information regarding the complexities and techniques of fraud investigations, see Vacca (2003), Abagnale (2001), Cauthen (2001), Mendell (2000), and IRS (1993).

Questions for Discussion and Review

1. What is a burglary? What are the major characteristics and trends of burglary?

2. How do burglars obtain information about their intended target? What are the investigative implications that relate to how information about the target is obtained?

3. What may a burglar's MO reveal about the burglar? What implications may this have on the investigation of burglary?

4. What are the ways in which burglars may dispose of property? What implications may this have on the conduct of burglary investigations?

5. What is motor vehicle theft? What are the major characteristics and trends in vehicle theft?

6. What are the various ways in which vehicles may be stolen?

7. What are the primary motivations for stealing vehicles?

8. How can stolen vehicles be converted into cash?

9. How did RATT and STATETF combat the problem of auto theft?

10. What is arson? What are the major trends and characteristics of arson?

11. What are the various causes of fires? How common is arson as a cause?

12. What is the importance of determining the point of origin of the fire at a fire scene?

13. What is the significance of the discovery of accelerants at a fire scene?

14. What are the major motivations for arson? Of what investigative value is this information?

15. What is larceny? What is fraud? What are the most common characteristics and varieties of larceny and fraud?

16. What are the difficulties associated with the investigation of larceny and fraud?

Related Internet Sites

www.nicb.org/index.shtml
This is the web site for the National Insurance Crime Bureau, a non-profit organization supported by property/casualty insurance companies. It engages in activities to prevent and detect fraud and theft.

www.callforaction.org
Call For Action, Inc., is a non-profit network of consumer hotlines available to assist individuals with consumer-related problems. The site provides useful information on how to prevent fraud, and how to prevent and deal with identity theft.

www.nfpa.org
This is the address for the National Fire Protection Association, an organization devoted to preventing fires and other related hazards. Click on Research and Reports for information on all sorts of fire-related topics, including arson

THE DOCUMENTATION AND PRESENTATION OF EVIDENCE

OBJECTIVES

After reading the chapter you will be able to

- Give examples of cases when there was an actual or perceived miscarriage of justice
- Explain why these, and other, miscarriages of justice occurred
- Describe the court process as an adversarial process
- Discuss the role of defense attorneys, prosecuting attorneys, judges, and the police in the adversarial process
- Discuss the importance and value of a vigorous defense for defendants
- Discuss in detail how police misconduct and incompetence can lead to miscarriages of justice
- Discuss how police perjury can lead to bad outcomes
- Discuss the role and importance of investigative reports in criminal investigations and the court process

- Discuss the role of lay and expert witnesses in court
- Discuss the controversies associated with the use of expert witnesses in court
- Discuss the purpose of the cross-examination of witnesses
- Identify four ways in which a defense attorney may attempt to "impeach" a police witness
- Discuss the role of the jury, and why the trial process and the jury system is a rather strange way to determine the truth
- Identify the factors that influence jurors' decisions

IMPORTANT TERMS

Adversarial process	Miscarriage of justice	Lay witness	Legal and extralegal factors in jury decision making
Role of the prosecuting attorney, police investigators, defense attorney, and judge in court	Police perjury	Expert witness	
	Incident report	Cross-examination	Trivial persuasion
	Supplemental report	Impeachment	
	Testimony	Voir dire process	

INTRODUCTION

In the overwhelming majority of cases, defendants actually committed the crimes for which they are charged, and they are found guilty of those crimes in a court of law (Dershowitz, 1996). But sometimes errors are made. When these errors occur, they have a devastating effect on defendants and on the integrity of the entire criminal justice process. Hundreds of such cases have been documented (see NIJ, 1996 and www.innocenceproject.org) and it seems that more are uncovered every day (see Dwyer and Flynn [2002]). Several examples are presented here.

In 1987, the residents of Huntington, West Virginia, were on edge. In separate incidents, two women were abducted at knife-point from a shopping mall parking lot. The perpetrator repeatedly raped each of the victims and both were robbed of jewelry. Although the perpetrator wore a ski mask and forced the victims to close their eyes, both victims caught glimpses of the attacker. One of the victims was able to provide a partial description of the perpetrator. Both victims were able to describe his clothing, and both told the police that the perpetrator was uncircumcised. As the police began their search for the rapist, their attention focused on Glen Woodall, who worked at a cemetery across the street from the mall where the abductions took place. The physical description of the perpetrator provided by the victims matched Woodall, and a police search of his house revealed clothing similar to that described by the victims. On the basis of this evidence, Woodall was arrested. During a pretrial hearing, Woodall's defense counsel requested that a DNA test be performed on the evidence in the case. The judge denied the request, because DNA analysis was not yet a proved science. At the trial, the prosecution presented additional evidence including chemical tests conducted by a state police chemist that showed Woodall's blood secretions matched secretions in the semen recovered from the victims, body and facial hair removed from a victim's car that was consistent with Woodall's hair, and that a unique smell of Woodall noted by the victims was consistent with the smell found at Woodall's workplace. Woodall's attorney presented a minimal defense. On the basis of the evidence, Woodall was convicted of sexual assault, sexual abuse, kidnaping, and aggravated battery and was sentenced to two life terms plus 203 to 335 years in prison. After the trial, Woodall's defense counsel once again requested that DNA tests be performed on the evidence in the case, and the request was granted. The results of the test, however, were determined to be inconclusive. On appeal, further DNA tests were conducted and these tests positively excluded Woodall as the perpetrator. As a result, in 1992, his conviction on all charges was vacated. Woodall was free after spending five years in prison for a crime he did not commit. Subsequent to the verdict reversal, the state police chemist who testified at the trial, Fred Zain, was investigated and indicted for providing perjured testimony in criminal cases, including Woodall's.

On July 17, 1982, a twenty-seven-year-old white woman was walking home from a shopping center in Hanover, Virginia, when a man riding a bicycle abducted her, carried her into a nearby woods, and brutally raped her. The victim reported to the police that one of statements made by the perpetrator during the assault was that he "had a white girl." A police officer suspected that the perpetrator might be Marvin Anderson because Anderson was the only black man the officer knew who lived with a white woman. The officer obtained a color photograph of Anderson from Anderson's employer. The photo of Anderson along with six other black-and-white mug shots of other individuals were shown to the victim. The victim identified Anderson as the man who attacked her. Within an hour of this identification, a lineup was conducted and she identified Anderson again. (Anderson was the only individual who was in the photo lineup as well as in the physical lineup.) Anderson was arrested. The case went to trial in 1983. At the trial, the victim testified in detail about the assault and again identified Anderson as the perpetrator. The serology analysis was uninformative; it could not include or exclude Anderson as the culprit. The defense presented an alibi for Anderson but failed to present evidence about a different suspect—John Lincoln—and the evidence that linked him to the stolen bicycle used by the perpetrator. The all-white jury convicted Anderson of rape, forcible sodomy, abduction, and robbery. He was sentenced to 210 years in prison. In the years after the conviction, Anderson requested that DNA analysis be performed on the evidence but he was told that the evidence in the case had been thrown away. In 1988, John Lincoln (the same man who was earlier linked to the crime) came forward and confessed to the crime but the judge (the same one who presided over the original trial) rejected his confession and refused to vacate Anderson's conviction. Anderson was paroled in 1997

Marvin Anderson shortly after his release from prison for a crime that he did not commit.
RICHMOND *TIMES-DISPATCH*

after spending fifteen years in prison. In 2001, Anderson's attorneys were advised that certain DNA evidence in the case was found; a request for DNA analysis on the evidence was then made. The request was denied. Later that year, another request was made and it was accepted. The results of the DNA analysis excluded Anderson as the perpetrator. Although never officially announced, the DNA profile was found to match John Lincoln, already in prison on an unrelated conviction (also see Krishnamurthy [2001]).

On January 24, 1984, Michelle Jackson, age sixteen, did not return to her Detroit home after school. Her family formed a search party and followed her path from the bus stop. They found her body in an abandoned garage. She was nude from the waist down and her long johns were twisted around her neck. The murder received much publicity, as did the fifty other assaults that occurred on young girls in the months prior to this murder. Shortly after the murder, Eddie Joe Lloyd, a psychiatric patient at a hospital in Detroit, began writing letters to the Detroit Police about the murder and provided suggestions to them about how to solve this, and other, homicides. The police interviewed Lloyd four times at the hospital, and they eventually obtained a confession from him about the murder of Michelle Jackson. The account he provided to the police contained details about the crime that only the killer (and the police) would have known (e.g., the type of jeans the victim was wearing, a description of her earrings, and other details about the crime scene). Lloyd signed a written confession and also provided a tape-recorded confession. The confession along with the physical evidence—a confirmation that semen was present on the long johns, on a bottle that was forced into the victim, and on a piece of paper that was stuck to the bottle—was presented by the prosecution at trial. Lloyd maintained that the details of the crime contained in his confession were provided to him by the detective on the case. According to Lloyd, detectives led him to believe that by confessing it would assist the police in finding the real killer. Not even Lloyd's attorney believed him. Lloyd's attorney provided a limited, and by most accounts pathetic, defense—limited to the unsuccessful attempt to have the confession ruled inadmissible, and an attempt to get Lloyd to plead insanity. His attorney conducted minimal cross-examination of prosecution witnesses and called no witnesses of his own. The jury deliberated less than an hour before finding Eddie Joe Lloyd guilty of first-degree felony murder. All his appeals failed. In 1995, the Innocence Project obtained the biological evidence in the case and had it subjected to DNA analysis. The DNA profiles obtained from each of the items matched each other but did not match Eddie Joe Lloyd. Lloyd was not the perpetrator. His conviction was vacated in 2002 after serving seventeen years of his life-without-parole sentence. A federal investigation of the police officers who investigated this case is ongoing. The perpetrator of the homicide is yet to be identified (Zeman and Schmitt, 2002).

On an early spring evening in 1989, a young woman, an investment banker, was jogging through Central Park in New York City when she was attacked, savagely beaten, and raped. She was found unconscious at 1:30 AM the next morning. She was close to death; her body temperature was eighty-four degrees and she had lost seventy-five percent of her blood. At the time the woman was discovered, five boys were already in police custody for harassing and robbing several people in the park the night the woman was attacked. Thirty-seven other teenagers were also questioned in the investigation. Five of the teenagers confessed to the robberies and to the assault of the woman. Although each of the boys tried to minimize their own role in the crimes, each provided details about the robberies, and about beating and raping the woman. The boys' confessions were the strongest evidence of their guilt presented in court by prosecutors. In addition, during several of the trials, the prosecutors presented hairs found on the subjects that were similar in their class characteristics to the head hair of the victim. The defense raised numerous questions about the evidence. Other than the non-DNA match of the head hair, there was no other physical evidence that linked any of the boys to the victim. The semen recovered from the victim did not match the DNA of any of the boys. The defense also raised questions about the confessions. The details of the crime provided by the boys were wrong regarding when, where, and how the rape took place. With most of the boys, the police did not begin taping the interrogations until they had admitted to the rape. Some of the boys had been taken back to the crime scene before their confessions were taped. According to the defense counsel, these peculiarities raised suspicions about police conduct in the case. The bottom line for the defense attorneys was that the confessions were coerced; their clients were tricked into confessing. Many observers were outraged at the arguments and tactics of the defense attorneys. How could defense attorneys represent these miserable, despicable, no-good kids? In separate trials, each boy was found guilty and sentenced to prison. More than thirteen years later, on December 5, 2002, the Manhattan district attorney asked a judge to dismiss the convictions of the men. The request was granted. Reportedly, police and prosecutors had been "reinvestigating" the case since 2001. The reinvestigation was prompted when Matias Reyes, a convicted and incarcerated serial rapist and murderer, came forward and confessed to the rape of the woman in the park. According to Reyes, he decided to confess after meeting in prison one of the men who was convicted of the rape. Tests revealed that the DNA of the semen recovered from the victim matched the DNA of Reyes. Reanalysis of the hair recovered from several of the boys revealed that the DNA profile did not match that of the victim. With this evidence, the district attorney has expressed confidence that the men, now in their late twenties, did not participate in the rape of the woman. Each of the men spent between seven and one-half years and thirteen and one-half years, their complete sentences, in prison (Dwyer and Flynn, 2002).

There are other cases for which a conviction was overturned without the benefit of DNA evidence. Consider the case of Jeffrey Hornoff. On August 11, 1989, Victoria Cushman was strangled and beaten to death in her Warwick, Rhode Island, apartment. When searching the crime scene, the police found a letter that she had written to Jeffrey Hornoff. In this letter, she had written about her refusal to break off their affair and she insisted that he leave his wife. In pursuing this possible lead, the police learned from some of Cushman's coworkers that Cushman believed that Hornoff was going to leave his wife for her. The police also discovered that several days before the murder, Hornoff told Cushman that the affair was over. Reportedly, Cushman was shocked and upset. Without fingerprints, DNA evidence, or witnesses, the prosecution case rested on the letter, the related testimony, and on Hornoff's own statements when he was questioned by the police. When he was initially questioned, he denied even knowing the victim, and his alibi differed from what his wife and brother told investigators. Later, he changed his story stating that he initially lied to hide the fact that he was having an extramarital affair with Cushman. He insisted that he did not kill her. In court, prosecutors argued that Hornoff killed Victoria Cushman to keep his wife from learning about the affair. The jury believed the prosecution and found him guilty of first-degree murder. He was given a sentence of life in prison. More than six years after his conviction, in November 2002, a man by the name of Todd Barry, age forty-five, came forward and confessed to killing Victoria Cushman. He provided a detailed account of what happened the night of the murder and some of the details of the confession were corroborated by his brother. No motive was provided but Barry and the victim had dated. Within hours of the confession, Hornoff was released from prison where he spent more than eight years for a crime he did not commit (Carovillo, 2002; Haskell, 2002).

Many people consider the verdict in the O.J. Simpson case another example of justice gone mad. As discussed in Chapters 6 and 8, investigators assembled—and prosecutors presented—a mountain of evidence that indicated Simpson murdered his ex-wife Nicole Brown Simpson and her friend Ron Goldman. The evidence was undercut by allegations made by Simpson's defense attorneys that investigators sloppily handled and fabricated evidence in the case. Simpson, of course, was found not guilty of the crimes for which he was charged.

All these case examples illustrate an important point: Justice in the criminal justice system is not a guarantee. Justice depends on the competent and conscientious efforts of everyone involved in the process: investigators, prosecuting attorneys, defense attorneys, judges, and juries. As discussed in this chapter, the police, in conducting criminal investigations and collecting evidence, find themselves at a critical stage of the process. Evidence is extremely influential in determining the final outcome of the case. Errors in evidence collection can have grave consequences. This chapter examines the nature of the court process and the role and contribution of investigators in it.

The Adversarial Process

The court process in the United States can be described as adversarial in nature. The process can be viewed as a contest or even a game (Dershowitz, 1982), albeit a serious one, in which defense attorneys and prosecuting attorneys are opponents. Indeed, defense attorneys and prosecuting attorneys present conflicting arguments, or conflicting versions of the truth, in court in an effort to win the "game." Ideally, the judge is supposed to represent a neutral referee in the contest, making sure that rules of the game are enforced fairly. Police investigators are a part of the prosecution team. The role of investigators is to collect the evidence in the case and, on the basis of probable cause, to identify and apprehend the individual who committed the crime. The prosecution then presents evidence collected by the police in court to convince a judge or jury, beyond a reasonable doubt, that a crime occurred and that the defendant committed it. The role of the defense attorney is to probe, test, and question the evidence presented by the prosecutor; to provide alternative explanations for the evidence; and to present other evidence in an attempt to establish reasonable doubt. It is in this way that the quality and integrity of the evidence in the case is tested, and that defendants are represented. As such, the provision of a legal defense is no less important for a guilty defendant than it is for an innocent one. After all, it is only through the legal process that it is determined who is guilty and who is not. As explained by Dershowitz (1982), "defending the guilty and the despised—even freeing some of them—is a small price to pay for our liberties. Imagine a system where the guilty and the despised—or at least those so regarded by the powers that be—were not entitled to representation!" (p. xiv).

At times it may seem that the prosecution team is at a disadvantage in the game. Defense attorneys do not have to prove anything to win; the burden of proof is entirely on the prosecution. In addition, the prosecution and the police have to follow and abide by numerous rules in collecting and presenting evidence. The police have to tell "the truth" in court or face the consequences of perjury. Defense attorneys get to develop "alternative explanations" for the evidence. The prosecution has to share all evidence in the case with the defense counsel. Indeed, defense attorneys do have some advantages, but most are on the side of the prosecution. The prosecution has the full authority and power of the government on its side. The prosecution usually has significantly more resources at their disposal for evidence collection, analysis, and presentation, including resources for trial consultants, expert witnesses, and a legal staff. Only with the relatively rare wealthy defendant are the players in equal standing in terms of resources available.

Police officers and investigators often express a fair amount of contempt toward the judicial process and defense attorneys in particular. Some studies have shown that dealing with the courts is one of the more stressful aspects of a police officer's job (see Brown and Campbell [1994]). One likely reason for this is that judges and defense attorneys are in a position and have the responsibility to review and question the actions of police officers. Defense attorneys often test the evidence in the case by testing the police. "In representing criminal defendants—especially guilty ones—it is often necessary to take the offensive against the government: to put the government on trial for *its* misconduct" (Dershowitz, 1982; p. xiv). As such, police officers may see defense attorneys as being on the side of criminals and an obstacle to justice. Clearly, defense attorneys are adversaries to the police/prosecution team.

Although problematic from the perspective of individual officers, from a bigger perspective, the process of testing the evidence is necessary to increase the chances of a fair and just outcome. The lack of a vigorous defense is one of the common features in many miscarriage-of-justice cases, as seen in the introduction to this chapter (and as discussed later). It must be noted, however, that an adequate test of the evidence through a vigorous defense is not a guarantee that fairness and justice will prevail. Defense attorneys may mount a vigorous defense and their clients may still be convicted for crimes they did not commit (e.g., the Central Park jogger case). In addition, on probably quite rare occasions, a vigorous test of the evidence can actually result in justice being denied—in a guilty subject being set free. Because all defendants—both guilty and innocent—are entitled to a vigorous test of the evidence, this is a risk that is inherent in the process and, as noted by Dershowitz (1982), a small price to pay for our civil liberties. It is the nature of the game.

Reasons for Errors in Justice Outcomes

Miscarriages of justice—be they in the form of innocent subjects being punished or guilty subjects going free—occur for a variety of reasons, the most significant of which are discussed in the following sections. The more of these circumstances that are present in a particular case, the more likely a bad outcome will result.

Police Misconduct and Incompetence

When the police are reckless or neglectful in searching for and collecting evidence; when they conduct illegal searches and seizures, conduct inadequate interviews of witnesses, use inappropriate or misleading methods of eyewitness identification; and when they use coercive interrogation techniques that lead to coerced confessions, the evidence collected in the case will be of poor quality. Bad investigations produce bad evidence, which may contribute to bad outcomes. Consider the case of Eddie Joe Lloyd presented in the introduction to this chapter. The police tricked (or otherwise coerced) Lloyd into confessing to the murder. The outcome was tragic—a man spent seventeen years in prison for a crime he did not commit. To understand the gravity of the situation, put yourself in the position of Lloyd. Seventeen years of your life spent in prison for a crime *that you did not commit*.

Police misconduct and incompetence is common in false conviction cases (see Conners et al. [1996], Rattner, [1988], and www.innocenceproject.org). Periodically, accounts of investigative misconduct by police officials come to light. The instances that are widely publicized are, not surprisingly, quite shocking. For instance, between 1984 and 1992, several state troopers from New York State were found to have falsified fingerprint evidence on a wide-scale basis. According to prosecutors, in one double-murder case, an investigator lifted a suspect's fingerprint from the metal rim of a fingerprint cardholder and then testified in court that he found the fingerprint on a countertop at the crime scene. The defendant was convicted and sentenced to fifty years to life in prison. The conviction has been subsequently vacated and a new trial has been set. In another case, a state trooper removed fragments of a bumper sticker from the defendant's car and then testified in court that they were found at the scene of the robbery (Dershowitz, 1996; Teitell, 1994).

Not only might *actual* investigative misconduct relating directly to a specific case and particular evidence lead to a bad or questionable outcome, so too might *perceived* misconduct on the part of the police and even in a case that does not relate directly to the one at hand. Consider the extraordinary example of the Simpson investigation. An overwhelming amount of evidence was collected in the investigation and it pointed to Simpson as the murderer. This mountain of evidence was undermined by police perjury and incompetence, and strategic lawyering on the part of the defense counsel team. As explained by Dershowitz (1996), two lies on the part of investigators cast a shadow on all the evidence in the case and eventually led to the acquittal of Simpson on all charges.

The first likely lie related to the reason for the detectives' initial search and seizure of evidence from Simpson's property. After the bodies were discovered outside Nicole Brown Simpson's house, detectives went to Simpson's house. Once at the house, they noticed blood on the white Bronco sport utility vehicle parked outside the property. Unable to gain entry to the property, Detective Fuhrman climbed the wall, then unlocked the gate and let the other detectives in. Additional evidence was then discovered and collected (including the bloody glove found by Detective Fuhrman). This search was conducted without a warrant because, as explained by Detective Vannatter in court, "O.J. Simpson was not considered a suspect at the time." The legality of the search without a warrant was questionable and the conclusion that Simpson was not a suspect was hard to believe. What better suspect could there have been than the ex-husband who was known to have been involved in domestic violence with the victim in the past? If Simpson was considered a suspect, as he really likely was, and the detectives entered the property to obtain evidence without a warrant, the defense argued that the search was unlawful and the resulting evidence should be excluded. The judge allowed the evidence to be included but the damage was already done—the jury had doubts about whether the detectives were telling the truth about the reasons for that initial search.

The second and more significant lie was when Detective Fuhrman denied under oath in the trial that he previously used the "n-word" and that he previously made statements about the appropriateness of racism and police brutality. The allegations were subsequently proved to be true by the defense counsel through witness accounts and audio tapes. (Fuhrman was subsequently charged with perjury. He pleaded no contest and was fined $200 and sentenced to three years of probation.) One of the more inflammatory statements made by Fuhrman on the tapes was as follows:

> Now it is funny because guys in Internal Affairs go, Mark, you can do just about anything. Get in a bar fight. We'd love to investigate just some good ol' boy beating up a nigger in a bar. No problem, not even any marks, Dana. Just body shots. Did you ever try to find a bruise on a nigger? It is pretty tough, huh? (Dershowitz, 1996; p. 54).

The critical question that the jurors had to consider was: If Fuhrman is a racist and he lied in court about his previous actions, what else is he lying about? Maybe he did plant the glove on Simpson's property. Maybe other evidence was planted too. Maybe Simpson *was* framed.

Along with the lies, or likely lies, told by the investigators in court, the sloppy evidence collection procedures compounded the problem. In particular, four significant mistakes were made in handling the physical evidence in the Simpson case. First, the police used a blanket from Nicole's house to cover the bodies. This cast doubt on the hair and fiber evidence said to have been recovered from the bodies. Second, from the records kept, it appeared that some of the blood drawn from Simpson for DNA analysis purposes was missing. Third, it was determined that Detective Vannatter took the blood drawn from Simpson back to the crime scene. Finally, some of the blood evidence at the crime scene was recovered only weeks after the homicides had occurred. Clearly, these errors, compounded with the lies, cast a shadow on the evidence. As explained by Dershowitz (1996), it is no wonder that the jurors found reasonable doubt.

Prosecutorial Misconduct and Incompetence

Another reason for justice gone bad is prosecutorial misconduct and incompetence. Prosecutors exercise considerable discretion in deciding how cases should be processed and prosecuted. When this discretion is abused—when exculpatory evidence is suppressed, when other evidence is destroyed, when witnesses who are known to be unreliable and to offer perjured testimony are used, and when evidence is fabricated—the rules of the game are violated and justice may likely be sacrificed. Rattner (1988) explains:

> If a single reason had to be isolated that pervades large numbers of [false conviction] cases, it could probably be described as police and prosecutorial overzealousness. . . . The desire to obtain a conviction when one believes that the man at the bar is guilty may lead to the temptation to use improper, unethical, and illegal means to obtain that conviction. (p. 289)

This is probably most true in high-profile, well-publicized cases for which the prosecution team is under heightened pressure and scrutiny to solve the crime and to deliver justice.

In addition, prosecutorial *incompetence* may also contribute to bad judicial outcomes. Consider once again, the case of O.J. Simpson. As stated by Vincent Bugliosi, a former lead prosecutor in the Los Angeles County District Attorney's Office, "The prosecution of O.J. Simpson was the most incompetent criminal prosecution that I have ever seen. By far" (Dershowitz, 1996; p. 179). In particular, one of the critical errors made by the prosecution included the decision to try the case in downtown Los Angeles, which led to the selection of a jury pool more likely to favor the defense. The jury that was selected by the attorneys to hear the case was probably more receptive to the defense position than the prosecution position even before opening statements were even presented. The jury in the case consisted of eight black women, two white women, one black man, and one Latino man. On the basis of a 264-item questionnaire completed by each member of the jury pool, it was known that the twelve jurors selected for the case were all Democrats, two were college graduates, only one read a newspaper regularly, five said that they or someone in their family had a negative experience with the police, and nine thought that Simpson was less likely to be a murderer because he had been a football star (Dershowitz, 1996). As argued by Dershowitiz (1996), the prosecution probably lost the case even before the trial began.

Several other critical mistakes were made by the prosecution team. For instance, the prosecution often used poor strategy in presenting evidence. For example, the decision was made to allow Detective Fuhrman to testify even though Marcia Clark, the lead prosecutor in the case, knew that he was going to have to perjure himself should he be asked about his racial views and previous related statements. In another instance, at one point in the trial Simpson was asked by one of the prosecuting attorneys to try on the leather glove allegedly found on his property. As he struggled with the glove, it was clear that it did not fit on his hand. This led to the then-famous mantra from Johnny Cochran to the jury, "If the glove doesn't fit, you must acquit." Other mistakes consisted of the prosecutors disregarding the jury consultant report that indicated that Clark would be unpopular among the jurors, and that Clark showed a high level of stress and frustration in the courtroom (Dershowitz, 1996).

Defense Attorney Misconduct and Incompetence

The U.S. Constitution requires that those individuals accused of crimes be afforded legal counsel and be provided a vigorous defense. As noted, without this ingredient, the adversarial process ceases to exist. The game becomes totally lopsided. Without even a possibility of the evidence being tested, police and prosecutors may (mis)behave with impunity. An unjust outcome may be the result. This issue is of most concern with defense attorneys who

Why was it a mistake on the part of the prosecution to have OJ try on the glove in court?
CORBIS

represent indigent clients. Common are incredible case loads that prevent attorneys from spending the time that each defendant deserves. Lack of time to prepare a defense may have obvious implications. A lack of a vigorous (or even informed) defense is evident in several of the cases highlighted in the introduction to the chapter.

At the other extreme, it may be reasonable to ask whether a vigorous defense can go too far. In the O.J. Simpson case, the defense attorneys were criticized a number of times for their actions. In particular, race was made a major issue; for some it was unjustifiably the central issue. One of the most controversial actions was when Johnny Cochran compared Mark Fuhrman with Adolf Hitler during his closing arguments:

> There was another man not too long ago in the world who had these same views, who wanted to burn people, who had racist views and ultimately had the power over people in his country. People didn't care. People said he is just crazy. He is just a half-baked painter. They didn't do anything about it. This man, this scourge, became one of the worst people in the history of this world. Adolf Hitler, because people didn't care or didn't try to stop him. He had the power over his racism and his anti-religion. Nobody wanted to stop him and it ended up in World War II. And so Fuhrman, Fuhrman wants to take all black people now and burn them or bomb them. That is genocidal racism (Dershowitz, 1996; p. 119).

Another example of a controversial action on the part of the defense counsel was that, for all practical purposes, Simpson's house was "staged" prior to the visit by the jurors. For instance, the picture of Simpson and his white girlfriend at the time, Paula Barbieri, was taken down and replaced with a Norman Rockwell picture of a black girl being escorted to a southern school by federal marshals. Pictures of Simpson and his white golfing buddies were replaced with pictures of black people. A bible was placed on a table in the living room. All these changes were part of a "redecoration" of Simpson's house (Dershowitz, 1996). Neither the reference to Adolf Hitler nor the redecoration, however, were ruled to be unlawful by the judge.

Inept Judges

We all know what happens when referees are biased and favor one team over the other. It is no longer a fair game. So it is with the game of justice. Judges who allow police, prosecutorial, and defense misconduct are working against the desired outcome of justice. Examples abound of uninformed and biased legal decisions made by judges. Most judges are elected and realize that "soft on crime" criticism from an opponent may lead to an unsuccessful reelection. Judges are generally reluctant to enforce the technicalities of the law and to take action against prosecutors and the police (e.g., for perjury). In the O.J. Simpson case, however, it has been suggested that the judge, Lance Ito, was too permissive with allowing defense counsel arguments, and it has been reported that the judge agreed to be assigned the trial despite a potential conflict of interest that may have affected his ability to rule fairly in the case. (Judge Ito's wife, a commander in the LAPD, had numerous run-ins with Detective Fuhrman, to the point that Judge Ito may have wished revenge on Fuhrman; see Fuhrman [1997].)

Incompetent and Corrupt Expert Witnesses

The testimony provided by experts in court can be quite influential on the final outcome of the case. In addition, because of the manner in which experts are often compensated and the process by which they are hired, they may have incentive to provide testimony that is not necessarily truthful. Case in point: Dr. Ralph Erdmann. Erdmann was a medical examiner who traveled from county to county in Texas to conduct autopsies. He claimed to have performed more than 400 autopsies a year for more than ten years. The case that exposed his misconduct involved a man who was found dead in his home. Erdmann indicated that the autopsy revealed that he died as a result of a cocaine overdose. The man's family questioned this finding. In reviewing the autopsy report, it was noted that the man's spleen had been examined and weighed. The only problem was . . . the man's spleen had been removed four years earlier! On further examination of the body, no autopsy incision marks were found. A subsequent autopsy showed that the man died of a heart attack. Investigation into other autopsies that he claimed to have had performed indicated that many were not conducted. In 1992, Erdmann pleaded no contest to seven felony counts involving fraudulent autopsies (Teitell, 1994). As another example, consider Fred Zain. Zain was a serologist in West Virginia and later in Texas who fabricated evidence regarding blood, hair, and semen samples. More than 1,000 convictions in the two states have come under review because of his documented perjured testimony (recall Zain was also the serologist involved in the Glen Woodall case summarized in the introduction to this chapter) (Teitell, 1994). There are numerous other examples of when expert witnesses have lied about their credentials to be retained by attorneys for purposes of expert testimony (e.g., Hansen [2001]). Lawyers and especially judges need to be aware of the potential problem and be able to identify fraudulent experts before they provide their testimony and before the damage is done.

Perjured and Unreliable Testimony Delivered by Lay Witnesses

Witnesses may have a variety of reasons for providing intentionally misleading or erroneous information to the police. The reasons range from desire to get revenge on an enemy, to covering their own illegal behaviors, to protecting someone they care about. In addition, as noted, even well-meaning witnesses have the ability to provide seriously misleading information, particularly through eyewitness identification testimony. Examples of faulty eyewitness testimony are plentiful, and the ramifications of those identifications are clear when reviewing cases of false convictions. In nearly every case in which there was a false conviction, excluding homicides, inaccurate eyewitness identifications played a role in the outcome. As discussed in Chapter 7, this problem can be at least partially remedied by changes in eyewitness identification procedures.

Inept Juries

Another reason for justice gone bad is inept juries. The trial process depends heavily on juries to consider the evidence in the case conscientiously and carefully and reach a decision based on instructions provided by the judge. In many respects, the jury is the final link in the justice chain. If the jurors do not make decisions in good faith, bad outcomes may result. Good faith may be inhibited by fear of their personal safety, fear of others' safety, or concern about the ramifications of their verdict. Jurors may also be affected by extraneous information and evidence. It is important to remember that juries play a passive role in the trial process. They are there to hear and consider the evidence as it is presented. As for the jury in the O.J. Simpson trial, if Simpson was in fact responsible for the murders, the verdict of not guilty should probably not be considered the fault of the jurors. More likely, the verdict was a result of the actions of the police and the prosecution. The strategy of the defense counsel also certainly played a role. As noted by one of the jurors in the case after the trial (quoted by Dershowitz, 1996), "As far as I am concerned, Mr. Simpson would have been behind bars if the police work had been done well" (p. 183). Another juror said "In spite of it all, I still feel he's guilty. But the evidence just was not there and I had no other choice. He did it, they just screwed up on the evidence" (p. 184). Jurors can only work with the evidence they are presented.

The Role of Investigative Reports

Reports are written documents that contain information relating to a criminal incident and investigation. They are used to document the particulars of the crime and the investigation. As illustrated in the reports included in the introduction to Chapters 7 and 12, incident reports typically contain basic information about the criminal incident (e.g., who, what, where, when, and maybe why) and the evidence in the case (e.g., witness statements, the presence of physical evidence, etc.). Incident reports may also include information on the offender's MO, and descriptions of the suspect, the suspect's vehicle, and the property taken. Incident reports are most often written by patrol officers at the conclusion of the initial investigation. Supplementary reports most often consist of a narrative that describes in more detail the leads in the case, the source of the leads, the result of the leads, and statements from suspects. Supplementary reports are most often completed by detectives on an ongoing basis throughout the duration of a follow-up investigation.

Across agencies, reporting and record-keeping processes vary considerably, as do the actual reports that are completed by investigators. In some agencies the process is largely computer automated, and in others it is not. The one consistent dimension across agencies regarding investigative reports is that much of investigators' time is spent reading and writing them.

The fact that much time is spent on reports speaks to the importance of reports in the investigative process. Reports have several functions. First, in documenting the nature of the crime and the evidence in the case, reports help provide continuity across investigators and assist investigators in making informed resource allocation decisions regarding cases, such as whether the case should receive a follow-up investigation. Another function of reports is to provide a basis on which prosecutors can become familiar with the details of the crime and ensuing investigation. Reports serve as a basis for prosecutorial decision making about whether to pursue charges against a suspect, and what those charges should be. Third, reports are used in court by investigators to help refresh their memories about the offense and the investigation. It is common that cases first go to trial months after arrests were made. As such, an investigator's testimony in court may only be as good as his or her reports (see *American Bar Association Journal*, [2002]). Finally, reports are used by defense attorneys to provide a means by which to become familiar with the nature of the investigation conducted by investigators. It is in this manner that poorly written reports can be used against officers who wrote them. Investigative reports are frequently used by defense attorneys in the cross-examination of police officers (Snortum et al., 1990). For all these reasons, it is critically important that reports be written well, that they be accurate, and that they be complete. Police officers and investigators typically receive numerous hours of training regarding the technical aspects and requirements of report writing in their respective agencies.

The Role of Testimony in Court

All evidence presented in court is delivered through or accompanied by testimony—statements made in court by individuals under oath to tell the truth. Witnesses provide testimony. Witnesses can be classified as either lay witnesses or expert witnesses. Lay witnesses can testify only to the facts of the case as they see them. Commonly, lay witnesses testify regarding their actions and observations. To the extent that judgments can be offered by lay witnesses, the judgments are related to the particular case at hand (e.g., "in my judgment, he was pretty drunk when he said he was going to kill her"). Police officers and investigators are usually considered lay witnesses in court. Expert witnesses on the other hand can express their opinions in court. Expert witnesses are usually persons who are skilled or knowledgeable in a particular subject. Their testimony is supposed to educate the jury (or judge) on a particular issue (e.g., battered women's syndrome). An expert's opinion is advisory to the jury.

Expert Testimony

The use of expert witnesses in court is quite controversial. Expert witnesses are most often hired and compensated by either the defense counsel or the prosecution. In trying to advocate either the guilt or innocence of the defendant, the attorneys would, of course, desire testimony from an expert that supports their respective position. It is likely that if an expert is unable to offer a supportive opinion, the attorney will look for a different expert who could provide such testimony. As such, if an expert witness cannot offer testimony to support the attorney's position, the expert will not be hired. Although one may legitimately question the appropriateness of this arrangement, what is even more problematic is that experts may have considerable "economic" reasons to conform their opinions to the position of the attorney who is requesting such testimony. Expert witnesses are often very well compensated. It is quite common for expert witnesses to receive $200 to $300 an hour or more relating to their work on a case. As a result, a relevant question is: Are expert witnesses conveyors of the truth or are they hired guns?

Rarely are scientific opinions uniformly and unambiguously supportive of a one-sided conclusion. Attorneys who request the testimony of experts must realize that this, in fact, is the case. Accordingly, the most desirable and ethically defensible role for the expert is that of an impartial educator who comes to a conclusion and provides testimony based on a well-informed understanding of the issue in question (McCloskey et al., 1986). In practice, the expert's testimony that is the most supportive of the desired position is usually elicited during the direct examination of the witness, and a more balanced view emerges as a result of the cross-examination. In addition, jurors (and judges) may find the background, experience, credentials, and expertise of expert witnesses relevant in judging their credibility and their believability.

The use of expert testimony in legal proceedings is also potentially problematic for other reasons as well. In particular, the sometimes complicated opinions offered by the expert may be misunderstood by jurors. Indeed, because testimony of an expert witness may be shaped by the questions asked by the prosecution and defense attorneys, there is considerable opportunity for testimony from even a well-intended "impartial educator" to be misunderstood. In addition, although it is possible that a fair, honest, and knowledgeable expert could provide an accurate opinion based on the available scientific research on the issue, it is also possible that this "truthful" opinion could be invalidated sometime in the future by subsequent research on the issue. In essence, how can experts testify regarding the "truth" when "truth" in science is always changing? An understanding of these issues may provide a better appreciation of the role of expert testimony in the legal process.

The Cross-Examination

As noted earlier, to test the evidence, defense attorneys often "test" the police. This "test" often occurs during a cross-examination of the police witness. Investigators almost always testify as part of the prosecution case. As such, the prosecuting attorney conducts a direct examination of the investigator to elicit the facts of the case and the corresponding evidence against the defendant. At the conclusion of the direct examination, the defense attorney has the opportunity to question the investigator, to conduct a cross-examination. The purpose of the cross-examination is to convince the jury that the investigator should not be believed or to convince the jury that certain evidence presented by the investigator should not be believed. In essense, the goal is to "impeach" the witness.

A defense attorney can attempt to impeach a police witness in several ways (Stutler, 1997). First, the defense attorney can question the witness about the legality of the actions

Preparation is critical in counter-ing a cross-examination.

taken, the investigator's knowledge of the law, and the legal justifications for the actions taken. This line of questioning can be used to lay a foundation for an argument that the evidence was collected unlawfully. An example of this line of questioning was the cross-examination of Detective Vannatter in the O.J. Simpson trial that related to the reasons for the initial search of Simpson's property without a warrant.

Second, the defense attorney can attempt to discredit the investigator by attacking the quality of the investigator's reports, the accuracy of those reports, inconsistencies that may be found within the reports, or inconsistencies between accounts provided by other officers, witnesses, or victims and the investigator's reports. Any testimony from anyone that is inconsistent with what is contained in investigators' reports is very likely to be an area of interest and questioning by defense attorneys. Consider the following exchange:

DEFENSE ATTORNEY: Officer, did you search for fingerprints at the time of your initial investigation of the robbery?

OFFICER: I did not.

DEFENSE ATTORNEY: Indeed, there is no such reference to such an activity in your report, is there?

OFFICER: No, there is not.

DEFENSE ATTORNEY: We heard from the bank manager, however, that you did dust for fingerprints. He was one hundred percent sure that you did. Why wasn't this in your report, officer? Do you not remember whether or not you conducted a thorough investigation in this robbery?

Clearly, the intent of such an exchange is to try to discredit the officer based on a perceived discrepancy between the victim's account and the officer's account. The discrepancy may be small, relatively insignificant, and even explainable, but it may be the focus of questioning nonetheless. Or, at the very least, the intent may be to confuse or fluster the investigator through the use of double negative, repetitive, or compound questions.

Another method used to "impeach" an investigator is to call into question statements of fact, opinions, and the justifications for those opinions, most often as those facts and opinions are stated in reports. Consider this exchange:

DEFENSE ATTORNEY: Officer, you wrote on page two of your report that "entry was gained through the bedroom window that was left unlocked." Is that correct?

OFFICER: Yes.

DEFENSE ATTORNEY: How do you know that the window was not locked?

OFFICER: Because it appeared to me that if the lock on the window was locked, the window would have to have been broken in order to open it. And the window was not broken.

DEFENSE ATTORNEY: Do you realize officer that the lock was broken prior to the incident in question?

OFFICER: No.

DEFENSE ATTORNEY: That window could not have been locked because the lock did not work. Did you put that in your report officer? What else didn't you put in your report officer?

During this exchange, the defense attorney is not even contesting whether the window was locked. The defense attorney is just highlighting the fact that the officer did not know that the lock was broken. From here, the defense attorney suggests that the investigation was incompetently performed. Even if objections are raised by the prosecuting attorney regarding this line of questioning, the intent on the part of the defense attorney is to discredit the officer by questioning a seemingly simple statement that may not have even had an important role in the investigation. The lesson here is that investigators should draw conclusions very carefully and should write reports carefully.

A final method of impeaching an investigator witness is to call into question the investigator's honesty and credibility. If the defense attorney can show that the investigator lacks honesty or lacks credibility, then the opportunity exists for the defense attorney to call into question the honesty and credibility of the officer in the current case. Consider how the defense attorneys cast a shadow on the evidence discovered by Mark Fuhrman in the O.J. Simpson investigation based on Fuhrman's past conduct and his attempt to cover that bad behavior through perjury. As another example, during the investigation of the kidnaping and murder of Danielle van Dam in San Diego in February 2002, the defendant's attorneys requested and received access to the personnel files of the police officers who conducted the investigation, apparently in an attempt to find evidence of previous misconduct that might relate to their conduct in the current investigation. Apparently, no useful information was found in the files because no such evidence was produced by defense attorneys during the trial. The lesson here is that past misconduct can come back to haunt you.

The strategies commonly used by defense attorneys in cross-examining investigators may help investigators in preparing for their testimony. "Indeed, the right time for law enforcement officers to contemplate the defense's strategy is at the beginning of an investigation, not while they are sitting on the witness stand" (Stutler, 1997; p. 5).

The Role of the Jury

Juries are sometimes much maligned, especially when they find a defendant not guilty. As discussed, the role of the jury is to hear and consider the evidence as it is presented and decide whether the prosecution proved beyond a reasonable doubt that a crime was committed and that the defendant committed it. It is important to understand that juries are *not* asked to decide if the defendant committed the crime; rather, they are asked to decide whether there is *proof* beyond a reasonable doubt that the defendant committed the crime. As such, a not guilty verdict does not necessarily mean that the defendant did not commit the crime, just that the prosecution did not present evidence beyond a reasonable doubt that the defendant committed the crime.

The trial process and the jury system is a rather strange way to determine the truth—a method unlike any other. It is, nonetheless, the way of the American justice system. It is an odd methodology of truth finding because the rules are so artificial. The exclusionary rule, double jeopardy, beyond a reasonable doubt—nowhere can we find a truth-finding methodology that is so infused with values. In the case of the trial (and criminal justice) process, the predominant value reflected by the process is freedom from government (Dershowitz, 1996). In addition, another oddity is that the evidence presented to the jury is not necessarily inclusive of all evidence collected. For example, in the Danielle van Dam case, jurors never heard that Westerfield, his attorneys, and the prosecuting attorneys were close to reaching a plea bargain for which Westerfield would tell authorities where to find the girl's body in exchange for a sentence of "life in prison without parole" instead of the death penalty. The tentative plea agreement was nixed when volunteer searchers found the body on a rural road three weeks after she disappeared. In the O.J. Simpson case, jurors did not hear anything about the interrogation of Simpson conducted by Lange and Vannatter (Chapter 8), nor did they hear the testimony from the pathologist who conducted the autopsies, and they heard nothing about the contents of the car in which Simpson rode when he was supposed to turn himself in to the police (the police found his passport, nearly $9,000 in cash and traveler's checks, a loaded gun, and a disguise in the car). For whatever reason, strategic or otherwise, this potentially influential evidence was not introduced at trial. Furthermore, the process of selecting jurors is a rather unusual one, at least in terms of a truth-finding methodology. Through the voir dire process—specifically, peremptory challenges—attorneys have some discretion in deciding who is to be included in the jury. In using the peremptory challenge, the objective is not to select a fair jury, but a biased one! Attorneys attempt to identify and reject individuals for the jury who they expect will be unsympathetic to their side. The only rule is that race is not to be used as a basis on which to make exclusions (*Batson* v. *Kentucky* 1986).

Numerous research studies have examined the factors that influence jury decision making. Some of the more notable findings are presented here. First, jurors' decisions are based on both legal (i.e., legally relevant; e.g., evidence) and extralegal (i.e., legally irrelevant; e.g., victim characteristics) factors. For instance, in a study conducted by Visher (1987), a series of rape trials were conducted with mock jurors. It was discovered that testimony regarding the victim's careless behavior was the most influential in verdicts, followed by an argument from the defense that the victim's story was implausible, the use of a weapon by the offender, evidence of force having been used against the victim, testimony relating to the victim's sexual activity outside of marriage, and physical evidence. Overall, physical evidence may have played a relatively small influence on the jurors' decisions because in rape, of course, consent is often the most critical element to be proved.

Second, the defendant's and victim's characteristics often affect jurors' decisions. In particular, attractive defendants have been found to be judged less severely than unattractive defendants. In addition, when victims are judged by jurors to have poor character or to exhibit poor judgment, the defendant is more likely to receive lenient treatment (see Visher [1987]).

Third, research has shown that detailed testimony from witnesses is more persuasive than general testimony, even if the details are about irrelevant information. Furthermore, the influence of detailed testimony is often generalized to other testimony. For example, detailed testimony from a witness about the things she purchased at the store prior to the robbery tends to make the eyewitness identification made by the witness more credible and influential in jurors' minds. The effect of detailed testimony is most pronounced when an opposing witness testifies that he or she cannot remember the same details. In essence, all else being equal, whoever provides the most detailed testimony tends to be the most believable. Bell and Loftus (1989) refer to this phenomenon as *trivial persuasion*.

Fourth, jurors tend to perceive testimony selectively. In general, jurors tend to pay more attention to testimony that confirms their original beliefs about the guilt or innocence of the defendant (Carlson and Edward, 2001). Jurors often have at least a tentative judgment about guilt or innocence after the opening statements have concluded. Evidence that supports their initial judgment is then perceived as most significant. This research finding clearly highlights the importance of well-articulated and comprehensive opening statements during the trial process.

Fifth, the research finding that eyewitness testimony is a strong determinant of verdicts, despite its unreliability, is well established in the empirical literature (see Cutler et al., 1990). In addition, research has also shown that jurors are insensitive to the various factors that may affect the reliability of eyewitness evidence. For instance, eyewitness identifications that involve suggestive lineup instructions are just as influential as identifications that involve nonsuggestive lineup instructions (Cutler et al., 1988).

Sixth, research has shown that physical evidence is more influential in determining verdicts than eyewitness testimony. The highest rate of guilty verdicts in mock trials was achieved when there was both strong physical evidence and strong eyewitness evidence (eighty-seven percent). The second highest rate of guilty verdicts was with strong physical evidence and weak eyewitness evidence (eighty-three percent), followed by weak physical evidence and strong eyewitness evidence (seventy percent), and weak physical and weak eyewitness evidence (thirty-seven percent) (Skolnick and Shaw, 2001).

Seventh, jurors' general demographic characteristics are not uniformly significant in determining their verdicts. Rather, demographic characteristics of jurors are more meaningful in case-specific situations (e.g., race of jurors is most influential when race is an issue in the case). In addition, demographic factors of jurors affect deliberation performance and ability to recall evidence. In particular, high social status and educated jurors tend to dominate the deliberation process and are more persuasive as a result (see Visher [1987]).

Finally, with regard to how jurors judge expert witnesses, Cooper and Neuhaus (2000), found that the experts *most* likely to be believed by jurors were those who were highly paid but who did not testify frequently. The least likely to be believed were experts who were highly paid and who testified frequently. These individuals were perceived as hired guns. Clearly, factors beside the testimony itself can have a substantial impact on how the testimony is viewed by jurors.

This chapter highlights issues relating to the nature of the court process and the investigator's role in it. There is often much misunderstanding among investigators in this area. Effective investigators must be able to understand the complexities of the process, recognize its pitfalls and booby traps, and they must be able to overcome the challenges that it presents.

Questions for Discussion and Review

1. Why did the court trials of Glen Woodall, Marvin Anderson, Eddie Joe Lloyd, and the Central Park rapists result in bad outcomes? What is an important lesson learned from these, and other, miscarriage-of-justice cases?

2. Why is it important that defense attorneys provide a vigorous defense for their clients? Can a vigorous defense go too far? Explain.

3. What are the reasons why justice sometimes "goes bad"?

4. Specifically, how can police misconduct and incompetence lead to bad judicial outcomes?

5. How can police perjury lead to bad outcomes?

6. What are the purposes of investigative reports?

7. What is the purpose of using expert witnesses in court? Why is the use of expert witnesses often controversial?

8. Beyond the controversies, why else may the use of experts in court be problematic?

9. What is the purpose of a cross-examination of a witness? In what ways may a defense attorney attempt to impeach a police witness?

10. Why is the trial process and jury system a rather strange way of determining the truth?

11. What are the factors that influence jury decision making? What are the implications of these findings with regard to the police who conduct criminal investigations and provide testimony in court?

12. What is trivial persuasion?

Related Internet Sites

www.innocenceproject.org.

This is the address of the Innocence Project, a non-profit legal clinic at the Benjamin N. Cardozo School of Law. The project handles cases for which postconviction DNA evidence can yield proof of innocence. Case profiles are provided for each of the cases for which a defendant was exonerated.

www.fbi.gov/publications/leb/leb.htm

Through this web site you can get free access to the *FBI Law Enforcement Bulletin*, a publication that contains articles on law enforcement and criminal investigation-related issues.

www.ojp.usdoj.gov/nij/

This is the address of the NIJ home page. NIJ is the research arm of the U.S. Department of Justice. The site contains a wealth of information on policing, criminal investigative issues, and the criminal justice system. Particularly informative is the publications link, where you can get free access to reports of research studies that have been funded by the NIJ.

www.uscourts.gov

This is the site of the federal judiciary with links to the U.S. Supreme Court as well as the other federal courts.

THE FUTURE OF CRIMINAL INVESTIGATION

OBJECTIVES

After reading this chapter you will be able to

- Summarize the investigation of the terrorist hijackings on September 11, 2001
- Discuss why an understanding of history is important in making predictions about the future
- Describe how the system of policing reflected society during the agricultural wave, industrial wave, and the information wave
- Identify the "crises" that prompted change in police systems during the mid 1850s, early 1920s, and the 1960s
- Identify the most significant "new" threats and demands being faced by the police today
- Discuss terrorism as a "new" criminal threat

- Discuss technology as a "new" demand on the police
- Discuss the Posse Comitatus Act and how it may relate to the future of policing
- Discuss what is meant by "the militarization of the police"
- Identify the most significant new technological tools of criminal investigation
- Discuss biometric technologies and how they relate to criminal investigation
- Discuss the relationship between technology of the future and privacy issues
- Discuss what is meant by a "maximum-security society"

IMPORTANT TERMS

Agricultural wave, industrial wave, information wave

Terrorism as a criminal threat

Technology as a demand on the police

Militarization of the police

Police paramilitary units

CODIS

Biometrics

Verichip

Facial recognition systems

Smart ID cards

Technological tools for "seeing"

Maximum-security society

INTRODUCTION

Nineteen motivated men. A few box-cutter knives. Four hijacked commercial airplanes. Sixty thousand gallons of jet fuel. Logistical and training support from the al-Qaida terrorist organization. Several hundred thousand dollars. The World Trade Center and the Pentagon, filled with people. On September 11, 2001, these ingredients came together to create a disaster of previously unseen proportions. The criminal investigation that has followed is arguably the largest and most complex investigation in our history. In fact, in many respects, "the" investigation has actually become a multitude of interrelated investigations, all of which represent the new "war on terrorism." More than 7,000 agents from the FBI and other agencies are assigned to the matter. Information uncovered as a result of the investigation has led investigators to numerous foreign countries and has led to U.S. military action in Afghanistan. Given the magnitude of the matter, summarizing it in just a few pages is difficult, to say the least. To complicate matters even more, many of the details of the investigation are of a classified nature. Given its significance, however, any informed discussion of the future of American policing and criminal investigation would be incomplete without it.

On September 11, 2001, at 7:59 AM American Airlines Flight 11 departed Boston Logan Airport en route to Los Angeles with ninety-two people aboard (passengers and crew). It crashed into the north tower of the World Trade Center at 8:45 AM. At 8:14 AM, United Airlines Flight 175 left Boston Logan en route to Los Angeles with sixty-five people aboard. It crashed into the south tower of the World Trade Center at 9:03 AM. At 8:10 AM, American Flight 77 left Dulles International Airport in Washington, DC, for Los Angeles with sixty-four people aboard. It crashed into the Pentagon at 9:39 AM. United Flight 93 left Newark International Airport en route to San Francisco at 8:01 AM with forty-four people aboard. It crashed in a cornfield in Pennsylvania at 10:03 AM. It is believed that it was headed for the White House before passengers attempted to take control of the aircraft from the hijackers. In total, more than 3,000 people were killed as a result of the terrorist acts.

It was known by authorities even before the first plane crashed into the World Trade Center that at least three planes were under the control of hijackers. Passengers and crew on the planes made phone calls to loved ones after the planes were hijacked. The phone calls made from the planes described the hijackers as "Arab men" with knives. One was said to have a red box strapped to his chest that was believed to be a bomb. Besides the frantic phone calls, it was also clear from communications received by air traffic controllers from some of the planes that hijackings were in progress. As the planes crashed, one by one, the enormity of the situation became obvious to everyone.

The first objective of investigators in the wake of the hijackings was to stop or interrupt any additional hijackings that were imminent. Air travel on September 11 was ordered to halt. Planes that were in the air were ordered to land and planes on the

Two of the hijackers, Atta and Alomari, are seen on videotape passing through airport security.

ground were prohibited from taking off. All grounded planes were then searched and passenger flight manifests were examined. As a result of the planes being searched, box cutters were found hidden on two other airplanes. Investigators believed at the time that, indeed, other planes were intended to be hijacked. It appeared that the hijackers had accomplices. Investigators discovered that two Arabic men who had been on a flight from Newark to San Antonio, but had landed in St. Louis because of the hijackings, boarded an Amtrak train from St. Louis to San Antonio. In Texas, these men were detained by the police. In their possession, the police found box cutters, a large quantity of cash, and hair coloring, among other items. Reportedly, these men were later released without charges. Other investigations began on airport workers in an effort to identify who may have assisted in the terrorist plot.

The second objective was to determine the identities of the presumed-dead hijackers. To do so, the passenger manifests from each of the hijacked planes were collected. From the information provided by passengers and crew before the planes crashed, investigators were already confident that they knew the hijackers were Middle Eastern men. On each of the manifests for Flight 93, Flight 11, Flight 175, and Flight 77 there were several Arabic names.[1] With the manifests in hand, investigators had names of suspects.[2] The airlines were also able to provide information to investigators about when and how these individuals purchased their tickets (all were one-way tickets, several were purchased with the same credit card, and most were purchased shortly before the flights). The credit card and flight manifests led investigators to addresses in Florida, New Jersey, and California. Investigations regarding these individuals were conducted in each of these places. Meanwhile, it was discovered that a suitcase checked for Flight 11 at Boston Logan by Mohamed Atta, one of the individuals identified as a hijacker, did not make the flight. The suitcase was opened and numerous items of interest were found including a suicide note, a copy of the Koran, an instructional video on flying commercial airliners, a fuel consumption calculator, a letter containing instructions to the hijackers in Arabic, and other personal belongings.

At about this same time, after hearing about the Arab hijackers, an individual contacted the police and told them about an argument that he had with several Arabic men in the parking lot at the Boston airport the morning of September 11. He described the car they were driving as a white Mitsubishi. The police found the car in the airport parking garage. Among the items of interest seized from the car was a flight training manual written in Arabic. Similarly, another vehicle identified as belonging to the hijackers was seized from Dulles Airport. Inside that vehicle the police found a Washington, DC, area map. Written on the map was the first name and phone number of Mohamed Abdi. When authorities contacted Abdi, he could not explain why his name was in the possession of the hijackers nor could investigators establish a link between Abdi and the hijackers. Also found in the car was a letter identical to the one found in Atta's suitcase. Days later, another copy of the same letter was found at the crash site of Flight 93 in Pennsylvania. A third rental car that was believed to be used by the hijackers was recovered from the Portland, Maine, airport (several hijackers made a connecting flight in Boston). Most leads led investigators to Florida. Searches of the hijackers' residences, along with interviews with landlords and neighbors, led to the discovery that many of the suspected hijackers had been enrolled in flight schools in Florida as well as other places in the country. It was discovered that the hijackers lived low-key, low-profile lives; they did not stand out in any significant way.

Further investigation of visa and immigration records revealed that none of the hijackers was born in America, nor were they American citizens. All were in the United States either legally with student or business travel visas, or illegally, with expired visas or without visas. At least one lived in the United States as far back as

---

[1] As it turned out, eighteen of the nineteen hijackers' names were listed on the manifests. Hani Seleh Hanjour was not listed on the Flight 77 manifest because he may not have even had a ticket.

[2] It was determined later that many of the hijackers used names obtained from stolen identities of individuals in Saudi Arabia, used aliases, or had common Arabic names. This factor in itself adds an extra dimension of complexity to the investigation.

1990, when he took an English class in Arizona, and another attended flight school in the United States as early as 1997.

As the investigation progressed, investigators realized that a man already in police custody was likely a player in the plot. Zacarias Moussaoui had been arrested by the INS on immigration charges August 17, 2001, after an instructor at a flight school in Minnesota became suspicious of him. Reportedly, Moussaoui was only interested in learning how to turn an aircraft; he was not interested in takeoffs or landings. It is now believed by investigators that Moussaoui was to be the fifth hijacker aboard Flight 93. As of 2003, Moussaoui is waiting trial on several counts of conspiracy to aid terrorists.

With the hijackers identified, analysts at the Central Intelligence Agency (CIA) realized that they had prior knowledge of several of these individuals and had actually been monitoring their foreign travels as far back as 2000. In the bombing of the U.S. Embassy in Nairobi, Africa, in 1998, one of the terrorists—the man who drove the truck filled with explosives to the embassy—was apprehended. He was questioned by the FBI and provided information about an al-Qaida safe house in Yemen, a "logistics center" of sorts where the African Embassy bombings were planned. The CIA monitored the house. The CIA intercepted phone conversations that alerted agents to a January 2000 meeting of al-Qaida terrorist operatives in Malaysia. Of the twelve individuals who attended the meeting, two were identified as Khalid Almihdhar and Nawaf Alhazmi. The CIA was aware that when Almihdhar and Alhazmi left the meeting in Malaysia, they were headed for the United States.[3]

In an attempt to identify other individuals who supported the hijackers, the FBI sent a notice to all U.S. banks requesting information on any transactions with twenty-one individuals identified on the FBI suspect list, nineteen of whom were believed to be the actual hijackers. Also included with this list were numerous addresses associated with the names. Reportedly, no large cash transfers were uncovered. Later attempts to "follow the money" were more productive. Most of the money received by the hijackers while in the United States appeared to have had a single overseas source.

In tracing the activities of each of the hijackers through credit card receipts, airline records, flight school records and enrollments, housing rental records, and INS

---

[3]Almihdhar and Alhazmi were two of the hijackers aboard Flight 77, which was flown into the Pentagon. Representatives of the FBI have said that they were not told by the CIA that these two individuals came to the United States. Representatives of the CIA have said that they did, in fact, relay this information to the FBI. Apparently, what neither the CIA nor the FBI knew at the time was that both these men were already living in San Diego for two months prior to the meeting in Malaysia. In mid 2000, Almihdhar left the United States for the Middle East. While he was away, his visa expired but the State Department consulate in Saudi Arabia issued him a new one. He returned to the United States on July 4, 2001. Meanwhile, Alhazmi moved to Phoenix and stayed with Hani Hanjour (who is believed to have piloted Flight 77). They moved to New Jersey on August 25.

records, investigators were led to Hamburg, Germany, where Atta and several of the other hijackers had earlier shared an apartment and attended the same university. The investigation in Germany led authorities to believe that the hijacking plan was probably first discussed and planned at that time. From there, travel by several of these individuals to Afghanistan and Pakistan, among other places, was uncovered. Links between the hijackers and the al-Qaida terrorist group led by Osama bin Laden became clear. In October 2001, the United States invaded Afghanistan in search of bin Laden and his associates.

During the course of the investigation, countless other leads, many of which were false or otherwise unexplained, were developed. For example, consider the following:

- Khalid S.S. Al Draibi was stopped by police ten miles north of Dulles Airport twelve hours after the planes crashed in New York and Washington. He was driving on the highway with a completely flat tire. When his car was searched, flight training manuals were found. Further investigation revealed that since he arrived in the United States in 1997, he used ten variations of his name, three social security numbers, and drivers' licenses from five different states. As of mid 2003, his possible role in the hijackings is still being investigated.

- It was discovered that two of the hijackers used credit cards that belonged to Dr. Al-Badr Al-Hazmi, a radiologist who lived in Texas, for various purchases. Interestingly, Al-Hazmi was missing from work on September 11 without explanation. It was eventually determined that he was a victim of theft and had no connection to the hijackers.

- Ahmed Badawi, a travel agent in Orlando who sold plane tickets to several of the hijackers, wired money on their behalf, and who cashed their checks, was also identified as a possible accomplice but he too was eventually released without charges.

- Nabil Almarabh was arrested September 30, 2001, in Chicago where he was working as a clerk in a liquor store. It was believed by the FBI that in the 1990s, Almarabh stayed at a home in Pakistan that was known to be used by terrorists. It was discovered by authorities that he lied about his relationship with a man sentenced to death in Jordan for plotting to blow up a hotel on New Year's Day in 2000. At the time he was arrested by the FBI, he was found to have in his possession $22,000 in cash and gems worth $25,000. It was determined that he entered the United States illegally at a crossing near Niagara Falls on June 27, 2001. He was deported on September 4, 2002, without further prosecution.

- In 2002, federal agents began investigating a fraudulent scheme whereby foreign (primarily Middle Eastern) students hired other people to take their "Test of English as a Foreign Language" exams—an exam often required of international students for admission into American colleges and universities. Agents conducted a search of a Virginia address where the suspected leader of the scheme, Fahad Alhajri, lived, and they found various items including flight manuals, flight school catalogs, a diagram of a plane striking the World Trade Center, a postcard with aerial pictures of the Pentagon, photos of people inside the World Trade Center, and a Rolodex of oil refineries. After extensive investigation, investigators came to the conclusion that Alhajri was not involved in the September 11th plot.

Of course, with associations between the hijackers and Osama bin Laden's al-Qaida terrorist group, the investigation into September 11 has become global in nature. As a result of the war in Afghanistan and raids of suspected terrorist hideouts in Afghanistan and Pakistan, several leaders and planners in the al-Qaida group have been apprehended or are believed to have been killed. As an example of such a raid, consider the capture of Ramzi Binalshibh. On September 11, 2002, authorities in Pakistan captured Binalshibh in a raid conducted by the FBI, CIA, and Pakistani police. Binalshibh was known by authorities as being instrumental in the planning of the September 11 hijackings and, at the time of his capture, he was wanted by the FBI. It is believed that he shared an apartment with Atta in Hamburg, that he wired money to Moussaoui and hijacker Marwan Al-Shehhi when they were in the United States, and that he attended the January 2000 meeting in Malaysia. It was also known that Binalshibh attempted to obtain a visa for entry into the United States four times between May and October 2000. In all likelihood, Binalshibh was to be the twentieth hijacker. But with Binalshibh unable to gain entry into the United States, it is believed that Moussaoui was then designated as the twentieth hijacker; however, as noted, Moussaoui could not fill this role because he was arrested on immigration charges in August 2001. As another example, in Yemen in October 2002, a U.S. Predator drone (an unmanned aerial aircraft) operated by the CIA fired a missile at a car in which Qaed Salim Sinan al-Harethi was an occupant, killing him and five others who were in the car. Al-Harethi was known to be Osama bin Laden's top lieutenant in Yemen.

Along with an ongoing arrests of suspected al-Qaida terrorists and commanders overseas, arrests have also been made in the United States. For example, based on information uncovered as a result of the arrest of Almarabh in Chicago, the police were led to a previous address of his in Detroit. Police raided the apartment in which he used to live and arrested several men. A search of the apartment revealed maps of the Detroit International Airport along with security passes for the airport. These men were eventually charged with conspiring to aid terrorists. In September 2002, the FBI arrested six men who allegedly comprised a terrorist cell in New York state. They were charged with supporting bin Laden's al-Qaida network. In October 2002, six additional U.S. citizens were arrested and accused of traveling to Afghanistan after September 11, 2001, for purposes of joining the al-Qaida fight against America. In December 2002, FBI agents raided a software firm in Boston because of suspicion that its owners were funneling money to terrorists while doing business with sensitive U.S. agencies, including the FBI, the North Atlantic Treaty Organization, and the IRS. In addition to these high-profile, well-publicized arrests, numerous other people in the United States have been arrested for immigration violations, and many have been deported. Furthermore, it has been reported that as of 2003, hundreds of people are being detained while awaiting further investigation and possible charges in connection to terrorist-related activities. The war on terror continues (Fainaru, 2002a, b; Isikoff and Klaidman, 2002; Schmidt and Eggen, 2002).

History as a Guide to the Future of Policing

As discussed in Chapter 2, one reason for studying history is that it may serve as a guide to the future (Gallie, 1985). According to Lichtman and French (1985), "the past provides our only source of information for evaluating current affairs and making predictions about the future" (p. 277). Indeed, as stated by American historian Charles Beard (1934), "all efforts . . . to guess the trends of the future . . . require some penetration into the depths of history" (p. 69). Scholars agree that making accurate predictions based on the past is always difficult, and sometimes impossible. Schlesinger (1985) explains:

> Most useful historical generalizations are statements about massive social and intellectual movements over a considerable period of time. They make large-scale, long-term prediction possible. But they do not justify small-scale, short-term prediction. For short-run prediction is the prediction of detail and, given the complex structure of social events, the difficulty of anticipating the intersection or collision of different events and the irreducible mystery, if not invincible freedom, of individual decision, there are simply too many variables to warrant exact forecasts of the immediate future. (p. 319)

In other words, the more specific the prediction, the more likely it is to be wrong.

Understanding these limitations, the purpose of this chapter is to use history to make general predictions about the future of American policing, and the future of criminal investigation in particular. The objective is to identify developments of the past that may continue as trends of the future. The basis for these predictions is an understanding of history; specifically, an understanding of the reasons that policing and investigative methods have changed during the course of history. As illustrated in this chapter, throughout history, changes in policing have been prompted by crises, which have been caused by dramatic changes in society. The crises that the police have faced are largely two-dimensional—new crime demands and new technological demands. A fundamental premise of the discussion is that organizations tend to reflect their social, political, and economic environments. As the social, political, and economic environments change, so too will organizations. Accordingly, to understand police organizations, one must appreciate the dynamic environments in which they operate. It must also be understood that policing cannot be separated from criminal investigation in history or in the future. The investigative function evolves hand in hand with the methods and tactics of policing.

The History of Policing

Three major "waves of change" can be identified in society: the agricultural wave, the industrial wave, and the information wave (Toffler, 1980). Precolonial and colonial America reflected the agricultural wave. At this time, the land and farming were at the center of the economy and life in general. The land was divided into farm parcels, and small villages and towns dotted the landscape. In the South, the land and, in particular, slave labor, were the main engines of the economy. Farmers, plantation keepers, and craftsmen represented important and common occupations of the agricultural era. For the most part, each household provided for its own needs. Health care, transportation, and communication systems were quite rudimentary, if they existed at all. Society was simple and so too was the system of policing. The policing function was not formalized. It consisted primarily of loosely organized groups of watchmen in the North and slave patrols in the South (Williams and Murphy, 1990). In whatever form it took, the police function was devoted to the maintenance of order—particularly the control of groups perceived to be threatening to those with economic advantage. Success took the form of squashed riots and smothered rebellions.

By the mid 1800s, America was in the firm grip of the Industrial Revolution. The economy was increasingly based on capital, energy, and raw materials. The Civil War marked the transition from the agricultural wave to the industrial wave (Toffler, 1980). Industrialism affected every aspect of human life. Giant advances in technology were made. Electrical power and the steam engine were invented. Mass production via assembly lines became the norm as machines were introduced into the manufacturing of goods. Coal and oil were used to power machines. Steel was a building block of the new economy and was used to build machines, machine tools, railroads, and to make other goods. Factories and corporations became the centerpieces of the new economy. With the construction of factories came the creation of cities as work centers. The population of cities grew rapidly through immigration and with people moving to cities to find work. For the first time, the "urban" problems of health, sanitation, and crime became a major concern to residents. With the Industrial Revolution, the police found themselves in the midst of a crisis. The old systems of policing were ill equipped to deal with the demands of the new society. Slave patrols of the South became irrelevant, and the watches of the North became outmoded. Policing did not work well in the face of the new demands. There were persistent and serious concerns about the social order among political and economic leaders. It was in this environment, and a result of this crisis, that the first formal police departments in the United States were created.

The first police departments in America were modeled after the London Metropolitan Police Department, which was established in 1829. Most important, departments were organized in a military manner and deployed officers on patrol with the intent of dealing with crime and disorder. Policing was conceived as a responsibility of local government. There were few federal laws and, correspondingly, there were few federal agents to enforce them. Policing during the mid 1800s was all about politics. Politicians controlled virtually every aspect of policing, including the hiring and firing of officers, and what officers did while they were at work. The police acted as an arm of the political machinery. With no formal system of communication between the police and citizens, or among the police themselves, the role of police supervisors was minimal. The police were corrupt and generally inefficient.

Into the early 1900s, another swell of change swept American society. Industrialism was cresting. By 1920, automobiles were widely used, as were radios, telephones, and other technologies. Charles Lindbergh's first trans-Atlantic flight in 1927 signaled a time of great promise, of great mobility. Along with advancing living standards for many, the new technology also provided increased demands on the police. With the use of automobiles in particular, criminals could commit crimes in one jurisdiction and easily flee to another, causing great difficulties for the police. In addition, automobiles created a need for traffic enforcement, a responsibility assigned to the police. Another element of technology that significantly affected the work demands of the police was the telephone. The telephone turned police organizations into twenty-four-hour-a-day agencies that were just a phone call away. Besides technology, the police were confronted with other demands as well. Concerns about crime became a major issue. With the 1920s came a rise (at least in perception, if not in fact) in serious crime. The kidnaping of Charles Lindbergh's infant son was the "crime of the century." The crimes of gangsters were front-page news. In 1919, the United States experienced a series of bombings with targets ranging from police departments to banks. These actions were believed to be the responsibility of communists and others who were deemed un-American. The bombings and their aftermath became known as the Red Scare. World War I, Prohibition, and The Great Depression also placed significant new demands on the police. In the face of these developments, the police were once again in the midst of another crisis. And yet again, the crisis led to change.

The new work demands and technology of the early 1900s led to the emergence of the reform era of policing (Kelling and Moore, 1988). The reform era was a response to the police crisis of the 1920s. The reform era was all about "the police as experts," "police professionalism," and about putting distance between the police and undesirable political influences. Technology was an important element of the reform era. Automobiles allowed the police to institute "preventive" patrols as a tactic and to offer fast response to crime scenes as a means by which to make more arrests. In addition, the patrol car provided the means by which officers could be removed from close day-to-day contact with citizens and to have them patrol anonymously through communities. The two-way radio provided a mechanism by which police supervisors could monitor and direct the activities of officers on the streets. Also in response to the crisis of the early 1900s, state and federal law enforcement agencies were created to assist local police departments with the new demands they faced. The Bureau of Investigation, later known as the FBI, was created in 1909. The FBI played a prominent role in law enforcement efforts. It led the war against the communists, gangsters, and kidnapers. The FBI developed a crime laboratory, collected crime information, developed fingerprinting on a large scale as a method of identification, and created the FBI National Academy to provide advanced training to police leaders across the country. With these new tools, the police presented themselves as experts, as professionals who had the knowledge and capabilities necessary to control crime, and who successfully overcame the challenges of the early 1900s.

This system of policing worked well until the 1960s came into focus, until the information wave began to take form. The information wave, as discussed by Toffler (1980), is characterized by an electronics explosion. Beginning in the 1960s, huge advances were made in space exploration, genetics, health care, computers, and in manufacturing processes, just to name a few. Also beginning in the 1960s, and associated with the movement from the industrial wave to the information wave, society began experiencing "a great disruption" (Fukuyama, 1999). Consider some of the events of the 1960s: President John F. Kennedy was assassinated, as was his brother, Senator and presidential candidate Robert F. Kennedy. Martin Luther King, Jr., was also murdered. The civil rights movement was in full gear; racially motivated riots and other demonstrations were occurring in most major American cities. The Vietnam War was being waged, as were protests against the war. The police found themselves on the front lines of these riots and demonstrations. In many places, the police were viewed as a white "occupying army" in ghetto neighborhoods. Drug use and the hippy movement were prominent counterculture movements. America was also in the grip of a crime wave: From 1960 to 1970 the crime rate doubled. Fear of crime was even worse. In addition, for the first time, systematic research was conducted on police operations and strategies, and much of this research came to the conclusion that the police had little or no impact on crime. Given the state of society, many people were not surprised by these conclusions. By the end of the 1960s, it was clear that policing was not working well. The police were once again in the midst of a crisis because the old system of policing was ill equipped to deal with the demands of the new society.

The crisis in the 1960s led to yet another paradigm shift in policing. As the notion of police professionalism dissolved, the community problem-solving era of policing began to form (Kelling and Moore, 1988). The community problem-solving era is considered to be the predominant style of policing today. During the community problem-solving era, deliberate efforts have been made by the police to recognize citizens as meaningful partners in crime prevention efforts. Community policing is the cornerstone of the community problem-solving era. Community policing represents many different things to many different people, but the core idea is that the police institute policies and practices that involve citizens in policing. According to the ideals of community policing, it is only when police and citizens work together that crime can be prevented.

In summary, policing in America has evolved through a series of stages or eras. The era of informal policing from precolonial and colonial America to the mid 1800s. The political era was in place from the 1850s to the early 1900s, the reform era from the early 1900s to the 1960s, and the community problem-solving era from the 1970s to the present. Each stage represented a new way of policing. Police organizations in each of these eras reflected the social, political, and economic environments in which they operated. Likewise, the emergence of each new era of policing—in the mid 1800s, early 1900s, and the 1960s—was prompted by major social, economic, and political changes. Each of these periods represented a time of major crises for the police and, as noted by Kuhn (1970), "crisis is a prerequisite to revolution" (p. 92).

The Future of Policing

As we begin the twenty-first century, we see the information wave building momentum. Computer technology has matured. Computer networking has taken the form of the Internet. Developments in genomics, alternative fuel sources, and space travel have continued unabated. With the adoption of technology (especially the Internet), individual citizens have widespread and immediate access to information, and citizens with information are citizens with power. As with the Industrial Revolution, the Information Revolution is affecting every aspect of human life, from the nature of education, to family structure, to the nature of occupations (see Toffler [1980]). With these changes, we see once again significant "new" demands on the police. We see continuing disruption in society. As explained by Toffler (1980):

> The period of transition (from the second to third wave) will be marked by extreme social disruption, as well as wild economic swings, sectional clashes, secession attempts, technological upsets or disasters, political turbulence, violence, wars, and threats of war . . . the clash of two civilizations presents titanic dangers. (p. 367)

Although the clash and resulting disruption may be "normal," it represents the latest crisis for the police because the police may not be prepared to deal with the new demands being placed on them. Given how extraordinary developments and demands have prompted changes in policing in the past, it may be reasonable to expect that these demands will once again lead to a paradigm shift in policing, to fundamental changes in the nature and style of policing.

The "New" Crime and Technological Demands

Just as in the past, many of the new demands on the police today are related to crime and technology. With regard to crime in particular, it is clear from history that as society becomes more complex, so too does crime. Indeed, crime has, in general, become more devious, organized, specialized, and complex (Marx, 1988). In addition, it may be reasonable to expect that as society becomes more global, so too will crime. Globalization is a firmly established trend as evidenced over time by imperialism, world wars, global and continental currencies, global trade agreements, and so forth. These two trends—increasingly sophisticated and devious crimes, and globalization (along with consideration of September 11, 2001, and related events)—point to organized international terrorism as the "new" most significant crime-related demand on the police.

Terrorism is hardly a new phenomenon, but it has taken on a new meaning since September 11. As reported by the U.S. Department of State (2001), terrorist incidents have become much more frequent since the late 1960s, and the frequency of such incidents has increased even further since the mid 1990s and even more since September 2001. According to the State Department, there were more than 150 significant terrorist incidents worldwide since 1968; however, only a few of them actually occurred in the United States: the 1975 bombing of a Wall Street bar by Puerto Rican nationalists that killed four and injured sixty, the 1995 bombing of the federal building in Oklahoma City by Timothy McVeigh that killed 166, the 1997 Empire State Building sniper attack by a Palestinian gunman that killed one, the 1993 bombing of the World Trade Center by Islamic extremists that left six people dead, the 1993 shooting deaths of two CIA employees outside of CIA headquarters by a Pakistani gunman, and, of course, the terrorist attacks of September 11, 2001, that killed more than 3,000. The still-unsolved October 2001 anthrax letters that killed five may also be added to this list. Several incidents directly involved Americans and American interests, but occurred overseas; for example, the Iranian hostage crisis of 1979, the bombing of the U.S. Marine barracks in Beirut in 1983, the *Achille Lauro* cruise ship hijacking of 1985, the Pan Am Flight 103 bombing in 1988, the U.S. Embassy bombings in east Africa in 1998, and the attack on the *U.S.S. Cole* in 2000.

Most terrorism is motivated by hate and revenge. Acts of terrorism directed against the United States by foreign interests is most directly related to American support for Israel, and American involvement in Middle Eastern political affairs. The United States is the global superpower, and attacks on it can glean attention for groups that wish to advance a particular cause (Kelley, 1998). Given the hatred of the United States by these foreign interests, acts of terrorism directed against the United States are not surprising. What is most odd, as explained by Kelley (1998) was that:

> [t]he United States has escaped major, externally based terrorist actions for so long, given this country's thousands of miles of open borders, porous immigration control service, easily accessible firearms, and the availability of unfettered travel. (p. 23)

Of course, on September 11, 2001, terrorism came to the United States in a big way. September 11 was what many have referred to as a blaring wake-up call. It is now realized that America is not immune to major terrorist actions, even on our own soil. It is realized that other serious threats may loom, and they are not hypothetical. If commercial airliners can be turned into missiles to destroy skyscrapers filled with people, then bioterrorism and the use of nuclear bombs for terrorist purposes could certainly be a possibility. Given the new threat, it is being realized that the current system of policing is ill equipped to deal with the new demands of society.

There are good reasons to believe that trends already in place will increase the terrorist threat to the United States. One such trend is the demographics of Middle Eastern countries. For instance, in Saudi Arabia, seventy percent of the population is twenty-five years of age or younger—the age group most likely to become involved in criminal activity. This situation will not change soon because almost one half the population is younger than the age of fifteen. In addition, the decline of central authority of political heads of state in Middle Eastern countries (Kaplan, 2002) is troubling. It is this type of political environment that can serve as a haven for terrorist groups. As explained by Kaplan (2002), "the experience of neighboring Yemen, with its brazen highwaymen and rampant kidnapings, may be what Saudi Arabia can look forward to—and that's the optimistic view" (p. 55). Furthermore,

American power, influence, and foreign policy, which is the source of much of the hatred directed against the United States, is not likely to change. As a result, the "new" terrorist threat is likely to be with us for awhile.

Right now, changes are being made at a rapid pace among American law enforcement agencies to deal with the threat and to prevent the police from looking impotent in the face of the new threat. Already, law enforcement agencies have received their share of criticism regarding the inability to foresee and prevent the recent terrorist incidents. For instance, many have argued that the warning signs for the terrorist act of September 11, 2001, were so obvious that they should not have been missed. Specifically, for years it was known that airplanes were planned to be used in terrorist plots. Consider these clues: The discovery and interruption of the 1995 terrorist plot to blow up eleven American jetliners over the Pacific Ocean and crash a light aircraft loaded with explosives into CIA headquarters. Consider as well the al-Qaida terrorists who hijacked an Air France flight as it prepared to leave Algeria for Paris (presumably to crash it into the Eiffel Tower), but commandos stormed the plane during a refueling stop and killed the terrorists. Consider that several informants in the investigation of the African Embassy bombings spoke of al-Qaida's interest in flight training. Consider that Islamic terrorists were planning to use an airplane to kill President Bush in July 2001 in Italy. And then there was the information that two known terrorists associated with al-Qaida entered the United States after the January 2000 terrorist planning meeting in Malaysia. If authorities would have monitored the activities of Almihdhar and Alhazmi when they were in the United States, then their meetings with other hijackers, along with their flying lessons, may have been discovered. It is likely that the entire September 11 plot would have been disrupted. Then there was the arrest of Moussaoui in flight school in Minnesota, and the multitude of intelligence reports that were received by the CIA that spoke of the interest of al-Qaida in hijacking American airplanes and flying them into various high-profile targets. The list of warning signs was a long one. Despite this knowledge, little seemed to have been done to prevent the disaster of September 11, 2001. Government officials described September 11 as "a new type of attack that had not been foreseen" (Fainaru, 2002a; p. A09).

Along with an increasingly devious, organized, and global terrorist threat, another trend that may have implications for crime, the future of policing, and the future of criminal investigations is the continued, rapid discovery and adoption of technology. Just as with electricity, the telephone, the automobile, and the airplane, the technology of today dramatically affects the nature of our lives. As seen throughout history, technology can place incredible demands on the police. Perhaps the most significant technology of today and of the future is the Internet. The Internet is a global computerized network that allows for the exchange and dissemination of information. With the good of the technology comes the bad. The Internet has created a multitude of criminal opportunities: It can be used to disseminate information of hate and other unlawful materials (e.g., child pornography), it can be used to perform acts of terrorism (e.g., cyberterrorism), it can be used to gain illegal access to and to steal protected governmental and corporate information (e.g., hacking), and it can be used to distribute computer viruses (see Damphousse and Smith [1998]).

The "New" Police

In the face of the "new" crime and technological demands, what may be the next adaptation of policing? As Marx (1988) has noted, not only does crime tend to reflect the nature of society, but methods of policing also tend to reflect the nature of the criminal threat in society. When crimes are simple and local, detection strategies are simple and local. When crimes are complex and global, detection strategies are complex and global. As such, at a minimum it seems reasonable to predict that policing of the future will likely be more complex and global than in the past. To support the increased scope of police operations, it is likely that more resources and authority will be provided to law enforcement agencies, particularly *federal* law enforcement agencies, to deal with global crime, particularly terrorism. Previous crises have led to an increased role and authority of federal agencies, and the current crisis may be no different. This point is obvious with the passage of the federal antiterror bill—the USA Patriot Act of 2001—that provides new police powers, including expanded authority to wiretap telephones, examine Internet use, conduct searches, combat money laundering, and detain foreigners suspected of terrorism. On signing the bill, President Bush stated:

> We're dealing with terrorists who operate by highly sophisticated methods and technologies, some of which were not even available when our existing laws were written. The bill before me takes into account the new realities and dangers posed by terrorists.

(See News Hour with Jim Lehrer, President Bush signs antiterrorism bill, October 21, 2001, www.pbs.org/newshour/bb/terrorism/bush_terrorism_bill.html.)

In addition, massive additional resources are being allocated to federal agencies for the purposes of enhancing homeland security. In 2002 and 2003 the estimated expenditures for homeland security will be more than $35 billion—and President Bush has called this a "down payment." The greatest proportion of the money will be spent on border security (INS), import security (U.S. Customs Service), national security (Department of Defense), and transportation security (Department of Transportation). It is estimated that homeland security will attract more than $100 billion in private and governmental spending by 2008 (Dow Jones Business News, 2002). The newly authorized Department of Homeland Security represents a massive reorganization of federal efforts to deal with domestic security threats. The department will include twenty-two agencies and employ 170,000 employees. The federal government has not seen such changes since 1947, when President Truman merged the Department of War and the Department of the Navy into the Department of Defense.

With the increased resources devoted to federal law enforcement efforts, it would not be surprising if there was a corresponding decline in federal funding to local police agencies. In particular, the $30 billion allocated for the Violent Crime Control and Law Enforcement Act of 1994 (the 1994 Crime Bill) may soon come to an end. This money provided local police departments with funds to hire additional community-policing officers, among other mostly local initiatives. The shift away from local law enforcement matters is also evidenced by the fact that, under the direction of Attorney General Ashcroft, the FBI is now focusing more on preventing terrorist acts and less on solving traditional crimes that "local police can handle" (Gullo, 2001).

Regardless of these shifting priorities, citizens will remain powerful players in the police enterprise and in crime fighting. Nowhere will this be more apparent than with citizens as sources of information. Reward and tip lines will be increasingly important as the police continue to rely on citizens for information about crimes and the people who committed them. A proposal of the Bush administration and the U.S. Department of Justice is the development of Operation TIPS—a national system for reporting suspicious and potentially terrorist-related activity. The participation of workers in several occupations— truck drivers, meter readers, taxicab drivers—is seen as critical to the success of the program. In the past, most crime tip programs have been administered at the local level (e.g., Crime Solvers). Operation TIPS takes the concept to the national level and is further evidence of the trend toward the federalization of law enforcement.

Policing of the future may also reflect the continuation of another trend already in place: The lines separating the police and the military will become increasingly blurry. In particular, the police will become more militarylike and the military will become more policelike. With regard to the military becoming more policelike, since September 11 there have been numerous instances of the military becoming involved in domestic law enforcement activities. For example, an immediate response to September 11 was the placement of fully equipped and armed National Guard personnel in airports to provide security. In addition, for several months, the U.S. Air Force operated air patrols over numerous cities in an effort to enforce airspace restrictions and to protect cities from any additional terrorist hijackings. In November 2002, the Department of Defense provided aircraft surveillance to assist federal, state, and local law enforcement authorities in the investigation of the sniper shootings in the Washington, DC, area. Of course, the precedent for military involvement in the "war on terrorism" is the "war on drugs," which has been fought for years by law enforcement and the military (see Duke and Gross [1993]).

The Posse Comitatus Act of 1878, amended in 1994, restricts the participation of the military in domestic law enforcement activities. It reads:

> Whoever, except in cases and under circumstances expressly authorized by the Constitution or Act of Congress, willfully uses any part of the Army or the Air Force as a posse comitatus or otherwise to execute the laws shall be fined not more than $10,000 or imprisonment not more than two years, or both.

The Navy and the Marines are included in the Posse Comitatus Act as a result of a 1992 Department of Defense regulation. The original intent of the Act was to end the use of federal troops in policing state elections of the former confederate states. There are several important exclusions to the Act. They include

- The use of National Guard forces
- The use of federal troops to quell domestic violence, by presidential order

- The use of military personnel to provide for aerial photographs and surveillance
- The use of military personnel to combat the "war on drugs"
- The use of the Coast Guard
- The use of Navy resources to assist the Coast Guard

As reported by Lindlaw (2002), in the wake of September 11, President Bush has called on Congress to review thoroughly the modern-day appropriateness of the Posse Comitatus Act.

Along with the military becoming more policelike, the police are also becoming more militarylike. Police organizations in America are, at their core, quasimilitary in structure and function; however, it appears that the parallels are becoming more clear and will likely become even stronger in the future. During the last few decades in America there has been a gradual and now more rapid adaptation of the police into military roles—in terms of rhetoric (e.g., "war" on drugs, "war" on crime, "war" on terrorism) and function (e.g., the use of paramilitary units and technology). The war on terrorism is being fought by police forces and the military. As the police function evolves, law enforcement agencies may be "democratic and participatory" (community oriented) in peacetime but "highly centralized and authoritarian" (militarylike) during times of unrest (Toffler, 1980). Zalman (2000) appears to concur: "This indicates that [in the next twenty to forty years] the criminal justice system will continue in its dualistic, quasi-authoritarian mode marking the United States as a flawed liberal democracy" (p. 182).

Indeed, military tactics and technologies are increasingly being used among police departments. This trend is what Kraska and Kappeler (1997) refer to as the "militarization of the police." Much law enforcement technology, and civilian technology for that matter, has its beginnings in defense contract work. Consider the development of technologies such as radar, two-way radios, night vision, sensor technologies (including gunshot detection), and even the Internet. All were born at least in part through defense grants and contracts (Rome Laboratory Law Enforcement Technology Team, 1996). In addition, the police occupation has traditionally been a magnet for former members of the military. Military service as a police officer usually counts toward retirement credits as a police officer. The "Troops to Cops" program of the Violent Crime Control and Law Enforcement Act of 1994 is a recent example of an attempt to bring former military personnel into local police departments. The program provided money to local agencies that hired former members of the U.S. Armed Forces.

The parallels are also striking when one considers the similarities between police and military tactics. In 1996, Kraska and Kappeler (1997) conducted a survey of all police departments in the United States that served cities of 50,000 people or more. Of the 548 agencies that responded to the survey (seventy-nine percent response rate), eighty-nine percent had a police paramilitary unit. This compares with approximately fifty-nine percent of the agencies in 1982. According to Kraska and Kappeler (1997), the mean number of callouts (deployments) of police paramilitary units per year in each agency has gone from thirteen in 1980, to forty-four in 1990, to fifty-three in 1995. With regard to police paramilitary unit deployments, the researchers found that police paramilitary units are increasingly being incorporated into "normal" police work. Seventy-five percent of call-outs were for purposes of "high-risk warrant work" and when the police paramilitary unit served as "a proactive tool through which the police gather evidence and crudely conduct an investigation into suspected illegal activity" (Kraska and Kappeler, 1997; p. 9). "Since 1982, there has been a 292 percent increase (from 24 to 94) in the number of departments using [police paramilitary units] for proactive patrol" (p. 9). As concluded by Kraska and Kappeler (1997), not only has there been a dramatic increase in paramilitary policing activity, but also a "movement toward the normalization of paramilitary groups" in police organizations (p. 9). Similar findings were also found among small departments in the United States (Kraska and Cubellis, 1997). On the basis of these two studies, the only available studies that have examined the use of paramilitary policing in the United States, it is clear that the trend toward a more harsh and "high-power" police strategy is firmly in place. It seems reasonable to expect that the events of September 2001 did not diminish the trend; if anything, they have accelerated it.

Technology and the Future of Crime Detection and Criminal Investigation

Technology not only makes certain types of crime possible, it also provides the police with new tools for fighting these, and other, crimes. It is likely that the discovery and adoption of technology for crime detection and investigative purposes will continue to progress at an accelerated "information age" pace. The impact of technologies under development and in early adoption stages are likely soon to be realized. Much of the significant new "crime fighting" technology will focus on identification (e.g., biometrics), "seeing," computer/Internet applications, and information access.

The Technology of Identification

As discussed in Chapter 6, DNA analysis was first applied to criminal investigations in the late 1980s. Since that time, it has become a widely used and extremely powerful tool in criminal investigations. However, one of the primary limitations of DNA analysis is that it is of limited value unless a suspect is available for comparison. With the development of CODIS, a nationwide DNA network that includes DNA samples from convicted offenders and crime scenes, DNA will become an even more powerful tool for identifying suspects. On the distant horizon may be the construction and operation of a massive DNA databank that would include samples of DNA from every individual who resides in the United States. The technology to store this amount of data is currently available; legal and ethical issues have inhibited the development of such a system. More immediate, progress continues to be made on the science of collecting and analyzing DNA. A number of new technologies are being developed that will allow DNA to be collected more efficiently and analyzed more quickly with lower cost (see Friedman [1999]).

Implantable microchips are another technology that could serve an important identification function. This technology is already in existence, but to date has only limited application. The "Verichip," made and marketed by Applied Digital, Inc., is about the size of a grain of rice and has been used in the United States to track and identify house pets, livestock, and fish. In 2002, the company applied to the Food and Drug Administration for approval to use the chip as a way of providing information about medical devices (e.g., pacemakers, artificial joints) to doctors who need quick access to patient information. The same technology has been incorporated into a wrist watch-type device that, when linked to a global positioning system, can transmit information on body temperature, pulse, and location of the person who is wearing it. This system is sold in the United States as a way to monitor the whereabouts of Alzheimer's patients, children, and parolees (Krolicki, 2001). It is conceivable that the next application of the technology will be under-the-skin placement, where the chip contains readable information on an individual's identity, whereabouts, and other critical information.

The technology that supports fingerprints as a method of identification is likely to continue to evolve. AFIS computers (Chapter 6) are being developed that provide for nationwide access to computerized fingerprint files. AFISs are also being improved to provide faster and more accurate search results. Fingerprints are likely to continue to be used in other applications as well. For instance, fingerprint scanning devices have been developed to take the place of passwords on computers and locks on doors (controlled access). Retinal scanning devices have also been developed for similar purposes.

Facial recognition systems are also being used as a method of identification. Facial recognition systems go beyond passive camera surveillance and include a link between the cameras and databases of photographs of wanted or known criminals. When a match between the facial image caught on camera and a facial image in the database is made, the operator of the system is alerted. Facial recognition systems have been deployed in casinos for several years, assisting security personnel in identifying and apprehending known gambling cheats and scam artists. More recently, facial recognition systems have been implemented in airports, public streets, and sports stadiums (Associated Press, 2001). Like the other technologies discussed earlier, these systems also raise a multitude of issues regarding privacy. In addition, the effectiveness of these systems has not yet been firmly established.

Another biometric technology is "smart" identification cards. Smart cards have been in existence for several decades (e.g., credit cards), but recent applications are "smarter" than previous ones. Such cards embed information either in a magnetic strip or in a computer chip. Smart cards are beginning to be used for driver's licenses, passports, computer authentication, and as control access devices. Smart cards are difficult to alter fraudulently. Future applications for smart cards may include global positioning satellite locators as well as personal, medical, and other identifying information.

The Technology of "Seeing"

Along with the biometric technologies discussed previously, technological advances are also being made in the technology of "seeing." Most significant is the use of low-level x rays or gamma rays to facilitate the detection of weapons, explosives, drugs, and other contraband.

For example, although we are all familiar with walk-through metal detectors, a more recent and beginning-to-be-deployed technology includes devices that allow one to see through clothing and to see items that may be hidden under clothing. As described by Phillips (2001),

> [i]n use, a passenger stands on a platform that moves past a scanner, producing a full body picture within ten seconds. . . . But the picture looks more like a skeleton with a fuzzy body around it and it does not show body parts vividly. Foreign objects stand out where ever they are, from belt buckles to plastic explosives to drug-filled condoms that have been swallowed. (p. E2)

Similar technologies have been developed that allow one to see through luggage for explosive detection, to see through walls, and to see through cargo containers. These technologies are most applicable to cargo, border, and airport and seaport security.

A technology with related applications is the electronic "sniffer" microchip. These electronic computer chips are designed to detect microscopic amounts of substances including chemicals, explosives, radiation, and drugs. Once the reliability of this passive technology has been established, it is likely that it will replace canines as "sniffers."

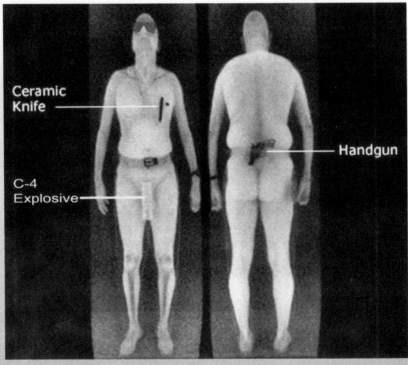

The image of a strip search using low level x-ray. RAPISCAN SECURITY PRODUCTS, INC.

Technologies for Computer and Internet Applications

Other investigative tools are also being developed and deployed to deal more effectively with Internet and computer-related crimes. For example, DCS 1000 (previously known as *Carnivore*) can search e-mail traffic for specific senders, recipients, and key words. "Magic Lantern" is a technology that can record keystrokes on identified computers. It is likely that related technologies will be developed and existing technologies will be improved to confront related crimes effectively.

Technologies for Information Access

One of the primary functions of technology in the workplace is to enhance productivity by making work tasks less time-consuming. Technology will continue to have such effects on policing and criminal investigations. Common today is the use of laptop computers in squad cars for communication and deployment purposes. In the future, police officers will likely have immediate access to a multitude of information through portable handheld computers—information such as photographs of suspects, photographs of stolen property, as well as fingerprint and DNA data.

The Implications of Technology on Crime Detection and Criminal Investigation

Little question, the technology discussed here, and the widespread adaptation of this technology, may produce a significant reaction, mostly as it relates to the issue of privacy. Indeed, it is likely that most legal challenges of the future that relate to technology will center on privacy issues. For example, the law relating to the constitutionality of strip and body cavity searches is well developed; however, do digital fifteen-second body examinations through the use of x rays alter notions of privacy and expectations of it? Do through-the-wall surveillance devices alter the meaning of search and seizure? What are the parameters of privacy in e-mail? The courts have begun to address these questions, but clearly the technology has opened a new set of issues relating to the reasonable expectation of privacy.

In 1988, Gary Marx (1988) posed the question: Are we moving toward a maximum security society? In addressing the question, he suggested that a maximum-security society is composed of five interrelated subsocieties:

1. A dossier society, in which computerized records play a major role
2. A predictive society, in which decisions are increasingly made on the basis of predictions about future behavior as a result of our membership in aggregate categories
3. An engineered society, in which our choices are increasingly limited and determined by the physical and social environment

4. A transparent society, in which the boundaries that traditionally protected privacy are weakened
5. A self-monitored society, in which surveillance plays a prominent role

Are we moving toward a maximum-security society? Given recent technological advances and adoptions, we seem to be well on our way, but we are not there . . . yet.

Questions for Discussion and Review

1. To consider the implications of September 11, 2001, on the police and criminal investigation is to consider the future of the police and criminal investigation.

2. What are the potential benefits and drawbacks of using history to predict the future?

3. What was the nature of society and the system of policing during the agricultural wave and the industrial wave?

4. What factors prompted changes in the way policing was conducted in the mid 1850s, early 1920s, and the 1960s?

5. How might the threat of terrorism and the demand posed by technology affect how policing is done in the future?

6. If current crime and technological trends continue, what will be the impact on policing and criminal investigation? Explain.

7. What is the Posse Comitatus Act? Do you think that it will have meaningful implications for the future of policing? Why or why not?

8. Discuss how the lines differentiating the police and the military are becoming increasingly blurry. Provide examples to support your position.

9. What are five "new" technologies that could be used to enhance the ability to detect crime and to identify offenders. Discuss how these technologies could be applied to make criminal investigations more effective.

10. What is the likely relationship between many of the "new" technological tools discussed in this chapter and privacy? Explain how these tools may affect one's right to privacy.

11. What is a maximum-security society? Is our society currently maximum security? Are we becoming a maximum-security society? Why or why not?

Related Internet Sites

www.choicepoint.net
This is the address for ChoicePoint, Inc., a company that is in the information business. Its services include providing information on individuals to assist in background checks, hiring decisions, and insurance and banking decisions.

www.biometricgroup.com
This link brings you to the web site of the International Biometric Group, a company that offers consulting services to agencies about biometric solutions. The site contains a lot of information about various biometric technologies.

www.forensic-evidence.com
This site offers information on a variety of topics relating to the role of evidence in criminal investigations. Most relevant is the information (and links) about biometric technologies and their impact on criminal investigations.

COURT CASES CITED

Aguilar v. Texas 378 U.S.108 (1964)

Arizona v. Evans 56 CRL 2175 (1995)

Arizona v. Fulminante 499 U.S. 279 (1991)

Arizona v. Hicks 480 U.S. 321 (1987)

Arizona v. Robertson 486 U.S. 675 (1988)

Batson v. Kentucky 476 U.S. 79 (1986)

Berkemer v. McCarty 468 U.S. 420 (1984)

Brewer v. Williams 430 U.S. 387 (1977)

Brinegar v. United States 338 U.S. 160 (1949)

Brown v. Illinois 422 U.S. 590 (1975)

Brown v. Mississippi 297 U.S. 278 (1936)

Brown v. Texas 433 U.S. 47 (1979)

California v. Acevedo 500 U.S. 565 (1991)

California v. Beheler 463 U.S. 1121 (1983)

California v. Carney 471 U.S. 386 (1985)

California v. Greenwood 486 U.S. 35 (1988)

California v. O.J. Simpson CA (1995)

California v. Prysock 453 U.S. 355 (1981)

Chambers v. Maroney 399 U.S. 42 (1970)

Chimel v. California 395 U.S. 752 (1969)

Colorado v. Bertine 479 U.S. 367 (1987)

Coolidge v. New Hampshire 403 U.S. 443 (1971)

Daubert v. Merrell Dow Pharmaceuticals 509 U.S. 579
(1993)

Davis v. Mississippi 394 U.S. 721 (1969)

Delaware v. Prouse 440 U.S. 648 (1979)

Dunaway v. New York 442 U.S. 200 (1979)

Edwards v. Arizona 451 U.S. 477 (1981)

Escobedo v. Illinois 378 U.S. 478 (1964)

Florida v. Jimeno 500 U.S. 248 (1991)

Florida v. J.L. 98–1993 U.S. (2002)

Florida v. Riley 488 U.S. 445 (1989)

Franks v. Delaware 438 U.S. 154 (1978)

Frye v. United States 293 F. 1013 (1923)

Gideon v. Wainright 372 U.S. 335 (1963)

Griffin v. California 380 U.S. 609 (1965)

Gustafson v. Florida 414 U.S. 260 (1973)

Harris v. New York 401 U.S. 222 (1971)

Hayes v. Florida 470 U.S. 811 (1985)

Horton v. California 496 U.S. 128 (1990)

Illinois v. Gates 462 U.S. 213 (1983)

Illinois v. Perkins 496 U.S. 292 (1990)

Illinois v. Rodriguez 497 U.S. 177 (1990)

Illinois v. Wardlow 120 S.Ct. 673 (2000)

Jacobson v. U.S. 503 U.S. 540 (1992)

Katz v. United States 389 U.S. 347 (1967)

Knowles v. Iowa 525 U.S. 113 (1998)

Mapp v. Ohio 367 U.S. 643 (1961)

Maryland v. Buie 494 U.S. 325 (1990)

Maryland v. Garrison 480 U.S. 79 (1987)

Maryland v. Wilson 519 U.S. 408 (1997)

Massiah v. United States 377 U.S. 201 (1964)

Michigan v. DeFillipo 443 U.S. 31 (1979)

Michigan v. Long 463 U.S. 1032 (1983)

Michigan v. Mosley 423 U.S. 96 (1975)

Michigan v. Tyler 436 U.S. 499 (1978)

Mincey v. Arizona 431 U.S. 385 (1978)

Minnesota v. Dickerson 508 U.S. 366 (1993)

Minnick v. Mississippi 498 U.S. 146 (1990)

Miranda v. Arizona 384 U.S. 436 (1966)

Moran v. *Burbine* 475 U.S. 412 (1986)

Neil v. *Biggers* 409 U.S. 188 (1972)

New York v. *Quarles* 467 U.S. 649 (1984)

Nix v. *Williams* 467 U.S. 431 (1984)

O'Conner v. *Ortega* 480 U.S. 709 (1987)

Oliver v. *United States* 466 U.S. 170 (1984)

Oregon v. *Haas* 420 U.S. 714 (1975)

Payton v. *New York* 445 U.S. 573 (1980)

Pennsylvania v. *Mimms* 434 U.S. 106 (1977)

Rhode Island v. *Innis* 446 U.S. 291 (1980)

Schneckloth v. *Bustamonte* 412 U.S. 218 (1973)

Schrember v. *California* 384 U.S. 757 (1966)

Schwartz v. *State* 447 N.W. 2d 422 (1989)

Smith v. *Illinois* 469 U.S. 91 (1984)

South Carolina v. *Washington* 14th Circuit, 97–2216 (1997)

South Dakota v. *Neville* 459 U.S. 553 (1983)

South Dakota v. *Opperman* 428 U.S. 364 (1976)

Stoner v. *California* 376 U.S. 483 (1964)

Terry v. *Ohio* 392 U.S. 1 (1968)

Texas v. *Brown* 460 U.S. 730 (1983)

Thompson v. *Louisiana* 469 U.S. 17 (1984)

United States v. *Arvizu* 1519 U.S. (2002)

United States v. *Crews* 455 U.S. 463 (1980)

United States v. *Leon* 468 U.S. 897 (1984)

United States v. *Miller* 425 U.S. 435 (1976)

United States v. *Ortiz* 422 U.S. 891 (1975)

United States v. *Santana* 427 U.S. 38 (1976)

Vale v. *Louisiana* 399 U.S. 30 (1970)

Warden v. *Hayden* 387 U.S. 294 (1967)

Washington v. *Chrisman* 455 U.S.1 (1982)

Weeks v. *United States* 232 U.S. 383 (1914)

Winston v. *Lee* 470 U.S. 753 (1985)

Wong Sun v. *United States* 371 U.S. 471 (1963)

Ybarra v. *Illinois* 444 U.S. 85 (1978)

REFERENCES

Abagnale, Frank W. (2001) *The Art of the Steal*. New York: Broadway Books.

Adams, Susan H. (1996) Statement Analysis: What Do Suspects' Words Really Reveal? *FBI Law Enforcement Bulletin* 65(10): 12–20.

Aiken, Margaret M., Ann Wolbert Burgess, and Robert R. Hazlewood. (1995) False Rape Allegations. In: Robert R. Hazlewood and Ann Wolbert Burgess, eds. *Practical Aspects of Rape Investigation: A Multidisciplinary Approach*. Boca Raton: CRC Press, pp. 219–240.

Ainsworth, Janet E. (1998) In a Different Register: The Pragmatics of Powerlessness in Police Interrogations. In: George C. Leo and George C. Thomas, eds. *The Miranda Debate: Law, Justice, and Policing*. Boston: Northeastern University Press.

Alter, Jonathan, and Mark Starr. (1990, January 22) Race and hype in a divided city. *Newsweek* 115: 2.

(2002) Arresting Behavior. *American Bar Association Journal* 88: 22.

(2001, July 1) High-Tech Security on Tampa Streets.

Baker, James, N. (1990, January 15) Boston: a deadly family affair. *Newsweek* 115: 3.

Baker, Liva. (1983) *Miranda: Crime, Law, and Politics*. New York: Atheneum.

Ball, Larry, D. (1978) *The United States Marshals of New Mexico and Arizona Territories, 1846–1912*. Albuquerque: University of New Mexico Press.

Band, Stephen R., and Donald C. Sheehan. (1999) Managing Undercover Stress: The Supervisor's Role. *FBI Law Enforcement Bulletin* 68(2): 1–6.

Beard, Charles. (1934) *The Nature of the Social Sciences*. New York: Scribner.

Becker, Eugene S., and Eric S. Rein. (2000) Field of Schemes. *Security Management* 44(7): 117–122.

Beekman, Mary Ellen, and Michael R. Daly. (1990) Motor Vehicle Theft Investigations: Emerging International Trends. *FBI Law Enforcement Bulletin* 59(9): 14–17.

Bell, Brad E., and Elizabeth F. Loftus. (1989) Trivial Persuasion in the Courtroom: The Power of (a Few) Minor Details. *Journal of Personality and Social Psychology* 56: 669–679.

Bennett, Wayne W., and Karen Hess. (1984) *Investigating Arson*. Springfield: Charles C. Thomas.

Bennett, Margo, and John E. Hess. (1991) Cognitive Interviewing. *FBI Law Enforcement Bulletin* 60(3): 8–12.

Berger, Margaret A. (2002) Raising the Bar: The Impact of DNA Testing on the Field of Forensics. *National Institute of Justice Perspectives on Crime and Justice* 5: 95–115.

Blackledge, Robert D. (1996) Condom Trace Evidence: A New Factor in Sexual Assault Investigations. *FBI Law Enforcement Bulletin* 65(5): 12–16.

Blinkhorn, Steve. (1988) Lie Detection as a Psychometric Procedure. In: Anthony Gale, ed. *The Polygraph Test: Lies, Truth, and Science*. London: Sage.

Brandl, Steven G. (1993) The Impact of Case Characteristics on Detectives' Decision Making. *Justice Quarterly* 10: 395–415.

Brandl, Steven G. (1991) *The Outcomes and Processes of Detective Decision-Making in Burglary and Robbery Investigations*. Ph.D. dissertation. Michigan State University, East Lansing, MI.

Brandl, Steven G., and Frank Horvath. (1991) Crime Victim Evaluation of Police Investigative Performance. *Journal of Criminal Justice* 19: 293–305.

Brandl, Steven G., and James Frank. (1994) The Relationship Between Evidence, Detective Effort, and the Disposition of Burglary and Robbery Investigations. *American Journal of Police* 13: 149–168.

Brandl, Steven G., James Frank, Robert E. Worden, and Timothy S. Bynum. (1994) Global and Specific Attitudes Toward the Police: Disentangling the Causal Relationship. *Justice Quarterly* 11: 119–134.

Breed, Allen G. (2002, October 21) Two Men in Custody in Sniper Hunt.

Brown, Jennifer M., and Elizabeth A. Campbell. (1994) *Stress and Policing: Sources and Strategies*. New York: John Wiley and Sons.

Browning, Norma Lee. (1970) *The Psychic World of Peter Hurkos*. Garden City, NY: Doubleday.

Buncombe, Andrew. (2001, October 23) Suspects May be Given Truth Serum. *The Independent*.

Bureau of Justice Statistics. (2002a) *Criminal Victimization, 2001*. Washington, DC: U.S. Department of Justice.

Bureau of Justice Statistics. (2002b) *Rape and Sexual Assault: Reporting to Police and Medical Attention, 1992–2000*. Washington, DC: U.S. Department of Justice.

Bureau of Justice Statistics. (2001a) *Criminal Victimization in the United States, 2000: Statistical Tables*. Washington DC: U.S. Department of Justice.

Bureau of Justice Statistics. (2001b) *Federal Law Enforcement Officers, 2000*. Washington, DC: U.S. Department of Justice.

Bureau of Justice Statistics. (2001c) *Local Police Departments, 1999*. Washington DC: U.S. Department of Justice.

Bureau of Justice Statistics. (2001d) *Sheriffs' Offices, 1999*. Washington, DC: U.S. Department of Justice.

Bureau of Justice Statistics. (2000) *Survey of DNA Crime Laboratories, 1998*. Washington, DC: U.S. Department of Justice.

Bureau of Justice Statistics. (1999) *Felony Defendants in Large Urban Counties, 1996*. Washington, DC: U.S. Department of Justice.

Bureau of Justice Statistics. (1997) *Criminal Victimization, 1995*. Washington DC: U.S. Department of Justice.

Bynum, Timothy S., Gary W. Cordner, and Jack R. Greene. (1982) Victim and Offense Characteristics: Impact on Police Investigative Decision Making. *Criminology* 20: 301–318.

Canter, Philip. (2000) Using a Geographic Information System for Tactical Crime Analysis. In: Victor Goldsmith, et al., eds. *Analyzing Crime Pattern: Frontiers of Practice*. Thousand Oaks: Sage.

Carlson, Kurt A., and J. Edward Russo. (2001) Biased Interpretation of Evidence by Mock Jurors. *Journal of Experimental Psychology: Applied* 7: 91–103.

Carovillo, Brian. (2002, November 24) Man in Prison for Murder Was Only Guilty of Adultery.

Carroll, Douglas. (1988) How Accurate is Polygraph Lie Detection? In: Anthony Gale, ed. *The Polygraph Test: Lies, Truth, and Science*. London: Sage.

Casey, Eoghan. (2002) *Handbook of Computer Crime Investigation: Forensic Tools and Technology*. San Diego: Academic Press.

Casey, Steven J. (1995) Car Thieves Smell a RATT. *FBI Law Enforcement Bulletin* 64(11): 1–4.

Cassell, Paul G. (1998) Miranda's Social Costs: An Empirical Reassessment. In: George C. Leo and George C. Thomas, eds. *The Miranda Debate: Law, Justice, and Policing*. Boston: Northeastern University Press.

Cassell, Paul G., and Bret S. Hayman. (1998) Police Interrogation in the 1990s: An Empirical Study of the Effects of Miranda. In: George C. Leo and George C. Thomas, eds. *The Miranda Debate: Law, Justice, and Policing*. Boston: Northeastern University Press.

Castleman, Terry L. (2000) *Death Investigation: A Handbook for Police Officers*. Springfield: Charles C. Thomas.

Cauthen, John. (2001) Investment Fraud. *FBI Law Enforcement Bulletin* 70(5): 13–17.

Chen, Huey-tsyh. (1991) Dropping In and Dropping Out: Judicial Decisionmaking in the Disposition of Felony Arrests. *Journal of Criminal Justice* 19: 1–17.

Christiaansen, R.E., J.D. Sweeny, and K. Ochalek. (1983) Influencing Eye-Witness Descriptions. *Law and Human Behavior* 7: 59–65.

Clarke, Ronald V. (2002) *Thefts of and From Cars in Parking Facilities. Problem-Oriented Guides for Police Series*, Vol. 10. Washington, DC: U.S. Department of Justice.

Clifford, Brian R., and Graham Davies. (1989) Procedures for Obtaining Identification Evidence. In: David C. Raskin, ed. *Psychological Methods in Criminal Investigation and Evidence*, New York: Springer.

Cohen, Bernard, and Jan Chaiken. (1987) *Investigators Who Perform Well*. Washington, DC: U.S. Department of Justice.

Cole, George F., and Christopher E. Smith. (2002) *Criminal Justice in America*. Belmont: Wadsworth.

Constable, George, ed. (1987) *Mysteries of the Unknown: Psychic Powers*. Alexandria, VA: Time-Life Books.

Conti, Philip M. (1977) *The Pennsylvania State Police: A History of Service to the Commonwealth, 1905 to Present*. Harrisburg, PA: Stackpole.

Cooper, Joel, and Isaac M. Neuhaus. (2000) The "Hired Gun" Effect: Assessing the Effect of Pay, Frequency of Testifying, and Credentials on the Perception of Expert Testimony. *Law and Human Behavior* 24: 149–171.

Council on Scientific Affairs. (1985) Scientific Status of Refreshing Recollection by the Use of Hypnosis. *Journal of the American Medical Association* 253: 1918–1923.

(2001) Agents Link Radicals to Northwest Arsons. *Crime Control Digest* 35(21): 4.

Crowley, Sharon R. (1999) *Sexual Assault: The Medical-Legal Examination*. Stamford, CT: Appleton and Lange.

Cunningham, Larry. (1999) Taking on Testilying: The Prosecutor's Response to In-Court Police Deception. *Criminal Justice Ethics* 18: 26–40.

Cutler, Brian L., Steven D. Penrod, and Hedy Red Dexter. (1990) Juror Sensitivity to Eyewitness Identification Evidence. *Law and Human Behavior* 14: 185–191.

Cutler, Brian L., Steven D. Penrod, and Thomas E. Stuve. (1988) Juror Decision Making in Eyewitness Identification Cases. *Law and Human Behavior* 12: 41–55.

Damphousse, Kelly R., and Brent L. Smith. (1998) The Internet: A Terrorist Medium for the 21st Century. In: Harvey W. Kushner, ed. *The Future of Terrorism: Violence in the New Millennium*. Thousand Oaks: Sage.

Daniels, Charles W. (2002) Legal Aspects of Polygraph Admissibility in the United States. In: Murray Kleiner, ed. *Handbook of Polygraph Testing*. San Diego: Academic Press.

Davis, Ann, Maureen Tkacik, and Andrea Petersen. (2002, November 21) Nation of Tipsters Answers FBI's Call. *The Wall Street Journal*.

del Carmen, Rolando V. (1995) *Criminal Procedure: Law and Practice*. Belmont: Wadsworth.

del Carmen, Rolando V. (2001) *Criminal Procedure: Law and Practice*. Belmont: Wadsworth.

Dershowitz, Alan M. (1982) *The Best Defense*. New York: Random House.

Dershowitz, Alan M. (1996) *Reasonable Doubts: The Criminal Justice System and the O.J. Simpson Case*. New York: Simon and Schuster.

Dillon, Jeff, and Steve Perez. (2002, June 12) On Tape, Westerfield Describes Meandering Trip. *San Diego Union Tribune*.

Dilworth, Donald C. (1977) *Identification Wanted: Development of the American Criminal Identification System 1893–1943*. Gaithersburg: International Association of Chiefs of Police.

Douglas, John. (2000) *The Cases That Haunt Us*. New York: Scribner.

Douglas, John. (1996) *Unabomber: On the Trail of America's Most Wanted Serial Killer*. New York: Pocket Books.

Douglas, John E., Ann W. Burgess, and Robert Ressler. (1992) *Crime Classification Manual*. New York: Lexington.

Douglas, John E., and Corine Munn. (1992) Violent Crime Scene Analysis: Modus Operandi. Signature, and Staging. *FBI Law Enforcement Bulletin* 61(2): 1–10.

Douglas, John, Robert K. Ressler, Ann W. Burgess, and Carol R. Hartman. (1986) Criminal Profiling from Crime Scene Analysis. *Behavioral Sciences and the Law* 4: 401–421.

(2002, August 29) Firms Rush to Fulfill Homeland Security Needs After 9/11. *Dow Jones Business News.*

Doyle, James M. (1989) Legal Issues in Eyewitness Evidence. In: David C. Raskin, ed. *Psychological Methods in Criminal Investigation and Evidence.* New York: Springer.

Duke, Steven B., and Albert C. Gross. (1993) *America's Longest War: Rethinking Our Tragic Crusade Against Drugs.* New York: Putnam.

Duyn, J. Van. (1990) *Automated Crime Information Systems.* Blue Ridge Summit, PA: TAB Books.

Dwyer, Jim, and Kevin Flynn. (2002, December 7) Prosecutor Is Said to Back Dismissals in '89 Jogger Rape. *The New York Times.*

Eck, John E. (1983) *Solving Crimes: The Investigation of Burglary and Robbery.* Washington, DC: Police Executive Research Forum.

Egger, Steven A. (1998) *The Killers Among Us: An Examination of Serial Murder and its Investigation.* Upper Saddle River, NJ: Prentice Hall.

Elaad, Eitan, and Murray Kliener. (1990) Effects of Polygraph Chart Interpreter Experience on Psychophysiological Detection of Deception. *Journal of Police Science and Administration* 17: 115–123.

Ellis, Hadyn D. (1984) Practical Aspects of Face Memory. In: Gery L. Wells and Elizabeth F. Loftus, eds. *Eyewitness Testimony: Psychological Perspectives.* Cambridge: Cambridge University Press.

Ericson, Richard V. (1981) *Making Crime: A Study of Detective Work.* Toronto: Butterworths.

Ethridge, Philip A., and Raul Gonzalez. (1996) Combating Vehicle Theft Along the Texas Border. *FBI Law Enforcement Bulletin* 65(1): 10–13.

Fainuru, Steve. (2002a, May 19) Clues Pointed to Changing Terrorist Tactics. *The Washington Post* p. A09.

Fainuru, Steve. (2002b, September 4) September 11 Detainee Is Ordered Deported. *The Washington Post* p. A10.

Federal Bureau of Investigation. (2002) *Crime in the United States: Uniform Crime Reports.* Washington, DC: U.S. Department of Justice.

Federal Bureau of Investigation, National Center for the Analysis of Violent Crime Homepage. (2001) URL: *www.fbi.gov/hq/isd/cirg/ncavc.htm*

Federal Bureau of Investigation. (1999b) *Your F.B.I.* Washington, DC: Office of Public and Congressional Affairs.

Federal Bureau of Investigation. (1999c) *Handbook of Forensic Services.* Washington, DC: U.S. Department of Justice.

Federal Bureau of Investigation. (1996) *National Crime Information Center: 30 Years on the Beat. The Investigator, December, 1996–January, 1997.* Washington, DC: U.S. Department of Justice.

Federal Bureau of Investigation. (1990) *FBI: Facts and History.* Washington, DC: US Department of Justice.

Feeney, Floyd. (1999) Robbers and Decision Makers. In: Paul Cromwell, ed. *In their Own Words: Criminals On Crime.* Los Angeles: Roxbury.

Ferkenhoff, Eric. (2002, June 9) Man Held Mistakenly Is Dropped as Suspect. *The Chicago Tribune.*

Fisher, Jim. (1994) *The Lindbergh Case.* New Brunswick: Rutgers University Press.

Fisher, Ronald P., R. Edward Geiselman, and Michael Amador. (1989) Field Test of the Cognitive Interview: Enhancing the Recollection of Actual Victims and Witnesses of Crime. *Journal of Applied Psychology* 74: 722–727.

Fisher, Ronald P., and R. Edward Geiselman. (1992) *Memory-Enhancing Techniques for Investigative Interviewing: The Cognitive Interview.* Springfield: Charles C. Thomas.

Fisher, Ronald P., R. Edward Geiselman, and David S. Raymond. (1987) Critical Analysis of Police Interview Techniques. *Journal of Police Science and Administration* 15: 177–185.

Fleming, Zachary. (1999) The Thrill of It All: Youthful Offenders and Auto Theft. In: Paul Cromwell, ed. *In their Own Words: Criminals On Crime.* Los Angeles: Roxbury.

Forst, Brian, Frank J. Leahy, Jr., Jean Shirhall, Herbert L. Tyson, and John Bartolomeo. (1982) *Arrest Convictability as a Measure of Police Performance.* Washington, DC: National Institute of Justice.

Forst, Brian, Judith Lucianovic, and Sarah J. Cox. (1977) *What Happens After Arrest?* Washington, DC: Institute for Law and Social Research.

Friedman, Alan L. (1999) Forensic DNA Profiling in the 21st Century. *International Journal of Offender Therapy and Comparative Criminology* 43: 168–179.

Fuhrman, Mark. (1997) *Murder in Brentwood.* Washington, DC: Regnery Publishing.

Fukuyama, F. (1999) *The Great Disruption: Human Nature and the Reconstitution of Social Order.* New York: The Free Press.

Gaines, Larry K., B. Lewis, and R. Swanagin. (1983) Case Screening in Criminal Investigations: A Case Study of Robberies. *Police Studies* 6: 22–29.

Gallie, W.B. (1985) The Uses and Abuses of History. In: Stephen Vaughn, ed. *The Vital Past: Writings on the Uses of History.* Athens: University of Georgia Press.

Garner, Brian A., ed. (2000) *Black's Law Dictionary.* St. Paul: West.

Garofalo, James. (1991) Police, Prosecutors, and Felony Case Attrition. *Journal of Criminal Justice* 19: 439–449.

Geberth, Vernon J. (1996) *Practical Homicide Investigation: Tactics, Procedures, and Forensic Techniques.* Boca Raton: CRC Press.

Geiselman, R. Edward, and Ronald P. Fisher. (1989) The Cognitive Interview Technique for Victims and Witnesses of Crime. In: David C. Raskin, ed. *Psychological Methods in Criminal Investigation and Evidence.* New York: Springer.

Geller, William A. (1998) Videotaping Interrogations and Confessions. In: George C. Leo and George C. Thomas, eds. *The Miranda Debate: Law, Justice, and Policing.* Boston: Northeastern University Press.

General Accounting Office. (1979) *Report of the Comptroller General of the United States, Impact of the Exclusionary Rule on Federal Criminal Prosecutions.* Washington, DC: Government Printing Office.

Gentry, Curt. (1991) *J. Edgar Hoover: The Man and the Secrets.* New York: Penguin Books.

Goff, M. Lee. (2000) *A Fly for the Prosecution: How Insect Evidence Helps Solve Crimes.* Cambridge: Harvard University Press.

Goldenson, Robert M. (1984) *Longman Dictionary of Psychology and Psychiatry.* New York: Longman.

Goldstein, Herman. (1987) Toward Community Oriented Policing: Potential, Basic Requirements, and Threshold Questions. *Crime and Delinquency* 33: 6–30.

Gonzalez, Richard, Phoebe C. Ellsworth, and Maceo Pembroke. (1993) Response Biases in Lineups and Showups. *Journal of Personality and Social Psychology* 64: 525–537.

Goodman, Gail S., and Annette Hahn. (1987) Evaluating Eyewitness Testimony. In: Irving B. Weiner and Allen K. Hess, eds. *Handbook of Forensic Psychology.* New York: John Wiley and Sons.

Greenwood, Peter W. (1970) *An Analysis of the Apprehension Activities of the New York City Police Department.* New York: RAND Corporation.

Greenwood, Peter W., Jan M. Chaiken, and Joan Petersilia. (1977) *The Criminal Investigation Process.* Lexington: D.C. Heath.

Greenwood, Peter W., Jan M. Chaiken, and Joan Petersilia. (1976) Response to: An Evaluation of the Rand Corporation's Analysis of the Criminal Investigation Process. *Police Chief* 12: 62–71.

Grispino, Robert J. (1990) Serological Evidence in Sexual Assault Investigations. *FBI Law Enforcement Bulletin* 59(10): 14–20.

Gudjonsson, Gisli H. (1992) *The Psychology of Interrogations, Confessions, and Testimony.* New York: John Wiley and Sons.

Gudjonsson, Gisli H. (1988) How to Defeat the Polygraph Tests. In: Anthony Gale, ed. *The Polygraph Test: Lies, Truth, and Science.* London: Sage.

Gullo, Karen. (2001, November 9) Justice, CIA Revamping for Security.

Haller, Mark H. (1976) Historical Roots of Police Behavior: Chicago, 1890–1925. *Law and Society Review* 10: 303–323.

Hansen, Mark. (2001) Inexpert Witness. *American Bar Association Journal* 87: 20.

Haskell, Dave. (2002, November 7) Ex-Rhode Island Cop Freed in Murder Case.

Haskell, Neal, and Christine Haskell. (2002) Forensic Entomology. *Law and Order* 50(5): 58–63.

Hazelwood, Robert R. (1995) Analyzing Rape and Profiling the Offender. In: Robert R. Hazelwood and Ann Wolbert Burgess, eds. *Practical Aspects of Rape Investigation: A Multidisciplinary Approach*. Boca Raton: CRC Press.

Hazelwood, Robert R., and Ann Wolbert Burgess. (1995) The Behavioral-Oriented Interview of Rape Victims: The Key to Profiling. In: Robert R. Hazelwood and Ann Wolbert Burgess, eds. *Practical Aspects of Rape Investigation: A Multidisciplinary Approach*. Boca Raton: CRC Press.

Hazelwood, Robert R., Park Elliot Dietz, and Janet Warren. (1992) The Criminal Sexual Sadist. *FBI Law Enforcement Bulletin* 61(2): 12–20.

Hazelwood, Robert R., and Janet Warren. (1989) The Serial Rapist: His Characteristics and Victims, Conclusion. *FBI Law Enforcement Bulletin* 58(2): 18–25.

Hendrie, Edward M. (1998) Warrantless Entries to Arrest: Constitutional Considerations. *FBI Law Enforcement Bulletin* 67(9): 25–32.

Holmes, Ronald M., and Stephen Holmes. (1996) *Profiling Violent Crimes: An Investigative Tool*. Beverly Hills: Sage.

Homant, Robert J., and Daniel B. Kennedy. (1998) Psychological Aspects of Crime Scene Profiling: Validity Research. *Criminal Justice and Behavior* 25: 319–343.

Horvath, Frank. (1982) Detecting Deception: The Promise and the Reality of Voice Stress Analysis. *Journal of Forensic Sciences* 27: 340–351.

Horwitz, Sari, and Steve Twomey. (2002, May 22) Remains Found in Park. *The Washington Post* p. A1.

Howlett, James B., Kenneth A. Hanfland, and Robert K. Ressler. (1986) The Violent Criminal Apprehension Program VICAP: A Progress Report. *FBI Law Enforcement Bulletin* 55(12): 14–22.

Imhoff, John J., and Stephen P. Cutler. (1998) INTERPOL: Extending Law Enforcement's Reach Around the World. *FBI Law Enforcement Bulletin* 67(12): 10–16.

Inbau, Fred E., Hohn E. Reid, and Joseph P. Buckley. (1986) *Criminal Interrogations and Confessions*. Baltimore: Williams and Wilkins.

Innocence Project, Innocence Project Homepage. (2001) URL: www.innocenceproject.org.

Internal Revenue Service. (1993) *Financial Investigations: A Financial Approach to Detecting and Resolving Crimes*. Washington, DC: Government Printing Office.

Isaacs, Herbert H. (1967) Police Operations—The Apprehension Process. [Chapter Two in The President's Commission on Law Enforcement and Administration of Justice.] *Task Force Report: Science and Technology*. Washington, DC: United States Printing Office.

Isenberg, Alice R., and Jodi M. Moore. (1999) Mitochondrial DNA Analysis at the F.B.I. Laboratory. In: *Forensic Science Communications*. Vol. 1. Washington, DC: U.S. Department of Justice.

Isikoff, Michael, and Daniel Klaidman. (2002, June 10) The Highjackers We Let Escape. *Newsweek* pp. 19–28.

James, Earl. (1991) *Catching Serial Killers: Learning From Past Killer Investigations*. Lansing, MI: International Forensic Services.

Jones, Charlotte-Foltz. (1991) *Mistakes That Worked: 40 Familiar Inventions and How They Came To Be*. New York: Doubleday.

Kaplan, Robert D. (2002) The World in 2005: Hidden in Plain Sight. *The Atlantic Monthly* 286(3): 54–56.

Kelling, George L., and Mark H. Moore. (1988) The Evolving Strategy of Policing. *Perspectives on Policing* 4: 1–15. Washington, DC: National Institute of Justice.

Kelling, George L., Tony Pate, Duane Dieckman, Charles E. Brown. (1974) *The Kansas City Preventive Patrol Experiment*. Washington, DC: Police Foundation.

Kelly, John F., and Phillip Wearne. (1998) *Tainting Evidence: Inside the Scandals at the FBI Crime Lab*. New York: Free Press.

Kelley, Robert J. (1998) Armed Prophets and Extremists: Islamic Fundamentalism. In: Harvey W. Kushner, ed. *The Future of Terrorism: Violence in the New Millennium*. Thousand Oaks: Sage.

Keppel, Robert, and Joseph Weiss. (1994) Time and Distance as Solvability Factors in Murder Cases. *Journal of Forensic Sciences* 39: 386–400.

Keppel, Robert D., and Joseph G. Weiss. (1993, August) *Improving the Investigation of Violent Crime: The Homicide Investigation and Tracking System. Research in Brief.* Washington, DC: National Institute of Justice.

Keyes, Edward. (1976) *Michigan Murders.* New York: Readers Digest Press.

Kiley, William P. (1998) The Advanced Criminal Investigation Course: An Innovative Approach to Detective In-Service Training. *FBI Law Enforcement Bulletin* 67(10): 16–18.

Klockars, Carl B. (1985) *The Idea of the Police.* Newbury Park: Sage.

Kocsis, R.N., and H.J. Irwin. (1998) The Psychological Profile of Serial Offenders and a Redefinition of the Misnomer of Serial Crime. *Psychiatry, Psychology and the Law* 5: 197–213.

Kovaleski, Serge F., and Sari Horwitz. (2002, October 26) In Letter, Killer Makes Demands and Threats. *Washington Post* p. A14.

Kraska, Peter B., and Louis J. Cubellis. (1997) Militarizing Mayberry and Beyond: Making Sense of American Paramilitary Policing. *Justice Quarterly* 14: 607–629.

Kraska, Peter B., and Victor E. Kappeler. (1997) Militarizing American Police: The Rise and Normalization of Paramilitary Units. *Social Problems* 44: 1–18.

Krishnamurthy, Kiran. (2001, December 8) Will the Truth Set Him Free? *Richmond Times-Dispatch.*

Krolicki, Kevin. (2001, December 22) Microchips Under the Skin Offer ID, Raise Questions.

Kuhn, Thomas S. (1970) *The Structure of Scientific Revolutions.* Chicago: University of Chicago Press.

Kuykendall, Jack. (1986) The Municipal Police Detective: An Historical Analysis. *Criminology* 24: 175–200.

Lane, Roger. (1967) *Policing the City: Boston 1822–1885.* Cambridge: Harvard University Press.

Laughery, Kenneth R., and Richard H. Fowler. (1980) Sketch Artist and Identi-Kit Procedures for Recalling Faces. *Journal of Applied Psychology* 65: 307–316.

Lavine, Emanuel. (1930) *The Third Degree: A Detailed and Appalling Exposé of Police Brutality.* New York: Garden City Publishing.

Lengel, Allan, and Sari Horwitz. (2001, July 16) Levy Looked Up Map of a Rock Creek Site. *The Washington Post* p. B1.

Leo, Richard A. (1998a) The Impact of Miranda Revisited. In: George C. Leo and George C. Thomas, eds. *The Miranda Debate: Law, Justice, and Policing.* Boston: Northeastern University Press.

Leo, Richard A. (1998b) Miranda and the Problem of False Confessions. In: George C. Leo and George C. Thomas, eds. *The Miranda Debate: Law, Justice, and Policing.* Boston: Northeastern University Press.

Leo, Richard A. (1996) Inside the Interrogation Room. *Journal of Criminal Law and Criminology* 86: 266–303.

Leo, Richard A. (1992) From Coercion to Deception: The Changing Nature of Police Interrogations in America. *Crime, Law, and Social Change* 18: 35–59.

Leo, Richard A., and Richard J. Ofshe. (1998) The Consequences of False Confessions: Deprivations of Liberty and Miscarriages of Justice in the Age of Psychological Interrogations. *Journal of Criminal Law and Criminology* 88: 429–496.

Lichtman, Allan J., and Valerie French. (1985) Past and Present: History and Contemporary Analysis. In: Stephen Vaughn, ed. *The Vital Past: Writings on the Uses of History.* Athens: University of Georgia Press.

Lindlaw, Scott. (2002, July 21) U.S. Mulls Military's Domestic Role.

Lindsay, D. Stephen. (1994) Memory Source Monitoring and Eyewitness Testimony. In: David Frank Ross, et al., eds. *Adult Eyewitness Testimony: Current Trends and Developments.* Cambridge: Cambridge University Press.

Loftus, Elizabeth F., Edith L. Greene, and James M. Doyle. (1989) The Psychology of Eyewitness Testimony. In: David C. Raskin, ed. *Psychological Methods in Criminal Investigation and Evidence.* New York: Springer.

Loftus, Elizabeth F., and John C. Palmer. (1974) Reconstruction of Automobile Destruction: An

Example of the Interaction Between Language and Memory. *Journal of Verbal Learning and Verbal Behavior* 13: 585–589.

Lumpkin, John J. (2002, February 28) U.S. Seeks bin Laden Family DNA Samples.

Lykken, David. (1988) The Case Against Polygraph Testing. In: Anthony Gale, ed. *The Polygraph Test: Lies, Truth, and Science*. London: Sage.

Lykken, David. (1981) *A Tremor in the Blood: Uses and Abuses of the Lie Detector*. New York: McGraw-Hill.

Malone, Patrick A. (1998) 'You Have the Right to Remain Silent': Miranda After Twenty Years. In: George C. Leo and George C. Thomas, eds. *The Miranda Debate: Law, Justice, and Policing*. Boston: Northeastern University Press.

Maltz, Michael D., Andrew C. Gordon, and Warren Friedman. (1991) *Mapping Crime in Its Community Setting*. New York: Springer-Verlag.

Martin, Christine. (1994) *Illinois Municipal Officers' Perceptions of Police Ethics*. Chicago: Criminal Justice Information Authority.

Martin, S.E., and Lawrence W. Sherman. (1986) Catching Career Criminals: Proactive Policing and Selective Apprehension. *Justice Quarterly* 3: 171–192.

Marx, Gary. (1988) *Undercover: Police Surveillance in America*. Berkeley: University of California Press.

McCloskey, Michael, Howard Egeth, and Judith McKenna. (1986) The Experimental Psychologist in Court: The Ethics of Expert Testimony. *Law and Human Behavior* 10: 1–13.

McDonald, John. (2002, July 20) How the Case Unfolded. *The Orange County Register*.

McDonald, W.F., H.H. Rossman, and J.A. Cramer. (1982) *Police–Prosecutor Relations in the United States*. Washington, DC: U.S. Department of Justice.

McGuire, Philip G. (2000) The New York City Police Department COMSTAT Process: Mapping for Analysis, Evaluation, and Accountability. In: Victor Goldsmith, et al., eds. *Analyzing Crime Patterns: Frontiers of Practice*. Thousand Oaks: Sage.

McIver, J.P. (1981) Criminal Mobility: A Review of Empirical Studies. In *Crime Spillover*, pp. 20–47. S. Hakim and G.F. Rengert, eds. Beverly Hills: Sage.

Mendell, Ronald L. (2000) *How to Do Financial Asset Investigations: A Practical Guide for Private Investigators, Collections Personnel, and Assets Recovery Specialists*. Springfield: Charles C. Thomas.

Merrill, William F. (1995) The Art of Interrogating Rapists. *FBI Law Enforcement Bulletin* 64(1): 8–12.

Miller, George I. (1987) Observations on Police Undercover Work. *Criminology* 25: 27–47.

Miron, Murray S., and John E. Douglas. (1979) Threat Analysis: The Psycholinguistic Approach. *FBI Law Enforcement Bulletin* 48(9): 5–9.

Morgan, Marcia K. (1995) *How to Interview Sexual Abuse Victims*. Thousand Oaks: Sage.

Morganthau, Tom, and Tom Masland. (1993, July 5) The New Terrorism. *Newsweek* p. 18.

Moreau, Dale M., and P. David Bigbee. (1995) Major Physical Evidence in Sexual Assault Investigations. In: Robert R. Hazelwood and Ann Wolbert Burgess, eds. *Practical Aspects of Rape Investigation: A Multidisciplinary Approach*. Boca Raton: CRC Press.

Mount, Harry A. (1990) Criminal Informants: An Administrator's Dream or Nightmare. *FBI Law Enforcement Bulletin* 59(12): 12–16.

Muller, Gallus. (1889) *Alphonse Bertillon's Instructions for Taking Descriptions for the Identification of Criminals and Others* [translation of 1889 work]. Chicago: American Bertillon Prison Bureau.

Murray, Robert K. (1955) *Red Scare*. New York: McGraw-Hill.

Napier, Michael R., and Susan H. Adams. (1998) Magic Words to Obtain Confessions. *FBI Law Enforcement Bulletin* 67(10): 11–15.

Nardulli, Peter F. (1983) The Societal Costs of the Exclusionary Rule: An Empirical Assessment. *American Bar Foundation Research Journal* 3: 585–609.

National Institute of Justice. (2001) *Understanding DNA Evidence: A Guide for Victim Service Providers*. Washington, DC: U.S. Department of Justice.

National Institute of Justice. (2000a) *Crime Scene Investigation: A Guide for Law Enforcement*. Washington, DC: U.S. Department of Justice.

National Institute of Justice. (2000b) *Fire and Arson Scene Evidence: A Guide for Public Safety Personnel.* Washington, DC: U.S. Department of Justice.

National Institute of Justice. (1999a) *Eyewitness Evidence: A Guide for Law Enforcement.* Washington, DC: U.S. Department of Justice.

National Institute of Justice. (1999b) *What Every Law Enforcement Officer Should Know About DNA Evidence.* Washington, DC: U.S. Department of Justice.

National Institute of Justice. (1998) *The Unrealized Potential of DNA Testing.* Research in Action. Washington, DC: U.S. Department of Justice.

National Institute of Justice. (1996) *Convicted by Juries, Exonerated by Science: Case Studies in the Use of DNA Evidence to Establish Innocence After Trial.* Washington, DC: U.S. Department of Justice.

Nelson, Scott A. (1989) Crime-Time Television. *FBI Law Enforcement Bulletin* 58(8): 1–9.

NewsHour with Jim Lehrer. (2001, October 21) President Bush Signs Anti-Terrorism Bill. URL: www.pbs.org/newshour/bb/terrorism/bush_terrorism_bill.html.

Newton, Christopher. (2002, August 9) FBI to Profile al-Qaida Prisoners.

Ney, Tara. (1988) Expressing Your Emotions and Controlling Feelings. In: Anthony Gale, ed. *The Polygraph Test: Lies, Truth, and Science.* London: Sage.

O'Hanlon, Michael E., et al. (2002) *Protecting the American Homeland: A Preliminary Analysis.* Washington, DC: Brookings Institution Press.

Organized Crime Digest. (2000) *Federal, State Agents Break Up Ring Stealing Cars for Russia, East Europe.* Vol. 21; pp. 1–2.

Orne, Martin T., David A. Soskis, David F. Dinges, and Emily Carota Orne. (1984) Hypnotically Induced Testimony. In: Gery L. Wells and Elizabeth F. Loftus, eds. *Eyewitness Testimony: Psychological Perspectives.* Cambridge: Cambridge University Press.

O'Toole, Mary Ellen. (1999) Criminal Profiling: The FBI Uses Criminal Investigative Analysis to Solve Crimes. *Corrections Today* 61: 44–47.

Owen, David. (2000) *Hidden Evidence: 40 True Crimes and How Forensic Science Helped Solved Them.* Buffalo: Firefly.

Parks, Roger B. (1984) Comparing Citizen and Observer Perceptions of Police-Citizen Encounters. In: Gordon P. Whitaker, ed. *Understanding Police Agency Performance.* Washington, DC: U.S. Department of Justice, pp. 121–135.

Percy, Stephen L. (1980) Response Time and Citizen Evaluation of the Police. *Journal of Police Science and Administration* 8: 75–86.

Petersilia, Joan, Allan Abrahamse, and James Q. Wilson. (1990) The Relationship Between Police Practice, Community Characteristics, and Case Attrition. *Policing and Society* 1: 23–38.

Peterson, Joseph L. (1987) *Use of Forensic Evidence by the Police and Courts.* Washington, DC: National Institute of Justice.

Peterson, Jonathan, and Robert L. Jackson. (2001, October 24) Look-Alike Letters Provide Clues. *Los Angeles Times.*

Peterson, Joseph L., Steven Mihajlovic, and Michael Gilliland. (1985) The Capabilities, Uses, and Effects of the Nation's Criminalistics Laboratories. *Journal of Forensic Sciences* 30: 10–23.

Peterson, Joseph L., Steven Mihajlovic, and Michael Gilliland. (1984) *Forensic Evidence and the Police: The Effects of Scientific Evidence on Criminal Investigations.* Washington, DC: National Institute of Justice.

Phillips, Don. (2001, October 26) FAA May Start Using Scanner That Looks Inside the Body. *The Washington Post* p. E2.

Pinizzotto, Anthony J. (1984) Forensic Psychology: Criminal Personality Profiling. *Journal of Police Science and Administration* 12: 32–39.

Pinizzotto, Anthony J., and Norman J. Finkel. (1990) Criminal Personality Profiling: An Outcome and Process Study. *Law and Human Behavior* 14: 215–232.

Poister, Theodore H., and James C. McDavid. (1978) Victims' Evaluation of Police Performance. *Journal of Criminal Justice* 6: 133–49.

Pope, Justin. (2001, September 12). Boston Airport Breaches Investigated.

Porter, Bruce. (1983, April) Mind Hunters. *Psychology Today.*

Porter, Stephen, and John C. Yuille. (1996) The Language of Deceit: An Investigation of the Verbal

Clues and Deception in the Interrogation Context. *Law and Human Behavior* 20: 443–458.

Potter, Angela. (2002, November 26) Who Will Get the Sniper Reward Money?

Powers, Richard G. (1983) *G-Men: Hoover's FBI in American Popular Culture*. Carbondale: Southern Illinois University Press.

Rabon, Don. (1994) *Investigative Discourse Analysis*. Durham: Carolina Academic Press.

Raskin, David C., and Charles R. Honts. (2002) *The Comparison Question Test*. In Handbook of Polygraph Testing, pp. 1–47. Murray Kleiner, ed. San Diego: Academic Press.

Rattner, Arye. (1988) Convicted But Innocent: Wrongful Conviction and the Criminal Justice System. *Law and Human Behavior* 12: 283–293.

Regini, Charles L. (1997) The Cold Case Concept. *FBI Law Enforcement Bulletin*. 66(8): 1–6.

Reiser, Martin. (1989) Investigative Hypnosis. In: David C. Raskin, ed. *Psychological Methods in Criminal Investigation and Evidence*. New York: Springer.

Reiser, Martin, Louise Ludwig, Susan Saxe, and Clare Wagner. (1979) An Evaluation of the Use of Psychics in the Investigation of Major Crimes. *Journal of Police Science and Administration* 7: 18–25.

Reiss, Albert. (1967) *Studies in Crime and Law Enforcement in Major Metropolitan Areas*. Washington, DC: U.S. Government Printing Office.

Ressler, Robert K., and Ann W. Burgess. (1985) Crime Scene and Profile Characteristics of Organized and Disorganized Murderers. *FBI Law Enforcement Bulletin* 54(8): 18–25.

Rhodes, Henry T.F. (1968) *Alphonse Bertillon: Father of Scientific Detection*. New York: Greenwood Press.

Rice, Thomas. (1998) When You're First at a Robbery Scene. *Police* 22(5): 38–41.

Rider, A. (1980a) The Firesetter: A Psychological Profile, Part I. *FBI Law Enforcement Bulletin* 49(6): 6–13.

Rider A. (1980b) The Firesetter: A Psychological Profile, Part II. *FBI Law Enforcement Bulletin* 49(7): 6–17.

Rising, David. (2002, August 22) German Officials Charge 9/11 Suspect.

Rome Laboratory Law Enforcement Technology Team. (1996) The New Horizon: Transferring Defense Technology to Law Enforcement. *FBI Law Enforcement Bulletin* 65(4): 10–17.

Rosenbaum, Dennis. (1994) *The Challenge of Community Policing: Testing the Promises*. Thousand Oaks: Sage.

Rosenbaum, Dennis P., Arthur J. Lurigio, and Paul P. Lavrakas. (1989) Enhancing Citizen Participation on Solving Serious Crime: A National Evaluation of Crime Stoppers Programs. *Crime and Delinquency* 35: 401–420.

Rossmo, D. Kim. (2000) *Geographic Profiling*. Boca Raton: CRC Press.

Roth, Alex. (2003, January 10) Westerfield Trial Papers Detail Home Videotapes. *San Diego Union Tribune.*

Roth, Alex. (2002a, March 14) Experts Agree Defense Team for Westerfield has a Hard Task. *San Diego Union Tribune.*

Roth, Alex. (2002b, June 12) Uncoiled Hose Aroused Suspicion, Police Testify. *San Diego Union Tribune.*

Sampson, Rana. (2002) *False Burglar Alarms*. Problem-Oriented Guides of Police Series, Number 5. Washington, DC: U.S. Department of Justice.

Sanders, Glenn S., and William L. Simmons. (1983) Use of Hypnosis to Enhance Eyewitness Accuracy: Does it Work? *Journal of Applied Psychology* 68: 70–77.

Sandoval, Vincent A., and Susan H. Adams (2001) Subtle Skills for Building Rapport: Using Neuro-Linguistic Programming in the Interview Room. *FBI Law Enforcement Bulletin* 70(8): 1–5.

Scheflin, Alan W., and Jerrold Lee Shapiro. (1989) *Trance on Trial*. New York: Guilford Press.

Schlesinger, Arthur M. (1985) The Inscrutability of History. In: Stephen Vaughn, ed. *The Vital Past: Writings on the Uses of History*. Athens: University of Georgia Press.

Schmidt, Janell, and Ellen Hochstedler–Steury. (1989) Prosecutorial discretion in filing charges in domestic violence cases. *Criminology* 27: 487–510.

Schmidt, Susan, and Dan Eggen. (2002, September 14) Suspected Planner of 9/11 Attacks Captured in Pakistan After Gunfight. *The Washington Post* p. A1.

Schulhofer, Stephen J. (1998) Miranda's Practical Effect: Substantial Benefits and Vanishingly Small Societal Costs. In: George C. Leo and George C. Thomas, eds. *The Miranda Debate: Law, Justice, and Policing.* Boston: Northeastern University Press.

Schulte, Brigid, and Sylvia Moreno. (2002, October 26) Who Will Get $500,000 for Tip Leading to Suspect? *The Washington Post* p. A16.

Serrano, Richard A. (1998) *One of Ours: Timothy McVeigh and the Oklahoma City Bombing.* New York: W.W. Norton.

Shapland, Joanna. (1983) Victim–Witness Services and Needs of the Victim. *Victimology* 8: 233–237.

Sherman, Lawrence W. (1990) Police Crackdowns: Initial and Residual Deterrence. In: M. Tonry and N. Morris, eds. *Crime and Justice: A Review of Research.* Vol. 12. Chicago: University of Chicago Press.

Sherman, Lawrence W., Patrick R. Gartin, and Michael E. Buerger. (1989) Hot Spots of Predatory Crime: Routine Activities and the Criminology of Place. *Criminology* 27: 27–55.

Sherman, Lawrence W., and Barry D. Glick. (1984) *The Quality of Police Arrest Statistics.* Washington, DC: Police Foundation.

Sherman, Lawrence W., and Dennis P. Rogan. (1995) Effects of Gun Seizures on Gun Violence: "Hot Spot" Patrol in Kansas City. *Justice Quarterly* 12: 673–693.

Sherman, Lawrence W., and David Weisburd. (1995) General Deterrent Effects of Police Patrol in Crime "Hot Spots": A Randomized, Controlled Trial. *Justice Quarterly* 12: 625–648.

Simon, David. (1998) Homicide: A Year on the Killing Streets. In: George C. Leo and George C. Thomas, eds. *The Miranda Debate: Law, Justice, and Policing.* Boston: Northeastern University Press.

Skogan, Wesley G., and George E. Antunes. (1979) Information, Apprehension, and Deterrence: Exploring the Limits of Police Productivity. *Journal of Criminal Justice* 7: 217–241.

Skolnick, Jerome H., and David H. Bayley. (1988) Theme and Variation in Community Policing.

In: Michael Tonry and Norval Morris, eds. *Crime and Justice.* Chicago: University of Chicago Press.

Skolnick, Jerome H., and James J. Fyfe. (1993) *Above the Law: Police and the Excessive Use of Force.* New York: The Free Press.

Skolnick, Paul, and Jerry I. Shaw. (2001) A Comparison of Eyewitness and Physical Evidence on Mock-Juror Decision Making. *Criminal Justice and Behavior* 28: 614–630.

Snortum, John R., Paul R. Riva, Dale E. Berger, and Thomas W. Mangione. (1990) Police Documentation of Drunk-Driving Arrests: Jury Verdicts and Guilty Pleas as a Function of Quantity and Quality of Evidence. *Journal of Criminal Justice* 18: 99–116.

Spelman, William, and Dale K. Brown. (1991) Response Time. In: Carl B. Klockars and Stephen D. Mastrofski, eds. *Thinking About Police: Contemporary Readings.* New York: McGraw Hill. pp. 163–169.

Spelman, William, and Dale K. Brown. (1984) *Calling the Police: Citizen Reporting of Serious Crime.* Washington, DC: U.S. Department of Justice.

Steblay, Nancy Mehrkens, and Robert K. Bothwell. (1994) Evidence for Hypnotically Refreshed Testimony: The View From the Laboratory. *Law and Human Behavior* 18: 635–651.

Stutler, Thomas R. (1997) Stand and Deliver: Cross-Examination Strategies for Law Enforcement. *FBI Law Enforcement Bulletin* 66(9): 1–5.

Sutton, Paul. (1986) The Fourth Amendment in Action: An Empirical View of the Search Warrant Process. *Criminal Law Bulletin* 22: 405–429.

Teitell, Beth. (1994, July 31) Experts: Faked Forensics 'Surprisingly Widespread.' *Boston Herald.*

Theoharis, Athan G. (1999) *The FBI: A Comprehensive Reference Guide.* Phoenix: Oryx Press.

Thomas, George C. (1998) Miranda: The Crime, The Man, and the Law of Confessions. In: George C. Leo and George C. Thomas, eds. *The Miranda Debate: Law, Justice, and Policing.* Boston: Northeastern University Press.

Toffler, Alvin. (1980) *The Third Wave.* New York: William Marrow.

Trager, Jennifer, and JoAnne Brewster. (2001) The Effectiveness of Psychological Profiles. *Journal of Police and Criminal Psychology* 16: 20–25.

Uchida, Craig D., and Timothy S. Bynum. (1991) Search Warrants, Motions to Suppress, and 'Lost Cases': the Effects of the Exclusionary Rule in Seven Jurisdictions. *Journal of Criminal Law and Criminology* 81: 1034–1066.

U.S. Department of Justice. (2001) *First Response to Victims of Crime*. Washington, DC: Office of Justice Programs, Office for Victims of Crime.

U.S. Department of State. (2001) *Significant Terrorists Incidents, 1961–2001: A Chronology*. Washington, DC: US Department of State.

Vacca, John R. (2003) *Identity Theft*. Upper Saddle River: Prentice Hall.

Vessel, David. (1998) Conducting Successful Interrogations. *FBI Law Enforcement Bulletin* 67(10): 1–6.

Visher, Christy A. (1987) Juror Decision Making: The Importance of Evidence. *Law and Human Behavior* 11: 1–16.

Voss, Frederick, and James Barber. (1981) *We Never Sleep: The First Fifty Years of the Pinkertons*. Washington, DC: Smithsonian Institution Press.

Vuong, Andy (2002, September 23) Software Offers Web of Clues for Cops Across the U.S. *The Denver Post*.

Waller, George. (1961) *Kidnap: The Story of the Lindbergh Case*. New York: Dial Press.

Walters, Stan B. (1996) *Principles of Kinesic Interview and Interrogation*. Boca Raton: CRC Press.

Waltz, Jon R. (1997) *Introduction to Criminal Evidence*. Chicago: Nelson Hall.

Wellford, Charles, and James Cronin. (1999) *An Analysis of Variables Affecting the Clearance of Homicides: A Multistate Study*. Washington, DC: Justice Research and Statistics Association.

Wells, Gary L. (1993) What Do We Know About Eyewitness Identification? *American Psychologist* 48: 553–571.

Wells, Gary L., and Amy L. Bradfield. (1998) "Good. You Identified the Suspect": Feedback to Eyewitnesses Distorts Their Reports of the Witnessing Experience. *Journal of Applied Psychology* 83: 360–376.

Wells, Gary L., Mark Small, Steven Penrod, Roy S. Malpass, Soloman M. Fulero, and C.A.E. Brima-

combe. (1998) Eyewitness Identification Procedures: Recommendations for Lineups and Photospreads. *Law and Human Behavior* 22: 603–647.

Wells, Jeffery D., Francesco Introna, Jr., Giancarlo Di Vella, Carlo P. Campobasso, Jack Hayes, and Felix A.H. Sperling. (2001) Human and Insect Mitochondrial DNA Analysis From Maggots. *Journal of Forensic Science* 46: 685–687.

West, Michael H., and Robert E. Barsley. (1992) Ultraviolet Forensic Imaging. *FBI Law Enforcement Bulletin* 61(5): 14–16.

White, Peter J. (1998) *Crime Scene to Court: The Essentials of Forensic Science*. Cambridge: Royal Society of Chemistry, Information Services.

Wikin G. (1996, April 22) How the FBI Paints Portraits of the Nation's Most Wanted. *U.S. News and World Report* p. 32.

Williams, Hubert, and Patrick V. Murphy. (1990) *The Evolving Strategy of Police: A Minority View. Perspectives on Policing* 13. Washington, DC: National Institute of Justice.

Willmer, M. (1970) *Crime and Information Theory*. Edinburgh: University of Edinburgh Press.

Wilson, James Q. (1968) *Varieties of Police Behavior*. Cambridge: Harvard University Press.

Wilson, James Q., and George L. Kelling. (1982) Broken Windows: The Police and Neighborhood Safety. *The Atlantic Monthly* 249: 29–38.

Worden, Robert E. (1993) Toward Equity and Efficiency in Law Enforcement: Differential Police Response. *American Journal of Police* 12: 1–32.

Worden, Robert E., Timothy S. Bynum, James Frank. (1994) Police Crackdowns on Drug Abuse and Trafficking. In: Doris Layton MacKenzie and Craig D. Uchida, eds. *Drugs and Crime: Evaluating Public Policy Initiatives*. Thousand Oaks: Sage.

Wright, Richard T., and Scott H. Decker. (1997) *Armed Robbers in Action*. Boston: Northeastern University Press.

Wright, Richard T., and Scott H. Decker. (1994) *Burglars on the Job: Street Life and Residential Break-ins*. Boston: Northeastern University Press.

Yarmey, A. Daniel, Meagan J. Yarmey, and A. Linda Yarmey. (1996) Accuracy of Eyewitness Identifications in Showups and Lineups. *Law and Human Behavior* 20: 459–476.

Zalman, Marvin. (2000) Criminal Justice and the Future of Civil Liberties. *Criminal Justice Review* 25: 181–206.

Zeman, David, and Ben Schmitt. (2002, October 24) How Justice Failed Eddie Joe Lloyd. *Detroit Free Press.*

Zuckerman, Miron, Richard Koestner, and Audrey O. Alton. (1984) Learning to Detect Deception. *Journal of Personality and Social Psychology* 3: 519–528.

Zulawski, David E., and Douglas E. Wicklander. (1992) *Practical Aspects of Interview and Interrogation.* New York: Elsevier.

INDEX